Around the World with Etiquette

A Practical Handbook to Culture and Manners Across Continents

Compiled by Sophia Lingham
and Dobrochna Giedwidz
Featuring Multiple Global Etiquette Experts

Around the World with Etiquette

A Practical Handbook to Culture and Manners
Across Continents

Olympia Publishers
London

www.olympiapublishers.com
OLYMPIA PAPERBACK EDITION

Copyright © Compiled by Sophia Lingham and Dobrochna Giedwidz Featuring Multiple Global Etiquette Experts 2024

The right of **Compiled by Sophia Lingham and Dobrochna Giedwidz Featuring Multiple Global Etiquette Experts** to be identified as author of this work has been asserted in accordance with sections 77 and 78 of the Copyright, Designs and Patents Act 1988.

All Rights Reserved

No reproduction, copy or transmission of this publication may be made without written permission.
No paragraph of this publication may be reproduced, copied or transmitted save with the written permission of the publisher, or in accordance with the provisions of the Copyright Act 1956 (as amended).

Any person who commits any unauthorised act in relation to this publication may be liable to criminal prosecution and civil claims for damage.

A CIP catalogue record for this title is available from the British Library.

ISBN: 978-1-80439-119-8

The information in this book has been compiled by way of general guidance only. Neither the author nor the publisher shall be liable or responsible for any loss or damage allegedly arising from any information or suggestion in this book.

First Published in 2024

Olympia Publishers
Tallis House
2 Tallis Street
London
EC4Y 0AB

Printed in Great Britain

Dedication

This book is dedicated to anyone who has ever taken bread from the wrong side plate.

Acknowledgements

Thank you to all those who read through different versions of our chapters along the way; to Jean Paul Wijers and Philip Sykes, who kindly read our work and composed the forewords, and to our illustrator, Lucrecia Palladino, who penned such beautiful illustrations. Thank you also to our clients, tutees and supporters who provided the inclination to write this book. Lastly, but not at all least, thank you to all our families and friends who proofread, supported us and made lots of tea during the writing of this book!

About This Book

This book is the brainchild of Dobrochna Giedwidz, Sophia Lingham, Ellyna He, Maria Campos and Victoria Thomas who made each other's acquaintance whilst attending a course at The British School of Etiquette (now The British School of Excellence) in London, England, in 2019. Whilst the idea for the book was not an immediate consequence pertaining to the course, over the weeks and months that followed, constant communication between these women led to a realisation: we all had different etiquette nuances and traditions in our countries, different cultures and languages, yet we were united by a desire to share with others the ability to feel at ease in each of our countries. And thus, the idea for a global etiquette book was born! The title of *Around the World with Etiquette* was an early suggestion which has remained the firm favourite ever since.

The project consisted of only a handful of countries to begin with, but by developing connections with etiquette instructors worldwide, we soon had over twenty countries contributing, and have since had requests from others to join the party. The fact that we are all women was completely coincidental, but this has led to the forming of a global sisterhood of like-minded, empowered women. Over the course of the last three years, each of these fabulous and talented ladies has been involved in developing the book, its contents, chapters, illustrations and social media promotion. Ergo, despite the genesis of the project being a desire to make others feel at ease, it has led to the creation of many new friendships and solidarity, as well as a growing thirst for knowledge.

Our book celebrates the culture, values, traditions and etiquette of twenty-five separate countries, spanning every populated continent in the world. Each of our amazing women are experts in soft skills, etiquette, protocol and diplomacy in each of their countries and write to provide insider knowledge on how these practices work in their country. With a wealth of experience working either in different countries to their homeland, or working with professionals internationally, teaching programmes of the highest quality, each of these incredible women are more than qualified in co-creating the first international etiquette book of its kind. Their chapter contributions each illustrate how to avoid faux pas and ignorance, creating a necessary guide for those travelling for business or pleasure alike. Each contributor has their own etiquette consultancy business, details of which can be seen at the end of this book.

This book by no means gives you all the answers to avoid every faux pas you could make whilst abroad but is intended to give first-hand knowledge and information both about the country's culture and its etiquette; this is often mixed with a personal admiration for the country we originate from or have adopted as our home. It is separated by country, in alphabetical order. Within this book are etiquette guides for the general culture of each country, body language, posture, meeting, greeting and conversation, gifting, dining, business, and weddings.

    We hope you find this book a fun and useful companion for your travels abroad, opening your eyes to the depth, richness and fascinating nuances which make each of our countries unique.
    Sophia and Dobrochna

Table of Contents

Foreword by Jean Paul Wijers, Founder of Protocolbureau and Co-author of *Protocol to Manage Relationship Today* 13

Foreword by Philip Sykes, Founder and Principal at The British School of Excellence 16

Argentina By Mabel Di Michele 19

Australia By Victoria Thomas 49

Botswana By Samantha Matlhagela 77

Brazil By Merely Siqueira Reis 103

Caribbean By Alice Thomas-Roberts 127

China By Ellyna He 159

France By France de Heere 185

Ghana By Sasha Oquaye 211

Hungary By Gabriella Kanyok 249

India By Niraalee Shah 277

Iran By Farno Rezaei 307

Italy By Dobrochna Giedwidz 335

Lebanon By Irma Vartanian Balian 367

Morocco By Mariam Filali Meknassi 397

Pakistan By Dr Sadia Javed Rajput 423

Poland By Dobrochna Giedwidz 449

Portugal By Maria Campos 477

The Russian Federation By Anastasia Martel 507

Slovenia By Simona Lečnik Očko 531

Switzerland By Julia Esteve Boyd 557

Turkey By Özgü Ergün 591

UAE By Andreea Stefanescu 619

United Kingdom By Sophia Lingham 643

United States of America By Nancy Hoogenboom 681

Vietnam By Mai O'Donnell 711

About the Authors 739

Foreword by Jean Paul Wijers, Founder of Protocolbureau and Co-author of *Protocol to Manage Relationship Today*

How to do business in another culture? How to become familiar with local customs? What are local dining manners? What is important to know when attending a wedding in another country? This multi-country guide is co-authored by professionals from all over the globe. These true experts in the fields of soft skills, etiquette, protocol and diplomacy cover all populated continents.

This wonderful book is meant to provide an insider's perspective. The book is aimed at professionals and purposeful travellers seeking a reliable guide about the country they are visiting. *The book celebrates cultures around the globe; Interacting with different cultures is a rewarding experience.*

In our open society, we are more connected than ever before—far beyond our own communities, countries or companies. Many of us are dealing with the complexity of interacting with a large variety of people all around the world and being part of multiple global networks. The significant challenges we will face this century will be global ones and cooperation across cultures is needed to make the world a fairer and safer place.

This book demonstrates the value of having a sound knowledge of local customs, etiquette and non-verbal communication. By understanding the local culture, it becomes easier to create mutual understanding and by doing so it enables us to build strong long-term relationships necessary to take strides in our interconnected global society.

In our current society there is much focus on transactional relationships. Transactional relationships are led by pragmatism: What is in it for me? The opposite of transactional relationships are symbolic relationships: relationships with a focus on common ground. By focusing on what both sides have in common, the relationship is able to gain value and become deeper.

In creating such common ground, a good understanding of the symbols described in this book are most helpful. The word 'symbol' stems from the Greek word *sumbolon*: that which connects people and allows them to create and maintain a community with others. Symbols reflect what we have in common, instead of focusing on our differences. By doing so, symbols are a binding force, even among people of very different backgrounds.

Many of the local customs described in this book have a symbolic value. For example, in Lebanon where the Arz (cedar tree) is the state emblem symbolising longevity and strength. Lebanon's cedars are thousands of years old and even mentioned in epics and Biblical stories. Or in Botswana where the Zebra – a wild animal and yet very soft, graceful and harmless – symbolises the peaceful, tranquil and harmless nature of the country.

It is important to understand the meaning of these customs or symbols; otherwise, they are worthless. In the United Kingdom, Queen Elizabeth II of Great Britain didn't expect anyone to bow to her. As the palace explains it, this was because it was not to her directly but to the office she carries. Those who understand this, understand that they are in effect showing respect to themselves; they are bowing to themselves.

Another example is the first incoming state visit after the election of the new president of the Portuguese Republic, traditionally made by Spain. State visits mostly take place in the Portuguese capital of Lisbon, but the current president and former law professor Marcelo Rebelo de Sousa chose the ancient city of Guimarães to welcome the king of Spain. Guimarães is the birthplace of Portugal. It became Portugal's first capital after Prince Afonso Henriques declared the independence of the country of Portugal in 1128 and established a new kingdom. Afonso became the first king of Portugal in 1139. Rebelo de Sousa chose Guimarães over Lisbon to symbolise his role as president of the entire country, but Guimarães also gave him the opportunity to symbolise the long-standing relationship with Spain since 1128.

Customs are not made up but rooted in history; in Hungary, twenty-three historical flags are put on display at official state events to symbolise the long history of the country from the Hungarian Conquest of the Carpathian Basin in the C.9th (895–96). It is important to explain history, because it will make people understand and they will start to want to protect it.

Customs expressed in symbols, rituals and ceremonies help to build strong relationships and good friendships. They are meant to facilitate trust and connection. This book helps the reader to understand the broader context of these local customs, but the book is also written in response to a need for new meaning. In a period where we see the declining influence of traditional institutions, people are looking for experiences that are significant. These local customs, etiquette and non-verbal communication transforms the moments into an experience to never forget.

This book is therefore essential for those travelling the world, either for business or pleasure, in order to understand the other's history, culture and symbols in order to build strong authentic relationships.

Jean Paul Wijers

Founder of Protocolbureau and co-author of *Protocol to Manage Relationship Today*

Foreword by Philip Sykes, Founder and Principal at The British School of Excellence

A book first written and published in 1926 by Lady Troubridge opened with the following quote:

"Etiquette may be defined as the technique of the art of social life. For various and good reasons certain traditions have been handed down, just as they are in any other art, science or department of life, and only very thoughtless persons could consider unworthy of notice that set of rules which guides us in our social relations to each other.

Please notice the word *guide,* for that is the very root of the matter. Books on etiquette are guides, not regulations to be followed blindly without understanding their meaning, and with a grasp only of the letter and not the spirit."

Almost a hundred years on and the above opening lines from Lady Troubridge could not be more relevant in today's modern world.

I would even go as far as to say that etiquette and manners have never been more relevant than they are right now. We are all dealing with the complexity of relationships in our personal and business lives. I feel the way to navigate this is to look at etiquette and manners as the traffic lights in our lives. They guide us and help us so that we don't crash into one another in everyday behaviour. They give us the confidence to put the correct foot forward.

Good etiquette and manners will always be accepted no matter where you are in the world. It is about standing out for the right reasons rather than the wrong reasons. For me, it is about being the person you would like to meet.

Around the World with Etiquette is written by some of the most incredible, wonderful people and is an essential, informative and easy-to-read guide to modern etiquette. If you take on board the guidance and advice in this book, it will stand you in good stead, wherever you go. It will give you the knowledge and help you with your confidence when travelling and meeting people from all over the world.

I have no doubt that this is a book that will stand the test of time and be passed on for generations to come. You cannot afford not to read this book, in doing so you have nothing to lose and everything to gain.

It is an honour and a privilege to have worked with each and every one of these incredible authors and contributors to life, to know you and to have worked with you has enriched my life to no end. I thank you for the opportunity to write this foreword to your valuable book.

My very best wishes.

Philip Sykes
Founder and Principal at The British School of Excellence

Argentina
By Mabel Di Michele

Chapter 1

Cultural Symbols

Additionally to my foundation in the teaching of etiquette, protocol and ceremonial procedures, I also promote the development of ethical and cultural values in each of my students. With great pride and respect, I want to show you the cultural icons of Argentina.

With our individual national features inherited mainly from immigration from Italy and Spain and from many other integrated cultures, I want to tell you about our soul. Generous and friendly, innovators and traditionalists, with a great hospitable spirit, we are the product of a magical mixture of what is inherited from the valuable townsfolk that arrived and inhabited our wonderful country.

Argentine Flag
Our beautiful official flag is made up of three horizontal stripes of equal size, two of them light blue and one white in the middle. In the centre of the white stripe is the sun in gold/yellow, a reminder of the first Argentine coin, with the thirty-two flamboyant and straight rays radiating from it.

Music: Tango / Folk Music
The culture of Argentina is marked by the multi-ethnic and multicultural character of our population. The variation can be found from the world-famous tango and folk music to the most varied national rock music groups. Outstanding personalities such as Carlos Gardel, and the world-renowned Astor Piazzolla, made the dance and musical style of the Argentine Tango stand out and have worldwide success and recognition today.

DRINKS: MATE AND MALBEC WINE

In those great moments with friends or family, when we travel or go on vacation, when we are at work, studying, or when we develop a project, Argentines have a faithful companion: 'el mate', an infusion that we share with family and friends. A herb grown in the north of the country is brewed and this infusion is sipped from a stainless steel straw out of a light bulb shaped vessel called a 'calabash'.

Among the alcoholic beverages, wine stands out. Argentina is the fifth largest world producer. The provinces of Mendoza and San Juan are the main producers but other mountain provinces and the south of the country also contribute. Among the characteristic wines of the country, Malbec stands out as a 'national variety'. It is currently the most planted red grape in the country. Wines from the high altitudes of Mendoza have attracted many foreign experts, such as Paul Hobbs, Michel Rolland, Herve Joyaux-Fabre, Roberto Cipresso and Alberto Antonini, and today there are several Malbec wines from the region that have c.95 points in the Wine Spectator and Robert Parker's The Wine Advocate. Herve Joyaux-Favre has gone so far as to say that 'the Malbec grapes in the area are the best in the world'.

Argentinian Asado

Empanadas

GASTRONOMY: ASADO, DULCE DE LECHE, EMPANADAS AND LOCRO

In gastronomy, we stand out for the quality of our beef, so our typical dish is 'the Argentine barbecue' which is nothing more than a barbecue with the meat held on a cross support and cooked over a low heat. We are large producers of beef.

I cannot fail to mention the 'empanadas' cooked with minced meat, and their regional varieties.

The 'Dulce de Leche' is an essential dessert. Composed of condensed milk cooked with sugar, and with a flavour similar to that of toffee, it is the inevitable gift that we usually make when paying tribute to a foreign guest!

Finally, I cannot fail to mention, as one of our typical meals, an exquisite stew called 'Locro', made with cereals, pork and beef. Argentinians usually cook it on national holidays.

TYPICAL CLOTHING: GAUCHO, PONCHO, TANGO AND SILVER GOLDSMITH

The typical clothing of Argentina is that of the 'gaucho'. The star accessory for this outfit is a 'poncho', and you cannot miss the red scarf tied with a knot at the front, around the neck. Other important details are a brown sash and boots, which always go over trousers, a hat or beret, a large knife at the back of the waist, and baggy trousers called bloomers.

The figure of the 'gaucho' emerged in Argentina in c.1600, after the Spanish brought the horse to the New World. Originally, the figure was a lonely, free-spirited person with few possessions other than his horse. To this day, the figure of the gaucho continues to occupy a very important place in Argentine folklore, especially in the agrarian sector, where men continue to dress in this outfit.

During Spanish colonisation, goldsmithing also began to emerge in the everyday utensils of wealthy families.

Tango costume:

Women's clothing is very sensual and feminine: a short dress, or a long dress with an opening down one leg, sometimes mesh stockings, without showing anything: 'suggest without showing'. Necklines and tight clothing that highlight the figure are used. For men, a black suit with thin white stripes and a white shirt (tie or bowtie are optional), are common. A hat, and braces for the trousers may also be worn.

Gaucho

CULTURAL AGENDA: THEATRES, LIBRARIES, SHOWS, MUSEUMS, AND MAFALDA

Buenos Aires is one of the main cultural metropolises of the West. Its cultural development can be seen in the large number of museums, theatres and libraries. The City of Buenos Aires is the city with the most theatres in the world and offers a wide variety of theatrical performances, both in its commercial state and independent rooms. The Teatro Colón is an opera theatre in the City of Buenos Aires. Due to its size, acoustics and trajectory, it has come to be considered as the best lyrical theatre in the world. The Teatro Colón has the best acoustic room for opera, and the second best for concerts, in the world. The City of Buenos Aires is undoubtedly one of the most fascinating, sensual and seductive metropolises in the entire South American continent. More than for its history or its cultural heritage, this city of tango, soccer, bowling alleys, and milongas, captures the bustle of its streets and the friendliness of the locals. In national culture, I have to mention the most important figures in Argentine literature Julio Cortázar, Victoria Ocampo, Adolfo Bioy Casares, Ernesto Sabato and Jorge Luis Borges. The latter was awarded numerous distinctions but was also controversial for his conservative political positions.

The comic strip in Argentina is one of the most important comic strip traditions worldwide and the most important one in Latin America. An example of this is the well-known character 'Mafalda' by Quino.

Tourism: North Area, Patagonia Autonomous City of Buenos Aires or Ciudad Autonoma de Buenos Aires

Argentina offers the traveller everything you can ask for, from being diverse and wild with incredible nature, from beaches to mountains, to a cultural mix, being fun, and also having the best meat in the world.

The Northern zone: Iguazú Falls. In the middle of the jungle, this immense force of nature appears violent and powerful. Visitable from Brazil and Argentina, the gateway system in the latter allows you to see a greater number of waterfalls. The famous Devil's Throat (Garganta del Diablo) is appreciated, a spectacle that hypnotises everyone.

Patagonia: the ice wall of the Perito Moreno Glacier. This is one of the best natural attractions to see in Argentina, and is thus a sufficient reason for you to make the long journey that takes you to El Calafate.

Valdez Peninsula: whales can be seen during a visit to the Valdés Peninsula, as well as penguins, sea lions and the harsh and inhospitable but beautiful nature in Puerto Madryn.

Bariloche: When you walk through the streets of Bariloche, you may think that you are in Switzerland. This town, surrounded by breathtaking natural beauty, features wooden houses, restaurants, chocolate shops and souvenir shops. In summer, the landscape of mountains and lakes will catch your breath for their great beauty. In winter, Bariloche will welcome you to the most famous ski resorts in South America.

Usuhaia: The southernmost city on the continent is very close to Antarctica, a place that can be visited on a cruise excursion. The most popular attractions to visit in Ushuaia are the Tierra del Fuego National Park and the Beagle Channel. In addition to these places, you must visit the Autonomous City of Buenos Aires: Buenos Aires is the great cosmopolitan capital of Argentina. Its centre is the Plaza de Mayo, surrounded by imposing C.19th buildings, including the Casa Rosada, the iconic presidential palace which has several balconies. Other major attractions include the Teatro Colón, a luxurious 1908 opera house with nearly 2,500 seats, and the modern Malba Museum, which exhibits Latin American art. Also, do not miss seeing the famous Obelisk in the city centre.

Wine Route: No trip to Argentina is complete without tasting the first-class wines offered by the province of Mendoza, for example, visiting the Uco Valley and its tour of three renowned wine houses in the company of an expert winemaker.

Pope Francisco

The Argentine Jorge Bergoglio, who adopted the name De Francisco (Pope Francis), is the first pope of the Catholic church born on the American continent.

We are also proud to have the first Argentinian to be crowned queen of the Netherlands. Warm and charismatic, when she became Queen Consort of the Netherlands on the 30th of April 2013, Her Majesty, Queen Maxima has enjoyed ever increasing popularity. Loved by her people, her sympathy and spontaneity not only modernised the country's monarchy but also drew the world's attention to the Netherlands.

Sports: Maradona and Messi

In sport, soccer is the most popular game in Argentina. Diego Armando Maradona is considered one of the greatest exponents in world history and as beloved as the famous Lionel Messi. He is considered 'the current best player in the world'.

Nobel Prize: The Five Argentines who received the Nobel Prize

1936 Nobel Prize in Peace: Carlos Saavedra Lamas (1878–1959)
1947 Nobel Prize in Medicine: Bernardo Alberto Houssay (1887–1971)
1970 Nobel Prize in Chemistry: Luis Federico Leloir (1906–1987)
1980 Nobel Prize in Peace: Adolfo Pérez Esquivel (1931)
1984 Nobel Prize in Medicine: César Milstein (1927–2002)

Chapter 2

Meeting, Greeting, Posture and Body Language

Argentines, as with many other Latin populations, tend to be very close, not only in terms of treatment but in terms of personal space. This is called *proxemia* or proxemic. Proxemics is the study of relationships and communication that we establish through space and through the distances we put between ourselves and the things around us. When Argentines have a conversation, we are likely to place ourselves very close to the person with whom we speak. It does not matter if these people are new to us; we still tend to be quite close.

We act the same when we have a conversation or when we give a simple explanation to a stranger on the street. It even surprises us if someone is bothered by this closeness and we might interpret this as a sign of mistrust, and even insecurity. In addition, if the person moves away, we will approach again, since we do not like to talk at a pronounced distance. Our body posture is very Latin and we have characteristics very similar to that of Italians.

GESTURES AND BODY LANGUAGE IN ARGENTINA
Argentinians gesture considerably when speaking. Sociable and friendly, we have the need to also communicate with gestures. As we come largely from Italians, and body expressions are not alien to us, we are expressive, emotional and passionate.

A well-known American YouTuber in love with Argentina, Dustin Luke, includes in his book a fun dictionary of gestures, expressions and words, because, according to him, Argentines take all their actions to the maximum expression. 'When Argentines speak to me, relationships are pure contact', he says in his book. "Talking with your hands is 'key' and almost 'obligatory'," he says.

'Argentines, when they speak to you, are communicating to you even more due to the fact that they are speaking with their hands and have another level of communication with body language'—Dustin Luke.

Argentines are people of moderate speech and a melodious tone of voice. Although we raise our voices when speaking, we don't like to do it excessively when we are in public places. We consider it very bad taste if we hear discussions/arguments between people in public.

For us, signs are common, such as the 'OK' sign or the raised thumb sign (as a symbol that everything is correct/everything went well). However, in formal settings we prefer not to use them.

Hitting the fist of one hand against the palm of the other, we usually do when we are surprised by what someone is telling us.

We dislike it if you/the interlocutor loses visual contact with the person who speaks as we feel you have little interest or have developed mistrust. Maintaining eye contact while speaking is important because it is a sign of interest and that we are paying attention to what you tell us.

When Argentines turn the palm of their open hand to the right and to the left, it means that they are undecided or that something does not completely convince them. If someone asks us: "Do you like…?" That is when we rock our hands to the right and to the left, with an open palm.

Another very characteristic gesture is placing the back of our fingers underneath our chin; it means that we do not know much about that topic.

If you rub your thumb and middle finger together creating a 'snap' sound, it means you want someone to hurry. Quick, quick, hurry up a bit! Sometimes, we do another gesture, waving our fingers with our hand partially open, which also requests speed.

When we are talking to others, putting our hands on our waist or hips, or in our pockets is inappropriate.

GREETINGS AND FORMAL MEETINGS

Introductions are made, as in many other countries in the world, through a third party who acts as a 'mediator' between both new parties. If it is not possible to have a third party (generally the host), then the presentations can be made directly by the interested parties themselves or through someone trusted by the hosts.

In any meeting, be it social or business, it is very important to make the corresponding presentations among all attendees. It is a way of making 'contacts' and starting conversations.

The usual greeting between men is a handshake and, if we want to give a little more 'formality' to the greeting, we can highlight this gesture with the slightest tilt of the head. When there is confidence, this greeting can be complemented by a hug, a pat on the back or a tap on the shoulder. Sometimes we make mistakes in protocol due to the spontaneity that characterises us.

Ladies greet each other with a kiss on the cheek. The greeting with men is a handshake. But we must bear in mind that it is the woman who reaches out and starts the greeting. Also, among women who do not know each other, it is correct to shake hands, if they do not want to kiss.

Greetings in the Informal Sphere – Trustworthy People

Amongst friends, family and acquaintances, it is more common to give a hug to men and a kiss on the cheek to women. Men, when they are very confident, also usually exchange kisses on the cheek with other men. This custom is so very common. The greeting with a kiss on the cheek is so frequent that we even forget other types of greetings when we are introduced to someone.

In Argentina, it is customary to give a kiss as a cordial greeting or as a sign of gratitude.

The man always greets the woman with a kiss, even if they do not know each other. Among men, when they are friends or family, they also kiss.

How Do We Make Formal Presentations in Argentina

We usually use only the first name and last name, nothing else.

The treatment we should use by default should be our treatment in the first moments. We must wait for the hosts to invite us to use their first name (proper name) and 'authorise' informality. But, once we gain confidence, we quickly use the word *'vos'*.

Whenever we enter a room or a meeting, we must greet all those present, and wait for them to introduce us to others. When leaving a meeting or room, it is also correct to say goodbye to everyone present. Depending on the number of people present, we can make a general farewell, or do it personally, one by one.

Argentinean Temperament

As Argentines, we are open, communicative, educated and proud of our country and culture. The economic problems of the past and present helped us develop an aspect of early adaptability to different situations to be faced.

Our ability to cope with very different professions is known. Nothing is impossible and we are ready to learn and face new challenges.

Most of the population have ancestors from European countries, such as Spain, Italy, France, Germany, Portugal, Switzerland and Poland, as well as Russia and even the Middle East. We also stand out for being tolerant of cultural diversity and we welcome foreigners who come to inhabit our lands. We integrate communities of different cultures and customs without discrimination.

Argentines are known as the 'Europeans of South America' for our customs and manners. There is an urban legend that says that Argentines are Italians, who speak Spanish, and live like the English, in Paris.

The Argentine population is mostly Catholic, and somewhat conservative in customs, especially when it comes to family issues.

Regarding education, etiquette and manners, we place great value on traditional customs, having respect for social and behavioural norms.

Our social life is of utmost importance and we often celebrate with gatherings where food is essential.

We are quite open-minded, affable, pleasant to deal with, and generally good communicators with good social skills.

The strong European influence differentiates Argentines in many ways from the inhabitants of other countries in the South American region.

Chapter 3

Conversation Dos and Don'ts

5 Tips for Conversation 'Dos and Don'ts'
1. Argentines have a very different way of speaking from the rest of Spanish-speaking countries, and sometimes quite particular. I am not only referring to our marked accent but rather to those words of '*lunfardo*' that mean not everyone can understand us.

What is '*lunfardo*'?

It was a jargon found in Buenos Aires at the end of the C.19th and the beginning of the C.20th, and which has words from the languages spoken by the immigrants who arrived at the Río de la Plata; many terms of this jargon are now part of the colloquial language of the River Plate areas.

Some examples of *lunfardo*:
– '*Morfar*' instead of saying 'eat'
– '*Bondi*' meaning 'by bus'
– '*Garpar*' meaning 'to pay'
– '*Pinta*': good appearance
– '*Chanta*': not a very credible person
– '*Guita*': money
– '*Pilcha*': clothing

2. What is remarkable is the intonation, Italian influence, and the conjugation of the second person singular.

The pronunciation of the letters 'll' and 'y' in the Río de la Plata area is very peculiar because it becomes 'sh'.

We usually use '*Che*' in a colloquial way to inspire confidence.

Example: "*Che, vení a mi comer a mi casa! Venite en bondi pero no te empilchés demasiado.*" (Che, come to my house to eat! Come by bus but dress casually).

3. We use the '*voseo*' (we try and say '*vos*').

The '*voseo*' is a linguistic phenomenon within the Spanish language in which the pronoun '*vos*' is used, together with certain particular verbal conjugations, to address the interlocutor to replace the pronoun 'tu' in familiar situations.

Main differences:

We often say '*vos*' for 'tu' or for 'ti', '*sos*' for 'you are', '*querés*' for 'you want'. '*Tenés*' for 'you have', '*Decime*' for 'tell me', '*podés*' for 'you can', '*decís*' for 'you say'.

4. Some rules when talking:

- Make eye contact. It is important for establishing reliability and trust.
- Tell us about family and personal matters. We take this aspect as a friendly, trustworthy and open gesture.
- Talk about football; known worldwide for the passion we profess in this sport, it is an inevitable topic when we enter into conversations. Other frequent topics: travel, food, wine, fashion and the latest premieres of artistic shows.
- We do not often talk of local politics with foreign visitors. With them we usually talk about lighter and more trivial topics.
- The '*porteños*' (natives of the Autonomous City of Buenos Aires) exaggerate, and sometimes fall into the mistake of saying that we have the best meat in the world, the best soccer players in the world, the most beautiful women, and even pizza that is richer than in Italy! So, do not be afraid to exaggerate things a little and praise us; a *porteño* will recognise you as an equal.

5. We don't like to talk about:

- Although we like to talk about the local and world economy, we prefer not to express or ask about salary figures.
- We are uncomfortable continuing to deal with the formal version of 'you' (*usted*) after a certain time after meeting a person. We need to establish a trust quickly and be able to talk informally.
- We do not like to hear opinions against immigrants, the poor, sexual freedom or social rights.
- We do not like to hear complaints against foreigners.
- In Argentina, as in the rest of the world, being politically correct is a sign of education that is always valued. However, some *porteños* are sometimes not so politically correct.

Chapter 4

Gift Giving

VISITING A FRIEND'S HOUSE
If we are invited to a house where Argentinians are hosting, or we go as guests to any other private house, we must bring the hosts a gift. If the host has young children, we would also appreciate it if you could bring something for the children.

A NICE TOUCH FOR THE HOSTS
Whiskeys, *cavas*, champagne and, in general, foreign liqueurs, are highly appreciated. In Argentina, there are geographical areas where some great wines of great quality are produced. But, rest assured, any gift that is appropriate will always be well received.

Leather products in Argentina are also of excellent quality. That is why we are very pleased to receive them, and it is a good idea to make a gift of this type: leather wallet, purse, suitcase, etcetera.

Flowers or chocolates are also well appreciated gifts. If there are children, a bag with sweets can be a nice touch. Also, gifts from the home country of the guest are usually welcome if they are a foreigner. Some type of local crafts, some gastronomic delights, books about art or monuments of the country, etcetera, are well received.

WEDDING GIFTS
In these times, it is frequent that the couple exhort those who want to give them something. The couple may provide a gift table at their wedding or instead ask for money, any amount being appreciated. Honestly, giving them the money directly makes it easier for everyone: it avoids the guest having to go to one or several shops and spend an hour deciding on the best gift, it avoids repeated gifts for the couple, and gives them the ability to decide if they want to spend the money on a food blender or save it and buy a washing machine!

How Much Money Should be Given to the Bride and Groom
Well, according to 'protocol', the minimum amount that should be given would have to be the equivalent of the cost they paid to invite you to the party.

In the wedding invitation you can find clues and have an idea whether it will be a simple party or not. If the invitation is elegant, if the party will be in a distinguished place, and if the dress code is formal, then you will attend an event for which the cost will surely be very high. Thus, this gives an orientation of how much to spend.

In addition to the type of event, other relevant factors to decide how much to spend on the wedding gift are:
- The relationship you have with the bride and groom.
- The commitment you have with them.
- The budget that is available.
- How many companions will come to the party.

The better relationship you have with the bride and groom, or if you have a moral commitment to them, and the more companions you take to the party with you, obviously, the greater the care in the gift would have to be.

Gifts for Girls Turning Fifteen
We usually celebrate the arrival of teenage girls' youth by holding unforgettable parties. The best gift goes straight to the emotions. All gifts keep an emotion and convey what kind of relationship you have with the girl whose birthday it is. Going straight to the emotion causes endless positive feelings.

What Do Argentines Give as Gifts When We Travel Abroad
- All *capybara* items that were ever manufactured (it is now a protected species, and is no longer manufactured).
- The typical *alpaca* objects: tea boxes, photo frames, etcetera.
- Portfolios, generally, from traditional businesses that sell high-quality leather goods.
- White leather belts, bracelets and necklaces, generally combined with silver. It may even be a 'true gaucho' tie that represents the Argentine tradition.

- Ponchos from the north of Argentina, *vicuña* shawls…
- 'Tourist' T-shirts with inscriptions from Puerto Madryn, 'End of the world' from Ushuaia, etcetera.
- '*Dulce de leche*' and '*alfajores*'. The preferred ones are those of the traditional and historic brands of Argentina.
- A bottle of Malbec wine. There are many varieties of wineries that represent this iconic wine from our country.
- A book with photos of Buenos Aires, and CD's of both the 'Misa Criolla' and the known musician Ástor Piazzolla.
- We also give away hats/caps from the highlands.
- Sometimes when you think of a typical Argentine gift, we visualise 'the mate', the lightbulb-shaped vessel called '*calabash*' for drinking the mate, and the ponchos or the leather… but there are the delicious *alcayota* fruit and the *mamon* (papaya in syrup).

Argentinian Mate

- We give away gaucho knives and leather souvenirs such as the map of Argentina, or an almanac where you can mark the date of your visit so that it will be left as a souvenir, or an almanac with prints by the painter Molina Campos…
- Football shirts in the colours of those used in the national football team or those of rugby teams.

• We love to give away objects with the typical '*fileteado porteño*'. It is the quintessential Buenos Aires style of painting that is recognised by its very particular letters, with romantic decorations and bright colours. Scattered throughout the city, this form of drawing and lettering is concentrated above all in the historic neighbourhoods.

• We also give away artistic products with the beautiful silkscreen of Argentina.

GIFTS FOR PUBLIC OFFICIALS
Can public officials receive gifts?
As a general principle, public officials may not receive gifts or donations, be they things, services or goods, for, or on the occasion of the performance of their duties.

EXCEPTIONS: GIFTS MAY BE ACCEPTED WHEN:
• Courtesy (expression of respect or affection due to an event in which it is usual to gift).
• Diplomatic custom (protocol acknowledgments from governments, international organisations or non-profit entities).

Can the gifts come from any source?
No. Regardless of whether it is courtesy or diplomatic custom, the gifts may never come from people who have any of these links with the body in which the official works:
• They are contractors.
• They are dealers or suppliers.
• Seek an agency decision.
• Who carry out activities regulated or controlled by the body.
• Who have interests that may be affected by a decision of the body.

In these cases, gifts must be rejected or returned, as appropriate.

What should be done with gifts that can be received?
They must be incorporated into the state assets up to a statutory value.

Regardless of their value, it is not necessary to incorporate groceries into the state's assets.

Chapter 5

Dining Etiquette

An excellent way to get to know Argentina is through its gastronomy, from the *'asado o barbacure'*, to the *'locro'* (typical stew) and other stews, from the *'centolla'* (crab) and the Patagonian Lamb, to the meat pie (pasty), or desserts: the flan with the sweet milk called *'dulce de leche'*, the *'alfajores'* and the sweet potatoes and cheese. Each place in the country has a traditional cuisine that is special and defines our culture and all of them together demonstrate the large variety of foods that can be eaten in our country.

The typical meals of Argentina are strengthened and popularised thanks to the strong influence of immigrants, especially Italian, Spanish, French, Greek, Arabs and Jews, added to the ancient traditions of the original peoples. Although these days Argentine gastronomy is recognised worldwide, largely because of the meat cuts, the truth is that the inhabitants of our soil did not always eat the same.

The recipes of the colonial era that do not change with fashions and are still consumed today are:
- *Locro*
- *Carbonada*
- *Pastel de papa*
- *Torta fritas*
- *Empanadas*

With the arrival of the C.20th and the different migratory currents, local gastronomy suffered a 180 degree turn. In a very short time, local recipes were enriched by those who brought the new goods from the ships: Italian and Spanish, mainly, and to a lesser extent, German and English.

ITALIAN INFLUENCE IN ARGENTINE CUISINE
Italians can boast of having revolutionised local gastronomy. Among the

most popular dishes of this cuisine that quickly began to be consumed also on the Rioplatese tables are:

- *Pizza:* Unlike the ones eaten in Europe, the pizzas in Argentina were always of greater thickness, a tradition that has remained up to the present day. In addition, the adaptations of this typical dish are not lacking. '*Fugazetta*' is a 100% local creation.
- *Pasta:* Another of the Italian specialties par excellence that the Argentines adopted was pasta. In addition to the 'tallarines' and 'gnocchi', 'ravioli' and other pasta parcel varieties also enjoyed great acceptance from the first moment.
- *Polenta:* This simple but substantial dish was part of the gastronomic legacy that northern Italians brought to our country.
- *Milanese:* A thin slice of veal, breaded and fried. At home, we eat it usually accompanied by a puree of potatoes and/or lettuce and tomato salad with a bit of onion (*Ensal Creaul*).

Restaurants add fries and one or two fried eggs and call it *Milanesa*: 'on horseback'. There is a variety of *Milanesa* that amuses Italian visitors, called the contradictory '*Milanesa Napolitana*', in which, added to the *Milanesa*, are cheese, tomato and oregano; this is then cooked for ten minutes in the oven.

- *Sweets:* In addition to the salty recipes, Italian cuisine also influenced the sweet part of our gastronomy. Ice cream and tiramisu, in addition to *sambayon*, are some of the delights for which we still should thank this immigrates current of the C.20th.

SPANISH INFLUENCE ON ARGENTINE CUISINE

Not only did the Italians leave their imprint on the River Plate area gastronomy, but the Spanish influence had also already been felt decades earlier. Before independence, some of the star dishes from this country were served on local tables. For example, rice, stews and the pot dishes (*puchero*).

In summary, with immigrants who arrived in the country in the C.20th, the Spanish influence in Argentine gastronomy deepened even more. The Argentine cuisine offers a complete variety of options. Depending on the province visited, the most popular dishes will be, although always delicious, very different and individual. If the gastronomic tour begins in the central area of the country (including, in addition to Buenos Aires, Córdoba, La Pampa, Santa Fé and Entre Ríos), a European influence in the cuisine must be particularly expected.

In addition to the contents mentioned above, the *Milanesas* and the famous local barbecue are some of the most popular options. '*Asado*' (Argentine meat) is the best and probably the favourite dish for foreigners who visit us. It constitutes the primary element of the diet of the Argentinians.

Those who have tested a juicy 'chorizo' know that this also is an unforgettable experience of pleasure. On the grill, the chorizos can be eaten in a sandwich with French bread; this is called *Choripan*. It is also very common to see a sweet blood sausage called *'morcilla a la vasca'* that includes nuts and raisins.

The *'hachuras'* are part of the menu: the liver and gizzard are dishes with extraordinary exquisiteness. The grills generally have a salad bar with varied types of vegetables and salads, which facilitates the coexistence between carnivores and vegetarians. Going up to the northern provinces, the gastronomic panorama is filled with new flavours. Among the delicacies that can be tested in this area of Argentina (which are prepared differently from those of the rest of the country) are the *'locro'* and the *'tamales'* (a mass of corn stuffed with meat or vegetables). In addition to its dream landscapes, Patagonia also has a thriving gastronomy that attracts both local and international palates. Lamb, spider crab and trout are three irresistible dishes, coupled with sausage, hams, salads, *longungans*, and cheeses.

In the provinces of La Rioja, Catamarca; olives and olive oil occur.

Argentine wines, especially the red (*Valy Malbec*), are among the best in the world, especially those of the Mendoza area where the best sparkling of the country also occurs.

The great diversity of grapes allows the growers to give flight to their creativity and achieve the best blends of all time. The most achieved types are Cabernet Sauvignon, Malbec and Malbec Cabernet Franc, although many also use pinches of Merlot and Petit Verdot. The wine production and export of that region constitutes one of the most important in South America.

Discerning travellers are quickly surprised by the number of flavours offered by our country, but the roasted meats are still the most popular dish with newcomers.

DINING ETIQUETTE

Most of the Etiquette rules that we follow in Argentina are those of the Western World. In the protocol area we have specific legislation and decrees to organise official events.

In diplomacy, we carry out action based on good diplomatic relationships and international communication.

In the informal sphere, we usually have some variations that characterise the etiquette and makes us unique. For example, in an informal meeting, we drink '*Mate*'. The etiquette indicates to serve the *Mate* in a round following the hands of a clock. The water with which is it served should not boil. It is drunk from a lightbulb-shaped vessel with a silver straw. Also, in informal settings, we usually get together to eat a barbecue ('*Asado*') and we enjoy sharing food with friends or family. It is generally outdoors.

Some customs for such occasions are:
- To be on time.
- To bring the host a gift.
- To bring a sweet cake to share with the '*mate*'.

These are habits that Argentines have to welcome friends and justify encounters.

We are proud of all this and we usually offer them to foreigners to make them feel at home.

Other rules of etiquette you need to know if you are invited to enjoy a dinner or lunch:

Table protocol posture at the table:
- Keep your back straight and place the feet together, not stretching or crossing the legs.
- Cutlery must ascend with the food to the mouth and not the other way around.
- Never place your elbows on the table.

- Avoid coughing, sneezing, sounding the nose, getting up, and answering/using the phone.
- Mobile phones will remain in silent mode in your pocket or wallet and you must not use it when sharing good moments with other people.
- We will not say 'good profit', '*bon appetit*', nor 'you can already start'. When the homeowner is served, takes their napkin and starts eating, the guests may start also, but not before.
- We will not say 'bless you' or 'good health' when someone sneezes.
- In the case of coughing, sneezing or yawning, it will suffice to cover the mouth with the inner part of the arm without needing to apologise.

Behaviour rules relevant to the table:
- The hosts will be the first to sit.
- The napkin is folded in two and is placed on the knees.
- Napkins may be used as many times as required and it is mandatory to use it before taking water or wine.
- When leaving the table, the napkin should be left on the right-hand side of the plate.
- Eating formally finishes when the hostess places her napkin on the right and clearly indicates to the guests where the coffee is being taken.
- If in a restaurant, we all wait for everyone to be served before we start eating.

Eating etiquette
- Break the bread with your hands, over the bread plate, rather than cut or bite it. Break off a small piece and eat it etcetera.
- The owner of the house will be attentive: if someone eats slowly, she will do the same to make everyone feel comfortable.
- Always aim to help fellow diners if they cannot reach something which is within your reach easily.
- If, during the meal, a lady should get up, the gentlemen will stand up too and again when she returns to the table.
- Eat slowly as it demonstrates education and elegance, in addition to aiding good digestion.
- Chew with your mouth closed, quietly.

- Liquids are silently taken.
- If you require the salt (for example), politely ask the diner who is closest to it to pass it to you. Never stretch over people to reach it.
- The salt and pepper are passed together.
- Do not reject a plate unless to observe any kind of diet or religious/ethical issue.
- Do not pour sauces onto your food; instead, place it on one side of the plate. However, you may pour liquid seasonings/gravy over the meat.
- When finished, place your cutlery in the form of a clock, five minutes to five, the knife with the edge in and on the right side. On the left side, the fork is placed. The tines can go up (English) or down (French).

Behaviours to avoid:
- Never say if you do not like the food.
- Do not put dirty cutlery on the table.
- Do not smoke.
- We will not talk to the service staff. The lady of the house will be attentive to all the details and ask for what we need.
- Do not speak whilst there is food in your mouth.
- We must not blow on hot drinks to cool them.
- A host should not try to find out why a guest does not eat a certain dish.

For toasts:
- Brief and emotive words.
- Guests will raise their glasses and listen in the attitude of silent participation.
- After the toast, all the glasses are raised to the height of the eyes and everyone drinks in unison for the expressed reason.

Who makes the toast or cheers:
- In a wedding: the godfather or father of the bride.
- At a business meal: the person who holds the highest charge.
- In a sports celebration: the president of the club.
- At a funeral: the organiser of the tribute.
- At a dinner: the toast occurs before dessert so that in between the meals you may digest different wines for each plate.

Chapter 6

Business Etiquette

Protocol and etiquette are important tools to achieve the prestige that companies seek. Every firm knows that having a good product is no longer enough and that the guidelines dictated by business protocol are increasingly important because they contribute to the corporate image and the company's positioning within the market. Etiquette is necessary because it helps to take care of the details in personal and corporate relationships.

Protocol and etiquette serve to achieve a good and harmonious coexistence in the workplace. It helps people understand the need to adapt and integrate whilst giving them the tools to do this by knowing the rules to follow and observing the correct treatment, both with superiors and colleagues.

In Argentina, things that seem unimportant are often left out, but those mistakes don't always hinder customer relationships later. I believe that many of the commercial agreements in Argentine companies are successful due to the personal communication capacity that characterises the company's human capital.

Soft skills and the use of emotional intelligence help the Argentine businessmen close business agreements.

The success of a company lies in its being different from the others, a differentiation that is achieved by establishing and maintaining good relationships and projecting a positive corporate image, which achieves the loyalty of customers.

CONVERSATIONS AND GREETINGS

Argentinians have mastered the art of conversation but get carried away by effusiveness in the workplace, and it is at that moment when physical contact occurs.

As for the formal handshake, the same thing happens. We know that we should not invade personal space and must avoid touching or patting the person we are greeting, and we make an effort to comply with this rule. In addition to not being correct, there are a considerable number of people from abroad who may feel annoyed by such behaviour. So, I always feel obliged to communicate and explain the friendly side of the Argentines.

A seasoned Argentine who knows how to be a very good host will welcome your company with open cordiality. They will take into account different customs so that everything is effective.

If an Argentine has to negotiate with foreigners who come to the country, they know how to act as hosts and are in charge of preparing, directing and managing the program of activities.

Argentine hosts will take care of even the smallest details so that guests feel at home. The most experienced entrepreneurs take care of everything, from arrival to departure:

Reception, luggage, security, transport, accommodation, visits, cocktails in the guest's honour, and any other type of activity.

Everything that surrounds a negotiation has to be properly studied also. That is why a good host will make sure that introductions, card exchanges, greetings or meals are optimal.

A good host will try to control the details of his clothing and, according to the culture that his guests belong to, has in mind the issue of the physical distances allowed between people. Although, we know that this is only fulfilled in formal settings.

In Argentina, it is understood that the one who begins the negotiation is the one who closes it. It is also known that an untimely or disproportionate gift can spoil the outcome of a negotiation. The most common business gifts are usually folk elements that represent us as a country.

Business lunches are frequent in the business world, which is why knowledge about table etiquette is increasingly in demand. During a negotiation in a restaurant, you do not usually approach the topic of interest at the beginning of the meeting. Only at the end of the main course is the topic of interest addressed.

Finally, I must add that physical image is very important, to complement good communication during negotiations. The names that are established and used to describe the 'dress code' often change according to the regions in South America. But even if they carry other names, Argentines will always try to fulfil them and dress appropriately on each occasion.

Chapter 7

Wedding Etiquette

The rules of etiquette at weddings have changed little in Argentina over the years. The traditions are still in force and although marriages are less and less frequent, when they are celebrated it is done with all the rites that this type of event requires.

WEDDING INVITATIONS
Traditionally, and depending on the formality of the celebration, they are sent by post or electronically. Invitees must always respond in a timely manner when the RSVP acronym exists.

DRESS CODE
Guests usually respect the code as indicated in the invitation. It differs a lot if the celebration is held in the day or night.

Etiquette dictates that it is a mistake to opt for a morning suit at an informal wedding, in the same way that it is a mistake to wear a normal suit in a formal ceremony. The morning suit is the most elegant garment for a wedding. By tradition, it was always used in morning ceremonies in some countries but now it is quite commonly also used in the afternoon. The same does not happen in Argentina, as the most used attire is the dark suit. The tuxedo is also in fashion. This marks the difference between what most people consider valid and what they should wear at a wedding according to the etiquette in Argentina.

As a rule for choosing the tone of the suit, the Argentine groom wears dark colours, where black, grey and navy blue dominate. The white suit is not common except for those weddings performed on the beach.

The use of a tie or bowtie is governed by the groom's style. In general, the Argentine groom is quite classic and he uses neutral colours for the tie/bowtie, with a white shirt. He always wears oxford type shoes.

It is classic to have a 'buttonhole' (a small bouquet of flowers in harmony with the bride's bouquet).

Weddings during the day have been frequent for several years. This greatly complicates the choice of clothing for guests and is a reason for constant consultation. The fear lies in not dressing appropriately, depending on whether the event is held in a field, for example, or in a more urban place. There are also doubts about the use of shoes with heels or the type of jewellery to wear.

The bride's dress:
If the couple are of the Catholic religion, low necklines are not allowed. That is why the wedding veil often helps to cover certain parts of the body.

The styles of dresses are very varied, and two are often required, one for the more modest church and another for the party (something sexier and more comfortable).

The Argentine bride wears makeup of a very natural style.

The jewellery is minimal and her entire look is extremely fine and delicate.

Civil weddings:
In Argentina, these events are usually very simple and when they take place in the morning everything is quite natural. The couple's closest family and friends attend. It is commonly performed at the location of the civil registry closest to the domicile of either the bride or groom.

ETIQUETTE IN THE CHURCH
Entrance:
Guests arrive at the church about fifteen minutes before the ceremony start time.

The bride's relatives are located on the left side and those of the groom on the right.

The first two rows are reserved for the most direct relatives.

The groom enters giving the godmother his right arm and waits by the altar for the arrival of the bride. The 'godmother' title is given to the groom's mother.

The bride enters holding her father's right arm (the title 'godfather' is given to the bride's father), with the procession of page boys and young ladies of honour in front of her. In Argentina, it is not customary to have bridesmaids.

The location scheme in front of the altar is: godfather/father of the bride, groom and godmother/mother of the groom.

Departure from the Church:
The bride and groom are the first to leave. The groom gives his right arm to the bride. This is followed by the godfather and godmother, and then the father of the groom with the mother of the bride. Then, and finally, the procession of pages and young ladies.

It is traditional to throw rice and rose petals at the newlyweds as a symbol of fertility, and heralding the arrival of many children.

RECEPTION PARTY
The best man and the bride usually open the dance, followed by the godmother and the groom, and finally the bride and groom. When the newlyweds finish their dance, all the guests must join in to celebrate.

It is common for children of families to be included in the parties.

Something that characterises Argentine weddings is the development of the party. Dinner is interrupted several times because the music changes rhythm and thus you are invited to dance between the different courses on the menu. This form of celebration is a deeply rooted custom in Argentina, as is the dance in the style of a Carioca carnival, this moment being the most fun of the night.

The wedding cake is cut by the bride and groom and then the bride throws the bouquet of flowers for the single ladies.

Finally, the guests are treated to a shared breakfast at the end of the wedding, in the early morning.

WEDDING GIFTS
The bride and groom have a wedding list which they send out with the invitation. Currently, it is most common to send money to a bank account number provided by the couple if they do not have a gift list.

Much of what is described in this chapter refers to Catholic ceremonies, since they are the majority in our population. But there are other celebrations, such as those governed by the Jewish or Evangelical religions, with various rituals and customs.

Australia
By Victoria Thomas

Chapter 1

Cultural Symbols

The lucky country, indeed!

I am immensely proud to be an Australian. Although I would be completely comfortable accepting an invitation from the Queen of England to join her for tea at Buckingham Palace, I am even more at home sitting on the lawn of the local sporting ground with a group of fellow Aussies cheering on our national side to win, lose or draw, eating a meat pie, sipping on sparkling wine (as I'm one of few who are not fond of beer), and having as many laughs as we can manage.

Being Australian is to be egalitarian, irreverent, multicultural, humble, authentic, laid-back, progressive and loyal to our team of fellow Australian citizens and residents. Our progressive attitude is reflected in our national symbols. The kangaroo and emu were chosen as unique and native to Australia and because they move forward.

We are fortunate enough to have largely been accepted by the true inhabitants of the sixth largest country in the world, being the oldest surviving civilisation on earth. Aboriginal and Torres Strait Islanders have inhabited the continent for 60,000 years, but unfortunately, were brutally and fatally forced to have us share in the richness of this extraordinary land. There are now 25,000,000 people sharing the wealth of one of the most prosperous nations on earth.

We are envied by many for our high standard of living, warm climate, abundance of natural resources, democratic political system, relaxed can-do attitude, diversity of cultures, and wealth of opportunities and experiences on offer.

The following are some of the key elements required to understand Australian culture.

We are:

EGALITARIAN

Australia is an egalitarian society that believes in a 'fair go' for all. We tend to be non-judgmental, open-minded forward thinkers who promote equal opportunities for all. We would be uncomfortable asking anyone to do anything we were unwilling to do ourselves. We have publicly funded health and education systems and were the second country in the world to allow women to vote. Recently, 62% of the population voted for gay marriage equality, regardless of their religious affiliations. This attitude stems primarily from our colonial heritage, whereby convicts were eventually able to take advantage of the opportunities to thrive and prosper in a developing nation.

MULTICULTURAL

We are a nation of diversity, which we celebrate and consider a great strength. In addition to the native Australians and British penal settlers, post-World War II saw many emigrates from Europe to take advantage of growth opportunities. 50% of our population were born overseas or have a parent born overseas. There are over 200 languages and dialects spoken. A large percentage of residents now emigrate from Asia, Africa and America. With so many diverse cultures, we benefit from exposure to a variety of opinions and attitudes, which stimulates healthy debate and fosters a progressive societal framework. We participate in a vast array of cultural events, and benefit from being able to indulge in eating numerous delicious international cuisines each day of the week. Australia is a foodie's paradise. We will eat anything from prawns to pies to *pide* to pasta to *pho*. Although we sell our national symbol, the kangaroo, for consumption at our local supermarkets, there is no traditional Australian cuisine. Absolutely anything goes. Our inquisitive natures and taste buds have constant sources of stimulation.

MATES
We tend to have a 'team' mentality and are loyal and giving to our friends. There is a strong comradery and sense of belonging. We rely on our mates to help in hard times, rather than always relying on family. We band together and drop everything to help friends in need. In saying that, we would be too uncomfortable to ask others to do things for us, that we would not be prepared to do for ourselves. We always rally to support the underdogs.

IRREVERENT
Australians tend not to take themselves too seriously. Laughter is a priority. We will take any opportunity to make fun of ourselves and others, with self-deprecation being a common practice. Offence is not intended. Simply laugh along, tease yourself and others, and you will feel comfortable and be accepted. I certainly need to be mindful of this natural instinct when travelling to other countries, as I am often misunderstood.

INFORMAL
We have a relaxed and casual attitude towards life, which has primarily been stimulated by our adventurous spirit, warm climate, beach culture (80% of us live within 100 kilometres of the coast), love of the outdoors and love of laughter.

Generally speaking, we tend to be quite lazy with our speech, taking any opportunity to abbreviate as many words as possible. Example: afternoon has become '*arvo*', and even the word 'Australian' has become '*Strayan*' (which drives me insane). Aussie 'slang' has become another language, which foreigners find difficult to understand, but rest assured, I will include an abbreviated reference guide. We also casualise peoples' names almost immediately, which is a sign of acceptance. I use the word casualise, as they are not always abbreviations. Often the name will be longer than the original. For instance, my name, Victoria, is too formal and has too many syllables for Australians to bother with. I often have to go by Tory instead, which is then turned into 'Torza', and often even 'Torzinator', which is more a reflection of my personality. David becomes 'Davo', and Sharon, 'Shazza'.

It is often difficult to distinguish those that are affluent from those that live comfortably, as the accent doesn't vary greatly, and nor does the dress sense. Australians tend not to 'overdress' and wear casual attire whenever possible (as a fashion stylist, I'm certainly not one of them). Shorts, a T-shirt and thongs/flip-flops are the favoured 'uniform'. Australians tend to be more casual and relaxed to suit the climate.

Sport-Obsessed

we are fiercely competitive and love to support an underdog to victory. Although having a small population for our land size, we are proud to be a breeding ground to many world champions. We will watch and gamble on almost any sport, even those we have created for our own amusement, such as cane toad racing (just another excuse to gamble and drink). Our sporting culture is a rich one, with many major international sporting events being held here, such as the Australian open tennis tournament, F1 motor racing, cricket, golf, surfing, sailing etcetera. We have four codes of football, inclusive of soccer. Even the annual Melbourne Cup horse racing event is a public holiday in the host state. All Australians stop work to watch this particular race as it is a time-honoured tradition to do so. There are countless numbers of sports Australians will support and participate in. We are fiercely loyal to our chosen team, and even if we aren't interested in a particular sport, we will still pack ourselves into the local pub to cheer Australia to victory—any excuse to drink beer together at the local pub will do.

Chapter 2

Meeting, Greeting, Posture and Body Language

SOCIAL

It is not always typical to shake hands when being introduced in social situations, which can be confusing. Always take the lead of the person you are being introduced to. We prefer a firm grip and eye contact for a few seconds to indicate sincerity, trustworthiness and confidence. Using eye contact makes you approachable, but ensure you break eye contact intermittently, as it can be perceived as staring, which is too intense and can cause discomfort and offence. Women don't often shake hands with one another upon being introduced. It is not frowned upon but is not typical. When in doubt, follow the lead of the local. When greeting those you have met previously, women tend to be more affectionate. They will often hug and 'kiss' (by connecting right cheeks) to show enthusiasm. Male friends may hug, back slap or just nod an acknowledgement. There are no definitive rules, which can be challenging and awkward, unfortunately. Offence is rarely taken for any greeting you choose to give, as long as it is warm and sincere.

In social situations, we use first names only to introduce one another, as it creates a sense of equality. We do not appreciate people mentioning personal, professional or academic titles as it is considered elitist and alienating. We prefer to discover those details organically over time. For instance, it is typical for a CEO to share a beer with a cleaner without judgement. I adore this characteristic of our culture.

When greeting an Australian, do not say 'G'Day' or 'G'Day (Good Day) mate', as not only is it rarely used, but is reserved for Australians only. You will be perceived as being overly familiar and as trying too hard to be accepted. Say, "Hello, how are you?" instead. Also note that the response should always be, "Well, thank you. How are you?" As it is meant as a polite greeting, rather than an invitation to discuss intimate details of your life.

BUSINESS

Both first names and surnames are used in a business greeting. We tend not to use titles, and only mention positions if necessary. Business cards can be exchanged upon introduction or at meeting close, although there is no need to be offended if one is not handed to you. Often people don't have one on hand in this contemporary digital age.

PERSONAL SPACE

Australians are fortunate to live within a huge continent with a relatively small population of twenty-five million people. As such, we value our space, and like to keep at least an arm's length between ourselves and others. If you stand too close to another person, you will often notice them take a step back to create a comfortable distance. It is not meant to offend, but purely a habit created by our luxury of space. Also try to leave spare seats in between yourself and strangers when in public spaces whenever possible. If you need to invade someone's personal space, always say 'excuse me' to be polite.

Be mindful not to block pathways or public areas. Use your common sense when forming queues to create a clearway for pedestrians. Forming a queue against a wall is preferable. We become annoyed when people gather in large groups on pathways which make it difficult for others to pass. It is disrespectful not to consider others. Try not to be self-absorbed in public especially. We prefer to always consider the rights and needs of others. If you have been blocking access, be sure to excuse yourself.

We stand to the left in Australia. When walking up staircases, do so on the left-hand side. Stand on the left-hand side of an escalator and overtake others by walking up the right-hand side. Ensure you allow people to exit elevators, buildings and public transport before you enter. Stand to the side to create a clearway. We become extremely annoyed if you don't adhere to this policy.

It is polite to hold doors open for people if they are only a few paces behind, although we will wait for an extended period for those who are carrying goods or for the elderly.

It is rare that we touch each other while communicating, although occasionally we will touch each other softly on the upper arm when trying to express genuine interest and engagement. Men never touch women unless they have been invited to do so. Never touch the arm of a man or woman or wink at them if their partner is present. Although it is purely a friendly gesture, this would be considered overstepping the boundary and could cause unnecessary friction.

HAND SIGNALS

The 'V' sign (index and middle finger with palm inward) is vulgar and meant to offend. On the other hand, the thumbs up is a positive gesture that means 'well done' or that you approve. People often point with their index fingers when expressing aggression and dominance which is best to avoid.

SERVICE

If you require attention in a restaurant, catch the eye of the waiter and raise your hand shoulder-high to beckon them over to the table. Never whistle, click your fingers or yell at service staff. It is considered the height of rudeness. Also be mindful to say please, thank you and excuse me when interacting with service professionals. Look them in the eye when speaking to them, as we prefer to treat each other as equals rather than servants.

When standing at a bar to order a drink or at a cafe to order coffee etcetera make sure you are mindful of the people who were waiting before you. If a bartender or barista has inadvertently overlooked the next person waiting, ensure they are served before you.

When waiting in any queue for service, never cut in front of others.

Ask where the end of the line is and join. Do not ever try to push ahead. Australians are very direct and will not hesitate to make you feel uncomfortable for trying to prioritise yourself over others. If it is an urgent situation, politely ask those in line if you can move ahead; otherwise, wait your turn.

Driving
Australians like to be acknowledged with a raised hand if they let you merge into traffic ahead of them. If they are doing you a favour, they appreciate simple acknowledgement for doing so.

Hygiene
The majority of Australians are very conscious of hygiene standards. Never clear your throat in public. Cough into your elbow and use a disposable tissue to sneeze or blow your nose. It is best to try to find privacy to do so when possible; otherwise, turn your head away from others. When yawning, cover your mouth. No one wishes to see your internal organs!

Public Displays of Affection
Passionate kissing in public is frowned upon. We prefer people exchange passion in private to avoid the discomfort of others. Holding hands is acceptable, as is kissing on cheeks or closed lips.

Chapter 3

Conversation Dos and Don'ts

As a general rule we are quite straight forward and uncomplicated people who are not easily offended. There are few conversational rules to consider as a result. As long as your intentions are good, most faux pas will be forgiven. If you have caused offence, just apologise and mention that you are still learning to grasp the cultural differences.

As a visitor, it can be considered a little patronising to use the words 'G'Day' and 'mate' as we are conscious of the stereotype. These words are rarely used by women, but you will often hear men use them in informal settings to create a relaxed atmosphere and a sense of familiarity with one another. Simply saying 'hello' and introducing yourself by using your first name only is preferred.

As with most cultures, meeting someone for the first time and discussing race, religion, politics and sex is unadvisable. It is always best to leave often controversial, intimate and potentially intense discussions for those you know well, who are less likely to pass judgement and more likely to respect your opinion. It is preferable to choose safe topics such as current events, sport, weather etcetera and allow the conversation to flow naturally from there. Undoubtedly the locals will ask where you are from, not only as a polite and easy conversation starter, but also out of genuine interest. We are curious people.

When conversing in social settings, ensure you listen for the same amount of time as you speak. It is important to show interest in others, as a courtesy if nothing else. You will become unpopular quickly if you choose to dominate the conversation and interrupt constantly. In saying that, use your judgement. It is important to be able to contribute to each discussion point, if you so desire, but without cutting someone off in order to do so.

We are a people who appreciate humility. Compliments are one of the complicated grey areas. I usually try to read the situation before responding.

In some cases, I will thank the other party for paying a compliment and return the sentiment in kind. On other occasions, it is better to make a self-deprecating remark to downplay the compliment and be seen as humble. My rule of thumb is, if I am in a group, I will play the compliment down, but if one on one, I will accept the compliment.

Australians are fiercely competitive and patriotic, which is especially prevalent within our international sporting rivalries. A great way to bond with an Australian is by watching competitive sport at a local pub. We welcome the rivalry and friendly taunts back and forth to create a competitive atmosphere, and a lot of laughs. If you keep your comments fair and light-hearted you will be welcomed no matter which team you support. If your comments come across as mean-spirited, you will be ostracised and become uncomfortable. I often take the opportunity to support the underdog, just to create an amusing rivalry, whether I'm genuinely interested or not. It's all part of the fun. We also often use the opportunity to gamble to increase the stakes and the level of interest. Money is not always at stake; often you will be required to perform a task for the winners' amusement.

On a more sensitive note, the colonisation of Australia and the plight of the Aboriginal and Torres Strait Islander people as a result, is a topic that should be treated with great care. If you wish to ask a member of the Torres Strait Islander or Aboriginal community to share their experience, just be mindful that it is a sensitive topic and can cause discomfort amongst a group, as we do not feel we ever have or will be able to compensate for the damage caused by past atrocities. It may be preferable to have your questions answered in private.

In business, Australians prefer a direct, no-nonsense approach. We do not appreciate playing games, as it is a waste of valuable time and energy. We respect honest reliable exchanges of information and choose to do business with those we can trust. Long winded, fanciful sales pitches tend to irritate us.

All in all, just feel free to be yourself. We acknowledge and embrace our imperfections and are an easy-going people. If you have good intentions, want to relax and have a good time, Australia is the perfect place for you to spend time.

Chapter 4

Gift Giving

Australians, generally speaking, are humble and modest people. They do not like to focus too much attention on themselves but enjoy partaking in social gatherings and celebrations; any excuse will do! That being the case, the focus is the celebration itself and to create lasting memories with friends and loved ones, rather than the need to be 'honoured' by the exchange of material gifts. In saying that, milestone lifetime celebrations for immediate family and close friends are considered special and worthy of gift giving. We tend not to focus on the value of the gift, but more the depth of thought that has been given to the choice of gift for the recipient. It is more important that it reflects the unique individual the gift is for. For this reason, it is advisable to ask close friends and family of the recipient for gift suggestions when in doubt.

When travelling abroad, it is wise to carry a number of small gifts to pass on to those who have hosted you over the course of your travels. Items that are unique and native to your homeland leave a lasting impression and help the hosts recall the time they shared with you.

Before purchasing gifts, always try make yourself aware of the recipient's cultural background, religion, and social and moral attitudes to help guide you in choosing an ideal gift. If you do not know the recipient well, try to seek advice from someone who does.

CONSIDERATIONS FOR SPECIFIC OCCASIONS

CHRISTMAS
One custom that is often adopted by both large families and professional workplaces is the '*Kris Kringle*' gift exchange. Many of us are mindful of the financial burden the Christmas holiday season can bring and adopt the *Kris Kringle* gift exchange. This is a tradition whereby the name of each member of the family or group are placed in a bowl and one name drawn

by each person. You are responsible for choosing a thoughtful gift for that specific individual only.

As Christmas falls within our summer season, we often eat outdoors and enjoy a seafood feast, usually for lunch. If you are invited to a Christmas lunch gathering, bringing a gourmet treat which is unique to your homeland would be a thoughtful gesture. Alternatively, there are very few Australians who don't appreciate alcohol as a gift to enjoy together over the course of the day.

Weddings
If you have been invited to share in such a momentous occasion, it is polite to purchase a gift, regardless of whether you are able or unable to attend.

It is common for a gift registry to be provided to simplify the decision. If not, it is often advisable to ask a close friend or family member of the bride and groom for suggestions. Many cultures prefer cash to be gifted, but you will be made aware of that.

Large Group Gatherings
Australians love to socialise frequently, and as we have a more informal and relaxed culture, often the gatherings will be hosted at a family home. In many cases, the host is providing a gathering place more so than catering. If the invitation doesn't specify what food and/or beverages to bring with you, always ask. Even if the host declines, it is polite to bring alcoholic beverages to share with the guests. Even if either you or the host do not drink alcohol, it will still be considered a thoughtful contribution.

Celebratory Events
Celebrations such as birthdays, anniversaries and christenings etcetera where you are an invited guest, are of course, fully funded by the host. You are expected to bring a gift to mark the importance of the occasion and honour the guest.

Lunch Or Dinner Invitation
If you have been invited to a family home for lunch or dinner, it is always polite to bring a gift as a token of gratitude for the effort that has been made to host you and welcome you into their home. A gourmet delicacy or craft or coffee table picture book from your homeland, a good bottle of wine, a scented candle or bunch of flowers (preferably in a vase or pot) would be

considered thoughtful gifts. Be mindful that you should never expect the gift you take to be shared with you; it is a gift after all.

Overnight Home Stays

If you have been welcomed to stay overnight in a family home or holiday home, it is customary to treat the hosts to lunch or dinner at a local restaurant as a token of appreciation. Otherwise, a gift basket with gourmet treats or a pamper package with bath salts, scented candles etcetera should be well received. A gift that will be useful to the hosts is also a good choice. In theory, anything that shows gratitude will be appreciated.

Business

Generally speaking, gifting is not part of Australian business culture, but can be used to promote goodwill and show gratitude. It is common practice to purchase a gift for a business associate or team that have achieved excellent results as recognition and a sign of appreciation. Christmas gifts are also given as part of an annual bonus or as a thank you for their contribution over the course of the year. Care needs to be taken to never give a gift to a potential client as that can be construed as a bribe. It is in poor taste to gift people with items with your corporate logo attached (they are not being paid to promote your business), except of course if they are useful at the time. Example: a cap and towel for a sporting day, a golf umbrella at a golf day and a pen etcetera at a business meeting.

Gift Giving

Unless at a large celebration such as a wedding where you will be expected to leave your gift in a designated spot, hand the gift directly to the recipient. They may be able to open the gift in front of you, but if there is a crowd, they may wait until they can open the gift in a more private setting, so don't be offended if this is the case.

Receiving Gifts

Try to open the gift in the presence of the person who chose it for you, although avoiding doing so in front of a crowd as it 'cheapens' the moment. They have taken time and effort to select a gift especially for you and would appreciate a positive response. Always look the gift giver in the eye and give a warm smile, even if you must feign sincerity. Occasionally you will exchange gifts at a gift opening ceremony, but fortunately this practice is losing favour as it is viewed as 'tacky'.

Obviously, you will always thank the gift giver verbally at the time it is received, but ensure you send a message the following day thanking them in writing. The rule of thumb is to send a handwritten 'thank you' note if you sent a handwritten invitation. Otherwise, an email or SMS to thank them is acceptable. In saying that, handwritten 'thank you' notes are rare, unfortunately, and considered special.

If you receive a gift in the mail or by courier, it is courteous to advise the gift giver as soon as you have received it. It saves them having to track and trace deliveries.

GIFT PACKAGING
It is thoughtful to place extra care and attention to the packaging of a gift but be mindful of managing expectations. If the gift wrapping is extravagant, the expectation will be that the contents are too. Try to match the wrapping to the contents to avoid potential disappointment.

Chapter 5

Dining Etiquette

Australia is renowned for its cultural diversity, and as such, offers a vast array of international dishes to savour as part of our regular diet. We tend to eat a different style of cuisine each day, from Italian to Vietnamese and Lebanese to Japanese to Indian; we are spoilt for choice and are used to stimulating our tastebuds with different sensations regularly.

It is difficult to define a uniquely Australian dish. As we are fortunate to be surrounded by sea, seafood is favoured by many, as it is fresh, of high quality, and relatively inexpensive. As we are a relaxed culture, so too are many of our dining preferences. We enjoy a casual barbecue with meat and seafood, Sunday brunch at our local cafe with smashed avocado (*avo*), feta, tomato and rocket on sourdough with a squeeze of lemon juice (a breakfast staple), a meat pie or sausage roll at a sporting event, or a chicken parmigiana (*Parmi*), which is crumbed fried chicken breast topped with tomato sauce and melted cheese, at our local pub. Don't let that fool you; we are a nation of 'foodies' and have an enviable international reputation for our high standard of cuisine. Although we do have a number of excellent fine dining restaurants which are normally reserved for special occasions, we have reduced the number over recent years, as Australians tend to prefer a more relaxed style of dining, which is indicative of our culture. Our local chefs create innovative and sophisticated dishes which often offer a fusion of international flavours. Tasting plates are popular in most restaurants as we enjoy trying as many different flavours as possible and sharing with friends.

As we enjoy warm temperatures for the most part, we dine outdoors regularly. Breakfast is usually consumed between six a.m. and nine a.m. lunch between twelve p.m. and three p.m. and dinner between six p.m. and nine p.m. As the most popular dinner reservation time is six-thirty p.m. (to coincide with the end of the working day), it is wise to reserve a table later, if possible, to ensure the service is more attentive and the atmosphere more relaxed.

As for table manners, all of the standard Western dining etiquette rules apply. When in doubt, follow the lead of the locals, although it would be unusual for foreigners to be judged harshly in a social setting if they are relaxed and being true to themselves. We tend not to be judgmental in that regard. In saying that, it is important to be aware of formal Western dining etiquette, and apply the rules whenever possible. I've never known anyone to be criticised for using impeccable manners. It will be noticed, although not mentioned, and you will be held in high esteem. Some of the most important rules to note include:

INVITATIONS AND THANK YOU

Most invitations are sent by SMS, email or through social media posts in this technological age. More formal occasions may warrant a handwritten or printed invitation. As it seems to be a dying art, it is worth adopting, to add instant impact and noteworthiness to your event. Always respect the host by responding to the RSVP on the specified date to allow them to plan and budget accurately and effectively. It is polite to not only thank the host in person before leaving the event, but to write a 'thank you' note within twenty-four hours post event, in the same form the invitation was received.

ARRIVAL TIME

Avoid arriving early. When attending a home-based dinner party or event, arriving ten minutes after the specified time is often appreciated to allow the hosts to collect themselves, but no more than twenty minutes, as it is disrespectful to interfere with the host's cooking schedule. When dining at a restaurant, if you arrive early, try to take a seat at the bar until the host arrives to allow them to be escorted ahead of you to the table, as a courtesy.

DRESS CODES

Usually, the invitation will note the appropriate dress code. If in doubt, online research is worthwhile. You can research the image gallery of the venue and get a sense of the standard of formality, or research suggestions on how to dress appropriately for the event type. The images posted of the previous years' event are a perfect guide. It is wise to place some accessories in your handbag for an instant outfit upgrade in case you feel underdressed.

SEATING

At a restaurant, allow the host to choose their seat and sit first. If at a dinner party, if there isn't a place card, ask the host where they would like you to be seated. Always leave the head of the table free for the host. Be aware if a waiter or gentlemen is wanting to pull the chair out and seat you; it is polite of them to do so and should be encouraged. In my opinion, there is no need for chivalry to die. They are aware you know how to seat yourself but are choosing to be courteous. I have no idea why that gesture needs to be eradicated (just my opinion).

Napkin

The napkin should be placed in your lap once you are seated. Be mindful that in more formal restaurants waiters may wish to place the napkin in your lap. When leaving your seat, place the napkin in your seat. Often waiters will fold the napkin and replace it on the table. Once you have finished your meal, fold the napkin and place it to the right of your plate.

Ordering

It is advisable to discuss how many courses you would like to eat before perusing the menu. If you aren't terribly hungry, but want the other guests to enjoy extra courses, you can recommend a selection of appetisers to share. This way you can eat a small amount to be polite without overindulging.

When to Commence Eating

Ensure you wait until each guest has their meal placed in front of them and for the host to lift their silverware before you do. It's best not to continue eating once the other guests have completed their meal. It is preferable to leave that course and move on. Place your knife and fork together in the middle of the plate facing up to indicate you have finished the course.

Ordering Wine

Australians are one of the biggest consumers of wine per capita and have a reputation for producing excellent wine. In saying that, we do not appreciate obnoxious wine snobs. We prefer people to be more subtle when sharing knowledge. Most of the wine produced in Australia is bottled with a screw top cap. As such, the wine will not be corked and is therefore unnecessary to taste. Many of us find it pretentious. If there is a cork, please do taste the wine, although be aware if you are at a restaurant with an in-house sommelier, they always taste the wine prior to serving to approve the quality, and it will be unnecessary for you to do so as well. You are unable to return the wine if you made a choice that does not suit your taste. If there are two people dining, it is advisable to order wine by the glass to allow you to enjoy a predinner cocktail or glass of champagne before moving on to wines that enhance the flavour of the dishes you have ordered. If in doubt, ask the sommelier for advice. If there is a group of diners, and you are ordering bottles, ensure each guest has an opportunity to discuss their preference to find a balance to suit as many palettes as possible.

THE BILL AND TIPPING

It is advisable to discuss splitting of the bill beforehand to avoid awkward moments. Australian restaurants normally use a wireless card machine that is brought to the table for processing transactions and has a function to split the bill equally between members of the group, including the nominated tip. It is convenient, but not discreet unfortunately. It's a good idea to have cash on hand just in case. 10% is the standard amount to leave as a tip, although it is not expected in Australia. Staff are paid well and do not rely on customers to supplement their wage. However, it is polite to leave a token if you have appreciated the level of service and hospitality.

ICONIC AUSTRALIAN FOOD

Although we have a wide array of gastronomic delights on offer, Australia is known for many iconic snack foods that may make their way into your luggage to take home with you. Some of these include:

Vegemite:
An unusual substance made from yeast and vegetable extract. It is a thick, salty dark-brown paste which most Australians are raised with, usually as a breakfast staple. We smear a layer on toast over butter, or in addition to avocado or cheese. It is definitely an acquired taste, but most Australians have a jar in their kitchen pantry. Be warned, we do love to have international visitors taste it and watch them wince. It amuses us.

Tim Tams:
A chocolate malted biscuit with a light chocolate filling. It is now produced in many different flavours and is another Australian staple.

Meat Pie:
Rather than pies made with sweet fillings that Americans tend to favour, we prefer savoury fillings. Mincemeat with a unique gravy encased in pastry is the original version, but we also enjoy steak pies with many additions such as mushroom, onion and bacon. Topping it with tomato sauce is standard. Meat pies are delicious and are a lunchtime favourite.

Pavlova:
This is a desert made of meringue topped with fruit and cream. It was created to celebrate the tour by prima ballerina, Anna Pavlova in 1920.

Lamingtons:
Another desert made of sponge, coated in chocolate and desiccated coconut, sometimes filled with jam and cream. Delicious!

Anzac Biscuits:
A biscuit made with oats, caster sugar, treacle and flour. It was created during wartime to send to soldiers as the ingredients were readily available and able to be preserved for long periods. ANZAC stands for Australia and New Zealand Army Corps.

Barramundi:
This is a popular fish similar to seabass that should be chosen when ordering fish and chips to eat by the beach.

Kangaroo:
It is a richly flavoured game meat that is found in all supermarket meat departments. It should be tried at least once on your visit.

GENERAL ADVICE
Don'ts:
    Do not chew with your mouth open.
    Do not speak while eating.
    Do not discuss controversial topics (unless you know the guests well).
    Turn your phone on silent and do not place it on the table. (It is best not to refer to it at all. If you are expecting an urgent call, notify the guests when you arrive, and excuse yourself from the table to take the call).

Do not ask to take leftovers with you.

Do not announce you are leaving the table to use the restroom. Simply excuse yourself.

Do not ask why someone is leaving the table.

Do not put your elbows on the table. Keep your hands in your lap when not eating.

Do not hunch over. Be mindful of your posture and sit with a straight back.

Do not apply makeup at the table. Go to the restroom. Blot lipstick before entering the venue to limit the amount of residue left on the glass.

Chapter 6

Business Etiquette

In keeping with our laid-back attitude and egalitarianism, it is important to conduct business in Australia with a direct, honest, and modest approach. Australians will be straightforward and to the point, so you will know exactly what they require and where you stand.

GREETINGS
We prefer informal greetings and will use first names only. You may introduce someone with their full name, but the first name will almost always be used. Do not introduce yourself or others with their business title as it is considered unnecessary and obnoxious. Business cards can be exchanged during introductions without formality.

We appreciate personal space, so try to keep at arms' length. Maintain eye contact to show respect and engagement and use a firm handshake.

Be punctual. Arriving five minutes early is advisable, but never be late. Respect that time is valuable.

ATTITUDES
Although we have a relaxed approach, rest assured we take business seriously. Use common sense and be clear, concise and direct, using facts and figures to support your position. Do not say more than is necessary to express your point as it wastes valuable time. We are more interested in your experience, results and reliability. Although we are diplomatic and polite, we will still be honest and straightforward.

Australians will be modest and humble and normally downplay their success. We believe results to speak for themselves and don't appreciate grandstanding. Having an inflated ego will be detrimental. By the same token, using a position of power to control a meeting is not appreciated. If you have been invited to attend a meeting, it is expected that your opinion and contribution is of value and deserves to be heard. Be mindful that this collaborative approach can slow down decision making, as many people will be included in the process.

We enjoy using humour whenever possible to lighten the mood of negotiations and bring pleasure to our relationships. Healthy debate is encouraged, and you will often find Australians making provocative comments to ignite them. You will gain instant respect if you respond with humour.

State the true value of your products and services as we do not wish to engage in haggling. Do not use aggressive sales techniques or attempt to mislead us with an emotional narrative. It is best to aim for a fair and equitable outcome for both parties to secure a deal. Greed will be frowned upon.

Australians value reliability and trustworthiness. If you do not follow through on promises made, it is unlikely that you will be able to maintain the relationship.

Dress Code

Standard business dress code normally applies. Always wear a quality tailored suit regardless of your gender. It indicates professionalism and respect for both yourself and others. Men should wear a tie for formal meetings. You can always remove it if appropriate to do so. With our warm temperatures and relaxed lifestyle, you will often find men in corporate dress without a tie, and jackets removed after introductions. Research the business before arriving to get a sense of the corporate culture. Image galleries and social pages are a valuable resource.

Social Meetings

If you are the person selling a product or service, put your best foot forward by meeting your client at a well-respected restaurant. As you are the person extending the business invitation, you are expected to pay, although this differs for outings with friends, as you will normally split the bill. Western table manners are used, so please refer to the dining etiquette chapter for advice.

If you are invited to a social gathering at a pub, you will be expected to buy a 'round' of drinks for the group. Each person within the group will take a turn to do so. If you don't partake in this ritual, you will lose respect. Don't be offended by any 'colourful' language that may be used throughout the conversation. It is common for Australians to do so, but rest assured no offense is intended.

Initial conversation should be kept light and social to build rapport. Don't discuss business immediately unless required by your guest. Sport and current events are good conversation starters so ensure you do a little research beforehand to help the conversation flow. When in doubt, ask questions. It allows the guest to steer the conversation and focus your attention on them while learning something about our culture.

Always ensure your phone is switched to silent and is not on the table. If you are expecting an urgent call, announce it at the commencement of your meeting and excuse yourself from the table to take the call.

Gift Giving
It is imperative that gifts not be construed as a bribe. Ensure your gift is of low monetary value. Something to reflect your own culture is advisable. It is even better to give a gift to celebrate the closure of a deal rather than an attempt to secure one. If you do wish to present a gift to government employees, declare it to the human resources or finance department before doing so.

Thank Yous
Remember to send a 'thank you' email or SMS within twenty-four hours of your meeting as a courtesy and sign of professionalism.

Business Hours
Standard business hours are considered to be between nine a.m. and five p.m. Monday to Friday. Keep in mind that business slows over the summer holiday period between mid-December and mid-January, so it's best to schedule outside of this period.

Chapter 7

Wedding Etiquette

Australian weddings do not adhere to any culturally specific traditions. Western traditions are followed for the most part, although we tend to tailor weddings to express the uniqueness of each partnership, even more so now that Australia has legalised same sex marriages.

The current trend is to marry in your thirties and upwards rather than in your twenties, as in decades past. As such, both the bride and groom have their own careers and incomes and have normally lived together for a period before choosing to formalise their partnership with a marriage licence. Many archaic traditions have been dispensed with for this reason, such as the brides' father 'giving her away'; therefore, it is not expected that the brides' parents pay for the wedding expenses. The cost is often split between the bride and groom and both families, although many couples choose to bear all expenses themselves to give them complete control of all decisions pertaining to their celebration. A bride can choose to walk down the aisle with her father, alone, or with a person who has a positive impact on her life. There is now freedom of expression in all regards. Most social traditions have been dispensed with.

There seems to be an even number of Australians who choose to elope, have small intimate weddings with close family and friends, and those who choose to have extravagant and expensive celebrations with large numbers of guests. The impact of social media has seen a rise in the average cost of an Australian wedding to approximately AUD $60,000. Brides have more exposure through social media to examples of wedding celebrations across the globe which seems to have created a spirit of competition amongst many. Great importance is placed on being able to post notable wedding 'events', which often comes at great expense.

Australian weddings take many forms, from formal black-tie events to small family gatherings at home, and destination weddings across the globe, to intimate gatherings on a local beach or in a garden. Almost nothing would seem unusual, as the occasion is an expression of the lives and interests of the bride and groom.

As we have such a culturally diverse population, many couples host weddings to celebrate their cultural heritage, with some even having two ceremonies; one to reflect their Australian culture and the other their genetic heritage.

Many brides still choose to wear white as a symbol of tradition rather than purity, so guests should ensure they do not wear white, allowing the bride to be the focus of attention. It is also advisable to make yourself aware of the colour worn by the bridal party and not wear a similar colour.

Invitations are usually beautifully printed on paper and posted, as a sign of the significance of the event. Always respect the RSVP as noted on the invitation and reply by the date set. If the invitation does not mention you are able to bring a guest, then don't. The bride and groom will have a valid reason for doing so, and their wishes need to be respected.

The type of gift preferred will always be indicated, so there will be no need to guess. As many couples have lived together for many years and established a home, cash gifts are often favoured to assist with the cost of the honeymoon or house deposit. Wedding gift registries are still popular and practical, but if there is nothing on the list that caters to your budget, choose a gift that you know will be meaningful and personal. Gifts are not often brought to the wedding reception but instead are delivered to the home of the couple up to three months after the event.

Be sure not to post any photos of the celebration on social media before the bride and groom have done so. It would be in poor taste to do so.

Always be mindful that it is a privilege to be invited to attend such a meaningful event and conduct yourself accordingly.

Botswana
By Samantha Matlhagela

Chapter 1

Culture Symbols

My Botswana, my pride. I was born and bred in Botswana and I feel blessed to have grown up in this beautiful land of peace and tranquillity. Botswana is in the southern part of Africa. It is a landlocked country and shares borders with South Africa, Zimbabwe, Zambia and Namibia. Botswana has a population of about 2.308 million people, most of which stay in Gaborone, the capital city of Botswana. The people of Botswana are called Batswana and the two official languages are Setswana and English. There are, however, other languages, though they are not recognised as official languages.

Like many other countries, Botswana has its own culture symbols that hold a very special meaning to its people and are held in high regard. These symbols are an iconic representation of the values and history of the people of Botswana. Below are some of the most recognised *culture symbols* in Botswana.

THE NATIONAL FLAG
Botswana has a very beautiful and simple national flag, consisting of blue, black and white. I talk of these colours with pride. These are the colours of our national flag and each one of them has a meaning. The blue represents the blue waters and skies that signify the centrality of rain in the semi-arid Botswana; the black and white represent the racial harmony of different nationalities living together peacefully in one country. The national flag is found everywhere, starting with the airport upon entering this beautiful laid-back country. It is found in all government institutions and some private businesses. Once in a while the national flag is displayed all around the country during celebrations of special national events or

to commemorate significant days like the President's Day and Independence Holiday. While Batswana love their country and are very patriotic, it is uncommon to find them displaying the national flag in their homes. The Botswana National Flag was adopted on the 30th of September 1966 when Botswana gained her independence, as before she was a British protectorate.

Coat of Arms

The Botswana coat of arms is an important culture symbol as it represents the life of Batswana. It is made up of a shield supported by two zebras, which hold a tusk of ivory and an ear of sorghum. At the bottom it has a blue sash, upon which is written '*Pula*'. All these symbolise different things. The zebra is the national animal which has also influenced the national flag colours (black and white); sorghum is an important crop of Botswana and here it represents agriculture and the self-sufficiency of the country through arable farming; the ivory tusks represent trade (ivory trade in the yesteryears). The shield houses three cog wheels that represent mining and different industries, three blue waves which represent water, and a bull's head which symbolises the importance of the cattle industry in the country's economy. Cattle rearing is one of the main long-standing cultural aspects. This explains why Botswana is a beef country and serves the best beef in the world. Last, but not least, the blue sash upon which is written '*pula*', which translates to 'rain', emphasises the importance of rain in the lives of Batswana. *Pula* is also our national motto, used at the beginning or end of speeches, presentations and just as blessings to say, 'Let

Botswana Coat of Arms

there be rain'. We Batswana believe that rain is life, and it brings with it good luck and blessings. The coat of arms is mostly seen in Botswana bank notes and coins. Botswana's coat of arms was adopted on January the 25th 1966.

The National Anthem

We also have a national anthem. It was adopted when Botswana gained her independence in 1966. The national anthem was composed by the late Dr Kgalemang Tumediso Motsete, popularly known as KTM. It is titled: '*Fatshe Leno la Rona*'. Our national anthem emphasises the importance of our land and that we should all (men and women) work hard to make it a better place for generations to come. The lyrics of '*Fatshe Leno la Rona*' alludes to God and his standing as the bestower of the nation's land. It also promotes values such as love of the country, and peace among the different ethnic groups residing in the state.

MOTTO: PULA

Our motto, *Pula*, as mentioned above, represents life itself, happiness, good health and prosperity, as well as warm greetings / a warm welcome, or wishing a good journey/bon voyage. *Pula* is also our national currency (BWP).

CATTLE

In Botswana, cattle are held in high regard. Cattle are an important part of the people of Botswana and their significance cannot be ignored. Firstly, rearing of cattle is part of our lives, most families have herds of cattle, some for family benefit and some for business purposes. Botswana is known to have the best beef in the world and exports its beef to most European countries through the Botswana Meat Commission. Cattle are also used to pay the bride price by a man seeking a woman's hand in marriage. The man's family is expected to gift the lady's family with cattle as a token of appreciation. Another fun fact to mention is that the first university of Botswana was built a long time ago through citizens contributing a cow each towards the national

project of building the University. The motto for contributing to this project was 'one man, one beast' referring to the expectation that each capable citizen was to donate a cow towards the building of the first university of Botswana.

National Animal: Zebra

While Botswana is famous for its variety of wild animals, especially the big five, its national animal is the zebra. The zebra is a wild animal and yet it is very soft, graceful and harmless. This makes it easier for Batswana to associate with. Botswana is known for its peace, tranquil and harmless nature, hence choosing the zebra as its national animal. It was also easy to choose the zebra as a national symbol because it is considered to be neutral in so far as tribal symbols go.

We see the zebra in the coat of arms, and its black and white stripes on the national flag as well. The zebra is among the abundant wildlife in Botswana and contributes immensely to the tourism sector. There are three species of zebra. These are the plains zebra, grevy's zebra and the mountain zebra. *A fun fact to note is that The Botswana National football team is called The Zebras, named after the national animal.*

NATIONAL TREE: MORULA (SCLEROCARYA BIRREA)

The Morula tree (Sclerocarya birrea) is said to be found in most areas around the country and is also known as the 'tree of life' due to its substantial benefits. Historically, the Morula tree was useful as its fruits were used to make juice and beer, while its barks were used for medicinal purposes. *A fun fact to note is that animals such as elephants and baboons do get drunk from eating a lot of Marula fruits.*

Botswana national tree: Morula

NATIONAL FLOWER: SENGAPARILE (HARPAGOPHYTUM PROCUMBENS)
The national flower, Sengaparile (Harpagophytum procumbens) or devil's claw, is found in the arid parts of the country and is said to symbolise Botswana as a strong nation. Sengaparile is famous for its medicinal capabilities in dealing with ailments such as arthritis, gout, muscle pains, liver and gall bladder problems, amongst others.

Botswana's National Flower: Sengaparile

National Beer: St Louis Lager

On a lighter note, just like in most countries, the citizens of Botswana love to have fun. Although Botswana does not have a very robust night life, there are a few night clubs and hang-out spots, plus other events that take place where people can let their hair down and party. For enjoyment, the people of Botswana love to patronise their own products and one such product is the local beer, St. Louis Lager. The St. louis Lager is brewed locally at Kgalagadi Breweries Limited. There is also the traditional beer '*Chibuku*' which is made from sorghum meal. Kgalagadi Breweries Limited has different products ranging from alcoholic beverages, traditional beers like *Chibuku* shown above, and non-alcoholic beverages: soft drinks and water.

Chapter 2

Meeting, Greeting, Posture and Body Language

MEETING AND GREETINGS

Batswana are very friendly people and easily embrace each other and strangers. For these reasons, greetings are a very important part of our tradition when it comes to meeting people.

One is expected to greet everyone, wherever they go. Greetings should not be overlooked; they are viewed as a sign of respect for others. We greet with a simple '*Dumela*' followed by '*mma*' (women) and '*rra*' (men) and '*Dumelang*' if it is a group of people; for example, if someone was to find me in a coffee shop or elevator, they would say, "*Dumela mma.*" Traditionally, greetings were extended by a way of a handshake if you were introduced to someone. However, in public spaces like elevators or buses, a handshake may not be necessary, but rather a nod or slight bow. Greetings are used as a way to acknowledge the presence of other people in your space. We greet everyone we meet, and you do not have to know the people to greet them.

In more social settings, people, especially ladies, tend to greet each other by hugging. One can hug family members as well as their closest friends. Men are allowed to hug ladies; however, it is not common to see men hugging other men. Before COVID-19, men would greet each other by the handshake; now they are expected to use the elbows or touch their shoe tips in a casual manner; otherwise, they use the thumbs up to acknowledge each other. Winking is not acceptable, especially if it is done by a stranger, as it is viewed as very offensive.

The people of Botswana are very relaxed and laid-back, and this sometimes tends to lead to a 'laissez-faire' attitude. It is very easy to make friends even on first encounter, like meeting at a party, concert or any other social event. All that one has to do is greet the other party, introduce themselves, and start small talk. As mentioned earlier, it is culturally expected that you must always make sure that you greet people irrespective of who they are or where you meet them. Young people are expected to greet older people first; however, if an older person enters a room and finds young people, they can greet them, but culturally the younger person is supposed to initiate the greeting; this is a sign of respect. When a young person enters a room and finds adults, the young person has to kneel down to greet them. It is also considered impolite to greet or address adults with hands in the pockets.

The habit of acknowledging other people through greeting can contribute to building solid relationships with one another. It is a habit that I grew up practicing and has become part of who I am. It is a good habit as it forces us to recognise the presence of other people and embrace them, which is something every human being needs: to be acknowledged. People warm up to you and you tend to get help easily when you need it from the people you greet.

POSTURES AND BODY LANGUAGE
Postures and body language represent non-verbal communication. Much of the non-verbal communication is normally influenced by our cultural values and background. It is therefore desirable for one to familiarise oneself with different cultures in order to improve intercultural communication and avoid misunderstanding. While most Batswana may seem unobservant of postures and body language, Botswana is similar to other countries in that there are postures and body language that are attributable to the Botswana culture. Public displays of affection are not so common and are usually frowned upon by elderly people; however, holding hands as a couple and a slight kiss are acceptable, especially in cities, but are still not a very familiar sight in rural areas.

When talking to someone, you are expected to look at them; that is, to look at their face, for there is the Setswana saying of '*mafoko a matlhong*', meaning that our words and truth lie in our eyes. However, it has to be a comfortable, social eye contact, as a straight gaze may cause discomfort or can be misconstrued as rudeness. It is regarded impolite or disrespectful to look at someone, especially an adult/elderly person, straight in the eye.

The lowering of the head or eyes when one is scolded is said to be an expression of remorse or showing that one is sorry.

Girls are taught at a tender age to sit 'properly'. Legs are brought together when sitting down or on a chair, so as not to expose the inner part of the thighs, as this is considered indecent.

The use of a left hand to give someone something is considered disrespectful, and to receive something with one hand, especially the left hand, is considered unappreciative or ungrateful. It is encouraged that one should use the right hand to give out something and both hands to receive.

Batswana are normally not particular about how close to them you stand, but of course with the new health protocols, one has to make sure that they stand a minimum of one metre apart.

Chapter 3

Conversation Dos and Don'ts

As mentioned in Chapter 2, Batswana are very friendly people and easily embrace each other and strangers. For these reasons, a very important part of our tradition when it comes to meeting people is the *greeting*.

In Botswana, you can never start a conversation before you greet someone, whether at home, work or public places like restaurants or parties. Greetings are considered an acknowledgement and first step in building a rapport with someone. Greetings are a first sign of good manners.

I cannot say there is a strict rule on how you greet other people, it depends on the relationship with them. Different settings and people require different ways of greeting. In business settings, greetings are more formal and professional, addressing people by their surnames; for example, at the office someone will say, "*Dumela Mma* Matlhagela." Meaning, "Good day Mrs Matlhagela." In informal settings, we operate on a first name basis and in a more casual manner; for example, at a party one would say, "Hi Sammy." However, as a sign of respect, the elderly are always addressed formally as '*rra*' or '*mma*' for a man or woman respectively, regardless of whether it is a formal or informal setting. Once you have greeted someone, especially someone you do not know, the safest way to start small talk is by talking about the weather. Often most people mention how hot the weather is (our summers tend to be extremely hot), then the conversation will progress easily.

In the northern part of Botswana, when a young person is greeting an elderly person who is seated, they must kneel down and give the person being greeted both hands clasped together as if clapping. If they are not seated, you can just bow a little and give them your clasped hands. In other places, you can greet another person by shaking hands. And in some cases, especially in the cities, women will give each other a kiss on each cheek, or they hug.

Batswana are easy going people and talk about anything and

everything, and they particularly find it easy to talk about the weather, sports (mainly soccer), current affairs and local events. Some Batswana may seem a bit on the reserved side, but this may be due to their discomfort with speaking a language that they are not good at, such as English. However, once they have met you and introduced themselves, they take a keen interest in knowing where you are from and the way of life in your country. They are always more than happy to talk about their culture and heritage and never miss an opportunity to talk about The Okavango Delta, which happens to be one of Prince Harry's favourite holiday destinations, and about the Botswana diamond which was used for Meghan Markle's engagement ring from Prince Harry. That is something they are really proud of. Batswana men are also proud of their livestock and are always happy to talk about their cattle posts and cattle farming.

For close associates, it is common to ask about their family and how they are doing. However, if you have just met someone for the first time, you may ask them if they have any family members living close by. Batswana are very much family oriented, hence the adults never fail to ask the younger ones when they intend to get married or when they will have kids. This is mostly common in rural villages where everything is just said innocently and with good intentions. Nowadays, especially in towns and cities, people get offended by such questions, as they may be uncomfortable to answer. They are viewed as too personal and invasive. My mum would sometimes ask me when I would be having a second child, and I knew she meant well because she enjoys being a grandmother. However, some people may not take it well due to their medical conditions or other personal choices.

While we enjoy talking about almost everything, it must be noted that there are other topics where one needs to tread carefully before discussing them. These include politics, religion, money, tribalism (some tribes think that they are treated as minority groups and they feel they are considered lesser Batswana), and racism. It is safe to talk about these when you are with your closest people or people you know will not take offence. Another topic that is not yet well received is of gay relationships, including gay marriages. Whilst we know they exist; gay marriages are not yet legal in Botswana. You cannot discuss your personal relationships with a person you have just met; they will wonder about your upbringing. And issues of sexual orientation are taboo; you cannot discuss them openly except with someone you trust.

Eye contact is expected during conversations; it determines a person's trustworthiness. This should be a steady eye contact but not staring. Batswana will not necessarily maintain constant eye contact because in some settings it is considered rude to look someone straight in the eye; on the other hand, it is considered a sign of dishonesty if a person refuses to or is reluctant to make eye contact.

While talking, men generally do not touch other men unless they know each other, even then this would be occasional. Friends are more likely to touch each other and, although they will often maintain a similar distance when speaking, the sphere of personal space around each person is not considered as private and inviolable. How much associates will touch each other or the distance they will keep apart depends on familiarity and level of comfort, but it is best to keep one's distance if unsure.

Batswana like to joke. If you want to make a joke, make sure it will not offend your listeners. Avoid jokes that deal with racism.

Chapter 4

Gift Giving

Giving gifts is a long-standing tradition in Botswana. Although it is not very popular, there are life events, milestones and occasions which we celebrate by giving gifts. Everyone loves receiving gifts; therefore, people go out of their way to look for perfect gifts. Gift giving is done by both personal and business associates.

Batswana love celebrating life events. The most common social events where gifts are often given include but are not limited to:

- *Birthdays* – Most people celebrate their birthdays either by hosting a big party or just going out for lunch or dinner with family or close friends. The choice of birthday gifts is normally informed by the receiver's hobbies and likes; for example, if they love reading, one can get them a book or two. If they love sports, one can get them gym gloves and gym towels. Otherwise, a birthday card, bouquet of flowers or a spa voucher are always appreciated.
- *Weddings* – Whenever people are invited to weddings, they are expected to bring gifts for the couple. It is good etiquette to bring a gift. Normally, wedding gifts are those that will make it easier for the couple to settle into their matrimonial home. These included household items like kitchenware, bedding, garden tools etcetera. Nowadays, couples make sure that they leave gift registries at several stores and indicate what they wish to receive as gifts. It is advisable for the couple to choose different price ranges for their choices so they give all an opportunity to buy what they can afford. Some people may not buy gifts but rather buy gift vouchers or give money on the day. There is normally a table manned by a designated family member or close friend to receive and register all gifts, including monetary gifts, on the day of the wedding.

In some local traditions, on the day after the wedding, wedding gifts are unwrapped for viewing and appreciation by close family members and friends. This is an old tradition and practised more in the rural areas where culture is still very much more intact than in the urban areas where weddings are often held at special venues like hotels and wedding gardens.

- *Bridal showers* – Normally before a wedding, family and friends of the bride-to-be come together to celebrate her. They do not only shower her with gifts to start her new home with, but they also share advice relating to marriage as well as what her in-laws would normally expect of her. Bridal shower gifts most of the time range from anything that is assumed would help the bride-to-be with her role as a wife and homemaker. Gifts such as kitchen utensils, bedlinen, home decor items, bathroom accessories like towels, are some of the gifts given at a bridal shower. Beauty spa vouchers are beginning to be popular gifts as well. Some people bring their gifts to the bridal shower so that they do not have to carry gifts to the wedding on the wedding day.

- *Baby showers* – Just like bridal showers, baby showers are also very popular. Babies are a blessing, and everyone loves babies. News of a new bundle of joy always bring excitement amongst family and friends. The common practice here in Botswana is that close family and friends (most of the time women, though the new trend is to have both men and women) will get together to organise a baby shower for the mother-to-be. At the baby shower ceremony, guests bring gifts.

- *Christmas* – While Christmas is celebrated, not everyone buys Christmas gifts. Normally people who buy Christmas gifts only buy for their close family and friends. Most families buy for small kids to create excitement and teach them the spirit of giving. Christmas gifts especially for kids are commonly toys and clothes, inexpensive items. Family members also buy each other gifts and normally just give Christmas cards to other extended family members and friends.

A trend that has also grown through the years is work colleagues buying each other Christmas gifts. This is done in a secret Santa fashion where one may write three gift options that they prefer so as to make it easier for the one who is buying for them. Writing gift preferences also helps in ensuring that everyone loves their gifts upon receipt of their gifts.

- *Business gifts/ corporate gifts* – In a business environment, gifts can either be given to clients by the company or employees can receive gifts from clients.

- *Gift prices* – There should be a cap/ceiling: If gifts are of a very high value, they can be considered manipulative or taken as a bribe, especially if they are from business associates. The price of the gifts should be such that they do not raise any eyebrows or bring feelings of discomfort.

- *Business gifts* – These should be work related and not be too personal, as this can send out the wrong message.
- *Should be branded* – Corporate gifts should be branded with the giving company's logo, tagline or any message that is attached to their business.
- *Gifts received by employees should be declared* – Employees are mandated to declare all gifts they receive from other business associates or their customers. Declaring them helps to curb undesirable practices like bribery or creating expectations.
- Some gifts are not necessarily for the individual employee but for company use.

Chapter 5

Dining Etiquette

Dining is a beautiful experience as it brings people together. Whether dining at home or at an event, everyone is always in a jovial mood. Food, just like sport and music, brings people together. Like all other topics discussed in previous chapters, dining has its own etiquette, ensuring that there is order around the dining table and everyone participates accordingly.

Like in other countries, Batswana (people of Botswana) have their way of dining that is often related to their food. We observe both formal and informal dining etiquette. However, it must be noted that most of the time we err on the side of informal more than formal.

FORMAL

Dining etiquette is something held in high regard especially at hotels and special events. Generally, most people practice formal dining etiquette when invited to weddings and other special and business events. This is where tables are beautifully set with beautiful shiny tableware and glassware. Normally, formal dining can go up to four courses, serving a carefully selected menu, and beverages include both red and white wine and champagne, sometimes rounded off with a cup of tea for those who may fancy it. In Botswana, it is not everyone who understands the formal dining table scape, only the elite and those who have been trained, including hotel staff. It is however, not a big deal for most Batswana because formal dining is rarely practiced at home. Some people get an opportunity to learn the art of formal dining when they are expecting visitors to host or are attending business events where formal lunch or dinner will be served. What I have observed is that most people are always confused by the napkin. They are never sure where to place it; on their lap or chest, whether to use it or not, especially as most napkins at hotels are white.

Formal dining cuisine is often served a la carte, where every individual is served whilst sitting, instead of serving themselves from a buffet.

INFORMAL

Informal dining is the most common and preferred style by Batswana families. While dining brings the family together, there are only two strict rules around the table: you do not talk with food in your mouth, and remain seated, rather than moving around. Our informal dining most of the time refers to a one or two course meal. There are few utensils used except for a dinner fork and knife, a teaspoon or tablespoon for the kids, and some adults even use their hands. Most of our staple food is eaten by hand, like maize meal and sorghum meal, so it is a very common practice to use our hands to eat, including for eating meat. Some families, especially in the rural areas, would have kids eating together from the same dish instead of serving them in individual plates. I must say this is a practice I have experienced too when I was young, and it encourages kids to eat their food before they find that others have eaten everything. It also teaches kids to share. With informal dining, people do not normally sit at the dining table; they sit anywhere they find comfortable and where the family can bond.

The interesting thing is that, while there is a difference between the formal and informal dining, the principles are similar. It is about respecting other diners and doing our best not to interrupt others whilst they are dining.

Chapter 6

Business Etiquette

Most businesses in Botswana are always keen to set and agree on values that are meant to guide the behaviour and conduct of employees. One key value for most companies in Botswana is '*Botho*' which may be translated to mean respect for one another, humaneness, and civility. In fact, *Botho* is a national value and it is also shared across the Southern African region, and mostly referred to as '*Ubuntu*'.

GENERAL MANNERS AND BEHAVIOUR

The value of *Botho* forms the cornerstone of the code of conduct for most companies in Botswana because if there is respect, not only among employees but also respect for customers, then one can be assured that employees will display good manners and appropriate behaviour at all levels of the organisation, as well as to external customers. Good conduct is a major component of business etiquette in Botswana. Everyone in the workplace is expected to respect one another and the customers they serve regardless of age. However, formality is more pronounced when dealing with older members of the business and those high up in the hierarchy; young employees normally display less formality with each other.

GREETINGS

As mentioned in previous chapters, Batswana consider greetings to be a very important part of day-to-day interactions, in both formal and informal settings. Greetings are regarded as a way of acknowledging another human being. Therefore, whenever one meets another person, they must greet them, whether they know them or not. Greetings are said to open up and facilitate pleasant interactions, hence being considered a desirable way to start business meetings and discussions. A customer is well received if he acknowledges those who are supposed to serve him by greeting them before requesting assistance; however, employees are also expected to greet customers with a smile as part of living the value of *Botho*. By so doing, they are each showing appreciation and respect for one another.

DRESS CODE

Most businesses in Botswana adhere to a formal code of dress: suits or formal jackets and ties for men and either trouser or skirt suits and formal dresses for women. Women are expected to wear knee length dresses or skirts instead short length (mini). However, where a mini dress or skirt is worn, it is considered decent to wear it with pantihose to give it a formal look. See-through clothing is discouraged, as some people view such clothing as a distraction or indecent. Batswana are not very particular with colours that are worn in the workplace, with some men wearing light blue or purple suits and printed or multicoloured shirts, as well as multicoloured socks. However, cleanliness, neatness and general good grooming are emphasised. Most businesses have adopted casual Fridays where employees are allowed to wear branded company golf/T-shirts with jeans or casual trousers.

Although formal wear is emphasised by most companies, some smaller companies that are individually owned are a bit more relaxed and allow smart casual wear for their employees.

TITLES AND HIERARCHY

In the business environment, just like in day-to-day traditional settings, authority is held in high regard; therefore, businesses accord great importance to seniority in the hierarchy of the organisation. Businesses in Botswana have a strong hierarchical culture and employees are normally addressed by their job titles or as Mr (surname) or Mrs (surname), especially those in senior positions or older members of staff. The business culture is normally based on formality as well as rank.

LANGUAGE

The official business language in Botswana is English. However, this is not to say that our language, Setswana, is not used. Whilst English is the official language, Setswana is mostly used day-to-day, especially because most of the population is Batswana, and the workforce is mostly comprised of locals. Sometimes it is dependent on the industry or the level of education whether a business wants to use English or Setswana. In some instances, some organisations deliver their information in both languages (English and Setswana) to accommodate everybody.

BUSINESS MEETINGS

Business meetings (before COVID-19) are mostly held in meeting rooms and boardrooms, depending on the number of people attending. Time is very important and must be respected, as it shows respect for all people. Meetings are held any time of day within working hours (seven-thirty a.m. to four-thirty p.m. or eight a.m. to five p.m. for most businesses). Normally there is a person who chairs the meeting and guides the proceedings of the meeting. There is also an assigned secretary who takes minutes of the discussions to later share with all people who were in attendance. People respect each other and give each other opportunity to voice their opinions, ideas and ask questions. The business dress code must also be respected.

There has been a new trend of having meetings outside the office, at a coffee shop, in hotels or restaurants. This is done by some organisations as a treat or just giving the meeting attendees a different environment, which may motivate them to be more relaxed and open to discussions.

COVID-19 then brought about the introduction of online meetings through different platforms like Zoom and Microsoft Teams. With these platforms, people are a bit more relaxed, and some choose not to turn their cameras on. Despite this, proper etiquette dictates that people must behave like they would behave in physical meetings: turn their cameras on, dress smartly, have clear voices and participate, all of which encourage concentration and participation by meeting attendees.

OFFICE ROMANCE

Office romances are not really encouraged in the business world; however, a lot of companies do not have any policies in place to shun office romances. Whilst it is uncommon, there are still employees who get involved in office romances. Should people find themselves in such a situation, they should make sure that the affair does not disturb work and does not offend fellow workers. They should maintain the professional high standards and not let their relationship interfere with their work. I must say though, I know of a few people who met at work, fell in love and got married. And who can blame them when they spend most of their time at work?

Chapter 7

Wedding Etiquette

In Botswana, a wedding is normally celebrated twice. A wedding celebration is first hosted at the bride's home, and similar festivities then following a few days later at the groom's home village. The first ceremony celebrates the couple's exchange of marriage vows, when they are pronounced husband and wife. The second celebration, known as '*kgoroso*', is hosted by the parents of the groom to welcome the bride into her new family. These traditional ceremonies usually take place regardless of where the vows are exchanged, whether at the church or at the district commissioner's office.

Whilst most Batswana families still insist on separate wedding celebrations at their respective homes, a joint celebration on a cost sharing basis at a neutral venue such as a wedding garden, lodge or a hotel is becoming increasingly common. The etiquette rules applied during such celebrations depend to a large extent on whether the celebration is at a hired venue or at home. The atmosphere at a home celebration is much more relaxed and the invitations are extended to many more guests than when the celebration is held at a hired venue.

WEDDING GUEST LIST ETIQUETTE

Whilst the couple usually expect to draw a guest list for their wedding celebration, the parents of both the groom and the bride also play a major role in deciding on who to invite, especially regarding relatives. If the celebration is held at home, the hosts, example: the bride and her parents or the groom and his parents, have a great influence on the guest list, that is, they decide on the number of invitees. When the bride and groom are happy with the guest list, in some cases the couple decide on when to send 'save the date' cards. The invitations are shared between the two families with the hosting family normally having more guests. Where the celebration is held at a neutral venue with costs shared, the capacity of the venue is taken into consideration and the invitations are normally split fifty-fifty between each of the two families. However, the couple normally indicate the number of friends and workmates they would like to invite.

INVITING CHILDREN TO THE WEDDING

To invite or not to invite children is a major consideration. In the past, wedding celebrations were normally hosted at home, with invitations open to the entire village, and the issue of inviting children was not a big deal. Modern day wedding celebrations require much more coordination and cost considerations. This issue can be a bit tricky because some of the invited guests might want to bring their children along, citing the excuse that they do not have babysitters; other guests are of the view that only children of the hosts should attend because some children behave inappropriately at formal events. In trying to strike a balance and in an attempt to be more inclusive, some families would normally have two or so tables designated for children old enough to take care of themselves, and not allow attendance by smaller children.

SEATING/TABLE ARRANGEMENT

Wedding celebrations hosted at home are usually held in a large marquee with well-arranged table settings and decorations, and this makes the setting for the ceremony not very different from that of a hotel or a wedding garden. Whether the celebration is hosted at a hired venue or at home, the tables are arranged such that there is a side for the groom's entourage and a side for the bride's family and their guests. The high/head table is for the bride, groom and the best man and best lady. The couple's parents as well as the rest of the bridal party sit at the tables closest to the high table. The ushers normally stand at strategic places so that they can easily take care of the guests and lead them to their tables.

FAMILY INTRODUCTIONS

Normally, the programme of ceremony starts with a prayer followed by welcome remarks by an uncle who would have been the designated head of the family. The introduction of family members on both sides is an especially important item of the wedding programme as it enables guests to be feel comfortable with one another. There are usually one or two people, close family members from each side, who are tasked with introducing the family, including the extended family members present. The introductions would then be followed by short speeches.

EATING ARRANGEMENTS

In order to ensure that the serving runs smoothly, several serving points are strategically placed within the wedding venue, and the number of these serving points is based on the number of the guests, as some of the celebrations attract many invitees. The serving starts with the bridal party, followed by the in-laws, that is, if the ceremony is hosted by the bride's family, then the groom's entourage would be served immediately after the bridal party and the rest of the guests would follow.

WEDDING GIFTS

Guests are expected to bring gifts for the couple on their wedding day, although some arrive after the wedding. Bringing gifts is considered proper etiquette as it is a way of celebrating the newlyweds and helping them to settle in their new home. Wedding gifts range from home/kitchen utensils and appliances to garden tools, bedding and blankets, money and even livestock such as chickens, goats and sheep. Most Batswana are farmers, so the livestock are a way of encouraging the newlyweds to either start farming or adding to their already existing livestock, or for enjoyment (meat).

DRESS CODE

Most weddings do not have a dress code; it is considered that guests know that they are expected to look smart for weddings. However, I must say that traditional weddings are the ones which always have a dress code, in the form of the colours chosen by the bride/groom and their families, or the printed fabric they prefer the guests to wear. This printed fabric is referred to as '*jeremane*', meaning 'German print'. It is a fabric that has been used for a long time in traditional weddings. It comes in different prints and colours; however, the original and most common colour used is blue. This dress code is normally followed by women making different dresses and skirts. Men do not necessarily follow it, though nowadays some men really try to incorporate the chosen fabrics in their outfits in the form of a pocket, pocket square, buttons, and shirts.

As for white weddings, normally the dress code is smart or elegant depending on the venue of the wedding, as different venues call for different dress codes. For hotel weddings, the dress code is more formal or black tie, while for garden weddings it is a bit more relaxed with summer inspired dresses and colours. Those hosted at home call for a more traditional feel to the attire. Generally, guests dress well to suit the wedding celebration. Long ago, it was shunned upon for a guest to wear an all-white outfit to a wedding, as this meant they would compete for attention with the bride wearing a white wedding dress. Nowadays, it does not matter because some brides also opt for non-white wedding dress.

Brazil
By Merely Siqueira Reis

Chapter 1

Cultural Symbols

Brazil is a country of continental proportions and with a broad cosmopolitan aspect. Its beautiful history since colonisation in 1500 characterises it as a very receptive and warm country and people. Its miscegenation makes it even more charming as multi-cultures create several countries within a single country. Endowed with a beautiful coastline and forests full of freshness and beauty, Brazil also has a lightness and joy complementing the scenic beauty.

Some national symbols characterise this vivacity in Brazil in a tangible way.

Among them are the following:

Cristo Redentor

CHRIST THE REDEEMER

Located in Rio de Janeiro, Christ the Redeemer is the largest and most famous art deco sculpture in the world. From the top of the Corcovado Hill and with open arms over the Bahia de Guanabara, it welcomes all visitors to the wonderful city.

He is considered a symbol of Brazilian Christianity. In 2007, Christ the Redeemer was considered a World Heritage Site by UNESCO.

AMAZON OR AMAZONIAN FOREST

60% of the world's largest rainforest is on Brazilian soil, stretching seven million kilometres^2 and covering nine Brazilian states. It is part of the Amazon Biome, one of the largest biomes in the world.

The forest comprises 53% of world's tropical forests. This makes preservation a matter of great care, as it requires protection to keep it healthy.

Thousands of rivers flow through the region. The Amazon River is the largest of them with an extent of more than six thousand kilometres. Its source is in the Andes (Peru) and flows through to the Brazilian coast.

The beauty of the biodiversity of the Amazon Forest enchants its visitors, containing one in ten known species globally, with 40,000 plant species according to the WWF.

A hot and humid environment dominates most of the time. The annual average temperatures vary between twenty-two and twenty-eight degrees Celsius and a rainfall index that varies from 1,400 to 3,500 mm per year; the relative humidity of the air exceeds 80%.

The forest is the heart of Brazil and the lungs of the world. If there is something Brazilians are proud of, it's having this beautiful forest in national territory.

The indigenous peoples that inhabit the forest make our nation a country of multifaceted history and culture.

GIRL FROM IPANEMA

Composed by Antônio Carlos Jobim and Vinicius de Moras in 1963, *Garota de Ipanema* is a Brazilian song in the style of Bossa Nova and MPB, Brazilian popular music known worldwide.

The song was created at the request of businessman Oscar Ornstein, to be integrated into the musical '*Dirigível*'. The play was in production, but never premiered. The song's original title was 'The girl who passes'. The first recording of the song took place in the same year by Pery Ribeiro.

The authors' inspiration to compose the music was Heloisa Menezes Paes Pinto, who at the time was a seventeen-year-old girl who lived in Ipanema, a coastal neighbourhood in the city of Rio de Janeiro. She passed daily by the Veloso bar cafe towards the beach, but sometimes entered the bar.

'*Garota de Ipanema*' competes with '*Yesterday*' by Paul McCartney, in the ranking of the most widely interpreted songs of the C.20th. It is almost impossible to compile a complete list of all versions published in recent decades. In a report to Deutsche Welle on the song's 50th anniversary, it says that 'the song was performed more than 200 times, forty times alone, between 1963 and 1965'.

THE CARNIVAL

Carnival is a celebration of Western Catholicism that precedes the period of Lent that typically occurs during February or early March. The period is known historically as the Seventieth (it is a Christian liturgical time of preparation for Easter).

Carnival involves a public party with parades, combining circus elements, masquerade and a street party. People make use of fantasies that allow them to lose their daily individuality and experience a heightened sense of social unity.

Characterised by the carnival are simulated battles, social satire, mockery of the authorities and a general inversion of day-to-day social norms. Excessive consumption of alcohol, meat and other prohibited foods during Lent is extremely common.

The word carnival comes from the Latin expression '*carne vale*', which means 'goodbye to meat', in reference to the fasting period that is approaching, but this interpretation has no philological evidence.

Carnival, as we know it today, with parades and costumes, is the product of Victorian society of the C.20th, with its main diffuser in the city of Paris. The Parisian carnival was a source of inspiration for other cities in the world, such as Rio de Janeiro, New Orleans and Toronto, to implement their new carnival parties.

The city of Rio de Janeiro created and exported the style of making carnival with parades and samba schools to other cities in the world such as São Paulo, Tokyo and Helsinki.

FOOTBALL

Football is now the most popular sport in the world, with more than 270 million players. The first records of football are from 4500 – 4000 BC in ancient Egypt where a board game called *Senet* was taken to the fields and the dice was used instead of a ball.

The modern model was created in England with The Football Association, which created the present rules in 1863 as the basis of the sport. FIFA (Fédération Internationale de Football Association, in French) is the highest normative entity of football and holds its main event, the FIFA World Cup, every four years.

Charles Miller, an Englishman, introduced football to Brazil in 1894 after returning from England. At the same time, the German professor Hans Noibiling founded Germânia – now Pinheiros – in São Paulo, and Oscar Cox founded Fluminense Football Club in Rio de Janeiro.

Cox organised, on 1st August 1901, the country's first soccer game at the Rio Cricket Association, in Niterói. From then on, Miller and Cox started to encourage the creation of clubs in São Paulo and Rio de Janeiro.

Today, football is considered a national passion in Brazil. Stadiums can hold more than 100,000 people. The fans cheer a lot with the goals and the country stops at the time of the World Cup.

JUNE PARTY IN BRAZIL

The June Party is a traditional popular festival which takes place in June throughout Brazil, especially in the north-east. The festivity was brought to Brazil in the C.16th by the Portuguese. Originally, the party was held in honour of saints like Santo Antônio and São João.

Studies indicate that the June festival originates from the pagan festivals held in Europe that celebrated the summer solstice when the passage from spring to summer occurs. We must consider that in the northern hemisphere the summer solstice occurs exactly in the month of June.

With the consolidation of Christianity as the main religion in Europe, several celebrations held by different pagan peoples were Christianised and incorporated into the festive calendar of Catholicism. This was a common practice of the Catholic church to facilitate the conversion of pagan peoples.

In Brazil, during the June festivities, dances are performed, such as the quadrille, and it is common to dress up as a hillbilly, in a caricatured way. Another characteristic is the production of foods based on corn and peanuts in addition to beverages such as *Quentao*.

Chapter 2

Meeting, Greeting, Posture And Body Language

POSTURE

The first impression is what remains. This is an old popular saying that represents the Brazilian view on image and personal presentation.

Keep the body firm and stand straight, with your shoulders back and chin always perpendicular to the body, as this shows elegance and sophistication.

When meeting people, always smile and be charismatic. When greeting women informally, always kiss them on the cheeks.

The look must be firm and focused on the interlocutor. This demonstrates character and attention. Brazilian people are very emotive and usually gesticulate a lot when communicating.

BODY LANGUAGE

Brazilians are very expressive in our body language. We gesture, smile and give hugs and kisses to people we have just met. This is a perfectly common behaviour. Cordiality is always expressed through a smile.

Some gestures have their own meanings, for instance:

- Pressing the earlobe with your index finger and thumb—that means 'very good'. Example: the person compliments the food and squeezes their earlobe.
- Hitting the palm of your hand in the back of the hand and alternating hands/wiping one hand with the other—this means you don't care.
- Closing the fingers of one hand and raising only the thumb—this indicates that everything is fine.
- With the palm of the hand up and fingers opening and closing—this means that the place is full.
- Closing one hand and touching the forehead—that indicates a person with little intelligence.

Informal Meetings

When meeting someone informally, do not be alarmed if they hug you or kiss your cheek. It is very common and a sign of affection. And believe me, each place in Brazil has a different number of kisses that you can receive. In Sao Paulo, it is one; in Rio, it is two; and in Minas Gerais, it is three.

Do not look into a woman's eyes for too long as you might cause her to feel embarrassed or harassed. Brazilian women touch their hair and smile a lot, but don't think that these are gestures of innuendo or invitation.

A pat on the back is a way of greeting, but it is exclusive amongst men.

When you are invited to a party, and if you do not know the people who are there, shake hands with each person, one by one. However, they may hold your hand and attempt to kiss your cheeks.

Foreigners are always well received. However, do not overdo the physical contact.

Formal Meetings

In formal moments, avoid speaking loudly, embracing who you know, and laughing.

Avoid crossing your arms as it creates a feeling of discouragement or denial.

When shaking hands, be firm. Do not use too much force, especially with women.

When introduced to others, keep the focus on looking into the eyes of those you have just met.

Women usually cross their legs when sitting and keep their posture straight. Men unbutton their jacket and then sit.

Bars and Restaurants

In informal settings, it is common to raise a hand and index finger to call the waiter.

To ask for the bill, the global gesture of pretending to write on the palm of your hand, is common.

Chapter 3

Conversation Dos and Don'ts

Like every culture, Brazil has some issues and behaviours that need care during interactions in the country. Aspects such as football, politics and religion are the most complex. There is a national popular saying which is: 'Politics, football and religion are not discussed'. These subjects yield many endless discussions.

- Politics

In recent years, politics has become polarised in Brazil. The left and right are radical. Issues such as corruption, the private life of politicians, and the position of the president are matters that require a lot of background and history to be discussed, so avoid these as much as possible. If you refer to Brasilia (Capital of Brazil), never refer to the 'land of corrupt people'; the inhabitants of this city are totally repelled by this. Do not judge a concept attributed to politicians with the population.

- Soccer

They say that Brazil is the land of football. The vast majority of our population is totally passionate about this sport. At the end of national championships or the world cup, the country stops. Shops are closed and elementary schools and universities have no classes, especially if the Brazilian team is participating. Thus, it is a very delicate topic to address. If you are not Brazilian, avoid rooting for a team. Always be neutral in discussions and never say that Maradona played better than Pele: always be impartial.

- Religion

Most religions in Brazil are of Christian origin. Catholics and Protestants are the majority, consisting of more than 80% of the over 210 million population. There are other religions and all live together peacefully. Although coming from the same origin (Christianity), do not think that these religions are the same or have the same practices. So, avoid this kind of subject as much as possible.

Chapter 4

Gift Giving

Who does not love receiving gifts? A gleam in the eye and smile are guaranteed when you see a beautiful package coming towards you. It is no different in Brazil. We love to give and receive gifts.

Giving a gift to a Brazilian is very easy, although, if you are receiving a gift, make sure you give a smile of gratitude, even if you do not like the gift.

To give gifts, it is important not to give anything personal. Perfumes and hygiene items, even if they are of excellent quality or rare, are not a good gift. They are always seen as suggesting the lack of personal hygiene of the person you are giving the gift to.

Never give home items to a young woman, unless it is her wedding. Older ladies tend to use this advice much more than younger ones.

If you come from another country and bring a gift that expresses your culture, you will certainly have a great deal of success in the present.

Religion

We are an extremely peaceful country with regard to religious freedom. We respect each other's religions and are not easily offended due to it. However, always observe when offering a gift, especially during religious holidays, the correct religion. Christianity is the religion with the greatest number of followers, however, within this religion there are three strands: Roman Catholicism, Eastern Orthodoxy and Protestantism. Christmas for Catholics and Protestants is celebrated on December the 25th. For the Orthodox, it is on January the 7th. When gifting, it is best to follow these general rules:

- When giving gifts to Protestants, never give any kind of image or sculptures related to the Bible.
- Orthodox people generally do not exchange gifts on these dates.

At Catholic Easter parties, there is a tradition of presenting people, especially children, with chocolate eggs. There are several options for

Easter eggs; you can even buy chocolate eggs with *Caipirinha*, which is a traditional Brazilian drink.

OTHER GIFTING OCCASIONS

Mother's day (second Sunday of May), parents' day (second Sunday of August), children's day (October the 12th), and Valentine's Day (June the 12th) are special moments, and there is always someone waiting for a gift. Halloween, however, *is not a date celebrated by Brazilian culture.*

On children's birthdays, normally children under twelve years of age do not need to open the gift at the time it is given to them, if there are other children nearby. The intention is that a party is not stopped to open gifts. Therefore, do not expect the child or parents to specifically thank you for the gift, but they will thank you at some point.

On the other hand, adults, when receiving gifts on their birthday, have to think about timing if they are having a celebration: if the celebration has many guests, it would not be practical to open each present with each gift giver. If there are fewer guests, and a certain interval between receiving the guests and opening gifts is possible, then opening gifts is acceptable.

In particular, I believe that a reception for thirty people is an adequate number for us to be able to receive guests and open gifts immediately. For this, I suggest that there are scissors nearby to facilitate this work and not leave the next guests expecting to be greeted for a long time. For celebrations with large numbers of guests, it is best to have someone to receive the gifts on behalf of the hosts, with a note to say who it is from, so the hosts may thank the giver later.

For big celebrations and weddings, we must not bring gifts on the day of the ceremony or party. Instead, have them delivered to the bride's house beforehand. Usually, the bride and groom have a list of gifts on websites of specific companies. These companies will deliver the purchased gifts to the bride's house, and send a digital gift receipt to those who bought the gifts.

Newborn babies always receive gifts in Brazil. Suggestions like clothes and toys are always acceptable. If you want to visit the family after the birth of a child, wait until the baby is at least a month old before scheduling an appointment to see the family. If you need to return to your country before this deadline, send the gift to the family home.

For academic graduations or professional awards, usually family members and closest friends give a gift to the honouree.

If you are invited to a dinner, bring flowers. However, flowers like bouquets are not a good option, as the hostess must then leave her guests, even if just for a short time, to find a vase to put them in. Potted flowers are always the best option in this case. Sweets and wines are always a great alternative.

RECEIVING GIFTS

If you have received a gift, open it in good time and thank the gift giver. Regardless of whether you like the present or not, it is good manners to say thank you: even if the gift is not something you would love, smile. After all, we assume that the person who presents us with it has taken the time to choose, with great affection, something that they believe we will like.

Chapter 5

Dining Etiquette

When we come together to celebrate the Brazilian soul, we are filled with joy. At home or in a restaurant, it does not matter, what matters is to celebrate life. Brazilians love celebrations. Brazilians take life more lightly, so we do not have much rigidity in our eating times.

As Brazil is a country of continental dimensions, we use an average of times for meals. Breakfast always from six a.m. to ten a.m. lunch from twelve p.m. to two p.m. afternoon coffees from three p.m. to five p.m. and dinners from eight p.m.

Food varies according to the region of the country. Brazil is a country that has an administrative division into five parts: north, south, north-east, south-east and mid-west.

I will talk specifically about each region.

NORTH

This region of Brazil is the one with the greatest influence of indigenous culture. In the state of Amazonas, we find most of the Amazon Forest, where the largest number of indigenous tribes in Brazil live.

Breakfast: The presence of a root called *Mandioca* is a consequence of the indigenous influence in gastronomy, not just in the north, in every area. Pure *Mandioca* cake and tapioca are part of breakfast in this region, in addition to roasted bananas, coconut, açai and juice from many tropical fruits such as *Cupuaçu* and *Graviola*, in addition to Pupunha which is eaten cooked.

At lunch and dinner, we still have the indigenous influence with the famous *Maniçoba*, filet of *Tucunaré*, Pirarucu and *Costela de Tambaqui* and *Vatapá*, which is a very common shrimp dish. Many fish are displayed in these dishes with absurdly tasty flavours. Northern Brazil has strong spices and unforgettable flavours.

Here, there is a specific food culture in relation to what we call lunch, which is at a typical afternoon coffee time. Even the foods are repeated at this time, especially *Tacacá* (a soup with shrimps and peppers). People gather in white houses and even in houses specializing in typical foods to eat in the afternoon.

NORTH-EAST

Breakfast: The very famous corn couscous is a very common dish in the morning for the people of north-eastern Brazil, served with butter from a bottle (clarified butter/ghee), dried meat and other foods that they add. In addition, *tapioca*, *biju* with dried meat, *coalho* cheese and cooked sweet potatoes are part of this breakfast, providing a lot of substance.

For lunch or dinner, we have several dishes based on shrimps, sea fish and crabs.

The afternoon coffee snack is not very common in this region.

The famous traditional north-eastern party, São João, which is celebrated in the month of June, has several typical foods. Among these foods are a sweet Peanut Brittle (*pé de moleque*), Souza Leão cake, roll cake, and *Pamonha* and *Canjica* desserts made from corn.

MID-WEST

In the typical breakfast of the central west of Brazil, we have the Chipa (which is a cheese bread), the Paraguayan coconut biscuit, rice cake, Pequi chestnut cake, and a wide variety of Cerrado fruits.

For lunch or dinner, Paraguayan soup (which is not a soup, but more of a cake/bread), and beef dishes are very typical in this region.

SOUTH-EAST

In this region, we have the largest number of internal migrants and immigrants in the country, so it is where we have the greatest variety of dishes. But coffee here is unanimous in all states. The famous cheese bread and baked bread are very characteristic products of Minas Gerais and São Paulo.

Lunches and dinners here have all the flavours from around the world. Some typical Brazilian dishes are *Moqueca Capixaba*, *Tropeiro* beans, *Filé a Osvaldo Aranha* ,and *Virado a Paulista.*

Afternoon snacks repeat the breakfast menu.

SOUTH

Breakfast in southern Brazil is very diverse, with a strong European influence that came with immigration from the peoples of Germany, Italy and Portugal. Fruit cakes, cheeses, sausages, jams and *Cuca* (a sweet bread). They have a meal called 'cafe colonial' which serves German inspired dishes as a lunch, in the afternoon.

On the other hand, lunch and dinner have red meats, as a reference to the famous barbecue. *Pinhão*, meat *Paçoca* are very typical dishes of the region.

At Christmas, it is customary to have turkey, ham or pork roasted on the table.

Dinner Etiquette

The host's attitude is always friendly and helpful. They must pay attention to all the guests during dinner and need to be on hand and ready to respond to anyone's request. The Brazilian host is lively, attentive and very polite.

As a host, part of your job is to introduce the guests to each other. You should initiate some common matter between them, because then, if there is a need for you to leave them alone and attend other guests, they will be able to continue conversing.

Do not be alarmed if you see personal or sanitary materials in the toilet or lavatory, such as absorbents, wet wipes, dental floss, amongst others. These materials must be visibly and elegantly displayed for use by the guest. Thus, the guest does not need to ask the hostess in front of the other guests, or in the form of a whisper, for any of these items.

Invitation

The invitation all depends on who we invite, the reason and the response time for the invitation.

Usually, for less formal receptions at home, emails, phone calls and WhatsApp messages are very easy to use, as long as they give enough time for the guest and host to plan. A minimum period of seven days is sufficient.

Within the invitation, especially for meetings with less than twenty people, it is important that some guests are mentioned so that the hostess can note, through the comments, the affinities between the guests and how the interaction will be during the party. So, if you are asked if you care about someone else going to the meeting, answer honestly and without embarrassment.

If you need to consult someone, ask for a deadline to respond to the invitation. But don't take more than forty-eight hours to answer.

If the meeting, the reason for the invitation, is a more formal event such as a wedding at home or a christening lunch, you will receive a printed invitation thirty days in advance. In it, it must contain the RSVP (*repondez s'ill vou plait*) information, by phone or email to confirm your presence.

The deadline for reply is forty-eight hours after receiving the invitation. If the guest does not respond, it is common for the hostess or a specialist company to call to confirm with the guest, if necessary.

But unfortunately, one thing is a fact: Brazilians are always late. Fifteen to thirty minutes of tolerance is critical before starting a dinner.

FOOD AND DRINKS

Knowing the people being invited presupposes knowing a little of their tastes, if they are allergic to any food and if they have any food restrictions. It is possible that the host, within the invitation, may ask if the guest has any food restrictions. It is very impolite to serve seafood to a guest who is allergic, or red meat to a guest who is vegetarian.

Food should not be served in excess to the point that the guest cannot taste everything that is served to him. The meal should follow in a harmonious way, where one dish completes the other and in the correct proportion, so that the guest can enjoy all the dishes without becoming full.

During a dinner or even a happy hour, guests are offered a bucket with ice, still and sparkling water, normal and diet soda, normal juice and diet. It can be served without constraint by the guest at all times.

During dinner, keep your voice down and if you need to leave to go to the toilet, excuse yourself and always put the chair back in place. When you return, listen to the subject that is being commented on by the other guests before speaking.

Always smile and be friendly. Brazilians feel uncomfortable when they do not see the guest excited or satisfied with the dinner.

Never make a table noise. Burps are not well regarded. Gesticulate little. Do not over drink. Brazilians love happy people, but they cannot stand inconsequential drunks.

Never talk about topics like Brazilian women in the sensual sense, the 'Brazilian way', or corruption. Most Brazilians do not agree with what is characteristic of a few people in our population.

During dinner will be served:
- Appetisers

- Starter
- Main course
- Dessert

Before dinner, a light cocktail is served during the aperitif, with light and refreshing foods in the summer and warm and light in the winter. Drinks are usually cold when the weather is warm. Usually beer, chop and vodka-based cocktails are very common.

There is precedence for serving in this order: children, women starting with the honouree or older to the hostess, and then men starting with the guest of honour, the eldest and the host last.

SERVING THE WINE

Traditionally, the wine is shown and served first to the host (in the restaurant) who will identify the label of the requested wine and, when tasting the wine, will approve it so that it can be served to the guests. The host will be the last to be served even if they are a woman. This is because the person who ordered the wine is offering the drink to all those present, so that it can be served later, showing education and respect to their friends and guests.

When talking about the service order, after the chosen drink is approved by the host, it will be served initially to women, respecting the order of age—first the older women, then the younger ones. Sequentially, men will be served, respecting the same age rule.

If dinner is at someone's home, the host is the one who serves the drink, and serves himself last (even if the wine was brought by a guest).

Never fill glasses fully. Beer is the only drink for which you can fill the glass to the brim. If not serving beer, for serving guests follow a standard: for red wine, serve 2/3 of the glass only, and if it is white, do not exceed half the glass.

There are glasses suitable for different types of wine. However, in general, whites should be served in smaller bowled glasses so that the drink does not heat up as quickly; reds, served in larger and wider bowled glasses, are allowed to breathe and release their aromas. Sparkling wines are always served in flutes because they keep the bubbles in the drink for longer.

The tasting of a wine can be a party of flavours, but in order to be truly appreciated, we must have an order: first the dry, then the sweet; the new wine before the old; the white is served before the red, the good before the very good. To finish, right after the coffee, sweet or liqueur wine, a digestif like a port wine, for example, is served.

This order is discussed and questioned among connoisseurs, but it all depends on the number of wines and dishes/courses to accompany the tastes, and sensitivity of the guests.

Acknowledgment

Thank you cards are a cordial and traditional way of thanking the hosts. They can be sent with gifts, but it is not a rule.

Today, we have several ways to communicate, such as email, WhatsApp and other social media platforms. However, the good old phone call is still the most elegant. The important thing is to thank those who dedicated time, money and knowledge to invite you.

Chapter 6

Business Etiquette

PERSONAL IMAGE

Brazilians are very visual, so always show a confident and beautiful image. The dress code determines your business segment. For example, if you are a lawyer, suits are always the best clothes to wear, but if you are a marketing or fashion entrepreneur you are completely free to wear something more creative. For city jobs, you must always be well dressed in impeccably aligned suits.

Personal hygiene counts a lot. Ensure your hair, nails and beards are well cut. Ensure you have a fresh breath also. For women, the use of a softly scented perfume is a nice touch.

POSTURAL LANGUAGE

Observe your posture. Keep your shoulders back; this also helps reduce tiredness and encourages productivity. Always be cheerful, with a sincere smile. Look into people's eyes, especially when you are talking to them. Brazilians are very friendly people, so be as pleasant as you can.

Don't gesticulate too much and always be elegant.

COMMUNICATION

The language of Brazil is Portuguese, not Spanish. Although, Brazilians are very patient and receptive to foreigners. If you are unsure of a word in Portuguese, do not worry; Brazilians will not care if you say something incorrectly, and will try their best to understand you.

Always use courteous and polite words.

Avoid using slang in any language.

INTRODUCTIONS

There is always precedence when introducing people. The social position, age and gender will always be observed when considering who should be introduced first.

Always have your personal or digital business card to exchange, especially in business meetings. The card must be easily read. If you receive a physical card, keep it in the inside pocket of your jacket or in your purse.

Always use a firm handshake when meeting someone. There is a custom to kiss the cheeks of women. However, between men, use a handshake or a friendly hug.

The kiss on the cheek has an exact number in each state, as described previously. Remember though that each state uses one kiss on each cheek.

INTERNET ETIQUETTE

Social networks like Instagram and Facebook are used a lot, so be careful what you post: avoid photos that compromise your image.

WhatsApp is another app which is useful for small talk and also for work, but always try to write the message rather than voice record it. In Brazil, there is a habit of recording voice messages instead of writing them, but this is not the best form.

Chapter 7

Wedding Etiquette

Usually, a wedding in Brazil has three different moments: the wedding in front of a judge, the wedding in a church or other religious ceremony, and the party after the wedding. This order is followed in most cases. When we talk about the main ceremony, we are referring to the moment of civil marriage or religious ceremony.

CIVIL MARRIAGE
Civil marriage is the most intimate moment, exclusive for the groom, the bride, and their families.

Dress in formal wear. Light suits of light colours are appropriate because this type of wedding is usually during the day. Women wear elegant knee-length dresses and carry a clutch bag. Colours should be discreet, but white must is not worn by guests.

RELIGIOUS WEDDING
Usually, the religious wedding and the wedding party are scheduled on the same day. First, the religious wedding and then the party.

Usually, the wedding invitation is received by the guest thirty days in advance. It contains the RSVP (*Répondez S'il Vous Plaît*). In the RSVP, there will be a phone number for the guest to answer, to confirm or not confirm their presence at the wedding. Whether you go to the wedding or not, remember to respond and thank the sender for the invitation.

LOOK OUT FOR THE DRESS CODE
Groomsmen must wear the same style of clothing as the groom, as well as a buttonhole. Bridesmaids can wear the same colour dresses if the bride requests. Always wear a formal outfit and never wear colours like black (which has a funeral symbolism), red (which has a very sexy symbolism)

or white which is the colour exclusive to the bride. Hats are exclusive for daytime weddings. Long dresses are suitable for night parties.

Arrive at the church at least fifteen minutes in advance. If you are late, look for a place at the back of the church and stay there until the end of the celebration.

Usually, the church's benches closest to the celebrant are reserved for the bride and groom's families, so avoid sitting in these spaces if you are not a family member. On the left of the church are the bride's guests and on the right are the bride and groom's guests.

Do not talk during the ceremony and avoid leaving your seat. Do not yawn or stretch as this creates a bad impression.

Never take someone as a partner who has not been invited by the bride.

WEDDING PARTY

When the bride and groom leave the religious wedding and go straight to the party, it is there that they will greet their guests, and the guests will congratulate them.

This is a time to relax and celebrate with the couple. But remember, the party is not yours… Beware of excess alcohol.

Avoid talking for a long time with the bride or groom.

Eat moderately and politely according to the service that the buffet will offer.

During the party, it is usual for the groom or his best man to sell off pieces of his tie, which he cuts, to sell and raise money for the honeymoon; so, take some cash with you.

If you are very tired, you can leave the party before the couple leave.

Caribbean
By Alice Thomas-Roberts

Chapter 1

Cultural Symbols

Caribbean Map

The Caribbean is that cultural 'melting pot' at the crossroads of the Western World. It was to this region five centuries ago that Spanish, Dutch, French and British sailors sailed in their quest to find another route to the Spice Isles of the east. But while the Caribbean was not the route to the east via sailing, it presented its own riches: rich, green, tropical lands, capable of producing wealth from agriculture: sugar cane, cocoa, bananas and other crops, which were not being produced in the temperate climate of Europe. But there was need for workers/labourers. Thus, began the movement of slavery, followed by that of indentured workers which brought peoples from Africa, India, China and other far eastern countries to live and work on plantations in the Caribbean.

As a result, the Caribbean is now one of the most diverse, yet culturally tolerant regions of the world. We are a 'melting pot' of descendants from different cultures: West African, Indian, Chinese, British, Spanish, Scottish, Dutch, French, Portuguese and others.

THE CARIBBEAN IS KNOWN FOR:
Its Integration Efforts
Political, as well as non-political efforts have been made for decades to connect the islands of the Caribbean, before as well as after independence. Many of the islands have been members of various intergovernmental associations, such as the West Indies Associated States (Statehood), the failed federation, as well as contemporary institutions such as The Caribbean Community (CARICOM), the Association of Caribbean States (ACS), and the Organization of Eastern Caribbean States (OECS). Both CARICOM and the ACS include English and non-English speaking member states, while the OECS consists only of English-speaking island nations.

The region also shares a Caribbean Court of Justice, a Regional Security System, the Caribbean Disaster Emergency Management Agency (CDEMA), and among other well-established institutions, the University of the West Indies with campuses on three islands, and open campus centres in all other member states.

Despite the organised political structures, non-political efforts at integration continue to surmount all barriers. These include the following:

Transport
The regional airline Leeward Islands Air Transport (LIAT), now renamed LIAT (1974) Ltd, has provided air connection for all islanders from Guyana in the South to Puerto Rico in the north. British West Indian Airways (BWIA), now Caribbean Airways, continue to connect the islands to larger metropolitan centres outside the region.

Established sea connections have not been consistent. Boats such as the Federal Maple and the Federal Palm, gifts of the Canadian government to the Region's Federation, provided great interisland travel and movement of cargo, but became unviable and eventually went out of service after Federation.

Interisland schooners can still be depended on to bring produce from one island to another.

Religions
Religions in the Caribbean are as diverse as the regions from which they originate, and these contribute to the cultural tolerance in the region. Roman

Catholicism is dominant in those countries with longer histories of French and Spanish colonialism, while in those countries with a strong British influence, Anglicans and Methodists are predominant. Islam and Hindi also have a significant following particularly in Guyana, Suriname and Trinidad and Tobago.

Non-traditional Christian faiths have also arisen in the last hundred years, and African religious traditions also find expression through Voodoo, and Spiritual Baptists also known as Pocomania in Jamaica. Rastafarianism, which started in Jamaica, has also become a religion of significance throughout the region.

Celebrations and Festivals
Caribbean people love to celebrate, and the various festivals held throughout the region are testimony to that. Christmas and Easter are Christian commemorations but are celebrated regionwide, regardless of religion. The Hindu festivals of Diwali and *Phagwah* and the Muslim observances of *Eid-ul-Fitr* and *Eid-ul-Azah* are prominent in Guyana, Suriname and Trinidad and Tobago. Fisherman's Birthday and Emancipation Day are also big celebrations.

Carnival
The biggest and better known of all festivities in the region, Carnival, tends to be a season, rather than a day. With preparation for activities and events beginning months before, Carnival culminates in a two-day celebration of street parades with costumes with drinking, dancing and wild abandon in the streets. Some of these activities include calypso and soca music competitions, Panorama and carnival queen shows. Words like '*J'Ouvert*', '*Mardigras*' and '*Jabjab*' are terms used to describe different events held during the season, particularly in Trinidad and Grenada.

Carnival is held at different times of the year in different countries of the region, and in some countries is called by different names, such as Crop Over in Barbados, Junkanoo in The Bahamas, *Mashramani* in Guyana and *Owruyari* in Suriname.

According to the Caribbean Secretariat, the influence and energies of the region's diaspora in North America and Europe have resulted in the Caribbean Carnival becoming a major festival in metropolitan centres, such as London's Notting Hill Carnival, Toronto's Caribana, New York's Labour Day Carnival, Washington DC's Carnival and the Miami Carnival.

The COVID-19 pandemic has had a crippling effect on the region's carnivals which usually draw thousands of visitors to the region. Grenada's Carnival, which culminates on the second Monday and Tuesday in August, was postponed in 2020, while Trinidad's 2021 Carnival, usually held in February, was also postponed.

Gift Giving

Sports
Sports are an integral part of Caribbean culture and a feature of life. In every island, young people can be seen playing cricket, football and volleyball, on beaches, playing fields, and wherever there are open spaces, including on quiet roads.

Cricket
Cricket came to the West Indies as 'the gentleman's game' as early as the first decade of the C.19th, being a game popular among the planters and soldiers. Cricket is so entrenched in the lives of Caribbean people that cricketing terms form a natural part of everyday life; people talk about being 'stumped' for an answer (meaning being unable to reply), 'batting in your own crease' (meaning minding your own business), or not wanting to 'bat first' (meaning not wanting to speak first at an event).

The Caribbean's team, the West Indies Cricket Team, has a history of being one of the most formidable at an international level. The WI Cricket Team consists of men, but there is also a West Indies Women's Cricket team, though not as popular. There is also a Windward Islands Cricket Team and there are junior cricket teams in individual islands. Retired recognised cricketers include Sir Garfield Sobers of Barbados, Sir Vivian Richards of Antigua, and Brian Lara of Trinidad and Tobago.

Football
Football is another widely played sport in the Caribbean Region which evokes great passion among Caribbean people. Though there isn't a West Indies Football Team, different countries have their own teams which compete on a regional level to qualify for participation in the World Cup; a significant number of Caribbean footballers play with distinction at the highest levels of club football throughout the world. Some also coach extra regional teams.

Athletics
Track and field events have brought great pride to the Caribbean Region which continues to produce world and Olympic champions. Though few in number, the Region's athletes have maintained a high standard of excellence at the international level, including in the Olympic games, winning gold, silver and bronze medals. Names which stand out among contemporary athletes include Usain Bolt of Jamaica, Kirani James of Grenada, Veronica Campbell-Brown of Jamaica and Shelly-Ann Fraser-Pryce.

Other Sports

Other sports in which the Caribbean people have been active and successfully involved include netball, boxing, wrestling, swimming, basketball, volleyball, lawn tennis and table tennis.

Tourism

With their beautiful white sand beaches, volcanic landscapes and waterfalls, it is no wonder that tourism is now the main foreign exchange earner in many of the islands.

In recent decades, the Caribbean has become increasingly dependent on tourism as a source of income and employment, and there has been considerable expansion in tourist-related infrastructure.

The Caribbean Tourism Organization (CTO) is the region's tourism development agency, with twenty-four Dutch, English, Spanish and French country members, and a myriad of private sector allied members. The Caribbean Hotel and Tourism Association (CHTA) also partners with hoteliers and hospitality businesses in promoting the region's beaches, ecotours, water sports, marine life and other activities.

Specialty Foods

The diversity of Caribbean heritage is reflected in its cuisine, and each country has developed its own signature dishes such as jerk meats (chicken and pork) and ackee and saltfish in Jamaica, flying fish and cou-cou in Barbados, pepperpot in Guyana, mountain chicken in Dominica, oil down in Grenada, and roti and curry in Trinidad and Tobago.

Music

Caribbean music has gained popularity and acceptance worldwide and has impacted other cultures. Most outstanding are reggae which originated in Jamaica, and calypso associated with Trinidad and Tobago. Many Caribbean musicians, such as the Mighty Sparrow and the late Bob Marley, have achieved worldwide fame.

Across the region, there are other indigenous musical forms. These include spouge from Barbados, Punta from Belize, Zouk from Haiti, dance hall from Jamaica, Frafra from Suriname, chutney from Trinidad and Tobago, and musical rituals such as big drum dancing in Carriacou (one of the sister isles of Grenada).

The Steel Pan cannot be left out when talking about Caribbean culture. Developed in Trinidad and Tobago, 'pan music' is now recognised and played throughout the world, including in schools, churches and universities.

Caribbean Drama, Poetry, Dance and Theatre
Caribbean people are very dramatic. A simple conversation or explanation to someone could elicit body movements, hand gestures and facial expressions. However, even serious situations can be seemingly made light of, as humour is an integral part of Caribbean drama. Humour and drama are woven into the work of Caribbean poets, playwrights, actors, singers and dancers.

The Edna Manley College of the Visual and Performing Arts in Jamaica is a popular school which draws many aspiring professional dancers and playwrights to the region. The region's painters and sculptors are not to be left out either, as their work is internationally recognised. Many of them participate in international expositions around the world, such as in China and Italy.

The region's film industry is also drawing attention. Cuba already has a vibrant film industry, and producers from other islands are beginning to test their potential by producing short films. Residents of Grenada and Barbados can boast about being involved in a 1957 Twentieth Century Fox film titled '*Island In the Sun*' which featured the fictitious British island colony of Santa Marta. Additionally, Grenadian Jennifer Hosten, the first black woman to win Miss World, in 1970, was featured in the recently released film '*Misbehaviour*' which premiered in London.

The Caribbean region is a good example of cultural intermingling and tolerance where diversity in ethnic backgrounds, religions, languages, music and cuisine blend together to create a unique culture.

Chapter 2

Meeting, Greeting, Postures and Body Language

BASIC COURTESIES

In the Caribbean, courtesies are taught from birth. Parents, grandparents or even older siblings begin teaching a child to be courteous once the child can hold and grasp items. Saying 'thanks' is therefore the first word that the child learns. It may sound like 'Taa'. When someone offers an item to the child, a parent or older sibling would instruct the child to say 'taa'. Some toddlers have learnt this the hard way, by being denied the item several times until they realise that getting it is conditioned on expressing that word or phrase.

By the time children become toddlers, they also learn that 'please', 'thank you', 'excuse me, please', 'I'm sorry', and other 'pleasantries' are part of interactions. If they have not learnt these when they are ready for school, they will have problems with their peers.

It is these same basic courtesies which adults depend on to interact better with their colleagues in their jobs, with their customers, and in social settings. These help to make our communities more pleasant and tolerant places.

THE GREETING

The greeting is perhaps the most familiar concept of Caribbean courtesies, and bidding someone a good day is therefore part of Caribbean culture. In many Caribbean islands, it is expected that one would say 'good morning' or 'good afternoon' when one enters a room where others are, or passes someone on the street, (though not a busy street). If someone enters a room and does not greet others, those already there may very well conclude that this person does not have good manners. The greeting sets the stage for starting new friendships and maintaining good relationships.

Despite being particular about the greeting, Caribbean people may still not be sure what to say when they greet. They may say 'good afternoon' when it is evening, or even 'good night' when they should be saying 'good evening'.

FRIENDLINESS OF CARIBBEAN PEOPLE

Another aspect of Caribbean culture and etiquette that visitors are often impressed with is the warmth and friendliness of the people. Caribbean people are good at striking up a conversation with strangers, offering to help, giving directions readily and even offering a ride to wherever the visitor is going. Some visitors may think this is strange and wonder if there is some other motive, but this is generally how Caribbean people are.

Despite their friendliness, some Caribbean people may feel more comfortable introducing themselves by a courtesy title, such as 'Mrs Brown' rather than 'Jane Brown'. The same would occur when speaking to or about strangers or older persons; they would add a courtesy title to older persons' first names to show friendliness, yet respect for them. For example, I could be addressed as 'Ms Alice' instead of 'Ms Roberts'. If they are not familiar with you, Caribbean people will never call you by your first name without adding Ms, Mrs or Mr in front.

CARIBBEAN TIME

Have you ever heard of Caribbean time? It is different from Atlantic Standard Time (AST) though we are in the AST zone. Caribbean people say that Caribbean time is 'any time', so that if you invite a Caribbean person to a social activity for a specific time, and they arrive half an hour later, you will understand. Their genuine excuse would be that they came late because 'no one else would be early'.

Despite that, professionals in the Caribbean make every effort to be prompt for their meetings and work-related activities.

HANDSHAKES

In the Western world, greetings are usually accompanied by handshakes. Caribbean people know that, and professionals use handshakes in their business interactions. Yet on the streets, you will see Caribbean men bouncing each other's fists. This is now quite appropriate for this time when we are facing COVID-19 pandemic restrictions and handshakes are restricted.

We now also use the elbow bump and waving to acknowledge others.

When it comes to children, young boys are taught to 'give me a five' (raising the open palm and slapping it to the other person's open palm), while young girls are taught to 'blow a kiss', by kissing the inside of one hand and blowing it across to the other person.

POSTURE AND BODY LANGUAGE

Life in the Caribbean tends to be casual outside of work environments, 'laid-back' some would say, as there seems to be a lot of sitting around and 'liming'. Men in particular may be seen sitting on benches by the rural roadsides or standing outside of rum shops. It is the place where they can share drinks and laugh with friends.

When it comes to body language, Caribbean people can be very dramatic. Even when they are not speaking, their body may very well be. They tend to use all aspects of body language: facial expressions, gestures or hand movements, and all-body movements. Pointing, waving, rolling the eyes, moving the head and flaying the arms to illustrate or express emotions are commonplace. These really should be reserved for social and familial settings, but some people tend to forget and use them in business also. This gives employers additional responsibility to provide their staff with appropriate training to help employees manage their body language whilst serving customers.

Many Caribbean people are unaware that some of their gestures such as the thumbs up sign, the peace sign, the victory sign, and hand gestures for calling others may very well have different interpretations in some other parts of the world. It is therefore wise for Caribbean people to manage their body language, as well as for peoples of other cultures to be a bit tolerant and not be offended when the gesture or body language of a Caribbean person seems out of place.

Chapter 3

Conversation Dos and Don'ts

It has always been proper etiquette to know what to say and what not to say to people, especially when you are not familiar with them.

The Caribbean consists of English, Dutch, French, Papiamento, Spanish, Creole (French and Spanish based), and a number of other dialect speakers. Many Caribbean people speak more than one language, though English is the common denominator.

When you travel to a Caribbean island, there are some things you must bear in mind.

GREET BEFORE YOU ASK QUESTIONS
Caribbean people are easy to talk to. Even in an English-speaking island you will find someone with at least a basic or intermediate understanding of French or Spanish who is ready to listen and give you directions, or advice on products or services. The same is the case if you are English and visit a French, Spanish or Dutch speaking island.

Be sure to greet before you ask for directions and generally when you approach someone even if you are passing them while walking on the road or beach, though not necessarily on a crowded street in the towns.

COURTESIES
The answer to 'How are you'? in the Caribbean, is usually 'fine, thank you' even if the person is not fine. It is just a formality which helps to lighten the atmosphere so conversation can continue. It is not an invitation to relate your personal troubles.

REFERRING TO PEOPLE BY FIRST NAMES
It is not okay to call or refer to someone by their first name except when that is the name they gave you. If someone says, "Hi, I'm Alice Roberts, how may I help you?" Your response should be, "Hi Ms Roberts..." and continue with your question.

NICKNAMES
In some places you may be referred to by a nickname. Do not be offended. Words like 'Sweetie', 'Honey', 'Love' and 'Man' are used to show appreciation and acceptance. You may hear phrases such as 'How may I help you, Sweetie'? 'Have a good day, Love', or 'Take it easy, Man'.

BODY LANGUAGE
Try not to be offended by the expressive nature of the Caribbean people, especially if someone is explaining something to you and is gesticulating. It seems that it helps them to feel confident.

PERSONAL QUESTIONS
In some countries, it is okay to get to know a stranger by asking personal questions as soon as you meet. However, in the Caribbean, it is considered quite rude. Don't ask personal questions, such as 'Are you married'? 'How much do you work for'? Or 'what type of car do you drive'? Despite this, some Caribbean people can readily talk about their personal achievements and material possessions. It is not an invitation for you to talk about yourself too; it is their way of seeking your acceptance, so just listen.

POLITICS
As a visitor, do not talk about political parties, even if you have been following them in the news. Try to be neutral. Caribbean people can be quite passionate about their political parties, and there can be intense discussions about one party against another. As a visitor, you do not want to offend anyone, so stay neutral.

DIALECT MIXED INTO STANDARD LANGUAGE
Because Caribbean people are descendants of people from different ethnic backgrounds and cultures, there is naturally a mixture of words in their communication. So although someone says they speak English or French, you will sometimes hear other words and phrases which don't belong to that language. For example, 'yes, *oui*' is a common phrase among people of the Eastern Caribbean meaning 'yes, indeed' or 'definitely so'.

CONVERSATION WHICH IS READILY WELCOMED
If you are wondering what topics make good and acceptable conversation, here are some examples:

The beauty of the islands: Caribbean people love when you talk about how much you enjoy the beaches, waterfalls, hiking trails, and marine excursions.

The weather is also a natural topic. Caribbean weather can be sometimes unpredictable, as island states are in the path of the constant north-east Trade Winds.

Caribbean people are also passionate about sports, as mentioned in Chapter 2, and will get into long animated discussions about their favourite teams locally, regionally and internationally.

Local people want you to enjoy their food and drink, so there can be long and animated conversations about who makes the best 'oil down', 'pepperpot' or whatever dish they prefer. Caribbean people are proud of their national dishes and there are websites and social media pages dedicated to their meals and recipes.

Do Not Speak Negatively About the Islands

Finally, do not speak negatively in your own language about the way of life of Caribbean people or anything you see that is different to your country. Never presume that the people cannot understand you. They may not be able to speak back to you fluently, but it is likely they understand, so do not let them hear you commenting negatively about their islands. Some are even building a basic knowledge of Chinese which is being taught in some of the islands.

Chapter 4

Gift Giving

Caribbean people love social interactions and celebrations, and on these occasions, gifts might very well be brought along or exchanged. Elderly people in the English-speaking Caribbean area have always said that 'one should not visit someone's house empty-handed'.

Gift giving can be formal or informal, and gifts do not have to be expensive. Gift giving for family and friends is usually informal. Someone might stop by your house to bring you some fruits, vegetables, or whatever they have more than enough of. On occasions like these, the giver is not expecting a gift in return. People are always heartened by the fact that they were thought of, and many hold the view of 'it's the thought that counts'. Gifts may be wrapped or bagged, as on formal occasions, but many informal gifts are not wrapped. Some people reuse gift wrapping paper and gift bags, but one must remember who one received a gift from, so as not to give back the bag or paper to the same person on another occasion.

One must also remember to remove the price tag on the gift, or the receiver might think you want them to see the price.

On some occasions, gifts are opened when received. Some people like to see your reaction and be pleased that you like their gift. However, if there are several people around, the gift may not be opened immediately.

It is important to express appreciation for the gift, even if you did not like it. Forgetting to say 'thanks' is an act that is not easily forgiven by some, especially if the gift was unexpected. Even if you did not open it in front of the giver, call or send a message afterward to express appreciation.

GIFTS FROM RELATIVES VISITING FROM ABROAD
There is a tendency for Caribbean people to expect family and friends visiting from abroad to bring gifts for them.

GIFTS FROM WORK-RELATED VISITORS
If you are visiting, bring gift items from your country, not items made in another. Something from your home country, reflecting your culture would

be best appreciated. Personal items should be avoided, except if the prospective receiver is a very close friend. Try not to give what pleases you, rather give what you think the person might be pleased with.

It might also be wise to get to know what the person does, such as their work, or their likes and habits, in order that a relevant gift can be obtained. Ladies tend to welcome perfumes, lotions, shawls and purses; while men can be offered wallets or ties; everyone would appreciate a diary, desk planner, pen or desk sets at the end of a year or start of a new one.

If invited to the home of a Caribbean person, bringing something would be welcome, but is not expected.

GIFTING AT CHRISTMAS TIME
It is tradition for family and close friends to exchange gifts at Christmas and birthdays. Not everyone may return a gift, so do not feel bad if you gave one and did not receive one from the same person.

When gift giving is planned, people tend to prefer practical gifts which they can use.

At workplaces, there is a tradition of gift exchange, where colleagues dip for a name and purchase a gift for that person. The price range of the gifts are agreed upon, and gifts are usually exchanged at a staff Christmas party. Some staff members may discretely try to find out what the person whose name they received would like, in order to get a gift that pleases them. On the other hand, some staff may opt out of the gift exchange, and therefore their names will not be included.

On the business level, many companies send cards and or gifts to their clients and some customers at Christmas or at the end of the year.

WHAT TO BRING
Dinner at someone's house might be the occasion for a gift of snacks, chocolates or wines, or something that contributes to the dessert.

If invited to a party, it may not be necessary to bring a gift for your host, but if you wish to, ask what would be suitable. Sometimes a bottle of wine, tin of nuts or snacks which can be passed around as an appetiser, might be appreciated.

GIFTS ON OTHER SPECIAL OCCASIONS
Mother's Day and Father's Day
Cards and gifts are usually given by children to mothers on Mother's Day, and gifts to fathers on Father's Day.

Valentine's Day
Gifts of chocolates, stuffed animals and flowers are usual choices; roses, in particular, are usually given by lovers on Valentine's Day.

Baby Showers
Baby showers are often held in the Caribbean, more especially for young or new mothers. Bridal showers are not as common but may be held amongst close friends. In both cases, invited guests are expected to bring along gifts.

Easter
Traditionally, some Caribbean people sent cards to family and close friends at Easter; now, this is no longer maintained, and these days sending actual paper cards for loved ones is reserved for the closest or oldest relatives.

Weddings
Details about giving gifts at weddings will be discussed in the Chapter on Weddings.

Chapter 5

Dining Etiquette

As I mentioned in Chapter 1, the Caribbean is at the crossroads of the Western World.

Many of the countries of our region were colonised by European powers over four hundred years ago, and as a result their protocol and etiquette have been passed on to us. In the English-speaking Caribbean, we dine the British way, though, with our proximity to the American continent, the ease of travel to the USA, and the influence of American television programmes, many of our young people confuse British and American dining etiquette.

In a large number of Caribbean homes, families can be seen dining informally. By this, I mean they do not sit around a table, perhaps because of the desire to sit in front of the television or at their computers. Some homes may not even have a dining table. When dining informally, many people eat with a fork only; some may even use a spoon only.

Despite this, formal dining out at restaurants or during an invitation to someone's home, have become increasingly important over the last two decades, and as a result, more people are interested in understanding dining etiquette, in order to feel more comfortable eating in public.

EATING WITH A KNIFE AND FORK
When dining out formally, people in the English-speaking Caribbean, usually follow the British and continental style, with the knife remaining in the right hand and the fork in the left throughout the meal. The knife is used to push food onto the fork, which is lifted to the mouth, with the tines facing downwards. On the contrary, when eating the 'American way' (also known as the 'zig-zag method'), one uses the knife to cut the food, but it is then put down and the fork transferred to the right hand to lift food to the mouth with the tines facing upwards.

UNDERSTAND YOUR PLACE SETTINGS

Because so many people dine informally, there is a tendency for someone to mistakenly take your bread plate or your glass, especially when the table is closely set, so be sure to understand your formal place setting.

Below are diagrams of two place settings, an informal one and a formal one. If you understand a simple place setting, it will be natural to know which utensils are yours and which are not when you sit down to a formal setting.

Even in a simple place setting, remember that your fork is always on your left and your knife is always on your right. Your soup spoon is always to the right of your knife, and your glass should be in front of your knife and spoon. Other utensils are added to this setting for formal dining. These include cutlery for various courses, such as your dessert cutlery, your side plate, and your wine and water glasses.

At a formal meal, the table is usually preset with every utensil the diner may possibly need. During the meal, what is not used is removed by the waiter or server. For example, if you choose to have salad rather than soup, your soup spoon might be removed after you have been served the salad.

BEHAVIOUR AT THE TABLE

At formal meals, people are expected to act and behave differently to when they are attending an informal meal. Here are some things to bear in mind when dining out formally:

The Napkin

When you get to your place at the table, you should unfold the napkin and place it on your lap. The napkin is not to be used as a bib so do not put it over your chest. You should also use the napkin properly to dab at stray food and juices at the sides of your mouth.

Personal Items

Personal items such as bags, purses, sunglasses, or cell phones should not be placed on the table. These items belong either on your lap, on the chair behind your back (if the chair has a full back) or on the floor beneath your chair.

Cell phones should also be turned off or put on silent while at the table, as it is impolite to talk or text on your phone while dining in the company of others.

Before Beginning to Eat
Before beginning to eat, even when food is in front of you, be sure to wait for everyone at your table to be served or for an indication from the host to begin, since at formal meals, everyone should begin and end together.

Serving Yourself When Dining Informally
In our Caribbean region, people tend to serve themselves when dining informally. But at a formal table, it is always proper to serve someone else and to expect someone to serve you. This does not always happen however, so there might be times when you will have to serve yourself.

Eating Bread with Soup
When eating bread at a formal meal, you should break, rather than bite into or cut bread. The piece that is broken off is buttered if needed, and the whole bite sized piece is put into the mouth.

When bread is served with soup, it is not acceptable to dip the bread into the soup.

Elbows off the Table
'Elbows off the table' is a common phrase every Caribbean child knows. Even whilst dining at home, parents have scolded their children about eating with their elbows on the table. In formal settings, elbows on the table are acceptable between courses, but not while eating.

Chew with Your Mouth Closed
In our culture, it is disrespectful to chew food with your mouth open, make loud burping or other sounds at the table, or to talk with food in your mouth. It is also not proper to slurp soup from your spoon, or to slurp noodles or spaghetti when you are eating them.

Avoid Actions That Could Offend Others
You should also avoid doing anything at the table which would offend others, such as clearing your throat, blowing your nose into the napkin, scratching any part of your body including your hair, ears, nose, or any other part.

Sharing Food and Drink
Friends dining informally sometimes share food and drink, but in formal settings, it is improper to share food.

Talking While at the Table
In our Western culture, it is okay to talk while at the table. People talk between the courses, as well as in between swallowing. It is also proper to engage those on either side of the table in conversation, even if you do not know them.

Raising a Toast at the Table
If there is a speech to be made, or toasts to be raised, these are usually done after the main course and before dessert. When a toast is raised you should raise your glass, listen and then take a sip of your drink.

NATIONAL DISHES
In every Caribbean island, there are special foods which mean a lot to the residents. These are their celebratory foods or their 'feel-good' foods, the foods they associate with being nationals of their country, foods which they eat on special days or when in a celebratory mood. Here are a few examples:
　Barbados – Cou-cou and Flying Fish are usually eaten on Fridays or national days.
　Dominica – *Callaloo* Soup is a must-have during independence season – September to November. But it is also eaten throughout the year.
　Grenada – Oil Down is a must-have on public holidays and especially on Independence Day but is also eaten whenever breadfruit is available.
　Guyana – In Guyana, with its six ethnic groups, there are foods associated with every group: 1) Garlic Pork represents the Portuguese ancestors; 2) Cook up rice and Fu-fu represent the African ancestors; 3) Curry and various types of roti represent the Indian ancestors; 4) Chow Mein represents the Chinese Ancestors; 5) Shepherd's Pie represents the English Ancestors; 6) Pepperpot is from the Amerindian ancestors.
　Jamaica – Ackee and saltfish can be eaten all year-round for any meal in Jamaica, sometimes together with a combination of any of the following: fried dumplings, green banana, fried plantain, breadfruit or bread.
　St. Vincent and the Grenadines – Here, it is roasted breadfruit and fried jack fish which are traditional. Much emphasis is put on this dish at

independence time and around their National Heroes Day on March the 14th, but people prepare this meal at other times according to their desire.

Trinidad and Tobago – Also a multicultural society, Trinidad and Tobago, like Guyana, have many special dishes. These include various Chinese dishes, curry and roti, doubles, pelau, crab and callaloo. Some of these dishes are eaten every day, and the last two can be found on the Sunday lunch menu in many homes of African descent.

Chapter 6

Business Etiquette

Business in the Caribbean is carried out in much the same way as in the Western World. People in business try to be as professional as possible in order to outdo their competition.

Many companies, especially large ones, have guidelines for their staff, so that professional standards will be kept high. Many also arrange training for their staff in areas of professionalism and customer service so their staff can keep up to date with industry standards.

GREETINGS AND COURTESIES
Etiquette and courtesy are considered very relevant in the Caribbean business world and are believed to affect one's professional image and acceptance.

Owners and managers expect their staff to engage in courteous and pleasant communication whilst interacting with both their internal and external customers. Courteous behaviour provides an atmosphere which helps people feel comfortable and relaxed around one another.

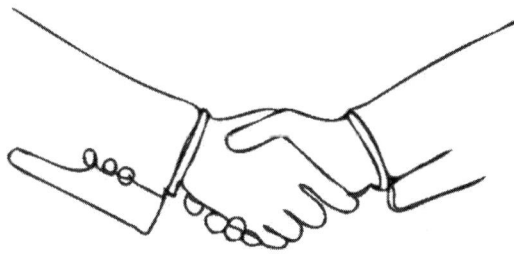

The Professional Handshake
If you are meeting someone to discuss business, you meet and greet in the usual western way with a handshake. As I write, the handshake is put on hold, due to the COVID-19 pandemic, but be prepared to shake hands again after this virus is under control. A proper handshake is conducting whilst standing as the two people face one another. It is firm, brief, and accompanied by eye contact and a smile.

The Caribbean Bounce
In informal situations, Caribbean men greet one another with a 'Bounce' (also called the 'fist bump'). It is a gentle touch of the fists by the two men as they approach one another or in passing. There are also other variations of bounce.

EXCHANGE OF BUSINESS CARDS
Many professionals still exchange business cards. Business cards should be offered with the writing facing the receiver. When you are given a business card, do not just put it away, look at it and say something about it or ask the giver a question. This will give the impression that you are genuinely interested in the exchange or the business transaction.

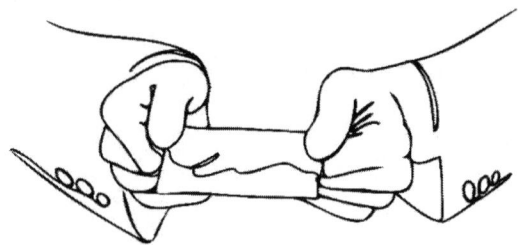

COMMUNICATION
Landline Phones
When calling a company landline, you should expect to hear a greeting according to the time of day, (for example: 'Good afternoon'), the name of the company, the name of the person answering and an offer to help. If you hear a simple 'hello', you may very well think you have reached a private home, or that the person on the other end was not expecting a business call.

Many staff answering company phones are trained to manage their tone and be pleasant, helpful and courteous to callers.

Cell Phone Etiquette
If a business uses a cell phone, you should expect to hear the receptionist reply as professionally as when on a landline. In the same way, if you are using your phone for business, you should answer with a greeting, your name or the name of your company, and offer to help.

Email Etiquette
When people use email for business, they must ensure that the

correspondence looks authentic. Formal business correspondence is expected to be on letterhead, signed, scanned and attached in the email. The standard form of the language should be used in the email and its attachments.

Social Media Etiquette

Like in other parts of the world, Caribbean professionals use social media to attract new customers/clients, but specific business is not carried out via public platforms. Some clients may prefer you to communicate with them via a social media platform which they are used to. In that case, the language used should be in its standard form, with words spelt out, not abbreviated, and the client's proper names should be used.

If you initiate business with a company you should start by using the official means, email or telephone, and once you have established contact, inform them that you can be more easily reached via whichever social media platform.

Body Language

As mentioned before, Caribbean people are very dramatic and communicate with their facial expressions, hand gestures and movements as they express themselves. Their feelings and intentions may be seen in their eyes, and they may even touch you to emphasise their point.

Because body language varies significantly with culture, visitors to the region should be tolerant, as the meaning of gestures may be totally different in their culture.

Caribbean people may sometimes laugh or joke when talking about a serious situation or accident which happened. They joke, not because they are glad it happened but because it is their way of dealing with the difficulty.

PERSONAL PRESENTATION AND APPEARANCE

Outfits

In the Caribbean, we still aim to dress like western professionals for work and other business-related occasions, such as conferences and official ceremonies.

Despite the tropical heat, some professionals dress in dark suits for business, some with blazers, while others dress in long-sleeved shirts and ties. For men, shirt colours for office work are solid colours (without patterns) and may range from maroons, blues and greens to more earthy and placid mustard, creams and, of course, white.

Women may wear skirts, trouser suits or dresses, some with jackets, for that extra 'punch', and some without.

If you plan to visit the Caribbean on business, be sure to find out before you leave your home country what occasions are on your agenda, so you can bring along appropriate clothes. Ladies should pack conservative outfits for meetings and ceremonies, such as referred to above; for dinners, an elegant or smart casual outfit will do, and for a formal evening session, an evening dress. Men must be sure to pack a lounge suit (matching jacket and trousers with an appropriate tie); a blazer which can be worn with any trousers will also come in handy, and a short-sleeved smart casual shirt. If invited to an evening function at a restaurant, note that jeans are not considered elegant or smart casual.

Accessories

Accessories for the business environment must be kept to a minimum: gold, silver, or perhaps a string of pearls, and a watch. Watches make a statement, so be sure to wear one for a business meeting.

Ladies must avoid jewellery that is flashy, jangles, or creates a noise, as these can be distracting in a professional setting. However, they can be worn to evening events.

Business outfits worn during the day can be enhanced with different accessories for an after work formal event.

Men must match their shoes with their belts, and their socks with their trousers in formal settings. White socks are not considered appropriate for business settings.

Shoes

You should also pay attention to your shoes. Different types of shoes are appropriate for different occasions. If you wear the wrong shoes for a business occasion, you might very well be judged by onlookers as not knowing what is appropriate.

For ladies, whole shoes with heels are appropriate for meetings and conferences. This includes shoes with either toes out or heels out, but not both. Many women also wear these with stockings. High heels and sandals are not considered appropriate for work.

Men should wear shoes with laces to the office and for other formal occasions.

Dress down Fridays
Many companies allow their staff to dress down on Fridays, with limitations. This could mean a polo shirt with or without the company logo, and a formal looking pair of jeans or chinos.

Hair
Hair is a powerful part of a person's presentation. How you wear your hair reflects your professional image. These days, a lot of Caribbean professionals want to reflect their heritage and as a result, wear their hair natural or follow the 'dreadlocks' hairstyle. They may look untidy, but this does not mean they do not perform professional work.

CARIBBEAN TIME AND TIME MANAGEMENT
Be prepared for social activities which do not start on time. Some people refer to this as 'Caribbean Time' (meaning 'any time'), and this can irritate many visitors who make every effort to arrive on time. Despite this, do not fail to be on time for your formal sessions, as business meetings and ceremonies usually start on time.

Chapter 7

Wedding Etiquette

Caribbean weddings are always beautiful experiences, with great memories. Whether it is a small family occasion or a large event with many friends and well-wishers, every effort is made to ensure it is beautiful.

RSVP

If you receive a wedding invitation, it is expected that you reply to indicate whether you will be attending. Many wedding invitations tend to include an RSVP card to be completed. It is necessary that you complete this and send it back as soon as possible so that the organiser can finalise arrangements for seating and catering.

GIFT LIST / GIFT REGISTRY

In the Caribbean, not all gift registries will be online. You may have to go to a store where the couple have compiled a list of items they wish their guests to purchase as gifts for them. Information relating to the gift list or gift registry is normally included in the wedding invitation, either at the bottom or the back of the invitation, or on a separate card. It is expected that invited guests will purchase a gift and one that the couple wished for.

Some people may request cash gifts, if they prefer to purchase heir own items, or for other reasons, such as to put the cash towards their honeymoon. The preference for cash gifts will also be indicated in the same invitation package.

THE CEREMONY

There are usually two parts to a wedding: the ceremony and the reception, and there could very well be a gap of at least an hour, sometimes more, between the ceremony and the reception as the bride and groom go somewhere to take pictures.

Weddings in the Caribbean are usually held in a church, though these days more couples are opting for non-church weddings such as at a hotel, in a garden or on a beach. Many tourist weddings have been held at waterfalls and historic sites. Non-church ceremonies tend to be more on the informal side.

OUTFITS AND DRESS CODES

Outfits for weddings tend to be very formal, especially if the ceremony is being held in a church. Men usually wear lounge suits, and ladies, long maxi dresses. Colours can range from mild and placid to bright and cheerful. In some cases, the bride and groom may include a dress code on their invitations, and guests are expected to comply.

A BEACH WEDDING

At a beach wedding, guests are not expected to wear suits, especially not dark suits. People wear lighter clothing in outdoor or seaside colours.

Men should consider wearing linen or cotton buttoned down shirts, even short sleeves, bearing in mind the dress code, if one was given. Trousers should always be long, never jeans or shorts. Shoes may be casual, like slip-ons.

Ladies should ensure their dresses are not too short or skirts too full, to cater for the wind, with elegant shoes.

GIFT TABLE OR ENVELOPE BOX

At the wedding reception, gifts and cards are usually handed directly to someone responsible to receive them, often a close relative of the bride or groom. For monetary gifts, a box might be placed in 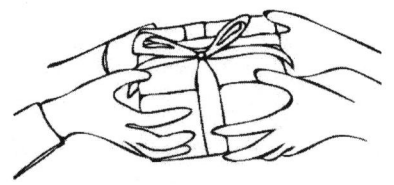 an accessible position, and there is usually a close relative of the couple nearby to assist guests or to ensure security.

BRINGING ALONG SOMEONE

It is not okay to bring along a friend or a child to a wedding to which you alone are invited. Neither is it okay to ask that your driver be allowed to remain for refreshments. In many Caribbean countries, weddings might be totally paid for by the bride and groom, and extra guests would affect the catering bill.

In the case of a young couple of middle to upper income, the parents might be the ones sponsoring the wedding costs. On the other hand, weddings in some rural areas might be a village affair, where family and close relatives contribute to food and drinks, and all are invited by word of mouth.

SEATING

If you are invited to a formal sit-down wedding, wait to see if there is a seating plan, as there might very well be. Your name might be placed on a table number.

FOOD AND DRINK

Watch to see what is expected here before you decide to head to the buffet table or to serve yourself. If it is an informal wedding, there might be servers, especially if the wedding is at a hotel. If it is a buffet, be disciplined and do not load up your plate or station yourself close to the bar.

TOASTING DURING THE RECEPTION

If called on to raise a toast to the bride or groom, do not make the mistake of giving a long story about how you met them or how they met. Make it short and simple, wish them all the best, and raise your glass in toasting.

TAKING PICTURES

Weddings usually have a professional photographer. If you take pictures for your personal benefit, do restrain yourself in posting them on social media until the bride and groom have posted theirs, or seek their permission. They may prefer to post pictures that put them in the best light possible, whereas your choice of pictures might be putting you in a better light. Remember this occasion is about them, not you.

Whatever type of wedding you are invited to, go, look your best, be on your best behaviour and enjoy yourself.

China
By Ellyna He

Chapter 1

Culture Symbols

CHINESE LANGUAGES

Chinese is one of the oldest languages in the world. Out of four great ancient civilizations, Chinese characters remain the only written system still used by human beings to this day.

Chinese language has played a significant part in shaping the Chinese mind and thinking. Compared to phonetic based languages, Chinese characters are pictorial based, and have a symbolic part that reflects the meaning.

For example, in Chinese, the word 'sun', in the old days would be written as below, resembling the shape of the sun, with the small dot in the middle meaning the sun is a luminous body. Overtime this has slowly transformed into to the character we use today: '日'.

'日'also becomes the component of other characters which are associated with the sun. For example, '旦 dan' can be translated as 'Dawn or Day break' which describes the pictures of sun rising above the mountain. '日' at the top means sun, '_' at the bottom represents the earth. The word of '旦 dan' simply displays the image of sun rising.

The reading and writing of pictorial characters and learning their various tones means that a Chinese person places a heavier reliance on the right brain thinking, the side of the brain connected to the visualisation, imagination and intuition. Some studies conducted in this area have revealed an interesting link between Chinese characters and Chinese thinking.

SILK ROAD

The ancient silk road is the transportation route that connected ancient

China with Central Asia, West Asia, Africa, and the Mediterranean. It derived its name from the trade routes primary commodity, distributing Chinese silk to Europe, and later becoming famous for the transportation of more exotic commodities.

Dating back to the Western Han dynasty (202 BC – 8 BC), the Silk road played a fundamental role in the development of the Chinese civilization, through the exchange of commodities, culture, science, technology, philosophy and religion between east and west. That significance has been reimagined with China's newest venture, The Belt and Road Initiative.

JADE

Jade is a natural stone, found in the colours green, purple, yellow and white. Merchants will normally buy the stone raw and unpolished, passing it to an artist who will cut and create designs from the stone. From there it will be polished into different styles and shapes and sold to jewellery stores throughout China. The Chinese desire for Jade has driven demand to record levels, driving up the price and in recent times outstripping the value of gold.

So why do Chinese people love Jade so much? In ancient times, Jade was used for sacrifices to heaven. The original symbol for Jade in Chinese characters meant ruler. In the Shang dynasty, Jade was to only be used by Royal nobles, giving it the symbol of authority and power, a meaning which has been carried on for thousands of years.

The great Chinese philosopher, Confucius, once said that jade has eleven virtues. Benevolence, intelligence, justice, manners, music, loyalty, credibility, heaven, earth, and mortality. These were virtues that he encouraged a person to follow.

'When I think of a wise man, his merits appear to be like Jade'. *Book of Odes*.

The Chinese love for Jade is also derived from its natural beauty, and you will find many idioms in the Chinese dictionary, using Jade to describe someone's beauty. For example, 花容玉貌 (*hua rong yu mao*), which directly translates as 'having the appearance like flower and beauty like jade'.

The symbolism and importance of Jade is etched deeply into Chinese history. In one of the most famous stories in China, 完壁归赵 'Jade

Returned to Zhao Region'. During a warring period (475—221 B.C), the empire of the Qin region, the most powerful kingdom during that period, wanted to exchange '和氏璧' *he shi bi*, a precious Jade artefact, with the Zhao region, in return for fifteen cities. The empire of Zhao sent the Lin minister to the Qin region to exchange the Jade. However, the empire of Qin did not intend to give up the fifteen cities. After using numerous diplomatic strategies, the Lin minister was successful in bringing back the Jade artefact without triggering war.

Later the king of the Qin region unified the whole country and carved his royal stamp from jade, passing it on to future generations and symbolising imperial power and status. This story has influenced Chinese history to this day and cemented the importance of Jade in Chinese culture.

THE FOUR NOBLE FLOWERS
Chinese culture is rich in flower symbolism and understanding the meaning of different flowers will help you to connect closely with the values that the Chinese hold dear to them.

Plum Blossom
Plum blossom has been described and shown in Chinese art and poetry for centuries. The Chinese love plum blossom, not only because of its beauty,

but also because of its spirit of strength and resilience because the plum blossom will bloom in the harshest of weather conditions. It represents the spirit of perseverance, courage and unremitting self-improvement.

Orchids

Orchids have often been used to describe nobility and scholarship. Growing in the mountains, they have a very subtle fragrance, light in colour, yet radiant and elegant, a symbol of purity and life lived without corruption. Orchids also represent love and friendship and you will often see them at weddings.

Bamboo

Bamboo has a deep strength; deeply rooted into the ground it will grow tall and straight. It represents the meaning of unyielding spirit and a humble heart. Bamboo also remains green throughout the four seasons, so it brings to the fore the spirit of extraordinary tenacity.

Chrysanthemums

The chrysanthemum blooms at the time of the traditional Chinese festival '重阳' (*Chong Yang*), which is the ninth day of the ninth month in the Chinese lunar calendar. During this festival, families will hold a ceremony to honour heaven and show respect to the elderly. Chrysanthemums are considered to have a cleansing quality, protecting against danger and giving longevity of life.

In some places, chrysanthemums are brought to the graves of the dead, when people visit their ancestors. In China, this is called '扫墓' (*Shao Mu*), which means to cleanse the grave of family members who have passed away. For this reason, you should use caution if gifting chrysanthemum flowers.

PAPER CUTTING: ART FROM SCISSORS

One of the traditional folk arts is paper cutting, with a history that can be dated back 1500 years ago. It has been popularly used in religious rituals, decoration and art.

There is an ancient story of an imperial concubine from the Han dynasty who died. The grieving emperor longed for his wife immensely and summoned a man called '李少翁' (*li shao wen*) to use paper to cut out a similar shape to that of his wife. With the paper shape in hand, the emperor used candlelight to project a silhouette of his wife on the wall, evoking her spirit.

Since the Tang Dynasty, paper cutting has been developed into sophisticated art which requires remarkable craftsmanship. The tools are very simple: paper, scissors, knife and a powerful imagination. The patterns are vivid and when unfolded will reveal the expressions of life, emotions and nature.

CONFUCIUS

One of the great pillars of Chinese civilization is the philosophy and teachings of Confucius, which often reinforce Chinese traditions and beliefs. Confucius is an ancient sage to the Chinese people, and like many great masters, his words and stories were recorded and scribed by his followers and passed on through generations in the 'The Analects' (*Lunyu*).

Confucius' teachings heavily promote a set of rules for social order, rules to follow which create harmony in society. As a great teacher, he championed the doctrine of '*Ren*' or 'the love of people' which centres around the values of strong family loyalty, and the respecting of elders by their children. He also pointed out the love should start with the parents as 'one without loving their parent does not know love to others'. He espoused the well-known principle 'do not do to others what you do not want done to yourself' (Confucius, Analects, chapter fourteen of book fifteen).

His teachings on morality and social correctness have had an impact even beyond China. Along with Daoism and Buddhism, Confucianism is a fundamental philosophy that has influenced Chinese and international culture to this day.

Chapter 2

Meeting, Greeting, Posture and Body Language

GENERAL SOCIAL CONTEXT

Having had the privilege of both living and working in both Chinese and Western cultures, I'm continually amazed at the subtle differences that can be found in how social dynamics play out. In Chinese culture, relationships and social interactions are often conducted with a view to 'Social Value'. Be it family, friendship or work circles, when you let your guard down and begin a new relationship, you are essentially giving privileged access to your network. So, getting to know a Chinese person for the first time can take a bit of effort.

In Chinese culture its customary to keep a little a bit of distance when you meet someone for the first time. If you're at the park and you meet a stranger, a simple head nod and gentle smile is a customary greeting and often, the gesture will be returned. If you've been invited to a party with a lot of new faces, you might find that people can act a little aloof or shy. They may even come across as stand-offish. Often the situation requires the introduction of a mutual friend to break the ice. More gregarious introductions are uncommon in Chinese culture and can make the receiver of such interactions uncomfortable. From personal experience and having lived in both Chinese and Western societies, I can tell you first-hand that while you might need to expend a little more energy in getting to know a Chinese individual, a successful interaction is often long lasting, fortunate and will quickly open you up to new friendship networks and possibilities.

In a social context, if you already know the person, the greeting can be quite direct. You may say, "Have you eaten?" "Where are you going?" Or "What are you doing?" This type of greeting can seem very strange or even rude, but it is in fact a very normal way to communicate for Chinese people and it even indicates that the relationship is very close. It differs from talking pleasantries, as is customary in many Western cultures, by asking,

"How's the weather?" Chinese people like to talk directly and somewhat pointedly. For example, when I go back to China to see my friends who I have not seen for a while, they normally say, "You look like you have gained some weight." Or "You look like you have lost weight." "You look not so well today, are you ok?" You might think it is intrusive for people to point out your weight, but for the Chinese, this is quite normal.

NAME AND TITLE

It is considered basic etiquette for the Chinese to call someone correctly with the correct title, especially if you are addressing someone who is older or more senior than you. Almost everyone who is older than you should not be called by their name directly; there is always a title after the person's surname.

Let us talk about the family title first. There is always one title to match with each individual in the family including your extended family, and the title can be very complicated to learn. For example, in the immediate family, you will call you older brother '*ge ge*' and older brother's wife as '*sao sao*'; you will call your younger brother '*di di*' and your younger brother's wife '*di mei*'.

In the social environment, if you don't know the person very well, and you don't know their career, you can address them respectfully in general terms according to estimated age. You can simply say the person's surname and followed by '*ni shi*' for females or followed by '*xian sheng*' for males.

If you already know the person's career, then it is very important to call them by their job title; for example, if Mr Zhang is a lawyer, we call him '*Zhāng lǜshī* 张律师'; '*lǜshī*' is translated as 'lawyer'. The reason we communicate in this way is mainly due to importance of social hierarchy in Chinese traditional history, where the title of what the person does reflects his or her social status.

Within a business network, if you have established a close relationship with your colleague or business partner, Mr Zhang, and he is younger than you, you can call him '*Xiǎo zhāng* 小张'; '*Xiǎo*' means small. On the other hand, if he is obviously older than you, you may call him '*Lǎo zhāng* 老张'; '*Lǎo*' means old. This shows your relationship is much closer.

BUSINESS CONTEXT

In a business environment, a formal handshake is very common in China.

It is similar to the western style of the handshake except the grip between hands can be a little softer and the duration can be shorter as well. You should always stand up before the handshake to show respect. If you are meeting someone in a senior position, they may not stand up for the handshake and it is acceptable for them not to do so.

Business cards are also very important for a successful business meeting. In almost every business meeting you go to, people will be handing out their cards. If you are doing business China, it is critical that you bring your own cards. How business cards are exchanged is equally important and you will need to show respect by handing out and receiving cards correctly, with both hands. Once you receive the card, take time to carefully read the details and give a few compliments; this will help you to ease any tensions or stress for both parties.

PUBLIC COURTESY

Displaying your affections in public, such as kissing and hugging is very uncommon in China and frowned upon, as most Chinese are raised with traditional values.

In the world of social media with Facebook and Instagram you would already have noticed that worldwide people love taking photos and sharing their experiences. In China, that goes to a different, almost over the top, level. Food shots and selfies are a very normal way in which many Chinese will express themselves and share their adventures. It also forms a big part of the 'social value' equivalency, so please don't judge or get offended when you see this.

SOMETIMES WE ARE TOO POLITE

'Harmony' is the core value of Chinese thinking. We try to 'devalue' ourselves during social interactions and place more 'value' on others to reach harmony. Most of the time it might seem too polite. For example, when you enter the room with someone, the Chinese like to let others in first, to make the other person feel above them and to help establish a great relationship. Quite often you might see two people spending quite a bit of time outside a door trying to let each other in first.

When your guest is leaving your house or your business, the Chinese like to send off the guest all the way to their car or other mode of transport to show respect. Once the guest gets into the car, the host generally stands there with their hand waving to say goodbye until the car drives off. In return, instead of saying 'thank you', the guest will show appreciation by saying '*Bu Ma Fan*', which means 'no need to make you trouble' to the host. This will be repeated often a few times until they get into the car. These back and forth interactions are ingrained in Chinese culture and whilst they may appear tedious to outsiders, they are critical for a harmonious relationship.

BE AWARE OF THE SOCIAL ORDERS

Influenced by Confucius' philosophy, some forms of ancient social ordering still playout in Chinese culture to this very day. The younger respects the older, the junior follows the senior, students obey teachers and so on. Here are some simple examples in daily practice:
- When you are passing things to the elderly or seniors, you will always use both your hands to show respect.
- You may find at schools, students generally like to listen to the teacher's lectures without questioning or challenging their teacher in front of other students.

Chapter 3

Conversational Dos and Don'ts

RESPONDING TO A COMPLIMENT

For Chinese people, accepting compliments can be considered offensive behaviour. Responding with a humble attitude and emphasising a deficiency in the complimented area is the culturally appropriate response. For example, your friends may compliment you by saying, "You look very pretty." Then you may politely disagree with them by saying, "没有，没有 *méi yǒu, méi yǒu.*" Which means, 'not at all, not at all'. This demonstrates your humility and reinforces the perception of the original compliment.

PERSONAL QUESTIONS ARE COMMON

My Western friends often mention to me that they are surprised at how directly I and other Chinese people ask personal questions, even if we are not close friends. Being asked personal questions is in fact quite common in China. For example, I am often asked, "Are you married?" "Have you got a child?" "Have you bought a house?" Or even, "How much did you pay for your house?" Private questions like this may seem extremely rude in other cultures but are acceptable and considered quite normal for Chinese people.

THE CHINESE ARE HOLISTIC THINKERS

There have been some interesting studies which have examined the differences between Chinese and Western thinking. The Chinese tend to look at things in context rather than specifics or instances. They tend to focus on the connectedness of different objects rather than analysing any significant one thing. I personally believe this is an important guideline for having a successful business conversation with Chinese companies or individuals. Lead with your vision and goal before delving into any intricate details.

THEY MAY BE 'HARD TO UNDERSTAND'
Most Chinese people like to withhold their opinion about things, so you may find it is hard to find where they really stand on a topic. One of my Western friends once mentioned to me that she found it extremely hard to take the conversation to the next level when talking with her Chinese colleagues.

The Chinese believe that people with wisdom do not easily reveal their thoughts, intentions or even their emotions. Sometimes behaving aloof or even foolish is preferred, even if you have knowledge and expertise in a matter.

In cases like employment relationships or client management, I suggest that learning to read body language and subtle signs will greatly assist you in getting to know your Chinese counterparts' true thoughts.

CONVERSATION TOPICS TO HELP YOU TO BREAK THE ICE
Chinese people often refer to China as 'Mother China', being deeply proud of the motherland with fifty-six different cultures and over 5000 years of history, art, language and customs. Showing that you are genuinely interested in China and its people will help you to set up a great connection in your conversation. Whilst this is true for most cultures, for Chinese people this display of genuine intent can be a game changer for developing a warm connection.

THINGS NOT TO MENTION
The Chinese are very sensitive to any politically related topic; any comments regarding the past or current political leaders or government should not be mentioned. Avoid having opinions about Taiwan, Tibet and Hong Kong issues; keep in mind that Taiwan, Tibet and Hong Kong are part of China. The Chinese often take strong pride towards the nation, so unless you are very close with the person you speak to, avoid having negative comments about the country and its people throughout the conversation.

Chapter 4

Gifts Giving

In China, gifts play an important role in building and strengthening the relationship between the giver and receiver. Giving appropriate gifts at the right occasions will ultimately improve the social relationship. Whilst it is common to wrap gifts in most cultures, the opposite is true in China and it is common for most Chinese not to wrap gifts. They may just put it in a bag and give it to you; so, don't be too offended should you receive such a gift.

When you present a gift to the host or the receiver, it is very important to hand it to them with both hands, to show respect. When you present the gift, you may say some wishes like, 'happy birthday' or 'Happy New Year'. In some cases, it is very common for the Chinese to show humbleness by devaluing the gift and say, 'This is a little something for you.' Continuing this important ritual of humility and respect, the receiver may reject the gift a few times by saying, "Please don't take the trouble, I am afraid of inviting you again next time." But this normally doesn't mean they don't want the gift and eventually they will accept. This back and forth effort may seem unnecessary and pointless to many other cultures; however, for the Chinese it represents the great value of '客气 *Ke Qi*' in China.

In Chinese, there is a saying '礼尚往来' which means 'Courtesy calls for reciprocity'. It presents the important value of reciprocity in Chinese relationships. If you receive a gift from someone, you may need to remember to have something in return. This is important to note in business relationships because on some business occasions people may reject your gift to protect their business interests. In that case, you will need to learn to read the clue to not insist on giving. Likewise, you may want to show some caution in accepting gifts from business associates. It is impossible to highlight every scenario and how to proceed; therefore, the recommendation is to be aware of the '礼尚往来' and the role it plays in Chinese culture. With that knowledge, you can use your judgement in proceedings.

Don't Open the Gift in Front of Others

If you are the receiver of a gift, it is not customary to open the gift in front of the sender. Part of the reason for this is to ease the tensions that may arise if the gift is not appropriate. In addition, one person may give a less valuable gift than the other, so by doing this you will avoid any embarrassment and save the face of the gift givers.

Cash Can Be a Gift

I remember when I visited China with my son, I received lots of cash for him from visitors. Most of the visitors would bring a red envelope with some money inside the envelope. A red envelope is a gift given to the parents as a gift for the child. Cash is also a common gift for weddings. You will normally give cash as a present to the new couple, and instead of a red envelope, there will be a registration table set up to collect the cash. A person will be assigned to write down the names and amount of money you give to the new couple which will then be reviewed after the wedding.

Gift Taboos

The number four in Chinese is pronounced '*Si*', which shares the same pronunciation as '死' which means 'die', so make sure to not gift in four pieces, and not have the number four printed on the gift.

The Chinese do not like the colours white and black for special occasions, as they are commonly used for funerals. So, try to avoid gifting things in white or black colours.

- *Clock:* A clock in Chinese is pronounced '*Zhong*', and it shares the same pronunciation as the word '终', which means 'termination'. So, it is considered as bad luck.
- *Pear:* Pear has the meaning of 'separation' in Chinese, so make sure you do not only give pears as a gift. If you mix pears with other fruit, it will be okay to give.
- *Umbrella:* In some areas, umbrellas are also considered an inappropriate gift, as umbrella in Chinese has the same pronunciation as '散 (*sàn*)' which can mean 'separation'. So, try to avoid this gift if you can.
- Green Hat: Men wearing green hats in Chinese are called '戴绿帽子 (*dài lǜ mào zī*)'. In Chinese, this means his wife has cheated on him. So, please bear in mind this saying in China.

Chapter 5

Dining Etiquette

If you ever want to do business in China, understanding Chinese dining etiquette is fundamental for success. The Chinese love to do business at the dinner table and matters become easier to negotiate when you start dining with your Chinese counterparts.

It all starts with punctuality. If you are invited to a dinner party by the host, it's important to be there on time, to show respect to the host.

SEATING ARRANGEMENTS

The Chinese normally use round tables to hold a dinner party, which comes down to the love of the round shape. Seating arrangements at the table reflect the social hierarchy and connections among attendees. The important seats are as follows: the middle seat facing the door and the seats either side of this. The host normally sits in the middle, facing the door, and the most important guest sits to the right of the host. Then, the next important guest sits to the left of the host. So, if you are hosting Chinese guests, keep this arrangement in mind when it comes to seating. The following diagram illustrates the Chinese seating etiquette.

ORDERING THE FOOD

If you are the host of the party and time permits, pass the menu around the table for each guest to look at. If the time is limited, you may ask if anyone has anything in particular that they would like to eat, or some dietary requirement that they need to manage, then you can order for all. When ordering, it is best to order a number of dishes that matches the total number of people at the table. Try to have good combination and keep a balance between vegetables and meat, cold and hot dishes. If you are a guest invited to order from the menu, choose dishes in the middle range of pricing and dishes popular to the area.

TABLEWARE

• *Chopsticks:* When you talk about Chinese dining it is hard to not mention chopsticks. Chopsticks have been central to the Chinese dining experience for three thousand years. Whilst many Asian cultures use some form of chopsticks, Chinese chopsticks can be identified by the following: one side is rounded in shape and the other side is a square shape. This reflects the Chinese traditional belief that the sky is round and that the earth is square.

When dining, never point your chopsticks at someone; it is considered extremely rude. When idle, never stick your chopsticks into a bowl of rice; the Chinese will only do this when they are praying to their ancestors. When you are dining at a restaurant, your table setting will normally come with a ceramic chopstick rest, so when you are not eating, you can rest the chopsticks on the top of the rest, with the end you eat from facing towards the table centre. If you are dining without the chopstick rest, then you can rest the chopsticks next to your plate or bowl. Resting the chopsticks whilst you are talking is recommended.

The purpose of using the chopstick is for eating, so do not wave the chopstick around the food to select the food, and also don't lick the chopstick with your tongue. Try to pick the food and carefully place it in your mouth.

In some formal dining settings, a serving chopstick is provided next to the personal chopstick. It is normally longer than the personal one. In this case, use the serving chopstick to pick the food on the table.

• *Spoon:* A spoon is normally placed to the left side of the chopstick; you will use the spoon to drink soup or use it as assistant to hold food with your left hand when picking food with chopstick from your right hand. It is to avoid the source from the food spilling on the table.

- *Towel plate:* Some restaurants will have a square shape of the towel plate presented on the table which is placed on the left side of the serving plate. A warm, sanitised wet towel will be handed by the waiters to this plate, it is for you to wash your hand before dining. Please don't use this to wash your face.
- *Teacup:* Teacups are normally presented on the right side next to the chopstick, tea is typically served before starting your meal as a way to cleanse your palate.
- *Rice wine glass:* Chinese love drinking rice wine and the rice wine glass is the smallest glass on the table. With a high alcohol content, a small serving is all that is required when drinking.
- *Bowl:* Bowls are used for eating rice or drinking soup. In the southern part of China, the bowl is also used for serving yourself with dishes. It normally seated on the top left of the dining plate. However, in some restaurants, if the serving plate is not served, the bowl may be presented on top of the dining plate.

DINING ETIQUETTE

As mentioned earlier in the chapter, Chinese normally like to have large round tables for dining, so when you dine reach out for the food closest to you first, do not stand up to reach for the food far from you. As a guest normally start the meal following this rule and as each plate is presented to you proceed to try a small portion.

There are slight differences between southern China and other parts of China when using bowl. In the south of China people pick the food from the table and eat the food from the bowl. They will spit the bones and other uneatable items on to their dining plate. While in other parts of China people normally pick the dishes to the dining plate and eat from dining plate. The bowl will be saved for fried rice or soup which will normally come after the main dishes. If you need steam rice, you will need to order it specifically.

When eating rice with a bowl, you may hold the bowl with your left hand and chopstick with your right hand, lift the bowl towards your mouth and push the rice to your mouth with your chopstick.

DRINKING ETIQUETTE

Apart from Western wines which may be displayed on your table, there is often a rice wine glass provided which is almost the same size as a shot glass. There may be a small rice wine jar which has prefilled with rice wine next to the rice wine glasses. Chinese like to have rice wine glasses filled full when toasting, so each toast you will need to drink the whole glass of wine and refill again. So, the rice wine jar is conveniently placed for refilling the wine.

Formal toasting starts after everyone is properly seated; it normally starts with the host. The host will start the meal with a toast accompanied with welcome speech.

Chapter 6

Business Etiquette

GREETINGS AND USING THE RIGHT TITLE

It is especially important to greet people with the correct business title in China, and to recognise their ranking within the organisation. You will normally start with the person's surname and follow with the person's title. For example, Mr Zhang is the manager in a finance department. Manager in Chinese is pronounced as '*jīng lǐ*'. Therefore, you will call him '*zhāng jīng lǐ*'. In Chinese culture, subtitles are not used in greetings as they may cause offence. For example, if Mr Zhang is the vice president of the company, you will need to call him '*zhāng Zǒng*', which means Zhang President. He is still the vice president, but we don't call him that when we greet him.

If you don't know the business title or organisational ranking, you may simply call someone by their surname and follow this with '女士 *nǚ shi*' for women, or '先生 *xiān sheng*' for men. Therefore, if you did not know Mr Zhang's title, you can call him '张先生 *zhāng xiān sheng*'. This has a very similar meaning to ladies and gentlemen in English.

BUSINESS CARD

Prepare your business card before meetings. If you are meeting with a Chinese client, make sure you have the content of your card translated into Chinese as most Chinese will have limited English. This is a great way to show respect. When giving someone your business card, do so with both hands; the same applies when receiving cards.

DRESS CODE

Professional business attire is recommended when conducting business in China; it also gives a great first impression to the people you are meeting with. Dress neatly and groom yourself well before any meeting. Choose plain colours instead of overly bright colours as you want to portray humility in your attire.

The Concept of Face: 'Miàn Zi'

It is very important to be aware of '*Miàn Zi*' which can be directly translated to 'face'. In Chinese culture, the concept of *Mian zi* does not relate to looks. Instead, it relates to social reputation or social status for this person or the social group this person belongs to.

Mian zi is akin to a social currency; you can give it to someone (给面子), lose it (丢面子), fight for it or gain it back (争面子), and it is also something you can save for someone (保住面子). In some ways *Mian zi* is one of the most important commodities of Chinese social dynamics.

For example, in a meeting, a person of junior ranking would not normally want to disagree with the opinion of a senior ranking person, as they would want to give *Mian zi* to that person. In the same way, if someone higher than you in the organisation invites you for a lunch, it is not a good idea to refuse them, as you want to give *Mian zi* to the senior.

As you begin to understand the weight of *Mian zi* on social and professional dynamics, it becomes easy to spot how peoples' behaviour may change in different scenarios.

Be Aware of The Hierarchy

When Chinese people enter a meeting room, it is always the person who is of the highest rank who will enter first. When greeting members of a group, you should greet the highest-ranking person first, followed by second highest ranking person and so on. By doing this you save the face of senior parties.

During business negotiations, you may find the leader will lead most of the discussions and subordinates normally will not disagree or raise their opinions in front of the person in charge. In this case you may find the meeting to be unproductive as it is hard to find out what alternate opinions are.

Be Ready for the Feast and Wine – After Hours Network

The Chinese believe that people are born connected and grow up in collective society. The Chinese value relationship building. So, spending time to build deeper relationships with their business partner(s) seems incredibly worthwhile for them. Additionally, if you are visiting China for the purpose of business, you will need to understand that successful business deals do not only come from business meetings. You may be invited to dinners or to karaoke; in these cases, you should attend those meetings, as the invitation itself reflects that the Chinese party is serious about building a long-term relationship with you. On most occasions, lots of drinking and toasting will be expected at the dinner table or in the karaoke room.

COMMUNICATION DIFFERENCES

They tend to be reserved in what they think

There is a famous saying in China: '大智若愚'; this means that 'a man of great wisdom appears slow-witted'. For this reason, you may find that the Chinese like to withhold their opinion towards things, especially during business negotiations. You will need to be patient and show your sincerity, and in the end, they will reveal their thoughts.

They focus more on the long-term goal than the specific action point

Conducting business meetings with Chinese people can be lengthy and unproductive, as often both parties have different approaches towards the goal. Westerners like to focus on specific issues and resolve them straight away. However, the Chinese like to find the connections on the issues with other subjects and slowly resolve them, as they believe everything is connected. Whilst this can be frustrating, a simple understanding that the approach is different is all that is needed to achieve a favourable outcome.

Research shows that the Chinese are more right-brain thinkers than left-brain. This leads to a more conceptual mind than analytical mind. They like to detect feelings and be a bystander first. Sometimes, they may make decisions from their intuition.

Sometimes 'Yes' is 'No'

Be cautious when Chinese people say 'yes' to you straightaway. Most likely it means they are still making decisions. As the decision-making process is a lengthy one, a premature 'yes' is better than 'I don't know yet'.

Chapter 7

Wedding Etiquette

Chinese weddings are lively, colourful, and extravagant events, and they are as much about the marrying couple as the families involved. Filled with time-honoured traditions, symbolism and blessings, Chinese weddings are events aimed to bestow abundance and happiness to the newly married couple from their family, friends and community.

Due to cultural and ethnic differences, there are many variations of traditional weddings across China, meaning that not all weddings are the same. Added to this is the influence of western culture which has also seen some young couples deciding to follow a more Western way of marriage. The most popular types of weddings in China are ones which combine the traditional Chinese wedding ceremony with the traditions of a Western wedding.

Weddings in China can take a whole day and in some places the celebration can take up to a few days. If you are invited to attend a Chinese wedding, be sure to block out at least a whole day off for the event.

INVITATIONS

Invitations for Chinese weddings are normally sent out in a red card imbedded with some gold colour. The most popular ones normally have a double happiness symbol printed on the front. The inside of the card will contain all the wedding information, which is very similar to a standard invitation letter.

DRESS CODE

For ladies, it is best to keep it classy and to maintain a low profile, whilst still showing off your best characteristics. Invitations generally will not have any specific dress requirements, so sticking to the safe and elegant options will be your best option, and above all, try not to outshine the bride.

Make sure not to wear red or white, as the bride may wear both a Chinese traditional red wedding dress and a traditional white wedding dress. It would be considered rude to clash colours with her. Also, black is to be avoided, as black is normally reserved for funerals. Choose simple and warm colour tones.

For men, a simple suit is enough for the wedding. You may find that some people will only wear smart casual, which is also acceptable at Chinese weddings.

WEDDING GIFT

Preparing gifts for Chinese weddings is simple and easy. The Chinese will normally provide cash as a gift, which will be placed into a red envelope. When you arrive at the reception, you can sign your name in the registry book and there will be a dedicated person to collect the cash from you and keep a ledger. They will count the money and write down the name and amount into the book. As part of Chinese reciprocity etiquette, the married couple will be expected to gift a similar amount back to the guest when they hold an event.

GENERAL PROCESS DURING THE DAY

Many rules and processes needed to be followed in traditional Chinese weddings. In recent times, the Chinese have adopted a more simplified way to celebrate. Below are some of the more popular customs.

- *The groom will pick up his wife-to-be*

The groom will come to bride's house to pick her up in the morning.

Traditionally, the groom will come in a wooden sedan chair which will be carried by four people. There will also be a group of traditional theatre players with drums and gongs playing along the way.

- *Breaking the door: the fun part starts*

When the groom arrives, he and his best men will need to open the door by way of passing different tests, designed by the bride's girlfriends. For example, he will be required to sing a song loudly until the bride's girlfriends are satisfied. Or he will need to answer questions which have been prepared beforehand. This is a fun tradition which is great to be part of and great to watch.

- *Tea Ceremony with parents and grandparents*

A traditional tea ceremony takes place with the new couple in which they get down on their knees facing their parents. A cup of tea is then passed from each of them to their parents to drink. This is a touching symbol that shows their appreciation for the many years of support in their upbringing. At the same time, the groom and bride will call their in-laws 'Mom' and 'Dad'. The symbolism of this is to announce they are officially part of the same family. After drinking tea, they will normally receive the red envelope filled with money from their parents in exchange; this is to wish them a happy marriage.

Moving to the Reception

The ceremony will continue during the reception. When the new couple arrive at the reception, they come in carrying red silk from two ends; in addition, the bride will have a red cloth covering her face. The couple will enter via a red carpet upon which a basket of fire is placed. Crossing over the flames means their lives will be filled, full of fire, full of passion, and fortune. Then they will come across a saddle which means that their life will be safe and healthy. Finally, they will enter onto the stage and bow three times to worship heaven, parents, and their spouse. After that, the groom can lift the bride's red face cloth so that she can then be seen by him.

Wedding Banquets

After you enter the banquet hall, you may find your name on the table and take a seat before bride and groom arrive. After the ceremony is finished, the host normally will announce that the dining will begin.

Although some couples have adopted the Western ceremony for the reception, the traditional Chinese banquet remains the same. It is very elaborate and normally comes with eight to nine courses. Those courses normally are symbolic courses that come with meaning. For example, fish will normally be served, and this means fertility and abundance in the couple's life.

During the meal, there is normally toasting involved. The bride and groom will come to each table and offer a toast to the guest. Rice wine is the common wine at a wedding event. For each toast, the bride and groom will drink the whole glass of wine to show their appreciation. The guest then may offer a toast back to the couple. In this case, they are also required to finish the whole glass in one go.

MULTIPLE DRESSES

In Chinese weddings, it is quite common for the bride to change multiple times throughout the event. The bride will change from three to even five times throughout the celebration, simply because most women think this is the day for them and a great way to show themselves off.

THE WESTERN ELEMENTS

It is more and more common to see that some Chinese weddings have adopted Western styles to become simpler. In some weddings, the bride will wear a white wedding gown instead of the traditional red gown. The morning session, which involves the tea ceremony will remain the same; however, for the reception part, a Western style will be adopted. The groom will wait for the bride on the stage, then the bride will enter the hall accompanied by her father. The wedding vows and rings are exchanged and then couple are officially married.

France
By France de Heere

Chapter 1

Culture's Symbols

OUR TRICOLOUR FLAG!
The national emblem of the fifth republic, the tricolour flag was born under the French Revolution, using the king's colour (white) and the Paris city colours (blue and red). Nowadays, the Tricolour flag is flown on all public buildings. It's used for the most official ceremonies, civil and military, and sporting events!

Before becoming a flag, the tricolour was a cockade. The Marquis de Lafayette wrote in his memoirs that three days after the storming of the Bastille (1789), he forced Louis XVI to wear the tricolour cockade to go to the city hall. It was the sign of 'August and eternal alliance between the king and the people'. The tricolour cockade's success, patriotic symbol, is already assured.

Others could say that Paris had imprisoned the king, so the blue and the red colours imprisoned the white, the royal colour. The tricolour flag takes took its definitive form in 1794 but disappeared during the comeback of the monarchy from 1814 to 1830.

The last king, Louis-Philippe, in 1830, gave it a second birth by associating it with the famous Gallic rooster.

THE GALLIC ROOSTER
The choice of the rooster is really historical, and the origin is etymological. In the middle-ages, inhabitants of Gaul were called *gallus* in Latin, but *gallus* in Latin also translates as rooster. Thus, it is essentially a pun (a play on words). Although often used as a French symbol, especially.

The noise made by a rooster, the 'cocorico' sound, is sometimes used familiarly to express our national pride!

LA MARSEILLAISE: THE NATIONAL SONG!
This is our anthem, and it is played at national events, sport oriented or not.

It was created by Mr Rouget de Liste in 1792, when France was at war against Austria. At this time, it was called the 'war's song for army of the Rhine' and was sung by the national guard of Marseille. In 1792, the revolt against the constitutional monarchy exploded in Paris, and the Marseillaise army came to aid the revolutionaries in singing this song. From then it was called 'la Marseillaise'. On the 14th of July 1795, it became the official national anthem of France.

LA TOUR EIFFEL: 'LA DAME DE FER', THE IRON LADY
The Eiffel Tower is the emblem of Paris, our capital! She is affectionately known as the 'Iron Lady'. She was built for the Universal Exhibition in 1889 to prove the industrial power of France. At a height of 324 metres, she was designed by the architect, Stephen Sauvestre, and built by the engineer Gustave Eiffel.

THE FRENCH BAGUETTE
The baguette is the king of bread and is characterised by its elongated form.

It is traditionally around 65 centimetres in length, with a weight of 250 grams. In 1993, a law was passed standardizing how a traditional baguette (a 'baguette de tradition') should be made, using only wheat flour, yeast, salt and water. The quality of the bread is most important, as a baguette should be crispy on the outside and fluffy on the inside, exuding that wonderful smell of freshly baked bread.

Note: Since 1994, Paris has organised an annual competition for the best baguette in the capital! This event is entitled the '*Grand Prix de la Baguette de la Ville de Paris*'. The judges decide according to these criteria: aspect, cooking and crumb, smell and taste!

Abroad, there are now a few places where you can find this famous French baguette, but if the baguette doesn't come to you, you must come to her!

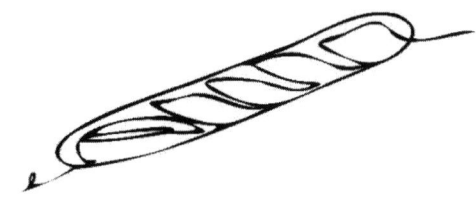

Our Good Local Products

Le champagne
This is an effervescent wine issued from the champagne area in the north-east region of France. It was the monk Dom Perignon in the C.17th who discovered many new winemaking techniques, such as increasing the ability of wines from the champagne region to keep more of their natural sugar content, enabling a second fermentation to naturally occur. Although, the main style of champagne wine production we recognise today occurred after his death.

It has international prestige and has become the national and international drink of choice for celebrations, feasts and ceremonies.

Le camembert
The camembert of Normandy is a cheese made from raw cow's milk, consisting of a soft doughy-like texture inside, surrounded by a floury soft crust. It is produced in Normandy (north-west France). The name comes from the village of Camembert, in Basse Normandy, where the cheese would originally have been produced.

Camembert is probably the most famous French cheese, but we have more cheeses in France than there are days of the year: more than 365 cheeses! France is considered as the country of cheese! The next item on the list makes a great accompaniment when eating cheese…

Wine
Red or white, it's a precious ally with our food!

In France, we have very nice areas where the vineyards are numerous: Bordeaux, Bourgogne, Champagne, Cote du Rhone, Chateau neuf du Pape, Jura, etcetera…

We serve it with our meals, and we are very proud of this heritage!

Dry sausage
Dry sausage or '*saucisson*' is a pork based cooked meat. There are many types of saucisson, such as *Saussison de Lacaune* or the *Sausisson de l'Ardeshe* and they are often enjoyed as an *hors-d'oevre* with an aperitif such as a glass of wine.

Le foie gras

Le foie gras is a cooking specialty consisting of full-fat liver from geese or ducks, a consequence of fattening them up by force-feeding, according to the law. The majority is prepared in three main areas: Périgord, Aquitaine and Alsace.

It is a luxury dish enjoyed at feasts like Christmas or Easter. Well-known in French cooking, it can be prepared in different ways. It is protected under the cultural and gastronomical heritage of France.

THE FRENCH MEAL

A French meal is very well-known because the French love eating, especially together, so the chance to have a meal together is very important. It is an occasion to be together around a table to exchange our points of view and to enjoy together our good cooking and local products. Indeed, the French gastronomic meal was recognised by UNESCO as an intangible cultural heritage of humanity in 2010, demonstrating the importance of this tradition to our culture.

During the meal, we appreciate and honour the quality of the cooking, *savoir-vivre* and good manners at table, the table's art, and the combination of food and wine which make every event special.

Le café et croissant

Foreigners may notice that our typical breakfast is coffee with a croissant! The croissant is a very typical pastry in France, formed in the shape of a half-moon. You can find it in every bakery in France; in fact, it is so popular that you can find them in bakeries across the globe!

FRENCH ELEGANCE

French Elegance is also very appreciated and envied all over the world. Since the C.18th, all of Europe looked towards French fashion for inspiration because it evocates elegance and refinement. That is why we can say that fashion is registered in the psyche of French people. Their style, their appearance and their sobriety give envy to other populations. Fashion designers such as Chanel, Yves St Laurent, Dior have maintained a reputation of French elegance for many years.

Also, French perfumes are very famous and appreciated all over the world.

L'ART DE VIVRE À LA FRANÇAISE

French lifestyle or *French art de vivre* is also very famous globally but it's a little bit difficult to define it. It is a general expression to describe our way of life.

This French style includes a certain attitude and a *savoir-vivre* which we are famous for internationally. I would go further and say it is a combination of elements which take the historic origins and France's culture, whilst revealing our taste, our esthetical research, a sense of detail, and also symbolises our freedom to make our own choices and the possibility to say what we think without fear.

LILY: THE FLOWER SYMBOL OF FRANCE

For historical reasons, the lily has become the flower symbol of France. The crown coat of arms of France represents the three flowers of the lily, evoking the Holy Trinity of Catholicism (the God, the Son and the Holy Spirit) and the theological virtues (faith, hope and charity).

The whiteness of the flower symbolises purity, innocence and virginity. This is why we find them in churches, and especially at weddings, and at funerals to give the idea of the soul's purification after death before going to paradise.

Chapter 2

Meeting, greeting, posture and body language

POSTURE
The French value good posture, as do most Europeans, as it indicates pride and self-respect.

A straight stance is essential! Stand up straight with your shoulders back, chin up (no one wants to highlight a double chin), hands by your sides, and legs shoulder width apart.

BODY LANGUAGE
Eye contact is very important to us, as we appreciate people expressing genuine interest.

If you don't maintain eye contact, we may think you are not interested, or have something to hide.

Here is a list of small gestures commonly used by the French:

a) Thumbs up, to indicate approval, and thumbs down to indicate disapproval.

b) Turning your wrist on your nose indicates you are drunk.

c) When you hold your palm to your forehead, you are fed up.

d) When you pass the thumb on your chin towards your interlocutor, it means, 'I understand; I'm right and you're not!'.

d) Pointing to your temple with your index finger indicates you think a person or comment is ridiculous.

TEMPERAMENT
The majority of French people are friendly, easy going and open. We also tend to be quite tactile, some more so than others. It tends to depend on the region you were raised in, and/or your upbringing.

Unfortunately, Parisians are considered quite rude and unfriendly, which is a problem for them rather than anyone else. When Parisians travel abroad, they tend to be indiscreet, loud and quite arrogant.

Generally, the French are considered to be proud, arrogant, chauvinistic, undisciplined and rebellious, but we aren't all bad! We like to share our opinions and create a convivial atmosphere, especially when socialising, by using humour. The French are known for their *art de vivre* (art of living). We enjoy creating pleasurable moments to share in beautiful environments.

French people from the south have more of a Latin temperament which is far warmer and more welcoming, especially with foreigners.

During the day, we like to greet everyone we meet with '*Bonjour*' (Good morning or hello) and kisses on the cheeks, but not a French kiss, of course!

SMILE

Parisians have a reputation for not smiling often, although those who live in the south smile regularly.

I like saying that the smile is a wonderful arm to welcome others with; I speak about the sincere smile though!

GREETINGS

In France, we can greet in four different ways:

1. By bowing one's head, making eye contact and greeting with 'Good morning, Sir/Madam/Paul'; 'Bonjour, Monsieur/Madame/Paul', (without physical contact) is a nice way to personalise the greeting.

2. By shaking hands and introducing yourself by name. You can add, 'I am delighted/pleased to meet you', to make the greeting even more polite: '*Bonjour, France de Heere, je suis enchanté(e) de faire votre connaissance*'.

If you are with a friend or friends ensure you introduce them too.

Be mindful that a man is always introduced to a lady, and it is the lady who dictates the type of greeting to be used.

3. If you are greeting family or friends, it is normal to kiss once on each cheek.

4. For gentlemen who wish to show their refined nature and respect for married and mature women (the '*baise-main*'), a feigned kiss on the hand is warranted. They will bring their lips close to the woman's hand without touching it. This practice is fading in popularity, but boys still learn the technique at the age of fifteen at 'French rallies' (a selective private party). This practice is sometimes used at an elegant and formal wedding or gala event.

Chapter 3

Conversation Dos and Don'ts

France is well known to be an international hub for freedom of speech. We like to discuss a broad range of topics and encourage healthy debate between those with opposing points of view. We all enjoy expressing our opinion and celebrate our freedom of expression, which is an important part of our cultural identity.

We often speak just for the sake of it, rather than remaining silent. We feel it is necessary to share our opinion on every topic of discussion, no matter how little knowledge we may have on the subject. Often our opinions are formed depending on the region of France we are from. We like to have our voices heard, which is often perceived as either arrogant or enthusiastic. Never be reluctant to disagree. We welcome it.

Many French people speak English, but not many other foreign languages. As this is the case, we are grateful if any visitors speak French. The effort is always appreciated.

The French are quite modest, and do not like to discuss their personal lives with people they do not know well. Safe topics of discussion vary depending on the region. Listed below are topics to discuss, and those to avoid.

SUGGESTED TOPICS OF CONVERSATION
In general, you will be well received if you ask questions and show interest in your interlocutor. To ensure pleasant conversation, consider discussing the following topics:

Food – Food is important to the French. We are proud of the quality of our local produce and enjoy cooking traditional dishes for family and friends at home as well as dining out. We also are obsessed with watching cooking programmes. Food is a source of joy, so it is always a welcome topic of conversation. As there are so many foods, dishes and traditions unique to different regions, asking about them is a safe conversation starter no matter who you meet.

Wine – We have a great reputation for the quality of our wine which is produced in different regions across France. We appreciate the pairings of great food and wine, so discussing and tasting wine is a good choice in a social setting. We have a lot of knowledge of wine and experience in drinking it, so we are happy to discuss this topic for a while!

Current affairs – We keep updated with news and current affairs locally and abroad over a diverse range of subjects. We are a country rich in contradictions and are known for labour strikes, protest and rallies which are common occurrences.

Culture and fashion – We are known for our love of culture. There are always many new exhibitions to attend across a range of cultural genres such as art, cinema, theatre, music and fashion. Attending exhibitions or asking for suggestions of which exhibitions to attend are great ways to start conversations and learn about different points of view. You will also have the benefit of enriching your senses by attending the exhibitions.

Weather – The weather is always a neutral and safe topic of discussion, as it something we all have in common.

Travel – The French travel regularly, so it is of interest to most people to compare travel stories and discuss different cultures and traditions.

Sports – Football (soccer), rugby, tennis, golf, handball, running, and skiing are all popular sports in France. Football is the most popular sport for French people (as it is in most countries), so we will be happy to engage in that conversation!

Topics to Avoid

There are a few topics that you would be wise to avoid.

Our country has a colonialist history which has allowed immigrants from many different countries to become residents and citizens of France, mainly after the Second World War. These immigrants include Algerian, Moroccan, Chinese, with 46% coming from Europe.

Religion

In France, we practice many different religions, as we have been a country of freedom of conscience since 1905. The French are predominantly of the Catholic faith (41%), with many other religions such as Judaism, Islam, Buddhism and Hinduism being practiced also. Interestingly, 40% of the French are not religious. Religion has always been a sensitive topic no matter what country you visit, so it is best to avoid.

Politics

We have a diverse range of political opinions and affiliations with strong convictions, so it is best not to discuss if you do not know the people you are socialising with well. It can often spark heated debate.

Money

It is always in poor taste to speak of money, especially if you are of the Catholic faith. We do not like to speak of our income or assets, or lack thereof, out of respect to others who may be suffering hardship. Money can be a cause of great stress to many, especially during periods of unemployment, so it is best to be gracious and not discuss it.

Immigration

France has been the victim of many terrorist attacks by fanatical Muslims over recent years, so immigration has become a sensitive topic best to be avoided.

Racism

Unfortunately, racism does exist between some people of different cultural backgrounds. It is always best not to get involved in discussions of such a delicate nature.

Social issues

There are many polarising social topics such as abortion, gay marriage, adoption, euthanasia etcetera. People tend to have strong opinions for and against, and therefore, debate on the subjects can be intense and become heated.

Chapter 4

Gifts Giving

There are specific guidelines to follow when gift giving in France, depending on the occasion and your relationship with the recipient. Relationships can be strengthened by showing your affection or appreciation with a small gift, even without a specific occasion to celebrate.

In general, no matter how big or small the gift may be, it is important to personalise the gift to make it meaningful. Take an interest in the recipient's tastes to assist you in selecting an appropriate gift but ensure you can exchange or return the gift if necessary.

Pay attention to the gift wrapping as it is as important as the gift itself, and do not forget to remove the price tag!

If you are the recipient of the gift, say 'thank you' before opening it and to be polite, mention that it was not necessary. Open the gift immediately in the presence of the donor in private, and always respond enthusiastically no matter what the gift may be. Even if you are disappointed, show appreciation.

Below is a gift giving guide for specific celebrations throughout the year. You do not need a specific celebration to offer a gift. You can offer a gift at any time to thank someone. Wine, gourmet food, chocolates or flowers are popular examples.

Dinner party – If you go to dinner at a friends' home whom you do not see very often, show your appreciation. It is a way to say thank you, especially if you cannot return the invitation quickly. This custom is relatively recent in France. *It has become customary, but not indispensable.* It is important to know that in our parents' time, they did not take a gift to a dinner party as they would return the invitation later. They would only give a gift if they were unable to return the invitation. Today however, do not feel like you must arrive with your hands full every time you have a dinner at a close friend's house. If you do not know your hosts well, please send flowers the day before or on the day of the party with your business card.

Passing the gift to the recipient – Your generosity must be discreet and be sure not to mention the cost! When you bring the gift, offer it at a time when you will be alone with the host, as you could embarrass the other guests who arrived empty-handed.

Cocktail party – The cocktail party is a reception with *hors d'oeuvres* and is served standing around a buffet between six p.m. and eight p.m. It makes it possible to show gratitude to large numbers of people at the same time. That is why it is not customary to bring gifts, except at a wedding cocktail party, of course.

Wedding – If you are invited to a wedding, it is customary to present a gift. It is essential if you accept invitations to the cocktail party and the dinner. Usually, the bride and groom have a bridal registry which allows you to deposit a sum of money once you choose your gift, otherwise you can bring a personalised gift on the wedding day. Be careful in this case, to attach a signed card to the gift to ensure they know the gift is from you.

Birth or baptism – If you receive a birth announcement, it is nice to respond by sending a gift for the baby. Similarly, if you are invited to the baptism, it is customary to attend with a gift for the baby. Do not forget to include a card.

Office – Whenever there is a celebratory event for a colleague such as a wedding, birthday, retirement etcetera, it is a good idea to organise a group gift. It stimulates comradery and humanises you amongst the group, which is important.

Home stays – Obviously, if you are invited to spend the weekend or several days at a friend's house or holiday home, present a gift to show gratitude. It shows you are touched by their generosity. The gift does not need to be expensive. Champagne, a decorative object such as a lantern or scented candle, a tray or vase, or product that represents your own country/region.

Thank your hosts – It is important to ensure you thank your host. It can even be done by SMS the next day. If you were at your friends' house on holiday, write your 'castle letter' (a handwritten letter) to thank them for the good time spent in their lovely home.

Chapter 5

Dining Etiquette

CORRECT TABLE SETTINGS

In France, you will notice numerous subtle differences in the way we lay our table settings, as compared with our European neighbours. We have been conscious of retaining our historical traditions.

When invited to a friends' house, be mindful that no matter the time noted on the invitation, you are expected to arrive fifteen minutes later to ensure the hostess is ready for you.

When you enter the dining room, the table should be laid in the traditional way. The spoon and knife should be on the right side, fork on the left side with prong-side down; the spoon is turned towards the table, and the knife is turned with the sharp side facing the plate. The reasons are twofold. Firstly, the hallmarks or engravings are visible on the top, which is the opposite of the English. Secondly, since the 17th century, the French have used tablecloths to set their tables, with forks facing prongs down to avoid any suggestion of aggression. As many of the French were of the Catholic faith, they believed the fork prongs symbolised a devil's blivet or tuning fork. Their fear of the devil and potential violence between guests prompted them to always place the prongs face down.

There are two ways to arrange the glasses at your table: either put them just in front of your plate in the middle or on the right side above the knife, as in gourmet restaurants.

Traditionally, bread plates are placed on the left side of the main plate but tend to only be used in restaurants. It is rare that you will now find them used in French homes. However, bread is still an important component in French meals. The most common way to eat bread as part of the meal is to use it instead of a knife to push the food onto the fork. It is also used on a fork to mop up gravy and sauces, as subtly as possible.

French Gastronomic Meal Recognised by UNESCO

In November 2010, UNESCO recognised the French gastronomic meal. It was registered as *Intangible Cultural Heritage of Humanity* by UNESCO. As such, it is important to us to incorporate the following characteristics in each meal to pay homage to our heritage:

- Conviviality.
- Savouring the quality of cooking.
- Sharing pleasant moments around the table.
- Honouring the quality of the local products our country produces.
- Expressing good manners at the table.
- Enjoying the pairing of food and wine.
- Appreciating the presentation of both the food and the table setting.

Traditional Meals

I believe the most traditional French food internationally is the French baguette, which can be eaten with every meal.

- Breakfast: our standard traditional breakfast is a cup of tea or coffee, with butter and jam or honey on toast, and perhaps orange juice and a croissant.
    - Breakfast time: until eleven a.m.
- Lunch: We prefer to have a substantial meal for lunch, time permitting. It may include:
    - Starter.
    - Main course, which is usually meat or fish with vegetables.
        - Cheese and dessert (fruits, cream, cakes).
        - Lunch time: Between twelve p.m. and one-thirty p.m.
- Dinner: We usually have another substantial meal of three courses for dinner.

- Starter: soup is a popular choice for dinner.
- Main course: usually a lighter dish than lunch, such as pasta or Quiche Lorraine (a French pie with bacon and eggs)
- Cheese and dessert (fruits, yoghurt, cakes)
- Dinner time: between seven p.m. and eight-thirty p.m.

TRADITIONAL FRENCH FOODS

We have many delicious traditional meals cooked regularly depending on the region we are from. You may be familiar with many of them. They include:

Quiche Lorraine, pot-au-feu, *veal blanquette*, cassoulet, sauerkraut, crêpes, beef bourguignon (burgundy beef), coq au vin, and many more.

TRADITIONS FOR SPECIAL OCCASIONS

Traditional Catholic feasts vary depending on your family. My family enjoy the following.

Christmas: Following midnight mass, we enjoy a celebratory meal of foie gras (of duck or goose), oysters, and orange salad with a special doughnut. In the area of Provence, they have the famous thirteen desserts: composed of various nuts, dried fruits (almonds, hazelnuts, dried figs, raisins), local sweets (flatbreads with jams, fruit pastes, *caliçons*, nougat) and fresh seasonal fruits (oranges, apples, clementines etcetera).

Christmas lunch: Oysters, turkey or game, followed by cheese and delicious Christmas chocolate cake.

Easter: Traditional lamb served with beans or green beans followed by a decadent cake. After mass, we hunt for Easter eggs with the children in the garden (chocolate eggs, that is)!

Candlemas and Shrove Tuesday: Crepes, of course!

Chapter 6

Business Etiquette

Although there has been a decline in social etiquette standards over recent years amongst the French, especially in the bigger cities such as Paris, this is not the case within our professional lives. Maintaining a respectful working relationship between colleagues is still considered important, fortunately. I do not believe all etiquette standards are maintained however, as these same standards would be replicated socially. That said, a positive working relationship between peers and clients is demonstrated and is considered essential to the function of successful business practice.

So how do the French behave in the workplace? The following are a few important considerations in order to adapt appropriately and thrive professionally in France.

PROFESSIONAL MANNERS AND RITUALS
Workplace rituals punctuate the professional day. It is advisable for foreigners to adopt these rituals as quickly as possible for professional acceptance. Regular coffee breaks, weekly meetings and casual Fridays are examples of rituals that need to be adhered to.

The first ritual of the day is to *greet everyone* you come into contact with each morning. When I say everyone, I mean everyone; from the person at the top of the corporate ladder (CEO) to those with entry level positions. It is a polite way to demonstrate respect for all colleagues and is also a way to highlight your presence.

The second important ritual is the morning coffee break with colleagues (73% of French people take it). It is an important time reserved to build rapport by discussing personal and social issues in addition to professional subjects. It is an informal way of networking, which is vital for professional success.

- If you work in an open-plan environment, discretion and self-control are essential, and should be adopted by all. Respect each person's professional output without being intrusive or overly curious.

- To foreigners, we can appear distant with our colleagues. We like to respect the boundaries between our professional and private lives. Nevertheless, among young professionals especially, we find many become personal friends.
- I will not deny that we also like to have a drink or two with colleagues to celebrate special occasions such as a retirement, promotion, an engagement or birth of a child etcetera.
- Casual Friday has also become a ritual in France, but beware of the potential trap, as explained below.

DRESS CODE

Corporate dress code varies greatly depending on the industry and company. In any case, it is recommended that you wear clean, pressed and appropriate clothing.

The following rules apply to *conservative professional companies such as* finance, aeronautics or the automobile industry.

- *For men* – Classic dark tailored suit, a plain or striped white or sky-blue shirt with a tie, and black or dark brown leather shoes and belt. Today, the tie is not compulsory, and often the top button of the shirt remains undone. Please be mindful of your sock choice. Under no circumstances should you wear sports socks (white for example), especially when your suit is grey. Socks should be the same colour as your trousers or shoes.
- *For women* – A conservative tailored suit (trousers or skirt with matching jacket) with a blouse that has sleeves. Wear closed toe shoes with no more than a mid-size heel. Colours should be dark or neutral and not too bright. Be mindful not to wear sexy outfits with plunging necklines, as people may forget your professional skills...

Small companies or start-ups – The outfit will probably be less classic or formal, especially if the employees are young. Young businessmen focus less on physical appearance and more on relaxed, authentic and friendly interaction. As such, it is up to you to adapt according to the first criteria being clean, pressed, well fitted and appropriate clothing. If you have a meeting with clients, you may wear something more corporate.

The casual day – Friday is the day you can express yourself in a 'cool' or fashion forward outfit. Do not push the boundaries too far as you are still in a professional environment, not on an evening out with friends! For men, a smart shirt (polo shirt or checked shirt) with chinos would be suitable. Obviously, there is no need to wear a tie. For women, a shirt with a jumper, trousers and flat shoes is suitable. Ensure you observe the dress code of your superiors as a guide, and do not wear clothing less formal than they do.

GREETING, TITLES AND HIERARCHY

Courtesy plays an integral part in our corporate culture. Being impolite can harm our image, our relationships and promotion potential. Acknowledging each person whom you cross paths with throughout your working day is essential.

A few things to consider:

The most senior person initiates the greeting. He/she will greet you by shaking hands (before the Covid period of course) holding their hand out first. They may instead choose to nod, look you in the eyes and say your name or surname, 'Hello Paul' or 'Hello Mr Dupont'.

If the president or CEO greets you, you will say his title: 'Hello President'. If he/she does not know your name, you will introduce yourself by adding your first name and surname. Note that in France we have a great respect for hierarchy, especially within large corporations. Do not be overly familiar with those who are senior to you, and keep your distance, being mindful not to discuss personal matters.

In smaller companies, the relationships between senior management and staff are more familiar. Greeting with kisses between colleagues (two kisses, one on each cheek) is standard.

Business cards are normally exchanged after the greeting.

MEETINGS

The French are known around the world to be obsessed with scheduling meetings. Whether or not it is a positive trait is for you to decide! Many foreigners believe our meetings to be too frequent and too lengthy, but as mentioned before, we love to have in-depth discussions, no matter what the circumstances.

Here is some useful advice:
- Be on time. Arriving a few minutes early is preferable.

- Turn off your phone.
- Don't be afraid to express yourself. Share your opinions and ideas no matter how different they may be. Stand up for what you believe in and you will be respected.
- Ask questions and show interest.

ORGANISING A BUSINESS MEAL

Mealtime is a priority for the French. It allows us to sit down together and share a delicious meal, usually comprising three courses, where we take time to get to know each other better without being interrupted. *It is of the utmost importance to create a meaningful relationship with your client and build trust.* The mealtime is used as an opportunity to build social rapport and then discuss professional points in a more intimate setting than the office. Be mindful of your manners by following these simple rules:

- Find a quality restaurant with a good reputation and recommend signature dishes if necessary.
- Arrive early to make sure everything is in place for your guest/s and to welcome them upon arrival. Thank them for coming and dedicating their valuable time to spend with you.
- You extended the invitation therefore you are the host. It is important to advise the responsible waiting staff that the bill is to be handed to you discreetly. It is usually best to excuse yourself from the table and pay the bill at the end of the meal once tea and coffee is served.
- Let your guest choose from the menu and adapt their order to their personal specifications. Try to select dishes in advance if you have invited a large group. If your guests do not want an appetiser, do not order one. You should enjoy your main course at the same time. If the waiter is late serving your dish, invite your guests to start, so their meals do not get cold.
- Be attentive and considerate and use a natural, confident tone.
- Conversation – make sure your clients are the focus of attention throughout the entire meal by asking questions, whether they be about professional topics or personal matters such as family, hobbies and special interests etcetera. Beware of discussing delicate topics. In France, politics, money and religion should be avoided. Business can be discussed between 'the pear and the cheese', that is, after the main course.

After the meal, send an email to thank your guests for having spent their time with you.

Professional Gifts

Bestowing gifts on clients is no longer common in France, as we are conscious of being accused of bribery. Tax rules have even been created to ensure gifts are declared if they exceed 100 € in value.

Nevertheless, the festive season at the end of the year is a good time to thank your customers and employees for their loyalty and show appreciation with gifts.

This allows a more personal expression of gratitude and appreciation to be extended in this virtual world. Personalising gift wrapping and cards is another way to express your esteem.

How do you choose an appropriate gift? It must be in line with your image, positioning and services offered, or relating to your native region or client's tastes.

In France, traditional gourmet baskets are always welcome (champagne, wine, foie gras, chocolate etcetera). Similar local specialties from your country will be greatly appreciated.

Finally, *relations between men and women* in the office are now more egalitarian, more so than in our personal lives. I recommend you invest in your professional relationships to gain the trust of your French colleagues, which must be earned over time. Do not hesitate to speak French. The effort will always be positively received.

Creating and fostering team spirit is an asset. Be positive, encouraging, complimentary and honest with your constructive feedback.

One last point is to be mindful not to discuss income. It is a subject that should remain confidential in France. I recommend you be discreet and wait for an appropriate moment to discuss the matter with your boss if necessary.

Chapter 7

Wedding Etiquette

The daughter of your French friends gets married, and they decide to have a beautiful wedding.

Here is how a classic and elegant wedding takes place in France, in a Catholic environment, and what will be expected of you as a guest.

It usually takes place on a Saturday afternoon until late in the evening, in a beautiful place such as a castle (rented or in the family home).

RECEIVE THE WEDDING ANNOUNCEMENT
You will receive an announcement; if it is composed in the traditional way, it will be in a card form (in vellum folded in the middle) in English lettering, and a double-page spread. On the first page, the bride's family invite you and announce the wedding. The grandparents are listed in the first line, and then the parents, who announce the marriage of their granddaughter and daughter who is marrying 'Mister X'. Titles and decorations may be mentioned, as well as the titles of certain professions. On the second page, the family of the fiancé announce their son's wedding to 'Miss Y'.

In this announcement you will find other cards because the announcement is there to announce the wedding but is not an invitation card. So, you can receive it without being invited to the wedding. If you find a Bristol card inside, you are invited to the reception that follows. It is the mothers of the bride and groom who receive and invite you to the different events, that is:

- To the cocktail party (until eight p.m.).
- To dinner (this means that you are invited to the cocktail party beforehand: the time is indicated, eight p.m. for example). The mention is written 'diner placed', under the mention of the cocktail.
- At the next day's brunch (if you are intimate, close).

The announcement is generally sent six to eight weeks before the big day.

You, as a guest, have only one duty when faced with the announcement: to reply! Even if you are not invited to the wedding because you are not very close to the family, as you were sent an invitation by post, you must send your congratulations in writing and wish the newlyweds your best wishes for happiness.

If you are invited to the cocktail party and/or dinner, you must respect the announced reply date. 'Please reply before June the 1st (often one month before the day). It is very important for the organisers to know the number of people who will be present at the cocktail and dinner. They must indicate the number of guests to the caterer!

Answering and respecting the given deadline is therefore the first form of politeness to achieve.

In your reply, you congratulate the parents, thank them for this beautiful invitation and inform them whether or not you are coming, without forgetting to wish the bride and groom your best wishes.

The card of the cocktail party or dinner often contains a (discreet) address for the wedding gift list. It is important to notice it so that you can choose your gift.

THE WEDDING GIFT

It is normal to take a wedding gift to the reception. There are three possibilities:

- You may choose it on the list by placing a sign, where indicated, on the card. This involves depositing a sum of money for an object of your choice preselected by the bride and groom.
- You may arrive with your gift at the wedding. A place will have been chosen and you will be informed to deposit it there. In this case, don't forget to leave your business card attached to the package (with a little note so that the bride and groom know whom to thank). Your note must not get lost!
- You may have your gift delivered or bring it yourself to your home a few days before the ceremony.

For an idea of the value of the gift, you can estimate that the longer you are invited to the wedding for (to dinner for example) the greater the value of your gift can be. For instance, if you and a guest are invited to dinner, your gift may be more expensive than if you are invited alone to the cocktail party.

Wedding Outfit

Do you want to honour the friends who invite you? Do you want to feel in harmony with the style, the place, the family? Dare to be elegant!

Until ten years ago, hats were very fashionable and made the day very elegant. Today, (unfortunately) the hat is less fashionable or only the very close family can wear one (the mother of the bride and groom, sisters, best friends). But a little detail in the hair can still be elegant such as a flower, a wreath, a headband, or a few feathers etcetera.

Your outfit can be colourful and in beautiful material. Weddings are a great opportunity to be very elegant, much more than at the office. But be careful, not in white!

The accessories are all important: high heels, the matching clutch or mini purse, your beautiful jewellery (but not too much)!

Men will always look very elegant in a beautiful white shirt, perfectly ironed, and in an impeccable suit. The shoes must be perfectly polished and the socks should be the same colour as the trousers.

You can find out if the groom and the fathers of the bride and groom will be in a tailcoat… it's an indication of elegance!

The Big Day

Of course, if you are invited to the wedding, you will attend the religious ceremony that begins the event. Being present at this public and sacred commitment and surrounding the bride and groom for this solemn moment is very important for them as well as for their parents. Plan to arrive fifteen minutes before the start of the ceremony. The entrance of the bride on her father's arm is often a very moving moment not to be missed!

At the end of the ceremony or at the beginning of the cocktail party, you will have to find the best moment to greet the bride and groom, to congratulate them, as well as the four parents.

And from then on, you can enjoy the party!

The Cocktail

It's a time to meet as many people as possible. Be open and ready to meet people. Be careful not to spend too much time at the buffet, or abuse the champagne glasses, as the evening is going to be long…

At the end of the cocktail, it is traditional that the fathers of the bride and groom give a speech. This is the opportunity for those who are invited only to the cocktail (and not to the dinner) to leave.

Dinner

Often this involves place settings, and your place is indicated on a board at the entrance to the dining venue (at the entrance to the tent, for example). Be sure to locate your table beforehand and know that you will not be able to change your place. You will find your name on the table quoted on the board, and you will wait until everyone is there to sit down.

The last piece of advice is that you will find a bun/bread roll next to your plate… you will find yours on the left side of your plate!

The Dancing Party

In the traditional way, it will start with a waltz danced by the bride and her father… there could be a few more according to the tastes of the bride and groom, then quickly the D.J. will move on to more rhythmic music (to dance rock) and more and more modern music according to the wishes of the bride and groom!

Enjoy this beautiful day of celebration and leave after thanking those who invited you.

A little message sent, one or two days later, even by SMS, to congratulate and thank again for the beautiful party, will be always very much appreciated.

Ghana
By Sasha Oquaye

Chapter 1

Cultural Symbols

THE 'ADAE KESE' FESTIVAL, THE ASHANTIS AND THE GOLDEN STOOL

The 'Adae' Festival is a cultural festival and celebration that has been performed in Ghana since the sixteenth century and is considered a formal state celebration. It was first celebrated to mark the attainment of statehood of a newly celebrated people in the aftermath of the Ashanti War of independence between 1697 and 1699. The *Adae Kese* festivals are magnified forms of the more frequent Sunday *Adae* festivals and are usually held to climax celebrations of specific milestones and achievements of the Asante/Ashanti kingdom of Ghana. The Ashanti/Asante people are an ethnic subgroup of the Akan-speaking people of Ghana. The Ashanti tribe is the largest tribe in Ghana and like many other tribes in Ghana, is known for its rich culture.

The *Adae Kese* Festival is a very important and elaborate celebration of the Ashanti people and every five years the festival is hosted by the ruler of the Asantes and can last up to two weeks, in the city of Kumasi. Kumasi is the regional capital of the Akan-speaking people and also the second largest city in Ghana after the country's capital, Accra. The smaller Adae festivals are held every six weeks in accordance with the calendar of the Akans people.

The festival has existed since the introduction of the Golden Stool in the sixteenth century and serves as the platform for pledging allegiance to the Ashanti kingdom and to affirm loyalty to the occupant of the Golden Stool (the occupant of the Golden Stool being whoever is the sitting ruler of the Asantes). The Adae festival represents the unity and embodiment of the Ashanti people and is also seen as a celebration to thank the ancestors for the new harvest. The celebration which parades colourful umbrellas amongst drummers, dancers, singers, etcetera generally coincides with the harvest season for yams, a staple starchy vegetable eaten widely throughout West Africa, and hence, centuries ago, the ritual was also informally called the 'yam custom' by Europeans.

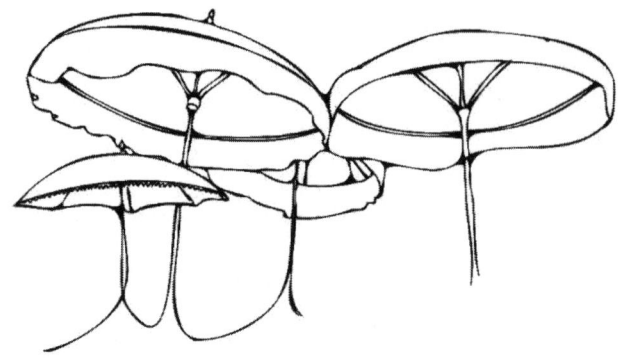

The elaborate version of the festival includes a parade of chiefs and queen mothers presided over by the Asantehene (the ruler of the Asantes) and involves a rich display of cherished regalia and paraphernalia accompanied by traditional drumming and dancing. The festival is embraced by Ashanti people from all walks of life and is now a tourist attraction, bringing tourists from all over the world to Ghana.

The Adae festival is a continuous demonstration of faith in the vision and heritage of the Asante Kingdom and the Golden Stool. The Golden Stool is considered the royal and divine throne of the king of the *Ashanti people* and the ultimate symbol of power. The Stool must never touch the ground and is therefore always placed on a blanket and is believed to house the spirit of the Asante nation (living, dead and yet to be born). It has not been seen by many and only the king, queen and trusted advisers know where the Stool is kept. The Stool represents the succession and power of the Asante empire.

The festival is a time when people pledge their confidence in the present king and awards of recognition are given to some during the occasion.

The timing of the *Adae/Adae Kese* festivals are not interchangeable as they have been fixed since ancient times. *Adae Kese* is translated into English means 'big resting place' and the day of the festival is considered a day of rest for the people.

The Ashanti kingdom of Ghana is considered the richest in Ghana in terms of resources, history and culture and notable among these are its range of minerals, rich cultural heritage, historic leaders and amazing tourist sites. The Asante King's position is entrenched in the Constitution of Ghana and his influence continues to exist alongside Ghana's democratic system.

THE KENTE FABRIC

For a number of reasons, the kente cloth can be considered as Ghana's national cloth and is indeed symbolic of the beauty of Ghana's culture.

Legend has it that the cloth was first made by two friends of the Akan tribe who went hunting and found a spider making its web. The friends watched the spider for two days then returned home and implemented what they saw, using fabric. It is also believed that the first ruler of the Ashanti Kingdom accepted the kente cloth as the Royal cloth to be worn at special royal occasions.

The kente fabric is an amazing textile and is one of the most intricate fabrics weaved in the world. The word 'kente' means 'basket' in the dialect of the Akan tribe of Ghana and the fabric is also known as *'nwentoma'* (translated as 'woven cloth' in English) in the local Ashanti communities of Ghana. The cloth is native to the Ashanti people and it can be dated back to the C.12th. Although the cloth was initially reserved for Ashanti royalty, as time went on it became more readily available to everyone and so today people from all walks of life adorn themselves with the fabric. Today the kente cloth is still held in high esteem and its significance to Ghana's history, culture and fashion remains.

Interestingly, the kente fabric has been adopted and is now widely accepted by diasporas of Africa as a symbol of not just Ghanaian heritage, but African heritage as a whole. The cloth, for example, is now commonly used in the design of academic and other types of stoles by African Americans in particular. Special ceremonies called 'Donning of the Kente' are conducted where the stoles are presented to the graduates and this ceremony is said to bring about a great sense of connection with their African heritage.

Over the years the kente cloth has also been modernised by designers adorning the fabric with beautiful stones and ornaments. This evolving trend has made the kente cloth very appealing to younger women, including traditional brides, in particular. Indeed, the modernization of the fabric has made it an attractive option for non-Ghanaians also.

More than three hundred patterns exist for the kente cloth, and each pattern has its own name and unique meaning. The meaning behind the patterns originates from either past events, religious beliefs, political ideas or social customs. The kente cloth, since the twelfth century, is worn for traditional ceremonies and festivals, including weddings, funerals, baby naming ceremonies, etcetera. It would be rare to find a Ghanaian lady, single or married, who does not own kente cloth and rarely would one meet a bride-to-be who doesn't include kente cloth in her dowry list. Should you attend a Ghanaian traditional wedding, the bride's dress would be made from luxurious, kente cloth of bright colours.

It is important to note that at certain ceremonies, a particular colour/colours may be specified or expected to be worn by those attending. For example, for baby naming ceremonies, guests will usually be asked to wear white or fabric which is a mixture of both white and black. For funerals, red and black are acceptable colours to wear. However, where the deceased is a very old person, it is common for families to request guest to wear white or a mixture of black and white as the ceremony will be seen as a celebration of life.

Below are examples of the meanings given to some colours, in the Ghanaian culture:
- Black: spirits of ancestors, passing rites and funerals.
- Blue: peacefulness, harmony and love.
- Green: planting, harvesting, growth, spiritual renewal.
- Gold: royalty, wealth, spiritual purity
- Grey: healing and cleansing rituals; associated with ash
- Maroon: the colour of mother earth; associated with healing
- Purple: associated with feminine aspects of life; usually worn by women
- Red: political and spiritual moods; bloodshed; sacrificial rites and death.
- White: purification, sanctification rites and festive occasions.
- Yellow: preciousness, royalty, wealth, fertility, beauty.

It is advisable to always ask the host/hostess or the invitee of any Ghanaian event you are invited to whether there is a specific colour/colours that should be worn to the event.

The Ghanian Flag

The three colours, red, gold and green were chosen for the flag of Ghana because of the country's geography, history and resources.

The green represents the rich vegetation and natural wealth of the country.

The gold was influenced by the mineral rich nature of the land, particularly gold as a mineral resource that is found in Ghana. Ghana was even previously called 'The Gold Coast' before its name was changed to 'Ghana'.

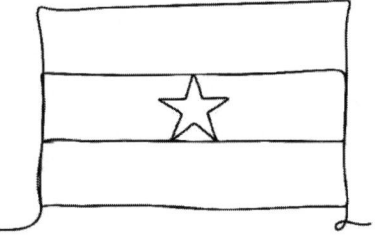

The red in the flag commemorates those who died or worked for the country's independence from Great Britain.

The black star was included in Ghana's flag. The five-pointed black star is seen as a symbol of African emancipation and unity in the struggle against colonialism. Over history it had become a symbol of the 'Lodestar of African Freedom'. With Ghana being the first country in sub-Saharan Africa to achieve independence from colonial rule, which served as an inspiration for many other countries in Africa to achieve independence, the black star symbol was indeed a perfect choice for the country's flag. You may hear Ghana being referred to as 'the black star of Africa' by some.

The nickname of Ghana's national football team is also the 'Black Stars'.

CAPE COAST CASTLE

Cape Coast Castle is located in the city of Cape Coast in Ghana and is one of approximately forty slave castles/large commercial forts built on the Gold Coast of West Africa (now Ghana) by European traders. Other well-known castles in Ghana are Elmina Castle and Ussher Fort.

Cape Coast castle was originally a Portuguese trading post that was established in 1555 and in 1653 the Swedish Africa Company constructed a timber fort at the site. The castle was then the centre for trading in timber and gold in Ghana and it later became a site for the transatlantic slave trade. That is, a location for imprisoning captured slaves who were later shipped to what was then known as the New World (the Americas and the Caribbean), under the most inhumane conditions. The castle also became a 'slave market' where transactions involving the buying and selling of slaves as commodities took place. Enslaved Africans were sadly a valuable commodity in America and elsewhere during this period and slaves eventually were the main trade in Cape Coast during this period. The castle had underground dungeons where the slaves were kept in extremely cramped and degrading conditions.

After Ghana gained independence in 1957, the castle underwent a restoration project sponsored by the 'Ghana Museum and Monuments Board'. Today, the castle is maintained as a historical museum and is open to the public for tours. Tourists from all over the world as well as official visitors to Ghana such as Barrack Obama and Melania Trump have visited the castle. The site is extremely popular among African American tourists due to their connection with its history.

FUFU

Fufu can be considered one of Ghana's better-known national dishes. It is essentially a starchy side dish which is eaten with soups such as groundnut soup, palm nut soup or light soup. Fufu requires ingredients such as plantains, cassava, or malanga and is prepared by grounding or mashing the ingredients and then cooking it overheat whilst forming it into a rich paste. It is eaten by hand and can also be found in different forms across west and central Africa as well as some parts of the Caribbean.

GHANAIAN ADINKRA SYMBOLS

Ghana's culture is full of symbolism and folklore and its adinkra symbols clearly depict this fact. These ancient symbols represent popular Ghanaian proverbs, historical events, values and traditional mythology. There are over 400 adinkra symbols in existence and each symbol conveys more meaning than just a single word. Some of the more popular adinkra symbols which are often used in the design of fabric, pottery, furniture, tattoos or jewellery design are *Sankofa, Gye Nyame and the Adinkrahene* adinkra symbols.

Sankofa means 'return and get it' and symbolises the importance of learning from the past. *Gye Nyame* means 'except for God'. It symbolises the supremacy of God and is also considered the most popular adinkra symbol used. It also reflects the deeply religious character of the Ghanaian people. *Adinkrahene* means 'chief of the adinkra symbols' and it signifies greatness, charisma and leadership.

Chapter 2

Meeting, Greeting, Posture and Body Language

POSTURE AND BODY LANGUAGE
People in Ghanaian society use body language (that is, eye contact, hand gestures, etcetera) to express emotions, thoughts, etcetera. It is important to note however, that body language does not actually count for a great deal within Ghanaian society as far as communication is concerned. In addition, hand gestures such as the 'peace' sign, 'thumbs up', etcetera are not often used in Ghanaian society. Therefore, one may find, for example, that in traditional, rural communities, residents may not be aware of what you mean if you should make such signs as a way of communicating. It is therefore advisable to avoid making such signs when in certain environments in the event that you may be misunderstood.

Eye Contact
A visitor to Ghana may notice that some Ghanaians may not give very direct eye contact when communicating and may appear timid, even if they are not, when conversing. This is particularly evident when communicating with children (including teenagers) who are raised in what may be considered as 'traditional homes' as, culturally, within such homes children are taught (directly/indirectly) from a young age that this displays one's respectfulness and humility, particularly when communicating with those older than themselves, etcetera. This is, however, changing within developed parts of Ghana such as within parts of the capital, Accra. In addition, differences with respect to eye contact or the lack thereof whilst conversing may also be based on the class of the individual, with younger people from lower class homes being raised to perceive less eye contact whilst conversing with individuals older than themselves as a sign of respectfulness more than young people from middle to upper class homes do.

On the other hand, foreigners may find that Ghanaians stare a lot and staring may not be considered by some as rude as it is considered in some Western societies. It is important that one does not take offense to this as this may be a 'positive' stare. That is, they may be staring as they may simply be observing you or perhaps it may be that they think you are very attractive. Whatever the reason, it is always better to think positively and smile rather than negatively if being stared at.

Facial Expressions
In Ghanaian society as in most societies, facial expressions can say a lot. Ghanaians are particularly very friendly and hospitable towards foreigners and may at times smile when they may be offended for the sake of being polite.

Gestures, etcetera on the Road
Visitors to Ghana may find that drivers are particularly emotive and a lot more impatient than what they are used to particularly if they have only previously driven in the West. Emotions can run high at times on the roads and it is therefore important to always practice as much patience as possible if you should choose to drive in Ghana, as a foreigner. As a driver in Ghana one may find that paying attention to as well as trying to predict the actions/decisions of other fellow drivers is necessary. You must drive with your eyes very much wide open.

As a pedestrian in Ghana, one must be vigilant as drivers may not always stop to give pedestrians priority unless it is at a traffic light and even then one must always look carefully to ensure that vehicles have come to a halt and drivers have seen you and have signalled to you that you should cross the street, including when at pedestrian crossings. Pedestrian crossings are relatively new in Ghana and a small number of these exist within the more developed cities in the country. Be certain that other cars will not, for example, overtake the motorist who has given you the signal to cross the street. Therefore, always be vigilant when crossing the street.

Car horns are used extensively by drivers as a way of communicating and alerting other drivers as well as pedestrians.

Should you find yourself in difficulty on the road as a pedestrian or as a driver, Ghanaians are always extremely helpful and would often quickly unite to assist anyone in difficulty.

MEETING AND GREETING

Greetings are generally an important aspect of Ghana's culture, socially, officially, professionally, etcetera.

Introductions

When someone is being introduced to you for the first time, they will most likely be introduced by their title (Mr, Mrs, Dr, Professor, etcetera) and surname as opposed to by their first name only, unless it is a very informal situation. It is best to refer to them as they were introduced to you until you are told differently as titles are important in the Ghanaian society.

Greetings

Greeting are usually always 'good morning', 'good afternoon' or 'good evening' and also when entering public places such as a hospital waiting area, a shop, restaurant, etcetera, these are the usual greetings that should be exchanged. In Ghana it is always important to greet those present as you enter a public area otherwise you may be left wondering why those present are looking at you; they are usually waiting for you to offer some form of greeting.

'Good morning', 'good afternoon' or 'good evening' is usually the common greeting that is exchanged with strangers or people you may not know very well. Another common greeting you will hear from your arrival at the airport as well as throughout your stay is '*Akwaba*' (which is a Twi word meaning 'you are welcome').

In Ghana, 'hello' or 'hi' are greetings which are exchanged between young people amongst themselves or between friends of any age. In answering the telephone however, 'hello' is an acceptable greeting, but you will find that this will more often than not follow with a 'good morning/afternoon/evening', especially where it is an official telephone call.

Kissing people on the cheeks as a greeting is not the usual custom in Ghana as in some other countries. Kissing on the cheek as a greeting is usually reserved for those who are romantically involved. Hugging is the more common form of greeting amongst close family/friends. Handshaking is often used in Ghanian culture amongst people you have either just met or do not know very well.

At an event where people are together in a group, especially if they are seated it is important to always greet with a 'hello' and shake hands with everyone, starting with the first person on your right and working your way to the last person on your left. Always follow this order regardless of the gender, age or status of the individuals present. The exception to this rule is when greeting a chief in a formal setting. In this case, the chief should be greeted first, where it is convenient to do so.

It is acceptable to interrupt a group of people in conversation in order to greet and shake hands with everyone within the group.

It is important that one remembers to never shake hands, eat, receive or give anything with the left hand. If you happen to be left-handed it is advisable to practice using your right hand as much as possible in order to get used to it.

West-African Handshake

When in Ghana it is important to know what the West African handshake is. This handshake is used in Ghana and other countries in West Africa and is done by snapping your middle finger with the middle finger of the person you are shaking hands with. This handshake is often exchanged as an expression of the person/persons shaking hands displaying their friendliness with each other and it is seen as a less informal and friendlier greeting than the traditional handshake. You will observe that people who already know each other very well use this handshake when reconnecting. This handshake is exchanged between males, or you may witness a male extending this greeting to a female to express a degree of friendliness towards the female. Interestingly, this handshake style is never exchanged between two females. Men may however extend this informal handshake with some women to express their level of friendliness with the woman or if they simply know the female very well.

Visitors/foreigners will find that Ghanaians are very hospitable by nature and the country and its people are also known for their peacefulness.

Chapter 3

Conversation Dos and Don'ts

GENERAL CONVERSATION
Ghanaians are largely very welcoming and friendly but may not take well to very personal questions being asked of them during a first meeting or if they do not know you very well.

Ghanaians are very polite by nature and in an attempt to not be impolite towards someone else may simply refrain from responding to negative remarks by simply smiling. If a Ghanaian does not know you very well, he/she may be hesitant to open up about his/her opinions on certain sensitive subject areas. It may therefore be best to keep your conversation as balanced as possible and perhaps restrict sensitive topics to people you know quite well and who may not misread your intentions.

The official language spoken in Ghana is English so you will find that most people in the larger cities speak English but this may not be the case however, within very rural parts of the country. Knowing a few words of any of the most widely spoken Ghanaian languages, such as 'Twi', would always make a good impression on the locals. '*Me da ase*' (thank you) and '*Wo ho te sen*' (how are you?) are a good start towards learning basic communication in Twi.

You will find that Ghanaians say 'please' a lot before most sentences, even when it is not a request. This is due to the fact that in many local languages the word meaning 'please' such as '*mepa wo kyew*', for example, is used at the start of most sentences even when the sentence is not a question but is a statement or a response to a question.

Don'ts
If doing business in Ghana as a foreigner, it is best to refrain from discussing politics during your professional and social engagements, particularly if you are uncertain of the political affiliations or political party preference of those you are engaging with.

As a guide, be careful when also discussing the following:
- Religion – Avoid speaking negatively about religion. Ghana is a particularly religious country, with Christianity and Islam being the main religions. Although Ghana's citizens are predominantly Christians, all religions live peacefully and respectfully together in the country.
- Sensitive topics such as gay rights, abortion, etcetera.
- Money – Unless the conversation at the time is along the lines of business.
- You will find that disrespectful, rude or vulgar jokes are not generally acceptable amongst Ghanaians particularly when such conversations are not amongst close friends. Ghana, although a relatively developed and embracing society when compared with some other West African countries, is still very much conservative and traditionally grounded. As a general rule when dealing with cross-cultural matters, always bear in mind that what may be seen as good humour in one culture may be considered offensive in another.
- Avoid cursing whilst speaking, even when in a relaxed, friendly, social environment. Ghanaians do tend to think before they speak and so, cursing is never perceived as good communication.

Dos – Good Conversation Topics

Questions or conversations about one's spouse or children are usually very welcomed as Ghana is a very family centred society. Questions such as "Do you have children?" Or "How many children do you have?" Are not considered too personal to ask during a first-time meeting. Additionally, discussing one's job, especially if there is some connection with those you are communicating with, is also a great conversation starter.

When being introduced to someone or meeting people for the first time do attempt to get the pronunciation of their names as accurate as possible. It may of course be difficult, as a foreigner, to get name pronunciations one hundred percent accurate. Nevertheless, displaying a good attempt to do so will always be appreciated by the individual whose name it is and should they giggle slightly at your mispronunciation, do take this in good faith.

As a foreigner, pointing out any similarities with your own culture and the Ghanaian culture is always a plus when it comes to forming a connection. Knowing a few things about Ghana's history, customs and geography would also always make for great conversation or ice breakers as well as for forming warm connections.

Ghanaians are very patriotic and proud of their country's achievements so the following will help for engaging in good conversation:

- Ghana was the first country in sub-Saharan Africa to gain independence from colonial rule.
- Ghana is literally located at the centre of the world. Geographically, Ghana is the country closest to the centre of the world where the equator and Greenwich Meridian meet at coordinate (O,O). The town, Tema, in Ghana is the closest land settlement to this point.
- Ghana has the biggest man-made lake in the world. The lake is called Lake Volta and is found in the Volta region of Ghana.
- Ghana is a multilingual country where approximately over eighty languages are spoken.
- Children are traditionally named based on the day of the week on which they were born.
- Kofi Annan is one of the most well-known Ghanaians; he served as secretary-general of the United Nations from 1997–2006.

(Fun fact: Kofi is the name given to boys born on a Friday).

- Sport is always a great topic which brings people together and Ghana is no exception. Most Ghanaians love football and are generally proud of their national football team, popularly known as 'The Black Stars'.

Finally, Ghanaians are well known for being very hospitable and visitors to the country often attest to this. They generally always aim to make visitors feel as comfortable as possible.

Chapter 4

Gift Giving

Gift giving is not a particularly complicated aspect of Ghanaian culture.

If giving gifts, do not be afraid to give gifts reflecting your own culture, country or tradition as this will always be appreciated and considered a well thought of gift.

Gifts need not be expensive. The general perception is that the fact that someone considered you enough to get a gift for you is much more important than the monetary value of the gift itself.

Gifts should be packaged or wrapped nicely and modestly.

It is important to know that gifts may not always be opened when received. Therefore, one should not get offended if the receiver of your gift does not open the gift in your presence and it doesn't necessarily mean that the receiver is not appreciative of the gift.

THE GIFT TABLE
At most events that you may attend in Ghana such as weddings, birthday parties, christenings, etcetera, you may find a table allocated for guests to place gifts which they wish to give to the celebrant. This table is referred to as the 'gift table', and it would be managed by an individual who would have been assigned by the host/hostess to monitor and take responsibility of all gifts, monetary or otherwise, brought to the event. The gift table is particularly important in instances where the host/hostess is unable to personally receive all guests and gifts and it also serves as a secure way of monitoring any monetary gifts as it is not unusual for large sums of money to be gifted by some guests during certain events. At some gift tables, guests who give monetary gifts may be asked to register their name and other personal details as well as the amount of money they are gifting.

Whether there is a gift table or not, it is important to ensure that your gift/envelope is always well labelled with your name so that the receiver will know who the gift/envelope is from.

DINNER GUEST

Although in Ghana it is not generally expected that a gift must be given if you are invited to someone's home for dinner or to visit a community/village you will always be thought well of if you do decide to take a gift to show appreciation to the host/hostess. The exception to this however may be when the one being invited is a foreigner. In this case, a gift/token of appreciation for the host/hostess will be expected and a bottle of wine or sparkling, alcoholic drink are perfectly acceptable gifts for such occasions. If you are not certain whether alcohol would be acceptable or not, non-alcoholic, sparkling versions are a nice gesture, or a nice selection of chocolates can also be given. If the host/hostess has children, simply taking along something for the children in the home would be warmly welcomed.

SPECIAL OCCASIONS, CEREMONIES/EVENTS

Baby Christenings (Also Called Outdooring / Naming Ceremony)
In Ghana a christening can take the form of a religious Christian ceremony, a traditional spiritual ceremony or a mixture of both of these in one ceremony. One should always take a gift for the baby/family during such ceremonies. A monetary gift is the usual tradition.

If you feel the need to visit a family who has just had a newly born baby, the tradition in Ghana is that you wait until the family has performed the outdooring of the baby before you can visit the family home to see the baby. This is a very significant aspect of Ghanaian culture with respect to new-borns as it is believed that it is spiritually and physically unsafe for the baby to be exposed to the outside world before the outdooring ceremony has been performed.

Weddings
For wedding gifts it's usually best to take a card/envelope with money especially if you are not sure what household items the bride and groom may already have or may also receive as a wedding gift. Receiving multiple sets of the same drinking glasses as wedding gifts is rarely exciting for any newlywed. (See Chapter 7 also for more on weddings).

Gifts to Chiefs
Should you be invited to visit a community/village bear in mind that you may get the privilege of also meeting the traditional leader (also known as

a chief) of the village. It is advisable to always take a gift during such visits. Traditionally, drinks such as 'schnapps' is given to the chiefs of some tribes. Livestock and money are also other types of gifts traditionally given to chiefs. Some tribes within certain regions of Ghana also have their specific traditional gifts, for example, amongst some tribes of the northern region of Ghana, it is traditional to present food and drink items, cola nuts or livestock to the chief of the village. Today, it is common for some visitors to villages to present to chiefs items which may represent their own culture or country or food items such as packaged rice, drinks, etcetera. It is advisable to liaise with the host who would have arranged your visit on what may be the best type of gift to present.

It is likely that someone working for the chief will receive the gift from you on the chief's behalf and it is also important to remember to always give items with your right hand, even if you are left-handed. If invited to meet the chief, you should stop just short of where they are seated and bow slightly. In Ghana, you need not go on your knees or lie prostrate as a sign of showing respect to a chief as may be done in some other African cultures. Do not offer your hand unless the chief invites you for a handshake. Do not cross your legs and try to keep your hands out of your pockets as signs of respect.

Funerals

If you are expected to attend a funeral, whether you know the family well or not, it is customary to bring a monetary gift/contribution for the family. This is done by everyone in the community to assist in the financing of the funeral as well as to support the family in general. Your contribution should be any amount that you can afford as it will always be appreciated.

Easter

In Ghana, Easter is very much a religious season celebrated by the Christian population of the country. The exchange of gifts such as chocolate eggs or chocolate bunnies, which is practiced during this period in the west is not done in Ghana. Therefore, associating rabbits, chicks, chocolate eggs etcetera with the Easter season may not be viewed enthusiastically by Christians as the focus of the season for them is its religious aspect.

Christmas

Gifts are not necessarily exchanged within families during Christmas as it is in the West. Christmas is more a time to spend with family members and friends who one may not have seen for some time. Beautifully wrapped gifts under the Christmas tree are not the focus during the Christmas season in Ghana. The focus and spirit of the season is one of togetherness more than anything else.

SOME DOS AND DON'TS
Dos
Gifts are generally always welcomed at any time of the year, particularly small token monetary gifts (tips) to those who may be assisting you or doing some form of service for you during your stay as a foreigner in Ghana. This may be more appropriately described as tips as opposed to gifts, however, and a visitor to Ghana must bear in mind that tips are not what is generally given only to waiters/waitresses at restaurants/bars, etcetera, but in Ghanaian culture tips are widely given by locals to individuals who may offer any type of assistance, be it assisting in parking your car, doing your laundry, etcetera. Should you be a foreigner in Ghana, you will be expected to do the same and do not be surprised when someone assisting you, even when you did not ask for their assistance, asks for a tip in return for their service.

Don'ts
Halloween is not celebrated in Ghana as in the West therefore it is advisable to refrain from giving gifts to anyone in support of this occasion.

Remember, as previously mentioned in Chapter 2, do not give or receive gifts or anything else with your left hand.

Receiving Gifts and Showing Appreciation
Always show appreciation and do not show if you dislike a gift as offense will probably be taken by this.

Even if you are the host of a large event and gifts were brought to you, some of which you may not be aware of, you must find a way to say thank you the following morning to everyone that brought you a gift even if you had said thank you during the event itself. It is appropriate to say thank you the following day, preferably before noon, if possible. Doing this shows that you appreciate the gift/gesture received and failure to do this may be interpreted as dislike or lack of appreciation of the gift/gesture. Saying thank you is always extremely powerful.

Chapter 5

Dining Etiquette

Food plays a very important role in Ghanaian culture where the act of dining itself is not specifically approached in a formal way, but rather dining is usually viewed and approached as a social and relaxed time where bonding with those present is much more significant than any of the formalities associated with the meal itself.

BREAKFAST
Breakfast meals usually consist of what is called *koko*, which is a type of porridge made from millet which has been soaked and blended with spices such as ginger, black pepper and cloves added to it for flavour. It is also popularly called '*Hausa koko*' as it is believed to have originated from the northern part of Ghana.

Other breakfast dishes include *koose* (a bean-based fried food where beans have been mashed and mixed and then fried in a ball-like shape) and '*bofrot*' (a ball shaped fried dough which tastes similar to a doughnut).

These breakfast dishes are considered not so heavy breakfast meals. However, heavier breakfast alternatives such as '*waakye*' (pronounced '*wachey*') are also eaten in Ghana and is usually the option chosen by those who may be involved in industrious work and/or long hours of work outdoors, for example, or those whose schedule may require them to skip or have a late lunch. *Waakye* is a rice and bean-based food which is eaten with a variety of spicy accompaniments such as spicy meat stew and/or *shito* (a chili pepper-based condiment unique to Ghanaian cuisine) and non-spicy accompaniments such as boiled eggs, salad, spaghetti, fried plantains. The choice of accompaniments is according to one's taste. When *waakye* is eaten at breakfast, lunch will usually then be eaten later in the afternoon as *waakye* is quite a heavy and filling meal. *Waakye* is traditionally a popular breakfast/brunch meal choice on Saturdays, however, it can also be eaten as a lunch meal any day of the week.

As life in the developed cities of Ghana is becoming increasingly fast-paced, these breakfast foods can now be found readily available and can be purchased as street foods, making it convenient for busy professionals, etcetera to grab breakfast on the go. It is common to see long queues of people waiting to purchase *waakye* from local vendors in the early mornings.

LUNCH

In Ghana, traditional lunch dishes consist of soup-based dishes such as groundnut soup, palm nut soup or light soup, which are eaten with starch-based foods such as fufu, rice, yams or *banku*. Fufu can be considered one of Ghana's better-known national dishes and is made from plantains or cassava. It is prepared by grounding or mashing the ingredients and then cooking it over heat whilst simultaneously forming it into a paste. It is eaten by hand and in fact, using any cutlery to eat this dish may be perceived as improper etiquette and it is therefore advisable to attempt, initially, to eat this meal and other similar meals with your hands as this would show your appreciation for the etiquette of eating the dish.

Rice dishes and vegetable-based stews are also common choices for lunch, especially for those who may require a quick and easy meal during the working or school hours.

DINNER

Dinner may not always be a particularly heavy meal in Ghana, particularly where one may have had a heavy lunch of fufu for example. Dinner usually consists of rice-based dishes such as jollof rice or boiled yams, chicken, fish or vegetable-based stews together with salads. The dishes consumed at dinner are very much similar to the dishes prepared for lunch.

SNACKS

Ghanaians are not particularly known for snacking in between the main meals of breakfast, lunch and dinner as may be the practice in other countries where afternoon tea, coffee breaks, and dessert courses for example are a part of one's daily dining habit.

BEVERAGES

Common beverages which have become unique to Ghana's cuisine include alcoholic drinks such as '*pito*' and 'palm wine' and non-alcoholic drinks such as '*bissap*' which is more popularly called '*sobolo*' in Ghana. *Bissap/sobolo* is an ideal drink for the hot, tropical climate due to its refreshing nature. It is made from the species of the hibiscus flower known as the roselle and ginger and sugar are added to the mixture for additional flavour and taste. The bissap drink can also be found in other African countries but it may be referred to by a different name.

TYPICAL MEALTIMES

Breakfast, if eaten, tends to be eaten very early, especially by those living in the rural farming areas where due to an early sunrise, the day begins particularly early. In the city and developed areas however, you may find that breakfast may be eaten around seven-eight a.m. with many opting to eat breakfast at their place of employment prior to starting their working day. This is often due to the fact that many people working in the city have long distances to commute and so leave their homes as early as five-thirty a.m. or six a.m. in order to beat the heavy rush hour traffic.

Lunch is eaten usually between noon and two p.m. However, where a heavy breakfast of *waakye* for example was eaten, lunch would probably then be pushed to a later time of around two-thirty or three p.m.

Dinner, if eaten, would usually be eaten around six-thirty p.m. to eight p.m. depending on one's lifestyle. Children would normally eat dinner around six p.m. as the school day in Ghana commences particularly early and children's bedtimes tend to be before seven-thirty p.m. A dinner meal may consist of something light as most Ghanaians tend to have the largest meal of the day during lunch.

SPECIAL MEALS / FOODS FOR SPECIFIC OCCASIONS OR EVENTS

Traditionally, on someone's birthday a special dish called '*eto*' or '*etor*' is prepared for the celebrant. This consists of mashed yam cooked in palm oil and is served with boiled eggs and slices of avocado. This is considered a celebratory meal.

During certain tribal-based festivals such as the '*Homowo*' festival of the Ga tribe of Ghana, specific foods are prepared as part of the rituals and celebration of the festival. At this festival, for example, the traditional food prepared is called *kpekple/kpokpoi* which is a mixture of steamed/fermented maize mixed with palm nut oil and served with palm nut soup and smoked fish.

COMMUNAL EATING

Communal eating, that is, family or friends eating from one bowl or plate, is not uncommon in Ghana. You will find people having lunch from the same bowl within some communities.

Should you be invited to dine with others in a communal eating setting, you can either decline respectfully or join in. In our recent times, it is acceptable to decline respectfully should you not feel comfortable with communal eating. However, should you choose to partake in communal dining, ensure to adhere to the following: wash your hands before eating, preferably where your co-diners can see that you have washed your hands. This is normally possible as where food is served where diners are expected to eat by hand, a wash basin, water and soap will be provided for washing your hands before you eat. Once again, remember to use your right hand for eating and also for receiving and passing anything. Traditionally it is considered respectful to wait for the oldest male to start eating before you begin to eat. You must only eat from the area of the bowl that is directly in front of you and you should not reach across to take from another part of the bowl.

In most cultures, eating together is socially significant and communal eating is no exception. Communal eating may also be indicative of the closeness of relationships between individuals, platonic or otherwise, and it may also be a sign of level of your trustworthiness should you be invited to join in communal eating.

GUESS WHO'S COMING TO DINNER

If your host/hostess should ask you what you would like to eat do leave it open to the host/hostess to make suggestions as that way you don't place too many restrictions or unrealistic demands on your host/hostess. However, if you should have any food allergies or other dietary restrictions this would be a good time to mention these.

When you are served food try not to refuse it unless it is contradictory to your religion for example, allergies/medical conditions or you may be vegan/vegetarian, etcetera. In these cases, it is acceptable to respectfully decline. However, where none of these apply, it is considered good manners to try a little of the food, at the least, in order to please your host/hostess. Comments with respect to food should always be favourable as this can be a sensitive area and always remain mindful of your facial expressions when tasting new foods. Additionally, remember that it is never appropriate to sniff food or beverages when in the company of others.

If you are invited to dinner to someone's home, it is good etiquette to take along a nice sparkling drink (non-alcoholic if you are not sure if they drink alcohol) or chocolates to show your appreciation of the invitation.

'You Are Invited'

When eating and there are other people in your presence, always invite them to join in your meal. The customary way of doing this is by saying, "You are invited," to the person. This is considered good etiquette, is widely practiced by all social classes and is the polite thing to do when in Ghana. It is important to note that this practice is more often than not a polite, customary gesture as opposed to a genuine invitation. Most people don't actually expect you to join them in their meal should they say, "You are invited," to you, and, vice versa, those you may invite to join in your meal would most often take the invitation as simply a customary, polite gesture.

Dietary Restrictions

Few Ghanaians are vegetarian or vegan, therefore, if you are invited to dine, whether for breakfast, lunch or dinner, do let your host/hostess know if you should be a nonmeat or nonmeat and non-dairy eater. Notwithstanding this, there will always be non-meat and non-dairy options available.

Alcohol

Any form of drunken behaviour is usually considered inappropriate, whether in a formal or informal setting, social or professional.

Other General Dining Etiquette Tips

Remember not to eat with, receive or pass food, etcetera with your left hand.

If you should personally invite someone to a bar/restaurant, it will most likely be implied that you will be covering the expenses of the night. That is the drinks and the meal, depending on the type of venue you take your guest to. This implied rule also applies where the relationship of those involved is purely a business one. (Also see Chapter 6 on business etiquette).

Chapter 6

Business Etiquette

There are two main scenarios when discussing the nature of business/professional etiquette in Ghana for the purposes of foreigners. One scenario being personnel employed as an expatriate within an organisation in Ghana and the second one being foreigners visiting Ghana to conduct business as an entrepreneur, for example. Notwithstanding that there may be some differences between these two main groups, we can look at some general factors that may pertain to both groups.

GREETINGS, TITLES AND HIERARCHY
When doing business in Ghana it is to one's advantage to be knowledgeable, mindful and respectful of the cultural nature of the country and to this end it is important to note a few points. Should you be working within a Ghanaian organisation you may find that it may be conservative in some ways, for example with respect to hierarchy, age, titles, etcetera.

It is important when introducing yourself to introduce yourself with both your first and last name. This is the usual expected introduction in Ghana in business settings.

Additionally, it is perhaps best not to refer to your professional colleagues or acquaintances by their first name unless you are asked to do so by them, or they were introduced to you on a first name basis. Colleagues and other professional acquaintances, particularly if they are older than you, should be referred to as Mr, Mrs or Ms, as appropriate, followed by their surname, or they can be addressed as Sir, Madame or Professor, etcetera, where you are not familiar with their surname or you do not know them.

It is not unusual to find some younger professionals address those older than themselves, even within a professional environment as 'Auntie' and their first name or 'Uncle' if they are male. This may be a result of some cultural practices infiltrating into the workplace, as culturally, in Ghana, as in some other west African countries, it is taught from an early age that one should address those older than themselves as either 'Auntie' or 'Uncle' rather than on a first name basis, as a sign of respect. Therefore, needless to say, always be sure to address those older than yourself appropriately regardless of whether they may be less qualified or less experienced than yourself.

Personal touch

As a people, Ghanaians usually prefer a personal or face to face initial meeting for the purposes of building a good, rapport/relationship with potential business partners, etcetera. Aiming to build good relationships is a very important factor and face to face connection has been found by most as the most effective way of achieving this in Ghana. Consequently, if you are used to communicating and doing business very quickly and effectively via virtual means you may find that you may need to make some adjustments with respect to your expectations in terms of speed of responses, etcetera. This has changed somewhat at the time of writing this book which is during the period of the global corona virus pandemic and it is yet to be seen whether this will in fact be a long-term change to this aspect of Ghana's business culture or not.

It is important to build a good rapport with your colleagues if you should be working for an organisation in Ghana. This is usually effectively done by enquiring and showing interest in the well-being of their family as well as their own well-being before delving into professional discussions. This is always very much appreciated.

Developing romantic relationships with colleagues in the workplace is generally not acceptable in the Ghanaian workplace as may be the case within many other societies.

WORKPLACE MANNERS AND RITUALS

Ghana's business hours can run from eight a.m. to six p.m. and most workers generally have one hour break for lunch. From personal experience, official coffee/tea breaks are not common practice during the typical working day in Ghana as it may be in some Western countries. Therefore, for some foreigners, it may take some time to adjust to not having routine daily coffee/tea breaks.

Due to a lack of developed public transport systems in the country, heavy traffic is a factor you are likely to experience when travelling within the capital, Accra, and it is therefore often the case that meetings may commence later than scheduled. Although most Ghanaians are understanding of this and are accustomed to frequent delays in meetings etcetera, it is still best to aim to be on time for your meetings in order to make a good impression, specifically where it will be the first time you will be meeting the other attendees. As I teach in etiquette, a good first, second or third impression will positively influence your professional image and integrity and indeed, punctuality is key to one displaying qualities of professionalism and reliability. It is also advisable to leave enough time between your scheduled meetings in the likely event that meetings overrun.

Business Meetings

Initial business meetings are usually seen as more a time to get those involved to get to know each other on a more personal level and to assess whether personalities allow for future business partnerships, etcetera. One should therefore expect at times to spend some time during meetings in rapport building during meetings before delving into business, as this is particularly important in Ghanaian culture.

Hierarchy based on age is quite typical in Ghana so you may find that in some settings the oldest person may be introduced first regardless of whether that person is more senior in the business realm or not.

Meetings may at times take quite a formal stance, particularly where it is within an organisation. More structured meetings, specifically large meetings within some public organisations may include some or all of the following:

- A general welcome followed by an opening prayer.
- Introductions would then be made, where necessary, which may include a public welcome announcement for any special guest/s.
- Purpose of the meeting may be announced by the host/hostess or the chairperson of the meeting. At this point you may also be asked to introduce yourself specifically if the purpose of the meeting is based on your attendance.

It is important to note that the format of meetings may of course vary depending upon whether it is the first meeting or not as well as how many people are in attendance, etcetera.

One should take any light humour in good nature as this is usually a good sign that those present are becoming more relaxed with you. On the other hand, it is always important to be mindful of telling jokes yourself particularly within business settings as jokes can be taken differently within different cultures. Therefore, until you have understood the sense of humour of those present it is always best to refrain from telling what may be considered sensitive or controversial jokes as well as getting involved in such discussions. Sensitive/controversial topics or jokes include for example those related to race, gender, religion, sexuality, tribalism etcetera. Although freedom of speech applies and is practiced in Ghana, in adhering to good etiquette practices, one must be mindful of such topics particularly when they are in a cross-cultural environment. Topics such as sports, the weather, travel, hobbies, etcetera on the other hand are generally considered a lot less controversial/sensitive.

Business Dining / Socialising
Discussing business over a nice lunch, dinner or a glass of wine or coffee is becoming increasingly common in Ghana. It is therefore now more important for one to have great dining and social etiquette skills or improve upon these in order to ensure that a good impression will be made and business relations are enhanced.

If you are the host, that is, you are organising the meal and/or inviting guests to the business meal or drink, etcetera, you must ensure to pay the bill. In such instances it may be more appropriate to make prior arrangements with the venue you will be dining or drinking at and advise them that you would be the one paying the bill. You may be asked to provide them with your payment card details beforehand, etcetera.

GIFT GIVING
One should always be careful when giving gifts in the business/official environment as gift giving is often seen as a form of communication and it is important to be careful not be seen to be giving bribes to professionals or officials particularly where it involves business with or related to a public organisation. One must consider factors such as, *is it the right gift*. That is, think carefully about the type of gift you are thinking about giving and how it may be perceived. It is important to also consider *the monetary value of the gift* as this also gives a message about the perceived intention of the gift-giver. Extravagant gifts should always be avoided as a business gift and one

must always consider *why the gift is being given.* It is also advisable to try and obtain information on an organisation's policies on gift giving, if possible.

BUSINESS DRESS CODES

Ghanaians place a lot of value on dressing and consider it disrespectful if someone is dressed inappropriately for an occasion/function; business dressing may be no exception to this.

Office dress sense may appear more conservative than it may be in the West and though the weather is very hot all year round you will find that men do wear long sleeve shirts and suits in the professional environment. A tie may not always be necessary for men, but it is important to always dress smartly for most professional face to face interactions. For men, smart trousers, a shirt and a jacket are acceptable and for women a nice skirt and shirt or blouse is acceptable. In instances where you are aware that the meeting will be an informal one, a jacket may not be required and in recent years more African businessmen wear traditional style suits which do not require a shirt but are acceptable for business meetings.

Friday business dress code in Ghana is different from Friday business dress code in the West. In 2004 the Government launched the 'National Friday Wear Programme' which was implemented to promote the use of local fabrics and local designers, etcetera. You will therefore witness professionals within many private and public organisations such as banks, hospitals and governmental organisations etcetera dressed in colourful local fabrics and designs. Some organisations even incorporate their organisation's logo onto locally made fabric which their staff would wear to work on Fridays. Men and women equally have equally embraced this trend of Friday business dressing. As a foreigner doing business or employed within an organisation in Ghana you may choose to purchase ready-made or made-to-order smart clothing that are made from African fabrics and designed locally which can be worn on Fridays as a way of showing some appreciation for the local culture, etcetera. Made-to-order clothing may take a few days therefore if you do not have much time, it may be best to indulge in the many ready-made options that will be available.

It is important to note that, in Ghana, jeans are never appropriate in any kind of business interaction whether you've met the person numerous times before or not or it's a Friday. The same rules also apply to wearing shorts in a formal or professional setting. Additionally, Friday business dress code never includes trainers/sneakers. However, some organisations may have T-shirts/polo shirts with the company's logo on it which staff will wear on Fridays or on specific business occasions/events.

It is important to always assess the policies of any organisation where you may be employed as some organisations may have their own specific requirements due to the nature of the business they perform or their unique work culture.

Chapter 7

Wedding Etiquette

Who doesn't love weddings and all things love-related? In most societies, whether Western or not, weddings are perhaps one of the most celebrated societal events, and Ghana is no exception.

THE TYPES OF MARRIAGES RECOGNISED IN GHANA
The way in which weddings are conducted in Ghana has changed from what it was hundreds of years ago as traditionally, and some would say before colonisation, the only marriage ceremony which was performed and recognised in Ghana was the customary form of marriage ceremony. I will explain and discuss this interesting ceremony, including the pre-marital ceremony and traditional rites that must be carried out in more detail below and I will refer to it as a 'traditional or customary marriage ceremony/wedding'. It is significant to add that the traditional/customary marriage was the first type of legally recognised marriage in Ghana in accordance with the country's traditional laws which were the laws of the land prior to the country being colonised by the British.

The second type of marriage which we can refer to as a 'white wedding' is the Western form of 'white wedding' which some consider to be a Christian-based marriage ceremony that is widely practiced in Ghana due to Western influence as well as due to the now large Christian population in Ghana.

The Islamic religious-based marriage is the third form of marriage that is widely practiced in Ghana.

Now let's discuss each type of wedding in more detail
We will firstly discuss the traditional/customary Ghanaian marriage ceremony which may be the most interesting of all in this chapter due to its uniqueness. Then we will look at some of the specifics of the other types of weddings performed in Ghana such as the 'white wedding' and the Islamic wedding.

The Ghanaian Traditional/Customary Marriage Ceremony
It is important to note that some of the customs and rites to be performed in the customary/traditional marriage ceremony may differ between the various tribes in Ghana. Nevertheless, there are some aspects which are common amongst the main tribes such as the bride price/dowry and how the actual marriage ceremony is conducted, which we will look at below.

Before the Ghanaian customary/traditional marriage can take place, some obligatory premarital rites must be performed by the groom-to-be in order to express and make known his desire to marry a particular lady.

The first step is for him to show his interest or commitment by introducing himself to the lady's family, particularly her farther or the patriarch of the family where this is possible. The gentleman must do this by visiting the lady's family home with close members of his own family to introduce himself and declare his interest in the lady in question and, as per tradition, request for the 'dowry' list of the lady. Such a request is deemed to be the gentleman's proposal for the lady's hand in marriage or what may be called 'an engagement' in Western terminology.

The Dowry
Once the premarital rite of the gentleman obtaining the dowry list occurs the arrangements for the traditional marriage ceremony can then take place.

In Ghana the dowry means the items which the bride's family expect the gentleman and his family to provide in order for the marriage to take effect as per traditional Ghanaian law. On the day which the gentleman and his family bring the items listed in the list is traditionally called the 'Knocking Ceremony' which is in essentially the traditional wedding ceremony. This ceremony will be explained in more detail below.

In Ghana, the dowry does not just include an amount of money to be given to the family of the bride but it also includes a list of items to be purchased by the groom and his family for the bride and her family. There may be some variations with respect to the items in the premarital list and today the bride's family's personal preferences may also influence what items are on a list. It has been said that some families have included top of the range technological items such as mobile telephones etcetera in a dowry list, to the dismay of some grooms-to-be.

Below is an example of some of the items which may typically be included in a dowry/bride list.

- A bottle of gin, schnapps or whiskey.
- Pieces of traditional wax print fabric for the bride (each piece of fabric must be about six yards).
- The bride price (usually in cash).
- Money and a pair of sandals for the mother of the bride.
- A bottle of whiskey for the father of the bride.
- Money and a piece of cloth for the father of the bride.
- Money for the bride's brothers or male cousins. This is known as the '*akontasekan*'.
- A Holy Bible is given where the families are Christians.
- An engagement ring.

If the bride to be is from the Ga-Adangbe tribe of Ghana the premarital/dowry list is traditionally divided into three parts as follows:

The first part includes items needed for the premarital ceremony and will typically include the following:

- A monetary fee, called '*Shiwo*', is given to notify the bride's parents of the man's intention to marry their daughter.
- A bottle of wine.
- The '*Kplemo*', which is the acceptance fee given by the gentleman to the woman's family upon him receiving the dowry list.

The second part of the list is called the '*Yoo Tuumo*' which includes items necessary for the actual engagement including items for the bride to be and these usually include the following:

- The engagement ring.

- A Bible and hymn book.
- Two bottles of wine, whiskey and gin.
- Two cartons of beer, two castle bridge and six bottles of soda drink.
- '*Hika*', which is the monetary gift given to the bride for her wedding dress, accessories, make-up and hair.
- '*Tuumo dan*' and '*Too shibimo*' are also cash gifts given to the bride to set up a business or support an existing career.

The third part of the list is what is considered the actual bride price is traditionally referred to as the '*Nihamo*'. This is a cash gift given to the parents and other relatives of the bride-to-be and additionally it is supported with other gift items for the bride, for example:
- Six half pieces of textiles with matching headgears and jewellery.
- Traditional kente fabric.
- Set of neck, waist and wrist beads.
- Two wristwatches.
- Two pairs of shoes and handbags.
- Underwear.
- Cosmetics.

The following can also be added to the items brought by the groom to the family of the bride:
- Gift for the bride's father regarded as '*Shaanuu*' which would include men's fabrics and a cash gift.
- Gift for the bride's mother regarded as '*Shaayoo*' which is a half piece of cloth and a cash gift.
- Gift for the brothers of the bride called '*Dhabi*' which would be in the form of cash gifts.
- Gifts given to the extended relatives as a token of appreciation for their support and for serving as witnesses. This would be in the form of cash or crates of wine.

Indeed, the dowry list and requirements for the groom can seem like a tall order for a gentleman who wishes to marry under the traditional marriage but should these requirements not be met in their entirety, the bride's family are within their right to refuse to accept a gentleman's offer of marriage.

The Ceremony
Should you have the honour of attending a Ghanaian traditional marriage ceremony, you will be delighted at the occasion as it is filled with very

interesting and entertaining playful banter between the two families involved. I would also highly recommend that you get someone, where possible, to translate the different stages of the ceremony as it occurs as half the fun is following what is being said between the respective families.

In the more common Ghanaian languages, the ceremony is called 'kɔkɔɔ kɔ' and 'agboshimo' which can be translated to the word 'knocking' in English. These words are a way of saying 'knocking on the door'. This stems from the traditional way of knocking at the entrance of someone's home before entering.

The ceremony would formally begin with the arrival of the groom and his family and friends at the bride's family home as they bring all the items listed on the bride's dowry list to the bride's family.

The traditional marriage ceremony is taken very seriously by the families involved and is often taken much more seriously by the families than a white wedding or any other type of marriage ceremony which the couple may choose to also perform. In fact, in some instances, some families may not consider a marriage between a couple as valid where a traditional Ghanaian marriage ceremony did not take place and only a white wedding took place. Such issues would however, only usually come to light should marital problems arise between the couple at a later date. This knocking ceremony which includes the handing over ceremony (that is, the giving of the bride to the groom), once completed, essentially constitutes a binding and legal marital agreement under Ghana's traditional law and the couple are now husband and wife. Once the family is satisfied that all traditional marital obligations have been performed during the traditional ceremony, there is a large celebration and dancing, accompanied by lots of food and drinks at the home of the bride. In previous years the knocking ceremony/traditional wedding ceremony would be conducted followed by a white/church wedding a few days later. Today, however, it is becoming increasingly common for couples to perform both a traditional wedding ceremony and a church/white wedding ceremony a day apart or even on the same day. The couple can choose to also register their marriage as stipulated by ordinance at the country's national registry department.

Next, we will describe the white or what is sometimes referred to as a 'church' wedding ceremony.

The White Wedding
White weddings in Ghana are pretty much conducted in the same way as

they are in the West as it is essentially an adoption of the Western way of conducting weddings. You will therefore find that the protocols and etiquette observed are therefore more or less the same as within the West. A few notable points, however, include the timing involved at white weddings in Ghana. Church weddings typically start a lot later than stated on the wedding invitation for example. It is therefore advisable to seek advice from others locally as to approximately what time would be the best time to arrive at a particular wedding ceremony and endeavour to stick with the suggested time as much as possible. Ceremonies held within church buildings tend to be much longer and may be a more formal ceremony than white weddings held at other locations such as hotels or resorts, seaside, etcetera.

Traditionally, a white wedding is usually conducted within a church, however, in recent years and as laws have changed, such Christian-based wedding ceremonies are now also conducted at locations such as, hotels, beach fronts, beautiful resorts or in some cases at the home of either the bride or the groom. The ceremonies within churches are conducted by an ordained religious leader whereas outside of the church building a civil ceremony can be conducted by either an ordained religious leader or a 'marriage officer'. That is, a person authorised by law to conduct marriages and present marriage licences to couples.

After the white wedding ceremony, a party will follow with lots of food, drink and dancing. This celebration may be held at a different venue to where the formal marriage ceremony took place, or some couples may choose to have the celebration at the same venue as the formal ceremony.

The Islamic Marriage

The Islamic marriage ceremony is a binding marriage based on the rules of Islam where certain processes must take place in order for such a marriage to be binding and recognised as marriage under Islamic law. If certain rites are not performed on time for example, the marriage could be at risk of being considered invalid.

Although all the above-mentioned marriages are recognised in Ghana as legally binding marriages, today couples are often strongly advised to also ensure that an official marriage licence is signed by themselves and witnessed accordingly in order to avoid any risk of possible grey areas with respect to the validity of their marriage.

Wedding Invitations
In Ghana invitations may be sent approximately a month before the wedding date but don't be surprised if you are given an invitation to a traditional wedding a few days or even a day before the wedding date by a bride or groom who have only just met you and takes a liking to you and wishes to invite you to their special day. This is not uncommon and traditional weddings for example can often be less informal in terms of restrictions on the number of guests attending, etcetera.

Save the dates are now frequently also sent by the couple to guests usually about a month or two before the official invitation is sent out. Should you receive a save the date request for a wedding, do try and actually save the date in your calendar as this most certainly means that you will receive the actual wedding invitation in due course. Upon receiving the official wedding invitation do RSVP if you are asked to do so as a sign of respect and thoughtfulness towards the couple's planning of their big day. The high level of stress experienced by couples whilst planning their weddings is no secret; therefore, honouring their request to RSVP will always be appreciated.

Another important point to note is that you should make note of which type of wedding ceremony you are invited to as in Ghana there are different types of marriage ceremonies which may be carried out by couples which may occur on different dates or all on the same day. You could for example be invited to the traditional wedding only or the white wedding only or perhaps both of these ceremonies. You may be invited to attend just the informal reception party, or you may be fortunate to be invited to all the ceremonies, formal and informal, including an intimate gathering of close family and friends which usually occurs on the first Sunday after the wedding ceremony takes place. This post wedding ceremony is usually conducted by Christian couples and includes a church service. It is considered to be a 'thanksgiving' service to give thanks to God for the couple's union. After the church service, lunch will be served, usually at the home of the groom and his family.

Gifts
More recently couples request for monetary gifts for their wedding gift as contribution towards their honeymoon or any other large expenses related to marital life. Gift registries are not common in Ghana as they are in the

West and so it is important not to take offence to any such request from couples and give whatever you can afford as it would always be appreciated.

Dress Codes

The different wedding ceremonies in Ghana may have different dress codes. For example, white may be freely worn by guests at a traditional wedding as the bride is usually dressed in beautifully coloured kente fabrics and rarely wears white for her traditional wedding. At traditional weddings, white is actually the preferred colour for guests to wear as white is considered a celebratory colour. With respect to the church/white wedding, as previously mentioned, protocol, including dress codes, is quite similar to that of the West, and so it is advisable not to wear white if you are female, to avoid any risk of upstaging the bride. Men may however, wear white to a white wedding in Ghana as in recent times men it has become acceptable for men to wear traditional African outfits to marriage ceremonies held in churches (white weddings) unless black tie/formal wear is specified on the wedding invitation.

Men should not wear shorts to any of the ceremonies described in this chapter, including ceremonies which may occur on the beach or at a holiday resort. Long trousers are always a lot more acceptable at such events.

Avoid wearing black to any type of marriage ceremony as in Ghana black is generally only worn to funerals. It is therefore not acceptable to wear black to any celebratory or happy event such as a wedding.

Other General Etiquette for Guests

As a wedding guest it is important to remember your good manners of course in terms of your dining, socialising, networking, etcetera. Whatever you do, avoid over drinking as, as mentioned in previous chapters, drunkenness and drunken behaviour is never seen in a good light in Ghanaian culture. Your focus should be on having as much fun as possible by enjoying a joyous, colourful event. If you enjoy dancing, there is likely to be a lot of lively music and dancing to partake in as well as lots of food and drink!

Hungary
By Gabriella Kanyok

Chapter 1

Cultural Symbols

NATIONAL SYMBOLS

As with most countries, Hungary's national symbols are as interesting and varied as its long and ever-changing history. Many of the symbols seen below are heavily influenced by key moments from Hungary's past, whilst others are an everyday part of life around the world, though some may be unfamiliar with their Hungarian origins.

Standard items include the flag, the coat of arms, and the national anthem.

Coat of Arms
Whereas we normally expect some stability when it comes to such national icons, official Hungarian symbols have changed all too frequently during the long C.20th. This testifies to the torrid history of the country. Hungary has had four different coats of arms and seven different official national

flags in the past 100 years. The current ones are the plain, red, white and green flag, and a coat of arms with the Holy Crown on top of it—this is what we call the '*koronás címer*'.

National Flag

Regarding the flag, red stands for power, white for loyalty, and green for hope. Although the three colours have been present on flags and coats of arms since the C.12th, the current layout first emerged during the 1848–49 Revolution and War of Independence.

National Anthem

Hungary has an official and an unofficial national anthem. The official one is played at the beginning of ceremonies, and the unofficial one played at the end of them. The anthem was written for a national competition in 1823 by Ferenc Kölcsey, and a musical score composed by Ferenc Erkel was added in 1844. It has served as our national anthem since 1903. What is unusual about the national anthem of Hungary is its name, '*Himnusz*' (Hymn, an invocation to God, the Hungarian word for anthem, too), and the fact that there is a public monument dedicated to it just outside of Budapest.

Unusual Items

Unusual ones include the Holy Crown of St. Stephen (the first king), a second national anthem, and twenty-three historical flags that are displayed at official ceremonies (state visits, inauguration of new government).

Holy Crown of St Stephen

The hectic history of Hungary over the centuries has contributed to a unique constitutional tradition called the doctrine of the Holy Crown, which

revolves around the supposed crown of Hungary's first Christian king, Saint Stephen. Additional coronation regalia include a sword, a sceptre, an orb, and a coronation robe. The robe is held in the National Museum; all other regalia are on public display in the National Parliament House. The coronation regalia have had an interesting history, particularly the bent cross on the crown which resulted from its custody in Fort Knox (1953–78), where the regalia were kept together with America's gold reserves. The regalia were last taken out of Hungary by the local Nazis (Arrow-Cross) at the end of World War II, in May 1945. They were then turned over to the US Army for safekeeping (from the hands of the Soviet Army) and were finally returned to Hungary in January 1978.

Twenty-Three Historical Flags

A most spectacular, and for foreigners perhaps most weird, sight is that of the twenty-three historical flags put on display at official state events. These flags span the history of the country from the Hungarian Conquest of the Carpathian Basin in the C.9th (895–96) to the tragically failed 1956 Revolution.

Symbolic Places

Hungary also has quite a few symbolic places. Two of the most important ones were memorialised in preparation for the millennial celebrations of the Conquest (895–96—1895–96): the Feszty Rotunda in Ópusztaszer and the Heroes' Square memorial. The former displays the history of the Hungarian conquest and you can view it from a revolving stage; the latter is a public square.

Unofficial National Anthem – Szózat

Hungary's unofficial national anthem is a poem from the same period, *Szózat* (Appeal) by Mihály Vörösmarty, written in 1836—an accompanying musical score was added by Béni Egressy seven years later. The unofficial anthem is played at the end of ceremonies.

HUNGARIKUM

Hungarikum is a strange word that refers to things identified specifically with Hungary or Hungarians. It can be anything from animals and plants, through to food products and even inventions. Some of these things are internationally recognised and protected brands: we are the only ones who can use brand names like Tokaji Aszú, Zwack Unicum, Herendi porcelán, or Pick szalámi. The concept has become a rallying call for mock pride projects to turn Túró Rudi (a chocolate-covered curd cheese candy) or *Szalacsi bácsi* (an internet meme hero) into national icons. *Hungarikumok* is a key part of Hungarian identity as well as production and marketing, as seen with annual awards and even web shops. Products that Hungarians are proud of include Unicum and *pálinka* (fruit brandy), wine, sausage (*gyulai* and *csabai*), Pick salami, red paprika and '*Erős Pista*' (a hot, spicy paprika mash), and the Rubik's cube.

PULI
Puli is a breed of Hungarian shepherd dog; however, many refer to them as 'mop dogs' due to the way their fur grows in a cord-like manner. They usually come in three colours: black, grey and white. The vast majority of them are black; only 2% of the pulis are white. Few people know that Mark Zuckerberg and his wife came to Hungary to visit a Hungarian Puli breeder a few years ago. They visited the 'Ludas Matyi Puli farm'. Mark Zuckerberg was in love with Hungarian shepherd dogs. Beast, the most famous representative of the world-famous Hungarian dog breed, naturally has his own Facebook page with 2.3 million followers.

FILM

Regarding Hungarian contributions to international film history, the list is endless, and the story is being written as we write. William Fox (born as Fried Vilmos in 1879) was the founder of the Fox Film Corporation. Though he went bankrupt in 1936, his name lives on in the Fox Television Network and 20th Century Fox companies. Béla Lugosi, who arrived in the United States in 1920, became famous for portraying Count Dracula. Escape artist Harry Houdini was Hungarian, as was Peter Lorre (born as László Lőwenstein), Tony Curtis and Johnny Weismüller (the original Tarzan). Directors Michael Curtiz and Michael Korda (another 1956 refugee) as well as multiple Oscar winning composer Miklós Rózsa were all Hungarians, as was legendary femme fatale Zsa zsa Gabor. The 1956 Revolution 'exported' the cameramen Vilmos Zsigmond and László Kovács, who contributed to such pieces as *Easy Rider, Ghost Busters, Free Willy 2,* and *Close Encounters of the Third Kind*. The list continues today with Andy Vajna and Joe Eszterhasy, and director Nimród Antal. Vajna (of *Rambo* and *Terminator* fame) returned to Hungary to produce a movie on the 1956 Revolution for its 50th anniversary in 2006 (Children of Glory) and he was served as government commissioner until his death in 2019.

Chapter 2

Meeting, Greeting, Posture and Body Language

While much of posture and body language is universal, there are of course particular quirks when it comes to Hungarian culture. Some of these actions can also be seen in countries across Europe; however, there is much here that remains unique to Hungary and its citizens.

POSTURE
What I would mention here in particular, is that it's considered good manners if your feet are kept facing the ground, in addition to not showing the soles of your shoes.

BODY LANGUAGE
Gestures
Index and middle fingers are crossed—this means we wish you luck, and a positive outcome in whatever situation are you facing (exam, job interview, date etc).

Hungarians don't often use the peace or victory sign, but when they do, the palm is always facing outwards.

If you want to indicate that something is going well, don't make the 'okay' sign (index and thumb forming an O) as this is considered as an obscene gesture in Hungary.

Use the simple 'thumb up' sign to signal that something is going well. This hand gesture is also used for showing 'one', as a quantity.

Using the index finger and shaking it back and forth is a sign for another person not to do what they intend to.

Facial Expressions
Pay attention to the non-verbal clues while talking with a Hungarian. We like to use facial expressions to express our dislike or confusion. If you are not sure what a Hungarian thinks, you shouldn't be afraid to ask for clarification, as Hungarians often are indirect, out of courtesy.

Hungarians smile or laugh when there is a reason for it. But even when laughing, it will not be laughing out loud. In fact, seeing someone laugh very loudly does not occur very often. Hungarians call these kind of people '*harsány*', and it is not that positive a word. Some Hungarians will accept it if you are like this, but they would never behave like it themselves. You can only see young people laughing this way, because not all teenagers care about the social norms. Well, you can also hear tourists laughing loudly and even worse, when there is a bachelor or hen party.

Speaking
Don't get offended or afraid if a Hungarian friend or colleague raises their voice or if they have very different opinions, as this is considered normal in Hungary, and it shouldn't be taken personally.

If someone is spoken down to or spoken to condescendingly, Hungarians view this as a sign of disrespect and will perceive it as arrogance.

Greeting
In Hungary we say, good morning, afternoon, evening, and good day, which would be '*Jó napot kívánok*'! '*Szia*'! is the casual Hungarian for '*Hello*'!, but we also use it to say '*Goodbye*'.

When greeting another person, don't ask the question '*How are you*'? In Hungary, this is not taken as a sentence that comes as greeting, but rather a personal question indicating you want to learn about the other person's family, health or work-related issues. It is implied that you have time to get into a ten-minute discussion that usually follows after this question. When a Hungarian replies, they would always say the truth, so you would know exactly how they feel, in including both the good and the bad. So, if you don't know the person very well, asking this question is inappropriate.

Kisses on the cheeks are reserved for family and close friends. Typically, it's two kisses starting with the left cheek.

Hungarians only hug people when they haven't seen each other for a long, long time, and when they offer their condolences.

Men normally shake hands in a causal relationship; it is just palm to palm, not a real shake. We still keep to traditions, so older men or the person with the higher rank offers their hand first. Women may decide to shake hands, and men should always wait to see whether the lady offers her hand or not, but if not, it is not an offense.

Introductions

When meeting somebody, you will be introduced with your family name followed by your first name. At first, you may be referred to by surname only. Hungarians do not usually use first names when meeting someone for the first time. Titles are considered important in Hungary, so if you know the title of the other person, I suggest that instead of addressing the person using their first or last name, only use their title and '*úr*' if it is a Mr, or '*nő*' if it is a Mrs. In Hungary, everybody who has finished law school is entitled to get the title of doctor, therefore lawyers should be also called doctors.

DRIVING

In Hungary, there is zero tolerance in regard to alcohol, so it's illegal to consume any alcohol and then drive. So don't even try to drink a glass of wine for lunch or a pinch of beer. Therefore, Hungarians are always sober while driving. They are usually calm on the road—only a traffic jam can make them 'lose their minds' and that is when they curse. Otherwise, it's safe to be a pedestrian in Hungary, as they always have the priority, and cars – in most cases – stop and let the pedestrians pass. Even when drivers see them approaching a zebra crossing, they will stop.

Chapter 3

Conversation Dos and Don'ts

Hungarians are very hospitable and nice people, and they like to get into conversations with foreigners if the language barriers allow it. I would like to highlight that in conversations with Hungarians, you should always make sure that you say what you mean, and you mean what you say, as Hungarians will take your words for granted. As an example: don't invite somebody over to your place if you don't mean it. The contrary is also true: if you are invited over, don't accept it unless you would really like to go. It's a huge offence to promise something and then to decline/forget.

Here are a few topics to be on the safe side:

Dos

Family is a major focus in Hungary, so Hungarians enjoy talking about theirs and hearing about yours.

Hungarian food and beverages you have experienced and tasted. Hungary is proud of its agriculture. So topics about around viniculture, *pálinka* and food are safe and always welcome. Note: *Gulyás* (*Gulash*) is a soup and not a stew!

Sport – Everybody knows Ferenc Puskás, the famous Hungarian football player, but unfortunately Hungary has not been very lucky in this sport in the past decades. *But* we have other sports that we are proud of such as: handball, water polo, fencing, canoe-kayak, wrestling, gymnastics, and swimming. Hungary is also pretty successful when it comes to the Olympic Games, with its 491 medals in total.

Culture

Hungarian inventions: there are many such inventions that people use in their everyday lives, but they often don't know that they were invented by a Hungarian. This a nice topic that could be discussed.

Few highlights:

Ballpoint pen/biro—by László Bíró – replacing the quill and fountain pens.

Binoculars and opera glasses—by József Petzval.

Safety match—by János Irinyi.

Vitamin C—by Albert Szentgyörgyi who won the Nobel Prize for medicine in 1937 for his discovery.

First helicopter—by Oszkár Asbóth.

'The father of the electric train'—by Kálmán Kandó, who designed the three-phase motor and generator needed for electric railways.

Telephone exchange—by Tivadar Puskás.

Digital computing—by conceptual inventor, János Neumann.

Colour TV—by Péter Károly Goldman in about 1940.

Holography, the process of creating 3D images—by Dénes Gábor, who won the Nobel Prize in physics for this in 1971.

Prezi, cloud-based presentation software—by Adam Somlai-Fischer, Peter Halacsy and Peter Arvai.

Nobel Prizes have gone to thirteen Hungarians. In fact, Hungary ranks 16th in the world for the number of these prizes won. Hungary's Nobel Prizes have been won in the fields of physics, chemistry, medicine, economics and literature. One prize-winner, Richard Adolf Zsigmondy, has a moon crater 'Zsigmondy' named in his honour.

DON'TS

Communism and politics – Talking about *politics with a Hungarian,* unless you absolutely agree on all historical, political, social and economic angles, is risky business. In particular, the communist years, in which Hungary spent forty years under communist regime, is one of those touchy topics to be avoided.

The Treaty of Trianon – After WW1, the Treaty annexed 2/3 of Hungary's land to neighbouring countries.

Minorities – The Roma issue.

Salaries and living costs.

Play around or mistake the capitals: Bucharest and Budapest – it's not funny, and a Hungarian can get very offended by this. The Hungarian capital is called Budapest. The same applies for *'Hungry Hungarians'* – don't joke around with this phrase because it's not funny either.

Chapter 4

Gifts Giving

It's part of life and culture to celebrate joyful events with the exchange or giving of gifts. Whichever end we are on, the act of gifting can be fun and exciting, especially if we know certain rules of gifting etiquette that should be followed in Hungary.

We all know that when we visit somebody, we never arrive empty-handed. If you are invited to someone's home in Hungary, the Hungarian gift giving custom dictates that you should always bring a small gift, such as a box of chocolates, some flowers, liquor or wine from your home country.

If you are in Hungary and you are invited to somebody's house, avoid brining *pálinka* to your host, because you send the unintended message that you already know that you are not going to like the *pálinka* they will serve you.

When giving a gift of flowers they should be given in odd numbers, with the exception of thirteen, which is considered an unlucky number. When choosing a gift of flowers, do not give lilies, chrysanthemums or red roses. To gain extra bonus points, bring flowers to all the females in the house, your partner's mother, sister or roommate—this a nice gesture to say thank you all for your kind hospitality.

When receiving a gift, you should open it immediately and in front of the gift giver.

BIRTHDAYS AND NAME DAYS
While early birthdays are huge festive occasions with presents, cakes and guests, the older we get, the less and less we celebrate our birthdays, simply because we don't want to advertise our age. The nature of a birthday present depends on the relationship we have with the person. Some items should be naturally avoided, for instance, anything that makes the celebrated person

feel embarrassed (for example: lingerie). If you don't have a very close relationship with that person, stay on the safe side and get some flowers, and/or chocolates; perhaps a gift card to a book shop could be a nice gesture.

Hungarians also celebrate their 'name' days, where people usually offer gifts, chocolates or flowers. Each first name has been assigned to one or more days of the calendar—these days are based on religious traditions, historical events, or the birthday of a famous person. The typical and popular name day present is a flower.

OFFICE CULTURE

Celebrations might take place at the workplace, and it's custom that the celebrated person brings some cakes or cookies to offer to their colleagues. It also occurs that the colleagues' chip in and get a joint birthday present for the celebrated person. Women are typically given flowers as a gift on their name day by their colleagues.

MOTHER'S DAY, FATHER'S DAY

In Hungary, Mother's Day is celebrated on the first Sunday of May. On this day, we don't only celebrate mothers per se, but also grandmothers as well. Gifts can vary from flowers to presents that are often handmade made by the children.

Hungarians usually don't celebrate Father's Day.

MIKULÁS AND CHRISTMAS TRADITION

Santa Claus Day (St. Nicolas or in Hungarian Szent Miklós or Mikulás)
This is a unique and small holiday in Hungary. This holiday is held in commemoration of Saint Nicholas (called *Szent Miklós* in Hungarian), well-known in Hungary as the patron saint of pálinka distillers, the town of Kecskemét, sailors, and merchants. Many European cultures have some version of Saint Nicholas or Santa Claus, and the Hungarian version, *Mikulás*, was introduced in the 1850s.

Mikulás visits the homes on the 6th of December, and leaves presents for everybody. The evening before, children clean their boots and place them in front of the window. According to tradition, *Mikulás* will leave tasty treats inside the shoes for the good children. Gifts may include fruits, but typically orange (*narancs*), chocolate (*csokoládé*), peanuts, or candies. On the morning of Santa Claus Day, Hungary is filled with children's excitement and wonder as they wake up to find these precious gifts in their shoes! Even among adults, it is quite common to gift something on this day by putting the gifts in someone's shoes as a surprise, or by simply wrapping the gift and handing it to them.

Children and adults that have not behaved well all year long will receive a pile of golden birch-rod (*virgács*) wrapped in red paper, as it symbolises punishment, or they may wake up to find coal in their shoes.

It's also a custom to prepare Santa's Packages (*Mikulás csomag*), a little red paper sack filled with different goodies, fruits, chocolates, candies etcetera. At schools, children are offered these packages for *Mikulás* as a gift from the local authorities. It's also common that children 'play' Santa's draw, another nice custom in Hungary. People put their names in a basket, and each person draws a name, and offers/puts together a gift for the drawn person. This is also a habit at some workplaces not only for *Mikulás*, but for Christmas gifting as well.

Christmas in Hungary

Christmas celebrations and the offering of presents in Hungary is largely similar to the way most Europeans celebrate this holy day. Hungarian tradition dictates that it's baby Jesus (*Jézuska*) who delivers the presents, not Santa Claus. Gifts are opened on the eve of the 24th of December.

Wedding Gifts

Weddings in Hungary are costly affairs nowadays, so most couples aim to cover the wedding costs with the money they receive as a gift, so *money* is the most useful and practical gift. Deciding on the exact amount is not easy, as it depends on your relationship with the couple and also on your financial status (it could be from 30–50 Euros to up to 500–1000 Euros). If you are not a close friend or relative, keep in mind that the money you give should at least cover your food and drink at the event.

At a certain point during the wedding, or at varying times throughout the event, people will place their envelopes into a dedicated box, basket or other vessel, along with a greeting card.

In Hungary we don't really have the custom of having a register or wish list, but usually couples give hints on what they would like to receive as a wedding gift. In case of any doubt, you could always ask their parents, or even the couple, on what they would prefer.

Apart from the money, if you want to offer anything else, it's up to you. This could be anything meaningful, from vintage wine to items for the home, but I would suggest choosing something that reminds you of the couple.

It's also fun to offer instant lottery tickets, aka scratch-off tickets, as a side present, as some of them give the chance to win millions of Hungarian forints.

Business Gifts

Gifts are usually not expected, but small presents like a souvenir representing your home country would be very much appreciated. A diary or nicely engraved pens with your company logo could also be a really nice gift.

If you want to offer a meaningful present to your Hungarian counterpart, and you have decided to go for a nice pen, always choose a blue inked pen. In Hungary, official documents are only accepted if they are signed in blue ink. This is a small detail, but you would certainly earn yourself some good points by knowing it.

Chapter 5

Dining Etiquette

Food is very important to Hungarians, as we take great pride in our delicacies and cuisine. In this chapter, I would like to share some interesting traditions and give you an insight into the Hungarian style of dining.

DINING IN HUNGARY

Hungarians dine in continental style, which means that the fork is in the left hand, knife in the right hand, and hands and wrists are visible on the table throughout the meal.

The custom is to have a three-course meal (soup made of a variety of ingredients or a starter, main course and dessert). When choosing a quite filling soup, a dessert as the second dish would make a complete meal.

Breakfast is a light meal, lunch is usually the main meal of the day, although from a family perspective dinner is important, as most of the time, this is the only occasion when families can sit and eat together.

In a business set-up, business lunch tends to be a more common practice, but the chosen type of business meal also depends on the nature of the meeting, the occasion and the relationship between the parties in question.

Hungarians eat a lot of bread, but there is no butter offered with it. (Bread served with butter before the meal could only happen in an elegant restaurant, but this is not a custom at all).

Red paprika and Hungarian-ness belong together. We can make many different Hungarian dishes from one single paprika-spiced fish soup base. What's more, we are able to cook at least twenty dishes from a paprika-spiced fat-fried onion base, and we are very proud of that.

The host often wishes the guests a hearty appetite at the start of each course and encourages them to eat more during the meal, therefore it is considered to be impolite to leave food on the plate. This could be interpreted in a way that you are dissatisfied with the food that was served. (The portions are huge in Hungary).

The tipping in restaurants is usually 10–15%, but in many places there is a so-called service fee already included in the bill, so it's up to you to decide whether you would like to tip on top of that or not.

Pig Slaughter and its Festivity

Tourists rarely experience a pig slaughter, which is a Hungarian tradition in the winter season. This event usually takes place between November and February, as cold weather is needed to preserve the large quantities of meat, and it also helps to minimise the bacteria multiplication. The event starts early around five to six in the morning (yes, in the freezing cold). The pig is first de-haired, scorched, and then some parts are skinned. Then, as the next step, the butcher divides the animal into the parts which will be processed to make black pudding (*véreshurka*), sausage (*kolbász*), ham (*sonka*), *hurka* (organ and rice sausage), crackling and cuts of meat.

Each and every part of the pig is useful; for instance, the minced meat is seasoned with paprika, salt and pepper and stuffed into sheep gut.

The traditional breakfast on that day is the roasted blood with onion, accompanied by plenty of *pálinka* and mulled wine. The first shot of *pálinka* is drunk before the feast begins to put people in the mood, the second shot is in honour of the slaughtered pig.

For lunch *orja* soup is served, which is made of the vertebral of the pig, followed by some pork fillet, roasted fresh liver with parsley potatoes. At the end of the day, a festive dinner closes the festivity with freshly prepared roasted *kolbász* and black pudding from the day's slaughter.

Bogrács

Cooking on open fire is a special episode in our gastronomy, and it's called '*bográcsozás*'. *Bogrács* is the kettle we use to cook the meals in, and several of our one-pot dishes originate from this tradition of outdoor cooking. The dish could be anything from goulash, fish soup to stew. This type of outdoor cooking is perfect for 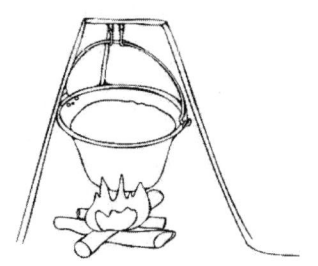 large gatherings, as the preparation of all the ingredients could be regarded as a great team-building activity as well. Although it takes practice to master a good *bogrács* dish, it's worth the effort, as the result will be divine!

SZALLONASÜTÉS AKA ROASTED BACON ON CAMPFIRE

The premise of the bacon roast is simple, everybody gathers around the fire pit with a pork belly on a stick, and roasts the bacon for around thirty minutes. This tradition can be real fun with friends and family, gathering together, drinking and talking while the bacon is being roasted. When the pork starts to glisten, we dab the grease on a piece of bread and continue roasting until the bacon is nice and crispy. We then chop it up, throw on some chopped onions, peppers, vegetables and other condiments on top of our grease covered bread, and enjoy our feast!

PÁLINKA AND DRINKS

You may have heard about '*Pálinka*', which is our traditional fruit brandy, often produced by the homeowner or family member, and if you are a houseguest in Hungary, as soon as you walk in the door, no matter what time of the day, a generous shot of *pálinka* will be immediately offered to you. It's very strong, so if you rarely drink alcohol, of course you can kindly decline the offer, but I recommend you try at least a tiny sip for the sake of your proud host, as a shot or a few is an integral part of Hungarian hospitality. Another drink I would recommend you try is called '*Unicum*', an alcoholic drink made of herbs.

Hungary is also extremely proud of its viticulture, so avoid making any negative comments on the wine, especially if it comes from the same region as your host or Hungarian counterpart.

On the same note, it's also good to keep in mind that the host often automatically refills the empty glasses, no matter what you drink, thus if you do not want to drink more, leave your glass half full.

During a toast or before a meal, Hungarians look at each other in the eye, clink glasses with wine or *pálinka*, and say '*Egészségedre*' ('Cheers').

We don't clink glasses if the beverage is beer. This is an old vow, which dates back to the 1848–49 Hungarian Revolution where the Hungarians got defeated, and while thirteen Hungarian generals were executed, the Austrians were clinking glasses filled with beer after each and every execution.

TYPICAL AND INTERESTING HUNGARIAN DISHES

Goulash; Stuffed cabbage with sour cream; catfish—stew with cottage cheese pasta and sour cream; fisherman's soup; stuffed cabbage leaves with sour cream; *Lángos*; chimney cake (*Kürtős kalács*); Hungarian trifle (*Somlói galuska*); plum dumplings; *Rákóczi* cottage cheese cake; Hungarian Gerbaud cake; Dobos Tarte.

Hungarians like to eat pastas topped with sweets and seeds, such as jam, walnut, fruits, powdered sugar, and poppy seeds.

Főzelék, which looks like a soup, but is like a thick vegetable stew, typically home cooked, but some restaurants list it on their menu, especially on weekdays, so this could be an ideal choice if you want to eat a quick and healthy meal, as well as a very Hungarian dining experience.

Chapter 6

Business Etiquette

The business culture in Hungary is quite formal, relationship oriented, and courteous. Personal relationships, contacts and networks are an essential part of doing business in Hungary. Business relationships are usually built on trust and familiarity, so we often socialise outside the workplace. Business lunches and dinners are common for getting to know people, but formal negotiations are not normally held over meals. In this chapter, I would like to guide you through the most important elements of the Hungarian business etiquette.

DRESS CODE
This varies depending on the level of the meeting and the sector. In general, traditional elegance is preferred in Hungary, so the dress code tends to be conservative amongst business people.

Neat appearance is a must; cleanliness and tidiness are an absolute necessity in the Hungarian business world.

Formal business clothes: for men, dark colours (black, blue, grey) are preferred, although during the spring and summer seasons, light coloured suits are appropriate as well; this would usually be with a white shirt and a tie. For women: business suits, skirts with a blouse and business jacket, or a dress, are the proper clothing.

As mentioned, depending on the business sector you are in or dealing with, business casual attire has become a trend in Hungary, especially in the IT sector.

During normal office hours, Hungarians dress less formally. In small or medium sized businesses, there is usually no official dress code and employees tend to wear casual business attire, for instance, jeans.

Shorts are not common in the city, and they are best reserved for the countryside or for the beaches of one of the lakes.

Hungarians enjoy dressing up for many formal events (tuxedo and evening gowns are popular), but standard business attire would be appropriate for any formal occasion, restaurants, the opera, or theatres.

BUSINESS GREETINGS AND TITLES

In the Hungarian business context, a firm handshake is customary, and not only upon greeting, but when departing too.

When greeting another person, extended eye contact is important as this is a sign that the person is trustworthy.

Hungarian organisations and companies often follow a hierarchical structure. It is therefore recommended to be respectful and formal towards executives and managers, who will make all major decisions.

The higher the rank, the humbler the person is, but titles and achievements are important.

In Hungary, the surname is listed before the first name. Close friends, relatives and young people usually call each other by, and use, their first names, but it's advisable to address adults by their titles and their surname until you are invited to do otherwise.

When addressing someone in Hungary, always use professional titles, such as Doctor, Minister, Director etcetera and either use a title with a surname, like Professor Kiss, or add Mr/Mrs/Miss to their surname.

BUSINESS MEETINGS AND NEGOTIATIONS

Business appointments should be requested by any means of communication as far in advance as possible.

It is often difficult to schedule meetings on a Friday afternoon in the periods between July to the end of August, as well as from mid-December to mid-January, as most people are on holiday.

The reconfirmation of a meeting the day before is a must.

Punctuality is extremely important, so it is expected in all business-related matters. It's advised to always arrive five to ten minutes before the scheduled meeting, but running a little late doesn't influence the final result of the business negations. (Compared to business meetings, public events never start on time, five to ten minute delays are quite common).

Business cards are exchanged without formal rituals. The cards are exchanged at the beginning of the meeting. The card doesn't need to be translated into Hungarian, as most people speak English and nowadays some other foreign languages as well.

In Hungary, meetings are an important part of the process of conducting any kind of business as they are regarded as the brainstorming phase of the process.

During negotiations, confrontational behaviour and high-pressure sales don't work often, but well-researched projects, accurate and convincing presentations do. Hungarians value facts, knowledge, and well-based background information.

Hungarians are goal oriented, well prepared, and flexible business negotiators, who don't mind compromising.

Promises made during meetings are usually respected, but agreements are rarely reached on the spot, and they are only binding when written.

BUSINESS ENTERTAINING

Hungarian hospitality is well-known, and meals are mainly social events, even at the workplace, so it's advisable to keep the business talk out while dining.

Business meals are formal events, and usually take place in restaurants. Being invited to a business contact's home is rare, and can be only accepted if the business relationship was based on a friendship, or if it later turned into a friendship.

In the case of a business dinner being more for entertaining rather than conducting business, the occasion is considered less formal and one should expect to be busy the whole evening, as most of the traditional Hungarian restaurants offer musicians or entertainment in the evening. If your schedule doesn't allow you to stay up late, then a business lunch would be a better choice.

We are also very proud of our traditions and our countryside, so a business partner could be invited for an excursion while in Hungary, such as a horse riding or wine tasting event.

Chapter 7

Wedding Etiquette

If you are invited to a Hungarian wedding, or you are planning to marry a Hungarian, there are some customs and traditions associated with this special day that you should know. Even though the typical, old Hungarian wedding traditions have faded away, some of them still remain and are practiced in the rural villages of Hungary. In this chapter, I would like to highlight and place the focus on modern Hungarian weddings that have some traditional touches.

WEDDINGS IN HUNGARY

In Hungary, for a marriage to be legal, couples must have a civil ceremony conducted by an official wedding registrar (*anyakönyvvezető*) working at the local municipality, as church weddings are not legally binding. Civil marriages are the only marriages that are legally recognised. Typically, but not always, couples will also have a church ceremony that follows the civil ceremony, and it is very common for a huge procession of guests to follow the couple from the municipality to the church.

Hungary by religion is predominantly a Roman Catholic country, so if the couple choose to tie the knot in a church as well, guests should be prepared to attend a religious ceremony and a mass.

Traditionally, the best man personally visits each guest and verbally invites them to the wedding ceremony (which is generally done in rhyme), and it is his responsibility to arrange for up to three days of wedding festivities. Even today, it is considered good manners for the *bride* and the *groom* to go as a couple to personally invite relatives, close friends, colleagues and neighbours to attend their wedding.

Wedding invitations will state which part of the festivities you are invited to. For instance, some couples invite their colleagues and acquaintances only for the official ceremonies, but not for the dinner and the party afterwards.

Weddings in Hungary nowadays are a *one-day event*, with the ceremony(ies), reception, dinner and the party all taking place within a day. (Having said this, the couple often chooses to have their civil wedding in private days or weeks before the actual wedding day with their two witnesses, and very often surrounded by close family and friends). Today, Hungarian weddings are typically less formal and follow a simple format: the bride and groom sit in special chairs up front, alongside their witnesses.

The symbol of the marriage, *the rings*, are traditionally worn on the right hand. (Engagement ring(s) are placed on the left hand, before being switched to the right hand after the marriage becomes official).

In Hungary, the *'vőfély'* is the master of ceremony, and assumes the role of best man. He is the official host, he coordinates, organises and entertains before, during and after the wedding. *Vőfély* can be a relative or a friend, but nowadays the couple will hire a professional for this role. You should not be surprised if you hear the *vőfély performing his roles while partly reciting in comic verse—this would be based on well-known traditional forms* and tailored to the couple and their families.

'Bridal send-off'—Before the wedding ceremony, it is a Hungarian tradition that the *vőfély*, in the name of the groom, goes to the nuptial house of the bride to thank the parents for raising their daughter, and ask them to allow the bride to leave the home. This Hungarian tradition might look a little bit old fashioned, but it serves the purpose of showing respect to the bride's family.

DRESS CODE

Hungarian brides traditionally wear *white wedding gowns*, white shoes and white accessories—this form of dress is observed on most occasions. The groom and his best man will wear a classic suit with some tiny floral decorations on their jackets.

After midnight, the bride goes to exchange her wedding gown for a so called *"new wife dress"* (*menyecskeruha* in Hungarian), which symbolises the transition of becoming a wife. Traditionally, the colour of *the new dress is red*, (but people today will choose to wear many different colours), and sometimes the groom will change his shirt to a red one.

The dress code for the guests is very simple: the couple will let you know if there is a special dress code required for their big day, but otherwise just *dress elegantly*. Once you choose the perfect outfit, follow one simple rule: it's not about you, it's about them. Everybody's focus should be on the bride and the groom, not on you. Female guests shouldn't wear red, white or black without the bride's consent.

If there is a ceremony at a church, it is essential for your clothes to be in accordance with the etiquette required at places of worship, however, at the very least, the shoulders and décolleté should be covered. Sometimes, the inside of a church can be really cold, so it's advisable to take this into consideration as well.

DANCE
Candle-light dance/waltz ('Gyertyafénykeringő')
If the bride changes her dress at midnight, she will say goodbye to the white dress with this dance by dancing with the groom while each holds a candle in their hands. The guests gather in a big circle around them while holding candles, which the newlyweds blow away while dancing. When all 'guest candles' are blown out, the couple will blow out their own and leave the room to change dresses. The dance itself used to be a waltz: Viennese Waltz (*'bécsi keringő'*) or English Waltz (*'angol keringő'*), and this is where the name originates from.

Bridal Dance / New Wife Dance – Money Dance – 'Bride for Sale'! ('Menyasszonytánc'/ 'Menyecsketánc')
The tradition of the bridal dance and 'new wife dance' varies from region to region, with different customs in each. As both dances essentially serve the same purpose, the two traditions often merge.

The *bridal dance* is the last dance of the bride on her wedding day in her wedding dress, that is, before midnight. According to old traditions, it is her last dance as a girl, since the wedding night has not yet taken place.

Either her father, the groom or the best man would announce that "The bride is for sale!" A bucket or a hat will be held out in order to collect money from all the guests to 'pay' for the privilege of dancing with the bride (usually only for a few seconds while spinning her around). This is the time when the guests 'throw' money into the bucket, usually in envelopes.

The last in line is the groom, who after the dance, picks up the bride and the money before running out to change into their other outfits.

Like the bridal dance, the *'new wife dance'* is also about collecting money, but, of course, it is done in a different dress. Its meaning is the opposite, as it is the bride's first dance as a new wife.

The best man or master of ceremony invites the guests to dance by shouting, "New bride for sale!" Often, according to the old traditions, the dance is followed by the bride being given change to sweep up with a broom. This would be collected in a bucket held by the newly-wed husband, symbolising their roles in the marriage.

Sometimes, the bride won't want to dance with all the guests in her white gown. Instead, she will only dance once during the night, after having changed into her 'new wife dress' which is typically *red* and always lighter in weight than the white one.

WEDDING MENU AND MIDNIGHT BUFFET

A small wedding reception usually takes place after the ceremonies, where different kinds of small *Hungarian savoury* (like *pogácsa) and sweet pastries*, and/or some canapés, are served with drinks.

The wedding menu normally consists of three to four dishes, but this will depend on the venue/restaurant/caterer, the style and the budget of the wedding, so you can expect to see many different menu options. There are two dishes which cannot be missing from any wedding menus, and that is the *Újházy style chicken soup and stuffed cabbage.*

The main *wedding cake* would be served to the guests by the bride and groom. Boxes of cake might be given out to the guests as they leave.

Hungarian weddings are all-night affairs with lots of music and dancing involved, so the *midnight buffet* is served to give guests some extra energy to keep the party going. The buffet usually consists of *stuffed cabbage*, and sometimes beef stew, and other typical Hungarian comfort foods.

Hungarians don't like to waste food, so the *leftovers* will be served as breakfast the next morning/lunch or packed up and given out to the guests to take home.

GIFTS

Wedding gifts are usually given personally to the bride and groom, or may be delivered personally to the home of the newlyweds after the wedding. Envelopes containing a nice card and cash are often gifted; the bride and groom's name will be the only written text on the outside of the envelope. Usually, the couple states in advance what kind of gifts they would like to receive (for example, household items or financial contributions to their new home or honeymoon etcetera).

A record of these gifts is important because a Hungarian custom requires that an equal gift is to be given back by the couple, should a similar event be hosted in the future by the giver or their family.

Engagement gifts and kerchief
There is a tradition that states that men should give a practical gift, such as a handmade or shop bought kerchief, comb, ring or gingerbread, to his beloved. Accepting the gift means that the proposal has been accepted. In order to reassure the future husband she has a gift to offer in return, the bride-to-be will give a kerchief to her fiancée with his name, or monogram, embroidered in it. (During a traditional wedding, this same kerchief would be wrapped around the bride's head by the eldest female guest. This act symbolises the bride becoming the wife during the ceremony.)

HUNGARIAN MOTIF
Several elements of the wedding can be decorated with Hungarian motives. For instance, this could be the famous 'Kalocsa embroidery' *('Kalocsai himzés')* or embroideries representative of other regions of the country *('Kalotaszeg', 'Matyó', 'Palóc', 'Sárköz')*. The decoration can be applied to invitation cards, dresses, seating cards or even on the wedding cake.

A draft scenario of a Hungarian wedding, some events are interchangeable:
- Ceremony.
- Wedding reception (few drinks, savoury and sweet pastries, canapés).
- While the newlyweds are being photographed.
- Throwing of the bride's bouquet.
- Group pictures, and pictures taken with the bride and groom.
- Festive dinner (three to four courses).
- Speeches.
- Opening dance by the bride and groom.
- Opening of the dance floor – party – and occasionally some games.
- Wedding cake.
- More party and drinking.
- Bride comes back as 'new wife' wearing her red dress.
- Bridal dance/money dance.
- Midnight buffet is being served.
- Party, party, party until dawn.

India
By Niraalee Shah

Chapter 1

Culture Symbols

LOTUS FLOWER

The lotus is the national flower of India. It is the symbol of purity, culture, virtues, benevolence, wealth, happiness and spiritual growth.

It is a sacred flower and occupies a unique position in the art and mythology of ancient India and has been an auspicious symbol of Indian culture since time immemorial.

The lotus grows in lakes, ponds and most stationery shallow water bodies. It grows in mud and yet is so beautiful, radiant, and doesn't smell of mud nor is it submerged in water. This is what the Indian culture believes creates strength of character; whatever the background, you should always rise above your surroundings and achieve high levels of virtue.

In the *Bhagavad Gita* (the Hindu scripture), a human is adjured to be like the lotus flower; they should work without attachment, dedicating their actions to God, untouched by sin, like water on a lotus leaf, like a beautiful flower standing high above the mud and water.

The lotus flower is deeply imbibed with the symbolism of Indian philosophy. It is considered sacred in both Hinduism and Buddhism. Many Hindu deities like Brahma, Lakshmi and Saraswati are depicted to be seated on a lotus flower. In Buddhist philosophy, the lotus represents the preservability of purity of one's soul amidst the grime of mortal life. The lotus flower is a symbol of divine beauty and is often used as a simile to describe someone with pure and delicate attributes.

The lotus is supposed to bring good luck and prosperity not only in a materialistic aspect but also a richness in beauty, lustre, and purity of thoughts, actions and growth of intellect, wisdom and spiritual merit, a symbol of youthfulness, joy and happiness. The lotus is one of the best symbols of everything good and thus has captured the imagination of Indians for so long.

It may be easily concluded that the importance of the lotus in India is nothing less than the soul of Indian culture itself.

Chapter 2

Meeting, Greeting, Posture and Body Language

A smile is the universally accepted facial expression for welcoming someone. However, India has some unique gestures and body languages which are sometimes too tricky to understand. Indian gestures are open, loud and highly expressive.

As a tourist, you may come across a lot of physical gestures when you visit India and wonder what they actually mean. Some of these gestures are inspired from different mudra (postures) in Indian Classical Dance. Having a thorough knowledge of Indian gestures can help you blend with the people and ensure you don't get offended or offend someone else.

IMPORTANCE OF INDIAN GESTURES: AN OVERVIEW
The literal Hindi pronunciation of 'gesture' is 'हाव-भाव' (*haav-bhaav*); whereas 'body language' in Hindi is 'शारीरिक हाव-भाव' (*saariirik haav-bhaav*).

With different Hindi gestures, people also express their sense of basic emotions, such as respect, joy, wonder, sadness, or disappointment. Relying on various gestures in India for emotional expression is so much a part of our culture that we do it all the time without even noticing it. For example, in India, body language is a great way to find out whether someone is really into the conversation or not. The fact may surprise you, but in India, gestures and greetings are mostly followed by a variety of typical Hindi words.

COMMON GESTURES IN INDIAN SOCIETY
In India, gestures reflect the state of mind. The moment you take your first step in this country, be ready to get pampered with lots of warmth and personal attention. Indian people leave no stone unturned when it comes to welcoming their guests.

Positive Gestures

Positive gestures are exchanged for sharing joy, positive vibes, and respect. All the positive gestures described below are completely okay to use in a public place.

- Joining Hands for *Namaste*

The first gesture we are going to talk about is how to greet in Hindi. It's also one of the most common hand gestures in Hindi. So, someone joined both their hands with open palms facing each other in front of you? No, they are not pleading or begging for something. This traditional Indian sign of bowing in front of someone and joining hands is a greeting of dignity and respect. This gesture is called '*Namaste*'. You will be glad to notice a gentle smile on the face of the people while they say *namaste*— that is exactly the sign of a warm welcome and acceptance. Accompanied with a slight bow, the *namaste* is practiced when welcoming someone, saying hello or during Hindu religious gatherings while praying to God.

– It's called नमस्ते *(NamaSTe)* or नमस्कार *(NamaSkaar)*.

– Whenever you meet an elder person or someone of the opposite gender, this is the perfect way to greet them.

– Whilst saying नमस्ते *(NamaSTe)*, join the palms of your hands in such a way that they're placed near your chest, then slightly bow your head with a gentle smile on your face.

Quick Tip

This gesture isn't required when you're meeting someone of your own age and gender. You can use a quick 'hello' for them, as well as for children.

Also keep in mind that in the Hindu religion, the same hand gesture is used when praying to God.

- Touching the Feet of Elders

Elderly people who are either close relatives, or parents/grandparents of your friends and spouse, are usually addressed by touching their feet. This is a symbol of your deep respect towards them and is yet another way to express your gratitude for older people, where a simple नमस्ते *(NamaSTe)* wouldn't suffice. The same gesture is also used to ask for their blessings.

– When meeting elderly people, stand at a comfortable distance.

– Slowly bend your upper body down and touch their feet. While doing so, you should say प्रणाम *(pranaam)*.

Quick Tip

The ideal way to do this is by using both hands. However, people aren't that particular about it nowadays and this gesture can be seen using just one hand as well. But one thing is for sure: touching the feet is a sure-fired way to melt their hearts!

– Blessing the young ones by placing your palm on their head.

Naturally, this comes as an immediate response to the gesture described above.

– The elders are supposed to lovingly touch the young ones by placing their palm on their head. By placing their palm, they intend to bless you with positive vibes as well as wish you joy.

– Usually, elderly people can be heard saying, जीते रहो *(jiiTe raho)* to males and जीती रहो *(jiiTii raho)* to females. The phrase means 'have a long and satisfying life'.

Quick Tip

If someone younger is touching your feet, you should respond by doing this gesture.

In case you're the one who's touching the feet, wait for a second to allow them enough time so that they can bless you.

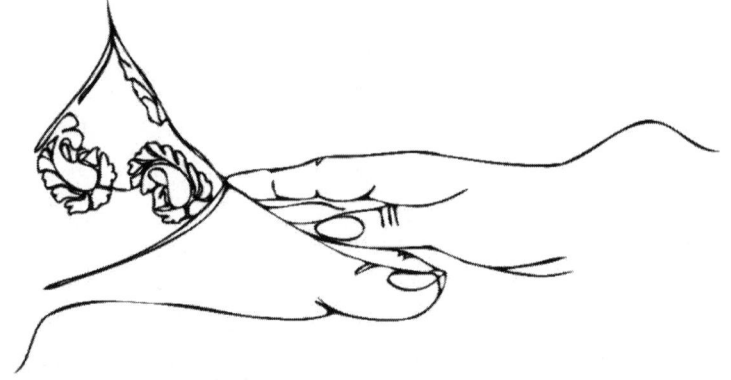

● Hugging

The hugging gesture is practiced by Indians as a tender display of affection. This is one of the most affectionate body language signs in Hindi.

– People hug their friends and cousins, those in the same age group, and those of the same gender.

– The elders show their love by hugging their kids and grandchildren.

– Festivals like Holi and Eid are especially celebrated by hugging each other.

Quick Tip

Whilst hugging, you can casually say कैसे हो *(kaiSe ho)* to men and कैसी हो *(kaiSii ho)* to women. Irrespective of the occasion and Indian traditions, we suggest that you don't share a hug with the opposite sex.

- Hand Gestures

In Hindi, hand gestures translate to हाथ के इशारे *(haaTH ke isaare)*.

Saying 'wow' or 'superb' using one hand.
– Hindi translations for these words are वाह! *(vaah!)* or ज़बरदस्त *(zabaraDaST)*.
– The gesture is made by touching the tips of the index finger and the thumb so that it forms a circle.

Quick Tip

It's a casual sign which serves the purpose of complimenting someone out of affection and is usually exchanged between friends and couples. The 'wow' sign is also used for praising someone's picture on social media.

– Thumbs Up

This is a good sign that confirms an approval, such as 'we're all set'! It's also used to wish luck. It's shared between classmates, often before exams, any competition, or a performance, in order to drive away nervousness. In short, with a 'thumbs up' sign, you're saying, "It's going to be great!" The Hindi translation for the phrase is सब बढ़िया होगा *(Sab badhiyaa hogaa)*.

- Subtle Nodding Along

This is a non-verbal communication which is really effective. It is a delicate way of assuring the speaker that you're listening intently.

Nodding the head also stands as a symbol of your warmth and empathy towards the other person. You should also maintain eye contact (but not too much!) to establish trust. Eye contact meaning in Hindi can vary, but in this case, it will be much appreciated. In such situations, you could always use Hindi phrases like, सही बात है *(Sahii baaT hai)* to say, "That's right," or expressions such as, "Hmm," *(हम्म hmm)*.

Quick Tip

This gesture is more powerful when it comes naturally to you. Indians are emotionally sensitive and thus their judgement depends quite a lot on non-verbal gestures. If you have a rather cold or stern body language, they might interpret it as disinterest in the conversation. It's good to keep warm facial expressions during Hindi conversation.

- Joining Palms Sideways When Prasad Is Given

Joining palms is a hand gesture that's displayed in particular situations only. With open palms facing upward, join them sideways. The palms should be gently curved so that anything offered doesn't fall out of your hands. Your head should be slightly tilted forward.

Quick Tip

This gesture is a common sight in temples and places of worship. People use this hand gesture when accepting sacred offerings (usually something sweet) after the worshipping is over. The sacred offering is known as प्रसाद *(praSaaD)*. It's not advised to perform the gesture during normal meals.

Negative Gestures

Negative gestures are used in extreme conditions, but they're better to stay away from in a public place.

- Showing the Slap Gesture

The slap gesture is given with a tilted but straight and open palm. In India, parents often use this gesture to warn their mischievous kids, and adults use the slap gesture to threaten each other during a serious verbal fight. It's more common to come up between two strangers as opposed to family members, as the gesture is too harsh to be practiced by adults within the family. It's better to avoid using it at all costs.

- Side-to-Side Head Shaking for a 'No'

Indians aren't offended by a 'no'. Still, they could do with a slightly softer tone. Body language that involves clear hand movements and side-to-side head nodding is considered quite harsh. If possible, don't be too direct in disagreeing with or rejecting an offer. Instead, go for gentler words that indicate your negation in a respectful way. Indians can quickly catch your 'no' even when that word hasn't even been uttered.

- Hands on Waist When Walking with Elders

Another posture that's better to stay clear of is the 'hands on waist' gesture. In plain words, it's only offensive during an argument with your elders. In other cases, it's quite a normal gesture. To be honest, a lot depends on the nature of the conversation. For instance, when talking to a friend or colleague about a neutral or pleasant topic, putting your hands on your waist indicates a sense of jolliness and frankness. It also shows that you're enjoying the talk.

Chapter 3

Conversation Dos and Don'ts

Greetings from India!

Namaste!

When first meeting someone, it is common to be introduced to them by a third party. Indian culture places a great deal of importance on personal relationships, and many business relationships will be built upon a personal foundation. Therefore, being introduced by a mutual acquaintance will stand you in good stead.

The British colonial influence has made handshakes the standard when greeting people in a business environment. Be aware, however, that in a lot of situations, it is not normal for men and women to shake hands with each other due to religious influence.

If meeting with a group of people, be sure to greet each person individually rather than addressing them as a group. Due to the influence of hierarchical Indian social structure, the oldest or most senior person present should be greeted first, followed by the next most senior, and so on.

First impressions are important wherever you go in India.

GREETING COLLEAGUES

A gracious greeting shows your new Indian acquaintances that you're committed to being respectful and courteous. The traditional Indian form of greeting is the *namaste,* which literally means, 'I bow to the divine in you'. The *namaste* is used for greeting, for taking leave, and also to seek forgiveness.

To greet someone with a *namaste,* bring your hands together with palms touching in front of your chest in a graceful fashion. Different languages may have different names for the *namaste,* but the gesture remains the same throughout India.

Greeting your Indian business colleagues with a *namaste* is considered a compliment. It sets the right tone for the rest of your meeting and shows that you've taken time to understand Indian exchanges. But offering a handshake isn't looked down upon. In fact, many Indian business people offer a handshake to show that they're familiar and comfortable with greeting foreigners.

MEET AND GREET POINTS

- Westerners may shake hands; however, greeting with '*namaste*' (placing both hands together with a slight bow) is appreciated and shows respect for Indian customs.
- When greeting elderly people, fold your hand, bow your head, and say '*Namaste*'.
- Please take note that physical contacts like a hug and a handshake are avoidable between men and women in India. Do not shake hands first; wait until the other person extends his hand first.
- Men shake hands with men when meeting or leaving. Men do not touch women when meeting or greeting. Western women may offer their hand to a Westernised Indian man, but not normally to others. Traditional Indian women may shake hands with foreign women but not usually with men.
- Now, in the professional world, all men and women are acceptable to a firm handshake and international business etiquette protocol.
- Business cards are exchanged, and Indians are very conscious of the protocol. Always present business cards when introduced. English is appropriate for business cards.

- It is considered rude to plunge into business discussions immediately. Ask about your counterpart's family, interests, hobbies, etcetera before beginning business discussions.
- Try to say goodbye to everyone when you leave.

Business cards are essential when conducting business in India and must be handled with respect. Make sure your card includes your name, company name, position and email address, all in English. Titles are important in India, and as such people should be addressed formally, that is, title (Mr, Dr, etcetera) and surname. Only use someone's given name if they have expressly given you permission to do so.

CORPORATE CULTURE

Depending on the type of Indian business you are dealing with, it is not common for middle management to have decision-making autonomy. Make sure the person you are negotiating with is senior enough to commit to business and partnership decisions. Do not begin business meetings by getting straight to the heart of the negotiation. Take a short time to ask personal questions about your contact's family and background, covering topics such as how long they have worked in the company or industry and where they grew up. Make a concerted effort to be on time for formal business meetings but be aware that they will not always start on time.

NOTE:

In some formal situations, at welcoming ceremonies for VIPs and important events, visitors are welcomed with garlands of marigolds or other flowers draped around their neck. If you are the guest of honour, you should wear the flowers for a while and then give them to somebody to hold. You should never casually drop them or leave them behind.

CONVERSATION DOS AND DON'TS

India has two official languages, Hindi and English, which are spoken very widely. However, there are also twenty-one other languages which are recognised by the Indian Constitution; overall, there are more than 1500 languages spoken across the country. Prominent languages include Telugu, Tamil, Bengali, Marathi, Urdu, Gujarati, Kannada, Malayalam, Odia, Punjabi and Assamese. If you are visiting India, it would be wise to look up which languages are widely spoken in the particular area that you will be spending time in, as learning a few words or greetings in those languages will stand you in good stead. Due to British colonial influence, English is spoken widely in the context of education, government and business. In north and central India, Hindi serves as the de facto lingua franca; however, in the south there has been some resistance to the promotion of Hindi as a national language, with southerners feeling that it will diminish the importance of their regional languages. As a result, in the south of India, English is the more commonly heard of the two official languages.

Five Key Conversation DOs
- Indian traditions, culture, architecture as well as that of other countries
- Families, friends and other interesting people
- Food is very important, and they enjoy discussing their traditional fare
- Cricket and other sports
- Religion and general politics (if you know what you are talking about)

Five Key Conversation DON'TS
- Personal matters or anything that might be considered overly intrusive
- Poverty or foreign aid in India
- Anything about India that you may have some unpleasant feelings towards
- Feet are considered unclean, so never point your feet at someone
- Pointing with your finger is considered impolite

UNCOMMON CONVERSATIONS
Here are a few strange ways Indians want to get conversations going with you and how to respond.

"Have you had your breakfast/lunch/dinner?" In the same way that Americans ask, "How are you?" without expecting a genuine response, Indians are not asking this question to find out the entire menu of your meal. It is just a polite way to start a conversation. You can respond with "yes" and ask them the same.

"Why are you looking dull today?" This is not a comment on your intellect or personality. Better to reinterpret this as "I appreciate you and am paying attention to your life. Today you don't look quite as cheerful as usual. Anything I can help with?"

"Why has your baby lost weight?" If you have a child in India, you will likely hear this at some point. You should translate this question as "I love your child very much and hope that he/she is healthy."

"You are getting a little fat." In India, comments about weight are sensitive. It is more of an observation than an insult.

Now you are ready to go out and have some great conversations!

Chapter 4

Gift Giving

India is a land of multiple cultures and rituals where people of different habits, castes, and religions live together in love and so much harmony. The numerous festivals celebrated across India work as a binding force that hold people together. They offer them a chance to create beautiful memories to cherish.

Gift giving has been an important part of Indian festivals since old times, and with the passing of time, it has evolved considerably.

In India, there is some etiquette related to gift giving. You must be aware of the traditions to ensure your gift is not going to be looked down upon. Before you give a gift to anyone, first take some time to understand the Indian gifting etiquette.

GIFT GIVING

Yellow, green and red are considered to be lucky colours and are often used to wrap gifts.

Different flowers have different connotations. Therefore, make sure to be aware of the connotations certain flowers have if you give them as gifts. Importantly, avoid giving frangipanis or white flowers. These are typically reserved for funerals and times of mourning.

Some gifts will be inappropriate depending on one's religious affiliation. For example, gifts made from leather may offend someone who identifies as Hindu. Gifts relating to alcohol or pigs, such as pork or pigskin, would be inappropriate to give to someone who identifies as Muslim.

If you are invited to an Indian household, the Indian gift giving custom is to bring the host a small gift of chocolates or flowers.

When giving money for some occasions, give an odd number value. For example, Rs 101 instead of just Rs100. This is understood to create good luck.

The Jain Community should not be given edible items as gifts which contain egg or gelatine.

Gifts such as electronic gadgets, computer games, crockery, flowers, and ready-made food items would be appreciated.

Chocolate, clothes, perfumes, toiletries, and *household items* such as *aluminium or steel containers* can also be welcome gifts.

Gifts are usually given to the head of the household and are presented on arrival at the host's house.

When giving gifts, present them with both hands.

WHAT TO AVOID WHILST GIVING GIFTS IN INDIA
Avoid giving expensive gifts, as the host may feel obliged to return the favour which may cause embarrassment.

So many Indians are vegetarian, so when you bring food products as gifts, make sure that it is free from non-vegetarian products and even eggs.

The gift of jewellery is seen as an intimate gift. Family members and women can exchange jewellery, but a gift of jewellery coming from a male can show a different intention.

Don't let any cheerful occasion pass away without involving gifts. Make a gift to your beloved parents, friends, or partners and see their smile grow!

Chapter 5

Dining Etiquette

Much like in different culinary cultures around the world, dining etiquette is very important in India. The convention of eating in India reflects the country's varied traditions and cultures. Though most parts of the country follow the same dining etiquette, you might find some dissimilarities in practices in the northern and southern regions. Here's a guide to basic Indian dining etiquette that you can follow when visiting an Indian friend or dining at an Indian restaurant.

BEFORE THE MEAL
'*Atithi Devo Bhava*', which means 'the guest is God', is something that Indians heartily believe in. So do not be surprised if you just casually visit an Indian friend and are then asked to stay for a meal because that's a gesture of respect and honour. However, if you've been invited for dinner, it's quite okay to arrive at your host's place fifteen to twenty minutes after the scheduled time. Arriving early or exactly on time might seem rude as your host will still be in mid-preparation. You will also notice that you won't be served your meal immediately after you arrive. There is a prior meal session, where you'll be offered a few drinks and some snacks accompanied by light chit-chat.

WHEN THE MEAL IS ANNOUNCED
After the meal is announced, you must wash and dry your hands. Washing your hands is the first step of dining as per Indian etiquette. In restaurants, hotels and urban homes, tables and chairs are arranged for dining; however, in rural areas, some families sit together in comfortable clothes on floor mats made for eating meals. In most Indian homes, generally, the homemaker arranges food for the family on the table and keeps an eye on who needs what, offering and bringing more food.

SEQUENCE OF FOOD

Unlike Western culture, there are no 'courses' when it comes to serving food in India. All the food is served in one go. However, you might get to see varying serving styles, depending on the country's regional cultures and different cuisines. Also, dishes will be served as opposed to individual portions, so the homemaker will either serve the food on your plate or you may help yourself.

STANDARD INDIAN FOOD

You would usually be served the standard Indian meal, which comprises of flatbreads (like naan, chapati, roti or paratha), daal, curries, raita, rice, pickles and some sweets. The food served might differ if you go to different regions of the country, like Punjab, Gujarat, Bengal, north-east India or south India.

USE OF CUTLERY

Indians don't usually use cutlery for eating food; they prefer eating with their fingers. There's also an inside joke that when eaten with fingers, food tastes much better. Eating with the fingers is done neatly and only the tips of the fingers are used. However, in urban areas and restaurants, spoons are used for eating liquid dishes like curries and daals. Indians do not encourage the use of a knife as cutlery because the food prepared here is generally bite-sized. Flatbreads, again, are eaten with hands only. A small piece is torn using the fingers and a boat-like shape is made; curries are then scooped and inserted in the mouth. Apart from bread and desserts, the rest of the food is served on one plate, either with little cups or without.

USE OF THE RIGHT HAND

When dining in India, always use your right hand. Even if you are left hand dominant, you must use your right hand for eating. Indians consider the use of the left hand to be unclean and offensive. Therefore, the left hand remains dry and is only used for drinking water or passing dishes. Do not place your left hand on the table, and do not pass food with your left hand. Banana-leaf food is eaten with your hands. These are vegetarian or meat curries, served with rice and sauce on a large banana leaf. Reach into the rice, take some with your fingers, gently roll it between your index and middle fingers and thumb (not in your palms!) into a kind of self-sticking ball, dip it into the sauce on the banana leaf, mix it with a vegetable or a piece of chicken, then pop the whole thing in your mouth. Most of these hands-on banana-leaf restaurants are Muslim or vegan (Hindu).

SHARING FOOD

Indian culture highly encourages sharing food with others. If you are dining at an Indian restaurant with a friend and both of you order different dishes, then it is customary to share your dish with the other. But keep in mind to share only from the serving dish or bowl and not from your plate. Similarly, taking food from someone else's plate is also considered bad manners. Also, do not dip your used spoon and fork into the other person's food or the main serving dish as it is considered highly unhygienic.

FINISHING FOOD

You must not leave anything on your plate as leftovers. Leaving food on your plate is not appreciated in Indian culture. It isn't necessary to taste each and every dish that is served, but whatever you place on your plate must be finished. Also, do not play with food or distort it in any way. You must keep in mind to eat your food at a medium pace. It might seem rude if you eat your food too quickly, and if you eat it too slowly, it may imply that you don't like the food.

PAYING COMPLIMENTS

After you've finished your meal, you must positively compliment your host for the food. Since food is prepared with great effort and care, expressing your admiration will make the host happy.

LEAVING THE TABLE

If you've finished your food early, then you must remain seated until the host or the eldest person at the table finishes their food. Getting up from the table when everybody else is still eating is considered ill-mannered.

DINING ETIQUETTE FOR SEATING

The host sits at the head of the table, with the honoured guest seated next to the host. (Spouses are usually not invited to business meals in restaurants. Do not ask if your spouse can join you: it will embarrass your Indian colleague into doing something that is uncomfortable for him; however, your spouse might be invited to a meal at your colleague's home, especially if the spouse of the host will be there, which will probably be the case). In addition, the honoured guest sits on the side of the table farthest from the door (in business meetings, the key people sit in the middle, flanked on either side in descending order by their aides, with the least important people sitting at the ends of the table farthest from the middle, and closest to the door; the arrangement is mirrored on the other side). Men and women eating at someone's home may dine in separate areas (and spend the entire evening separated) or at separate times, with the men dining first.

Dining Etiquette for Discussing Business

Business meals are generally not good times to discuss business or make business decisions; however, take your cue from your Indian associates: if they bring up business, then it's okay to discuss it, but wait to take your lead from their conversation.

Dining Etiquette for Tipping

Tipping is universally required. Tips in restaurants are usually expected to be about ten percent of the total bill.

Chapter 6

Business Etiquette

Building good business relationships and trust are important in India, so you should expect to spend plenty of time at meetings, dinners and social clubs with potential business partners. In a first meeting, let the Indian host guide the initial stages of the conversation. As in some other Asian cultures, Indians like to develop a personal connection first. Therefore, expect to be asked, and prepare to ask your own questions, about family.

GREETINGS AND TITLE
A handshake is the standard way to greet men and women in a business setting, whatever their age or seniority. When meeting with small independent retailers in non-urban areas, you may be greeted by your potential partner with the word *namaste* (pronounced nah-mas-tay). You may reciprocate by repeating the word, with the palms of your hands together and a slight bow or nod of the head. Often people will slightly nod or bow their heads when shaking hands, particularly with senior figures. The left hand is considered unclean and as such, should never be used alone to offer or accept a handshake, drink, food, money, gifts or business cards.

BUSINESS CARDS
These are essential when conducting business in India and must be handled with respect. Make sure your card includes your name, company name, position and email address, all in English. If you have a higher degree such as a masters or a PhD, you may wish to disclose it on your business card, as it will earn you greater respect in India.

When presenting your card, do so with both hands holding the card at the top in between your thumb and index finger with the writing facing the recipient. After receiving a business card, spend a few moments examining it, providing positive feedback with a smile, before placing it either in your chest pocket or in front of you on the table.

BODY LANGUAGE

Indians tend to value their personal space and are generally not prone to making much physical contact. However, it is common for Indian men to engage in friendly back patting. This is a sign of friendship and a positive signal for your working relationship. Indians are generally expressive and use body language to convey messages that are not always verbal.

Showing the soles of your feet or your shoes, or pointing your feet towards anyone, is considered highly disrespectful and insulting in India, as is stepping on or over papers, books, religious offerings on the ground, and especially people.

It is rude to touch anyone's head. Pointing with fingers is also disrespectful; if you must point, use your thumb, with the rest of your fingers curled into a fist, palm facing upward.

CORPORATE CULTURE

Depending on the type of Indian business you are dealing with, it is not common for middle management to have decision-making autonomy. Make sure the person you are negotiating with is senior enough to commit to business and partnership decisions. Do not begin business meetings by getting straight to the heart of the negotiation. Take a short time to ask personal questions about your contact's family and background, covering topics such as how long they have worked in the company or industry and where they grew up. Make a concerted effort to be on time for formal business meetings but be aware that they will not always start on time. Indians are less constrained by time than Australians.

DRESS CODE

Conservative, professional attire is expected in the business setting, although this can differ depending on the season and the city. Men should generally wear a suit (with a tie) and women should wear a business dress or a suit with a blouse (not low-cut and, in the case of skirts, not too short). In summer, however, it is more acceptable for men to not wear a jacket. Women should avoid wearing short outfits or exposing their shoulders.

BUSINESS LANGUAGE AND COMMUNICATION IN INDIA

English is widely spoken in business and is one of India's official languages. Many Indians and business managers speak it fluently, though of course meaning can vary across cultures and countries. Indians may have a particular difficulty saying 'no', as it can convey an offensive message. Instead, they will prefer making statements such as 'we'll see', 'yes, but it may be difficult', or 'I will try' when they likely mean 'no'. Listen carefully and be aware of the meaning behind these answers. Do not attempt to compel your contact to be more direct, as this can be counterproductive.

A good way to seek a more positive answer is to rephrase the question; for instance, if you are trying to secure a meeting and there is some evasion, one approach is to ask what day and time would be convenient to meet. Similarly, if there is resistance in providing a purchase order, the question could be asked when it is likely that a purchase order will be raised. This type of questioning may provide a more meaningful response.

INDIAN BUSINESS MEETINGS AND NEGOTIATIONS

Give as much warning as possible of your intended dates of travel and try to schedule your meetings well in advance. If you require help with your India trip, our business advisors based in your hometown or India can help source qualified leads, set up introductions, and arrange business meetings as well as plan productive business trips to India. Do bear in mind that the arrangements may change several times and may not be confirmed until the day of the meeting itself. Although punctuality is expected, be prepared for meetings to start and finish late and for interruptions to occur on a regular basis. Be patient and demonstrate good character; forcefulness will likely drive your contact away.

UNDERSTANDING BUSINESS RELATIONSHIPS IN INDIA

Business relationships are of the utmost importance. Indians will base their decisions on trust and intuition as much as on statistics and data, so be mindful of the importance of a good working relationship. Take the time to engage in small talk and get to know your prospective partner. Rushing straight into the business issue could be perceived as rudeness.

THE ROLE OF HIERARCHY IN INDIAN BUSINESS

Indian businesses are often very hierarchically structured. In negotiations, decisions are generally made at the highest of levels. Therefore, unless the company director, owner or a very senior manager is present at a meeting, a decision is not likely to occur at that stage. Roles are well defined and tasks such as manual labour will only be carried out by a specific person. An Indian manager is typically not expected to carry out tasks that could otherwise be undertaken by someone at a lower level in the organisation.

A QUICK GUIDE TO INDIAN BUSINESS CULTURE

- There are many India's within India. India is a multilingual, multi-ethnic and pluralistic society, and vast cultural differences can be seen between north and south India.
- Be aware of the cultural diversity and be cautious about generalisations. The great Cambridge economist Joan Robinson once observed: 'Whatever you can rightly say about India, the opposite is also true'.
- English is the official language of business.
- Be prepared for meetings to start and finish late and for interruptions to occur on a regular basis.
- There is a more formal and hierarchical relationship between managers and staff in India.
- Indians place great value on relationships: take the time to develop contacts and relationships.

Chapter 7

Wedding Etiquette

With over five hundred languages and six thousand dialects, the diverse cultures and religions of India shape today's wedding ceremonies, and so Indian weddings vary based on their region of origin. Many different rituals that are part of an Indian wedding ceremony also can take place over several days. As one of the world's most religiously and ethnically diverse lands, India boasts unique, culturally rich wedding ceremonies that run from the elegant and sophisticated to the beautifully intricate. Part of the complexity stems from the concept that when an Indian couple marries, entire families and communities are involved. Indian weddings have traditionally been considered a marriage of two families, rather than just a marriage of the bride and groom. The wedding can be anywhere from three days to one week-long and typically includes several events. The engagement is the first of many steps in what tends to be a lengthy process and serves as the agreement between the families of the future bride and groom. At this stage, the wedding date is also set. The wedding rituals themselves begin fifteen days before the wedding, with *Barni Band-hwana*, where a piece of thread, called *Mauli*, is tied to the hands of both the groom and his parents to humbly request a safe wedding day from the gods.

SANGEET AND MEHENDI

"Sangeet is a chance for relatives and friends of both the bride and the groom to get together," Sunita continues. "They play instruments, dance, sing and interact with each other. Sometimes, they even poke fun at the bride and groom." The party is hosted by the bride and bridegroom family and is also a time for introducing members of the families to each other.

At the Sangeet, an Indian bride takes part in a *Mehendi* ceremony, during which she and her female family members and friends gather for *henna*. The artists create intricate designs on the hands or feet of the bride and her friends and family using a paste of dried ground henna leaves. The henna is believed to ward off evil, promote fertility, and attract good energy for the soon-to-be wedded couple. The names of both the bride and the groom are 'hidden' in the bride's artwork and the groom is meant to find the names. There is also a saying that the deeper the colour of the henna, the stronger the bond between husband and wife and the better the bride will get along with her mother-in-law. So, brides often let the henna dry for up to eight hours!

Henna

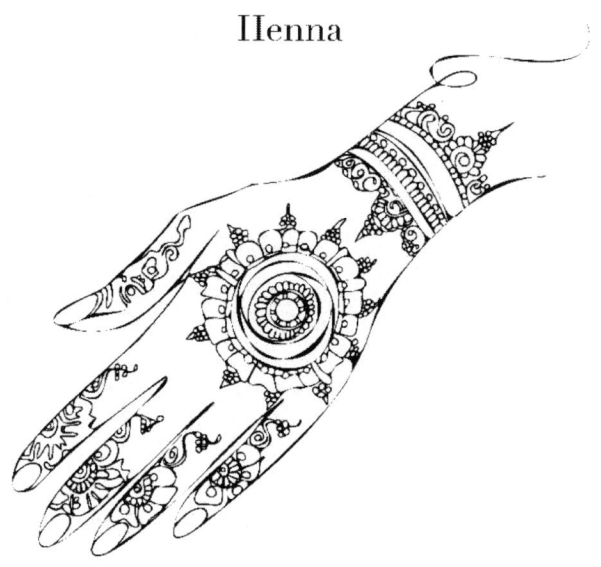

THE WEDDING PROCESSION

In most Indian wedding celebrations, the day begins with the groom's procession, as his entire family and friends all lead him to the wedding altar. This is called the Baraat! This 'ceremony within a ceremony' is where the groom, riding on a white horse or arriving in a vintage car, makes his grand entrance. He is ushered in by a long line of his family and friends, who are all singing, dancing, and shouting out traditional Indian well wishes. It is a rousing spectacle! The bride and her family greet the groom and the couple exchange *Milni Malas*, floral garlands, to wear around their necks. These symbolise their acceptance of one another. In the Baraat, the groom is dressed in a long jacket called a *Sherwani* or *Jodhpuri* and fitted trousers called Churidars. He wears a *Safa*, a turban, on his head, with a big fancy brooch called *Kalgi* pinned onto it. The bride's parents and family, including uncles and aunts, all welcome the groom and his entire family. Then they escort the groom and his immediate family to their place of honour at the altar.

The Ceremony under the Mandap

Hindu weddings take place outside under a canopy known as a *Mandap*, but if the *Mandap* cannot be placed outdoors, it is built inside. Each of the four pillars of the bridal canopy represents one of the four parents. Both sets of parents and any siblings stand up at the *Mandap* during the ceremony. Since the father is already at the altar, it is often the bride's maternal uncle who escorts her down the aisle. The bride's brother also plays a role in the ceremony. He places rice in the hands of the bride and groom, and they, in turn, throw it into the ceremonial fire pit. The officiant, bride, groom, and bride's parents sit beneath the Mandap, which is beautifully decorated towers or pipes enhanced with curtains, fabric, and flowers. Front and centre under the *Mandap* is the sacred fire. The fire can be small and confined to a brazier or dish for safety. 'Agni', the god of fire, is said to sustain life and thus gives life to the marriage. The ceremony starts off with the bride's parents giving away the bride in a ritual called *Kanya Daan*. The bride and groom then join hands and circle around the enclosed fire in a ritual called the *Mangalphera*, the walk around the fire. The bride and groom walk around the fire four times, with each turn representing a major goal in life: *Dharma*, morality; *Artha*, prosperity; *Kama*, personal gratification; and *Moksha*, spirituality.

As they perform the *Mangalphera*, the Pandit, who chants verses during the ceremony, ties them together. Once they finish their walk around the fire, the couple rush to their seats, since it is said that whoever sits down first will be the dominant one in the marriage. In another ritual, the priest takes the scarves the bride and groom are wearing and ties them together before walking them around the fire. They all are given a mix of flowers, rice, and herbs to offer to the holy fire, which is in the centre of the *mandap*, to complete the prayers. This practice is called *Havan*. Seven steps are taken as they vow to support each other and live happily together; this is the *Saptapadi*. Each step represents a marital vow, a promise to be committed to each other and to take care of each other. The priest offers blessings for an abundance of food, prosperity, eternal happiness, children, harmony, and friendship. The groom will apply a red powder to the centre of the bride's forehead and tie a necklace made of gold and black beads, and sometimes diamonds as well, around her neck, symbolising that she's now a married woman. This is called the *Mangalsutra*, the groom's gift to the bride. For happiness and prosperity, friends and families also throw flowers after the couple is married.

WEDDING FASHIONS

Bride and groom attire is different to that of Western cultures where black tuxedos and white dresses are the norm. Indian brides and grooms instead wear bright, vibrant colours and are usually decked out in gold jewellery. Jewellery will also adorn a bride's head and face. Not just one dress will do for an Indian bride; at least three or four dresses are worn for all the different rituals involved. On their wedding day, many Indian brides wear a traditional red sari, since red represents happiness and good luck. The traditional red sari is a six-foot fabric draped in a specific way and adorned with crystals and real twenty-four-karat gold thread. White is avoided since it's a colour reserved for mourning. Then the bride will change into a different sari for the reception. Indian brides typically mix red or pink with gold. Their wedding garment is called a *Lehenga*, which is a long skirt with a matching top and scarf. After the ceremony, they also change into a different *Lehenga*. The groom wears a *Kafni*, a long shirt extending to the knees, with *Pijamo*, leggings. The groom might also wear a turban. Traditionally, Indian weddings do not include bridesmaids, groomsmen, flower girls, or ring bearers, but now some couples are adding American-English traditions and including a wedding party, maid of honour, and best man. The bridesmaids typically wear Indian saris of the same colour or pattern.

THE RECEPTION FEAST

An Indian wedding menu is often served buffet style since many items involve a gravy sauce or 'Makhani' and would be difficult to serve pre-plated. A typical menu might feature seven to ten appetisers followed by four or five main entrées, plus rice, yogurt, salad, and naan (a type of bread). At the end of the meal, a wide variety of Indian cookies and sweets are served, such as silver-wrapped cashews, *kaju*, which is a fig-filled cookie, halva, and others made from heavy cream, cheese, and nuts.

Parents and friends also make special toasts, like at most other weddings. 'Similar to American receptions, there also is the DJ, photographer, cinematographer, flowers, food, cake, favours, and guests, but all on a much grander scale. Anywhere from 300 to 500 people are usually invited to a typical Indian reception. To them, it's a celebration with family and friends and the people within their society. The food never ends! Once the buffet is opened, it's replenished all night, as are the desserts. The grander scale also is apparent in the way the bride and groom are showcased at the reception. In American and English weddings, we often see a bride and groom sitting at a sweetheart table, sometimes with their respective bridal party sitting to the right and left of them. Indian couples are typically seated on a raised stage, which is beautifully decorated. Elaborate structures, backdrops, drapes, fabric, flowers, and candles are all involved in bringing attention to the special couple. It's a photo op, if you will, for all the important pictures that will last a lifetime! Another special ritual occurs during the reception. At some point when the couple is dancing, family and friends throw money at the bridal couple to wish them prosperity. The *Bou Bhat* takes place on the afternoon following the wedding day. The groom's family and friends are invited for lunch, and the close relatives of the bride are also invited. At this event, the bride is formally invited into the family, the groom pledges responsibility for her food and clothing, and as a sign of fulfilling that pledge, he gives her a new sari and serves her food.

BLESSINGS: THE AASHIRWAD

Sometime after the wedding, the families hold the *Aashirwad* ceremony, where they exchange gifts. The bride's parents, close relatives, and family friends go to the groom's house and give him their blessings, maybe along with a token gift. In a like manner, the groom's family goes to the bride's house and offers their blessings. Usually, the bride is given gold or diamonds on this occasion by his parents. But *Aashirwad* is really about the blessings. Aunts and uncles from both sides come to give their blessings to the new couple. In a culture that highly values the input of the elder family members, this is perhaps the most appropriate way to begin married life. Ultimately, with all their multi-day splendour and magnificence, Indian weddings are deceptively simple. Inter-twining rituals and traditions, they provide lessons full of unpretentious wisdom for a newly married couple. That, in essence, is the unique spirit of an Indian wedding.

Iran
By Farno Rezaei

Chapter 1

Culture Symbols

If you're looking for a country full of surprises, then Iran is the place to go. Travelling in Iran can be an eye-opening and rewarding experience, especially for curious travellers who want to understand the country and learn about its people and their culture beyond political issues and news headlines. As soon as you're here, you'll find that the reality is far removed from the stereotypes: it's a country desperate to be seen for what it is, rather than what it is often depicted as in the media.

Iranians are undoubtedly the friendliest people in the world; I have lost count of the number of times I have been invited to a stranger's home or was treated to an endless flow of tea from a shop vendor. The people of Iran truly move me with their genuine generosity and kindness.

If you're open to seeing Iran beyond the headlines, here are some of my tips on local culture that can help you better understand the country and its people.

Ancient Persian symbols are known to be both mystic and majestic, seen dominantly in ancient lithographic scriptures. These have carried their legacy into the modern times as well, gaining popularity over the years.

Ancient Persia was located in the Middle East, covering large swaths of land that have since fragmented into several countries. When we say Persia today, we refer to Iran, which was the heart of the Persian empire.

Here, we'll be taking a look at some of the most popular Persian symbols. These symbols came to be regarded as significant pillars of the history of ancient Persia and some of them are still used in Iran and around the world.

THE FARAVAHAR
Also called the 'falcon', it is the best-known ancient symbol of Persia, comprising of a winged sun disk with a seated male figure at its centre. Although the ancient Persians created this symbol, what it actually meant

to them is still unknown to this day. According to Zarathustra, the seated male figure in the Faravahar is that of an old man, who is said to represent *wisdom of age* and three main feathers on each of the wings represent three symbols of *good deeds, good words* and *good thoughts*. The Faravahar is the most powerful spiritual symbol of Iran: a secular cultural and national symbol.

SOURCE
Anahita is the ancient Indo-Iranian Persian goddess of all the waters upon the Earth.

Her name means *'the immaculate one'*. Associated with waters, rivers and lakes of birth, she is a war goddess and the patroness of women.

THE SUN AND THE LION
The Sun and the Lion is an ancient Persian symbol; it was formerly an important element of the national flag until the Iranian Revolution in 1979. The sun symbolises the ruler of heaven, while the lion symbolises the lineage of kings as well as royalty and divinity.

HUMA: THE BIRD OF PARADISE
Huma is a legendary mythical bird from the Iranian legends. Huma never rests on the ground but circles high above the Earth its entire life. It is

completely invisible and impossible to spot by human eyes. Today, the Farsi/Persian acronym for the 'Iran National Airline' is HOMA and the emblem of the national airline depicts a stylised version of the Huma bird.

Botehh Jeghe

The boteh jeghe is a tear-drop shaped design with a curved upper end. Boteh is a Persian word meaning bush or plant. This pattern is extremely popular and is used around the world as a textile pattern for clothing, artwork and carpets. The boteh jeghe is believed to be a stylised representation of a cypress tree and a floral spray, which are symbols of life and eternity in the Zoroastrian faith.

Achaemenid Bracelet

The Shirdal

The Shirdal (*the 'Lion-Eagle'*) is legendary. The Shirdal was thought to be an especially majestic and powerful creature, since the lion was considered the king of the beasts and the eagle the king of birds. Symbolic of leadership, power, courage and wisdom, the Shirdal has appeared in ancient art of Persia since the 2nd millennium BC. It was also a common motif in the North and North-West region of Iran during the Iron Age and appeared in the art of the Achaemenid Persian Empire, symbolising Iranian wisdom. The Shirdal is traditionally known for guarding gold and treasure and later on in the medieval era, it became a symbol of monogamous marriage which discouraged infidelity. Shirdal were strictly loyal to their partner and if one of them died, the other Shirdal would never mate again. Shirdal are said to protect from witchcraft, slander and evil.

SIMURG

The Simurg is a mythical flying creature in Persian mythology. This bird is considered to be immortal and is usually depicted with the head and foreparts of a dog, the claws of a lion and the wings and tail of a peacock. It's sometimes portrayed with a human face. In Iranian art, the Simurg is depicted as a gigantic bird that's large enough to carry a whale or an elephant. It's an inherently benevolent creature and is believed to be female.

The Simurg was considered to be a guardian figure with healing powers and the ability to purify the waters and land and bestowing fertility. It appears in many ancient tales of creation and according to Persian legends, it was an extremely old creature that had witnessed the destruction of the world three times.

MOUNT DAMAVAND

Mount Damavand is the highest mountain peak in Iran and the highest volcano in all of Asia. Damavand is significant in the mythology and folklore of Persia and is said to hold magical powers due to its many hot water springs which are believed to treat wounds and chronic skin ailments. Today, this mountain is known as the mother of Persian myths.

Chapter 2

Meeting, Greeting, Posture and Body Language

In Iran, the person with the lower status issues the first greeting. In the reverse logic of ta'arof, this means that a person who wants to be polite will make a point of this, using the universal Islamic *salaam* or the extended *salaam aleikum*. The universal phrase for leave-taking is *khoda hafez* — "God protect".

Iranians can be quite physically intimate with same-sex friends, even in public. Physical contact is expected and is not erotic. In restaurants and on buses and other public places, people are seated much closer than in the West. Both sexes can be excessively tender and doting toward their same-sex friends with no intention of eroticism. Kissing and hand-holding between members of the same sex is common. On the other hand, even the slightest physical contact with non-family members of the opposite sex, unless they are very young children, is taboo.

A downward gaze in Iran is a sign of respect. Foreigners addressing Iranians often think them disinterested or rude when they answer a question without looking at the questioner. This is a cross-cultural mistake. For men, downcast eyes are a defence measure, since staring at a woman is usually taken as a sign of interest and can cause difficulties. On the other hand, staring directly into the eyes of a friend is a sign of affection and intimacy.

In social situations, it is good form to offer a portion of what one is about to eat to anyone nearby, even if they show no interest. One sees this behaviour even in very small children. It is polite to refuse such an offer, but the one making the offer will be sensitive to the slightest hint of interest and will continue to press the offer if it is indicated.

Western men offering to shake a traditional Iranian woman's hand may see her struggling between a desire to be polite, and a desire not to breech standards of decency. The solution for many a woman is to cover her hand with part of her chador and shake hands that way. Under no circumstances should a proper man or woman willingly find themselves alone in a closed room with a member of the opposite sex (except for his or her spouse).

One must be very careful about praising any possession of another. The owner will likely offer it immediately as a present. Greater danger still lies in praising a child. Such praise bespeaks envy, which is the essence of the "evil eye". The parent will be alarmed, fearing for the child's life. The correct formula for praising anything is *ma sha'Allah*, literally, "What God wills".

Iranians use separate slippers for the toilette. These slippers are only for the washroom. Don't forget to remove your toilet slippers after usage inside the restroom.

TA'AROF

The social lubricant of Iranian life is a system known as *ta'arof*, literally "meeting together". This is a ritualised system of linguistic and behavioural interactional strategies allowing individuals to interrelate in a harmonious fashion. The system marks the differences between *andaruni* and *biruni* situations, and also marks differences in relative social status. In general, higher status persons are older and have important jobs, or command respect because of their learning, artistic accomplishments or erudition.

Linguistically, ta'arof involves a series of lexical substitutions for pronouns and verbs whereby persons of lower status address persons of higher status with elevated forms. By contrast, they refer to themselves with humble forms. Both partners in an interaction may simultaneously use other-raising and self-lowering forms towards each other. Ritual greetings and leave-takings such as *ghorban-e shoma* (literally, "your sacrifice") underscore this sensibility.

Taarof is a system of politeness that includes both verbal and non-verbal communication.

Iranians protest compliments and attempt to appear vulnerable in public.

They will belittle their own accomplishments in an attempt to appear humble, although other Iranians understand that this is merely courtesy and do not take the words at face value.

In adherence to ta'arof, if you are ever offered something, like a tea or sweet, even if you want it, at first decline it until their insistence becomes greater.

Dress Code

Iran observes the Islamic dress code, which calls for women to cover their hair, neck and arms. This doesn't mean you need to cover up your entire body with a chador (a black cloth that covers the whole body), you simply need to cover your head and hair with a hijab or loose scarf.

For men, shorts and flip-flops are not allowed. Stick to t-shirts and long pairs of pants or trousers, as well as covered shoes. You'll need to pay special attention at the airport and at land border crossings — be sure to put on a long-sleeved shirt, pants/trousers and proper shoes.

Iranian Bathrooms and Toilets

There are two types of toilets in Iran: Iranian-style and Western-style.

Iranians use water instead of toilet paper. So, usually in public washrooms, there is no toilet paper. Therefore, always carry a small package of tissue with you.

Spitting

Spitting is considered to be rude and an offense. Never spit on the ground, especially at historic and religious places.

Secular Celebrations

Most holidays in Iran are religious in nature. The few secular holidays relate to pre-Islamic practices, or modern political events.

The Iranian New Year's Celebration (*Now Ruz*) is the nation's principal secular holiday. The Now Ruz celebration is replete with pre-Islamic symbolism, beginning with the practice of jumping over bonfires on the Wednesday before the equinox. An array of symbols emphasising agricultural renewal are displayed throughout the long period of celebration, which lasts for thirteen days.

Accompanying the festivities is the celebratory presence of a black-faced clown, *Hajji Firouz*. In some parts of the country, a "king" of the New Year is selected and catered to during the holiday. On the thirteenth day he is ritually sacrificed.

In some parts of Iran, the winter solstice is celebrated in a special manner. Watermelons are saved from the summer and hung in a protected place. On the longest night of the year, family and friends stay up all night, tell stories and eat the watermelons.

The nation also celebrates Islamic Republic Day on 1st April to mark the 1979 Revolution.

PUBLIC VS PRIVATE

Iranians see themselves as having two distinct identities: "zaher" (public) and "batin" (private).

When they are in public, they must conform to accepted modes of behaviour. It is only within their homes and among their inner circle that they feel free to be themselves. Family members are always part of the inner circle.

The inner circle forms the basis of a person's social and business network. Friendship is very important and extends into business. The people from the inner circle can be relied upon to offer advice, help find a job or cut through bureaucracy.

POSTURE AND BODY LANGUAGE

Feet: Displaying the soles of one's feet to another person is improper. Similarly, placing one's feet on top of the table is not acceptable.

Expressions: People tend to smile less whilst in public in Iran. To smile casually while passing a stranger of the opposite gender on the street could easily be interpreted as provocative and escalate to questions quickly. Therefore, try not to be intimidated by an Iranian's apparent 'serious' demeanour. It is not necessarily a reflection on you, but the social expectation.

Therefore, if an Iranian avoids eye contact during interaction, consider that it is usually done as a defence mechanism to remain respectful and modest and does not necessarily mean they are disinterested.

Chapter 3

Conversation Dos and Don'ts

Dos

• Acknowledge the achievements of Iran and the country's cultural heritage. If you show an understanding of Iran's culture and history, your interlocutors will likely be impressed.

• Take care not to give the impression that you assume the West to be superior. Iranians are likely to respond negatively if they feel that you have an elitist understanding of the Middle East.

• Respect an Iranian's intelligence if they show evidence of a higher education. It is likely that an Iranian in Australia is very educated and technically trained. Many hold one or multiple university degrees.

• Make sure your actions and your words correspond. Iranians may notice if you are hypocritical or contradict yourself.

• Remain humble about your success and achievements. In Iran, people generally tone down their own success and self-deprecate out of politeness.

• Respect an Iranian's privacy. Avoid asking questions that could compromise their discretion—you can expect an urban and educated Iranian to know quite a lot about your cultural background. They are generally very well informed about the world.

Don'ts

• Do not confuse Persians with Arabs. This is a quick way to annoy Iranians and indicates that you are poorly informed about the Middle East.

• Avoid assuming that all Iranians are Muslims because they come from an Islamic Middle Eastern country—many are not.

• Do not criticise an Iranian for the actions of their government. Doing so is insensitive considering that many Iranians have faced persecution by the authoritarian regime.

• Similarly, do not blame the Iranian government's restrictions and exclusions on Islam. The situation is more complex than most understand. Iranians recognise the current Islamic political culture to be different from their own interpretations of the religion.

- Avoid mentioning divisive topics between the West and Iran (such as women's rights, civil liberties and Iran's nuclear power programme). If you must do so, make sure it is in a sensitive way that doesn't disparage your Iranian counterpart.
- Avoid talking down to an Iranian for having poor English skills or assuming that they can't understand deep concepts. It is a good idea to talk slower if English is their second language, but they may find it patronising if they notice you over-simplifying conversation for them.
- Avoid telling dirty jokes or jokes that are at the expense of someone else. This is considered to be unintelligent humour.

Chapter 4

Gift Giving

Iranians give gifts at various social occasions such as returning from a trip or if someone achieves a major success in their personal or business life.

On birthdays, businesspeople bring sweets and cakes to the office and do not expect to receive gifts themselves.

It is common to give monetary gifts to servants or others who have provided services during the year on No Ruz (The Iranian New Year). Money should be new bank notes or gold coins.

Guests bring honour to a household and are eagerly sought. When invited as a guest, a small present is appreciated, but often received with a show of embarrassment. It will usually not be unwrapped in front of the giver.

If you are invited to an Iranian's house, bring flowers or pastries to the hosts. When giving a gift, always apologise for its inadequacy.

Gifts should be elegantly wrapped—most shops will wrap them for you.

Gifts are not generally opened when received. In fact, they may be put on a table and not mentioned.

TAKING AND GIVING OBJECTS
When taking or delivering an object, use both hands as this is respectful.

Chapter 5

Dining Etiquette

FOOD IN DAILY LIFE

As one might expect from Iran's geographic situation, its food strikes a medium between Greek and Indian preparations. It is more varied than Greek food, and less spicy and subtler than Indian food, with a greater use of fresh ingredients.

Iranians have a healthy diet centred on fresh fruits, greens and vegetables. Meat (usually lamb, goat or chicken) is used as a condiment rather than as the centrepiece of a meal. Rice and fresh unleavened or semi-leavened whole-grain bread are staple starches. The primary beverage is black tea. The principal dietary taboo is the Islamic prohibition of pork.

Breakfast

Breakfast is a light meal consisting of fresh unleavened bread, tea and perhaps butter, white (feta-style) cheese and jam. Eggs may also be eaten— fried or boiled. Meat is not common at breakfast.

Main Meal

The main meal of the day is eaten at around one o'clock in the afternoon. In a middle-class household, it usually starts with a plate of fresh greens— scallions, radishes, fresh basil, mint, coriander and others in season. This is served with unleavened bread and white cheese. The main dish is steamed aromatic rice (*chelow*) served with one or more stews made of meat and a fresh vegetable or fruit. This stew, called *khoresht,* resembles a mild curry. It centres on a central ingredient such as eggplant, okra, spinach, quince, celery or a myriad of other possibilities. One particularly renowned *khoresht, fesenjun*, consists of lamb, chicken, duck or pheasant cooked in a sauce of onions, ground walnuts and pomegranate molasses. In addition to its preparation as chelow, rice may also be prepared as a pilaf (*polow*) by mixing in fresh herbs, vegetables, fruit or meat after it is boiled, but before it is steamed.

The Iranian national dish, called *chelow kabab*, consists of filet of lamb marinated in lemon juice or yogurt, onions and saffron, pounded with a knife on a flat skewer until fork tender and grilled over a hot fire. This is served with grilled onions and tomatoes on a bed of *chelow* to which has been added a lump of butter and a raw egg yolk. The butter and egg are mixed with the hot rice (which cooks the egg), and ground sumac berries are sprinkled on top. A common drink with a meal is *dough*, a yogurt and salted water preparation that is similar to Turkish ayran, Lebanese lebni and Indian lassi.

Sweets are more likely to be consumed with tea in the afternoon than as dessert. Every region of the country has special confections prized as travel souvenirs and served casually to guests. Amongst the most famous are *gaz*, a natural nougat made with rose water, and *sohan*, a saffron, butter, and pistachio praline. After a meal, Iranians prefer fresh fruit and tea. In fact, fruit is served before the meal and after the meal—indeed, at any time.

Evening Meal
The evening meal is likely to be a light meal consisting of leftover food from the main afternoon meal, or a little bread, cheese, fruit and tea. Urban dwellers may eat a light meal at a café or restaurant in the evening.

Outside large cities, restaurants are not very common in Iran. On the other hand, teahouses are ubiquitous and widely frequented at all times of day. One can always get some kind of meal there.

Alcoholic beverages are officially forbidden in Iran today under the Islamic republic, but their consumption is still widely practiced. Armenian, Jewish and Zoroastrian communities still produce wine, and local moonshine is found everywhere in rural areas. The principal alcoholic beverage is "vodka" distilled from grain, grapes or, more commonly, raisins. It is consumed almost exclusively by men in the evening or at celebrations such as weddings.

Food Customs at Ceremonial Occasions
Ritual foods fall into two categories—foods that are eaten in celebration, and foods that are prepared and consumed as a charitable religious act.

A few foods are traditional for the New Year's celebration. Fish is widely consumed as the first meal of the New Year, along with a *polow* made with greens. One food appears on the ritual New Year's table but is rarely eaten: this is a kind of sweet pudding made of ground sprouted wheat called *samanou*.

During the Islamic month of fasting, Ramadan, no food or drink is consumed from sunrise to sunset. Families rise before dawn to prepare heavy breakfasts that look like the noon meal. The process is repeated at sundown. Special crispy fried sweets made from a yogurt batter and soaked in syrup are frequently served. Two forms are popular: *zulbia*, which looks a bit like a multi stranded pretzel, and *bamieh*, which looks a bit like the okra pods it is named after.

Food is frequently prepared for distribution to the community as a charitable religious act. When a sheep is slaughtered for a special occasion, it is common to give meat to all of one's neighbours. To give thanks for fulfilment of a desire, a community meal is frequently prepared. Likewise, during the mourning ceremonies for Hossein during the months of Muharram and Safar, communal meals are paid for by charitable individuals. The most common food served on these occasions is a *polow* made with yellow peas and meat.

A folk belief prevalent in Iran revolves around dietary practice. This philosophy tries to maintain balance between the four humors of the body—blood, phlegm, yellow bile, and black bile—through judicious combinations of foods. Although more sophisticated Iranians use the full range of four humors in their dietary calculations, most adhere to a two-category system: hot and cold. For example, visitors quickly learn that their friends will not allow the simultaneous consumption of watermelon and yogurt (both cold foods), for fear that this combination will cause immediate death.

IF YOU ARE INVITED TO AN IRANIAN'S HOUSE
- Check to see if the host is wearing shoes. If not, remove yours at the door.
    - Dress conservatively.
    - Try to arrive at the invited time. Punctuality is appreciated.

- Show respect for the elders by greeting them first.
- Check to see if your spouse is included in the invitation as conservative Iranians do not entertain mixed-sex groups.
- Expect to be shown into the guests' room. It is usually lavishly furnished with European furniture.
- Shake everyone's hand individually.
- Accept any offer of food or drink. Remember to do 'ta'arof'.
- Table manners: Iranians are rather formal. Although some meals in the home are served on the floor and without eating utensils, it does not indicate a lack of decorum. In more modern homes, meals are served on a dining table with place settings.
- Wait to be told where to sit. An honoured guest is always placed at the head of a room or a table, and the highest status person is always served first. It is proper form to refuse these honours and press them on another.
- Try a bit of everything that is served.
- Most tables are set with a spoon and fork only. It is common to use the right hand to eat with but if you do not feel comfortable using your hands to eat, you may use the utensils.
- There is often more food than you can eat. Part of Iranian hospitality is to shower guests with abundance.
- Expect to be offered second and even third helpings. Initial refusals will be assumed to be polite gestures (ta'arof again!) and are not taken seriously.
- Leave some food on your plate when you have finished eating.
- Restaurants generally have two sections—"family" where women and families dine and "men only".

Chapter 6

Business Etiquette

Although Iran is considered as a part of the Middle East, it is important that you do not confuse Iranians with Arabs. They have different languages, cultures and histories.

IRANIANS ARE PREDOMINANTLY SHIA MUSLIMS
The official language of Iran is Persian – known as 'Farsi' to Iranians. Although it borrows many words from Arabic, it is a unique language. Some people speak Azeris, Kurds, Lor, Beluchis and other ethnic minorities in Iran speak with their own languages.

- Males in business must dress smartly and conservatively. A suit is standard, although wearing a tie is not necessary.
- People should always be mindful of their behaviour in public. Clothes should be conservative and non-revealing.
- Avoid talking loudly. Do not hold hands with the opposite sex in public, unless these are children or older members of the family.
- Women should wear conservative clothing that covers arms, legs and hair.
- When in public, women must cover their hair with a scarf. However, the last few years has seen incredible changes in what the authorities are willing to tolerate.
- Building a relationship with your Iranian counterparts is crucial. The first meeting should be focused solely on getting to know each other. Once a relationship has been established, you can move on to business matters.
- Iranians are astute businesspeople. They enjoy haggling and getting concessions, so prepare for longer negotiations.
- As such, decision making can be slow. It is most likely that you will meet and negotiate with less senior people first. Once you are seen

as trustworthy and your proposal financially viable, you will move on to meet more senior members.
- When negotiating, Iranians will start at extremes in order to gauge your response. Prior to negotiations, know your target figure and work slowly towards it through meaningful concessions.
- Business hours are Saturday to Thursday, nine a.m. to five p.m. Lunch is usually an hour at around one p.m. No business is done on Fridays.
- Although many Iranians in business will have a good understanding of English, it is best to arrange for your own interpreter to accompany you.

BUSINESS ETIQUETTE AND PROTOCOL IN IRAN
Relationships and Communication

Iranians prefer to do business with those they know and respect, therefore they expect to spend time cultivating a personal relationship before business is conducted.

Who you know is often more important than what you know, so it is important to network and cultivate a number of contacts.

Expect to be offered tea whenever you meet someone, as this demonstrates hospitality.

Since Iranians judge people on appearances, dress appropriately and stay in a high standard hotel.

Business Meeting Etiquette

It is a good idea to avoid scheduling meetings during Ramazan (Ramadan) as the need to fast would preclude your business colleagues from offering you hospitality.

Arrive at meetings on time since punctuality is seen as a virtue.

The first meeting with an Iranian company is generally not business-focused. Expect your colleagues to spend time getting to know you as a person over tea and snacks.

Be patient—meetings are frequently interrupted.

Written materials should be available in both Farsi and English.

Do not look at your watch or try to rush the meeting. If you appear fixated on the amount of time the meeting is taking, you will not be trusted.

Business Negotiating

It takes time for Iranians to become warm towards foreign businesspeople. Until then, they may appear somewhat stiff and formal.

Personal relationships form the basis of business dealings.

Decisions are made slowly.

Iranians are deliberate negotiators who can drive a hard bargain.

Do not use high-pressure tactics. They will work against you.

Iranians may display emotion, or even walk out of the meeting, or threaten to terminate the relationship in an attempt to convince you to change your position.

Iranians often use time as a negotiating tactic, especially if they know that you have a deadline. Be cautious about letting your business colleagues know that you are under time pressure.

Companies are hierarchical. Decisions are made at the top of the company, either by one person or a small council.

Dress Etiquette

Business attire is formal and conservative.

Men should wear dark-coloured conservative business suits.

Ties are not worn by Iranians but it would not be seen as negative if you did so.

Women should always dress modestly and cover their hair. Although it's not essential, it's advisable to wear a long tunic which is baggy on the top and extends down to the knees.

Titles

Address your Iranian business associates by their title and their surname.

The title "doktor" is used for both MDs and PhDs. Engineers are called "mohandis". These titles are preceded by the formal titles listed below and are used with the surname.

The title "agha" (sir) is used when addressing men. It may be used before or after the first name. The phrase "agha-yeh" is put before a surname.

The title "khanoom" (madam) is used when addressing women. It may be used before or after the first name. The phrase "khanom-eh" is used before the surname.

Wait to be invited before moving to first names. Only close friends and family use this informal form of address.

Business Cards
Business cards are only exchanged by senior-level people.

Since rank and position are very important, make sure your business card includes your title.

Have one side of your card translated into Farsi.

Chapter 7

Wedding Etiquette

Marriage within the family is a common strategy. The father is the disciplinarian of the family. Whereas most fathers dote on their small children, they can become fierce and stern as children approach puberty. It is the father's responsibility to protect the honour of the family, and this means keeping close watch on the women and their activities. A girl is literally a treasure for the family. If she remains chaste, virginal, modest and has other attributes such as beauty and education, she has an excellent chance of making a marriage that will benefit everyone. If she falls short of this ideal, she can ruin not only her own life, but also the reputation of her family.

The wedding celebration is held after the signing of the contract. It is really a prelude to the consummation of the marriage, which takes place typically at the end of the evening, or, in rural areas, at the end of several days' celebration. In many areas of Iran, it is still important that the bride be virginal. The new couple may live with their relatives for a time until they can set up their own household. This is more common in rural than in urban areas.

Divorce is less common in Iran than in the West. Families prefer to stay together even under difficult circumstances, since it is extremely difficult to disentangle the close network of interrelationships between the two extended families of the marriage pair; also, children of a marriage belong to the father.

Marriage is undoubtedly one of the most important events for Iranian families. The *aroosi* (or wedding) involves an abundance of perfectly arranged florals, elegant fruit and dessert displays, lavish décor and a perpetually packed dance floor. But beyond the extravagances Persian weddings so often entail, there existed (and still exists, to some extent) the ancient tradition of *khastegari* (or courtship).

In the olden times, it was customary for Iranians to partake in this formality in which the man (the *khastegar*) and his family would search for potential brides who were from families of similar standing in the community. After finding eligible women, the families were to meet and decide if an engagement was the next step. In modern Iran, men and women are able to more freely date and arrange their own *khastegari*.

The *aghd* is the ceremony portion of the wedding in which the bride and groom sit in front of an assorted *sofreh* (or table) full of items that have meanings behind them. The *sofreh aghd* represents the symbolic and traditional union of the bride and groom. It is an intricate spread of items that stand for the shared journey of life and marriage the couple is about to embark on. Some of the elements you'll find on a *sofreh* include a mirror that signifies eternity, two candlesticks that signify light, nuts and eggs for fertility and coins for wealth and prosperity.

Esfand (or incense) is a combination of spices and herbs that symbolise the unwelcoming of negative energy. Burning *esfand* is an important part of the Iranian culture that's meant to deter the "evil eye" from causing any harm, particularly as one is about to embark on a new journey or milestone. At a Persian wedding, the *esfand* is burned just as the bride walks down the aisle.

Canopies have served as a long-standing wedding tradition as well as traditional Persian weddings. In traditional Persian weddings, the canopy symbolises unity and is customarily held by four females in the family who are close to the couple.

Consent Ritual
The consent tradition is the "I do" part of the wedding. First, the officiant asks the groom for consent, and he quickly obliges. Next, the officiant asks the bride for her consent. "It is customary for the bride to be asked for her consent three times before she answers—this is to symbolise the groom's journey of earning his wife's love," says Enayati. The crowd gets involved by yelling reasons why the bride can't consent yet, such as "*aroos rafteh gol behshineh!*" or "the bride has left to plant flowers". Enayati explains that the consent tradition creates excitement and anticipation in the audience until the final moment the bride finally agrees by saying "*baleh!*" or "yes".

Dipping Fingers in Honey
At Persian weddings, a bowl of honey is placed on the *sofreh aghd* signifying sweetness for the couple. After the couple has consented and they

are officially married, it is customary for the groom to hold the bowl of honey as they each dip one finger (the pinky or little finger) inside and feed it to each other. This symbolises the idea that the couple will feed each other sweetness as they begin their lives as one.

For Iranians marriage is an event, which must be celebrated not quietly but with glory and distinction. It is the most conspicuous of all the occasions and is celebrated in the presence of a fairly large assembly. In the past, the parents and older members of the family arranged almost all marriages. This is still the case in rural areas and with traditional families. Modern couples, however, choose their own mate but their parents' consent is still very important and is considered by both sides. Even with modern Iranians, after the couple have decided themselves, it is normally the grooms' parents or other relatives who take the initiative and formally ask for the bride and her family's consent. Once this is done, then the marriage will be announced. In the ancient times, the musicians playing at marriage gatherings used drums to announce the marriage to the people of the town or village. The group that gathered for the marriage was called the assembly for the queenly bride. Traditionally, both the bride and the bridegroom dressed in white with garlands of flower on their necks. The colour white is a symbol of purity, innocence and faithfulness. Today, most modern Iranians follow the European dress code and style.

Once the groom and his family express their desire for the union, they go to the bride's home with flowers, sweets and sometimes gold coins or jewellery and ask for her hand. If accepted, more presents will follow. The couple becomes engaged in a reasonably lavish party. Rings are exchanged; the engagement rings are simple, mainly gold with no stones. The wedding ring presented to the bride will be lavishly expensive with precious stones. The engagement ring is sent to the bride's house with female relatives of the groom. A few days before the actual ceremony, again more presents are taken to the bride's house. Men dressed up in festive costumes would carry the presents in elaborately decorated large flat containers on their heads. The container is called *tabagh* and the whole thing with the presents is called *khoncheh*. Many of these customs are still followed by the more traditional families and in the provinces. The modern Iranians normally bypass some stages like sending the ring through relatives and outside Iran, *tabagh* and *khoncheh* are hardly used. However, ceremonial objects are still present.

The mirror and candelabras are amongst the most important ceremonial objects that are taken to the brides' home and they are reminiscence of the Zoroastrian religious believes. Grooms' families are expected to pay for all expenses and if they cannot, they will be looked down upon. The higher the status and social standing of the bride, the more lavish will be the banquets and the presents, especially the jewellery.

All financial details are sorted out before marriage and the couple's parents, mainly fathers, will carry out negotiations. With prosperous families, the issue is settled rather quickly. However, families without enough means may drag the negotiations for a while, bargaining about how much should be paid and what should be included in the marriage contract.

Three days before the actual wedding, the bride would be taken to female beauticians or visited by them at home for the ritual of removing body hair. A significant rite of passage, this marks the passage from girlhood to womanhood. Unmarried women would not remove their body hair or pluck their eyebrows—the most visible sign that a woman was married.

This is done three days before to make sure any allergic reaction and redness of face and body parts would be healed by wedding day. Facial hair, all hair from under arms, legs even stomach and back hair are removed by using special threads that once moved in certain fashion would remove the hair right from the root. This is called *band andazi* and is still practiced by traditional families and in the rural areas. In recent times with the more restrict and traditional parents moving to the western countries, shaving legs and plucking eyebrows has become a source of conflict with their teenage girls. For the teenagers, these are part of beautifying process common in modern societies, while for their parents this is an obvious indication of becoming a woman without being married.

Traditionally, mirrors and candelabra with *espand* (a popular incense), large decorated sugar cones, cardamom seeds, rosewater, henna, dress fabrics, a prayer mat (*janamaz*) and candles are sent at this time to the bride's house. Included is a specially decorated bread called *khoncheh*, placed on the wedding spread. These are carried on *tabagh* with singing and clapping and accompanied by male musicians if they can be afforded. All the males stop by the entrance to the bride's house and women take over from this point on. The day before the wedding is the bathing day. The bride and other female relatives go to the bathhouses. She is thoroughly cleaned, massaged and all dead skin on her body is removed by scrubbing (*kisseh keshi*). The hair is washed and her entire body is rubbed with oils and perfumes. On the morning of the wedding, the beauticians arrive again to apply the makeup. The groom also has his pre-marital bath; however, his is a lot simpler. What matters is the bride being accepted by the groom and not the other way around.

Today, still many of these traditions are kept and carried out even though they might be ceremonial. The wedding is almost identical to the past and all brides will have the mirror and candelabra, if not the other items. The mirrors were always full-size, and a pair of candelabra is placed on either side of the mirror with lit candles: one for each of the bride and the groom. However, the cost of living has forced many to settle with smaller mirrors and candelabras.

A very important part of the pre-wedding activities is dowry preparation by the bride's family. The bride's family will buy household items for the dowry. The higher the social status, the more elaborate will be the dowry and it could include properties as well. The very modern professional couples with means do not follow this tradition. On the whole, this is still very important and is practiced by the majority and at times it becomes a source of major conflict between the two families.

Paghosha parties will be happening for the next few weeks. There are no special foods for these parties at the present. In the 19 century, a number of foods including special soup called ash was prepared by the groom's mother and rich families put a few gold coins in the ash and it was sent to the bride the day after the wedding. Afterwards, the dishes would be sent back, cleaned and filled with flowers, sweets, nuts and cardamom seeds for their perfume.

It is customary for the newlyweds to be the first to visit their parents on No Ruz and to be visited by other relatives because it is their first New Year as a couple. The couple would normally receive special gifts such as flowers, sweets, fruits and expensive fabrics. Iranian Muslims do not marry at certain Islamic months like Muharram and Safar. The first one is a month of mourning for Imam Husayn, and his cheleh or fortieth day of death happens in Safar. No celebrations normally take place in Muharram. Until recently, if the wedding happened to be on the same day or close to the festival of sacrifice, the groom's family would send a live sheep decorated with gold, silver and expensive shawls for the newly wed. The sheep would be slaughtered, and the presents remained with the couple.

Italy
By Dobrochna Giedwidz

Chapter 1

Cultural Symbols

COFFEE

It is no secret that Italians love their coffee! Venice was one of the first European ports to import coffee beans in C.16th and the first European city to open a coffee shop. As a result, coffee has developed its own culture in Italy. Coffee rituals define the typical Italian day: cappuccino in the morning, followed by a 'pick-me-up' throughout the day, which can be defined in hundreds of different ways: espresso, ristretto, lungo, macchiato, shakerato, corretto, affogato... Often a quick *espresso* is required in the evening, too. If you order a cappuccino after eleven a.m. you risk an instant 'tourist' label and if you ask for a *'latte'*, you get a glass of milk. In some parts of the country, especially in the south, if you order a tea, the barman will look at you in wonder as if you've lost your sanity.

GELATO

Who doesn't love sweet and creamy *gelato* or ice cream? Well, the Italians certainly do. The history of 'modern *gelato*' goes back to C.16th. Florence claims the invention, which first used milk and eggs—a delicious innovation credited to the architect Bernardo Buontalenti. Another great populariser of ice cream was a fine gentleman from Palermo, Francesco

Procopio dei Coltelli, who moved to Paris and opened a café where he served his ice cream. The cafe is called Procope and still exists today, delighting the taste buds of locals and tourists alike.

If you see a queue outside a shop in Italy in the summer, it's surely for a *gelato*, even though a good *gelato* knows no climate or season. Some people think that ice cream is only for kids, but honestly, in Italy everyone eats it: children; parents; grandparents; businessmen, policemen… just everybody. People in Italy say gelato is healthy… let's believe that's so!

Pizza

As you may have noticed already, most of the things that Italians really care about are either things you can eat or things you can drink. Many consider that the real symbol of Italy is pizza, especially pizza Margherita, which owes its name to the queen of Italy, Margherita of Savoy. In 1889, Queen Margherita visited the Pizzeria Brandi in Naples. The *pizzaiolo* (pizza maker) on duty that day created a pizza for the queen that contained the three colours of the new Italian flag: red tomato, white mozzarella and fresh green basil. It proved an instant hit with the queen and the rest of the world. Some say that if Italy could get a cent for every pizza eaten in the world, they would be the richest country on earth. Pizza is also the 'happy' food for Italians; it boosts your mood no matter what else is going on!

Renaissance and Baroque

It's a matter of great national pride to Italians that two of the most important architectural and artistic trends of C.15th and C.18th, which have defined so much the culture of Europe, came from Italy (or, at least, from what is now Italy but was in the past territorial states around important cities such as Florence, Venice, or Naples). The masterpieces created during these periods still inspire and provoke us. Two distinctive but vibrant styles, the Renaissance celebrated balance and harmony, while the Baroque embraced asymmetry and drama. These trends completely changed the way Europeans live and think by putting the human being at the centre of interest.

Azzurro

It is the colour seen on the sports field when Italy competes, and the athletes representing the country are called *Azzurri*. Why blue, one might ask. Could it be because the colour is associated with the sky and the blue Italian sea? Well, the story goes that this intense shade of blue was chosen during a football match between Italy and Hungary in 1911 in honour of the House of Savoy—a dynasty that ruled Italy at the time. Since then, in football and other sports, blue has become the colour that represents Italy.

LA GAZZETTA DELLO SPORT

This is a pink Italian national newspaper about sports. Italians love sports and *La Gazzetta* can be found in every bar in the country. Contrary to popular belief, Italians don't just follow football. Cycling is also very popular (especially in the summer when the *Giro d'Italia* takes place), as is Formula one (where everyone gets excited about Ferrari) and motorcycle racing. The Italian sports tradition is almost as long as the history of the country and in most sports, Italy has had many successes, in particular fencing, swimming and Alpine skiing.

ITALIAN NATIONAL ANTHEM, OR *IL CANTO DEGLI ITALIANI*

This is best known among Italians as *Inno di Mameli*, after the author of its lyrics. The music of the anthem is uplifting, composed to a marching beat. It has a catchy character and a simple melodic line that makes it easy to memorise and perform. A few years ago, however, there was a minor scandal when some players on the national football team didn't know the words, which was obvious as the television cameras panned across the players' faces, and this raised some serious questions about their sense of patriotism. Nowadays, everyone makes sure to learn the words before the game and sing with a unique intensity and passion.

SAPER VIVERE

From the French, the phrase *savoir vivre* is defined as 'knowledge of life', or familiarity with the customs of good society. *Saper vivere* is a philosophy that defines not only the etiquette and rules of Italian society, but also the harmony and enjoyment of life. As one of the historical Neapolitan authors, Matilde Serao, wrote: 'You must know how to live if you want to live, if you want to carry out your whole life in harmony with people, in harmony with your thoughts and feelings'. Italians have special attention to the good things in life. They dress well, eat exquisitely and are, for the most part, naturally friendly (as long as one doesn't criticise their cooking). It is easy in Italy to strike up a conversation or a make a joke with a stranger.

OLIVE BRANCH

Symbolises the nation's desire for peace, both in the sense of internal harmony and international kinship. It is found in many national symbols, including as the emblem of the Italian Republic. Italians also live for olive oil (did I mention that they like their food?), which is the main source of essential fats in the Mediterranean diet. This golden elixir is healthy, tasty and beautiful. The simplest meal is bread dipped in rich and tasty olive oil—basic, yet delicious!

TURRETED ITALY OR *ITALIA TURRITA*

Italy is often represented in art and sculpture as a young woman wearing a mural crown decorated with towers. This imagery, which has its origins in ancient Rome, is typical of Italian civic heraldry, so much so that the distinctive design of the crown is also the symbol of the cities of Italy.

Chapter 2

Meeting, Greeting, Posture and Body Language

POSTURE
- As we know, a strong and upright posture not only boosts self-esteem, but also makes us more self-assured and charismatic. In fact, Italian men and women like to look distinct, and a straight back helps to show confidence. Even so, they never appear stiff, and women are quite sensual in their movements. When sitting, it is polite to keep your legs parallel or crossed but ladies tend to always keep their knees together.

GREETINGS
- When meeting for the first time, especially in a formal situation, a handshake accompanied by eye contact and a smile is the perfect greeting. There is, however, a superstition of sorts that you should avoid shaking hands over other people's handshake or across a table.
- In an informal setting, if you are a woman and know the other person even a little bit, you can expect to get two kisses, one on each cheek. If you don't get a kiss from a long-time friend, you know something is wrong! Men usually exchange a handshake, but if they are good friends, they also greet each other with two kisses and a warm hug. Traditionally, you kiss on both cheeks, starting with the right side.
- In southern Italy, even if you meet a large group of friends, you usually kiss everyone, which can take a while! With young children, instead of kissing them directly, you would touch their cheek and then kiss your own hand to show your affection.

BODY LANGUAGE
- Gestures are a big part of what makes an Italian, well… an Italian! Is it good etiquette though? It's hard to say and depends on the situation, but gestures are definitely an important communication tool, so much so that you don't have to know Italian to communicate with Italians. Lengthy

books have been written about their use of hand gestures and their various meanings. There's even a famous joke that goes, 'You know how to shut Italians up? Tie their hands'. Symbolic hand gestures can be used to express all sorts of emotions, from anger and annoyance to joy, or excitement. Body language experts have identified around 250 gestures used by Italians. Here are some of them, not all 'well mannered', but it is useful to know them all the same…

- Pinching all fingers together and moving the hand up and down forms the famous 'what do you want'? gesture.
- Brushing the upper part of your fingers against the underside of your chin says 'I don't care' or 'I'm not interested'.
- To express 'Are you out of your mind'? one simply waves one's hand in front of one's face as if swatting away a particularly annoying fly.
- When dining on something exquisite, placing your index finger on your cheek and twisting it means that you really appreciate the dish.
- In contrast, placing the index finger to the eye is a warning, which says to others: 'watch it', or 'be aware'.
- Finally, if the thumb is rested gently against the cheek, with the index finger clenched and the little finger pointing outwards, it means 'smart move'.
- Driving in Italy can be more 'creative' than in other parts of Europe and the further south you go, the more you have to keep your eyes open and remain alert at all times! There are, of course, also a few gestures you should know. They are not exactly friendly and usually express irritation, but are not to be taken too personally:
- 'Horns' play a big part in Italian sign language and are formed by extending the index finger and little finger while keeping the others clenched. Even though horns often used as a superstitious gesture, when you are stuck in traffic and someone is miming them derisively at you it implies that you've been cheated on (*cornuto*)…
- You can respond to this by stretching your arm with your palm open, with an appropriate dramatic facial expression of course, which means 'get lost' or worse…

Personal Space
- As for personal space, it shrinks down the more you know each other.

Hugging and personal closeness is often used as an amicable way of showing openness. Indeed, someone might be offended if you move further away from them whilst talking, as it appears as though you're trying to avoid them. In a friendly conversation, people may frequently touch your arm or nudge you to demonstrate their engagement in the discussion. Direct eye contact is expected during the conversation.

Temperament
- Italians are generally very open and friendly. They are not afraid to talk about their feelings and can often ask what might be perceived as direct and impertinent questions. If you feel uncomfortable about discussing a particular subject, it is best to avoid ambiguity and simply say in a friendly way that you would rather not discuss the matter.
- It is fair to say that prolonged silences make Italians uncomfortable. When you are with Italian friends, there will be very few 'silent' moments, as they usually always fill them with chatter and laughter.
- Italians like humour and jokes. Usually, conversations are quite light and through jokes they speak their mind quite openly. When good friends meet, they often make fun of each other as a way of showing affection.
- Italians often raise their voices during conversation. This is not necessarily a sign of anger but can often be an expression of excitement or conviction. When they argue, Italians often speak at the same time.
- *'Boh'* is a common expression in Italian; it's slang and is used very often to mean 'I don't know'.

Restaurants
- In Italy, being a waiter is a respected job and people train for it and make it their profession. It is, therefore, good manners to treat them with respect, especially since their expertise can always help to explain unconventional dishes or recommend the best wines to accompany your food. Usually, to call the waiter's attention you just raise your hand and make eye contact.

Chapter 3

Conversation Dos and Don'ts

Italians are talkative, chatty, long-winded, voluminous, loquacious, and any other adjective that describes people who like to talk a lot.

Italians are normally also a pleasure to talk with because they genuinely enjoy conversation and are typically very friendly and personable. It's common to have a simple conversation with strangers at the local bar or chat at the local shop. If you learn to say a few Italian words, it will be greatly appreciated.

HERE ARE A FEW TOPICS TO START A NICE CONVERSATION

Food
Italians love to talk about food! Not only do they love to eat, try new flavours and cook, but they also enjoy discussing dishes, deepening their knowledge and sharing ideas with relatives and friends. Almost every time people get together for a meal, there is an extensive conversation about where the dish comes from, how they are cooked in different households, what the best ingredients are and where one should buy them.

Keep in mind that almost every smallest town in Italy has a special and unique dish or dessert, many of which have interesting histories associated with them. People are very proud of their local traditions as well as the variety of food in their region, so be prepared to answer questions about traditional dishes from your country, how you prepare them, and the occasions in which you serve them.

If you're a visitor, you're likely to get lots of tips about local restaurants and the best places to go for a drink. An easy addition to the conversation about food is a discussion about wine. Italy is one of the top wine-producing countries and home to many well-known types of wine, including Barolo, Chianti and Franciacorta. Be careful, however—it is not a good idea to criticise Italian food or make suggestions on how to change and improve it! Italians are very proud of their cuisine, and you will quickly find out how passionate they can be about it.

Football
Yes, football is huge in Italy. It's a very passionate topic but be careful which team you support because a friendly conversation could quickly become more colourful. It's a good idea to avoid making any provocative or teasing comments when discussing football, even if it's meant in a friendly way.

Sometimes it seems as though, on almost any given night of the year, there is another 'absolutely crucial' football match taking place. Italy's top national league is known as 'Serie A' and the most passionate competition is always between teams from the same city or traditional rivals like Juventus, Naples, Inter or Milan. Mostly, however, football matches are just another reason for Italians to get together with friends or family and enjoy the simple pleasures of food, companionship and life.

Fashion
There is a famous saying, 'speak English, kiss French, drive German, and dress Italian'. What can you say to that? Italians have always had a sense of 'beauty' and they like to look good and often take great pride in their appearance. This doesn't mean you have to be overdressed, but make sure you don't wear beach clothes around town or shorts to a meeting, and dress moderately or smartly when visiting places of worship. Dressing inappropriately can make you look uncultured or disrespectful. You rarely see people in extremely casual clothing, even in the supermarket. Italians typically just look dapper for any kind of outing. A question of *'Che bello! Where did that come from'*? in reference to your bag or top is quite common and it's up to you to answer with a simple *'grazie'* or give a few more details about the item.

Travel
Italy is full of breathtaking nature, beautiful beaches and magnificent architecture. Italians are very proud of these treasures. They also, however, love to travel abroad; so, when they meet foreign people, they are curious and interested in their different cultures, traditions and food. Don't be

offended if they ask personal questions about your family or love life, as this is not considered rude or intrusive but is seen as a way of showing consideration and thoughtfulness towards others.

Colosseum

Vatican

AVOID OR BE CAREFUL WHEN DISCUSSING TOPICS LIKE

Fascism
Touchy subject is the period of fascism in Italy. Italians are often offended that the strong movement of partisans (*partigiani*) that sprang up during the Second World War in response to fascism is not commonly recognised by the rest of the world. Moreover, there are still unfortunately some who sympathise with the movement and mentioning fascism could trigger some uncomfortable discussions.

Mafia
There is a strong cultural tradition, expressed particularly clearly through cinematography, of portraying certain groups of Italians as violent, brutal, or simply '*Mafiosi*'. It is not a good idea to use these stereotypes when talking to Italians, especially since their post-war history is filled with crimes committed by the mafia and the subject can be very sensitive.

Chapter 4

Gift Giving

The Italians are very generous, not only when they invite others to their homes, but also when they themselves are guests.

Of course, the question of whether to bring a gift or not always depends on the formality of the event. If the event is formal, such as a reception or charity event, etiquette dictates not to bring gifts, but it's polite to send flowers to the hostess the next day, or a small gift that reflects the character of the evening or a conversation you had with the hosts. A thank you card with a personal note is also recommended.

For less formal occasions, such as a dinner or party at a friend's house, it's quite common to ask if one can contribute in some way. One might, for example, be asked to bring a dessert or a bottle of '*bollicine*', which is a sparkling wine like Prosecco or Franciacorta, or perhaps something for *antipasto* or dessert.

Often the hosts will say that nothing is necessary and, in this case, you can always opt for the classic gifts such as a bottle of wine, chocolates or a local delicacy (remember these can also make for interesting topics of conversation whilst having food). It is important to note that gifts may not end up being served during a dinner. Often the host will choose the right wines to accompany the meal or have a dessert prepared already, so he or she doesn't have to open yours.

'Knocking with your feet', or '*bussare coi piedi*', is a common saying in some regions of Italy. The phrase is a reminder of the obligation for guests not to come empty-handed, so they are forced to knock on the door with their feet.

As for flowers, it is classier to send the bouquet a few hours before the dinner or the next day with a thank you note, rather than bringing them. If that's not possible, however, bring a bouquet that's easy to handle or already has a vase.

One must also pay attention to the 'language of flowers', especially if you are not in love with the person you are giving the flowers to and you don't want to send the wrong message! The safe and 'neutral' choices for colours are orange, blue or pink. Yellow, depending on the circumstances, can mean jealousy, but it can also mean purity, intellect, and truth.

The type of flower chosen is also significant. For instance, tulips are one of the first flowers to bloom, heralding spring, and are generally associated with love, but their meaning varies by colour. Red ones are considered 'flames of passion', while yellow ones are a safe choice and represent happiness. On the other hand, roses are a symbol of love and beauty, of passion and desire, making them the quintessential Valentine's Day flower. If in doubt, the safest option is to choose seasonal flowers and avoid the colour red.

Flowers can also be given to men. They may, for example, be given on special occasions, such as graduation or birthdays, but the bouquet should be smaller and more discreet than for a woman. The colour of the flowers should also be chosen accordingly, avoiding pastel or pink tones and opting for eye-catching and intense colours instead. Great flowers to choose from can be yellow or orange tulips, daffodils or roses. If you have an Italian father-in-law, carnations are traditionally the most appropriate flowers, even though they have gone a bit out of fashion. Sunflowers can be a great alternative.

A souvenir or specialty from your country of origin is a great choice of gift. Again, food or drink will be particularly well-received; even though Italians are very proud of their gastronomy, they like to try and experience new flavours. Still, you must be careful however: giving a decorative item for the home or something personal could be a mistake, especially if you don't know the person very well or if the person is very particular about their tastes.

The best gifts are symbolic and either reflect something you have in common with your host or a special interest of the host. They should not be too expensive, otherwise they may cause inconvenience and embarrassment.

It is important to note that if you are in the lucky position of being invited to someone's summer residence or country house, you are not obliged to bring gifts. Instead, it is customary to invite the host to a dinner in town or to share in the expenses, depending on the arrangement and the length of the stay. If you have been given the keys to the house without the hosts being present, you should invite them to dinner on their return. It is also good manners to send a 'thank you' note or flowers after the visit.

When it comes to items that should not be given as gifts, there are a number of accessories that should never be donated as they may affect the sensibilities of the recipient. These objects include brooches, knives, scissors, or anything that is pointed, as well as pearls for young women because they represent tears. You should also generally avoid gifts that are associated with money, such as wallets, although if you really want to do so, put a coin inside as a symbol of prosperity and a good wish that the wallet will never be empty in the future.

Chapter 5

Dining Etiquette

Italy is renowned globally as having an outstanding cultural, historic and architectural heritage, but this is not its only claim to fame. The *Bel paese* (the classical poetical appellative for Italy, meaning the 'beautiful country') is also renowned for its certified and protected products.

From the famous *Parma Ham* and *Parmigiano Reggiano*, to niche geographical products such as the *Patata del Fucino* PGI, Italy has the highest number of registrations in the European catalogue of quality foods that are classified as having either a protected designation of origin or a protected geographical indication, which recognise products (typically food or drink) that are unique to a certain region and are typically an indication of quality and authenticity.

Italian cuisine has always been synonymous with excellence and authenticity and it might be the most famous in the world. Many people travel to Italy just to sample the exquisite local food. There is certainly a lot to try, as even the smallest towns generally have their own local specialty. There are hundreds of traditional Italian dishes and each region has a wide range of recipes passed down from generation to generation. It is no surprise that Italy is truly unique in the world of gastronomy.

Dining etiquette only changes in formality depending on whether you're eating in a trattoria or a Michelin-starred restaurant and is based largely on customary European or 'continental' table manners.

TABLE SETTING – TRADITIONS AND HISTORY
Table setting in Italy, as in the rest of Europe, must above all be functional and follow the menu. Italians generally take their cue from English table setting with some exceptions, in the north of the country, where French *mise en place* is found. The general arrangement of forks on the left and knives and spoons on the right is maintained. In the English place setting, the

glasses are on the right side of the place setting directly above the knife point; in the French *mise en place*, the glasses are in the centre above the plate. Another difference is that in the English mise en place the fork tines point upwards, whereas in the French one they point downwards.

If one of the meals is pasta or risotto, eaten only with a fork, the fork is still placed on the left side of the plate. Napkins are either placed on the left side of the setting or directly on the plate.

The popular use of forks in Europe actually began in Italy. Their first use is attributed to a Byzantine Princess who married a son of the Doge of Venice in 1004. She allegedly scandalised guests by using a fork to eat as the fork was considered 'a tool of the devil' at that time. Later, Catherina de Medici brought the fork to the French court after marrying the future King Henry II in 1533. Around 1770, the fork as we typically know it today, with four tines, was allegedly designed in Naples. The story says that Chamberlain Gennaro Spadaccini had the idea of creating a shorter fork, which was less pointed and had four tines instead of three, to make it easier for the king and courtiers to eat spaghetti.

Another interesting fact is that Leonardo da Vinci possibly invented the use of napkin. According to his diaries, while working for the Duke of Milan, Ludovico Sforza, as master of ceremonies, da Vinci thought about giving guests an alternative way to wipe their hands at banquets. In 1491 he began giving guests a cloth instead of them having to use common tablecloth or the fur of rabbits tied to the chairs to clean their fingers.

MEALS, MENU AND THE ETIQUETTE

A typical lunch or dinner menu consists of an *antipasto*—appetiser, the *primo piatto*, which is usually some kind of pasta or risotto, and the *secondo piatto*, which is usually a fish or meat dish with a side of vegetables (contorno). Italians like to finish their meal with a dessert, fruit or coffee. Let's take a look at the typical meals of the day.

Breakfast – In Italy, the morning routine is to get a shot of sugar and caffeine. Usually, it's a cappuccino and brioche or cornetto (as it's called in the south). It's not the healthiest option but it's very tasty.

Lunch – The time for lunch is quite fixed, at around one p.m. For people who work in bigger cities, it's usually an hour break where they either eat something very simple like a salad or sandwich, or else sit in a restaurant and enjoy a menu consisting of *primo*, *secondo* and maybe a small dessert with coffee or fruit. Italians would never order a cappuccino or café latte after lunch. If you find a shot of espresso too strong, you can add a drop of milk and ask for a *café macchiato*.

Aperitivo – A quick drink and an appetiser, usually after work with friends, to 'open' the stomach for dinner. Of course, great importance is placed on drinks with a wide selection to choose from, including sparkling wine (Prosecco or Franciacorta), wine, beer or cocktails.

Dinner – In Italy, this is the most important meal of the day and is the special occasion to which Italians usually invite their friends. Dinner in Italy is eaten between eight p.m. in the north and ten p.m. in the south. If you are invited to someone's house, you can expect to be greeted with a cocktail or a glass of wine and a small aperitif before sitting down. Once everyone has arrived, and after a little chat, the guests make their way to the table. The host is the first to place their napkin on their lap after which everyone follows suit. The most important part of the dinner is the conversation and just catching up on news. Avoid controversial political topics or mentioning your health problems or diets. At the end of the meal, the host places his/her napkin on the left side of their plate which indicates that the meal is over. It is quite common to then move to the sofa or even stay at the table to continue talking and have a digestive drink.

A few etiquette tips if you're invited for a meal or while dining in a restaurant:

- If at home, always arrive a few minutes after the appointed time. In the restaurant, however, be sure to be on time!
- In Italy it is not customary for guests to take off their shoes when they enter the house for dinner.
- The hostess or host always serves the first portion so when you sit down to eat wait until the host serves or starts passing a dish.
- You shouldn't really say '*buon appetito*'. Even if it's the first phrase you learn and many people use it, from an etiquette point of view, it should be avoided. The reason for this is because, in Italian courts in the Middle Ages, the prince would sometimes arrange a banquet for his servants and wish them '*buon appetito*'—meaning, 'eat as much as you can, because you may not be invited to another banquet if you do not behave'. This isn't quite the right sentiment for a dinner party!

- When seated at the table, your wrists should always be visible and propped up on the table.
- Keep your napkin folded in half on your lap throughout the meal. Clean the corners of your mouth with the inside part of the napkin before drinking from a glass. If you need to leave the table, the napkin should be left on the chair. At the end of the meal, it should be placed, unfolded, on the left of your plate.
- Wine glass or flutes are held by the stem.
- When eating pasta or risotto, use only the fork in your dominant hand, with the tines facing upwards.
- Sometimes, you see people using bread to help getting some food, for example salad, on the fork. This comes from the French style of dining and is common in less formal settings.
- When eating meat with *secondo piatto*, the English style is followed, where the fork is in the left hand, with the tines down, and the knife is in the right hand the whole time.
- If fish is served as a fillet, it can be eaten only with a fork or you help yourself with a piece of bread if necessary. Bony fish should be served with fish cutlery (fork and fish knife), using the knife not to cut the fish but to separate it from bones or skin.
- Italians are big bread eaters and bread is always present on the table during a meal. Remember to break it off with your hands rather than cutting it with a knife and do not eat it before the dishes come to the table.
- In a very, and I repeat very, informal or family situation, Italians do '*scarpetta*' which means they scoop all the sauce left on the plate with a piece of bread.
- Do not clear the dishes from the table after the meal without asking if you can lend a hand.
- Never leave immediately after the meal has ended, it is considered quite rude if you do not stay and chat for a while.

A few more notes:
- Eat pasta or risotto only with your fork. Do not ask for a tablespoon to help you swirl spaghetti onto your fork. Only a non-Italian would ever do that.
- If a pasta sauce contains fish or seafood, it is forbidden to put any kind of cheese on it.

- Do not add salt or pepper to your dish until you have tasted it first. Ketchup also has no place on an authentic Italian table.
- Sometimes it's okay to eat pizza with a knife and fork, even though in less formal situations everyone eats with their hands and only use their forks to pick up any tasty morsels that fall off the pizza.
- As a general rule, soup, cheese, salad, fruit or coffee should not be served twice.
- Salad in Italy is served after the main course.
- Dessert is served before fruit.

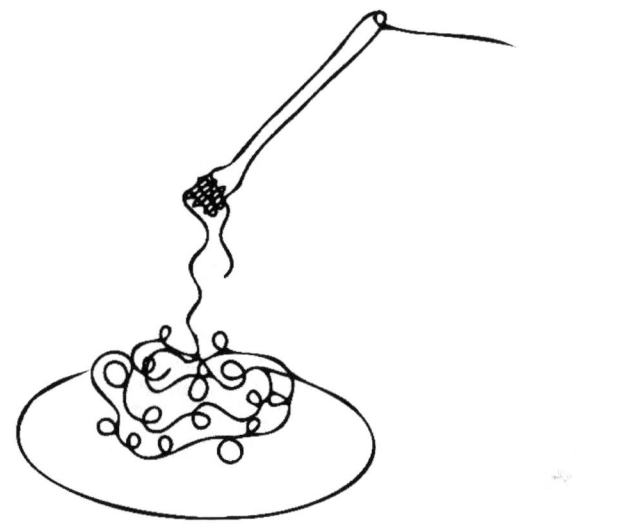

WHAT TO TRY – ONE SPECIALITY FROM EACH REGION

Abruzzo: Arrosticini, which is typically made from castrated sheep meat, or lamb, cut into chunks and pierced by a skewer. It is cooked on a brazier with a characteristic elongated shape, called '*furnacella*' as it resembles a gutter.

Basilicata: La Lucanica, which comes from Ancient Roman cuisine. Real *lucanica* is made from selected pieces of pork and fat, both of which are cut by hand into small cubes, spiced with salt, pepper, ground peperone dolce (from peperoni *cruschi*), and wild fennel seeds.

Calabria: Lagane e ceci—a type of wide pasta made with chickpeas, garlic, and oil.

Campania: Spaghetti con le vongole (spaghetti with clams) and of course Neapolitan Pizza.

Emilia Romagna: Tortellini, which are ring-shaped pasta, traditionally stuffed with a mix of meat, *Parmigiano Reggiano*, cheese, egg and nutmeg and served in a capon broth.

Friuli Venezia Giulia: Frico, which is a heated cheese which might include other ingredients such as potatoes.

Lazio: Amatriciana, which is a traditional Italian pasta sauce based on guanciale, pecorino cheese from Amatrice, tomato, and in some variations, onion.

Liguria: Trofie al pesto, which is short, thin, twisted pasta served with a sauce traditionally consisting of crushed garlic, European pine nuts, coarse salt, basil leaves, and hard cheese such as *Parmigiano-Reggiano* or *Pecorino Sardo*, all blended with olive oil.

Lombardia: Risotto alla Milanese, whose recipe calls for rice, fat, beef marrow, saffron, nutmeg and stock, flavoured at the end with grated cheese.

Marche: Olive ascolane, which is traditionally made using these fine local green olives stuffed with a meat filling, before being coated in bread and deep fried.

Molise: Composta Molisana, which is a fruit and vegetable conserve made with pears, grapes, tomatoes, onions, peppers and carrots.

Piemonte: Risotto al Barolo is a risotto made with butter, chopped onions, rice, stock, and *Barolo* wine, which gives it an intense pink colour.

Puglia: Orecchiette alle cime di rapa (Orecchiette with turnip tops), the name of which is derived from its shape: a concave disk, smooth on one side and rough on the other, reminiscent a small ear.

Sardinia: Seafood f*regola* with saffron. *Fregola*, which means breadcrumbs, is a typical Sardinian pasta made of semolina and rolled into small balls.

Sicily: Caponata, which consists of chopped and fried aubergine and other vegetables, seasoned with olive oil, tomato sauce, celery, olives, and capers cooked in sweet and sour sauce.

Toscana: Bistecca alla Fiorentina, which is a 'T' shaped bone with fillet steak on one side and sirloin on the other. It's normally 3–4 cm high and 1.5–2 kg in weight. This very special cut is commonly sourced from the big *Chianina* cattle breed.

Umbria: Porchetta, which is a savoury, fatty, and moist boneless pork roast.

Valle d'Aosta: Polenta concia, which consists of polenta mixed with butter, milk and the region's famous *Fontina* cheese.

Veneto: Risi e bisi, which simply means rice and peas!

Wine

Wine is a very important part of Italian culture and cuisine and is produced in every region of Italy. The history is ancient: Etruscan and Greek settlers produced wine before the Romans began planting their own vineyards in the second century AD.

Food and wine are thought of in Italy like the yin and yang of Eastern traditions and complement each other perfectly.

Italy is the home of delicate, refreshing white wines, strong and powerful red wines and, of course, delicious sparkling wines to be enjoyed as an aperitivo or with dessert.

You should feel free to be adventurous with wines when in Italy: do not be afraid to ask for lesser-known varieties and take the opportunity to try something new or rare. If you sample the local varieties, you might just end up with a bottle without a fancy label but containing the most amazing wine!

A few important names to recognise, however, are: *Barbera, Barolo, Moscato* from Piemont; *Valpolicella* from Veneto; *Chianti Classico* and *Brunello* from Toscany; *Lambrusco* from Emilia Romagna; *Montepulciano* from Abruzzo; *Taurasi, Fiano* di Avellino and *Greco di Tufo* from Campania; *Primitivo* from Puglia *Moscato* from Sicily.

As for sparkling wine, one of the best is *Franciacorta*, which only allows the 'classical method', where fermentation takes place in the bottle. This is the same technique used to make Champagne.

Coffee

Coffee is the quintessential Italian ritual and the most commonly drunk beverage in Italy. People drink coffee in a bar, usually in the morning, but often during the day as well. It is well worth spending some time enjoying your coffee at a bar and watching as the barman deals with all the orders at lightning speed.

Coffee is also served after lunch or dinner, but usually at a separate small table. One might also however simply be invited for coffee during the day. If at home, the coffee is brought to the table in a mocha or coffee pot and served in front of the guests by the host. The sugar bowl and milk jug are also placed on the table along with some small sweets or chocolates. Pouring the coffee for others is an act of courtesy and the first cup is given to the most important guest.

Chapter 6

Business Etiquette

A country like Italy with outstanding natural beauty, historic wonders and a rich culture may be the perfect place for a vacation, but it is not the most obvious destination for work. If one wants to work in Italy, some knowledge of the language would be required for professional reasons but also to make friendships. However, knowledge of English or other foreign languages is always greatly appreciated.

The Italian economy is one of the largest in the world and relies heavily on manufacturing and services. In fact, the service sector dominates the economy with a strong focus on wholesale, retail and transportation. Driven by the production of luxury goods such as fashion, automobiles and furniture, industry also contributes a large share to Italy's economic output. In terms of agriculture, Italy is one of the world's largest producers of wine, olive oil and fruit.

The number of multinational companies in Italy may be smaller than in other European countries, but strong Italian brands include automobiles such as Fiat and Lamborghini, and the fashion designers Gucci, Prada, Versace, and Armani.

It is important to remember, however, that there is still a large contrast between the north and the south; northern Italy is more industrialised and is known for its wealth of private businesses, while the south relies heavily on agriculture and farming.

Italians are hard-working, but they also try to find a healthy work-life balance. Work tends to be very structured: Italians typically work Monday to Friday from eight or nine a.m. until one p.m. take a one or two-hour lunch break, before returning to work until six or seven p.m.

MEETING & GREETING
A polished and polite demeanour is highly valued in a work environment, but it does not have to be rigid. Italians like to joke and participate in small talk even in a business setting.

When you first introduce yourself, shake hands with everyone in a group one at a time and maintain direct eye contact. Italians do not hesitate to greet people they know with a warm hug. Otherwise, the usual greeting between women or between a man and a woman is two kisses—one on each cheek.

You are expected to say 'Signore' (Mr) or 'Signora' (Ms) plus the surname when introduced to Italian executives. Use last names and appropriate titles until specifically asked to use first names by your Italian host or colleague.

Meetings usually began with a little chat. Do not be surprised if your Italian colleagues speak simultaneously or interrupt one another; it is a common trait in Italian communication.

Exchanging business cards is common and usually done at the end of a meeting.

PUNCTUALITY

It is fair to say that punctuality is not always a priority for Italians, so don't interpret a little lateness as a sign of lack of respect. Be prepared to wait a few minutes for your Italian counterpart to show up or let you into the office, especially if they are executives in higher positions than you. Having said that, you are expected and advised to be always punctual. It's an unfair world sometimes!

BUSINESS DRESS CODE

Style is probably more important to Italians than to most other nations and first impressions are crucial in the developing of business relationships. Your attire is perceived as a reflection of your social standing and relative success.

For formal business meetings, formal attire is expected. For businessmen, dark colours such as grey or blue are a classic choice, but the choice of fabric design may also vary. Lighter shades are quite common in the warmer months, paired with a bright shirt and tie which are often either unconventional in style or an eye-catching colour choice. This helps to emphasise the wearer's individuality. Let's keep in mind that Italian tailored suites have their own style and, in keeping with the Mediterranean climate, are considerably lighter to wear.

There are two main sartorial schools in Italy: the Neapolitan style and that from Milan. The Neapolitan suit is the most unique. The distinction begins at the shoulder, which is unpadded and natural, and features a so-called 'shirt-shoulder', which is folded slightly, where the sleeve merges into the armhole. It may also have patch pockets, indicating the more casual nature of the style.

The suits made in Milan, on the other hand, are more structured, similar to a typical British cut and distinguished by a greater emphasis on a stronger shoulder, rather than a natural one, albeit still designed with little padding.

Businesswomen also tend to wear elegant and modest trouser suits or skirt suits in formal situations, with much significance placed on high-quality fabrics such as lightweight wool and silk. Clothing is typically accented with jewellery, make-up or fashionable accessories.

Despite the importance of fashion, however, Italians always dress with a certain nonchalance; they like to add colour to their look and Italian men in particular always know how to appear casually sophisticated. This is the hallmark of '*sprezzatura*'—the art of dressing effortlessly.

More informal dress is also common, especially in creative environments and outside of large corporate, financial or legal circles. Still, you don't have to feel like you're 'competing' with fashion details; if you're not particularly interested in such things, you can also play it safe and just choose tastefully coordinated clothing instead.

GIFT GIVING

In Italian business culture, it is not particularly customary to give gifts. Only when you are familiar with someone it might seem natural to give a small and not obviously expensive gift as a token of friendship, or as a thank you on completion of a project.

A small gift may also be appropriate as a thank you for Italian hospitality. In such a case, the choice of gift may include liqueurs, delicacies or handicrafts from the visitor's country.

BUSINESS MEALS

As you might have realised by now, food and hospitality are central to Italian culture, and when it comes to doing business, Italians often invite potential business partners over for a meal. It is important for Italians to know who they are doing business with, after all! Declining an invitation of this kind is likely to cause offence.

Italians place a high value on etiquette, so if you plan to do business in Italy, it's important that you understand it. Please read the chapter on 'Dining Etiquette' for a detailed insight.

Chapter 7

Wedding Etiquette

Italy is one of the most popular destinations for weddings abroad. With so many breathtaking and diverse landscapes, as well as beautiful villas and stunning castles where you can tie the knot, it is easy to understand why. Being invited to a wedding in Italy can also be an amazing experience.

But what does it actually mean to attend an Italian wedding? As with many things, wedding celebrations and their associated rituals change from the north to the south of the country. The south is known for a more traditional approach with larger, busy weddings, characterised by food and excess, while in the north people opt for simpler and more practical celebrations instead.

Every wedding is different and special in its own way, but there is nevertheless some general advice and guidance which it's useful to bear in mind.

INVITATIONS

Traditionally, it is customary for two cards to be sent to guests of a wedding. One is sent to all family members and friends, in which the parents of the future couple announce the wedding. The other is an invitation for those who are requested to also attend the reception, which is sent along with the announcement.

Although the announcement is not as popular anymore, you still sometimes see this formality and it is worth remembering the ground rules. The people who only receive the announcement may or may not be present at the church (or other location) and are not required to give a gift. If they wish, they may send a card, telegram or flowers with congratulations. For those who have also received an invitation, it is mandatory to give a gift, even if they do not attend the ceremony.

It is good manners, as well as common sense, to respond to the invitation as soon as possible. In some cases, the invitations have special reply cards that must be filled out and returned, but if they are not there, it is enough to call the couple to confirm you can attend. You might also want to contact them if you have allergies.

Church Wedding

Most weddings in Italy still take place in a church, partly because a wedding in a Catholic church can also be registered as a civil marriage.

According to etiquette, the guests enter the place of ceremony on their arrival, observing that the front seats near the altar must be occupied by the closest relatives of the couple.

The order of the wedding procession can vary from region to region or according to the taste of the spouses and the formality of the ceremony.

Traditionally, the groom is the first to enter the church and is at least twenty minutes early. He arrives arm-in-arm with his mother. The groomsmen, the bride's mother and the groom's father turn up after him. The bride will then arrive a few minutes late with her father, who entrusts her daughter to her future husband at the altar, gives her a kiss on the forehead and shakes hands with her future husband.

An alternative which is becoming more popular, however, is that the groom waits for the bride in the churchyard and helps her get out of the car when she arrives, handing her the bouquet then walking her down the aisle.

In Italy, if bridesmaids are present, they will follow the bride.

You should be careful to follow church etiquette during the wedding ceremony. Enter the church quietly and show respect whilst you are inside. Put your mobile phone on 'silent' and avoid the temptation to take pictures the entire time. Remember to dress appropriately, cover bare shoulders and do not wear clothing that is too revealing. Men must remove their hats at the church entrance. Sunglasses should also be removed indoors.

The wedding mass usually lasts about an hour, so make sure you are wearing something comfortable.

Finally, it is a common tradition to throw rice at the spouses outside the church at the end of the ceremony. You might ask for what purpose. Sometimes, it's best to just go with things and not to question tradition too much!

Civil Wedding

Civil weddings are usually shorter and less formal than church weddings.

Still the guests should dress with elegance, as 'civil' is not synonymous with 'informal'!

Just as in a wedding ceremony, the guests are already in the room before the bride enters for a civil wedding. Traditionally, the bride's guests are seated on the left of the room and those of the groom are on the right.

In Italy, also couples of the same sex can marry through a civil union. During the ceremony, there are no special seats for those on the left and right. Spouses or brides may come to the altar together or be accompanied by a relative or parent.

GIFTS

The subject of what to buy as a gift for the bride and groom is a frequently debated and complex topic. What to give, how to give it and when? Nowadays, it is common for couples who are about to say 'yes' to give hints as to what would be most beneficial or pleasing to them, perhaps by creating a wedding or travel list. Others, however, prefer the more classic approach of gifting, of simply offering money sealed in an envelope. This practice is still quite common in the south of Italy.

When choosing a gift, make sure you consider your budget and also the nature of the relationship that you have with the couple. If you are a close family member or best friend, your gift should be more substantial and valuable. If you know the couple well, you can also buy something personal that isn't included on the wedding list. Also, if you are accompanied by a plus one, it is tactful to spend a little more on the gift, although there is no specific rule that demands this or indicates how much more should be spent.

DRESS CODE

The dress code of the wedding is always determined by the bride and groom, but the most important rule is that no one should try to outshine the bride. For this reason, it is okay to choose a beautiful dress that emphasises the figure, but at the same time one should be careful not to overdo it or choose an outfit that is too extravagant or revealing.

The etiquette of the wedding dress code for women is clear: in the evening, the dress should be as formal as possible, perhaps a long gown or a mid-length cocktail dress. For a semi-formal ceremony during the day, it is fine to opt for a skirt or cocktail dress, whilst for a formal ceremony, a long dress in lighter colours is required.

Let's remember, however, that there are also some rules regarding what to avoid. Black clothes are a bad idea because these are commonly associated with mourning. White is the colour of the bride and red is considered too flashy and provocative. Purple is also a colour to avoid because it is associated with superstition and considered a colour that brings bad luck.

These days, however, the rules are more relaxed, and a compromise is often acceptable. Red should not be too garish; black can be used but only in small doses and is best suited to a ceremony that takes place in the late afternoon or evening. White clothing with colourful prints is considered acceptable. Purple should, however, still be avoided.

For men, it is always important to consider the season and time of day. A dark suit – preferably grey or blue/dark blue – accompanied by a white shirt, dark shoes and tie is the safe way to go unless the invitation specifies a particular dress code.

THE RECEPTION

Upon arrival, guests are usually greeted with a welcome drink, often a sparkling wine or cocktail and a small aperitif.

In the area where the aperitif takes place, the *tableau de mariage* is usually set up so that all guests can freely consult it to find out which table they should sit at. It is important to remember that the seating plan cannot be changed and sometimes couples might, as a result, end up being separated.

Guests enter the banquet hall and take their seats before the bride and groom arrive. Only after the arrival of the couple is the first toast given and the food served.

Usually, a lunch menu is always richer than an evening menu and includes foods such as pasta, meats and cheeses. It is, however, best to be prepared to eat a lot and avoid snacking before the ceremony.

The wedding meal is officially concluded with the opening of the dessert buffet and the cutting of the cake. This is an important moment in the ceremony in which the happy couple cuts the first slice of the cake together. The first portions are always served in turn to the parents, groomsmen and bridesmaids by the couple. The other guests are served by the waiting staff.

Shortly after the cake is finished, guests gather for the famous throwing of the bride's bouquet, after which the party can begin in earnest.

Bomboniera and Confetti

The giving of party favours, or *bomboniera*, takes place at the end of the reception and after the cutting of the cake. Usually, small and simple gifts are offered to remember the wedding by. Sometimes they are sent after the wedding.

Confetti, on the other hand, are candies that are simply almonds covered in white sugar icing. Traditionally, they represent fertility and are given away in odd numbers during or after the wedding ceremony (if you receive them beforehand, don't open them until after the wedding). They may also be presented in a bowl during a wedding from which guests are invited to serve themselves.

Lebanon
By Irma Vartanian Balian

Chapter 1

Cultural Symbols

Lebanon dates back to ancient times with over six thousand years of history and is situated in the Levantine region of the Middle East. With significantly high literacy rates, the overall population is estimated at over four million inhabitants. Lebanon is a relatively small country and its capital city is densely populated. With a reputation bigger than its surface area, it has been widely known as the Switzerland of the Middle East, and home to the most fascinating cultural facts.

Ethnically the population is made of Muslim and Christian Arabs, Armenians, Greeks and Kurds. Most Lebanese Christians are Maronite and among them, some explain their racial roots as descendants of Phoenicians (ancient Canaanites who inhabited the Lebanese coast and the South Syrian regions, around the second millennium BC).

Lebanon is a secular country with no one religion dominating the faith of the population. However, there are eighteen confessional communities officially recognised, including four Muslim sects, Druze, twelve Christian sects, and Judaism. The variety of these ethnic societies have shaped the social and political structures of the country and have created a rich, unique and diversified culture for a nation which prides itself on them.

The pluralistic society and the openness of the people to both Western and Arab worlds make Lebanon culturally popular in various ways. The Lebanese are extremely sociable, helpful and warm-hearted people. With a significant number of people living abroad, they hold on to their roots and keep the family ties sacred. When it comes to culture, it is often difficult to frame it within couple of symbols. Even so, here are key features:

THE CEDARS OF LEBANON – AL ARZ
The *Arz* (cedar) is a species of tree that grows in the rocky mountain areas of Lebanon. It is the state emblem symbolising longevity and strength, represented in the centre of the national flag, along with the coat of arms

and the national airline. As the main insignia of the Lebanese culture, it may also be used to authenticate or endorse local products. Lebanon's cedars are thousands of years old and even mentioned in epics and Biblical stories.

The Arz

FAYROUZ

A world-famous Lebanese singer, Fayrouz is regarded as the ambassador of Lebanese art and culture. She has spread the soul of Lebanon worldwide through her international concerts, has been awarded medals of honour from various countries, and gained an unparalleled rank as a world class entertainer. After the 2020 explosion of Beirut port, French President, Macron came to Lebanon in support of the Lebanese nation and started his journey by visiting Fayrouz before meeting with country leaders. Her voice and songs are a symbol of nationalism and unity amongst the multi-confessional Lebanese citizens.

LEBANESE COFFEE

Ahwé Lebnaniyeh or Lebanese coffee is a national drink, served traditionally in *shaffé* cups. Households wake up to the smell of coffee, housewives start the day having a *finjen ahwé* (cup of coffee) with the neighbour, and working people make sure to have it at least once daily. It is served at happy and sad occasions, to reinforce friendships, to show warmth and hospitality, and to build new relationships and business agreements.

Coffee is an important aspect of hospitality and generosity in all Arab societies; thereby, it is best not to refuse it.

Lebanese Coffee

'Ibri'q

A jug, traditionally made of clay pottery but also made of glass, is used only for water drinking. It entails a similar experience to drinking water from a bottle in an upheld position without letting the spout touch the lips. The clay jug keeps the water naturally chilled and fresh with no need for refrigeration. The volume capacity is about one litre where the level of the water must not cross over the spout's lower part. It is a cultural characteristic which stems from Lebanese villages.

'IBRI'Q A Jug

LEBANESE CUISINE
Lebanon is world-famous for its copious cuisine. The variety of flavours,

the herbs, and the unique ingredients are a staple of its culture. When Lebanese expatriates are asked what they miss the most about the country, often the answer is the same: 'The food'! However, more details about the Lebanese food etiquette will be discussed in a later chapter.

Man'ouché (Za'atar)

Besides these famous dishes, the renowned *Man'ouché* is in a class of its own. This popular flatbread topped with an aromatic blend of *za'atar* (Lebanese thyme), sumac and sesame seeds, pure olive oil, is traditionally eaten for a casual breakfast on the go. It also comes in different flavours, but the legendary one remains the original *za'atar man'ouché*, with its famous accompaniments of tomatoes, olives, fresh mint, and cucumbers. Whenever expatriates get homesick, they become nostalgic about the taste of a *man'ouché*. Sometimes they even ask close friends and family members to bring some frozen ones with them when visiting them.

LANDMARKS

The Lebanese Landmarks are many, but the focus will remain on two sights which highlight the cultural features rather than the historical ones.

Our Lady OF LEBANON in Harissa

Our Lady of Lebanon is a Maronite church with an impressive shrine. It is highly respected and visited by both Christians and Muslims. It is located in an area called Harissa, twenty kilometres from Beirut, attracts both pilgrims and tourists, and represents one of the most important places in the world to honour the Virgin Mary. As a key Christian pilgrimage site, it highlights the vital role that Christians of Lebanon play in the Middle East.

Mohammad Al-Amin Mosque and the St George's Cathedral

Mohammad Al-Amin Jami', also known as the Blue Mosque, is a Sunni mosque, built by the former Prime Minister Rafic Hariri who is also buried beside it. It is located adjacent to a Christian house of worship, namely the St George's Cathedral. Its cultural symbol was re-emphasised during the 2019 Revolution because it represents the coexistence of Christians and Muslims, the religious tolerance and acceptance of *the other,* and the important role religion plays in the multicultural society Lebanon enjoys.

LANGUAGE

Locals speak what they call '*Lebanese*' as a colloquial language rather than Arabic. Taxi drivers, hotel staff, police officers, salespeople, restaurant staff and everyone you will communicate with in Lebanon speak the *Lebanese* Levantine Arabic dialect. Nevertheless, Modern Standard Arabic (MSA), or *al Fusha* is used in all formal and official documents. Hence, for diplomats, politicians, lawyers and professionals, MSA is vital. English and French are also spoken widely, since most Lebanese are at least bilingual. Another locally heard language is Armenian, spoken by the Armenian community.

Mixing Three Languages in One Sentence
Oftentimes Lebanese mix French and English words while speaking the local colloquial language. One very famous sentence which is even found in souvenir shops is the phrase '*Hi, Kifak? Ça va*'? meaning 'Hi, how are you? Fine'? Moreover, the French/English common terms such as *bonjour, bonsoir, merci, pardon, hi, sorry, ok, please, bye,* and *ciao* are so frequently used that most locals consider them as part of the Lebanese vocabulary, so much so that even greeting and invitation cards are printed with a mix of these three languages.

'Lebanising' Foreign Words
The Lebanese have come up with expressions unique to them which they then add to the local vocabulary. For instance, when referring to saving a document on computer, they use the term *sayyavta*, meaning 'I saved it'. Not only do they use foreign words as part of their dialect, but they also transform them into Lebanese terms. The trick, however, is knowing which words are *Lebanised* and which aren't. For that of course, you must come to Lebanon to find out!

Compliments and Praise
You know you're around a Lebanese when you hear expressions such as *habibi* (my love), *albi* (my heart), *te'berni'* (bury me), and *hayeti* (my life), all of which are used either for a loved one or sarcastically. People show warmth through hospitality but also with words. They are friendly and generous with their verbal expressions, so praising and honouring commendably is the norm.

Beirut Nightlife

No description of Lebanese culture is complete without a reference to Beirut's nightlife which takes place all week long, every night till daylight. Beirut is 'the' place to party. There is something to suit all budgets. Nightlife starts quite late with stylish ladies dressing up for the notion of *see and be seen*. You're overindulged with the choices available, from rooftop trendy restaurants with loud music to state-of-the-art cocktail bars, fashionable pubs and cigar lounges. The funky nightclubs offer exquisite food and create a dynamic atmosphere blending the popular music of the West with a Middle Eastern twist till sunrise, from where night owls continue straight to eat *Knéfé* or *Sahlab* (breakfast sweets at cafes or restaurants).

Lebanese Jokes and Sense of Humour

The Lebanese people have gone through numerous dark pages in their modern history, witnessing a devastating civil war, conflicts with neighbouring countries, a struggle for survival in dire economic conditions and the most dangerous explosion in modern history which took place on the 4 August 2020, destroying the houses and the lives of innocent people. Nevertheless, they continue to enjoy life to its maximum through resilience, inner strength, passion for life and commitment to progress. Besides these essential characteristics, the Lebanese have a witty sense of humour. They never miss the chance to laugh and joke about corruption and harsh times as a stress coping mechanism. They embrace humour in a unique way, which only a Lebanese could understand and laugh at.

Lebanon is a blend of the East and the West. Its special characteristics combined with its unique culture give rise to a country known as a 'must see location', to see at least once in a lifetime.

Chapter 2

Meeting, Greeting, Posture and Body Language

Talking with the hands is a common practice for the Lebanese, whether they're upset, excited or motivated. Moreover, hand gestures and facial expressions are so common that they sometimes replace words. As such, often the complete reliance on non-verbal communication must be interpreted as a cultural notion rather than disrespect.

NON-VERBAL EXPRESSIONS
To Say or Mean Yes/No
- To say 'yes', oftentimes people nod with the head downwards once or more as a sign of eagerness.
- The Lebanese lift the head up once, while raising the eyebrows, along with a click sound of the tong like 'tzso' to mean 'no' or 'I disagree'. This could be accompanied with a shake of the left or right index finger while pointing it upwards.

Eye Contact
Eye contact conveys a message of trust and respect. In most cases, the norm is to keep it long enough to acknowledge someone with sincerity and short enough to keep it decent and respectful. Socially, an extended eye contact is interpreted as scrutinizing the person. With the opposite gender, a prolonged eye contact beyond a brief glance is perceived as inappropriate. It may also be interpreted as confrontational or aggressive, especially if extended whilst communicating with a more senior person, either in age or rank.

Hand Gestures
Holding all five fingers or three of them together in a pear shape with the tips pointing upwards, while moving the hand slightly up and down, signals another person to 'slow down', or 'wait a little bit', referring to an idea or an action.

Holding the right hand forward with the palm facing up, while rolling it inwards towards the chest, is used to ask 'why'? or 'what'?

Forming a circle with the thumb and the index finger is used in a negative way, to warn someone, as if to watch out for a wrongdoing.

Raising both hands up with the palms facing the interlocutor signifies transparency and honesty. When people get upset however, they use this gesture with intensity as a reaction to a disliked conversation, as a way of meaning 'enough', or 'stop, I don't want to hear any more'.

For beckoning, one places the hand slightly out with the palm facing the ground and curling the fingers in a clawing motion back to oneself. Unlike other cultures, beckoning with the index finger is considered rude and condescending.

Placing the hand out, with the palm sideways and the hand in a clawing motion waving away from oneself is used either to ask someone to leave the premises or to indicate that one is busy.

Shrugging of the shoulders is used either to imply carelessness or to replace the verbal expression of 'I don't know', even amongst many adults.

Personal Space

Personal space is less than an arm's-length in most situations. Social distance between people is rather short in Lebanon, as people stand much closer together than in the West and sit or stand at proximities that make Westerners feel slightly uncomfortable. You may come across restaurant staff or boutique salespeople who get into your personal space whilst assisting you. In business and formal situations, the distance is slightly greater. With women however, this concept should be treated more delicately, by allowing them even more space, especially given the circumstances or the context.

Another common concept is that of touch between people of the same gender. Tapping someone on the shoulder, the upper back or the arm whilst conversing is perceived as a friendly and warm gesture. However, publicly displaying emotions of attraction with the opposite gender is disapproved.

Sitting Posture

While seated, slouching is considered disrespectful and gives the impression of being careless. Having the torso turned away while talking to someone is also impolite. Undoubtedly, sitting up straight with an open upper body is appreciated. In worship houses, faithful believers and even visitors are expected to sit appropriately without curling the shoulders or crossing the legs, and to wear clothes suitable for churches or mosques.

In general, crossing the legs is acceptable as long as the soles of the shoes or the feet are not showing, especially around the elderly. Moreover, raising the feet and placing them on a table or a desk is also considered ill-mannered and disrespectful.

Greeting and Meeting

In most cases the greeting norms are similar to those of the Western world. A proper handshake entails a vertical shake, slightly longer than that of the West, with a firm grip.

Hierarchy is an important factor. Elders are greeted first, out of respect. Handshakes may be complemented by three kisses. This warm gesture is referred to as kissing '*à la Libanaise*' (the Lebanese way), with three alternating kisses starting from the right side. Even men do cheek kissing amongst friends, and this is interpreted as a friendly and warm gesture. It is very common to see people of the same gender kiss and hug friends and relatives. In open and non-conservative communities, the cheek kissing extends to the opposite gender in a casual way but only after the initial meeting. However, first time encounters are treated formally without kisses in all circumstances.

Special Cases

In some Muslim communities, you may come across people who refrain from shaking hands with the opposite gender. To greet, they would fold the right hand over the chest, smile and nod with their head using the phrase *Assalamu 'Aleykon* (Peace be upon you). In this situation, one should reciprocate the hand gesture and reply with *Wa Aleykon Assalam* (Peace be upon you as well).

In a traditionally Muslim setting, a non-Muslim man must only shake a Muslim woman's hand if, and only if, she offers it. A non-Muslim woman must use the same rationale when meeting people from the opposite gender. Otherwise, it is perfectly fine to assume the Western norms, even with non-conservative Muslims who are open to handshake greetings with the opposite gender. If this sounds complicated, simply wait and greet according to the way you are greeted by a local.

Chapter 3

Communication Dos and Don'ts

Communication tends to be indirect and mostly non-confrontational in Lebanon. Non-verbal cues are crucial because locals rely on hand gestures, tone of voice and facial expressions instead of verbal language. Indirect speech is also common when someone needs to share bad news, because the bare truth would be viewed as blunt and insensitive in such cases.

Often, the Lebanese mix ideas and topics while chatting, leading to off-subject conversations. Therefore, it helps to ask close-ended questions politely, to have a precise and quick answer to your request.

It is common to display emotions of anger or enthusiasm publicly and loudly. Local people are passionate and governed by their intuitions. It is perfectly acceptable to gesticulate and voice anger by yelling or speaking with excitement without any reservation. On the other hand, silence may be perceived as a negative reaction, especially when people get upset.

INSHALLAH

Inshallah, meaning God willing, is used to link projections or upcoming tasks to faith in God. Locals say *Inshallah* to come across as humble and prudent about their future commitments, to do whatever is in their power and leave the outcome into God's own hands. Therefore, should local counterparts use this expression, foreigners mustn't regard it as an excuse nor assume that a given task will not be completed. *Inshallah* conveys humility and reliance on faith.

YALLA

Perhaps the most common word in the Arabic language is the word *Yalla*. Depending on the context, the implication of the sentence and the intensity of it, the meaning can vary. To name only a few, *Yalla* could stand for 'quickly, come on, let's go', 'let's start', 'hurry up', 'come down', 'come up', 'go on', 'waiting for you', and 'shall we'?

Khalas

Khalas is another popular word which foreigners seem to pick up easily. Again, depending on the context, it could stand for a lot of expressions. To name a few: 'enough', 'stop it', 'no more', 'finished', 'I don't want to talk about it anymore', 'forget it'.

Interruptions

Interruptions are a given medium during conversations. It is often interpreted as a sign of engagement, enthusiasm and even warmth at times. Don't get surprised when several people talk at once, especially if the discussion is a heated one. Loudness and interruptions should not be taken as sign of rudeness, especially among people of the same age and social status.

Politics

Politics is a hot topic in Lebanon. Most people are quite comfortable engaging in political debates with friends and even acquaintances. Besides family, social and business circles, it is even common to hear people discuss politics in the supermarket, at hair salons, doctors' clinics and even formal occasions. Nevertheless, it is best to be mindful about the people with whom politics is discussed. Approaching such conversations wisely with empathy, with mindfulness and maturity is key.

Domestic Economic and Financial Situation

Discussing topics related to the monetary condition of the country is a common theme in all social circles. The electricity or water supply in a given region, the welfare of the citizens and the banking sector are comfortable subjects among the Lebanese.

Conversational Dos

Family Matters and Status

Family is an integral part of Lebanese culture. Asking about the general well-being of the family is a sensible thing to do, out of courtesy. Family events and activities such as beach days, new venues, luncheons, hikes, and sightseeing within the country are all agreeable topics enjoyed by everyone.

You may be asked about your marital status, where you live and what line of business you are in, as a way of getting to know you better.

Health Matters
The Lebanese like to discuss, sometimes in detail, about issues affecting their health conditions. Staying fit, eating healthily and working out are all subjects openly conversed.

FASHION AND NEW TRENDS
Lebanese women are stylish and elegant. Most of them dress in modern and westernised ways. Dressing up for an occasion is the trend amongst women. They are up to date with the latest developments in the fashion world and discussing them is a hot topic among friends.

Travel
Whether visiting family members abroad, discovering touristic places or enjoying shopping destinations, the Lebanese love sharing their travel experiences as part of pleasant discussions and often ask each other about vacation and holiday ideas.

CONVERSATION DON'TS
Religion
Do not assume people's religion. As most people are dressed in Western style, it might be difficult to predict their religious preference. One must bear in mind that there are eighteen religious confessions recognised in Lebanon and that the number of interreligious or interracial marriages keeps growing significantly. Although Lebanese often discuss current issues relating to religion, avoid guessing and most importantly avoid asking about someone's religion, even out of curiosity, as you might come across as judgmental and intolerant.

What to call the Southern Frontier?
Most locals refer to the southern border of Lebanon as Palestine or occupied Palestinian territories. Even if you believe that it is rational to call the southern border Israel, eschew sharing your thoughts altogether about this matter, for this could lead to seriously intense discussions with some people. It is therefore wiser to keep the conversations impartial and steer them away from this matter.

Saving Face

The Arab culture does not appreciate criticism, blame or insults, especially when it is personal, against a family member or in front of subordinates. It is best to avoid it at all costs. You will notice that the Lebanese portray an honourable image of themselves and their loved ones, all the while aiming to save face with everyone. Any negative comments about topics that are dear to them might deeply offend them. Should you find yourself having offended a Lebanese person, you must make an effort to show genuine remorse and compensate for your misconduct as soon as you get the chance to do so.

Chapter 4

Gift Giving

When it comes to presents, the Lebanese enjoy offering as much as receiving. They're so generous that they may be perceived as looking for excuses to offer gifts! Besides the common occasions, such as childbirth, anniversaries, birthdays, graduations, weddings, bridal and baby occasions, Valentine's Day, house-warming, travelling etcetera, the Lebanese offer gifts whenever they see it fit.

SOCIAL GIFTS

People often get invited to homes for luncheons and dinners. Choose an appropriate gift that's suitable for the event. You can also ask for suggestions from someone closer to that person to help you choose according to the likes and dislikes of your host. You may offer a neutral gift of sweets, a bottle of wine or champagne, scented candles or decorative ornaments. In most communities, it is perfectly all right to offer alcoholic beverages. Even so, don't expect your hosts to serve what you brought them, as the menu would be set already along with the paired beverages. On the other hand, refrain from offering alcohol-based gifts to Muslim communities, including chocolate or candies filled with liqueur. It is also common for guests to offer a common gift by sharing its cost or by offering a gift card. The best presents are the thoughtful ones, appropriate to the person or occasion and coming from the heart.

If the invitations take place around a casual meal among close friends or family members, it is perfectly acceptable to show up without gifts when the gatherings happen often. In this case, it's best to reciprocate the invitation, within a couple of months at most.

RELIGIOUS OCCASIONS
Christmas
Personal gifts such as clothes, jewellery and accessories are appropriate

amongst close friends and family members for Christmas celebrations. Even when adults decide to opt out of exchanging gifts, children and youngsters are still offered presents such as toys and cash in envelopes.

First Holy Communion
Catholic communities celebrate the first Eucharist of children, around the month of May. After the Church ceremony, parents invite the family and close friends to commemorate this occasion. Guests must take into account the spiritual importance of the occasion and avoid presents commonly offered otherwise. Possible gifts include jewellery including a gold necklace with a Christian cross, a silver frame with which to cherish this memorable event, a personalised Bible or even an envelope of monetary gift with the consent of the parents.

Eid Al-Fitr
Once the month of Ramadan ends, Muslims begin the celebration period with Eid Al Fitr. Children are eager to visit the elderly members of the family who offer them monetary gifts according to their budget, whilst adults may offer their loved ones and close friends personal gifts similar to the ones offered during the Christmas season.

Eid Al-Adha
Muslims returning from the Al Hajj pilgrimage made to al *Ka'aba*, bring precious gifts as a way of sharing this beautiful experience with their loved ones who visit them upon their way back from Mecca. Upon returning from pilgrimage, Hajji people offer dates and nuts, blessed *Zamzam* water, white musk, prayer rug (*sejjad al sala'*), Qur'an or a *Zikir Subha*, namely prayer beads for the purpose of the *zikir* or *Tasbeeh*.

GIFT OFFERING TIPS
Sometimes, invitees send their gifts to the hosts prior to the occasion. In this case, it is essential to send it with a gift note addressed to the receiver. Personal notes are different than business notes or cards. Therefore, it is best not to use them interchangeably.

When offering gifts, hold it with both hands and offer it discreetly with a genuine smile. It's also important not to overspend or exceed expectations, for it may be interpreted as an enticement.

Gift Receiving Tips

Upon receiving a gift, it is well mannered to appreciate the gesture, show gratitude and accept it with humility. Refusal of gifts are taken negatively, sometimes as a disdainful gesture. When a present is delivered beforehand, one should immediately inform the sender of its receipt and thank the person for the gesture.

When social gatherings take place in big crowds, it might not be practical to open gifts in front of everyone. However, gifts received among small groups of less than eight guests can be opened before everyone leaves, to show appreciation and thank the guest for what was offered. Most importantly, the receiver remembers that it's the thought that counts.

Thank You Notes

Handwritten thank you notes still remain the most proper and respectful way to show appreciation for a gift or an invitation. Socially savvy and well-mannered Lebanese use personal cards printed with their names, which they use for gifting and thanking occasions. Nevertheless, with the norms changing and the widespread use of technology, people find it practical to thank the host via an email, a phone call or a digital message, depending on how the invitation was extended initially. However, human interaction remains the favoured way of showing gratitude.

Chapter 5

Dining Etiquette

Lebanese cuisine is world-famous for its aromatic, colourful and flavourful *mezzés*. As a national identity it has elevated the country to prominent gastronomic standards. It is inspired by regional cuisines as well as ancient civilizations and occupying powers that controlled its territories throughout history.

Breakfast
The Lebanese breakfast is rich with a variety of salty and sweet dishes. It takes place anywhere between six a.m. and ten-thirty a.m. depending on a person's schedule and circumstances. The most famous breakfast is the *Man'ouché* which was already mentioned in an earlier chapter. The variety of its toppings include the famous Lebanese thyme and olive oil, the cheese assortments, or the *Kishk* (a mixture of cracked wheat and yogurt). It is a street food traditionally but can also be found at restaurants as a variation on pizzas.

The traditional breakfast includes choices from the *Ful Mudammas* (fava beans) and *Balilah* (marinated and cooked chickpeas), Labneh (Lebanese yogurt), *Jebneh* (cheese), *Knefé bil jeben* (cheese pastry) topped with sugar syrup and eaten with its *Ka'ak* (round shaped biscuit bread), and the *Ka'aké Asrouniyé* (dry and soft biscuit bread, topped with sesame seeds, eaten with spreadable cheese, thyme and sumac). Usually, drinks accompanying these dishes are tea or coffee and fruit juices.

Lunch
Lunchtime varies between one p.m. and two-thirty p.m. The traditional lunch consists of cold and hot *mezzés*, followed by main courses. The lavish cuisine consists of more than forty types of *mezzés*. They correspond to the starters/*entrées* on the Western menus, but some could also be served as an appetiser whilst drinks are served prior to the mealtime.

Dinner

The Lebanese usually dine late. People show up at restaurants not before nine p.m. or nine-thirty p.m. By the time they order and eat, it is probably around ten p.m. Guests invited to homes are also expected to show up at around nine p.m.

Table Manners

Mezzé platters are shared by everyone at the table, providing a delightful way of socialising around food. With each portion intended to serve between two to four people, the proper way to eat is to start with the cold *mezzés* first, followed by the hot ones. Most of these dishes are accompanied by the Arabic bread *Khobz Arabi*, also known as the pita flatbread.

For health reasons and good manners approach, personal utensils must not be used with the shared *mezzé* plates. Moreover, one must avoid double dipping at all times!

Unlike other Arab cultures, the Lebanese enjoy chatting at mealtimes. Conversations can easily shift from travel, sightseeing, fashion and TV shows to heated domestic political discussions in a civilised manner, relying on good laughs and a sense of humour.

Most *mezzés* are eaten with Arabic bread. The traditional Lebanese table setting does not include a bread plate, however. Therefore, once the bread is broken by hand, it is best to place it on the side of the plate rather than on the tablecloth.

When guests are not familiar with some ingredients offered by the host, it is good manners not to refuse the suggestions, unless for health reasons, and savour them graciously, as much as possible, for this shows humility, kindness and appreciation to the hosts' efforts. At the end of the meal, one places the used cutlery together at five to five o'clock, with the knife blades inwards and on top of the fork.

Cold Mezzés

The popular classic cold *mezzés* include:
- The hummus (a tahini dip made of made of chickpeas) and the *Baba Ghanoosh*, also known as *Moutabbal Batingen* (roasted eggplant and tahini dip), eaten with the pita bread.
- Tabboulé: salad of parsley, tomato, onion and buckwheat, eaten with romaine lettuce, cabbage or iceberg leaves.

- Fattoush: Lebanese vegetable salad, prepared with garlic and sumac, eaten as a regular salad. Traditionally, Fattoush salad is served with dried bread pieces sprinkled on top of the serving bowl right before offering it to the guest.
- *Kebbé Nayé*: Raw minced lamb or beef, mixed with fine bulgur. Often it is accompanied by onions, mint, parsley and olive oil, and regarded as the Lebanese steak tartare.

Hot Mezzés

Hot classic Lebanese *mezzés*, similar to regional dishes, come in different flavours and textures. To name only a few:
- Falafel: seasoned deep-fried balls of chickpeas and fava beans.
- *Batata harra*: spicy baked potatoes.
- *Fatayer and Mou'ajjanet*: spinach and cheese rolls, fried or grilled.
- *Kebbé*: minced meat balls of beef stuffed and fried.
- *Shawerma*: marinated thin slices of meat, with sesame sauce and vegetables.

As for the main dishes, they include the *Mashéwé*, mixed grills of marinated lamb, beef and chicken meat, *Kafta Kebabs* (minced and marinated beef grilled), and *Shish Tawouk* (spiced chicken kebabs) accompanied by a garlic dip. The list is long but these are the basic dishes you are most likely to come across.

ARAK

Arak is a national alcoholic drink made from anise seed. Arak is a colourless beverage with a high alcohol percentage. It must be mixed with water right before serving it in small glasses with an ice cube, hence the shiny and milky colour of the drink. Traditionally, it is paired with the *mezzé* dishes.

DESSERT

The list of Lebanese and Arabic desserts is obviously endless:
Baklava is a famous Middle Eastern sweet made of pastry, honey and assorted nuts. Another choice is the cheese tart of *kenefeh bil jebbenh* with orange blossom cider syrup which can is also eaten for breakfast.

Sweets for Special Occasions
Meghli: to celebrate the birth of a child, a Lebanese traditional sweet

pudding is served to guests who visit the newborn child. It is based on cinnamon and aniseed, topped with a variety of nuts and shredded coconut and offered to guests in individual elegant bowls.

Ma'amoul: a traditional Middle Eastern aromatically flavoured cookie, stuffed with pistachios, walnuts or dates, served in Lebanon on religious holidays, such as Easter, Christmas and Ramadan.

Kellej Ramadan: to break the fasting period of Ramadan, Muslims prepare feasts of *iftar* which comprise a variety of delicious plates, including Baklavas and *Kellej* for dessert. *Kellej* is such a popular dessert during this period that it is often called *Kellej* Ramadan. It is made of fine layers of pastry with a creamy filling and scented sugar syrup.

Barbara Porridge: barley-based porridge, prepared with aniseed, pomegranate seeds, assorted nuts and sugar. This sweet dish is eaten at various special occasions: on the Feast of St. Barbara, for *Snayniyeh* which is celebrated for the appearance of a baby's first tooth, and as a dessert on the New Year's menu to symbolise prosperity, peace and happiness.

Atayef: a Middle Eastern version of a pancake, fried or baked, with crushed walnuts or *kashta* cream or soft cheese, sprinkled with pistachios and topped with syrup. It is served at the Feast of St. Barbara, at Ramadan or any other religious holiday.

Bûche de Noël: Lebanese Christmas dinners are characterised by copious meals. Members of the whole extended family get together and enjoy the most lavish menu of the year. Besides the delicious Lebanese food, people eat a variety of desserts including the famous log cake which comes in different flavours and versions.

'Aweymet and Mushabbak: a small ball and colourful entwisted dough deep fried or baked, dipped in sugar syrup, crunchy from the outside and soft from the inside. They are prepared for many yearly religious celebrations.

After dinner, coffee is served. Some dessert plates accompanying the Lebanese coffee are the famous turmeric tea cakes, called *Sfouf*, or a semolina-based sweet cake, soaked in aromatic sugar syrup, called *namoura*.

COFFEE

At the end of a meal, Lebanese coffee is served. Another interesting type of coffee is the 'white coffee' or *Ahwé Bayda*, which is prepared by pouring hot water on couple of droplets of orange blossom water, representing an aromatised warm water. Many people who don't drink Lebanese traditional black coffee opt for the white coffee instead, especially at the end of a heavy meal. It is worth mentioning that the Lebanese coffee is different from the Arabic coffee, otherwise known as the 'blond coffee' or *Ahwé Sha'kra* in the Arab world.

Chapter 6

Business Etiquette

As mentioned before, Arabic is the official language of the country, but many business contracts can also be written in French or English whenever international counterparts are involved. With the high literacy rate of the Lebanese, foreigners can easily communicate in English or French throughout meetings.

Being the most diverse country in the Middle East, working conditions, meetings and business connections may vary from one entity to another. The Lebanese are hard-working, serious and formal, all the while creating a warm and approachable working environment.

Timing
Business settings tend to be formal and are taken seriously. The Lebanese are punctual and expect their counterparts to respect the meeting schedule as well. Traffic occurs frequently in the city; therefore, anticipate that likelihood and leave slightly earlier to arrive on time to the destination.

Beirut is full of surprises even to its locals, where the only constant is change and the unexpected is expected. Whenever unavoidable force majeure arises, professionals ought to reschedule meetings or handle agreements virtually or by phone as much as possible, to prevent delays in the business process.

Business Handshakes
In business contexts, the most common form of greeting is the handshake. Should you come across people who refrain from shaking hands with the opposite gender due to their religious beliefs, then simply mirror the greeting form, as mentioned in an earlier chapter.

Handshakes take place both at the start and at the end of each business encounter. To be respectful, one must take into account the hierarchy of the group. This takes place by either greeting the most senior person in position first, the eldest person in the room, or even the host of the meeting first, and proceeds next to right of the most important person in the room.

When walking into a business area, people are expected to greet everyone with a handshake regardless of how large the group of people may be, as it is expected that all will stand up to greet.

MEETINGS

Interruptions take place frequently during office meetings, for the Lebanese tend to have an open-door policy where colleagues, team members or personal assistants walk in and out of the room, telephone calls get answered, and even documents are brought in for a quick look or a signature. It may happen that an unexpected visitor stops by the office where the meeting is held and sticks around for a while, bringing up unrelated topics or sharing pleasantries. In such cases, one may tactfully redirect the conversations to ensure a fruitful outcome. When the meeting comes to an end, everyone stands up to shake hands once again before leaving.

NETWORKING

Networking has been a fundamental fact in doing business the *Lebanese way*. Locals prefer to collaborate with people they trust and rely considerably on references made by their trustworthy circle of contacts. Likeability, warmth, reputation, personal qualities, as well as credibility, are decisive factors when choosing business counterparts, more than aptitude, competence and calibre.

Moreover, socialising and building personal rapport is often the most reliable way to build strong ties with potential partners. Therefore, expanding the social net is key to developing both friendships and business relations.

SMALL TALK

Almost always, Lebanese professional relations and meetings start with small talk. Often topics related to the weather, current affairs, the economy, politics, children and holidays are suitable for small talk. As long as one speaks English or French, it may not be necessary to hire a translator, since most Lebanese are at least bilingual.

Jokes are part of the Lebanese culture, so don't be surprised if your local counterparts slip in a joke or two about politicians, the governing system or any other serious matter. A sense of humour is part of the norm, even in most elite circles and in almost all circumstances.

Business Cards

Formal business cards are printed in two languages, namely Arabic on the main side, and French or English on the reverse side.

The Lebanese offer and receive business cards with the right hand at the start of meetings. The proper exchange takes place by offering it first to the most senior person, with the Arabic writing facing the receiver. They must always be presented and handled with respect, in a similar way to Western countries.

Business Attire

In all business situations being well groomed is essential, as the Lebanese tend to be stylish and chic all the time. The classic professional attire entails dark coloured suits and ties. Nevertheless, business casual dress code is becoming popular in various industries, especially amongst millennials and in tech industries.

Professional women tend to choose elegant and fashionable wardrobes. Trousers are acceptable in most communities and western style clothing is part of the norm for most of them. Women at work usually wear accessories and make-up. Moreover, in religiously conservative professional settings, women are advised to respect the dress code and cover their hair with a scarf before an encounter.

Family-Owned Businesses

As in most Arab cultures, respect, consideration and loyalty to the family are a priority for the Lebanese patriarchal society. The security offered by the family is regarded as the nucleus that strengthens its members, gives them peace of mind, leads them to self-growth, and ultimately to success.

Many successful businesses and corporations are family-owned, with key positions held by family members, due either to merit or to nepotism. It is best to eschew any form of disapproval regarding this matter. Foreigners should suggest their professional recommendations sensibly, making sure to mention praise and high regard first, in order to save face and preserve harmony and the family's dignity.

Honorifics

Courtesy titles and honorifics based on position and status are widely used in Lebanon. It is therefore important to address people respectfully according to their social, professional, religious or political ranks, such as 'Monsieur', 'Sheikh', 'Beik', 'Hajj', 'Madame', 'Mademoiselle', or 'Dr'. Honorifics are usually followed by the first name of people rather than the title followed by the last name.

Corporate Gifts

Corporate gifts are offered among business establishments and to valued customers. Most of the gift exchanges take place around the New Year and sometimes to valued customers during special occasions such as Mother's Day, Father's Day, Ramadan period and sales transactions related to exceptional asset purchases. Common corporate gifts generally include leather notebooks, desk clocks, company pens, desktop calendars, as well as gifts from select hampers supporting local charity organisations and national industries. When sending a corporate gift, send it with a handwritten note and make sure it suits the context and the cultural background of the recipient.

Chapter 7

Wedding etiquette

Most Lebanese favour lavish wedding celebrations over simple or minimalist ones. From the most financially comfortable families to the ones with limited budgets, they all consider this occasion worth spending on. Lebanese weddings are generally paid for by the groom or his family.

Invitation cards are sent four to six weeks in advance, taking into account the relatives and friends living abroad who need to organise their schedule and make the necessary travel arrangements to not miss the big day.

Guests must arrive at least ten minutes before the ceremony and half an hour before the reception, to not miss the bride's entrance, and ensure enough time to network and get seated before the *zaffé* begins.

The wedding day is marked by long sessions of photo shoots, enough to make every second of it memorable forever. Lebanese families are large in number, so adding that to invited friends and possibly public figures, the guest list is never a short one. Regardless of the budget, overindulgent food is offered generously, energizing the invitees for non-stop dancing to Arabic and Western songs played all throughout the evening. Those who can, invite prominent singers to create a lively atmosphere where the dancing and the singing become the high point of the evening. These receptions start late at night and last till dawn of the next day at least.

Lebanese weddings are truly a feast consisting of fine dining, live entertainment, and dancing till dawn. These celebrations also highlight family ties, friendships and the chance to appear generous, joyful and impressive.

Moreover, by law, all ceremonies are religious-based, and all marriages must be performed by religious authorities. Civil marriages are not yet performed in the country.

Ululation

Throughout the wedding, a loud high-pitched sound is voiced by some women, to express joy and excitement for the occasion. Usually, it takes place whilst the bride is getting ready, leaving her house by car, and at the reception with her newly-wed husband. It begins with a few verses of blessings and compliments to the bride for her character, her beauty, and the fine family she's marrying into, followed by the jubilation sounds.

Zaffé

Zaffé is an old tradition which now takes place with a modern twist. Today, it consists of a group of professional dancers and drummers wearing traditional folkloric costumes, who escort the newlywed couple to make a grand entrance into the reception hall where the guests are waiting, ushering the bride and groom to the dance floor. Once that performance is over, the couple is ready to have their first dance as 'Mr and Mrs' *groom's last name*.

Sometimes *zaffé* can also take place in front of the bride's house, before she and her family head to the wedding ceremony, where the *zaffé* group escorts her and the bridesmaids to her car.

In all cases, the tradition of tossing rice on the bride and groom at the end of the ceremony continues to this day, to symbolise fertility, good health and prosperity. In some communities, white pigeons are released as soon as the couple come out of the ceremony.

The Wedding Gift

Most of the time, weddings have a registered list or sometimes a bank account for the guests to make their contributions in lieu of gifts. The proper way is to get the gift or make the contribution before rather than after attending the wedding.

The invitation cards sent to those who are not close to the couple will not include a wedding list. As a sensible guest, one must still make the effort to offer something to the newly-wed, either by finding out about the list indirectly or by offering a heartfelt present when attending the wedding.

The Dress Code

Wedding dress code varies according to the religious and cultural factors affecting the ceremony, the reception, and how formal the occasion is overall. Timing and venue are good indicators to help make the right choice.

Formal receptions take place in the evening. With conservative religious weddings, one must respect traditions and wear clothes which cover the cleavage completely, ensure a height which is below the knee level and cover bare shoulders and upper arms.

Most formal weddings entail a black-tie dress code. Guests are welcomed to wear long evening gowns, should the dress code indicate it on the invitation card. Otherwise, for grand weddings, the long dresses and the tuxedos are worn by the immediate families of the couple. Lady guests may wear cocktail dresses with elegant accessories, and gentlemen may wear a dark suit with a white shirt and classic tie. For semi-formal receptions, besides short dresses, ladies can choose a classy trouser suit or even dressy skirts or trousers. In warmer weather, ladies can choose lighter fabrics and flowery dresses.

THE WEDDING CAKE

Modern day traditions include cutting the cake using a sword instead of a knife, with music and special lighting effects creating a spectacular scene for the photos. The groom places his hand on top of the bride's to cut the multi-tiered cake together to symbolise unity and feed each other the first bite of cake to represent a shared future. With this final ritual, guests are able to thank the couple and leave the reception!

This brings us to the end of the section about Lebanon! I'm confident that you'll find Lebanon an unforgettable destination and a unique blend of the East and West, once you get the chance to visit it!

Morocco
By Mariam Filali Meknassi

Chapter 1

Culture Symbols

Morocco is a modern country that has kept its traditions rooted in the mentality of Moroccans.

This first chapter brings together the Moroccan way of life and practices. This said, one should not imagine that customs and habits are absolutely uniform throughout the country. Moroccans living in the same city often differ more or less in their customs, as well as in their accent or dialect.

RECEPTION

The Moroccan is very welcoming and can invite you into his home by offering you a good mint tea with traditional cakes (*Mlouza*, *ghribiya*, gazelle horns…) or for a traditional meal (couscous, tagine, pastilla). Moroccan civility and politeness appear in all manifestations of life. The Moroccan has always sought to be polite and to act in such a way to make others feel comfortable.

Generally speaking, in Morocco, I would advise a man to wait for a woman to hold out her hand to greet, whether in the professional or social world. Several misunderstandings occur at that time, although today more and more Moroccan women are business leaders and even they know that in business etiquette, gender does not exist.

Tip: If you decide to reach out your hand spontaneously and the person in front of you does not respond to salutation by reaching out his or her hand, join your left hand to your right and put your right hand on your heart. The message you are sending is: *I respect your decision not to salute*.

The handshake is very warm and can end with a hug and kiss between men and also between women.

Women can refuse the handshake. To avoid any misunderstanding, it is preferable to wait for the woman to hold out her hand, especially in social situations.

HAND-KISSING

This custom can attract the attention of foreigners who come to Morocco. One kisses the hand out of respect for the elderly, whether female or male, or to a scholar (*Alem*) or the sovereign.

LOCAL CUISINE

Moroccan cuisine is rich in new flavours. Each region has its own dishes and there are many opportunities to discover them.

Couscous with seven vegetables or sweet and salty chicken, pastilla with chicken or fish, different tagines, *tanjiamarrackchi* are a few examples.

Renowned Moroccan chefs have modernised Moroccan cuisine. In different cities you can find local dishes revisited by chefs in gourmet restaurants.

Tip: If you invite a Moroccan into your home, remember to offer halal and alcohol-free food.

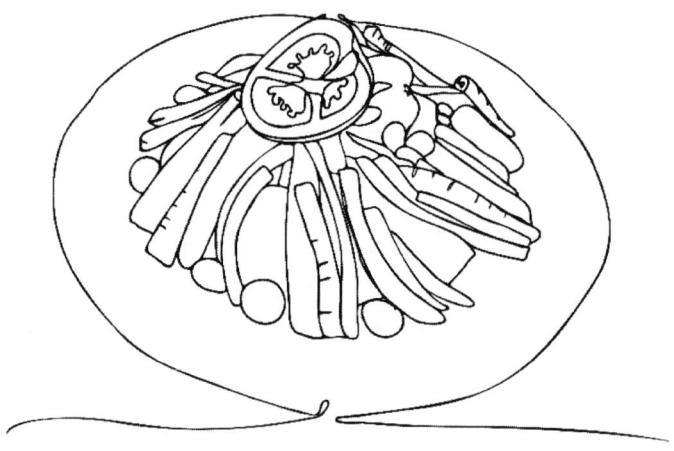

To Avoid!

If you have a dog, avoid bringing it close to a Moroccan. If necessary, do not allow the dog to sit on the same sofa as your Moroccan guest.

PUNCTUALITY

It must be recognised that Moroccan punctuality is almost non-existent except for new Moroccan entrepreneurs who have understood that time is worth its weight in gold. To understand this punctuality, I invite you to listen to Ismail Boukili, a Moroccan mathematician who did his research on this famous '*Moroccan rendez-vous*'. He concludes that 35.7 minutes should be considered as a lapse of time during a Moroccan appointment!

THE PERIOD OF RAMADAN

As Morocco is a Muslim country, Moroccans cannot eat on the day of Ramadan because it is illegal. It is good manners not to feast in front of Moroccans or to smoke in front of them. If you do not fast with them, be discreet when you are eating during the daytime, from dawn to dusk. Ramadan lasts one month. The date of the beginning and end of Ramadan is random and is proclaimed by the Ministry of *Habous* through an official communiqué.

THE MEAL DURING RAMADAN

The Moroccan always likes to be a great lord, very hospitable and likes to offer, even to the poor. He may invite you to break the fast with him during the period of Ramadan. Each region has its own ritual. The round coffee table will be decorated with the most beautiful table services including an embroidered tablecloth and matching napkins. The tureen in the middle and individual bowls will complete the service. You will find dates, honey cakes, and hard-boiled eggs. Afterwards, tea and coffee will be served with *Sellou* and salty food. Upon return from prayer, dinner is served.

The foreigner may be surprised by the quantity and richness of the food offered, but it is a ritual during the whole month of Ramadan where the Moroccan enjoys a good meal with his family.

To Avoid!

Do not criticise the way the country is governed, nor its leaders, by making fun of them, even if your thoughts diverge; do not look to impose your own habits and customs.

Moroccans are endowed with a certain humour; they love jokes; irony has an important place in Moroccan society but within limits.

FESTIVE PERIODS

The Muslim calendar is a lunar calendar. The Muslim holidays that use this calendar as a basis for setting the day of their celebration vary from year to year. The Ministry of *Habous* communicates the date of the celebration of religious holidays following the observation of the moon.

'Aïd Al-Fitr' (the small feast)
This is the feast of the breaking of the fast celebrated the day after Ramadan. It is a holiday. It is a day of relaxation where the family gathers around a copious and festive breakfast. Alms are distributed early in the morning on this day, called *'fetra'*, which means 'breaking the fast'. For each member of the family, a sum of money decided in advance is given. For example, one euro per person, per household.

'Aïd Al-Kébir' (the great feast)
The celebration of this festival coincides with the season of pilgrimage to Mecca. The tradition is that sheep are sacrificed in all Moroccan households according to ancestral customs.

Some tourists or foreigners may be surprised that such traditions can still be followed, when modern life has forced many families to leave the big houses for apartments in buildings. But the attachment to traditions knows no obstacle and we often see, on the eve of the festival, surrealist scenes such as a sheep in the bathroom or on the balcony, or a man in a city costume pushing a recalcitrant sheep in front of him in the street.

The 'Mouloud' (the Nativity of the Prophet Mohammed), the 12th Rabia the First, 570 AD
This is a holiday in most Muslim countries. The Moroccan family gathers and visits relatives and friends to exchange wishes and renew ties that could be strained by too long an absence.

The 1st Moharrem.
This is the Muslim New Year's Day and is a holiday in Morocco. The first Moharrem marks the beginning of the Muslim year. This year we celebrated the year 1440 *Anno Hegirae*.

Achoura
Achoura is not a holiday. It remains a simple day of recollection which corresponds to the tenth day of the 1st of Moharrem. The tradition allows children to receive gifts on this day; also, the souks are installed with *'kermesses'* where toys and sweets based on nougats and almonds are sold.

TRADITIONAL DRESS
The traditional dress is worn at a wedding or a baptism. The man can,

however, wear the traditional dress on a Friday, a sacred day in Morocco, to go pray at the mosque during lunch break. The woman will be satisfied with the shorter and sober modern djellaba to wear at work.

The traditional dress for men: Jellaba, shirt, *seroualkandrissa*, red *tarbouch* '*Le Fez*', babouche or traditional yellow '*belgha*'.

The traditional dress for women: *Takchita* composed of *Qmiss* (a tunic that slips under the caftan), *dfina* (caftan) which covers the whole body in addition to a belt (*mdama*).

Tip: A few words to remember.
- *Salam Alekum/Msal'khir*: Hello or good evening.
- *Labass*: How are you?
- *Smahli*: Sorry.
- *Bsslama*: Goodbye.
- *Choukran* (*bezaf*): Thank you (very much).
- *Ouakha/lae*: Yes/no.
- *Chhal*: How much?

Traditional Dress

- *Marhba*: Welcome.

I will conclude this chapter by quoting Mohamed El Alami who wrote in his book '*Protocol, habits and customs in Morocco*': 'If modern life attracts the Moroccan, if he dreams of being motorised and gadgetised at will, existence would be priceless in his eyes if it was devoid of the old-fashioned charms of his ancestral way of life, from tasting a good glass of mint tea prepared according to the rules, to the sybaritic spreading on these Moorish sofas stuffed with wool that he carries with him, even in his migrations abroad'.

Chapter 2

Meeting, Greeting, Posture and Body Language

HAND KISSING AND GREETING
In our country, we don't practice the kissing of a woman's hand, as in some European countries, but instead we kiss the hand of an elderly person, whether female or male, or the hand of a scientist.

It is common to also see men kissing each other and holding hands in the street.

Women can kiss each other two, three, four or five times at a time. It all depends on the region; you can even be kissed on the head out of respect.

Generally speaking, in Morocco, I would advise a man to wait for the woman to hold out her hand to greet him, whether in the professional or social world. Several misunderstandings take place at that time, although today more and more Moroccan women are becoming business leaders and they know that in business etiquette, gender does not exist.

A SALAM'OU ALAYKOUM!
When a person enters a room, they can say '*a salam'ou alaykoum*' (good morning to all) by sweeping their hand from right to left. This is a way to greet everyone without bothering to approach the people in the room.

The answer will simply be '*Alaykoum Assalam*'.

RECEPTION OF MOROCCANS
Moroccan civility and politeness appear in all manifestations of life. Moroccans have always sought to be decent and act with honour towards others.

Men have always worked, often unsuccessfully, to own a luxuriously decorated and furnished home. Whoever manages to achieve this opens it to friends and spends money to receive guests.

Hospitality

Moroccans always like to be good people. That is why they like to offer even to the poor. They will always offer you a cup of tea, accompanied by cakes or bread with olive oil when receiving you.

Humour

Moroccans are endowed with a certain humour; they like jokes, irony and have a perfect sense of ridicule. Irony, therefore, has an important place in Moroccan society. Incorrectness, impertinence, insolence and snobbery are ruthlessly attacked and ridiculed.

Religion

Young people are inculcated with a religious education. Young people are asked to be dignified, respectful of grown-ups, good to others, and charitable to the needy; they are required also not to smoke, drink alcohol, raise their voices, eat pork, or eat during *Ramadan*. In short, they must be a good Muslim who does not commit impropriety, impertinence or insolence when dealing with others.

Moroccan society is also characterised by its acute awareness of what is illicit and indecent (*Hchouma*).

Delicacy

Moroccans act as they would like others to act with them.

Chapter 3

Conversation Dos and Don'ts

Moroccans are warm and welcoming people who love to talk about their country and its history. Many cities have historical heritages. Moroccans have lived through historical events and are proud to talk about them and relate the customs of the past.

However, there are some topics to avoid.

Dos

Discussions revolving around family, traditions and customs. Moroccans are proud of their country and can talk for hours about Morocco.

The presence of foreign languages is limited to French and, to a lesser extent, Spanish.

English (or other languages, especially German) is confined to the educational space as a second foreign language.

Often the women get together to talk over tea and traditional cakes. We call these 'reunions' '*darat*' which take place once a month. Activities at these reunions include conversations, sharing of anecdotes, intimate discussions, charitable donations.

As for the men, they often get together in a cafe to discuss soccer. Soccer is an integral part of Moroccan life. We must take this into account before planning an event, otherwise we risk being alone!

Don'ts

Religion

Islam is the state religion. All Moroccans are born and die Muslim. The 'religion of the prophet' is omnipresent in the daily life of Moroccans.

'*Inch'Allah*' and '*Hamdoulilah*' come up very frequently during a discussion. It is therefore possible to talk about Islam with a Moroccan, ensuring avoidance of criticisms of the religion.

The King
Mohammed VI is very much appreciated by the Moroccan people. In addition to the political power he holds, the king is the leader of the believers and a direct descendant of the prophet, Mohammed. He is therefore fully legitimate in all that he does and can only be respected by his subjects.

If you want to criticise him or ask Moroccans what they think of their sovereign, the answer can only be positive!

Alcohol, Homosexuality and Sexuality
Often, people hide behind the notion of *'Lharam'* and *'hchouma'* to talk publicly about taboo subjects such as alcohol, homosexuality and sexuality.

Politics of the Country
This discussion remains generally avoided. The Moroccan will turn the discussion into derision and humour so as not to upset the other.

Personal Life
Moroccans will not easily open up about their personal life. The image of a perfect family life is linked to education and respects the members of the family and the name of family.

Chapter 4

Gift Giving

Giving a gift is an art, and if it is done well, an excellent social relationship is established.

The intention when you are given a gift is:
- To thank you.
- To please you.
- To congratulate you.
- To return a gift.

In Morocco, gifts are more decorative objects, like sets of silver trays, large vases, or a set of glasses. The more important the person is, the more expensive the gift.

The person receiving the gift will probably not open it right away.

As an expert, I educate people on how to make an impact when giving a gift: the timing, the card, the size, the packaging etcetera. Giving a gift requires the art of intuition and sensitivity. It requires you to know the person well. When giving and receiving a gift, do so with both hands and always be grateful. If you do not like a gift, you should not show this emotion. If you receive a package of sweets or cakes, you should share it with your guests.

WHAT TO OFFER
- Beautiful books on the different regions of Morocco or Moroccan cuisine.
- Paintings by Moroccan painters.
- Sculptures by Moroccan artists.
- Sets of pottery made by Moroccan creators.
- Purely Moroccan creations (the confinement allowed to put forward Moroccan creators).
- Beautiful bottles of *argan* oil, olive oil, rose oil…

THE DIFFERENT TYPES OF GIFTS
- Gift of thanks: if a person offers a gift, it is a positive gesture, and we must return the gesture. This gift must be discreet and not too expensive, being around the same price as the one received.
- Courtesy gift: a gift that we will give if we are invited to someone's home. It is an affectionate gesture for a good relationship.
- Institutional gift: corporate gift. In Morocco, on the 8th of March (the festival to celebrate Women's day), at the end of the year, and on retirement, gifts are given.
- Sentimental gifts: gifts for friends, relatives, lovers etcetera.
- Wedding gifts: gifts given to the bride and groom. These days, a wedding list is set up. Some will prefer to receive money, whilst others prefer objects of decoration for their future house.

GENERAL CONDITIONS TO OFFER A GIFT
- The type of gift will depend on the level of trust you have with the person. You must pay attention to their tastes and preferences.
- Find the best time to give the gift.
- The price of the gift should not be visible.
- Evaluate each situation to assess the budget.
- Avoid giving perfumes and creams unless you know the person well.
- Gifts must not be anonymous.
- When giving a book, read it first to see if it is fit for the person's taste.
- Do not give what you have been given.
- Do not give animals.
- Do not give a last minute gift because the receiver will feel it.

Chapter 5

Dining Etiquette

EVOLUTION OF SAVOIR-VIVRE IN MOROCCO
Even for the most hurried visitor, Morocco appears as a country different from others. One has the impression that there is a strange overlap between the modern and traditional.

In recent years, Moroccan society has witnessed the modification of certain customs, or even their disappearance.

In the space of a single generation, the customs of Moroccans have undergone almost revolutionary changes. Before, it was impossible for us to see older ladies breaking the fast outside their homes during *Ramadan* or spending the feast of the sacrifice of the sheep (*Aid El-Kbir*) in hotels!

Moroccan society is changing. The evolution is visible in all areas, and this is for several reasons. I quote two main ones that I have noted:
- Mixed marriages.
- The craze for French culture in some families reaches the point of abandoning the Arabic language.

The Moroccan youth has the right to reject customs and traditions that offend modern tastes for many reasons, for instance the excessive spending on feasts, and disappearance of the family in the broadest sense.

The large family houses in the *Medina* have been transformed into guest houses by foreigners and have given way to apartments in the city.

Concerning the uses of the table in Morocco, these have also been refined. Forks and knives made their appearance on round coffee tables, and plates now accompany the main dish placed in the middle.

During *Ramadan,* we see a mixture of the *tagine* dish and earthenware plates: a beautiful mixture between the modern and the traditional.

Moroccan working women revisit traditional dishes and lighten them, being inspired by chefs to create new flavours.

Another example is the fate of the *Djellaba* and the traditional *Caftan* which have been transformed into brightly coloured and sometimes even garish mini-djellabas and mini-caftans.

FORMAL MEAL

In Moroccan protocol, the meal table must be a place marked by *conviviality* allowing for exchange and sharing. A precise idea of the final presentation of a dish on the plate that will be served to the guests makes it possible to imagine a harmonious decor by reconciling colours and aromas.

It is advisable to provide enough space between each guest so that they can feel comfortably seated at the table (about 40 centimetres between each guest's plates). All this depends on the number of guests who will be seated at the table and the width of the chairs.

The cutlery is always installed according to the order of arrival of the different dishes planned during a meal. Forks are placed on the left side of the plate, whilst knives and spoons are placed on the right. The knives have the blade facing the plate. Forks and spoons are placed flat: the tines and the hollow are positioned upwards.

In the diplomatic missions of Morocco, the cutlery is generally placed on a round table.

The plates are aligned so that they are strictly facing each other. Traditionally, they are arranged as follows:

- Presentation plates will be arranged first, when available. These plates are large subplates that will be kept on site to prevent the table from becoming bare between meals. If table space is limited, it is preferable not to use the presentation plates because their diameter is particularly large (about 28 centimetres in diameter).
- A plate is placed on the presentation plate.
- Then the bread plate is placed at the top left of the setting.
- The salad plate is placed on the first plate.
- The guest's napkin is placed on the last flat plate.
- If the last plate is hollow, the napkin will be placed on the left before the forks.
- Two glasses will be placed on the right of the guest:
- A juice glass.
- A water glass.

The glasses are arranged with the largest glass on the left and smallest on the right.

Novelty

I introduced the tea glass on the official table; it will be placed behind the two glasses.

Tea is a drink that accompanies the various dishes in Morocco. Depending on the region, the infusion time differs. In the north, you will be offered a light and fragrant tea, whilst in other regions it will be more full-bodied and with bubbles.

The Dimensions of the Plates According to Their Function

The flat plate: the diameter of the flat plate is between 23 and 25 centimetres.
- The dessert plate: the diameter of the dessert plate is about 21 centimetres.
- The cake plate: the diameter of the cake plate is 19 centimetres.
- The bread plate: 16 centimetres.
- Soup plates and bowls:
- The classic soup plate with a rim: it is used for reception/occasion meals.
- The soup plate without rim: it is rather used for family meals.
- The broth bowl.
- Salad bowl.

The Centrepiece

A pretty flowered centrepiece will be placed in the centre of the table.

The Dress

The traditional dress will be worn in official and protocolary receptions in Morocco.

The traditional dress for men will be composed of the *Djellaba*, shirt, *saroual kandrissa*, red *tarbouche* '*Le Fez*', *babouche* or traditional yellow '*belgha*', and white socks.

The traditional dress for women will be composed of the *Qmiss* (a tunic which slips under the *caftan*), and the *mansouria* (*caftan* which covers the whole, in addition to a belt; it is also called *Dfina*).

The Music

Music is very present in our culture. We can find three musical styles in modern Morocco: classical music called Andalusian music, folk music and modern music.

Perfume

Sandalwood resin is burnt in a perfume lamp called '*mricha*', which is made of copper.

Service
- The service will be done in English.
- The hostess or a waiter will serve food directly to your plate.

Perfume Lamp

INFORMAL MEAL

In Morocco, the house is the women's domain, their secret garden. Their happiness and their satisfaction depends on how they occupy this space and how they furnish it.

To understand our culture, it is necessary to admit that the beautiful replaces the useful.

WELCOME

When you are invited, the hostess will receive you in a large Moroccan lounge decorated with coloured fabrics and chandeliers.

Our culture does not neglect the superfluous and everything is put in its place. It is not done in a spirit of display but in the pure tradition to keep this warm and exceptional welcome.

A round table will be privileged. The modern Moroccan table has introduced forks and knives, plates, and the main course will remain in the middle.

THE MENU

The Menu Will Be Composed Of Moroccan Dishes. The Moroccan Cuisine

Is Rich In Colours and spices. When receiving, the hostess will be delighted to prepare the great festive dishes. It is unsurprising that the Moroccans always provide quantities that go beyond the number of guests. The presence of bread at the table is as important as rice for the Chinese. Moroccan salads will be placed around the main course.

In an informal meal, Moroccans will use their index finger and thumb to eat directly from the main dish placed in the centre of the table, aided by a piece of bread.

Only one glass will be placed on the table to serve with water or soda.

THE TEA CEREMONY

A tea after the meal will be offered, with Moroccan cakes to conclude. The cakes are meticulously prepared by the mistress of the house or bought in a pastry shop. You will also be offered to take the cakes with you to enjoy them quietly, especially after a meal.

Chapter 6

Business Etiquette

Today, in politics or in daily business life, Moroccans strive to apply the rules of good conduct and good manners, so as not to embarrass people. Since cultures are different, it is necessary to have good knowledge of the rules that are in force in each country with which a Moroccan deals. The important thing is to find a balance of an international nature. Moroccans are very observant and quick to learn. When working with people from different cultures, they realise that there is an effort to be made to offer courteous service and they understand that a solid knowledge of the rules of etiquette will influence the outcome of the business. The 'business etiquette' module is not yet part of the university curriculum. One of my challenges is to introduce it as a 'module' in the last year of the student's course (of any discipline) before entering the business world!

THE PRESENTATIONS

Moroccans respect hierarchy. They will proudly introduce you to their superior.

The customer is '*king*'. In the business world, Moroccans will make an exception to their normal hierarchical rules and consider the customer as if they were '*the most important person on earth*'.

The Moroccan women hold important positions in the business world and are aware that gender does not exist in this environment. She may invite you to a meal, open the door for you, or offer you a coffee, like any other businessman.

To introduce themselves, a Moroccan will use their first and last names, the family name to honour their father. The presentation will be brief and they will use abbreviations out of habit; for example, 'I work at OCP' (*Office Chérifien du Pétrole*). Do not hesitate to ask the meaning of the initials to know the institution in which they work.

Do not be surprised if they also call you by your first name, as being addressed formally is not automatic, just awkward. Our culture is very welcoming and our main goal is to make the other person feel comfortable.

EXCHANGING HANDSHAKES

Moroccans are very warm, and their handshake is soft and lasts longer than in other cultures and may end with a hug and kiss between the men. If you withdraw your hand too quickly, this gesture can be considered as a lack of politeness and as a refusal.

Women may refuse the handshake. To avoid misunderstanding, it is better to wait for the woman to extend her hand.

The Moroccan will remain seated if you extend your hand.

In the event that you extend your hand and the other does not respond, join your left hand to your right hand and place your right hand over your heart. You will convey a message of respect to the person.

The look is shy, this is due to the education received to establish respect for the other.

THE USE OF TITLES DURING OFFICIAL MEETINGS

A Moroccan may preface their name with '*Sidi*' or '*Lalla*'. These 'titles' are a form of respect for the family.

TELEPHONE CONVERSATIONS AND NETIQUETTE

The use of the telephone is a fast and efficient tool for the Moroccan.

A Moroccan will be very spontaneous and respond in a friendly manner. He will forget to introduce himself or send his name in messages.

They may use 'short' formulas to answer a message (example: SMS, WhatsApp)…

The response of an email or a message will not be automatic and is not yet well anchored. Don't be surprised if they do not answer; it will only be because they do not know the etiquette rule.

THE HANDING OVER OF THE BUSINESS CARD

The business card is always available and do not be surprised if the Moroccan gives it to you at any time. In the luxury service, you will receive it with both hands. This is a way to distinguish yourself.

When you give a business card, a Moroccan will take the time to read it and compliment it.

The follow-up by email or phone will be done the next day, to arrange to make a courtesy visit in the professional place of each.

BUSINESS MEALS
- Business meals are frequently organised. You will find restaurants that offer '*business lunch*' menus.
- The managers of a company will invite their clients and suppliers to talk about a negotiation or a future collaboration over a meal.
- The employees of companies go once a week to the restaurant to de-stress after work, and you will often find a team with their manager.
- The atmosphere is relaxed and '*bon enfant*'.
- The Moroccan will choose renowned gastronomic restaurants.
- In the gastronomic restaurants, the proposed menus are international and Moroccan. Alcohol may also be offered.

TIPPING
Tips are a way to thank for the service. On average, they correspond to 10% of the total amount of the bill. They are not obligatory but are customary.

DRESS CODE
There is no real importance given to the dress code. Business attire is worn by managers, bankers and high-ranking civil servants (male or female).

Friday is a casual day; some employees may wear traditional dress (*jellaba*).

THE RAMADAN PERIOD
As Morocco is a Muslim country, Moroccans cannot eat on the days of Ramadan because it is illegal.

As mentioned before, it is good manners not to eat in front of Moroccans and not to smoke in front of them during this time.

If you do not fast with them, be discreet when you eat, during the day, from dawn to dusk.

Ramadan lasts one month. The date of the beginning and the end of Ramadan is random and it is proclaimed by the Ministry of *Habous* through an official communiqué.

NETWORKS AND ASSOCIATIONS
Several professional networks allow foreigners to meet around via

networking to develop their business, to have more visibility, and to expand their contacts. We can mention the *French Chamber of Commerce, the Spanish Chamber of Commerce, the Moroccan Chamber of Commerce*, the *Entreprendre Network,* and the Business International Networking (BNI) as notable networking hubs.

Associations are also present to welcome French speakers: *Tanger Accueil, Casa Accueil, Rabat Accueil, Maroc Amitié*. These associations offer activities such as discovering the city, learning the *Darija* language, and discovering Moroccan culture (dance workshop, cooking).

The Moroccan society is in full mutation. The installation of the LGV (the Moroccan high speed line trains) has saved time for entrepreneurs who wish to work outside their city and to move easily. Foreign companies are settling in and draining the economy. The will to modernise is evident in the construction of roads, ports (*Tangier Med I* and *Tangier Med II*), bridges and the opening of airlines by various low-cost companies to Europe.

Chapter 7

Wedding Etiquette

Wedding ceremonies are practices that are specific to each city and region.

I will only cover the important ceremonies, as it would take a whole book to cover such a very large subject in detail.

The bride performs the '*hina*' (henna) ceremony three days before the wedding.

After a *hammam*, the bride is surrounded by young girls and her family, and they talk and have tea. A '*m'alma l'hanaya*', a woman whose profession is to dye women using henna, makes a drawing on the bride's hands and feet called '*l'hanna bet-taqwissa*'; this is only done for brides.

Henna

The next day, '*nagaguef*' (the nagaguef are women who help the bride get ready) come to dress the bride. When she is dressed, she is taken to the living room, where the guests have come to admire her.

The *nagaguefs* put her on a low table and onto their shoulders, where the bride can dance whilst they sing:

'*ha hya ya lalla, ha hiya fi darna*', meaning 'here she is Ö madam, here she is, in our house'.

This ceremony, called '*d-dora*', takes place in the evening and during the whole time it lasts, the '*tabbalat*' musicians play and the other women sing traditional songs.

The formula '*tbark allah*', 'may God be blessed', is a common charm against the evil eye.

The bride usually keeps her eyes closed out of modesty.

The mother of the bride places a small amount of money in the cup which one of the '*ngaguef*' holds in their hands and lifts the tulle that covers her daughter's face and kisses her on both cheeks; then she makes her drink some milk from a container held by another '*nagaguef*', and takes a date from a bowl held by a third.

All the women present do the same, one after the other. This is called '*slam*' (greetings). The money is intended to pay the '*ngaguefs*'; the purpose of the milk is to make the bride's life 'white', and the dates symbolise fortune.

The next day, we celebrate '*lila kbira*'. The men of the bride's family and other friends are invited. They are received to the sound of *Andalusian* music. They are offered food and delicacies. They remain seated until the groom's people come for the bride.

Moroccan weddings can last all night. A hearty dinner is offered to the guests followed by tea and Moroccan cakes.

Close family may offer money or gifts for the bride and groom's future home.

The dress code is traditional Moroccan dress. Women will wear their most beautiful *caftan*, adorned with sumptuous jewellery and a gold belt.

The men may wear the traditional *djellaba* or his business suit and tie.

The bride will change several times during the evening, highlighting the traditions of several regions by wearing several outfits.

The bride will close the ceremony with a modern white dress or a white *caftan*.

Her wedding *trousseau*, composed of beautiful hand embroidered pieces, is sent to the bridal room to prepare the bed.

It is true that today these traditions are somewhat discarded and young people are content with a beautiful mixed party where the bride enjoys eating and dancing with her husband and guests.

Pakistan
By Dr Sadia Javed Rajput

Chapter 1

Cultural Symbols

'*Pakistan ka Matlab Kiya, La illa ha illal lah*' means: 'What do you mean by Pakistan? There is no God except Allah'. These were the words glued to the tongues of Muslim freedom fighters back in 1947, who sacrificed their lives, valuables and properties at the time of partition of India and Pakistan. The only notion in their minds was to have an independent piece of land, where they could practice their religion freely. They left half of their families back in India, lost the blood of their siblings and small children on their way, and only a small group of people managed to reach this much longed-for homeland safely. That is how our forefathers entered the boundaries of Pakistan.

FLAG

After the Second World War, when Muslims and Hindus lived under rule of the British Raj, Indian Viceroy, Louis Mountbatten, proposed a design for Pakistan flag, which was the flag of the Muslim League but with a Union Jack in the corner. It was rejected by the Muslim League leader, Muhammad Ali Jinnah because he felt that the Muslims of Pakistan would not accept a flag featuring a Christian Cross alongside the Islamic Crescent. Hence, a new flag proposed by the Muslim League, fresh green and white with a crescent and a star, inspired from the flag of the Sultanate of Delhi, the flag of Ottoman Empire and the Flag of the Mughal Empire, was accepted.

The green colour represents Muslims, who are undoubtedly in the majority, and the white portion demonstrates the religious minorities. The crescent is a symbol of progress, and a five-pointed star represents light and knowledge. It embodies the commitment of Pakistan to Islam and the rights of non-Muslims, which are undoubtedly protected and taken special care of.

Language

Urdu, a vibrant language, which is quickly spoken and understood all over the country, is the official language and medium of communication between all the provinces of Pakistan. Other languages spoken are Sindhi, Punjabi, Balochi, Pashto, Siraiki and English.

Literature and Poetry

Poetry has always proved to not just affect but transform the hearts and minds of people. Sufi poets occupy an honoured place as Data Ganj Bakhsh, Lal Shahbaz, Shah Abdul Lateef, Hazrat Sultan Bahu and Waris Shah rendered meritorious services for the spread of Islam in the subcontinent.

Dress

Though all the provinces have their traditional dress, *Shalwar Kameez* is the national dress. Since Pakistan is an amalgam of a very diversified population and has been under the British Raj, western clothes are equally welcomed.

Food

All the food available in Pakistan is strictly halal, under the Islamic rules. Wine is only allowed to be consumed by religious minorities. There is no national dish, but all love 'biryani', 'pulao' and 'chicken tika'.

Tourism

Pakistan is a land of great adventure and nature. Trekking, mountaineering, skiing, white water rafting, wild boar hunting, mountain and desert jeep safaris, camel and yak safaris, trout fishing and bird watching are a few activities which lure the adventure and nature lovers to Pakistan.

PLACES TO VISIT
The point where the Indian Plate meets the Eurasian Plate:

In Gilgit Baltistan, around 130 million years ago, when the Indian plate moved northwards as continents drifted, it collided with the Eurasian plate which was already present in the north. From the day of the collision, the movement of the Indian plate hasn't stopped, and slowly and gradually momentum continues. The rate of Indian plate movement is 45 millimetres a year nowadays, increasing the height of the Karakoram Range mountains.

Kaghan Valley, Naran Valley, Hunza Valley, and Shangirlla are a few of the beautiful gems of Pakistan nature.

Mohenjo-Daro:
'The Mound of the Dead', from around 2500 BC, is an archaeological site in the province of Sindh. It was one of the largest settlements of the ancient Indus Valley Civilization, and one of the world's earliest major cities, contemporaneous with the civilizations of ancient Egypt, Mesopotamia, Minoan Crete, and Norte Chico.

Chapter 2

Meeting, Greeting, Posture and Body Language

Over a thousand years before the Western psychology was constructed, the psychological language of the Quran (The Holy book of Muslims) described destructive emotions. It provides guidance to overcome the inner turmoil and bring a peaceful self into being. It gives the primordial soup for success and lays a great emphasis on having good mental health and emotional well-being; hence, a good posture and body language is a serendipitous result of maintaining a well-balanced inner self.

In Pakistan, predominantly, people have a joint family system; the head of the family is the oldest person, and they educate their grandchildren. Children spend their childhood listening to stories about heroes who move around with vigour and confidence and carry themselves flawlessly. 'Stand up tall, do not slouch, do not slump at your desk', are the common words heard by the children and are hence no more different than western etiquette. Besides, children are told that they should stand tall because of their religion and that this is something that they should be proud of; otherwise, people will think less of them. People pick up on messages we often don't even realise we're sending through small changes in our body language.

It is recommended you stand in a way that if you were to draw an imaginary line falling from the earlobes, it should land on the shoulders. Neuroscience research has proven that the mind controls the body, and the body influences the mind; therefore, if you want to keep a good state of mind, the best way to attain this is to keep a straight posture.

The same rule applies for your posture when sitting.

BODY LANGUAGE
It can be broken down into three core elements: presence, power and warmth. These elements depend both on our conscious behaviours and on factors we do not consciously control. To be charismatic, we need to choose

mental states that make our body language, words, and behaviours flow together.

Presence:

Presence means being fully present in the moments of our interactions. We may think that we can fake presence. We may feel that we can pretend to listen. We believe that as long as we seem attentive, it's okay to let our brains churn over other things. But we are very wrong. When we are not fully present in an interaction, people will see it. Our body language sends a clear message that other people read and react to, at least on a subconscious level. We have a specialised set of neurons (brain cells) called mirror neurons. The word mirror defines their salience because of their ability to reflect the other persons' mind. It also helps us build intuition.

Since the human mind can read facial expressions in as little as seventeen milliseconds[1], the person you are speaking with will likely notice even the tiniest delays in your reactions.

Not only is the lack of presence visible, it can also be perceived as inauthentic, which has even worse emotional consequences. When you are perceived as such, it is almost impossible to build trust, rapport and connect with people.

The good news is that presence is a learnable skill. You can increase it with practice and patience. In Islam, God asks his believers to pray five times a day and follow the etiquette religiously.

Regarding etiquette of prayer, the most prominent is to focus entirely on the presence of God and stop thinking about the worldly matters; this, in turn, facilitates an enduring control over the normal functioning of the brain and ability to build presence.

Olivia Fox writes in her book, *Charisma Myth*: 'The very next time you're in a conversation, try to regularly check whether your mind is fully engaged or whether it is wandering elsewhere (including preparing your following sentence). Aim to bring yourself back to the present moment as often as you can by focusing on your breath or your toes for just a second, and then get back to focusing on the other person'.

---

[1] Neural and behavioural evidence for effective priming from unconsciously perceived emotional facial expressions and the influence of trait anxiety, *Journal of cognitive neuroscience*: 20, 2003. 95–107).

Power and Warmth:

The word power is perceived as having authority, and we see it in someone's appearance and in their reaction to others. Most prominent is their body language, which acts as a mirror and reflects their inner self.

Warmth, on the other hand, is someone's goodwill towards others. The warmth gives us an impression of whether people will want to use whatever power they have in our favour. Being seen as warm in the world means people believe you are caring, loving and impact the world in a positive way.

When it comes to etiquette and creating an unforgettable first impression, warmth works like an enchanting spell over the person you interact with. Figuring out who might help us and who is in our favour has always been critical to our survival since the time of cavemen, hence our inherited instinct is deeply wired in our brains.

Portraying impeccable body language is a serendipitous result of a profound control over brainwork. It is not hard for others to pick up on a fake or genuine smile, and they can spot the difference in mere milliseconds. So, charismatic behaviours should originate at your brain level, otherwise all your efforts will be in vain.

Here again, the balance between the inner peace and the intention to impact the world positively helps you make memorable first impressions, as what your mind believes, your body manifests.

Visiting a Pakistani House

In Pakistan, it is advisable to wear clothes that adequately cover your body. Our national dress is a *Shalwar* (pants) and *Kameez* (top). Though the younger generation prefer to wear western clothes, it is considered indecent to put on an immodest outfit. Covering the head is not a requisite.

Whenever you meet someone for the first time or encounter your family in the morning, the first thing to do is say '*Assalam o alikum*' which means, 'peace be upon you'. If one wishes to cast a better impression and show warmth, you may place your right hand over your chest and say '*Asalam o alikum*'.

'Make eye contact, smile and handshake' are the old rules of meeting someone and remain unchanged in Pakistan. Your eyes are the window to your soul; they reflect your inner psychology because they are the most mobile part of the entire face, and so, the most expressive. Good eye contact is incredibly important. Profound eye contact can have a powerful impact on people; it can communicate empathy and give an impression of thoughtfulness, wisdom, and intelligence. You cannot make a great impression on anyone without eye contact. Anthropologist Helen Fisher explains that when you stare with intensity at someone, it can speed up their heart rate and send a hormone called phenylethylamine, or PEA, coursing through their bloodstream. PEA is the same hormone that produces the phenomenon we call 'love at first sight'.

SMILE

Our facial expressions, voice, posture, and all the other components of body language reflect our mental and emotional condition every second. Smiling is considered as a micro-expression which can tell our internal mental state straight away. In a genuine smile, eyes widen, while the outer corners of the mouth lift, and the inner corners of the eyebrows soften and fall down. In a fake smile, only the mouth-corner muscle (the zygomatic major) is used. The smile does not reach the eyes, or at least not in the same way a real smile would[2], and people can spot the difference.

HANDSHAKE

In more formal situations, the handshake plays a vital role in building a strong rapport. Its rules follow the same pattern as a western handshake:
- The fingers together and thumb is positioned at the right angle.
- The hand web meets the hand web of the other.
- Firm hand grip.

Through emotional contagion, your emotions can spread to other people. As a leader, the emotions conveyed by your body language, even during brief, casual encounters, can have a ripple effect on your team or even your entire company.

---

[2] P. Ekman, R. J. Davidson, and W. V. Friesen, 'The Duchenne Smile: Emotional Expression and Brain Physiology: II', Journal of Personality and Social Psychology 58, no. 2 (1990): 342–53.

Chapter 3

Conversation Dos and Don'ts

As we have seen, body language and other non-verbal clues can emit various messages that we can use to communicate even before a single word is spoken. In this chapter, we will learn tips to portray your presence and good mental state by listening, warmth and power, as well as throw light upon the dos and don'ts of conversations in Pakistan.

Being a great listener can make people feel ultimately heard and understood without saying a word. It's remarkably easy to impress people just by listening attentively.

LISTENING ATTENTIVELY
John F Kennedy was known to be a superb listener; his excellent listening skills helped him pay close attention to the feelings of whomever he was interacting with, enabling him to establish rapport on an intense, emotional level[3].

Tips to avoid the mind wandering whilst listening:
• If zoning out is the issue, bring yourself back to moment by focusing on physical sensations, like the feeling in your toes, or your breath flowing in and out of your body.
• If impatience is the issue, handle it by delving into the subtle physical sensations you're feeling. Then get back to the person.

To be a good listener, you must never interrupt people whilst they are talking, no matter how excited you are. And when other people interrupt you, no matter how wrong it was, never make them feel wrong; always make them feel right/at ease. If you see the other person repeatedly wishes to interrupt, keep your sentences short and give frequent pauses to allow them to interrupt.

---

[3] Ronald E. Riggio, *The Charisma Quotient: What It Is, How to Get It, How to Use It* (New York: Dodd Mead: 1988), 76

Master listeners know one extra trick, one simple but extraordinarily effective habit that will make people feel genuinely listened to and understood: they pause before they answer. The pianist, Artur Schnabel once said, "The notes I handle no better than many pianists. But the pauses between the notes—ah, that is where the art resides." [4]

When someone has finished speaking, show facial expressions intentionally to make them feel that you have absorbed everything like a sponge; use your zygomatic muscles and eye muscles to show them that they are adequately understood.

So, the sequence goes something like: when someone finishes talking:
- Your face absorbs.
- Then your face reacts.
- Count to three in your mind.
- Then, and only then, should you speak.

SPEAK TO DAZZLE

Choosing the right words circumspectly at the right moment is a real art in communication. Dale Carnegie said, "You can make more friends in two months by becoming truly interested in other people than you can in two years by trying to get other people interested in you."[5]

Dos of Conversation:

Throughout childhood, children are taught in Pakistan to follow the following rules as implemented by God in the Quran.

- When a (courteous) greeting is offered to you, meet it with a more courteous greeting or at least of equal courtesy. God takes careful account of all things (Quran: 4:86).
- Whenever you speak, speak justly, even if a near relative is concerned (Quran: 6:152). In the Quran, it is also written, 'O you who believe! Stand out firmly for God, as witnesses to fair dealing, and let not the hatred of others to you make you swerve to wrong and depart from justice. Be just; that is next to piety, and fear God. For God is well-acquainted with all that you do' (Quran 5:8).

---

[4] (Artur Schnabel, in *Chicago Daily News*, June 11, 1958).

[5] Dale Carnegie, *How to Win Friends and Influence People* (New York: Simon & Schuster, 1936).

- Whenever you speak, do not follow your vain desires. Conscientiously, choose the right words that will leave an impact on the world around you.
- Keep your voice low, 'And be moderate in your pace (walk humbly), and lower your voice' (Quran 31:19).
- The way to respond to evil in accordance with Quran (41: 34–35) is: 'Nor can goodness and evil be equal. Repel the evil deed with the best possible response. Then the one between whom and you there was enmity will your best friend and intimate'!
- If someone compliments you, stop, absorb the compliment, enjoy it if you can, let that second of absorption show on your face, and show the person that they've had an impact. Thank them. Saying, "Thank you very much" is enough, but you can take it a step further by thanking them for their thoughtfulness or telling them that they've made your day.

Don'ts of Conversation in Pakistan:
- Do not mock others. About mockery, the Quran (49:11) states, 'O you who believe! Let not some men among you laugh at others, it may be that the latter are better than the former; nor let some women laugh at others, it may be that the latter are better than the former; nor defame nor be sarcastic to each other, nor call each other by offensive nicknames; ill-seeming is a name connoting wickedness, to be used of one after he has believed. And those who do not desist are indeed doing wrong'.
- The Quran writes also about spying and backbiting: 'O you who believe! Avoid suspicion as much as possible; for suspicion in some cases is a sin. And do not spy on each other behind their backs nor shall you backbite one another' (Quran 49:12).

The temptation to gossip can be immense. Gossiping, at its best, is unproductive. It doesn't achieve anything other than to spread a story or personal information about someone who probably doesn't want it shared—true or not. At its worst, it can hurt people's feelings, their careers, or their relationships with others.

What is the difference between sharing an anecdote involving other people and gossiping? In the former, you're telling a story you know to be true, that you would have no problem telling in front of the people in it. Gossiping, on the other hand, is relaying rumours, or even true stories about someone, that are somewhat personal or at least not things that you would ever say in front of that person. If whatever you're saying might be embarrassing to the person it relates to, or they might want it kept private for any reason whatsoever, then it's gossip. Imagine that person is right next to you as you are telling your story. Would you be embarrassed if they overheard you? If the answer is yes, don't gossip.

Moreover, gossip sows the seed of negative thoughts which grows like an embryo. It is much easier to not to sow a seed rather than pulling out a deep-rooted oak tree.

Chapter 4

Gifts Giving

The experience of watching someone's eyes widening and the upward curling of the mouth corners is hugely gratifying, especially if it is due to a gift you gave them! But choosing a gift is not always easy. Choosing the right gift for the right occasion sometimes turns out to be an impregnable barrier, if not worked out cautiously and under the culture's social and religious norms. Giving a perfect gift does not require spending a lot of money. It is more a case of thinking about the recipient and what they like, what they value, and what memories you have together.

We often receive what we desire for others. Having a big heart, with generous intentions to add value in the lives of the people that cross your path, is the greatest gift. Prophet (peace be upon him) said, 'smiling in your brother's face is an act of charity' (At-Tirmidhi; Declared Authentic by Al-Albani). At another place, Abu Hurairah (Prophet's companion) narrated that the messenger of Allah said: 'You cannot satisfy people with your wealth but satisfy them with your cheerful faces and good morals'.

Seen in this light, our noblest intentions alone can do the job for gifting. Still, our visceral drive to purchase an appropriate gift for the right occasion can work wonders for building an unfathomable trust and connection.

People in Pakistan usually exchange gifts at almost every occasion. This plays a vital role in strengthening relationships at different events, from paying a visit, to weddings and business meetups.

If you want to give a present when you visit someone's house, a beautiful bunch of flowers can be enough. Additionally, if the person you are visiting is more than a mere acquaintance, then a gift (non-alcoholic) priced between PKR 2000 to PKR 5000 is adequate. It could be just a small souvenir, a decoration piece or chocolates and sweets.

When it comes to weddings, rules change. Pakistani culture is a vast canvas weaved from of various historic invasions and emblazoned with rich religious colours. Weddings are one of the most widely celebrated events. People in remote areas keep a record of the amount of money given as a gift by the giver and the recipient. They are either supposed to add to the amount received or return the same amount received when reciprocating.

Remember that while paying to travel to your friend's wedding is incredibly kind of you, you do so because you love them and want to be present to support them; it does not count as a gift for the bride and groom.

Office-oriented gift giving is a little different. You by no means have to give your boss a gift for the holidays or their birthday, but if you like them, you might genuinely want to. If you are unsure what to do, ask a co-worker what the office culture is. There might be rules against gift giving, or your team might like to pitch in for group gifts.

If you do end up buying one on your own, small and thoughtful gifts are the way to go. Simple leather office products are pretty safe choices.

If you want to buy gifts for your co-workers, small and thoughtful are again the key. When you are buying for your whole office or team, you can give the presents at the office party. If you're only buying for one or two close friends, give them the gifts privately, so no one's feelings get hurt.

If you are on the receiving end of a gift, no matter who it is from or if you love it or hate it, be delighted that someone thought of you and gave you something. Your reaction should not be to the gift itself so much as the lovely, thoughtful gesture of someone giving you a gift. A warm 'thank you', and a compliment about the gift or a simple 'This is so thoughtful'! will make you a gracious gift recipient.

Chapter 5

Dining Etiquette

Whether it's a new co-worker, acquaintance, date or your business partner, we often get to know them over a dining table. Having considerable knowledge of table manners provides you with an upper edge over your peers, eases your apprehensions, and builds confidence to close business deals.

Etiquette is not about having fixed codes of behaviour; it's more about making the other person feel comfortable in your presence. Someone very nicely stated, 'treat others the way you would want to be treated'.

A few etiquette tips are universally applicable, and few differ vastly with geographical borders and religious norms. The first half of the chapter will deal with basic etiquette rules and the latter half with where the Islamic ideology clashes with the western dining etiquette.

BASIC ETIQUETTE TIPS
- Before you walk into a restaurant or a dinner party, make sure you switch off your mobile phone or at least silence it in respect to the host and other invitees: what the host is asking from you is your moment-to-moment awareness of what is happening, that is, your attention, and our chief distraction is our mobile phone. It is a good rule to follow when with your friends, but almost mandatory when you are in a business meeting.
- When you sit at the table, place the napkin on your lap. The napkin stays in place as long as you are seated; the minute you get up from your seat, pick up the napkin and place it on the table in a way that it stays clean, and when you return to your seat, place the napkin on your lap again. When you finish eating, place it to the left side of your plate; this lets the server know when to clear your place.
- Cut one bite of the food at one time and chew it well.
- Do not season the food with salt and pepper until you have tasted the food.

- Wait until everyone is seated and has been served.
- Pass the plates of food in a counterclockwise fashion.
- Follow your host's lead if you are in doubt of how to eat something.
- Break the 'chapati' or bread in two halves first, then break it into small pieces and eat with curry, either directly with the hand or you can eat the curry filling with the help of a fork.
- Say you like the food if you do like it, and sit politely smiling if you don't like it. Do not show your dislike at the table.
- If you have dietary restrictions, let your host know beforehand or call the restaurant before you go to make sure they can accommodate you. Don't wait until you sit down to tell everyone you can't eat anything on offer.
- If you have to leave the table in the middle of the meal, wait for a lull in the conversation and say, "Please excuse me for a moment." No details or further explanation are necessary. Place your napkin on your chair and attend to your business quickly. Try to come back to the table in no more than a few minutes.
- Catch the server's eye and nod or wave lightly if you need something. Don't ever snap your fingers to get the attention of the server.

How Islam Differs With Western Etiquette?
Use of Right Hand for Eating and Drinking:
"When anyone eats, let him eat with his right hand and when he drinks let him drink with his right hand," said Prophet Muhammad, peace be upon him. At another place, he said, "When a man enters his house, he should enter with his right foot first and then his left and say '*bismillah*', when eating he should use his right hand and say '*bismillah*'." And if you don't want to do this, then Satan says to the other devils, that you have a house to live in and a place to eat here (Quoted by Imam Muslim). This way, we invite the devil to share our home and eat with us.

So, whenever you dine in a Pakistani house, one needs to mindful of this etiquette.

Eating Rice
Again, there is a great deal of controversy when eating rice, and many prefer eating with their hands directly and not using any spoon or fork. It doesn't matter; whether you use any utensils or eat with your right hand, the correct way is to take small mouthfuls and chew the food properly before

swallowing. We should be thankful to God that he has provided us with the opportunity to tantalise our taste buds. If we do not chew the food nicely, then we are intentionally depriving ourselves of gratification.

How to Eat With Fork and Knife?
Ideally, the knife is held in the right hand and fork in the left in the western world, and you eat with the left hand. But when it comes to Pakistan, you may hold the utensils vice versa, and still eat with the right hand.

Bohra Muslims Wedding Cuisines and Etiquette
Bohra Muslims, who migrated from Yamen to Gujarat, have a firm belief that 'families who do not eat together, don't stay together'. Keeping this notion, all the family members eat from one huge plate called the '*thaal*'. They begin the meal by passing the salt. And it is when each partaker, eight on each table, have seated around the big platter and tasted it that the first course has begun. The *thaal* is never left unattended, so it is placed when everyone has taken their seats.

All their heads should be covered when they eat, veils on women's heads and small white caps '*topi*' on the heads of the males.

They have to eat with the right hand only, and using a left hand even for an ice cream scoop is a taboo. Bohra Muslims have a stringent no-wastage policy and make sure that no grain is left in the *thali* after they are done. In their homes, they may eat in separate *thalis*.

Chapter 6

Business Etiquette

Deploying etiquette at your workplace helps you perform better, allows you to put your best foot forward and saves you from disappointments. Etiquette in the workplace is no more different in Pakistan than any other part of this planet. Let's take a quick look at the business etiquette in my country.

SHOWING UP ON TIME
Going to official meetings or even just entering the workplace in time is the most basic rule. Someone has very nicely stated, 'reaching one hour earlier is always better than a minute late'. Showing up doesn't mean only bringing your body but also your mind. This simple rule plays a pertinent role in creating a sense of warm engagement.

DON'T 'GHOST' ON YOUR JOB
As the cornerstone of etiquette is to be respectful and courteous, it is your duty to communicate to your boss if you have to go somewhere unexpectedly.
When you do, you'll feel proud of yourself instead of having that troublesome sense of dread that comes with slacking off when you know people are counting on you. The day will also go more quickly when you're engaged and working. It's when you're doing nothing that the clock stands still. And, of course, doing well will help you get ahead when the time comes for bonuses and raises.

HOW TO DRESS AT THE JOB
Islam is very strict about covering the intimate parts of the body. If we go back in Islamic history, when Adam and Eve were told by Allah (God) not to taste a specific fruit in heaven, they were adequately dressed up. After they disobeyed Allah and ate the fruit upon the devil's insistence, Allah immediately removed their clothes, and they had to cover their bodies with leaves ashamedly. So, exposing your body is like a punishment from God.

Therefore, dress appropriately, covering your whole body. In Islam, the females wear a *hijab* or a scarf on their head, but not many follow this in Pakistan. So, as a woman, when you go to a workplace, you should wear anything covering your entire body, especially the breasts, and avoid low necklines. If you dress inappropriately, you will get noticed, and there are high chances you will not be remembered in the right way.

If you have a dress code at your office, be sure to follow it even if some of your colleagues do not. Formal business attire means a suit for men and women: matching jacket and slacks, a button-up shirt, and dress shoes. Men should wear a tie and a belt. Ladies have the option to wear tailored *shalwar kameez* or suits.

For men, 'business casual' means you can ditch the jacket, and the tie is optional. A sweater over your button-up shirt is a sharp look. You can also wear chinos or khakis instead of dress slacks, and polo shirts instead of dress shirts.

Some very informal offices allow jeans, T-shirts, and sneakers. If that's the case, make sure you still look presentable. You want your outfits to stand out for all the right reasons, especially in the beginning.

Whatever you choose to wear, make sure that you follow the following basic rules:

- Your clothes should be clean and wrinkle-free.
- Your clothes should be comfortable.
- Wearing slightly loose clothes is always a good idea. Skintight ones attract the unwanted attention of your colleagues.
- Your hair should be dry when you reach the office.
- For ladies, you should not wear a lot of make-up or jewellery. The colour red is seductive and gives the wrong impression that you are not professional and probably intend hidden meanings. Hence, it is advisable to wear neutral colours in make-up.
- Wear deodorants—you should smell good when you go to work, but make sure to not to have strong smelling perfumes. Nails should be properly polished, with no chip offs.
- All shoes should be kept in perfect shape. Even if they are sneakers, make sure that they are not dirty.
  - Your boss is not your best friend. Even if they are your friend, in the office setting, it is highly advisable to call them by their first name or last name correctly, as per the office codes of behaviour.

COMMUNICATION

No matter with whom you are communicating, treat them with respect. Bosses, interns, and people with the same job title as you all deserve the same consideration. This is not just how professionals act; it is how good humans work. All you need to do to show a basic level of respect is pay attention to people when they speak and do not interrupt them.

If you do not agree with someone, voice your opinion, but be kind about it. On the flip side, if you feel like someone is ignoring or disrespecting you, don't sink to their level. You can let them know that you feel like you're not being heard, but treat others how you'd like to be treated when you say it.

MEETING ETIQUETTE

Meetings are a place where you have a chance to meet with not just your higher-ups but also your clients. In these situations, it is always a good idea to have a plan for how you're going to act.

The first rule is always to show up on time. Go to the bathroom before entering your meeting room, so you don't have to interrupt anyone to excuse yourself. Have your talking points or questions written in your notebook. It is always better to document and take notes down while listening. Deep listening is an art that can be mastered with practice.

It might be tempting to whip out your phone or laptop and get some work done, but that isn't polite, and the people you want to impress will likely notice. Put your phone away during a meeting (and make sure it is on silent). If you are waiting for an urgent work-related call or text, at least keep it face-down on the table.

Your body language also says a lot. Do not slump in the chair or look at the time; it gives an impression of disinterest. If you maintain good posture and look like you are paying attention, it multiplies your chances of success.

Do not eat in the forums; remember you are in a meeting and not there for dinner.

BUSINESS GIFTS

There is no better gift than a book or a pen in the business setting. Remember, alcohol is strictly prohibited in Pakistan. Wallets, key chains or diaries are other good choices.

QUITTING THE JOB

No matter how you quit, give your employer as much notice as you can. During your last weeks and days at a job, continue to show up on time and do your work.

Wrap up whatever loose ends you can and put together detailed notes about the state of your projects. That way, whoever is taking them over can jump in without drowning. If your replacement starts before you leave, offer to train them. You'll impress your boss, and the new person will always remember you fondly.

Make sure you stay connected with your old co-workers, whether through email or sites like LinkedIn. You never know where your career paths may lead you!

THE POWER OF A WRITTEN 'THANK YOU' NOTE

Though it might sound old school, the power of a handwritten 'thank you' note can do wonders. Even if you have just attended an interview for a job application at your dream office, writing a small note or a postcard is a beautiful gesture. It is also a polite way to remind them about you while deciding on your job, as it is just these small gestures and attention to detail that matters most at the end of the day.

Chapter 7

Wedding Etiquette

In the torrid Lahore summers of 2001, my grandfather came to me and said, 'I have chosen this guy for you to marry'. My mouth was agape and didn't know what to say. I had no other choice than to say 'yes' to him. He gave me his photograph to have a look and the minute I saw his picture my heart started thumping like never before; some unexplainable attraction pulled me towards him and I knew that he is the one for me. I still remember my grandfather hiding behind the door to see my expressions. Yes, this is the way marriages are arranged in Pakistan.

A Pakistani wedding, often called '*Shaddi*', is the ancient custom representing majesty, ritual, colours and decorative celebrations connected through the sacred occasion. In Pakistan, the wedding is celebrated as the ritual where a secure and robust union between two souls is combined. Marriage denotes the foundation of two bonds between them and the bonding of their two families as well.

There is something truly exceptional and enthralling about weddings in Pakistan that strikes a chord with everyone. Be it children, adults or teenagers who dreamily imagine themselves in a fairy-tale wedding, it is an occasion of social funfair for all. The ones married obviously cannot stop gushing and remembering their marriage, and the elderly smile with care and a lot of blessings for the new couple.

Of course, Pakistani weddings take revelry to an entirely different level, and almost all Pakistani weddings that follow the traditional route are expensive, a food fest, a fun riot, and of course a means of a grand family gathering.

In Islam, weddings are supposed to be simple, like a one-day event with no exorbitant costs. But since many people who migrated to Pakistan from India at the time of partition were converts from Hinduism, they still feel proud to carry the colourful culture. It is not easy to untwine the fun-loving part from the hearts of the Muslims of Pakistan. Hence, wedding events and preparations begin almost a month before the actual wedding day.

Dholki
These are a series of small gatherings hosted by the bride and groom's friends and relatives. They usually invite the youngsters for the dance choreographic preparations, followed by a delicious dinner.

Mayon
This ceremony is full of fun for both the bride and groom and their family members. During my *Mayon* ceremony, I remember each and every one played *Mayon*. It was so much fun to see everyone smiling and giggling around; it was a moment of mixed emotions for me. On this day, I was told to wear a yellow-coloured dress, and not go outside the house unnecessarily until the actual wedding day.

Mayon is held a week or just a few days before the wedding. This ceremony can be conducted separately at the bride's and the groom's place. The ritual begins with preparing the magical paste. The family members usually do this, and they make it using the soaked raw *Haldi* (Turmeric) and then grinding it to a fine paste using the traditional mortar and pestle. Many other ingredients are also added to this paste, like milk, sandalwood powder and rose water. Once the paste is prepared, it is applied by the near and dear ones and onto the bodies of the bride-to-be and the groom to-be (face, hands, feet and neck).

Mehndi
One or two days before the wedding, we conduct an exciting ceremony called '*Mehndi*'. On this day, the bride's hands and feet are decorated with beautiful motifs. These motifs are usually traditional mango and flowers. *Mehndi* is a get-together party organised by the bride's family for her friends and relatives; the groom with his family and friends are also invited. They bring beautifully decorated *mehndi thaals* and *methai* (traditional sweet) for the bride. You can find girls enjoying their day singing, dancing and playing, followed by a delicious dinner.

Barat
Barat is the actual wedding day that precedes the '*Nikah*' which is the legal marriage contract between the bride and the groom.

'*Mahr*', a gift of money or another possession by the groom to the bride, is agreed upon before the ceremony. This is a binding gift that legally becomes the bride's property. The *mahr* is often money but could also be jewellery or a residential dwelling. The *mahr* is usually specified in the marriage contract, signed during the marriage process and traditionally is expected to be of sufficient monetary value to allow the wife to live comfortably if the husband should die or divorce her. The groom is supposed to give the *mahr* amount to the bride immediately after the *nikah*.

The *nikah* ceremony is when the marriage contract is made official by the signing of the document, indicating she has accepted it of her own free will. Although the document itself must be agreed upon by the groom, the bride, and the bride's father or another of her male family members, the bride's consent is required for the marriage to proceed.

After an official with religious qualifications gives a short sermon, the couple officially become man and wife by reciting the following brief dialogue in Arabic:

The bride says '*Qabool hai*' three times ('I have given away myself in *nikah* to you, on the agreed *mahr*'.)

The groom immediately says, '*Qabool hai*' '*Qabool hai*' '*Qabool hai*' ('I have accepted the *nikah*'.)

At that moment, the couple becomes husband and wife. The groom brings the bride to his house with his family.

RITUALS AT GROOM'S HOUSE

The bride's feet are washed with milk by the groom's family. A large plate with sweet rice is brought from which every married man takes a bite with the new bride.

VALIMA

This is a grand dinner hosted by the groom, where the bride's family are the prominent guests, and everyone enjoys the tantalizing dinner.

POST-WEDDING DINNERS

These are a series of dinners given by friends and close family members after the wedding ceremony.

Poland
By Dobrochna Giedwidz

Chapter 1

Cultural Symbols

SEA WHITE-TAILED EAGLE
Poles have always lived very close to nature. From the Tatra Mountains to the beaches of the Baltic Sea, nature provides food, shelter and inspiration for the Polish people. That is why there are so many animals in Polish symbology. The beautiful white eagle with open wings has been the national symbol of Poland since the end of the thirteenth century, but the legend begins far earlier than that. According to the story, while resting one evening, the legendary founder of the state of Poland, who was called Lech, saw a large nest in a tree. Inside was a white eagle with three chicks. As Lech watched them, the eagle spread its wings against the crimson-red evening sky. Lech was so thrilled by this dramatic sight that he decided to settle down in that very place. He added the eagle to his coat of arms and named the place Gniezno, from the word 'nest'. Even today, a white-tailed eagle wearing a golden crown is the national coat of arms of Poland.

BISON
Poland's pride and the king of Polish fauna, the European bison, or Żubr, is the most imposing land animal on the continent. Adults can reach 700 kg in weight and a length of 3.5 metres. This makes the European bison larger than its famous relative, the American bison. There are only a few  thousand specimens of this majestic animal left and most of them live in the Puszcza Białowieska. European bison have been protected since 1529 and, thanks to a long period of protective laws established during various regiments, the animals still survive in the wild to the present day.

The Białowieska forest where many bison are found is itself a unique and magical place; one of the last and largest remaining parts of the vast virgin forests that once stretched across the European Plain.

STORK

In Poland, the white stork is a symbol of happiness, fertility and wisdom. For centuries, homesteads with stork nests on their roofs stirred envy among their neighbours and were an indicator of happiness within the household. The stork's nest was supposed to be a natural lightning rod, as it was believed that lightning would not hit the area nearby a stork sitting on its nest. There is probably no other wild bird so strongly associated with Polish villages and their folklore.

POPPY

Although the poppy is not an official symbol, it is found throughout the country and is considered archetypal in the Polish flora. It was considered an exceptional product even in ancient Slavic culture—known for its drowsy, almost hallucinogenic properties—and was used in ancestral worship to make strong decoctions. Nowadays, one of the dishes during a traditional Polish Christmas dinner must contain poppy seeds. The poppy is also a symbol of the blood that was shed by Polish soldiers who died in the battle of Monte Casino during World War II in Italy and is depicted in the popular military song '*Red Poppies on Monte Casino*'.

OAK

The oak is valued for its mighty size and impressive bearing. To the ancient Slavs the oak was the centre of the universe – the most important of all trees—and a symbol of longevity. In ancient beliefs the tree supported the sky and its roots reached into the deepest underground regions. In Poland, we still admire beautiful specimens of old oaks and give them names. The best known is Bartek (about 685 years old); it grows in the Świętokrzyskie Mountains, anglicised to Holy Cross Mountains. This mountain range is located in south-central Poland and is one of the oldest mountains in Europe.

Oak Tree

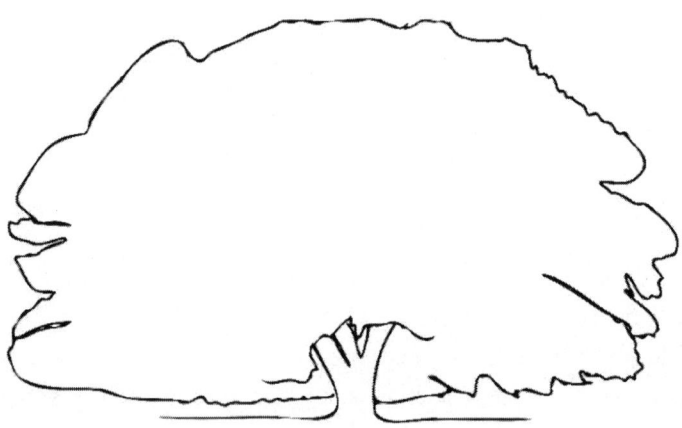

Vodka

The most famous Polish liquid. Although vodka is produced all over the world, there is something about Polish Vodka that makes it unique. The first written mention of the word 'vodka' was in the C.14th in a part of what was then Poland but is now Western Ukraine. Poland has an almost unmanageable number of vodka brands, not to mention some of the rarest vodkas with specific aromas and flavours. Vodka is drunk in a small glass called a 'shot glass'. Traditionally, before one drinks vodka, you say '*Na Zdrowie*'! Then afterwards you take a bite of a pickle. One of the most famous vodkas is Żubrówka, which has a picture of European Bison on the label and a piece of bison grass from the Białowieska forest inside the bottle. It is said that this is the piece of grass on which the bison has relieved itself on, but do not let that put you off!

PIEROGI

The best are made at home, of course! Traditionally, these savoury, stuffed treats were only prepared on special occasions like Christmas or important family reunions, mainly because making them at home is quite time-consuming. Nowadays there are many specialised shops and restaurants that serve them as the

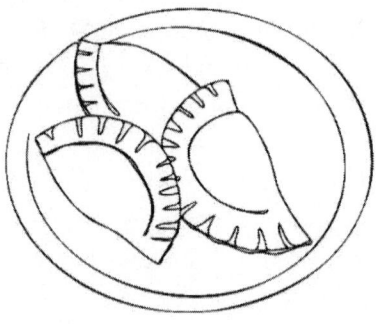

'main dish of the day'. Pierogi have been made in Poland since the C.13th and first appeared in Polish cookbooks and literature in the second half of the C.17th. They may have arrived during the Marco Polo expeditions from China via Italy or with the Tatars from the former Russian Empire, but today they are considered a national dish and one of the most recognizable Polish foods. Pierogi ruskie are made with cottage cheese (called *twaróg*), potatoes and fried onions. The other 'classics' are filled with sauerkraut, mushrooms and meat.

Pączki

You may ask what the distinguishes between *pączki* and American donuts? Well, the most obvious difference is the shape; donuts usually have a hole in the middle, while *pączki* do not, and instead are rounded like a small ball. They are made from very rich, sweet yeast dough with eggs, butter and milk, deep-fried and filled with a big blob of jam (traditionally rose jam). Although not very healthy, they are certainly delicious. Traditionally, *pączki* are eaten on 'fat Thursday', the last Thursday before Ash Wednesday and the beginning of Lent. The historical reason for making *pączki* was to use up all the lard, sugar, eggs and fruit in the house, as their consumption was forbidden during the season of Lent.

Folk

Folklore is a part of Polish tradition and culture. For many years it was considered 'backward', being an archaic, rural culture, but recently it has enjoyed something of a revival. Folk elements can be found in architecture, art and costumes, but also in songs, proverbs and legends. It is a rich part of Polish culture that has survived to this day. Each region is very specific and there are many factors that influence the folklore of a particular area, ranging from the influence of other neighbouring communities to the wealth of the local population or geographical conditions. Polish folklore has great variety, with almost one hundred costumes. Other important and popular aspects of this culture are traditional dances, for example the Krakowiak from Kraków or Oberek.

CONSONANTS

In general, Polish is a very difficult language to pronounce and understand, as is the orthography and spelling. When learning Polish, people are always surprised at how many consonants a word can contain. Some of these words are difficult even for Poles themselves: *źdźbło* (grain), *bezwzględny* (reckless), *żółć* (bile—a word formed entirely from letters not found in foreign alphabets). In the 1970s comedy '*How I Unleashed World War II*', the story is told of a Polish soldier who, by comic coincidence, becomes convinced that he started World War II. In one famous scene, he is asked his name by a German-speaking Gestapo officer and answers 'Grzegorz Brzęczyszczykiewicz'. The officer, of course, becomes increasingly frustrated trying to write the fictitious Polish name…

Chapter 2

Meeting, Greeting, Posture and Body Language

In many ways, Poland is somewhat more traditional than other European countries and it is still quite important to show courtesy to women out of respect. However, some gestures, which once were very common, such as pulling the chair or kissing the hand are slowly becoming a thing of the past.

POSTURE
- Men and women are taught to keep a straight back and shoulders from a young age in order to present themselves in an elegant and appealing manner.

BODY LANGUAGE
- Typically, gesticulating excessively during a conversation has always been considered bad manners. There are, however, some popular hand signs, not always tactful, that might be interesting to explore and get to know:
    - Making a fist with the thumb sticking out between the index and middle fingers is called a 'fig' and means 'you get nothing'. The expression comes from the fact that, during communist times, figs were very hard to find in Poland. The expression is generally used by older generations.
    - Connecting the thumb with the index finger to create circlet, simply means 'perfect'!
    - Tapping your index finger on your head means that you don't agree with what the other person is saying, and you think it is stupid…
    - Holding the thumbs in a fist, for example, during a game or contest, is a gesture said to bring good luck or victory!
    - Making a gesture of striking the neck with the edge of the hand is an invitation to drink, or a way of saying that someone is drunk.
    - As for personal space, Polish people are not very tactile and an arm's

length distance is generally respected. Physical contact tends to only be shown between people who are in close association, such as good friends, couples, or children. Friends might walk arm in arm and parents usually show open affection to their children, even if they are not babies. Kissing or excessive hugging in public places is generally frowned upon.

- Eye contact is direct and expected during a conversation; however, take care to ensure it is not too fixed. It is okay to break the connection from time to time.

Temperament

- Polish people are quite comfortable with directness, and on occasion they correct people or criticise them outright. This straightforward approach is natural in Poland and a sign of familiarity, so one should not be offended or dismissive if criticised but continue the conversation in a conventional way.
- It may not be the first impression one has of Poles, but they really do have a good and rather sarcastic sense of humour and are pretty good at laughing at themselves. Unfortunately, this humour is often quite nuanced and not always obvious when translated into other languages.

Smiling

- At first sight, it might seem that Polish people are very serious and severe. In general, smiling at strangers on the street or in public places is not normal social behaviour, although this is slowly changing. So if you smile at someone you do not know, it can make people uncomfortable. However, everyone becomes much more spirited once they get to know you—or once a few vodkas have been consumed—and everyone likes a good laugh.

Greetings

- Salutations in Poland can be a bit confusing as there are different ways to greet others depending on the relationship. Official introductions are polite and reserved and people are more formal when meeting strangers for the first time. In Poland, a proper handshake takes about two to three shakes and a moment of prolonged handholding. In general, a handshake is the safest way to greet when meeting new people, even in informal situations. Of course, not during COVID times when you greet people form a distance.

- The fashion of greeting with kisses on the cheeks is relatively new in Poland. In the past, this custom was reserved only for those in love or close family members. Nowadays, for new introductions, a handshake is usually the most appropriate greeting, unless you are meeting very young people in an informal setting.
- If cheek-kissing does end up taking place, it is traditional to kiss three times, beginning on the right cheek and ending again on the right cheek. When kissing a large group, however (such as when receiving guests), people usually only give one kiss on the cheek. Also, in cities, friends often greet each other with just one kiss. This could, of course, get quite confusing, so it is best to always be prepared for three kisses and then go with the flow…
- It is customary for men to greet women with a proper handshake, which can seem very formal, but is actually considered friendly and polite. Usually, people shake hands with women first before addressing men as a mark of respect. It is important to remember that until the early 1990s, it was common for men to kiss a lady on the hand. This may still be a common practise for people of the older generation.
- Men always greet each other with a handshake and occasionally a hug if they are very good friends or family members.
- Finally, always remember never to shake hands in the doorway. Polish people believe that this brings bad luck.

OTHER CONSIDERATIONS

- Navigating roads in Poland can be a challenge! Although Poles are quite careful when behind the wheel, they are not always very respectful of pedestrians and often do not stop at intersections if there are no traffic lights, so you have to be cautious whilst crossing the street.
- As for the manner of speaking, Poles do not as a rule raise their voices in public situations or in the street. In good company it is common to speak louder, especially if they are talking about something close to their heart. Poles can get very passionate when talking about topics they care about, and enthusiastic discussions are common. This is why you often see people who look like they are arguing, when in fact they are just debating passionately.

Chapter 3

Conversation Dos and Don'ts

The Polish people are extremely hospitable. They are very proud of their country and want to make a good impression on visitors. While welcoming, however, Poles can also sometimes be shy when they have to speak in a foreign language, so stay patient as they usually understand quite a lot and just need a little extra encouragement. Once you make friends with Polish people, however, you can get into amazing and mind-blowing conversations. One thing to note is that Poles like to speak very matter-of-factly and are quite enthusiastic about their opinions and beliefs. In fact, conversations can become very expressive and, when viewed from the outside, might look and sound argumentative, whereas the truth is that the participants are just being passionate about the topic at hand.

A few considerations for a great conversation:

- Understand a little bit about Polish history before travelling to the country. Poland is located in a very specific position between Germany and Russia and many consider it just a small and ordinary country, but nothing could be further from the truth. Poland has a very rich and complex history and knowing some facts can impress Polish people and also help with understanding their complicated politics. The Polish are conscious of their recent history and many social attitudes remain influenced and motivated by past events. Below are a few facts worth mentioning:
- The state of Poland was created in 966 AD.
- The C.16th and the first decades of the C.17th are known as the Polish Golden Age. The country's political system evolved into an early democratic monarchy and became one of the first multicultural states in history, with minorities' rights protected by the Union's laws.
- The Polish Constitution of the 3rd of May 1791 is generally considered to be Europe's first, and the World's second, modern written national constitution, after the United States.

- In 1772, 1793 and 1795 the three partitions of the Polish-Lithuanian Commonwealth took place. The country was divided between Russia, Prussia, and Austria. Poland vanished from maps for 123 years.
- Poland regained its independence on the 11th of November 1918.
- On the 1st of September 1939, the German army launched an invasion of Poland. This was followed by the Soviet invasion on the 17th of September. World War II was devastating for the country, killing five million inhabitants and leaving the country morally and culturally devastated. During the war, Poles provided significant contributions to the allied effort by joining the fighting on land, air, sea and helping with intelligence.
- Even though Poland ended the war on the winning side and was re-established as a state, it fell under the influence of the Soviet Union and was forced to adopt communism as its political system.
- During the communist era, almost every ten years there was some kind of uprising against the system. In December 1981, the regime declared martial law in Poland, under which the army and special police forces attempted to crush solidarity (*Solidarność*), the first independent labour union in a soviet bloc. They did not, however, succeed.
- From 1989–1991, Poland engaged in a democratic transition, which led to the foundation of The Third Polish Republic. After ten years of democratic consolidation, Poland joined NATO in 1999 and the European Union in 2004.
- Poland is also home to many amazing artists in all creative fields. The literary canon of Poland is admirable in its achievements, winning the Nobel Prize for literature six times. Some of its better known authors include Czeslaw Milosz and Wislawa Szymborska. A more recent literary phenomenon is Andrzej Sapkowski, author of the fantasy novel, *The Witcher* (*Wiedźmin*), which was translated into thirty-seven languages and has sold over fifteen million copies worldwide as of December 2019. *The Witcher* has also been adapted into a film, two television series and a trilogy of video games.

Polish cinema is widely appreciated, with famous names including Krzysztof Kieślowski, Andrzej Wajda, Agnieszka Holland and Paweł

Pawlikowski. We cannot also forget to mention also Fryderyk Chopin and Maria Skłodowska Curie (who were Polish, not French) as well as Copernicus, Artur Rubinstein and many more…

- It is important to add that if you ask a Pole how they are doing, the response will be… honest. Be prepared to hear about bad weather, annoying politicians or problems with irritating colleagues at work.
- In more formal settings, Polish people are cordial and can be quite chivalrous. Some traditional manners are still present: it is, for example, considered impolite to ask a woman her age.

Be careful with the following topics or concepts:

- Avoid confusing Poland with its neighbours or suggest that it is part of Russia…
- Poles also do not like being called 'Eastern Europeans', as this is sometimes associated with the stereotype of the 'Eastern Bloc'. Calling Poland a Central European country is much more appreciated.
- Avoid being overly enthusiastic and complimentary of Russians or Germans because of the complicated history between the countries. Also, do not presume that everyone hated the communist era.
- Do not assume that all Poles are Catholic but always be respectful as the religion has been a strong cultural force in Poland. The cult of the Polish Pope John Paul II is still very much alive.
- Unfortunately, you may find that inappropriate jokes (sexist undertones or slurring of racial/ethnic minorities) are still common in some parts of Poland.
- There are also many delicate issues, which cause political debates, regarding gay rights or abortion. Tread with caution if conversation strays to these topics!

Chapter 4

Gift Giving

By giving a gift to someone, we typically want to demonstrate warm feelings, care, sympathy or remembrance. In the case of Poland, giving a gift is a gesture steeped in a very rich history. Giving presents to one another was once considered a duty and gifts had different names depending on the occasion on which they were given; for name days – *wiązanie*, for good news—*nowinne*, a suitor's gift—*zalotne*, etcetera.

Nowadays, the reasons for giving gifts relate to the most common occasions, such as Christmas (in Poland, gifts are given also on the 6th of December, which is related to the strong cult of Saint Nicholas who became famous for his extraordinary generosity), important events in a person's life (baptism, wedding) or annual occasions (name day, birthday).

Gift giving ideas and traditions for different occasions:

- When invited to a house for a visit, it is always worthwhile to think of a little something for the host. A symbolic gift is very appropriate, for it gives pleasure and leaves a favourable impression. A little something with a universal character is always perfect: bouquets of flowers, a bottle of good alcohol, pralines, or, if you are visiting from another country, a delicacy or a regional speciality are more than welcome.

- As for the flowers, in Poland it is very popular to bring those for the hostess, but always remember that there must be an odd number of blooms, they must be unwrapped, and you should avoid buying callas or chrysanthemums, which are usually only given at funerals. In general, it is also better to avoid white flowers, and for generations it has been believed that only a lover can give red flowers to women, especially roses and carnations. Any bouquet, regardless of size (even a single flower), is handed with the stems down. Usually, when presenting the flowers, one holds them in the left hand, which makes it possible to say a few words or wishes, do the handshake or give a hug, and then hand over the bouquet. It is the duty of the host to place the flowers in a visible place as a gesture of appreciation for the gift.

- Etiquette states that it is always men who gives flowers to women in social settings. When a couple go for dinner to a friends' house the man would be expected to give flowers to the lady of the house. If an additional gift is brought, the flowers are presented by the man and the gift is presented by the woman. The only exception is if the owner of the house is a man and it is his birthday. In this case it is appropriate for the woman to present the flowers. If partygoers arrive with flowers and a bottle of alcohol, it is normal for the man to give the bouquet to the woman of the household, before handing the drink to the host.
- The packaging of the gift is also important as it shows additional consideration towards the recipient of the gift. Normally, white and black packaging is avoided; white for the practical reason of not getting dirty and black because it is associated with mourning. Needless to say, the price tag should not be attached.
- When visiting friends or family, it is usually nice to think of the youngest family members as well. A small gift such as a chocolate or candy or a little toy will be appreciated, but don't overdo it with gifts that might be expensive or age inappropriate.
- Finally, it is worth attaching a greeting card to the gift, especially in situations where the recipient receives many gifts at once, such as at a wedding.

Traditionally, in Poland, the gift should be opened immediately upon receipt. Thanks to that, the person who chose it can immediately see our reaction to the selected gift. The only exception is when there are so many gifts that it would take too long to open them, which would lead to the host neglecting other guests. Then they will just say thank you and set the gifts aside to unwrap later. It is important for Polish people that they always thank someone twice for the gift they have received: once when it is presented, and the second time after unwrapping. If the gift is not unwrapped immediately, therefore, Poles will usually always write or call the person who gave us the gift to thank them a second time.

Chapter 5

Dining Etiquette

In Poland, cuisine is an important part of the national identity, deep rooted in the culture, and Poles show a strong attachment to their cooking. No wonder that a Pole, when asked about his or her favourite dish, will proudly name something based on a Polish recipe.

If one had to describe Polish cuisine in just one word, 'genuine' might be the most appropriate choice, as many of the popular recipes of Polish cuisine date back centuries and they preserve delicious and generous flavours.

TABLE SETTING AND MANNERS
Nowadays, we can afford to take a lot more liberties with meals at the table than in the past. However, it is extremely important to adapt to the situation and this often requires some skill. People eat differently in a fast food bar, also called '*bar mleczy*', an elegant restaurant, or during a special celebration. The rank of the event and the place of the meeting are of great importance.

Generally, in Polish homes people set the table quite informally; for everyday meals you will find a simple runner and casual, often colourful crockery. For special occasions, however, such as Christmas, Easter or anniversaries, an elegant and traditional table setting is expected.

As for the cutlery and glasses, the arrangement follows European, continental standards. Cutlery is placed on either side of the plate in the same order as the food is served. Forks are placed on the left side of the plate, spoons and knives on the right. Glasses are placed on the right side, above the knives and/or spoons. As for the drinks, nowadays the meal is usually accompanied by wine, but very often beer or even vodka are served, in which case instead of wine glasses, one will find goblet glasses for the beer or shot glasses for the strong liquor.

In Polish homes, *family-style dining* is the most popular, which means that different dishes of a meal are served on the table at the same time and guests help themselves from the serving bowls. The dishes are passed to the right.

At the table, Poles are usually quite relaxed and focus on conversation and laughter.

At daily meals, the question of who should sit where is not a problem. However, at important dinners, the guests of honour should be seated as close as possible to the hosts on the right. The hosts may sit either at opposite ends of the table (as in the English style of dining) or in the middle of the longer edges (as in the French way). It is preferable that men and women sit alternately next to each other.

At the table:
- The host usually won't take a seat until all the guests are seated.
- It is customary to rest the hands on the table between the dishes served, but never the elbows.
- One waits until everyone is served before starting to eat, unless the hostess specifically asks guests not to wait.
- The hostess gives a signal that diners can start eating by taking the napkin and starting to eat.
- As for drinking alcohol, the signal to start comes from the host.
- Do not ask for another glass of alcohol; wait until another round is served for everyone.
- Bread often accompanies the meals and is always broken with the hands. Sometimes it can be accompanied by butter and in which case you should place a little butter on your plate and then spread it onto a small piece of bread with your knife.
- Soup is almost always on the menu. To eat it, spoon the soup away from you in the bowl. To finish it, you can tip the plate, but always angled away from you.
- Also, avoid blowing on your soup, or any food, to cool it. Allow your food to cool naturally.
- Note that people often do not eat meat on Fridays because of religious traditions. It is however fine to eat fish instead.

MEALS
Polish eating habits are surprising in many ways.

First of all, it is strange to admit that in Poland there are no very strict times for meals. Usually during the week, people work according to different schedules and the lunch break can vary from twelve to four p.m. On weekends, people usually meet for lunch between one and three p.m. As for dinner, Poles eat a fairly light meal at around seven or eight p.m.

Also, unlike much of Europe, a traditional daily menu includes five meals, not three. Let's look at all more in detail:

Breakfast – *śniadanie* (between six and eight a.m.) – Poles like to start the day with a real meal, which might include eggs or a sandwich, often with a side dish of kefir or cottage cheese. As a rule, Poles are not afraid of strong tastes, even in the morning!

Second breakfast (around eleven a.m.) – this usually consists of another slice of bread with ham or cheese. This is a meal that is often eaten on the go, so it must be easy to carry.

Lunch – *obiad* (around two p.m.) – the midday meal was traditionally the main meal of the day in Poland. Nowadays, however, people usually do not have time for a substantial meal and many workplaces do not even allow a one-hour break. During the week, hard-working Poles usually only have a quick sandwich or a set menu from a local canteen, *bistrot* or *bar mleczy*. Weekend lunches are a family affair and a multi-course meal, especially on Sundays. If you are invited to someone's house, it is usually for lunch.

Evening snack – *podwieczorek* (around five p.m.) – this is often a time for cakes and pastries, especially for children

Dinner – *kolacja* (around seven or eight p.m.) – depending on the evening, this may be a very simple meal including several sandwiches, or a main meal for those who have not had time to eat properly during the day, but usually consisting of just a small dish with a side salad.

Is it fair to say that the Polish menu opens and closes with sandwiches, which Poles like to eat for breakfast, lunch and dinner? Probably yes, at least if there is very little time for experimentation.

The daily menu of the Poles, however, also includes some iconic items and dishes prepared according to old time-tested recipes. It is also worth mentioning that, due to the complicated and rich history, Polish cuisine consists of many influences, from Jewish to Italian (thanks to Bona Sforza), as well as Russian and Austrian.

Soup is at the heart of the Polish menu and you will always find it on the menu. It is not only a daily dish, but also festive: at Christmas, mushroom, *borscht* or fish soup, and at Easter, *żur* (sour soup). In winter, a plate of hot soup warms things up, and in summer a delicious cold soup called *chłodnik* cools things down. Sometimes Poles even eat soup for breakfast—milk soup, with boiled noodles, rice or porridge.

The king of the second course is meat. Poles love minced meat like *gołąbki* ('little pigeons', made by filling white cabbage leaves, stuffed with rice and minced meat), pork chops, baked poultry and *kiełbasa* (sausages). For side dishes, they usually opt for carrots with peas or roasted beetroot. Poles also appreciate dumplings, pierogi and fish dishes. Many of the traditional dishes are time consuming and some are prepared only on weekends or special occasions.

Vegetarians in Poland, do not, however, need to worry! Many people do not know that Poland has the highest rate of fruit and vegetable consumption in Europe. You will not see a dinner plate in Poland that does not come with a heap of shredded cabbage salad, a rainbow beetroot salad, or a luminous orange carrot salad.

For multicourse dining, the meals should be served in the following order: cold starters; hot starters; soups; fish and meat dishes; cheese; dessert; fruit; coffee, and tea. Following which a good nap might be needed.

Tea

Tea has a very important role in Polish culture. You are sure to be offered a cup of tea when you visit, no matter what time of day it is.

Tea came to Poland from France in 1664, supposedly brought by Marie Louise Gonzaga, who was particularly notable for being both the Queen of Poland and Grand Duchess of Lithuania by marriage to two kings, the brothers Władysław IV and John II Casimir. The habit of drinking tea did not, however, spread until the second half of the C.18th, helped by good trade relations between Poland and England and by learning to brew it from the Russians. Today, tea is one of the most popular drinks in Poland, even though coffee houses can now be found on every street corner and every kind of drink is available.

Coffee

Coffee has become one of the most popular drinks in the world and this is no different in Poland. Today, Poles attach great importance to quality and preparation methods, but this was not always the case. In the C. 19th, coffee houses—called *kawiarnia* in Polish—gained importance. As in many other European cities, they became the centre for local personalities and intellectuals who met there to talk and observe. After World War II coffee was no longer available to everyone and became a luxury product offered as a name day gift or sometimes as a means of payment. A very popular way of drinking coffee at that time was the so-called Turkish coffee, which simply involved pouring hot water over ground coffee.

VODKA

Many foreigners may be surprised by the drinking culture in Poland but there is no denying that the country produces delicious liquors. Polish vodka is included on the list of protected geographical indicators, and drinking vodka has it habits, the most common of which is the toast '*na zdrowie*', which means 'for the health'!

Also, the Poles have invented excellent ways to drink without fuss. Pickled cucumbers, herring and tartar cannot be missing at any drinking party.

Chapter 6

Business Etiquette

Since the economic and political transition in the early 1990s, Poland has undergone many changes. Joining the European Union in 2004 improved the Polish economy and made it more attractive to foreign companies. Poland became one of the main destinations for foreign direct investment in Eastern and Central Europe. Even during the recent world economic crises, Poland has remained a good and stable location for foreign capital.

In general, Poland has been influenced by Western trends and business culture. Poland has embraced capitalism and the younger generation especially has internalised values and a work ethic not too far removed from those in Western Europe or the United States. In fact, a difference can be noticed between the older and younger generations. While the younger ones have a more relaxed work style, the older generation's management style is more formal and hierarchical.

BUSINESS CULTURE

The business culture in Poland is quite formal, with a fairly strong respect for the rules and a particular respect for those in higher positions. While the Poles are quite reserved, the communication style when doing business is direct and colleagues are expected to address things openly. It is worth keeping in mind that business relationships are very much based on trust, so it is important to build them with care. Sometimes, as a foreigner, it is advisable to make the first contact through a third party who can help build that trusting relationship. Unlike other countries where business can be done by phone or email, in Poland it is better to meet potential partners or collaborators face to face and discuss things in person. Women have the same business opportunities in Poland as men. Visiting businesswomen should encounter little or no gender bias and are judged on their professional skills.

Greetings and Titles

It is customary to greet people with a firm handshake and it is considered very important to maintain eye contact during meetings. It is also advisable to shake hands with everyone when arriving and leaving a meeting. Men should wait until a woman extends her hand before extending his own. Some older businessmen may still kiss the hand of a female employee at a meeting as a sign of respect, but it is rare these days.

Titles are quite important in Poland and it is recommended to use the person's title and last name until asked to use their first name. An appropriate way to address Polish employees would be to use *Pan* (Mr) for men and *Pani* (Mrs) for women, along with their last names.

Meetings and Punctuality

Business meetings usually start with some small talk, but Polish associates can also dive into negotiations quite quickly. If you are negotiating with Poles, it is recommended that you let them start and end so as not to appear too hasty. Find out in advance if an interpreter is needed, as not all business people are fluent in English.

Also note that Polish business people are known to communicate quite directly, and the degree of openness may seem blunt to some foreigners, but there is no need to worry. In fact, it is advisable to match this direct style of communication by expressing your views clearly and openly.

Punctuality is taken quite seriously. People in higher positions may be late for a meeting to demonstrate their status and importance within the company hierarchy. In general, however, it is advisable to be on time for a business meeting.

Business cards are usually exchanged at the end of a first meeting. Having a translation into Polish on one side will always be appreciated.

Business Dress Code

The dress code in the workplace tends to be formal and conservative. In meetings, most managers wear formal attire; that is, dark suits with jackets and ties for men, and suits with smart trousers or skirts for women. During normal office hours the dress code may be a little less formal, but you should still maintain a neat appearance. First impressions are always very important in the Polish business world.

Large organisations set a dress code for their employees to show respect to their business partners, customers, and the public. Some companies have, however, introduced casual Fridays when employees can wear more comfortable clothes.

Small and medium-sized companies often do not have a formal policy but will expect one to dress appropriately for your position and the environment in which you work. For example, if one works in an advertising agency, a start-up or an IT company, a suit is not required for meetings. Here one can adapt to the casual working atmosphere with a more personal and relaxed look.

GIFT GIVING

In Poland, gifts are expected to be presented at the start of a business relationship and at the conclusion of an agreement. Small offerings, such as a corporate gift (without company logo or branding) or a souvenir representing the country from you are visiting would be acceptable. Other suitable gifts include high-quality chocolates, flowers, wine or spirits from your home country that are either not available or difficult to obtain in Poland.

If you are invited to a business partner's home, or that of your boss, it is good form to bring flowers, sweets or a bottle of wine.

Chapter 7

Wedding Etiquette

Traditionally, Polish weddings lasted several days, involving a large feast with lots of food and dancing, during which many specific customs were observed. Over time, however, many traditions have been lost and new ways of celebrating are becoming more prevalent, especially in cities where the pace of life is faster and there is not much time for long and lavish celebrations.

INVITATIONS
In Poland, the invitation for the wedding should arrive about three months before the ceremony.

Chances are high that the wedding will take place during a month that contains the letter 'r' (in Polish, these are March, June, August, September, October, and December). These months are believed to bring good luck to a marriage and are therefore the most popular times to plan a wedding. Typically, weddings are organised on Saturdays.

It is important to pay careful attention to what part of the wedding you are invited to. Is it just the ceremony in a church or municipality or also the reception? The Polish word '*ślub*' refers to a ceremony in a church and '*wesele*' refers to the wedding party. Remember, the good news is that if you are invited only to the ceremony and not to the reception, you are not obliged to buy a wedding gift.

You should also make sure you note:
- The names on the invitation.
- Whether you are invited 'with children' or without.
- The RSVP date (and make sure you reply in time).

THE CEREMONY
Most of the Polish people still get married in a church, following the

Catholic tradition, but this is slowly changing and is no longer a standard. If the ceremony takes place in a church, it is usually accompanied by a mass, which can be a full mass or a shorter adapted version.

Guests enter the church before the ceremony and take their seats. The spaces closest to the altar are reserved for close family and friends.

Often the priest greets the future couple at the entrance of the church and, according to Polish custom, the couple walks through the knave, led by the priest and altar boys.

Nowadays, however, it is quite common for the bride to follow the U.S. American example and be led down the aisle by her father.

The ceremony begins when the young couple stand together at the altar.

After the blessing and formalities, the bride and groom may step aside as they often go to pray for a while by themselves.

As for leaving the church, usually the guests go first and the couple last. However, the guests often wait in the pews and the young people go through the line of applauding guests. You have to keep an eye out and, in particular, see what the parents of the couple are doing.

An interesting fact is that in Poland you wear the wedding ring on the right hand. Before the January Uprising in 1863, the wedding ring was worn on the left hand and only widows placed it on the right hand, but after the defeat married women also began transferring the rings to their right hands as a sign of mourning and things ended up staying that way.

Greetings

After both a church wedding and a civil wedding, it is traditional to greet the newlyweds at the exit. It used to be customary for guests to bring a bouquet of flowers to the ceremony, but more and more often, couples inform in advance that they prefer to get, for example, wine instead of flowers. It is, therefore, important to check the invitation for guidance. The traditional colours for a wedding bouquet are white and soft pink and the flowers chosen should follow this colour palette. The most popular are peonies and dahlias, lilies, lily of the valley, tulips and roses. Inappropriate flowers are callas, red roses and carnations (with the exception of a large bouquet of white carnations), as well as chrysanthemums and potted plants.

Remember to pay attention to the order in which guests greet the bride and groom. First to greet are the best men, then the parents, grandparents, close and distant family, and finally friends and acquaintances.

Sometimes it may happen that if the weather is capricious, or it is deemed convenient for the people gathered, wishes are made directly in the wedding hall. In this case, guests will be informed about it.

WEDDING RECEPTION

The traditional Polish wedding is not what it used to be. For centuries, a wedding in Poland was a three-day affair that included many unique traditions, several hundred guests, and a long party with music, vodka, plenty of food and dancing into the morning.

Having said that, the modern ceremonies are still very festive and entertaining.

Many Polish wedding celebrations are still opened with the traditional presentation of bread and salt, given to the bride and groom by their parents upon their arrival. The bread is often specially prepared and decorated with the couples' names. This gift is symbolic—the bread is offered so that the couple will never go hungry, whilst the salt reminds them of life's difficulties and the importance of learning to deal with them. The bride and groom tear off a piece of bread, dip it in the salt and eat it. Then the couple are offered two glasses to make a toast, one glass contains vodka and the other water. According to superstition, the one who gets the vodka will rule the marriage. After the toast, the couple throw their glasses; if they break, it is a sign of good luck.

Around this time, you may notice that guests have begun handing envelopes of money to the bride and groom. While some couples have begun to create gift registries, giving cash is still more common. Make sure to check the couples' preference before the ceremony.

Now the party begins, and the guests can look forward to the start of a very long, very filling evening. The meal traditionally starts with chicken broth (in Polish, '*rosół*') and there is much more to come. So if you're done with the first course and think it wasn't too filling, just wait... At some weddings a hot meal will be served approximately every three hours. After the main meal, '*zakąski*', a kind of Polish tapas, is served. Do not even think about trying to count calories at a Polish wedding; greasy food will help you get along with vodka. Following the global trend, however, more and more couples nowadays are changing the menu and opting for healthier and 'greener' options.

Dancing is another important part of a Polish wedding. Poles dance a lot, especially with a partner. The weddings are often accompanied by a live band that usually plays Polish songs. Be prepared for hours of dancing and don't worry if you don't have a partner for the wedding; it is very common to change dance partners and dance with everyone. If you are a man, it is mandatory to dance with the bride.

Whilst many weddings come to an end around midnight, a Polish wedding is just approaching one of its most traditional moments—the removal of the bridal veil. This ceremony, called '*oczepiny*', traditionally represented the transitional moment for the bride as she moved from her single youth towards her married future. For many years it was associated only with kitsch and embarrassing games, but today couples are opting for games that will only put guests in a good mood.

THE PARTY CONTINUES... A SECOND DAY

Often Polish weddings may include a second day of partying. This follow-up reception is called '*poprawiny*' and begins around one p.m. on Sunday, usually lasting until seven or eight p.m. It is very similar to the first day, but less formal—typically an opportunity to drink the remaining vodka and eat the leftovers from the reception dinner.

Portugal
By Maria Campos

Chapter 1

Cultural Symbols

Portugal is situated in the most western point of Europe and is the oldest country in the world to have the same borders since its foundation. It was founded in the 12th century, in 1143, by King D. Afonso Henriques and, since then, its borders have remained the same.

Portuguese is the official language of a total of ten countries.

In almost a thousand years of history, Portugal has gone through periods of great splendour, such as the era of the Portuguese discoveries; hence, the Portuguese are proud of their culture and heritage connected with the sea.

In Portugal, you can find elements classified by UNESCO as world heritage, intangible cultural heritage and underwater cultural heritage.

THE PORTUGUESE FLAG

The Portuguese flag is loaded with symbolism, which illustrates the country's history.

It was adopted in 1911 after the fall of the monarchy in 1910. The flag is composed of the Portuguese shield, an armillary sphere, and the colours red and green.

The Portuguese shield has been used for centuries, although with different presentations. On the shield, we find seven castles representing the castles that King Afonso Henriques conquered from the moors, five blue shields representing the five Moorish kings defeated by King Afonso Henriques at the Battle of Ourique, and five white dots on each shield representing the five wounds of Christ.

The armillary sphere, upon which the Portuguese shield rests, represents the routes discovered by the Portuguese navigators in the 15th and 16th centuries.

The two base colours, green and red, represent hope and the blood of the Portuguese heroes, respectively.

Rooster of Barcelos

THE ROOSTER OF BARCELOS (*GALO DE BARCELOS*)
The legend says that people in Barcelos were scared about a crime that had been committed in the city. One day a stranger came to the city on his way to Santiago de Compostela and everybody suspected him to be the murderer. The man said he was just passing by as a pilgrim because he was going to pay a promise, but no one believed him.

Although he claimed his innocence, the authorities took him away and he was sentenced to be hanged.

He asked to be taken to the presence of the judge that had sentenced him. The judge was surrounded by friends, having a feast drinking wine and eating roasted roosters.

The man pointed to one of the roosters on the table and said, "It is so true that I am innocent, that it is true that this rooster will sing when I am hanged!" Everybody laughed but no one dared to touch that one rooster.

At the very moment the man was hanged, the rooster came to life and sang! The man was innocent! The judge ran to the man to rescue him. Fortunately, or miraculously (?), the knot was lame, and the man was still alive. He was released and went on to Santiago de Compostela to pay his promise. Years after, the man returned to Barcelos and erected a monument in honour of Santiago and the Virgin Mary.

The rooster of Barcelos is usually found in every home; although, it is seen as a folklore item. The revival of old traditions brought the rooster back again and today we can find it in many homes and public spaces as a national symbol.

F ADO / P ORTUGUESE G UITAR (*F ADO / G UITARRA PORTUGUESA*)
The word *Fado* means fate, fatality, or destiny. *Fado* music has its origin in the 19th century, among the bohemian and marginal classes of society. It was sung in streets, alleys and places such as taverns and brothels. It was originally an improvised song. During the 1930s, *Fado* started gradually to be present in restaurants called *Fado* houses, where people would go to have dinner and listen to *Fado*. These would be mainly concentrated in the historic city centre and neighbourhoods.

Fado is usually sung by one person (called *fadista*) and accompanied by the classical guitar and Portuguese guitar. The Portuguese guitar has also become a symbol of Portugal due to its unique sound from its twelve strings. Any Portuguese anywhere in the world recognises the sound of this instrument.

We can hear *Fado* in *Fado* houses and popular festivals as well as in concerts of great *Fado* singers and musicians. The perfect environment for listening to *Fado* requires a room with dimmed lights and... silence! In former times you could hear someone in the room say, "Silence! *Fado* is about to be sung!" Before the show started.

Fado is a UNESCO Intangible Cultural Heritage of Humanity.

SARDINE / CODFISH (*SARDINHA/BACALHAU*)

The Portuguese love food and love to gather and feast around a table with friends and family. Sardines and codfish are two prominent symbols of the Portuguese cuisine. The Portuguese have eaten codfish for centuries, since the time of the discoveries.

Cod was preserved in salt so it could be preserved for months on the high seas, hence traditionally we eat mainly dry salted codfish. It is also the traditional Christmas food in most of the country. There are at least 365 ways of cooking codfish: one for each day of the year.

Sardines are the symbol of summer, and of the summer popular festivities mainly in the capital city, Lisboa, and also in Porto, the second main city in the country. Summer is not summer without sardines.

They are also a symbol of the canning industry that once was one of the largest industries in the country. Once considered as food for troops and the poor, some canned fish today achieves the status of gourmet food and can be found in many souvenir and gourmet shops.

There are no strict rules but, to many, *sardinha assada* (roasted sardine) should rest on a slice of bread. However, you should keep some room in your stomach before you are full because you will also want to eat the bread which has been impregnated with the sardines' oil. After all, you need to have Omega-3.

The popular festivities are an exception to normal etiquette and good manners because you are allowed to eat with your hands, should you wish to keep it traditional: Sardine on the bread in one hand, red wine in the other hand and you are ready to enjoy the night! You will never, ever be served roasted sardines at a formal event. No one would dare…

FILIGREE (*FILIGRANA*)

The word *filigrana* derives from the Latin words *filium* (string) and *granum* (grain). It is the art of working delicate strings of gold or silver together and was a sign of wealth, prosperity and luck.

The *filigree* has been used in jewellery for centuries since the pre-Roman civilisations that inhabited the Iberian Peninsula and is still used today to create the most beautiful jewellery. *Filigree* is an *ex libris* of the Portuguese jewellery.

Filigree can be found mostly in the north region of Alto Minho, namely Viana do Castelo, where the brides use their traditional dress and adorn it with *filigree*.

For centuries, women in this region like to wear precious fancy earrings to look like a queen. The so called 'queen's earrings' symbolise female fertility, hence they are an important adornment to a bride. The bigger the earrings, the better.

Another symbol of the art of *filigree* as well as a symbol of the country is the 'heart of Viana'. One might think it appeared as a symbol of love, but the real origin is believed to be religious. It symbolises the sacred heart of Christ.

Queen D. Maria used a big heart crafted in *filigree* as a sign of gratefulness for having been granted a son. Be it a pendant or an earring, the *filigree* heart is one of the symbols of the country.

Heart of Viana

PORT WINE (VINHO DO PORTO)

Port wine is one of the most known and appreciated wines in the world.

Only the liqueur wine produced in the Douro Demarcated Region can be called 'port wine'. The Douro Demarcated Region is located in the *Alto Douro Vinhateiro* area that is the oldest regulated wine region in the world and is considered a UNESCO world heritage site.

This wine is different from the others due to unique characteristics such as a high alcohol content (up to 22%), colour, sweetness and aroma. These characteristics vary according to the different types of port wine that exist.

Despite being known as a sweet wine, port wine can vary from very sweet to extra dry. The difference depends on the degree of sweetness which itself is determined by how long the manufacturer allows it to ferment.

Traditionally served as an aperitif and digestif wine, port wine has emerged as an alternative to traditional 'table wines', bringing elegance, finesse and sophistication to any meal. Like most wines, port should be stored in a cool place (not excessively cold), with little humidity.

There is nothing better to warm the body in winter, and the soul in any season, than a glass of port wine. With a unique colour, texture and aroma, port is a wine that cannot be compared to any other, and when served as an aperitif or after meals, it is always able to please and enchant people, adding a touch of refinement and good taste to any occasion.

How to drink Port Wine:

- It is usually served at a temperature between 15°C and 20°C, except for white and tawny types, which can be tasted a little colder.
- Port wine is served in small quantities, in a glass slightly smaller than the traditional white wine, with the upper part narrower than the body.
- The glass should only be filled to half, to allow a better oxygenation of the wine and thus to take greater advantage of the taste and aroma.
- Always hold your glass by the stem as you do not want to warm the wine with your hands.

Welcome to Portugal!

Chapter 2

Meeting, greeting, posture and body language

GREETINGS

Greeting is an act of courtesy that plays a very important role in social relationships. It is not only a form of politeness, but also a way of attracting the empathy of others.

The Portuguese greet everyone with whom, even if they don't have a close relationship, they cross paths with on a daily basis, such as neighbours or people who work in the same building. Passing by a neighbour or a colleague and not greeting him/her is frowned upon.

The Portuguese are very expressive in their communication amongst family and friends, with whom they freely show their emotions. Not that the Portuguese are exaggerated in their gestures but, amongst friends, body language is more relaxed and, therefore, the use of gestures is more expressive. It is common for a family or friend reunion to be quite lively; this is as opposed to having formal settings, or being in the presence of strangers, when the Portuguese often adopt a more reserved posture/gestures.

In Portugal, the most common form of greeting is two kisses, one on each cheek. This greeting is widespread but should be reserved for informal relationships.

Although this greeting may be used between co-workers, it should be limited to colleagues with whom one has worked for a long time, and with whom there is an informal and/or close relationship. In the workplace, it is always better to adopt a more reserved posture.

Ladies greet each other with two kisses, which is also the informal greeting between ladies and men. Men always greet each other with a handshake. In close relationships, the handshake may be paired with a hug. Younger generations may use the kiss and/or the hug as a greeting.

A variation of the 'two kisses' greeting is the one kiss on one cheek, which is usually used amongst family and close friends, in a more traditional family environment.

In formal occasions and in a corporate environment, the handshake is the most used, and most expected, between both men, ladies, and ladies and men. The handshake should be firm and eye-to-eye. Outside of the corporate world, in a private setting, to give a handshake to someone you have been introduced to, instead of two kisses, may seem strange or may be seen as a sign of arrogancy.

The rule of introductions is that the youngest person should be introduced to the oldest, men to women, and the person with the lowest rank to his or her superior. It should be the older person, the lady or the superior who extends the hand to greet or determines the form of greeting. Even though the man should wait for the lady to make the first move for the handshake, this rule is inverted if the man is undoubtedly older or of a higher rank.

POSTURE AND BODY LANGUAGE

Posture and body language are very important forms of non-verbal communication which must be observed in order to transmit, whenever possible, a correct and positive image.

When greeting someone, you should be careful not to have your arms crossed or your hands in your pockets, as this conveys, respectively, a lack of interest and disrespect.

Do not point, especially directly, at someone. If you want to mention a person who is across the room, describe them, but do not point at the person in question.

Don't squint in front of others, even in an informal setting.

Personal space gets *personal* on public transport. Everybody tries not to touch other people and, if they do, they should, and usually do, rush to apologise or to immediately shrink themselves to their space. Staring is rude and to be avoided. Portuguese are usually orderly and respectful people in queues. This attitude became even more pronounced during the pandemic times, when people respected each other's space even more.

However, do not think that someone who gets closer to your back in a queue is being disrespectful. Not everybody is sensible enough to leave some space.

Portugal, being a coastal country, has many kilometres of beaches that are widely frequented by many people, both Portuguese and foreigners. The beach, being a place of relaxation, where people keep an informal posture, is often the place where one's manners are revealed.

On the beach one should avoid sitting too close to other people. A distance should be maintained so that everyone's privacy is protected as much as possible. Listening to loud music (an attitude unnecessary nowadays, given the technology available) is very frowned upon, as are games and beach activities that may disturb other people's rest.

When shaking your towel, care should be taken not to throw sand on others. This is perhaps the greatest proof of good manners (or lack of it) we can give on the beach.

Chapter 3

Conversation Dos and Don'ts

When we visit a foreign country, we must prepare for the journey. Reading about the culture, language and history of the country we are visiting is as important as booking flights, hotels and tours. This not only shows good manners and respect for the country we are visiting, but also it can avoid us being unwittingly rude or getting in trouble by approaching the wrong topics.

Amongst friends and family, a topic of conversation easily arises, because everyone knows each other and knows what subjects can be discussed. With strangers, however, good manners dictate that subjects like politics, money or religion should be avoided, as these are delicate subjects that may upset someone with a different way of thinking.

Also, do not give in to the temptation to be permanently making jokes during a conversation. Monopolizing a conversation with jokes, besides being unpleasant for the listener, may show that you are not acquainted with the subject being talked about.

THE LANGUAGE: IN PORTUGAL, SPEAK PORTUGUESE
Trying to speak the language of the country you are visiting is a good way to narrow down barriers and show respect. The Portuguese are very tolerant with, and appreciate the effort of, foreign people who try to speak their language (they know what you have been through…). Also, most of the people in Portugal speak at least basic English.

Some foreigners either greet the Portuguese in Spanish or assume that Portuguese speak Spanish. Assuming that and approaching a Portuguese person in Spanish is a big *faux pas* and it is usually seen as disrespectful. Besides, it shows someone's knowledge about the country is fairly scarce. The same applies the other way around; one should never approach a Spanish in Portuguese.

Portugal and Spain are different countries, with different cultures and distinct languages. Although similar and with the same Romanic origin, Portuguese has its own grammar and vocabulary. Being a Romanic language, Portuguese is also related to other Latin languages in Europe such as French and Italian.

Portugal has two official languages: Portuguese and Mirandese. The latter is spoken by a few thousand, in the north region of Miranda do Douro. This could be an interesting topic to talk about with a Portuguese. Mind you, as only some people speak Mirandese, if you want to adventure yourself into the study of this wonderful (not easy) language, you will score points with the Portuguese.

HISTORY: PORTUGUESE HISTORY

The Portuguese are proud of their history. The achievements of their navigators and conquerors are a good topic for a conversation. On the other hand, subjects such as the dictatorship and colonial war are not peaceful. Portugal became a democracy in 1974, after the Carnation Revolution. Not much time has passed since this event; therefore, some wounds have not yet healed. Unless it is just an exchange of points of view, these topics can quickly slide into a political conflict which is not good manners when one wants to socialise.

FOOD AND DRINK: PORTUGUESE CUISINE / PORTUGUESE WINE

This is one of the best conversation topics for a Portuguese. Portuguese cuisine and Portuguese wine are safe topics on any occasion and every Portuguese will be happy and proud to talk about them. Anyone will tell you about the best dish and the best place to eat it, the best wine and the best dish that goes with it, their favourite restaurant and their favourite wine. The Portuguese are proud of their culture, so any topic on these subjects is welcome. All in all, any small talk can end in a conversation around a table with a good meal and one of the many very good Portuguese wines.

SPORTS: SOCCER

The Portuguese are fairly tolerant of soccer as long as you do not say anything offensive either about a favourite team, or the Portuguese soccer team, which the Portuguese defend passionately, even those who are not soccer fans. Almost all Portuguese are supporters of a football team, even if they are not members. There are three main football teams in Portugal and their supporters can be quite fanatic. Police are always strongly present whenever there is a match between these teams, as things can get serious amongst fans and cheerleaders.

Even amongst friends, the Portuguese are cautious in their approach to this subject with supporters of different clubs. This is a conversation topic that you should avoid, unless you know the others' thoughts on the subject, or you share the passion for the same team.

Religion: Fatima

One of the most known places in the country is the sanctuary of Fatima. It is the place where, in 1917, the Virgin Mary allegedly appeared to three shepherd children, making it one of the most important shrines in the world dedicated to the Virgin Mary. Every year in May, thousands of pilgrims (mostly Catholics, but also people of other faiths) gather in the sanctuary of Fatima to pray, to show their gratitude towards the Virgin Mary and to ask for miracles.

Although Portugal is a secular country, the great majority of the people who practice a religion are Catholics. Portugal is tolerant and welcoming of other faiths. Unless you know the other person is a devout Catholic (or other faith) with whom it would be bold to talk about religion, this is a pacific topic with Portuguese. The Portuguese, even those who do not believe in the apparition of the Virgin Mary, say that Fatima is always looking over Portugal. One never knows…

Chapter 4

Gift Giving

The Portuguese love to gift as much as they like to receive. This is not only to do with gifts on occasions like birthdays, but with anything that we think the other person will like. It is common, among colleagues, for example, for someone to bring 'those' cakes that are so well known from 'that' bakery, or to bring biscuits that they made at home. Among female friends/colleagues it is also common to offer small handicrafts that one of them has made. No special occasion is needed to give a gift to someone. If we find something, however trivial it may be, that we know that a family member or friend likes, we buy it and give it as a gift.

SOCIAL GIFTING ETIQUETTE
When you are invited to someone's home, for an informal event, a present to the hosts is not expected, but it is a common habit and always appreciated by those who receive it.

For an informal occasion, among friends who see each other regularly and when we are invited to a close friend's house, we are expected to ask the hosts whether they need or want us to take something. In this case, the hosts may simply say that they do not want us to take anything or say 'yes' and ask us to take, let's say, the pudding.

If the host/hostess says that nothing is needed, we may just take a bottle of wine, a cake that we make and know everybody likes, or homemade products such as jam or cookies. A flower in a vase is always a good gift for the hostess. A flower bouquet will require your hostess to prepare a vase to put them in, and thus a plant in a pot is more appropriate.

As for the bottle of wine, it would probably be a wine we had and loved and thus wanted to share with our friends, or one we know our friends are particularly fond of. As Portugal is such a wine producing country, it is a cultural norm for the Portuguese to offer wine to friends and visitors.

If the occasion is somehow formal, a box of good quality chocolates or a beautifully presented scented candle are good examples of gifts to give your hostess. For the host, a bottle of high-quality wine, old whisky or Cognac/Armagnac are usually appreciated, unless you know your host does not drink alcohol, in which case you can always offer a good coffee table book.

A gift to both hostess and host is not mandatory. Giving a gift only to the hostess is perfectly acceptable.

The gift will be opened the moment it is received, as to show appreciation and interest.

BIRTHDAYS

If you are invited to a birthday party, you should take a gift to the host. If the lunch/dinner party takes place in a restaurant chosen by the host, and each guest pays for her/his meal; your presence is the gift, hence a gift should not be expected. Most of the invitees have a gift for the host despite this, though.

CHRISTMAS

In Portugal, Christmas presents are opened mostly on Christmas Eve, after dinner, at midnight, or later if people attend the mass (which takes place at midnight). Some people open their presents on Christmas day in the morning, though.

Christmas is the only time when you are allowed to not open a present the moment it is given to you. If someone gives you a Christmas present days before Christmas, you may choose to open it only on Christmas Eve. In this situation it will not be seen as bad manners. Obviously, a thank you phone call should be made very soon after opening the present.

BUSINESS ETIQUETTE

Business meetings do not require gifts. However, gifts may be exchanged when hosting a foreign business partner.

Giving a gift to customers and partners is common, although these are usually not exchanged at first meetings. Company merchandise can be exchanged anytime. High-quality merchandise is usually exchanged amongst CEOs and directors. It is also gifted to customers and partners, especially during Christmas time.

Very expensive presents should be avoided, unless appropriate to the situation and the status of the person receiving the gift. Some companies have strict rules concerning the value of the gifts their collaborators are allowed to accept.

If in doubt, a beautiful coffee table book is always a good gift for any occasion.

Some companies offer gifts to the people who come into most contact with them or who make business decisions. This is a courtesy and should be viewed as such. If, by company policy, you cannot accept gifts, inform those giving the gift of this policy and thank them for their kindness.

The gifting etiquette golden rule is to never gift very personal items, like clothes or scents, unless you are gifting someone close whom you know very well and surely will appreciate these presents.

To thank for a gift is, obviously, mandatory for any occasion. It is usually done verbally but, if not done previously, a written note or, at least, a phone call to thank for a present is highly appreciated and is a manifestation of etiquette and good manners.

Chapter 5

Dining Etiquette

Whether as a host or as a guest, a gathering of people around a dining table should always be a pleasant occasion. As hosts, we should make our guests feel at ease and provide them with a pleasant atmosphere. As guests, we should behave in an exemplary manner and show our gratitude for our hosts' kindness in welcoming us.

The Portuguese love to entertain. A dinner arrangement may not require more than twenty-four hours warning. Except for weddings, christenings and other special occasions that require previous preparation, among close friends, the Portuguese do not need to schedule a dinner in advance for it to happen. We just need to come across a friend in the street or walk by a friend's door and we have what is needed for a gathering.

In a spontaneous situation, good manners become even more important, as the guests must think about giving the hosts the least possible disturbance. In this very informal situation, the guests are expected to help prepare the meal, set the table and clear the table, unless, as host, you tell them not to.

A full meal, with much preparation, is not expected. This kind of gathering usually ends up in a couple of morsels and titbits, what we call '*petisco*'. Still, the table setting is usually regarded, as a basic setting is mandatory whatever the occasion.

A spontaneous gathering implies an earlier end. One must be mindful that the hosts unexpectedly gave up their private time to have us in their home, and so one must not impose one's presence beyond the spontaneity of the situation.

INFORMAL DINING ETIQUETTE
For an informal dinner, the standard etiquette rules apply.

Be it in an informal or formal dinner, punctuality should always be regarded. In Portugal, the most common dinner time is between eight and nine p.m.

A delay of up to ten minutes is acceptable. More than this, and you must call your hosts to let them know you are going to be late and when you expect to arrive. One must keep in mind that our hosts have planned the dinner to flow in a way that must be met. Maybe there is an oven dish or pudding that cannot wait to be served beyond some time, who knows?

A gift to the hosts is not expected, but it is appreciated.

The table is set with the informal table setting composed of plate, cutlery with tines facing up (fork on the left and knife on the right, and soup spoon on the right, next to the knife), one or two glasses (water and wine, or only water or wine) and a napkin (either on the left or on the plate). Cutlery for pudding is usually placed on the top of the plate (spoon facing left, and the fork under the spoon facing right) with tines facing up. A salad plate/crescent may be used and is placed in the left upper part of the place.

Drinks and appetisers are usually served before the meal.

If there are starters served before the meal, these can come prepared from the kitchen. In this case, the cutlery may not be on the table, but come with the starter.

The food is commonly served on platters that are placed on the table and each person serves himself unless the hostess prefers to do it herself. No one should start eating until everybody has been served food, and the hostess has started. The hosts should be the last to finish, so to not hurry the guests.

Coffee is usually served after pudding and can be served either at the table or in the sitting room with digestifs.

Even for an informal occasion, the right time to leave should always be regarded by the guests.

Formal Dining Etiquette

The main difference between informal and formal dining lies in the table setting and the dress code, as good manners and etiquette rules are expected to always be present and suited to the given situation. Punctuality is mandatory. There are no excuses. Unless otherwise stated by the hosts, the dress code should be smart.

In a private household, a formal dinner requires the presence of at least one member of staff, so the hostess does not need to leave the room or can leave the room for the least time possible.

Drinks and appetisers are offered before the meal.

The table is thoughtfully decorated and is set with plate and cutlery (forks on the left and knives on the right, and spoons on the right next to the knives). The glasses are placed on the upper right side of the place, and the napkin is placed either on the plate or on the bread plate. The bread plate is placed either on the upper left side of the place, or, depending on the space, on the left of the place, aligned with the plate. A butter knife is placed on the bread plate. A salad plate/crescent may be used, in which case it should be placed on the upper left side of the place.

In a formal dinner, special cutlery may be used, such as antique silver cutlery. If it has a coat of arms or an engraved monogram on the back, it may be placed with tines facing down, to show what is engraved on the back of the cutlery.

Portugal Coat of Arms

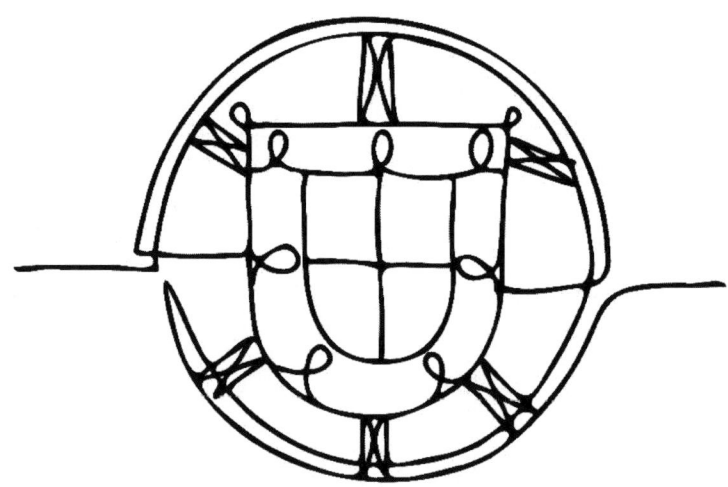

Cutlery for pudding can be set either aligned with the rest of the cutlery, or on the top of the place (spoon facing left, and the fork under the spoon facing right), depending on the space there is on the table.

Water should be in small glasses. The wine may be served either from the bottle or from a decanter. If served from the bottle, the wine should be opened hours before being served; if a decanter is used, this time may be reduced.

Coffee and digestives are served in the sitting room.

It is up to the guests to read the atmosphere, to perceive when it is the right time to leave.

Table setting in a common restaurant is basic (plate, knife, fork, napkin and one glass), whilst in a smart restaurant the formal dining setting is usual, except for the cutlery and glasses, the combinations of which cannot prepare for all the possible choices of the diner.

Mealtimes in restaurants/*cafes* in Portugal are the same as in most countries. Breakfast goes from six a.m. to eleven a.m. lunch from noon to two p.m. (usually kitchens close at three p.m.), and dinner from seven p.m. to ten p.m. Some places like *cafes* do not serve dinner, as these will generally close at seven p.m. or eight p.m. It is good manners not to arrive at the *cafe*/restaurant at the last minute before it closes.

In private households, the schedule will be like the ones described above but, obviously, adapted to the family lifestyle. The typical 'on the run' breakfast in a *cafe* is composed of one espresso or café latte and a pastry or a piece of toast, or a glass of milk with coffee and toast or a croissant. Obviously, choices change from person to person, but this is the classic basic breakfast version of someone who goes to a *cafe* quickly before going to work.

There are special meals for special days, such as Christmas and Easter which, depending in which part of the country you are, require different types of food. Formality on any of these dates depends on the household, but Christmas Eve and Easter lunch usually require some care regarding table setting and dress code.

Codfish is the main presence at the dinner table on Christmas Eve all over the country, but kid, rooster and octopus are also typical from some regions. You can find only codfish or both fish and meat at a Christmas Eve dinner.

On Christmas Day, a dish with the leftovers of the codfish is traditional for a Christmas lunch. It is called '*roupa velha*' (old clothes). Fortunately for those who do not appreciate this, there are other options available within the Christmas tradition like turkey, lamb and pork.

Pudding is always composed of typical Christmas sweets such as the '*bolo rei*' (in English, 'king cake') and different typical Christmas pastries, which are usually fried and made with ingredients such as pumpkin, chickpea, cinnamon and huge quantities of egg yolks and sugar. The traditional Portuguese Christmas sweets mostly come from old recipes from the monks and nuns, used in the monasteries.

For Easter Sunday lunch, fish, is not a frequent choice due to Lent, the period during which abstinence from meat prevails, and so meat is the favourite food. Lamb, kid, or goat are among the favourites depending on the region of the country you are in.

A special type of bread called *'folar'* is mandatory for an Easter meal. It can be sweet (tasting like fennel) or salty (made with meat inside).

Also, sweets and candy are much appreciated at this time of the year, like chocolate eggs and bunnies, and roasted almonds covered in all sorts of sweet coats and colours.

Good table manners must apply in whatever situation mentioned above.

As in most western countries, Portuguese teach the children the basics of good table manners from a very young age: to wash hands before going to the table, to sit straight, elbows off the table, to eat with mouth shut and ask permission to leave the table when they finish.

Portuguese etiquette does not contemplate putting food on the back of the fork. One would not even be able to do it with some types of food.

Dining is of great importance to the Portuguese. Be it a birthday, anniversary, graduation, football match, or a business meeting, anything can be the perfect excuse for dining.

Chapter 6

Business Etiquette

The main goal in business is to sell. Etiquette and good manners sell!

It is important that, from the first moment, the client perceives the other side as a professional. No matter what country you are in, the working day of a professional should start at the moment the clock chimes in the morning. One must do whatever is needed to look one's best.

Even though, in this day and age, things are getting more relaxed in relation to dress codes, the dress code must suit the function and the situation. Knowing how to dress according to the situation is a matter of etiquette and manners, as well as self-respect.

The dress code in a business environment depends on the company, but a smart dress code is expected. Casual clothes should be avoided, unless it is tacitly authorised by the company, considering that this type of dress code may represent the type of image the company wants to transmit.

In the corporate world, the Portuguese use their academic titles. '*Prof/Prof^a*' (a doctorate who is a professor in university or polytechnic education), '*Dr/Dra*' (for doctors and/or anyone holding a degree), '*Eng/Eng^a*' (for engineers) and '*Arqt/Arqt^a*' (for architects), are common.

In a business environment, these titles should be used when addressing someone of whom you know the title, and with whom a formal relationship is required. Address the person by the title followed by the surname(s) for a gentleman, and by the title followed by the first name and surname, for a lady. Thereafter, the person may be addressed only by his/her title, like *Senhor(a) professor(a)/Senhora doutor(a)*, etcetera.

If you introduce one person to another, use their academic titles to introduce them. As always, introduce the person with the lowest rank to the person with the highest rank.

You should not use your academic title to introduce yourself, though. Your name starts with your first name, not your academic title.

If you are making a presentation about your work, you should introduce yourself by your name, and then, mention your academic background. This way, the other persons know how they should address you.

To use your academic title to introduce yourself to someone in person, or to identify yourself on the phone, is frowned upon and may be seen as snobbish or as a sign of arrogance.

A lady who does not have an academic title but with whom you have a formal relationship, should be addressed by '*Sra D*' (*Senhora Dona*) followed by her first name(s). A gentleman should be addressed by '*Sr*' (*Senhor*) followed by his surname(s).

Invitations for business meals are common. The purpose of a business lunch/dinner is to discuss business, so that will be the topic of the meal. In a formal occasion, the subject should not be raised at least until everyone has chosen the main course. In the case of a business meal with people you already know, this rule may not apply, depending on the formality amongst those present.

The person who hosts the other guests pays the bill, even if it is a woman.

If you are the host of a business meal in a restaurant, you should arrive some time prior to the time scheduled for the event. This allows you time to check if everything is the way you expect it to be and make any last minute changes you find necessary.

If you are the invitee, arrive on time. Do not forget to call your host should you be delayed (but do not be, if at all possible). Unless you are expecting a 'life-or-death type' phone call, you should put your phone on silent mode, or better still, on flight mode. Your phone should never be laid on the table. Not only it is bad manners, but it is also, nowadays, unhygienic.

The host will be the one to tell when the meeting is finished. If you have your time limited by another meeting, do let your host know this beforehand.

When a business visit is expected, the reception desk or the secretary should be advised of the name of the person and the time the person is expected. The visitor should be met at the entrance of the office, or taken to the meeting room, by the staff. Whenever you have someone visiting in your office room, you should get up and welcome your visitor at the door.

When foreign visitors are expected, the host should provide all the information concerning the company, such as address and contact details, but also the name and contact of the person who will be waiting for the visitor at the arrival point, if applicable.

The host should offer to help plan the visitor's trip and stay.

Persons that will have contact with the visitor should be informed of the visit in advance, in order to let them prepare any meetings or documents that may be necessary.

If you are applying for a job, make sure to do your homework. Read about the company you are applying to. Check the company's website and social media for its history and its culture; this shows your interest in the company. Prepare a verbal presentation of your CV, as you will most probably be confronted with it in the interview. Also prepare the answers to the questions you know or believe you are going to be asked.

Prepare yourself to look polished and professional. Your clothes should be spotless. Make sure to have a fresh breath. If using a fragrance, it should be fresh, light and discreet. The dress code should be smart. Conservative colours like blue or black are safe choices for an interview. Depending on the type of company you are applying to, the colour chart may be used fully or in a more discreet way.

For ladies, the hair should be washed and styled, the make-up should be visible but discreet (opt for neutral colours and light sheens or matt), your hands must be immaculate (opt for clear or pastel shades of nail polish). For gentlemen, your hair should be groomed, and your beard should not look like you have just started letting it grow (either you have a beard or not, and if you do, it must be trimmed); make sure your nails are trimmed and tidy.

Before entering the building, put your phone on silent mode. Make sure you arrive early, so you have time to present yourself at the reception desk and to compose yourself. Be aware that your interviewer may check the time you arrived, as punctuality says a lot about a person as a professional.

The handshake and eye contact are crucial. These are the main features when building rapport. Smile!

Business cards usually mention, in addition to the name, the academic title and the position the person holds in the company.

If the card is attached to documents that will be sent to a known client/supplier, it is usual to write a few words of courtesy by hand on the card itself. In the case of someone with whom there is some intimacy, the surname(s) should be crossed out.

In business writing, dates will appear in day/month/year format. The use of red ink in written documents, for whatever reason, is seen as rude.

In Portugal, business and business meetings take place throughout the year. However, arranging a meeting during the months of July and August can be very difficult. It's considered a holiday time par excellence and many companies close, if not completely, at least some of their areas, for a whole month.

Chapter 7

Wedding Etiquette

A wedding is a unique party; everyone wants to be perfect. From the making of the invitations to the end of the party, everything must be thought through with time ahead and carefully prepared. Family and close friends should be the first to be informed, preferably in person. Invitations should be issued two months in advance. For guests living abroad, this period should be extended, in order to let people make the necessary arrangements.

Traditionally it is the respective parents of the bride and groom who issue the invitation, stating that they '*have the pleasure to invite you to the marriage of their daughter/son to…*', but it can also be issued in the name of the bride and groom (more common in second marriages).

Invitations should, preferably, be printed. Although, in this day and age, people may want to save costs, or have an ecological approach, and send them by email. To family and close friends, the invitation should be delivered in person. For the other guests it is sent by post.

The invitation should contain all the relevant information such as date and time, place, web page of the wedding (if any), deadline for replying to the invitation and contact for replies. Responses must be given at least two weeks before the ceremony.

A wedding list is organised, listing gifts that the bride and groom would like to receive to help them start their life in their new home, or a crowd funding website is increasingly common, to help finance a dream trip, for example. The wedding list should not be sent with the invitation. It is up to the guests to contact the bride and groom's parents, the bridesmaids or best men, and find out what has been defined by the couple. Nowadays, it is common for the bride and groom to create a wedding webpage on a social network, where all the information regarding the ceremony, including the wedding list, is published. If an invitee is not able to attend the wedding, he/she should still send a present to the bride and groom.

Small gifts for the guests will also be prepared. It is a way to show gratitude for their presence.

Traditionally, the bride's parents pay for the wedding reception, hence they should be the ones to define the final number of guests. However, nowadays, expenses are often shared between the parents of the bride and groom or, in cases of a second marriage, supported by the bride and groom themselves.

In times gone by, tradition dictated that the bride was responsible for the trousseau and the groom was responsible for the house and the furniture. Nowadays, these tasks and expenses are usually shared between the bride and groom, and their parents.

Before the wedding, it is common to have a bachelor party, which consists of informal gatherings between the bride and her friends, and the groom and his friends. These parties usually consist of a dinner, at home or in a restaurant, and/or a night out.

The time of day for a wedding depends on what the bride and groom want to offer after the ceremony.

A wedding celebrated in the morning will require a reception, that is, lunch, whereas a wedding celebrated in the afternoon, or at the end of the day, will be followed by a cocktail party or a dinner.

In classical and traditional ceremonies, the use of morning dress is expected. In less formal weddings, men present themselves in dark suits and the ladies in a dress or suit. In either case, guests should refrain from wearing totally black or white looks.

The non-use of a tie has become common at informal weddings.

In Portugal, both in civil and religious marriages, the presence of two witnesses, called 'godparents', is mandatory. These are chosen by the bride and groom from amongst their friends: the bride chooses the godmother, and the groom chooses the best man. There can be more than one couple of godparents. In modern wedding ceremonies, some brides choose to also have one or more bridesmaids.

The role of the godmother and/or bridesmaid(s) is to help the bride with the wedding organisation, and also to support her on the day itself, whether it is putting on the dress, holding the veil when entering the church, receiving guests, or dealing with any unforeseen events that arise during the day, sparing the bride any worries.

The rings are bought by the groom or the best man.

The rings are placed on a small silver tray which is handed to the priest (or celebrant, in a civil wedding) before the exchange of rings. The rings are given to the priest by a child, usually a family member or the daughter/son of close friends. There may be one or more children chosen by the bride and groom to perform small tasks such as carrying the rings to the priest or holding the tail of the bride's dress. These children are commonly called 'ring children' (direct translation).

The bride's entrance in the church is made on the arm of her father, or any other person chosen by her. Nowadays, the bride's entrance alone is also an option.

At the place of the ceremony, the bride's guests sit on the left side of the venue, and the groom's guests on the right.

At the end of the religious ceremony, and after leaving the sacristy, the bride and groom leave the church, followed by their parents and godparents. The guests should wait in the church and only leave after the bride and groom, but presently everybody waits outside the church to see the married couple leaving the church and greet them by throwing petals or rice at the newlyweds, to wish them good fortune.

THE LUNCH ('COPO D'ÁGUA')

After a ceremony celebrated in the morning, a lunch is offered. This is what in Portugal is called *'Copo d'Água'* (meaning 'glass of water', in an *ipsis verbis* translation). The origin of the expression is lost in time, but the dictionary describes it as 'a meal of sweets and liqueurs with which visitors or guests of a solemn act were obliged', *in Dicionário Priberam da Língua Portuguesa*.

That's when the wedding party begins. The most common version is to offer lunch to the guests and, at the end of the day, allow a buffet to be available until the end of the party, which is usually late at night.

Nowadays, the bride and groom may opt for more discreet ceremonies with fewer people, but not less refined. Some people are opting for late afternoon weddings. In this case, either a cocktail or dinner is offered. In any case, the guests expect a meal to be offered, and a party where good food and drinks cannot be lacking.

In a less formal and modern version of a wedding, held in the morning, a brunch can be served, and a specific time can be set for the end of the party.

Most commonly, the tables at a wedding party are round, with a long table reserved for the bride and groom, their parents and godparents.

Nowadays, the type of tables and the presentation of the room depends on the type of venue, and the creativity of the bride and groom and/or the organising company.

When the bride and groom are not in charge of the task, the organising company manages the seating of the guests in order to guarantee a good distribution of people by family groups, friends and avoiding any possible incompatibility.

For weddings with many people, there is a map of the tables at the entrance of the room where both the table and the seat assigned to each guest are displayed. In more intimate parties, with fewer people, the seats are reserved at the table. It is up to the parents, or the godparents, to receive the guests in the room.

No one is assigned the task of giving the speeches, but they are mandatory for the bride and groom, and the bride's and groom's parents. Usually, the first to speak is the father of the bride, the groom being the last one to speak.

The high points in a wedding party are usually the speeches, the cutting of the wedding cake and the opening of the ball.

After this, people enjoy the party until late in the evening, or even until dawn.

Tradition regarding the cutting of the cake is very funny, regarding the single ladies. The first slice of cake is given by the bride to one of her single friends. After that, and because there is but one 'first slice', the other single ladies will eat their cake slice under the bride's veil so they too can find a husband quickly.

During the party, young ladies gather for the throw of the bouquet. The bride turns her back to the group and throws the bouquet towards them. Tradition says the young lady who catches it will be the next to get married.

After returning from the honeymoon, or not more than a month after the wedding, the couple should address their guests and thank them, both for their presence at the wedding and for the gift they offered. This should be done, preferably in writing, on a thank you note where the newlyweds' address should be included, as a way of 'offering' their new home to their friends.

The Russian Federation
By Anastasia Martel

Chapter 1

Cultural Symbols

If you were to ask me to describe Russia in one sentence, with all the bias in my head and heart I could say my home country is the most beautiful place on earth, a country of remarkable culture, people and contrasts. It is the biggest country in the world, stretching throughout vast parts of Europe and Asia, covering eleven time zones, home to the most extraordinary and picturesque nature.

From Saint Petersburg (our very own northern Venice) to Far East Vladivostok, the megacity of Moscow to the tranquil wilderness of Altai, artic temperatures of Siberia to the sunshine and golden beaches of Sochi, the Trans-Siberian Express, vodka, Saint Basil's Cathedral, Red Square, Chernobyl, huskies, Cold War and of course Rocky IV, it is indeed a country of controversy and contrasts. Have you ever heard the famous saying, 'You can't grasp Russia with your mind'?

In this chapter, I would like to tell you more about Russia, Russian people, their culture and some prominent cultural symbols, which will give you great insight and spark your interest to visit this great country.

As someone who lived for fourteen years in Yorkshire, in the United Kingdom, I can certainly say that Russian people and culture profoundly differs from most Western cultures and this, in my opinion, is what makes our world interesting, journeys worth taking, places worth seeing and people worth meeting.

Russian people are an exceptionally proud nation. By nature, we are very reserved, private, resilient, tenacious, with a strong proclivity to what may seem like secrecy to the Western world. On the other hand, we are amongst the most family orientated people, always welcoming and certainly people who know how to have a good time.

Russians are a highly educated, philosophical and clever nation, with great problem solving and survival skills that were transcendent into our personalities and lifestyles through the centuries. We seldomly share or talk about issues or problems; we tend to solve them. This phenomenon can be witnessed across the wide spectrum of people from university intellectuals to simple folk in the countryside. You can say that Russians know how to live and just get on with it.

At times, Russians may seem to be lacking in manners or pleasantries. This is due to us being very straight forward and to-the-point people. Not ones for small talk or ice breakers, Russians prefer to get to the point, leaving no room for misunderstandings. This shouldn't be mistaken as rudeness; it is just our way of doing things. It is advisable to refrain from personal questions about family, health, religion, finances or politics during the first or second conversation; as already mentioned, Russians are private people and reluctant to disclose any personal details, especially to foreign nationals or anyone outside their inner circle and they wouldn't hesitate to ask 'why do you need to know this' even if the intention was to start a conversation or simply to be polite and show interest.

Whilst Russia is a mostly Christian country, belonging to the Eastern Orthodox Church, there are large populations of Muslims, Jews and Buddhists. Due to the size of this country, it has a varied demography of people of all races and religions—something Russians are very proud of. In almost every city you will find churches, mosques, synagogues and other temples. It is worth mentioning that Russia is a very patriarchal country, where more traditional family roles are assigned to women and fathers; older brothers or husbands tend to be the head of the family and main decision-makers.

Talking about the national symbol and at the risk of sounding redundant, Russians are known for their vodka and the ritual of drinking it.

VODKA

Yes, Russians are a heavy drinking nation and we have a reputation to that extent. Au contraire to most heavy drinking nations, like the United Kingdom, Russians don't binge drink and there isn't a 'pub crawl' culture. As a rule, a typical Russian person prefers their spirit at least 40% with good food, good conversations and company. There are many customs and rituals surrounding drinking vodka in Russia, occasions when vodka is gifted, the snacks that go along best with it and of course the occasions. If you consume alcohol in the first place, drinking Russian style is highly contagious practice, as it all based on having a great time with your friends and family and simply having a laugh. Rules are pretty straight forward: remember, first is the vodka, followed by the toast, and is finished by '*Zakuska*', which is Russian for a snack.

We never drink without a reason or an occasion, both a happy one or less joyful. A wide range of occasions present the opportunity to crack open a bottle of vodka, such as a birthday, wedding, funeral, national holiday and many more, pretty much any reason one might think, to a Russian it would be an appropriate reason to have a drink. However, it doesn't need to be so pretentious; you can always make up a good reason for drinking, much more important is that you should always have one.

The best description of the true Russian way of drinking vodka was given by Anton Chekhov, the Russian classic writer:

'And you don't drink a vodka right away. No, Sir. First, you take a deep breath, wipe your hands and glance up at the ceiling to demonstrate your indifference. Only then you raise your vodka slowly to your lips and suddenly: Sparks! They fly from your stomach to the furthest reaches of your body'!

It is integral in Russian tradition and culture to propose a toast each time you take a shot. Generally, the first toast is a longer one; all the following ones are simple '*na zdorovie*', or '*za zdorovie*' that literally translates into English as 'for the good health'. Another common toast is 'for friendship', which is simply '*za druzhbu*'!. As I mentioned earlier in this chapter, Russians are philosophical and quite sentimental people, which means that we don't drink to material things or money, but rather to love, family, friends, health and good times. The general etiquette rule of pouring yourself last applies in vodka drinking customs as well. It is considered very impolite to pour yourself first or take a shot of vodka before all other people are ready.

Before you begin drinking, make sure you have something to eat or at least to smell. In Russia we call it '*zakuska*', which literally means 'snack'. It can range from pickles, salads; my very favourite and most famous of them is Olivier salad: grilled and smoked meats, anchovies, salamis—you get the idea; we like salty snacks. You should never drink vodka without eating something immediately afterwards; whilst not many people know the purpose behind this tradition, I will let you in on a secret. The smelling and eating right after drinking lines stomach to pervert hangovers, and also when one loses a sense of smell or taste it's time to stop.

The terminology of '*Zastolye*' refers to drinking alcohol at the table with friends and family, which is a very common Russian way to celebrate holidays or any occasion, the most prominent being New Year's Eve. '*Zastolye*' is a highly respected Russian tradition of socialising, usually in a private home with plenty of traditional food and drink. If you ever find yourself at one of these table parties, you're in for a long evening of great food, drink and laughs.

Russian Soul

We are famous for our deep Russian souls. Both religious and non-religious Russians have a deep sense of purpose, immortal soul and spirituality. At first, this may seem extraordinarily confusing and baffling, as Russian people are full of contrasts and dualities in pretty much every aspect of their lives. We don't care for social acceptance or popularity but have more friends than any other nation; we dispense of most social pleasantries and don't smile a lot, but we have a great sense of humour, laugh a lot and once we make a friend, it's for life. We are a nation of people who do not overthink; as history proved again and again, no amounts of regret will change the past and no amounts of worrying will change the future.

The Russian soul is a very superstitious one. Even the younger generations still blindly believe most superstitious stories told by their grandmas. The funny thing is, usually there is a lot of truth in old wisdom. The Russian soul is in a way an old soul; we tend to put things in a perspective of a whole lifetime, rather than here and now. We place incredible value to advise from seniors and their life experience. There is something incredibly comforting about this dark and secretive, Gogol like disposition and view on life. Self-reflective people, we always hope for the best but expect the worst.

The Russian Dolls

And yes, I am talking about the beautifully authentic and colourful Russian Matryoshka doll, also called a nesting doll. This is unquestionably the best known symbol of Russia around the world. In Russia, the doll is thought to symbolise traditional values of Russian society: respect for the elderly, unity of the extended family, fertility and abundance, and the search for truth and meaning.

Russian Dolls

USHANKA
With our harsh winters and arctic climates of Siberia, Ushanka, the traditional thick and warm hat with earflaps, is not only the fashion statement of any Russian but also one of the most widely recognised Russian symbols.

Russian Hat

Brown Bear

As true as it was centuries ago, today the Brown Russian Bear is the ultimate symbol of Russia. Representing both the good (strength, power and sheer might), and the bad (ferocity and club-footedness), it's perhaps the only accurate likeness of the enigma that is Russia. The bear is an integral part of Russian culture from traditional inspiration or children's stories and folk superstitions. As a country with a large population of brown bears, it is not surprising that power, dominance and strength-loving Russians see this majestic animal as the truest reflection of what we are.

Chapter 2

Meeting, Greeting, Posture and Body Language

POSTURE

The way you carry yourself is immensely important in Russia. From a young age, children are taught that 'you wear your clothes, not the other way around', along with a strong importance placed towards confident body language. Whilst people in many countries would exude more of a friendly and gentle impression, Russian people tend to go for a 'it is better to be feared than to be loved' kind of mentality and then mellow down as they get to know people and get more familiar with the situation or the environment they encounter. Generally speaking, body language is very alpha dominant, assertive, confident and strong for both men and women. We are a rather tall nation and take great pride in this, hence we always try to present ourselves with a straight back and chin up posture. This may come across as very intimidating or even arrogant to some people, but rest assured there is no aggression in that kind of body language per se.

BODY LANGUAGE

Russians aren't crazy for overly expressive hand gestures or even facial micro-expressions, which makes them extremely hard to read. If you are familiar with the expressive gestures of Italian or Latin American people, Russians are quite frankly the opposite.

A strong handshake and eye contact are essential in every introduction or greeting. When meeting unfamiliar people, Russians will not get too close or invade personal space; however, once you know them or if you are introduced by a close friend or a family member, expect a big hug and a tap on a back. It is important to not get disheartened or offended by the stand-offish aura, as like discussed in the previous chapter, Russians are very reserved people, who take a little longer to connect with others, especially foreign nationals. I would always advise to act in a regular, familiar manner and be patient with Russians.

Temperament

I will not sugar coat this; we do have a temper on us and a short fuse, which is commonly and comically referred to as 'putting the fear of God' into someone. As a nation, we demand a high level of respect, loyalty, solidarity and don't suffer fools gladly. Russian people are very straight to the point, with a strong proclivity to 'my way or no way' mindset. This makes Russians very 'right here, right now', hot-headed people, rather arrogant and often outright bad and dangerous drivers. To elaborate further on this point, drink driving is very common in Russia and roads are not particularly safe due to younger generations opting for fast cars. I must admit, on many occasions I hear close people telling me 'here's the Russian in you coming out', which is funny retrospectively.

Smile

This is on ration I'm afraid. We are not a smiling nation, unless we are surrounded by friends or family. Overly friendly and smiley people (abroad, for example) usually make Russian people very uncomfortable, which is very funny to watch.

Greetings

These are always on the official side. It is either good morning—Доброе утро (*Dobroye utro*), good day—Добрый день (*Dobryy den*), or good evening—Добрый вечер (*Dobryy vecher*). The interesting aspect of Russian names is that we include a form of father's name as a middle name when introducing ourselves in an official or unfamiliar environment. For example, my father's name is Kristoff, hence I would introduce myself and expect to be referred to as Anastasia Kristoffovna or Anastasia Kristoffovna Martel. A male example might be Vladimir Fedorov, whose father would be called Vladimir as well. In Russia he would be referred to as Vladimir Vladimirovich or Vladimir Vladimirovich Fedorov.

Unless you find yourself in a romantic setting, there is not much difference in greeting for men and women. Au contraire to common misperception, Russian men, in general, are very gallant, respectful and gentle towards women.

The universal etiquette rules apply when introducing, and women are the ones who initiate the preferred method of greeting, whether it is a handshake or handshake with a kiss on both cheeks three times—left, right and left again. This is more common between females, but not limited only to women.

Chapter 3

Conversation Dos and Don'ts

Whether you're on a lighter side and prefer easy conversation or a deeper side and prefer more philosophical debates, Russia is the best place for this. Whilst technology is sweeping the world, making people interact less and message more, the good news is that a good conversation and good live company is still very much at the top of social life in Russia.

If you're not easily put off by the initial frostiness of Russian people and willing not only start a conversation but also persevere with what may feel like a monologue at the beginning, you're in for a treat. Slow to open up and get going, once Russians feel comfortable, they are extremely educational, entertaining and understanding.

Apart from the delicate subjects already discussed in the previous chapters, like religion, health, money, politics and personal relationships, there are a few more nuances I would strongly advise you to avoid. Firstly, to make a good impression and build strong relationships, it is integral to respect the history and not to pass any comments even on the most questionable historic figures like Lenin, Stalin or Putin. Many people are still very fond and nostalgic of the Soviet era and loyal to the current state of affairs. Delicate subjects, like the matter of Ukraine, Georgia or the Russian alliance with China, should be avoided. Whilst this, at first glance, may fall into the politics category, bear in mind that these topics can easily sneak into casual conversations and cause friction.

Avoid name dropping or any form of showing off, as this will be perceived as nothing more than posing. Conversations should flow very organically and easily if started from very general things and then narrowed down to the point at which both sides are comfortable. Be a good listener and always make effort to follow the conversation. If you find yourself at the point when you do not wish to disclose any kind of information, do not attempt to lie; a simple 'I'd rather not say' will earn you deep respect and no further questions will be asked on the subject.

Regardless of the topic of your conversation, always show genuine interest and do not disparage other opinions. Russians are a proud nation and would not pass a chance to tell you their perspective on life and interesting facts about their country. Avoid any dubious sexual innuendos and questionable remarks. If you are compelled to compliment a Russian person, always start with a compliment about their intellect, wit or character. Whilst it is always pleasant to be complimented on one's appearance, this is regraded the lowest form of compliment if you're not too familiar with that person. This also can be interpreted in the wrong way.

We all like to indulge in a few stereotypes now and then, and of course, the most common one is the vodka and cold Russian winters. This may be a light conversation starter, however, please keep in mind that a large population of Russia are of an Islamic faith, hence it will be highly inappropriate to suggest having a shot or two with a Muslim person.

Lastly, if you come across a person in Russia, who speaks Russian, but if called a Russian that person corrects you to Chechnyan or Dagestani, please take note of that and respect it. In the same way that a person from the UK may prefer specifically to be referred to as English, Scottish, Welsh or Northern Irish, due to the vastness of republics within the Russian Federation, certain people maybe be more loyal to the region they are from.

Chapter 4

Gift Giving

In Russia, gifting is more than a sign of appreciation or congratulations. There are some very deep-rooted gifting traditions in this country, which I will discuss in this chapter.

Yes, indeed it is the thought that counts when giving someone a gift, but in Russia, we don't do things by half measures when it comes to gifting. On top of the sentiment expressed to a recipient of a gift, there is an important element of expressing one's status through the gifts we buy. Even people from more modest echelons of society will give a high-value gift on occasions like weddings, christenings New Year's Eve celebrations (we give gifts on New Year's Eve, due to Eastern Orthodox Christmas usually taking place on the 7th of January) or milestone birthdays.

When invited to a dinner, it is not only polite but rather mandatory to bring flowers to the hostess and a bottle of strong alcohol to a host. Flowers should be elaborate, preferably a bouquet or an odd number of flowers. Choose higher-end flowers like roses, orchids, peonies or lilies, as even though my favourite flowers are irises and tulips, these are generally viewed as unsuitable for occasions. Choose alcohol on the premium side as well. It is always very polite and welcomed if a foreign guest brings something from their country, as this means a lot to Russian people, who are naturally very curious about overseas foods and things. This can be a box of chocolates, a premium tea or any national article. Always remember to bring something little for the children of the house, like sweets, which are usually handed to a mother.

If you happen to be more familiar with the host and you specialise in cooking or baking something, it is always very welcomed if you bring a homemade cake, cookies or even savoury dish.

When holding a gift you are about to present, a man needs to hold the alcohol and a woman should hold the flowers or chocolates. On the other hand, if no alcohol is presented and the occasion calls for a monetary gift, it is a man who gives it to a host or the hostess. The important thing to remember is discretion when giving money. The cash funds should be placed in a money envelope, in tidy banknotes and this does not get opened in front of the guest. When giving any gift you can expect a wholehearted appreciation and gratitude; it is customary to wish people health, happiness and love when presenting your gift. Also, it is worth mentioning that follow up handwritten 'Thank you' cards are not common in Russia and may be viewed as outright unnecessary; guests thank hosts for the invitation and the host thanks the guest for coming during the visit, and that is sufficient.

As a standard of international rules, remember to discard any price tags or receipts and never discuss the value of your gift. I would strongly suggest avoiding gifts that may indicate any shortfalls of a person, even if this is not intentional. For example, anti-ageing skincare, teeth whitening, soaps or deodorants, cooking class or hairdressers' vouchers, unless specifically requested in advance.

If the party you are attending includes several guests, your gift may be opened, but if the gathering is on a larger scale, the opening of the gifts will be done in private.

If you are visiting someone's home for a casual occasion, it is customary to bring a cake or a box of chocolates/biscuits, to go with tea and coffee. Generally, visiting someone empty-handed isn't viewed as having good manners.

Chapter 5

Dining Etiquette

Welcome to the tastiest chapter where we will discuss interesting aspects of Russian dining and any nuances surrounding this topic. As eating, and more so dining, is an integral part of any culture and almost a centre of social life, when visiting Russia, you should know the Russian way of eating.

Dining etiquette, in its essence, is pretty relaxed in Russia. Main international rules apply like:
- Always maintain a good posture whilst sitting—make minimal noise.
- Effortlessly lay a napkin on your knees with its crease towards you, without drawing attention to the process.
- Start eating only when the host has, or you have been asked to start.
- If there is no host, wait for everyone to be ready to eat.
- Keep your mouth closed whilst chewing.
- Eat quietly, keeping your area clean and tidy.
- Ensure that you rest frequently and maintain the flow of the conversation.
- If your lunch partner is speaking, rest your utensils and listen carefully
- Do not concentrate on food too much. If lunch or dinner is significantly important to you, ensure that you are not starving.
- Say 'excuse me' if you must leave the table for a short time; do not specify that you are going to the bathroom.

However, in general, unless visiting a certain calibre of event or high-end restaurant, Russians don't worry too much regarding which side to pass the bread basket or to pass the salt and pepper together, when they are surrounded by friends or family. All meal times, especially dinner, are a family time and it is common to make dinner time the main family gathering around the table.

Breakfast:

The first and arguably most important meal of the day may take place as early as five a.m. or as late as ten a.m. depending on one's lifestyle and work commitments. Usually, children have their breakfast around seven-thirty a.m. before heading off to school. For most adults, days begin with strong, black coffee or tea with honey and a slice of lemon. Russian breakfast, in general, is on the sweet side. The nation's favourite, '*Syrniki*', which are cottage cheese dumplings accompanied by crème fraiche, fruits and jam, rank at the very top of the list. It is closely followed by traditional oatmeal or semolina porridge, simple sandwiches or crepes. It is worth remembering that due to the vastness of this country and numerous cultures, breakfast, like any other meal, may vary. For example, in the Caucasus or Tatar regions, it will be different depending on the season of the year, opting for fresh fruit in summertime and gravitating towards dairy-based products in the winter.

Lunch:

For people who perform physical work, lunch is the most important meal of the day. Russian lunch time is around one p.m. to two p.m. and is rarely skipped. Traditionally, lunch is a three-course meal and is regarded as a necessary break from the working day to recharge. Typically, lunch consists of soup and bread as a first course, meat and a potato-based main course, and finished with something light and sweet for dessert. Soup is a must in a Russian lunch, as even children in preschool are served soup every day, to help with the digestive system and to help us warm up nicely during long winter months. Some legendary soup-based dishes are '*Kholodets*' and '*Borscht*', popular not only in Russia, but in all former soviet countries. Even though recently strong western culinary influence is felt in Russian kitchens, when it comes to main courses you may expect to be served '*Kotlety*' (our version of meatballs), Beef Stroganoff, '*Pelemeni*' (our version of ravioli with endless filling possibilities), or my very favourite, Ukrainian Chicken Kiev. If you chose to go all-in on tradition, lunch beverages are '*Kompot*' and '*Kisel*'. The two divine, non-alcoholic beverages are made from seasonal fruit, and are very tasty and refreshing.

Dinner:

As already mentioned, dinner time is a family and social affair in Russian households and usually the only time of the day when the entire family gathers together. This in mind, the dinner time is on the late side, around seven p.m. or even as late as eight p.m. depending on when all family members arrive home from work. Younger children are usually fed early, but similarly to French culture, children are introduced to the variety of foods at a young age, and generally eat the same meals as their parents. At the centre of the dinner is usually rye bread, which is a must, followed by a heavy, potato-based Olivier salad and a hearty main dish. The main course is not much different from main courses at lunch time, apart from hotpots, '*Golubtsy*', which is meat and rice stuffed cabbage leaf rolls, or herring.

As a nation, Russian people like big substantial hot meals. Not ones for snacking during the day, proper mealtimes are very important in this culture. At times, the amount of food consumed comes as a surprise to foreigners, compared to a generally very slender population. This is due to most meals being very traditional, minimally processed, fresh and slow cooked. Made with surprisingly simple ingredients, Russian dishes are very flavoursome, comforting and rich in carbs to keep people warm and healthy during long winters. Russians like to feel 'full' after each meal and aren't shy to ask for second serving if in family or close friend environment. Men, generally, are served bigger portions than women. Also, traditionally all cooking is done by women.

Two dishes, which deserve a special mention in Russian culture, are Shashlik and *Shuba Herring*. Shashlik 'Шашлык', is unquestionably the favourite and most anticipated Russian dish across the country. Essentially, it's a type of shish kebab meat skewer; traditionally, Russian Shashlik is cooked on a long narrow open style barbecue (without wire grills). Metal skewers are required, called *shampuri*. You can't use bamboo skewers for this meal, due to a slow cooking process over the open fire. This dish is cooked outdoors, during the big gathering, celebrations and social occasions and usually is a day-long affair.

Shuba Herring is Russia's favourite, but at the same time a very acquired taste. I think to truly appreciate this dish one has to be born in Russian culture. Russian herring salad 'under a coat' is made of finely chopped pickled herring, eggs, beetroot, carrots, potatoes, and dressing. The traditional layered salad, known as '*Shuba*' or '*Seledka pod shuboi*' takes its name from the outer layer that completely covers the salad. Some people choose mayonnaise dressing to cover the preparation, so it looks like a white fur coat, while others use beetroot. Prepare this dish at least six hours before serving so it can be chilled properly and nicely sliced to show off the layers. This dish can be found in pretty much every home or restaurant in Russia, also being very popular with Russians abroad.

Lastly, the preferred beverages may vary, but if you find yourself invited to a Russian New Year's celebration or Shashlik, most likely the strong spirits will be served, with non-alcoholic alternatives. In general, Russians aren't picky eaters, and huge meat lovers. Vegetarianism and veganism aren't as popular here as in the Western world, hence if you aren't one for meat or dairy dishes, please ensure you inform your host beforehand to accommodate your dietary requirements.

Chapter 6

Business Etiquette

If you are lucky enough to visit this remarkable country and conduct business with Russian nationals or work for a Russian company, there are many nuances you must know, as conducting business in Russia is as different from western ways as the Middle East, China or Japan. In this chapter, more than ever, it is paramount to recognise the cultural differences and employ your best EQ (emotional intelligence) in order to recognise the individuals you work with and all the cultural differences that may come into play.

There are two reasons why business etiquette in Russia is more in alignment to the core values within the team of colleagues or business rather than the internationally accepted codes of conduct.

Whilst the general business code of conduct applies, due to the vastness of the country and its history, one must remember that the ways business is conducted in Saint Petersburg is different to the way business is conducted in Yakuts or Vladivostok. This is due to the vast distances between the cities, regions, demographics and religions. To put this into geographical perspective, the distance between Saint Petersburg and Vladivostok is a staggering 6,500 miles (10,460 kilometres), one city being the most western point of Europe and the other, the most eastern point of Asia, a ferry trip away from Japan.

Secondary elements to consider when conducting business in Russia are the age of your colleagues, which will ultimately give a very accurate indication of whether the individual is from the Soviet Era (SE) or post 1992, modern, so to speak. Many individuals of a respectable age will fall under SE, which means that this group of individuals expect utmost respect at all times, very little to no familiarity at all, addressing in third person, always using the father's name as a middle name and never addressing by first name only (we have discussed this in previous chapters), with a dominant patriarchal ideology. This segment of businesspeople is very to the point, result driven, with a clear hierarchal divide between positions within the business. You will seldomly see them mixing with the general workforce and almost never working in open space offices, old school bosses having private offices. On the other hand, if you were to encounter a younger, progressive and global business environment, this will be easily recognisable, and this will resemble the general western structure of the business place. The modern businesses are more workforce talent-driven, with a strong work-life balance and a much less rigid approach to every aspect of the business.

As already mentioned, the general business etiquette rules apply across the Federation. Business dress codes must be appropriate, clean and smart. If unsure about the exact dress code policy, always opt for a conservative, smart suit for gentlemen, a smart suit with trousers or knee-length skirt for ladies, and immaculately polished footwear. In Russia, there is less emphasis on brands or trends of clothing, but rather cleanliness or tidiness, hence always ensure that your clothes are clean and perfectly ironed. Once you have worked for a day or two within the environment of the workplace you will be able to sense any fluctuations in dress codes, but for day one and especially for interviews, always ensure you look smart and conservative, which will ultimately show your commitment, high standards and respect for yourself and others. If you are doing business in a Muslim or a Buddhist region of the country, please dress more modestly and use your common sense, refraining from asking colleagues out for an alcoholic drink etcetera.

I would like to note that more and more business is conducted over lunch or dinner, hence always ensure that you are on top of your dining skills. It is commonly regarded that the ability to conduct yourself properly at the dinner table as well as hold a conversation will indicate a lot about your background and upbringing. Remember, whoever invites must cover the bill.

Whilst a work-life balance is respected in Russia, this applies to work hours only. It is not unusual for close workplace friendships to develop and colleagues working closely together becoming good friends. Always practice your best manners with all colleagues regardless of their position within the company. Always greet each person you come across; try to make small talk and in time try to remember a few things about that person, like their children's names or planned holidays, as this will make integration easier. And always remember the strong handshake, eye contact and smile.

In the cold time of the year, remember to always take your gloves off before shaking hands. At all costs, please refrain from engaging in romantic relationships at work, as they are highly frowned upon and can lead to irreparable damage to one's reputation, or even dismissal. The gender-neutral approach within the business world is common practice; however, the vast majority of the time, gentlemen will still hold the door open for a lady or assist her if needed.

Gifts are a common occurrence in the business world. If a colleague travels to a foreign country, it is polite and expected to bring a box of biscuits and sweets for one's colleagues to enjoy over a cup of tea or coffee whilst sharing memories of the holiday. Also, gift giving is common on the New Year's Eve celebration (if you remember, in Russia, Christmas is celebrated on the 7th of January, but gifts are given on New Year's Eve); these are usually more symbolic items or a bottle of VSOP or XO cognac for one's supervisor, but this isn't mandatory. Due to general social conventions and strict anti-corruption laws in the country, avoid giving a substantial gift within the business environment.

Always exercise discretion and diplomacy within the business environment, avoiding any taboo topics, especially politics and personal views on politicians. If you are asked any uncomfortable questions, like your salary or details of your personal life you don't wish to disclose, respond with a polite 'I don't discuss my personal matters/life'.

I would like to expand in greater detail about expected levels of adaptability within the Russian workforce and business environments. Employees or business partners often will be expected to be very flexible in their abilities or perform different tasks and be fast learners, as this is one of the most valued qualities in the workplace. 'Thinking on your feet', gumption and resourcefulness are also greatly valued within the individual, hence job descriptions often can vary in actual tasks expected to be done.

Lastly, when planning to work or conduct business in Russia, ensure you do your research into local history and origins of the company. Endeavour to learn a few phrases in Russian, or at least 'good morning', 'good afternoon', 'my name is *Anastasia*', 'it's nice to meet you'. The effort and interest in the Russian country will never go unappreciated and will immensely help to break the ice and build strong relationships from day one.

Chapter 7

Wedding Etiquette

Many nations know how to throw a great wedding, filled with culture, traditions and great entertainment. In this chapter, we will delve into Russian weddings and discuss the main traditions, customs and nuances to ensure that if you are invited to a Russian wedding you will have a great time and know what to expect.

In this chapter, we will talk about modern weddings rather than 'old custom' ones (not to be mistaken with traditional weddings) that include so-called kidnapping and capturing of the bride, wearing the wedding crowns for eight days and paying ransoms for a bride. Old custom wedding rituals are a very seldom occurrence these days, not actively practised for several decades.

When attending a Russian wedding, the same as with any wedding, the general western wedding etiquette rules apply. Guests should always RSVP on time, stating any dietary preferences, never bring people who aren't invited (plus ones or children), not to wear white or black and obey any dress code requested on the invitations, do not swap place cards, be respectful of any cultural differences, and of course, always be on your best behaviour. Also, remember to be on time, switch all the gadgets off, and under no circumstances post pictures of the bride or groom on social media without their permission.

Russian weddings, as a rule even today, usually are a two-day affair. This makes them different from western weddings. Couples either opt for a traditional religious ceremony in an Eastern Orthodox church or a traditional Muslim wedding. Alternatively, couples can get married in the registration office of a city hall, also known as the ZAGS (*Zapis Aktov Grazhdanskogo Sostoyaniya*), followed by a more casual and low-key reception or a party.

If the wedding is of a religious nature, long ceremonies are to be expected and certain modest dress codes must be respected, like a scarf over the head and covered shoulders for women, in an Orthodox church. Please note that the religious ceremony holds no official or legal status, and newlyweds have to register the marriage in ZAGS. However, this is still seen as the marriage in the 'eyes of the God' and therefore usually is the central and most prominent part of the celebration.

Traditionally, both the groom and bride enter the church together after leaving their family homes, where they take a bite of bread with salt. Bread and Salt is an old Russian wedding tradition; this custom symbolises, 'bread is the head of everything'. A proverb which explains the importance of bread in Russia for many centuries is the following:

'Bread is life and bread is hospitality. Salt is a symbol of wealth and prosperity'.

Once the bride and groom leave their parents' homes, they are closely followed and assisted by 'The Witnesses', which are the best man and maid of honour, in the Western terms. During the two-hour religious ceremony and symbolic crowning of the newlyweds, prayers are offered by the priest on the behalf of two families, the groom and bride are crowned with the words: 'in the name of the Father and of the Son and of the Holy Spirit' and 'O Lord, our God, crown them in glory and in honour'.

After the religious ceremony is finished, guests usually head for the reception and the couple take several hours to take pictures in their town or city, visiting the most famous landmarks or picturesque landscapes. They later join the guests at the venue, followed by a first toast to the newlyweds. The couple take a sip of champagne, or a shot of vodka, followed by a long kiss whilst all guest shout, 'Горько' (*gorka*). In Russian, this translates to 'bitter', which metaphorically means that the bitter alcohol will be soothed by the kiss of the couple in love.

There are different preferences to gift receiving by the couple. Some couples will greet each guest and thank them for coming whilst receiving a gift. The alternative may be a gift table or a box in which to post the envelopes with cards and any monetary value. Usually, the newlyweds will note on the invitation their preference for the gift; however, even if it is not specified, you must always come to a wedding with a gift and exquisite bouquet of flowers, if possible. We have already discussed the importance of substantial gifting on occasions like jubilees or christenings in the previous chapters and weddings are no exception. It will be seen as indecorous and rather disrespectful if the value of the gift (whether the actual item or a monetary amount) is on the lower side; hence, if you are in doubt, it is always best to ask close people for an indication of value.

All the formalities aside, during the reception part of the occasion, at a Russian wedding you will most certainly be well fed and entertained until the early hours, hence, make sure you wear comfortable shoes. Most weddings are so-called 'open bar' which basically means that an unlimited amount of alcohol will be served to ensure all guests have a great time. At this point in the celebration, each guest needs to know their limits and not to get overly intoxicated, even if people around keep serving drinks. In both higher and lower echelons of society, it is regarded as rude to refuse a drink or state that 'I don't drink'. If you are offered a drink and you'd rather not drink it, please take the drink and either hold it for some time in your hand or leave it on the table.

During the second day of the wedding celebrations, the groom and the bride will be dressed smartly but will not be wearing their official wedding attire. Guests may dress in similar attire and ladies may wear more casual but still dressy and smart outfits. Please note that the attendance of the second day isn't mandatory and usually the bride and groom will ask you to RSVP and specify if you wish to stay for the second day's celebrations, as the overnight accommodation may be provided. If accommodation isn't provided by the newlyweds, please ensure to make your own arrangements, and cover the costs yourself.

Lastly, a Russian wedding is a great social event, where people tend to mix and mingle. For anyone from a foreign country, it is by far the best opportunity to make new friends and connections. Even if generally Russians may seem rather stand-offish and reserved people, this most certainly isn't the case during weddings, as being a guest at the wedding is seen as a great honour. Since you are at the wedding, this will mean you are somehow connected to the bride or groom, which will break the ice in any conversation, and you will be guaranteed to have a great time.

Slovenia
By Simona Lečnik Očko

Chapter 1

Cultural Symbols

Slovenia is a colourful land of diversity in Central Europe. A paradise nestled between the Alps and the Adriatic. The best way to learn and understand about the country is to visit and see all the beauty in person. I would strongly recommend visiting Lake Bled. A traditional wooden boat will take you to the island situated in the middle of the lake, and after climbing ninety-nine stairs to reach the Assumption of Mary Church, you will ring a bell to make a wish, which will mysteriously come true. Even today, there is an old custom, where the bridegroom must carry the bride all ninety-nine steps if the couple wants to get married in the church on the island.

Character Kurent

PTUJ
The oldest town in Slovenia, Ptuj, would be the next recommended destination. The castle above the town has the oldest wine cellars. The

largest Slovenian Shrovetide celebration is in Ptuj, called *Kurentovanje*. It is an ethnographic carnival of national importance, where a typical Shrovetide character called *Kurent* plays the main role.

POSTOJNA CAVE

Postojna cave is an excellent attraction, where a cave railway has been operating for 140 years and more than thirty-eight million visitors from all over the world have visited. Here you can see human fish, who can live for up to 100 years and can survive more than eight years without food. The legend says that a dragon lived in Postojna cave, and that the human fish are its offspring.

Human Fish

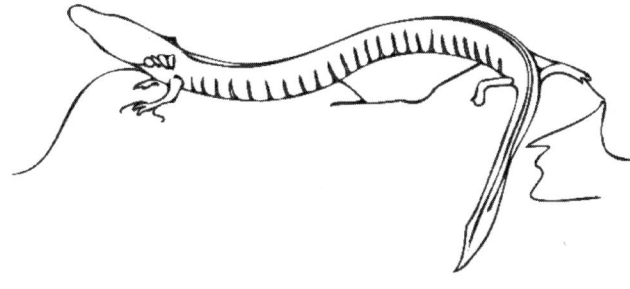

Influences

The mix of influences is something very specific to Slovenia. This has much to do with its history and geography. Slovenia was part of the Habsburg Empire for many centuries, evidence of which can be seen in the architecture of the cities. There is also strong Italian influence in the west by the coast. Furthermore, there is the Slavic influence, which is the basis for the name of the Slovenian ethnic group. The blending of all these influences is what makes Slovenia such an intriguing place to visit. Approximately two million speakers worldwide speak the unique Slovene language. Considering the number of speakers, Slovene has relatively many dialects. Such a language variety is the result of geographical, political, historical, social and other reasons. Slovene is also one of the rare Indo-European languages to have retained the dual grammatical number. People are proud of the dual, given that we can name 'just the two of us'. Official languages in addition to Slovene are also Hungarian and Italian in their respective ethnical minorities.

The first texts in Slovene date back to the turn of the first millennium AD, that is, the Freising Manuscripts, which are also the oldest texts in any Slavic language written in the Latin alphabet. They are still archived at the Bavarian State Archives in Munich. A special place in Slovenian literature belongs to Primož Trubar, who published the first book in Slovene, and to the poet France Prešeren, whose patriotic poem *Zdravljica* (A Toast) was declared the national anthem of Slovenia in 1989. Visually, you can see that it was actually written so that each of the eight stanzas mimicked the shape of a wine glass.

Potica Cake

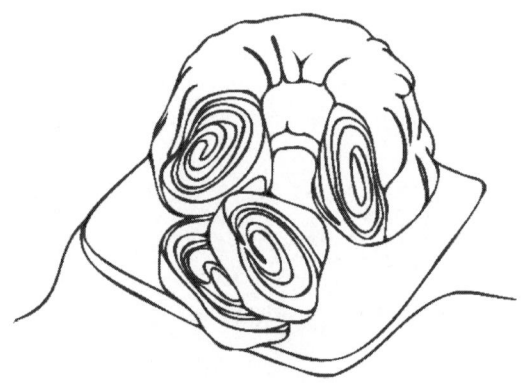

GASTRONOMY

Despite the fact that you can see the influence of neighbouring countries in Slovenian gastronomy, there are many things which are specific to our country. Carniola (*Kranjska*) sausage is taut, crunchy and juicy, with a full aroma that is characteristic of desalinated, specifically seasoned and smoked pork. It is cooked before eating, eaten hot, together with sour or cooked cabbage or sour turnip. Potica is one of the most typical Slovenian desserts and a truly sweet ambassador of Slovenia, made of dough and filled with various fillings, usually walnut. Next to potica and *štruklji*, there is also *prekmurska gibanica* (prekmurian layer cake), a juicy dessert, stuffed with poppy seeds, cottage cheese, walnuts and apples. It is not a light dessert, but worth trying. We Slovenes like to joke that it is an 'over-Mura moving cake', which would be funny if literally translated.

Another culinary specialty is pumpkin seed oil, which is not only a delicious condiment on salads, but also for soups, poured on ice cream or other desserts. Speaking of etiquette, because of its distinctive dark colour, I do not personally recommend it at business lunches or dinners, as it stains around the mouth or on clothing, and can be a very unpleasant experience if sufficient care is not taken.

In Maribor, the second largest Slovenian town, you can find the oldest wine in the world. The confirmed age of this vine is around 450 years, and it won a place in the Guinness Book of Records as the oldest noble vine in the world still bearing grapes. Every November (11th), people in Maribor celebrate St. Martin's Day, and it is like a second New Year celebration.

Oldest Wine in the World

SPORT

Despite being such a small country, Slovenia has so many top athletes with whom we achieve such good results on a global scale. Hard work, perseverance, dedication and diligence are just some of the values that distinguish Slovenia's versatile athletes. Slovenia has long outgrown the framework of a ski country and has become famous in all sports fields.

People nationally unite and support athletes during the international competitions, which cannot be said for local competitions, where club affiliation prevails. As a geographically diverse country, Slovenia offers a wide range of opportunities for sports activities.

SOME INTERESTING EXTRA FACTS

Should you wish to, you can stay in a prison, since a former military prison was refurbished into a hostel Celica, with a unique interior design: twenty unique, artistically designed prison cells and nine comfortable rooms.

There are more than 500 brown bears living in the Slovenian forests.

Slovenia has more than 90,000 beekeepers (out of two million people).

Hayracks are a unique cultural symbol of Slovenia.

The oldest (*Najevnik*) linden tree is in Slovenia; it is 700 years old and has a circumference of ten metres (over thirty feet).

There are more than 10,000 caves in Slovenia.

The most beautiful town on the Slovenian coast, Piran, is known for its salt pans, where the world-class flower of salt is still produced today using age-old methods.

They filmed some of the scenes from The Chronicles of Narnia in the Slovenian Soča Valley.

Chapter 2

Posture and Body Language, Meetings and Greetings

More and more individuals should recognise the importance of non-verbal communication in the process of communicating with other people. When we travel to a foreign country and do not speak the language of the natives, we can still communicate with them. No one can hide facial expressions, eye contact or waving with their hands when talking to someone. We communicate all the time, even if we are not aware of it, and largely the communication is non-verbal. With our posture and body language, we reveal a lot about ourselves or notice and learn about others.

If I had to assess the posture of the average Slovene, I wish it would be a bit straighter. Although many young people, especially when looking down at smart phones, have a bent spine, I cannot say that only smartphones are to blame for this bad posture, since many people have a slightly bent posture despite this. Gladly, I would recommend everyone to adopt a straight, confident posture.

Slovenians are probably slightly similar to the Austrians during public communication, where more closed body postures during conversation occurs, and much less expressive hands. We do not express ourselves excessively with the limbs. Furthermore, we also have some non-verbal peculiarities. For example, we hug less than our southern and western neighbours do. I originally come from Bosnia and Herzegovina where we hug and kiss on cheeks more often. When expressing themselves, Slovenes hold back rather than exaggerate when presenting themselves to others, and do not passionately show how they feel.

If someone in Slovenia invites you to their home, it is normal that they will offer you guest slippers at the front door. The fact that, especially for women, shoes can be a key part of their appearance is subordinate to the hygiene factor when entering someone's home.

MEETING AND GREETING

When meeting new people, there is always a possibility of feeling some kind of discomfort while communicating for the first time. People in Slovenia generally tend to create a distance between themselves and people they do not know. Greetings are initially quite formal and reserved. Slovenians, unlike most other Slavs, are not touchy-feely. When meeting someone for the first time, the most common greeting would be a handshake and a welcoming smile. It is customary to maintain eye contact during the greeting process, polite eye contact, not staring in any way. This may be followed by a 'Nice to meet you' (*Me veseli*). Unlike in Portugal or Spain, hugging and kissing when meeting someone for the first time is not customary, and should be avoided, as it may produce an uncomfortable atmosphere. Only close friends and family may kiss twice on the cheek and give each other a little hug. We first kiss on the right cheek. In Slovenia, the greeting kiss does not have a long tradition. It is slowly gaining ground nowadays, especially through young people, who embrace much more when greeting.

It is better to respect people's personal space when meeting people from Slovenia and wait for them to initiate physical contact first than to be too invasive. In Slovenia, acquaintances usually greet each other with a simple 'hello' (*Zdravo/Živjo*) or the more formal 'good day' (*Dober dan/Pozdravljeni*) and a wave. Among academic associates, Slovenians greet each other by smiling and saying, 'good day'. Colleagues of the same professional level might be more informal with each other, but a considerable physical distance usually stays. Unless otherwise instructed, Slovenians address their superiors such as college professors and bosses, with the formal pronoun (*Vi* instead of *Ti*) and do not call them by their first name. We use first names mostly among close friends and family, so do not use a person's first name until invited to do so. Addressing others, we use the honour titles '*Gospa*' (Madam) for younger women, '*Gospodična*' (Miss), and '*Gospod*' (Sir). In addition, it is important to arrive on time when meeting with someone. Being late when meeting someone, without any logical excuse, is not something to be proud of.

Most of Slovenians strive to be good. They must 'look' good in the eyes of others around them and be decent citizens in society. This has evolved in European culture over the centuries. Slovenians are considered as very friendly and kind.

Slovenians are egalitarian, yet interestingly, their natural communication style tends to be indirect with people whom they do not know well but can moderate their behaviour when dealing with people who come from cultures where communication is more direct. Slovenians are naturally soft-spoken and do not raise their voices when conversing. They are also polite, courteous, and respectful to others. Attitudes to business and professionalism in Slovenia are very similar to those in Germany and Austria. Learning a few basic words in the local language is always a good idea and the ability to say something like '*Zdravo*' or '*Dober dan*', would be a pleasant surprise to your host and local residents. Although Slovenians have a good sense of humour, they are certainly more restrained compared to their southern neighbours.

Chapter 3

Conversation Dos and Don'ts

At meetings, gatherings and events where we may not know all the guests, we should be careful when choosing the topic of conversation we are starting. With a thoughtless topic, we can inadvertently offend someone. Being a bit careful when choosing the topic would be a better choice in Slovenia.

HERE ARE THE TOPICS WE PREFER TO AVOID IN CONVERSATION
- *Politics:* let us not open the topic of political definition, the names of politicians and their actions. Everyone has the right to sympathise with any political party he or she wishes and, given the large number of parties and different orientations, any condemnation or disagreement about political decisions, could be a cause for possible discomfort and quarrel.
- *Religion:* cultural and religious diversity in the Slovenian environment enable the free choice of each individual. We should always leave aside sensitive religious topics to avoid interfering with intimate issues. Directly questioning people, or any condemnation of their religious affiliation, or even convincing them of our right, would be extremely reckless and offensive.
- *Intimate family matters and sexual orientation:* we never mention during the conversation any personal things that might interfere too much with an individual's intimacy. Private family matters or an individual's sexual orientation should remain private. The interlocutor may be confused when asked, or we could easily trigger discomfort and the person might withdrawal from the conversation. It is more important to make people feel good around us, than to prove our right in every way.
- *Health condition:* conversations about various diseases and health conditions are not a matter of public debate. Many people associate illness with their personal failures, making them reluctant to talk about it. Even if we have a good intention, or might even like to help, we do not open these topics with people with whom we are not in close relations.
- *Finance:* "How much did you earn with this project?" "How high

was the commission?" "Are you satisfied with your salary in this company?" Let us not open topics that concern the finances of our interlocutors. If there are any results of projects whose analyses are publicly available, this topic of conversation is acceptable. However, we do not mention personal finances and do not ask questions.

- *Unpleasant topics:* questions like "You're not married yet?" "No kids yet? You are not getting younger." "Do you still live with your parents and not on your own?" We do not know their background or their story, and it would be wrong if to ask questions or be judgemental just because we believe our thinking is the only right way.

- We should never brag, never curse, never tell unsavoury jokes, and never flirt with interlocutors of the opposite sex. We also do not talk about people who are not present or if we do not even know them personally. We need to be careful if we want to get along with someone, show ourselves in the best light during a conversation, and not exaggerate or flatter ourselves. Let us be careful not to interrupt when our interlocutor is speaking, but to listen politely, respectfully, and actively. We do not speak quietly or too loudly. In general, we should never whisper in someone's ear in company as this would be extremely offensive to everyone present.

SAFE TOPICS

On the other hand, we can easily start a conversation about some safe topics and never make a mistake choosing them. Small talk is not always easy to start with. Always come prepared when attending social or formal gatherings and events.

- In Slovenia, people like to talk about sports and the achievements of our successful individuals and teams. Especially when it is a period of matches and competitions, sport is one of the popular national topics.

- Food and culinary delights are always a safe topic to share experiences.

- In general, people like to talk about themselves. Ask them where they come from or what they do. It is very helpful if we find a common ground with our interlocutor. Always listen to the person talking to you. Pay attention and show respect.

- Nothing ends chatting faster than a closed type of question to which the answer can only be 'yes' or 'no'. Make sure your questions bring interesting answers, not just one-syllable words.

- When starting a conversation with the person we meet for the first time, it is better to choose light topics. The proverbially light topic is, of course, a popular conversation about the weather, which does not require deep thinking, and where we can divert the conversation at any time, like discussing road conditions or something similar.

- I would recommend people show interest in current news, cultural events etcetera, before attending meetings or social events. That is a great way to start a conversation and show general knowledge.
- In addition, most of all, never forget about eye contact and smiling. Make the conversation a pleasant experience for everyone.

Chapter 4

Gift Giving

The art of gifting is as old as humanity and is still the best way to show friendship, respect, gratitude, and strengthen interpersonal bonds. Business gifts have also grown on this tradition. With a business gift, we indirectly determine the place of the business partner on the value scale in relation to our company, so business gifts are a sensitive area to which we must pay more attention and creativity, and above all we must know why, when, to whom and how we give them.

We show affection and respect with a gift, so it is right to devote enough time to this form of business communication and follow five simple rules:
- Choosing the right gift.
- For the right person.
- Delivering and receiving the gift in the right way.
- Choosing the right value.
- Deliver the gift at the right time.

The biggest drawback to gifting is the lack of imagination and taste. Many individuals choose unwisely, with the result being the accumulation of insignificant dust collectors, which have achieved nothing.

Choosing the right gift can be quite a problem for every one of us. Even if we have all the rules of gift etiquette on our little finger, it is hard to find the 'right one'. Gift planning is most important. Make an effort; collect information about the person you are about to give a gift to. We should use our imagination if we want to make a good impression on someone. People like to talk about things they like. Pay attention. This way we can avoid the battle of not knowing what to give them.

In Slovenia, it is common to bring at least a bottle of wine and a box of chocolates when visiting someone.

SOME IDEAS FOR SUITABLE AND ORIGINAL GIFTS IN SLOVENIA:
- Food – Delicacies, cheeses, fruits, pastries, different sorts of tea,

special coffee. Do not forget the decoration of the chosen gift. The recipient can also share this kind of gift with his team and co-workers. In Slovenia, we have a diverse offer of gastronomic specialities.

- Flowers – A gift suitable for both men and women, if given in an appropriate and relaxed way.
- Tickets for sports, cultural events, entertainment events.
- Gift vouchers for fitness and wellness centres, massages, treatments etcetera.

Slovenia is a wine-growing country and wine is the most common gift on various occasions. Let me add two more hints. We should never give only a bottle of wine, but in combination with an opening set of two or more wine glasses. We should not write the name of recipient companies on wine bottles. The name of the company should only be written on the special card attached to the bottle.

THERE ARE ALSO SOME GIFTS CONSIDERED INAPPROPRIATE:
- Cosmetic accessories: a very personal thing for each individual (colognes, creams, soaps, shampoos).
- Jewellery, decorative scarves and ties. A matter of personal taste. Besides, everyone has his or her own colour scale.
- Perfumes are also a matter of personal choice. Not every skin reacts and smells the same. In addition, we cannot be sure if a person maybe has any allergies.
- When talking about inappropriate personal gifts, we should not forget underwear, which is always an intimate thing. Even if we have the best intentions, it is something we should rather avoid.
- We should never give our personal portrait, especially in relation to business partners. It is acceptable to like ourselves, but I do not know if a business partner would hang us on the wall in his office and watch us every day. Just skip that thought.
- Money is also not an option, unless relatives are collecting for a specific gift that they know is someone's wish. In business, giving money can be misunderstood as bribery.
- If we are handing over a gift prepared or purchased by someone else, we need to become familiar with its content and not give gifts we do not know anything about.

We should always give gifts with our right hand. When doing so, look the recipient in the eyes. If you are sending a gift by post, make sure to add a 'thank you' card with handwritten text. At a business meeting, gifts are given at the end of the meeting. If, at the end of the meeting, we take guests to lunch or dinner, we can give the gift after the main course. We also never give gifts right across the table, leaning over with all our weight. We always approach the recipient, shake his or her hand and say a few words. The old rule still applies, that we always open a gift as soon as we receive it. The exception is at strict business gatherings, where there is usually no time to open a gift, dedicate a few minutes to it, and talk about it. We also do not open gifts when we receive a large number of them at the same time, but they must remain in the eyes of the guests. While receiving gifts, we stand calmly and listen carefully to the wishes, we accept the gift with both hands, and we thank politely. Please forget things like "You shouldn't have…" "Just how will I repay you?" Or, "I brought you a book… but you can exchange it for something else!" By doing so, we kill the charm of the gifting.

A simple and sincere 'thank you' is always good enough. Most of all, enjoy buying gifts and enjoy receiving them, with a smile on your face.

Chapter 5

Dining Etiquette

You are welcome to taste the exceptional delicacies of Slovenia.

What is special about the gastronomic image of Slovenia? Without doubt the answer to this is her place on the world map at the crossroads of the European Alps, the Karst, the Mediterranean and Pannonia lowlands. This creates a wealth of diversity. Each region has its own rounded gastronomic areas. Slovenia has more than 150 recognisable dishes and their characteristic is that they are prepared from locally grown ingredients. I will try to describe just a few of them, the rest you will have to try when visiting our country. Slovenia is also a wine-growing country, but in recent years you can also try beer from many boutique breweries.

Typical Slovenian dishes are served in typical inns (*gostilna*) in all parts of Slovenia. That is the perfect chance for you to taste local cuisine. Dishes cooked from homemade ingredients are offered on tourist farms as well as at stops along hiking, mountaineering, and cycling trails. Slovene cuisine draws on Austrian, Italian and Balkan influences. However, there is a native tradition too.

In kindergartens and schools, we tend to support the tradition of the Slovenian breakfast, which normally consists of milk, bread, butter, honey, and apples, which are produced or processed in Slovenia. The purpose is to inform children and youngsters about the importance of breakfast as well as the importance and benefits of locally produced food. The goal is to emphasise the importance of agriculture and beekeeping for food processing, and its impact on the environment.

MEALTIMES

The usual time for breakfast is between seven and nine a.m. People generally eat lunch between twelve and two p.m. it depends on whether people eat out or after work at their home, in which case it is usually a bit later. Many people have snacks, at a snacks bar, guesthouses or a takeaway during work. Affordable and pre-prepared meals, most often eaten by the spoon or in the form of sandwiches, are available from ten until twelve p.m. Dinners are normally eaten between six and eight p.m.

Traditional Slovene žlikrofi

GASTRONOMY

Among all delicious Slovenian gastronomy possibilities, I would like to highlight some traditional dishes, which I recommend everyone to try when visiting our beautiful country:

You should taste the original Carniola sausage, which has a protected geographic indication. It is made according to a special recipe and has been present since the second half of C.19th.

Karst wind (*burja*) dries meat in the most natural way. Karst prosciutto, pancetta, and the Karst *zašinek* (dried shoulder of pork), in combination with some local cheese and a glass of quality wine, pampers the soul.

If you are heading to Idrija, treat yourself with some '*žlikrofi*'. They are made of pasta dough with a potato filling and a distinctive shape. You may try them as a starter, a side dish, or also as a main dish. They can be dressed with crackling or with typical Idrija '*bakalca*', a special lamb and vegetable sauce. People like to say that there is a proper way of eating them; one is held in the mouth, another is held in front of the nose on the fork, and a third is viewed in the bowl as the future morsel.

One of the most recognizable dishes known throughout Slovenia are 'Štruklji' dumplings. They are prepared from different types of dough, with a range of different fillings, baked or cooked, sweet or salty. You can taste them with tarragon, cottage cheese, walnuts, apples, poppyseeds, and many others.

The number one among Slovenian traditional holiday pastries is 'potica'. The most typical are walnut, hazelnut, tarragon, poppyseed and cheese. There are around eighty different flavours and it is a typical holiday dessert.

A sweet dessert called 'Prekmurska gibanica' is the top quality, juicy and most widespread Slovenian dessert from Prekmurje, stuffed with poppy seeds, cottage cheese, walnuts, and apples. 'Potica' is protected by the 'recognised designation of traditional reputation' status.

Despite the fact that drinking tea is present in Slovenia and that the presence of different types delights all tea lovers, there is still more coffee drinking in Slovenia. Daytime drinking takes place in small cafe bars, or in a 'kavarna', where a range of cakes, pastries and ice cream is also usually on offer.

Having a traditional Sunday lunch in Slovenia, at a restaurant or if you are invited to someone's home, can be a delightful experience. If you have been invited to a Slovenian's house or restaurant, arrive on time, and show respect to your hosts. They will probably offer you an aperitif first. After that, soup is served first. Typical soups include beef soup with noodles, seasonal vegetable soup, and very often, mushroom soup. This is then followed by meat with a side dish and a salad served together. A typical Sunday meat dish includes a roast or fried chicken. A very typical Slovenian side dish served with a meat dish is roast potatoes. A salad is necessary for Slovenians and should not be eaten before the main course is served, but together with main course. Many places offer Slovenian pumpkin seed oil or olive oil as a dressing.

DINING ETIQUETTE

When it comes to dining etiquette, in Slovenia we practice the continental style, especially on formal occasions. If you have a business meeting, do not drink alcohol, or only one glass of wine. You can refuse alcohol and have a different beverage. When it comes to tipping, you are not obligated to tip as it is not yet common, but it is appropriate and highly recommended if you are satisfied with the meal and the service. Do not ever ask to try the food on someone else's plate. Wait until they get to know you or offer to share.

Here are some general rules for table etiquette to keep in mind:
- Turn off your mobile phone before sitting down at the table.
- We sit on the chair from the left.
- We put the napkin in our lap, and it stays there throughout the whole meal.
- Never start eating before all guests are served.
- Do not rush to eat, do not blow hot food, and eat with your mouth closed.
- If we are not sure how to eat certain food, wait for someone else to start, and copy them.
- Never lick a knife even though delicious sauces remain on it.
- Do not use a toothpick or fix lipstick at the table.
- Do not assist the waiting staff in clearing the table.

All concluding actions in a business meeting most often take place right behind the table, after food and drink, which is supposed to have a unifying, social effect. Let us try not to create the exact opposite atmosphere. All the responsibility is on ourselves. We need to make sure that in our company, others feel good and treat their interlocutors with respect.

Slovenia has three wine-growing regions, and they rank highly in terms of quality globally. You are welcome to experience tastings in local wine cellars or visit some of the many wine festivals. '*Na zdravje*'—Cheers!

Chapter 6

Business Etiquette

If you ever get a chance to do business with Slovenian people, it should mostly be a positive and a very pleasant experience. In Slovenia, we are considered very professional, which means that people are trustworthy, determined, and straightforward. Attitudes to business and professionalism in Slovenia are very similar to those of Germany and Austria. Slovenian society is more formal in its approach to business and it is a good idea to try to act more formal and wait for the relationship to develop into a friendship before allowing too much familiarity and relaxation in the conversation.

In business etiquette in Slovenia, there is one main rule to remember. It is not the gender or age that matters, but only the hierarchy. The one who is higher on the hierarchical scale always has the advantage.

Let me list some of the key characteristics that are crucial for business etiquette in Slovenia.

OUR APPEARANCE—BUSINESS DRESS CODE
A person should always keep in mind that our business appearance must be in line with the area in which they operate. The clothes do not make the man, but they do create an extremely strong impression. We should ask ourselves what kind of impression we would like to make on the people we meet and on those surrounding us. After all, people are visual beings and since we never get the second chance to make a first impression, the way we stand, look, dress, smell etcetera, affects what impression we make. We will not go wrong if we choose conservative business attire and avoid bright colours when attending a business meeting, especially if we want people to take us seriously. For men, a dark coloured suit (black, dark blue or grey) or jacket and trousers with tie is appropriate business wear. Businesswomen should wear outfits similarly formal. Definitely skip and avoid anything that might be considered provocative, such as short skirts, anything mesh or transparent, or too much jewellery.

PUNCTUALITY, INTRODUCTIONS AND BUSINESS CARDS

Slovenian businesspeople are very punctual and are not fond of those who either keep them waiting or do not come on time. If we are late and do not let others know, we are showing a lack of respect for them. It does not mean we must arrive half an hour earlier, as is it treated as impolite and careless, but be on time and show respect to business partners and clients.

Before the first meeting, it is normal for Slovenians to exchange business cards. When there are two or three participants, this occurs before the meeting. If there are more participants, then the exchange occurs afterwards, since it would take too much time to check all cards beforehand. We must ensure to take good care of our cards, because they represent us and are treated like our identity card. They should always include our academic titles and position in the company we work at.

Introducing ourselves and leaving a good first impression depends on many factors: confident body language, posture, making eye contact, a smile on the face, a firm handshake, correct and clear pronunciation of our name and surname. The subordinate person is always the one who is introduced first.

GIFTS

Do not be surprised if you receive a bottle of wine, or some type of branded corporate gift when you first come to a business meeting. Any gifts are usually given at the end of a meeting, or during the business lunch. Many companies prepare promotion gifts of lower values, since there is a limit on the value of a gift that someone can accept. The gift should be opened immediately, accepted with honour and gratitude, without using words like, 'oh, you didn't have to'. We give the gift using our right hand, saying a few words about the gift we are delivering, and accept gift with both our hands, saying sincere thanks.

MEETINGS

Business meetings are usually held between nine a.m. and twelve p.m. right before lunch. The host arranges the venue, including the arrangement of any technical equipment, facilities and refreshments that may be required. The host should be waiting for your arrival and escort you to the meeting room. Always wait for them to offer you a seat or find a table tag with your name written on it. Passionate conversations and debates in the Slovenian environment are not an established practice; rather, a calm voice and quiet tones are used. We never interrupt the speaker.

EMAIL AND ONLINE COMMUNICATION

Since most of our communication takes place by email nowadays, there are a few simple rules to follow to create respect, dignity and build trust among partners. Always respond, the sooner the better. Do not leave people waiting and create the wrong impression of not receiving an answer. Never use 'caps lock', nor any exclamation marks because that would mean we are yelling, and that is not something to look for in business communication. Never forget to use polite phrases and double check everything, before hitting the 'send' button. It is desirable for emails to be short and concise, due to time constraints. During online meetings, we should consider all basic manners: greetings, respectful dialogue, not doing any other tasks, never eating, clean the background behind us and remove all possible distractions.

BUSINESS MEALS

Business meals are very popular in Slovenia. They give participants a chance to discuss business in a more informal environment. It is also a great opportunity to find out more about partners on a personal level. However, everyone must take care to not cross the line between personal life and business matters, which is easy to cross, especially if alcohol is involved. That is why only one unit of alcohol per person is welcomed during a business lunch. That is also the reason brunches are even more popular, so many can avoid drinking alcohol. The ones that invite guests, pays the bill. The guests should always be seated in a way which gives them a better view of the restaurant, such as by the window or opposite a wall with nice paintings, and never looking at a door. The dress code for lunch and dinner is typically formal for both men and women. You will not get an invitation to visit your business partner's home in Slovenia very soon. Only relationships that outgrow business onto a personal level will open the door to private homes of the average Slovenian business person.

The ideals that are valued amongst Slovenian businessmen are trust, integrity, respect and dignity.

Chapter 7

Wedding Etiquette

We do not attend weddings daily, so it is a good idea to think about some basic rules to follow and refresh the memory on our appropriate behaviour to make sure we do not embarrass ourselves or someone else. If you get invitation to a Slovenian wedding, here are some useful tips to follow.

Always respond (RSVP) by the due date and write how many members will be attending the wedding.

Guests should always dress appropriately for the occasion. That means we must follow any wishes or dress codes the newlyweds might have, making sure we do not stand out or overshadow the newlyweds with our choice of clothes. We are not the ones who are supposed to be the centre of attention.

Everyone should always arrive on time or a few minutes earlier and make sure not to be late for the ceremony. Leave home early enough and check the route before leaving.

No matter what kind of ceremony we attend, we must show our respect. If we do not know the custom and traditions, we can find out about them in advance; otherwise, we can imitate the people around us by observing.

Before the feast begins, take a moment to greet the parents and relatives of the newlyweds. If we do not already know them, we can introduce ourselves to them. We can also find time to present the wedding gift during the ceremony and celebration unless we have agreed otherwise or have already given the gift. Always congratulate the bride and groom after the ceremony.

The seating order is a decision of the newlyweds that needs to be considered prior to the wedding and we must respect the plan. When the wedding atmosphere warms up, the bride and groom normally mix themselves between their guests.

It is common for the groom to thank to all guests present. When it comes to speeches and toasts in Slovenia, it is most appropriate for the groom's best man to perform the first toast, followed by the father of the bride. The maid of honour takes care of the bride's handkerchiefs, tears, and bouquet, etcetera. Newlyweds do not always stick to traditional, classic scenarios, so there might be more or less than two toasts in a more relaxed atmosphere. This is especially so if a best man or the bride's father are not good at/do not like making speeches, or if the bride or groom does not have a parent.

Speeches are not necessary, but these things have always turned out to be welcome, adding some extra value to the event. During speeches, we must always be respectful and never talk to our neighbours. It is nice to be invited to speak but consider not making too long a speech.

We must never eat and drink everything we see at once. Knowing what appropriate table manners are is undoubtedly a great advantage and we should behave our best.

You might witness several customs and funny wedding games if the wedding is traditional. Keeping that in mind, bring some cash with you, if you do not want to blush and apologise for just having a card.

At the farewell, we should always thank the newlyweds before saying goodbye.

WEDDING GIFTS

An eternal question is whether we should give money as a wedding gift. The answer is no, unless it is specifically stated and perhaps even written, that the newlyweds would much rather accept our money contribution to their honeymoon, than a household appliance. If we decide for ourselves to give money, we should combine it with some little gift, and implement it in a nice story behind our decision, rather than just giving the money in a white envelope.

Vouchers are out of fashion now, but if we know that would be something they really wish for, we should consider buying them vouchers. The gifting culture, however, advises not to buy too many of them, especially if they are time-limited vouchers.

If we, as guests constantly record and make photographs, we demonstrate rudeness. When it comes to festive events, such as weddings, there are simply no phones. Etiquette has nothing against electronic devices, but we came to the wedding to meet and socialise with other guests rather than to play with our smartphones. We must put a little effort in socialising with everyone present. There is nothing wrong with taking a picture or two for our personal memory, and then putting our phones away. Newlyweds are the only ones who can publish any pictures from the wedding, not the guests.

Enjoy the weddings, as they are happy and cheerful events; take care of limits with drinking alcohol, accept invitations to dance, and have fun in polite conversations.

Switzerland
By Julia Esteve Boyd

Chapter 1

Cultural Symbols

Welcome to Switzerland! Also known as...
Schweiz (German), *Suisse* (French), *Svizzera* (Italian), *Svizzra* (Romansh).

MOTTO
'*Unus pro omnibus, omnes pro uno*'.
('*One for all, all for one*').
translated as...
German (*Einer für alle, alle für einen*), French (*un pour tous, tous pour un*), Italian (*Uno per tutti, tutti per uno*) and Romansh (*In per tuts, tuts per in*).

Switzerland is a very diverse country with four different cultures and four different languages, and each region is proud to have its own customs, common courtesies and cuisine. When thinking of Switzerland, one normally envisages picturesque scenery of mountains, lakes and alpine fields, and that's exactly what one would find if visiting. It is a beautiful country which is clean, well maintained and peaceful. Switzerland is home to many multinational companies such as the International Olympic Committee, has the highest concentration of Fortune 500 companies in the world and is also very proud to be the birthplace of the International Red Cross. It is a country with prosperity and has one of the highest standards of living in Europe.

The Swiss Confederation (the official name of Switzerland) is divided into twenty-six cantons, each one largely autonomous, retaining their individual identity and having responsibility for their own budget, taxes and other key areas. Although each canton has equal status, they each have their own flag, car licence plate identifications and speak different languages, with some cantons speaking more than one language. These differences, along with the high numbers of international expats, is why Switzerland is such a diverse and interesting country.

The Swiss are proud of their differences and embrace them whole heartedly. Despite the diversity between cantons there are many well-known cultural symbols which are embedded in Swiss culture and are symbolic of Switzerland around the world.

THE FLAG

The Nation's Flag: do you know that the Swiss flag is distinctly different from all the other national flags in the world? It's the only square flag in the world other than the Vatican City, therefore the only square flag to fly outside the United Nations headquarters building in New York. Occasionally, the square flag does have to conform to international standards—for example the rules of the International Olympic Committee state that all national flags must have the same dimensions, so for most sporting events the Swiss flag will be rectangular to conform to international regulations.

The Swiss flag also bears a strong resemblance to the official flag of the International Committee of the Red Cross, and it's not a coincidence; it's exactly the same flag with the colours inverted. The emblem of a red cross on a white background is one of the most recognised symbols in the world. It is a recognition of the historic connection between Switzerland and the Geneva Convention of 1864.

The Canton Flags: all of the twenty-six cantons have their own flag which will be proudly displayed at every opportunity, either alone or alongside the country flag, depending on the occasion. Each flag has a special meaning and significance for the canton and incorporates animals, stars, eagles, letters and colours to differentiate themselves. The canton flags are also square.

THE NATIONAL FLOWER

The edelweiss is an iconic image of Switzerland and is depicted on the logo of the Swiss Tourism board, the five-franc coin and many Swiss products. The flower is quite rare and has a protected status. It grows high in the Alps and became a symbol of courage and love because legend tells of a brave suitor who risked his life by climbing a steep rock face to pluck the white flower as a gift for his beloved. It is used in many Swiss skincare products because of its antioxidants and anti-ageing properties.

The Matterhorn
One of the world's most famous mountains in the world, the Matterhorn is an iconic symbol of Switzerland. It is the best-known peak of the Alps because of its distinctive pyramid shape. Nestled between the Swiss and Italian border, the four sides of the pyramid align perfectly with the cardinal directions.

It rises more than 4,000 metres high, and every year thousands of people successfully climb to the summit. At the top of the peak, a metal cross commemorates the ones who were not successful in their climb and lost their lives on the mountain. Visitors come to see the Matterhorn at all times of the year even if they do not wish to climb it.

The Matterhorn image is used to sell many Swiss products such as Toblerone chocolate, fondue and water.

Fun Fact: the first woman to successfully climb the Matterhorn was Lucy Walker in 1871 and she did so wearing a long, wool skirt!

Animals – Cows, Bears and Dogs
Although Switzerland doesn't have an official national animal, there are three which are very symbolic of the country.

- *Cows* – During the summer months throughout Switzerland thousands of cows can been seen grazing in the pastures. At the end of spring, hundreds of thousands of cows are walked to the fields and autumn begins with the Swiss cow parade, an annual tradition of the cows coming back down the mountains for the winter. Farmers and children are dressed in traditional costumes and the cows are typically decorated with colourful floral crowns on their heads and large bells around their necks. The cow is symbolic of Swiss traditions and agricultural heritage. Nowadays, the image of the Swiss cow is used for marketing many Swiss brands and for tourism. Cows actually have an impact on the Swiss economy as they generate a very high revenue in the milk and cheese industries each year.

- *Bears* – The Bernese bears are kept in a historic bear park on the bank of the river Aare that runs through the city of Bern. Since medieval times there have been stories of warriors hunting bears around the city. The bear park is a large well-designed enclosure and considered a monument of national importance. It has tunnels, trees to climb, water pools and an opening to the river for the bears to swim and catch fish. Images of the bear are proudly displayed all around the city and on the canton's own flag.

- *Dogs* – The St Bernard is a breed of dog that originated in the mountain ranges of Switzerland. Due to their good sense of direction and resistance to cold, these dogs were used during the 18th century by monks to help travellers to pass through The Saint Bernard Pass, a route that passes throughout the Alps between Switzerland and Italy. They were also used as search and rescue dogs and would even dig down through the snow to find lost travellers. Often the dogs would work in pairs and if a traveller was found and in need of help, one dog would remain to guard the victim and the other would return to raise the alarm with the monks. Although the most famous images of the dog show it with a cask of brandy or whisky strapped to the collar, the dogs never carried such barrels; the collar keg stuck in the public's imagination after an artist in the 1800's painted the dogs wearing them.

THE ALPENHORN

This unique musical instrument is an emblem of traditional Swiss music. Although, it was not originally intended for music. It is made from wood and looks like a long smoking pipe, ranging from one to four metres in length. It is a very simple instrument which consists of a very long tube with a mouthpiece.

Historically, the alpenhorn was used by shepherds in the mountains to call cows and herdsmen from the pastures in the valley to return to the farm at the end of the day. It is sometimes referred to as the original mobile phone! The sound of the alpenhorn can be heard up to ten kilometres away depending on the wind. Although the traditional use of the alpenhorn is no longer necessary, it's widely used as musical entertainment at festivals such the Swiss Yodelling Festival, and it takes a minimum of two years to learn how to play it!

Alperhorn

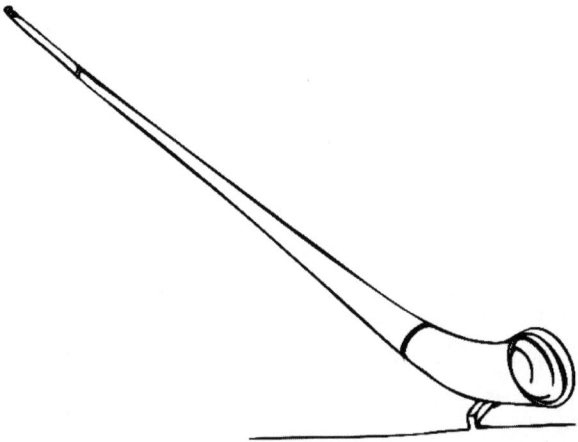

THE SWISS ARMY KNIFE
In the 1880s, the Swiss Army asked a German knife manufacturer to create folding pocketknives for their soldiers to help open canned foods and assemble and disassemble the service rifles. They supplied a pocketknife which had a single blade, a can opener and a screwdriver. Later, a Swiss cutlery company reproduced the folding knives and began adding more elements and design, resulting in what we know now as the Swiss Army Knife. Today, there are now over one hundred different models available and to this day, upon joining the Swiss military service (which is compulsory in Switzerland), each recruit receives their very own Swiss Army Knife.

FONDUE AND RACLETTE
There are so many traditional foods enjoyed throughout Switzerland (meringues, muesli, rösti etcetera) but fondue and raclette are iconic of Swiss food. Fondue originates from the canton of Fribourg and it's a simple tradition of dipping bread or potatoes into a pot of hot melting, bubbling cheese. It's so popular in Switzerland and there is an abundance of vending machines selling everything you need to enjoy the dish—the cheese, the bread, the potatoes, and even the meringues and cream for dessert! Raclette, which originated in the canton of Valais, is more complex than fondue. In a restaurant, a half-round wheel of cheese is presented, and the melted cheese is scraped directly onto the plate and is served with traditional accompaniments such as potatoes, pickles, hams and green salad. At home,

individual serving spoons/trays are filled with slices of cheese and placed under a grill to melt. The cheese is then scraped onto the plate and the spoon/tray is refilled with more cheese to place under the grill again.

Both raclette and fondue are enjoyed throughout the country with each canton proudly favouring their own variations, with or without potatoes, truffle or herb infused cheese, all of which are mouth-watering! What's not to love about cheese?

FUN FACTS ABOUT SWITZERLAND

- Stairs – Switzerland's Niesen Mountain has the world's highest stairs of 11,674 steps and reaching a height of 1,669 metres.
- Tunnels – Switzerland has many tunnels including the longest tunnel in the world, the Gotthard tunnel, which is 57 kilometres long.
- Toblerone is a popular Swiss chocolate which is enjoyed throughout the world. The image on the packaging shows the iconic Matterhorn Mountain covered in snow. The next time you enjoy a Toblerone, look a little closer at the mountain and find the hidden bear. The bear represents the capital city, Bern, the birthplace of the chocolate.
- Urban Swimming – It's a thing! The city of Bern has the longest river in Switzerland, the River Aare, running through the middle. The river is enriched with rock minerals that have turned the water a beautiful shade of turquoise blue, so it's quite remarkable. During the summer months, local workers in the city will change their clothing at the side of the river, place their clothes in a waterproof backpack and swim home, or just float and let the river currents pull them along. There are several entry and exit points along the river banks for the swimmers. The waterproof bags are sold in many stores around the city. Passers-by can watch from the bridge and observe the swimmers and floaters holding on to their colourful bags heading home from work; it's rather entertaining!

Chapter 2

Meeting, Greeting, Posture and Body Language

Switzerland has four official languages, German, French, Italian and Romansh, and two unofficial languages, English and... body language! The Swiss have been strongly influenced by their surrounding countries; however, despite some regional differences there is an air of conservatism throughout the country. Understanding the cultural body language of other countries is very important in order to manage efficient communication, particularly in business situations. A nod of the head, incorrect eye contact or even a smile at the wrong moment can result in disaster and this type of miscommunication can cause great offence or even ruin a business relationship. Switzerland typically follows the Northern European standards when it comes to facial expressions, gestures, mannerisms and degree of eye contact. The perceptions of personal space and the use of mannerisms are more reserved in comparison to Southern Europe.

GREETINGS

In Switzerland, greetings are an important part of the culture, and a fairly formal approach is taken to acknowledging one another. There are regional variations to be expected because of the influences of the close surrounding cultures, all of which are quite different in their own ways.

Upon meeting a Swiss person, it would be considered impolite and presumptuous to use his or her first name. Should the person wish to invite you to call them by their first name they will do so, otherwise, stick to formality. In the French-speaking part, people are usually addressed as *Monsieur* or *Madame* followed by the family surname if known. The German equivalent is *Herr* or *Frau* and the Italian is *Signore* or *Signora*.

A greeting such as 'good morning', 'good afternoon', 'good evening', 'good bye' (in the local language, of course) is always followed by a title even when passing a stranger in the street; for example, if walking in the street and you pass another person, you would say 'Bonjour plus Monsieur/Madame'. This greeting is typically used throughout the day, when you pass people in the village streets, in supermarkets and shops, anywhere you cross paths with another person, even while hiking (with the exception of the larger towns or cities of course). If you enter a shop, you will always be greeted with a 'good day' in the local language and you are expected to reciprocate immediately. If you don't respond, it is quite likely that they will patiently wait for your response before continuing with any further interaction. A farewell greeting is also expected by proprietors of shops, bars and cafes. Before leaving any private event, it's considered polite to offer a handshake and say goodbye to everyone who is present, individually, whenever possible.

Until recently, the handshake was the common gesture to accompany a verbal greeting. In fact, people would shake hands many times throughout the day. Children are taught from a young age to shake hands with adults such as house guests, teachers and even their sport coaches or teachers of after school activities.

Between friends the '*bise*' was commonplace, three or sometimes four air kisses, starting by offering the right cheek first. Nowadays, there is no real distinction between business greetings and greeting friends, due to social distancing and wearing masks. Some people add a very obvious and controlled nod of their head for emphasis and acknowledgement of a greeting, and eye contact is more important than ever. When seated, traditionally a man would always rise to greet a woman; however, nowadays, women should also rise to greet a man as this is just good manners.

Eye Contact

Eye contact is very important in Switzerland, particularly when greeting someone. It is considered a sign of attentiveness; in other words, why would you not look at the person you are talking to? If you are talking with a Swiss person and look away from them whilst talking, they will form the opinion that you are disinterested. More recently, eye contact has become even more important. In the absence of a handshake, eye contact is held momentarily longer than previously. Eye contact during conversation should be frequent as this conveys sincerity and helps build trust.

Personal Space

The Swiss will keep a respectful distance from others in social and business situations. Standing too close to someone will make them feel uncomfortable or perhaps even intimidated, so a respectful distance of approximately an arm's-length is the safest option to avoid any awkwardness. Closer proximity is too personal, and any form of touching is considered invasive.

Body Language and Non-verbal Communication

The body language used by the Swiss is similar to other Northern European countries and is generally more reserved and less demonstrative than Southern European regions. However, you should expect the Swiss to quietly pay close attention to body language. Having good posture is very important as it implies good breeding and confidence. Gesturing whilst speaking tends to be more conservative, particularly in the German speaking regions, whilst the French and Italian areas are somewhat more expressive. That said, there is still a distinct difference between a Swiss Italian and an Italian when it comes to gesticulating! When it comes to physical contact, the same differences apply depending on the region, the German regions slightly more reserved than their French and Italian counterparts.

Gestures and Actions – Dos and Don'ts

- Pointing at another person is rude. Using one's full hand to gesture towards a person is preferable.
- The OK sign with the thumb and index finger forming a circle is also considered rude by most Swiss people, although the thumbs up gesture generally means approval so is acceptable to use.
- Talking to someone with one's hands in one's pockets is rude.
- Crossing one's arms during a discussion may be seen as boredom, disagreement or a sign of closure.
- Avoid gesticulating too much unless you visit the Italian speaking region of course! Even then, don't expect the same level of hand movements as you would find in Italy; the people are still Swiss.
- Chewing gum in public is frowned upon although teenagers do it much to the dislike of the adult population.
- Avoid touching another person; it's an invasion of personal space and is too intimate for a normal interaction.

In Switzerland, children are taught good manners from a young age. They are taught to acknowledge adults, use eye contact, shake hands and thank others. One interesting gesture of thanks in Switzerland is the 'hand up' gesture (raising one's hand to the shoulder). This gesture is used by young children and adults alike when crossing the road! When using a pedestrian crossing it's only polite to thank the driver for stopping, so in order to be polite the non-verbal way— 'hand up'!

To summarise, David Hampshire, the author of the book, *'Living and Working in Switzerland'* accurately describes the Swiss in the following way:

'*Scrupulously honest, narrow-minded, industrious, pessimistic, boring, hygienic, taciturn, healthy, insular, tidy, frugal, sober, selfish, spotless, educated, insecure, introverted, hard-working, perfect, religious, rigid, arrogant, affluent, conservative, isolated, private, strait-laced, neutral, authoritarian, formal, responsible, self-critical, unfriendly, stoical, materialistic, impatient, ambitious, intolerant, unromantic, reliable, conscientious, obstinate, efficient, square, enterprising, humourless, unloved (too rich), obedient, liberal, thrifty, stolid, orderly, staid, placid, insensitive, patriotic, xenophobic, courteous, meticulous, inventive, prejudiced, conventional, intelligent, virtuous, smug, loyal, punctual, egotistical, serious, bourgeois, cautious, dependable, polite, reserved or shy, law-abiding and a good skier*'.

He then continues to explain:

'*You may have noticed that the above list contains a 'few' contradictions, which is hardly surprising as there's no such thing as a typical Swiss*'!

Chapter 3

Conversational Do's and Don'ts

When visiting a new country, meeting or working with someone from a different culture, there are some conversational topics that will be acceptable for one and not acceptable for the other. It's always recommended to do some research beforehand when travelling and if you unexpectedly end up in a conversation with someone from another culture that you are unfamiliar with, then be sure to keep the conversation light, neutral and impersonal to avoid causing any offence.

In Switzerland, as it is generally a polite country, there is a real possibility of making a mistake during conversation. That said, the Swiss are educated enough to know that any error is just a mistake, and they would be unlikely to judge you too harshly; however, as a result, it can cause an awkwardness in the conversation.

The Swiss are polite yet direct conversationalists who listen intently without many interruptions. This can be perceived as coldness by others, but for the Swiss, directness is considered an honest approach and therefore preferable to anything else. Professional lives are kept entirely separate from personal lives and this is reflected during conversations. Personal questions and topics are best avoided until a closer relationship has been firmly established.

Typical small talk is common in Switzerland, both socially and in business, and serves as an introduction to a deeper or more relevant conversation. Safe or fail proof topics to kick-start a conversation could include subjects such as something about the local area you may be visiting, something new you have recently learned about the culture, or which canton the Swiss person is from. Avoid talking about the weather—this is so boring!

There are some subjects that are good to steer away from in Switzerland to avoid coming across as rude or nosy.

TOPICS TO AVOID
- *Neutrality in World War II* – There is always reluctance to talk about this subject, particularly with a foreigner, so it's best to avoid all reference to the topic.
- *Swiss Military* – Switzerland has mandatory military service so it's best to steer clear of this subject as it can lead to some raised emotions during conversations. The Swiss people voted to keep military conscription not so long ago so it's something that most feel strongly about and is best avoided.
- *Salaries and personal finances* – This topic is rarely discussed even between friends. The Swiss are not great for showing any wealth, preferring to display modesty instead of any riches they may have. Switzerland is a wealthy country but not everyone is rich. Salaries are higher than the rest of Europe but so is the cost of living.
- *Personal questions* – The Swiss are very private people, so don't ask personal questions as this can be quite offensive and impolite. Avoid asking questions about someone's occupation (unless in a business environment of course), age, marital status, religion, number of children they have etcetera. In some circles, particularly with the younger generations, personal topics are being spoken about more openly, although it's still recommended to approach personal affairs with caution until certain relationship boundaries have been established.

SOME GENERAL DON'TS:
- Don't finish another person's sentence.
- Don't interrupt another person whilst they are speaking.
- Don't correct a person's grammar.
- Don't talk too much
- Don't brag about oneself and never gossip! You would not be perceived as well mannered!

There are many 'safe' topics in Switzerland and here are just a few particularly good subjects to get a conversation off to a good start with a local.

TOPICS TO DISCUSS:
- *Swiss wines* – The Swiss are very proud of their wines. There are 240 grape varieties grown in the country, 30% of which are local

grape varieties, such as the famous Chasselas which is the second most popular in Switzerland after Pinot Noir. However, very little of the wine is actually exported as the Swiss drink most of it themselves!

- *Travel* – Particularly in Switzerland. The natural beauty of Switzerland and the variety of beautiful, interesting and unusual destinations is a great topic. Open all year round for tourism, it has everything from lakes, rivers and waterfalls, alpine countryside and mountains. The Swiss enjoy travelling in their own country and each season is full of activities to be enjoyed. They will be happy to talk about their country. Talking about other travels is also accepted but avoid 'bragging' about too many personal trips as this can be seen as uncouth.

- *Swiss cuisine* – Food is always a good option particularly to get a conversation started. There are so many different types of cuisine in Switzerland, some with strong European influences and therefore will be quite distinct for each region. Within each of the twenty-six cantons there is much more to the food than cheese and chocolate, potato dishes, risottos, sausages, spätzle and charcuterie to name just a few.

- *Current world affairs* – (with caution) It's always interesting to talk about world affairs and the Swiss are no different. However, using caution with certain topics would be advised so as to avoid any debates.

- *Sports* – A welcome topic of discussion around the world and in Switzerland too, especially talking about winter sports! Switzerland is well known for being a country of sport and the Swiss particularly enjoy their outdoor activities all year around, so any questions about sport will always lead to interesting and safe conversations.

It's important to note that the Italian conversation style may be slightly more open, the German style slightly more closed, and the French style somewhere in the middle!

Don't forget the importance of eye contact during a conversation in Switzerland and make sure to keep some personal space, an arm's distance is the norm, certainly never any closer in business settings (although during the current pandemic that space is obviously much larger).

These conversational guidelines still apply to the younger generations albeit less so, perhaps due to more mixing of cultures in families, but nevertheless they are a good example for everyone to follow.

LAST, BUT NOT LEAST

Be an active listener – Listening is a key conversational skill. It allows you to find out a few things about the other person and then use the information to keep the conversation going.

Ask open-ended questions – This means that the other person must give an answer other than a simple yes or no and then that's it… let the conversation flow.

Use humour with caution – It doesn't always translate well so be sure that it will be understood.

Chapter 4

Gift Giving

When it comes to gift giving in Switzerland, politeness and propriety are the most important factors. In order to be polite, a gift must be given at the right time, and in order to keep within boundaries of propriety it should be appropriate for the occasion. This applies both to social and business gifts. Should a gift seem overly expensive or too personal then this can be deemed inappropriate. Modest is the way to go.

SOCIAL GIFT GIVING

Gifts are generally given for births, christenings, engagements, weddings, as a dinner guest or house guest, for birthdays, Christmas and sometimes for business. There are many good examples of social gifts and a few that can be offensive and therefore should be avoided. One should always offer a gift that the recipient will really appreciate and understand the thought that was put into choosing it.

• *Wine* – A bottle of wine is a standard gift when invited for dinner to someone's home so it's nice to think outside the box and really consider your hosts preferences. Try to find out what they like and select something a little more special accordingly. Also, it's a good idea to let the host know that you don't expect them to open the wine during the meal, as they may feel obliged to do so. Remember the gift is for them, not to be shared with you!

• *Other alcohol* – Brandies, cognacs, whiskies and other similar spirits will always be appreciated but caution should be used as these could be considered somewhat excessive. However, for a special occasion these would be acceptable, especially if the recipient is a connoisseur!

• *Chocolate* – Who doesn't enjoy chocolate? In Switzerland, it's nice to take handcrafted chocolates from a local village or one's hometown for your host to enjoy. Avoid the typical well known Swiss brands which are considered 'every day' chocolates and avoid Belgian chocolates for obvious reasons.

- Flowers are accepted with pleasure in a Swiss household, just remember to bring them already prepared so the host doesn't have to find a vase and arrange them in. Avoid red roses and red carnations, which symbolise romance, and white lilies and chrysanthemums, which are reserved for funerals. Traditionally, flowers were only given in odd numbers, but nowadays I don't believe anyone actually counts them; however, if you don't know your host very well and believe they may be quite traditional then it would be a good idea to count them just to be on the safe side—maybe you'll have one flower left over that you can keep for yourself! Bonus!
- *Cultural gifts* – Bringing a gift from your home country is a great idea if you can. It could be a coffee table book, a delicacy, a traditional item, a sweet treat, alcohol, almost anything. The fact that you have taken the trouble to select something from your culture to share with your host will be greatly welcomed.
- Sometimes flowers and/or chocolates can be sent in advance of an event or immediately after, as a thank you; this also a nice alternative.
- Avoid giving a Swiss Army Knife as the host will more than likely have one and avoid other sharp objects such as scissors, as they symbolise the severing of a friendship.
-

Christenings and Weddings

Gifts are given before the occasion or on the day. At some Swiss weddings, the gifts are taken to the wedding reception. If invited to a Christening or wedding, the best thing to do is to ask the preferences.

Business Gift Giving

In Switzerland, exchanging gifts is not very appropriate at the beginning of business relationships, rather, if gifts are to be exchanged this will be done at the end of certain negotiations or collaborations. Business gift giving in Switzerland is not as important as it is in other countries. However, Swiss companies recognise this and will arrange appropriate gifts to be exchanged at the appropriate times when dealing with international clients if they know it is an important part of the culture.

Many companies have a policy that prevent employees giving or receiving gifts, so if you travel to Switzerland for business, it is a good idea to check beforehand with the company policies, and if they do accept gifts, you can be prepared by bringing a few items from your own country that you can offer if necessary.

- *Company logos* – Gifts with company logos are considered acceptable but they should be of good quality.
- *Personal items* – Items such as clothing, jewellery or perfumes should always be avoided in business situations. A personal item can be viewed as inappropriate and may raise more than a few eyebrows.
- *Expensive gifts* – Don't offer any Swiss business an expensive item as this can be seen as a form of bribery and will be perceived as excessive. Quality, however, is important.
- Wine and nice alcohols can be offered in Switzerland and will be appreciated if they are of high-quality.
- As with social gift giving, avoid sharp objects such as penknives or letter-openers as these are considered unlucky and a severing of ties.

Chapter 5

Dining Etiquette

The Swiss are generally polite and are quite conscious of their manners at all times; therefore, at the dining table is no exception. Western dining etiquette is far from universal, particularly in a multicultural country like Switzerland. Therefore, there are a few variations of the styles of dining; however, generally speaking the Swiss use the Continental European style, which is quite an informal way of dining in comparison to the British or Continental styles.

Lunch is generally taken between twelve noon and two p.m. and dinner is eaten between six-thirty p.m. and seven-thirty p.m. Any evening meal with friends or colleagues always begins with an apéritif, whether in a restaurant or a private home. The '*apéro*' as it is known, is a short time for introductions and small talk over a glass of wine and some light snacks such as nuts or hams. It's often the time when a toast will take place as a way to start off the evening. This is an important ritual when each person raises their glass to every individual present as a form of acknowledging their presence. Raising your glass without observing eye contact or to miss raising your glass to someone is considered very impolite.

TABLE MANNERS (INFORMAL)
The continental European style of dining is observed by most Swiss people in day-to-day life.

- Hands and wrists are visible on the table throughout the meal and not on one's lap.
- The fork is the main utensil. Knives are only used to cut hard foods; instead, the side of the fork is used to cut foods and scoop it into one's mouth. Typically, the fork is switched to the right hand and held in the same way you would hold a spoon. The knife remains on the plate when not in use. After cutting a harder food, the knife is placed

back on the plate and the fork is switched back to the other hand again. Cutting soft food such as potatoes with a knife implies that the food is incorrectly cooked. In informal dining, bread can be used to push the food onto the fork.

- Don't start to eat your food until everybody has been served or the host tells you to start eating. The host may say '*bon appetit*' in French, '*guten appetit*' in German or '*buon appetito*' in Italian and you should respond with the same.
- Utensils – There are two important positions for placing your cutlery during the meal and the end of the meal.
- The resting position shows your host or server that you are not yet finished eating. The knife is placed at the top right of the plate above the food because it is only used occasionally, and as the fork is typically used in the right hand it is placed on the lower right of the plate.
- Placing your cutlery parallel together as if they were the hands on a clock, with the tip of the knife and tines of the fork pointing to eleven and the hands to five indicates that you have finished the meal.

Bread is always broken with one's fingers and eaten bite by bite; it should never be cut with a knife.

- Do not add salt or pepper to your food unless you have tasted first.
- Fingers are only used at the table for bread, fresh fruit will be served with cutlery.
- Your host will appreciate that you finish your meal and don't leave any food on your plate. Leaving leftovers on your plate is considered rude—waste not want not!
- When toasting, raise your glass to everybody at the table and hold eye contact momentarily before drinking.
- As with all cultures, don't forget 'please' and 'thank you'.

Table Manners (Formal)

In more formal situations, the continental style of dining should be used. This means no switching of cutlery between hands.

- Keep the fork in one hand and the knife in the other for the duration of the meal.
- Do not use bread to push food onto the fork.

- Hands and wrists should remain visible on the table throughout the meal.
- The utensil positions will change when resting and will form an inverted V on the plate instead. The reason is logical: if you are always holding the fork in one hand and the knife in the other then if you wish to pause for a moment it's the best position to place them (cutlery should never touch the table again after they have lifted; they should always be place on the plate).

OTHER BASIC TABLE MANNERS:
- Don't sit at the table until your host tells you; they may have a seating plan.
- Don't ask for ketchup, Coca Cola, Tabasco etcetera. This is a huge insult to the chef/host!
- Ladies, don't put your handbag on the table even if it is a clutch.
- Napkin etiquette: in a restaurant, you may place the napkin on your lap as soon as you sit down at the table. In a private home, wait for your host to do so first.
- Avoid gesticulating with the knife and fork in your hands.
- Don't talk with food in your mouth.

CONVERSATION AT THE TABLE

Everyone at the table has a responsibility to keep the conversation pleasant. Avoid controversial topics, such as religion, politics, Swiss neutrality, and topics that could seem overly personal. Make an effort to talk with everyone around you and include others in conversations as much as possible. Polite conversation at the dinner table is important in Switzerland.

FONDUE ETIQUETTE

One of the most commonly enjoyed meals, particularly in the French speaking cantons of Switzerland, is fondue. A combination of Swiss cheeses is melted with white wine and cornstarch and served in a caquelon (a clay pot). Long forks are used to dip bread (or potatoes depending on the region) into the communal caquelon of melting cheese. That's it... although there are a few rules of etiquette when it comes to eating fondue correctly and without causing offence:

- Use the fork to pierce the crust of the bread as this gives it a better hold.

- No double dipping one's bread for obvious hygiene reasons.
- Use front teeth to remove the bread from the fork so as to prevent the mouth from actually touching the fork at all.
- Try to avoid touching someone else's fork in the pot.
- The long forks with bread are also used to stir the fondue to stop it from burning.
- As with all foods, taste your fondue before seasoning.
- Warm tea or wine are the traditional drinks to serve with fondue. These are the best for aiding digestion; after all, it is quite a heavy meal. Nowadays, many people drink beers or soft drinks but the locals will spot you a mile away as a 'foreigner'.
- *'Le coup du milieu'* or *'the shot in the middle'* is a tradition still observed by some. This is an alcoholic shot in the middle of meal which is also meant to ease digestion. Typically, this would be Kirsch, a cherry brandy. Therefore, if you visit a traditional fondue restaurant, don't be surprised if you're offered a shot right in the middle of your meal!
- *'La religieuse'* is the name given to the golden crust at the bottom of the pot when the fondue is finished. It's delicious and considered by many to be the best part of the fondue and is a crime not to devour it. This is scraped off with a knife and enjoyed by everyone at the end of the meal.
- One last word: don't ask for chocolate fondue as it is not a traditional Swiss dish.

Tipping

A service charge is often included in the bill in Switzerland; therefore, tipping is not commonplace. Sometimes 'rounding up' the bill takes place, but larger tips are generally only given for outstanding service.

Some More Fun Facts

- When sharing fondue, if a woman drops a piece of bread in the pot, she must kiss all of the men, and if a man drops his bread, the drinks are on him!
- Grill Parties! You may be invited to a barbecue and asked to bring your own meat. It may seem strange, but this is not impolite in Switzerland; it is the normal way of grill parties, particularly when large numbers are involved.

- You will be expected to remove your shoes upon entering a Swiss home, so make sure you don't have holes in your socks!
- Don't be surprised to see dogs inside restaurants; they are welcome everywhere.

Chapter 6

Business Etiquette

When faced with business situations, it's particularly important to remember that not all companies in Switzerland are operated by Swiss nationals. There are many multinational businesses with employees from all over the world. As a result, the corporate culture of companies will vary, and depending on whether they are based in the German, French or Italian area of Switzerland, this will also need to be taken into consideration. Overall, hierarchy is quietly observed in most Swiss businesses, whereas many international companies are somewhat less hierarchic. There is no 'one rule fits all' in Swiss business. However, there are a few guidelines that are extremely important to know that flow throughout the different regions in the country. The way you first connect and thereafter continue to connect with someone in business, especially with those from a different culture, is critical to establishing a relationship. This chapter will focus on the Swiss expectations based on traditional business values which still remain relevant in today's corporate world.

DRESS CODES
Dressing well for any business is important and the same standards are expected in Switzerland. There are different levels of formality depending on the type of business, and professionals working in more conservative industries still wear smart business attire to work every day.

Many companies do take a more semi-formal view of dress codes but in Switzerland this does not translate to casual. Even if one is not expected to wear a suit to work, being well-dressed is of the utmost importance. It is not about wearing high-end designer outfits; in fact, this would be considered ostentatious and not be perceived well. Being well-groomed and conservatively dressed is expected of men and women, whatever the working environment may be.

- Dress according to the industry you will meet. Dress modestly and appropriately for the occasion. It will always be better to arrive slightly overdressed than underdressed as you can always remove a jacket or tie if you feel it necessary.

- Jeans and casual attire should always be avoided, even when meeting with industries that have adopted a very casual dress code. In order to form a good impression, wear something a little smarter than they do. It's a good idea to research the company dress code if you're not sure.
- Colours in business are generally neutral and muted (blues, greys, brown etcetera). Of course, touches of colour are fine but bright or loud clothing will attract attention for the wrong reasons. Incorporating colours into accessories is a great way to avoid being boring when it comes conservative dress codes!
- Finishing touches won't go unnoticed in Switzerland. For example, shoes for men should always be clean and/or polished, and for women, high heels should be understated for business. Jewellery should be subtle, and accessories should be tasteful.

Here are some examples of business dress codes by industry:

Formal: (suits & ties for men, suits or trousers/dress with jacket for women): *banking, financial, insurance industries, hotels, hotel/hospitality schools, embassies/consulates, private/international schools…*

Semi-formal / business casual: (trousers, shirts, no tie, for men; trousers/skirt with blouse/top or dress for women, no jackets needed):
international organisations, local authorities, universities, IT companies…

Businesses with casual dress codes: (anything not mentioned above apart from sportswear):
local small businesses, schools, agriculture, arts, entertainment…

PUNCTUALITY

Time keeping in Switzerland is extremely important (both in business and social situations) and failing to observe punctuality is a sign of bad manners. This is especially important in the German speaking areas, as people in the French and Italian speaking areas may be slightly more forgiving if someone is a few minutes late. However, punctuality remains one of the most important points to be aware of if you want to make a positive impression.

Meetings in Switzerland, like most things in the country, are very well organised. They will start on time and end on time. They are arranged in advance by appointment and will rarely ever be spontaneous. Arriving a little early, approximately fifteen to twenty minutes before a meeting, will give a good impression and show that you take the business matter seriously, while giving you  time to get acquainted with your surroundings and greet people before the meeting starts... on time!

Greetings

In all business environments, the first greetings will always be formal. Everyone is addressed by their title in the language of business (in English, Mr or Ms, in French, *Monsieur* or *Madame*, in German, *Herr* or *Frau*, and in Italian, *Signore* or *Signora*) followed by their last name. In most Swiss business situations this formality will continue for a long time, perhaps never even changing to first name terms. Direct eye contact during a greeting is equally as important as the spoken word.

Until recent times, the handshake would always accompany a greeting, and also when leaving. Now, even in the absence of the handshake, the vocal greeting remains the same, although eye contact tends to be held longer, perhaps in replacement of the missing handshake.

Communication

Face to Face

The first impression is extremely important; therefore, if you master the art of a polished appearance and a polite greeting, you'll be starting well. Good posture along with positive, controlled body language play a vital role in Swiss business. The Swiss are always polite, formal and slightly reserved. They do of course enjoy light-hearted small talk it remains impersonal. They maintain clear boundaries between their professional and personal lives, so topics such as family matters, age and religion should be avoided. After some initial small talk, it's straight to the business matter at hand. Business communication is taken very seriously, and only minimal humour is used occasionally.

Written
Emails and letters are the preferred forms of written communication, and they should always be formally addressed and composed. Never use the person's first name in a business email or letter unless you have been invited to do so. Doing so is considered impolite and presumptuous. Emails should remain professional and polite, unlike some other cultures that quickly move on to more casual terms. Keep written communication short but sweet! Don't waste a Swiss person's time with exaggerated small talk! Always reply within twenty-four hours.

Digital Etiquette
As modern technology evolves, the Swiss evolve accordingly, yet manage to maintain a high level of formality. WhatsApp and other platforms are becoming more common in business communication, but grammar and punctuation are uncompromised and the use of acronyms is certainly avoided. Titles will still be used in business messages!

Corporate Culture
A typical Swiss business environment is conservative and holds high regard for hierarchy. Hierarchy and rank are more important in the German-speaking area; however, individuals with seniority hold their positions modestly. Decision-making processes may seem slow, but they are methodical. The Swiss use a direct and honest communication style whilst remaining polite… of course!

The protocol for exchanging business cards is the standard international protocol; there are no additional rules to observe as there are in other countries such as Japan. Gift giving in business is done with caution to avoid any misconceptions of bribery. The cost of the gift, the reason for the gift and the type of gift should be considered.

Overall, the culture of business can vary depending on the region but the traditional Swiss values of politeness, mutual respect and of course punctuality remain engrained throughout the country.

Business Dining
Business meals are an important part of the Swiss business culture, and a business dinner is the most common form of entertaining. The general rules of international business dining etiquette will apply but here are a few important considerations for Switzerland.

Dress appropriately
You may have to dress up or dress down from the daywear! Depending on the reason for the business meal you could be dining at a ridiculously expensive five-star hotel or a nice simple bistro around the corner from the office. Know before you go!

The host (who has offered the invitation) will pay
There is no need to offer to pay for the meal but a 'thank you' and offer to reciprocate will be expected. A follow up 'thank you' the next day by email will be received with appreciation. There is no need to send a handwritten note.

Introduce yourself to others
This shows politeness and confidence, both of which are extremely important. Introduce yourself to everyone before sitting down as you may not have another opportunity to do so later if there are many people.

Don't take your seat without asking where you sit first
Quite often there is a seating plan and even without the use of place cards on the table the host and/or Maître d'hôtel will know by memory where all the guests should be seated.

Table manners are important for the Swiss
It would be advisable to use the continental style or the European style (see dining etiquette chapter), otherwise you may be perceived as uneducated. If you are unsure about anything, quietly observe your host and follow suit!

Don't even think about drinking before the toast!
The host will raise a glass to toast the start of the meal. After you have raised your glass and made eye contact with everyone at the table, then you may sip your drink!

When it comes to business dining, it is extremely rare to receive an invitation to someone's private home. If you do receive an invitation, it is a great, great honour.

Last words on Swiss business etiquette…

'*You can never be overdressed or overeducated.*'
Oscar Wilde

Chapter 7

Wedding Etiquette

Welcome to the wonderful world of weddings in Switzerland.

In this chapter, we'll start with the prewedding preparations and discuss interesting customs that take place on the wedding day. Then we shall look at some important etiquette tips you should know as a guest attending a Swiss wedding.

THE LEGALITIES

In Switzerland, the religious ceremony must be separate from the legal ceremony. This means that if a couple wish to marry in a church or have any type of religious ceremony then they will need to have a legal ceremony beforehand. Couples can arrange for the civil ceremony to be conducted anywhere, such as by a lakeside, a castle or even a mountain igloo depending on the season, although church weddings are still popular. Wherever the ceremony is conducted, it will usually be followed by an aperitif, dinner and dancing.

Prior to a ceremony, the couple must publicly declare their intention marry, in order to allow anyone to notify the registrar of any legal reason why the marriage should not take place. This intention to marry must be publicly declared for approximately five weeks and then the civil ceremony can take place. There is a time limit for this, and the wedding should take place within three months or the intention to marry must be publicly declared again. Weddings cannot take place on a Sunday or public holiday.

SAME-SEX MARRIAGES

Same-sex marriages are classified as civil or registered partnerships and are considered legally binding in the same way as heterosexual marriages. Whether same-sex marriage or heterosexual, the couple must be over eighteen, not part of a civil partnership and unmarried in order to legally proceed.

Female spouses keep their original surnames although many women prefer to change their name to their husband's or hyphenate the two names.

SWISS WEDDING TRADITIONS

There are many traditional elements to a Swiss wedding; however, with such a large international community, weddings are nowadays much more a mix of other non-Swiss customs than ever before. Here are a few fun, typically Swiss traditions that you may not have heard of… some perhaps more popular than others!

- The night before the wedding, the couple may have what's known as a wedding shower. The guests often bring some old porcelain with them which then they throw on the floor to break. It is believed that the broken porcelain will bring good luck to the newlyweds.
- A popular tradition is 'walking the gauntlet' or *'faire la haie'*. Upon emerging from the church or registry office as a married couple, the bride and groom hold hands and walk together between two rows of work colleagues, friends and family members. Sometimes the guests will hold up some ski poles in the air or something else to form a tunnel that the couple walk under. This custom is meant to symbolise the challenges awaiting the married couple.
- As the couple leave the church or registry office, the guests sometimes throw sweets instead of rice or confetti. These are made especially for weddings and are wrapped in papers which have special words of wisdom for the newlyweds. They are not so easy to find nowadays but can still be sourced.
- The Swiss couple may plant something together after the ceremony, perhaps at the reception venue. Traditionally, this would have been a pine tree but nowadays the custom is continued by planting anything of their choice in a plant pot. This custom symbolises fertility and luck for the bride and groom.
- At the wedding reception, the bridesmaids give coloured handkerchiefs to each of the guests. The handkerchief is a symbol of good luck, and the guests give the bride some money in return for it.
- Sometimes, the Swiss bride chooses to wear a traditional crown or wreath on her head and after the wedding the crown is removed and burned. If it burns quickly then it's good luck.
- Horn blowing takes place after the ceremony when the guests

will follow the bride and groom in their cars to the wedding venue. All the cars will follow behind the wedding car in succession, each car decorated with a flower, and will blow their horns non-stop until they reach their destination. Other cars passing by will blow their horns in recognition of the couple.

- Wedding games are arranged by the best man and maid of honour to involve the guests and the newlyweds. These games usually take place after the aperitif and before the evening meal. They organise sing-songs, charades and play jokes on the bride and groom depending on the ages of the couple.

THE WEDDING DAY

Whether the couple decide on a civil ceremony or both civil and religious, after the vows the celebrations follow, starting with the apéro.

The guests that attended the wedding will follow the couple to share their first celebration as a married couple at the apéro. They may invite more guests to join them if the venue for the ceremony was small. The apéro usually is champagne and some light foods and allows the bride and groom some time to mingle with the guests before dinner and dancing.

After the apéro and perhaps some games, there will be a reception dinner and party and dancing afterwards. Sometimes, many of the guests will leave after the apéro and only the family and closest friends will stay to continue the celebrations. This depends entirely on the couple and their budget.

The evening events are quite typical of any other western style wedding with dinner, slicing of the cake, and of course the couple's first dance.

GENERAL SWISS WEDDING ETIQUETTE FOR GUESTS

Swiss wedding traditions are very similar to other Northern European countries; therefore, the following tips should be taken into consideration if invited to a Swiss wedding.

The RSVP

A wedding RSVP should be answered according to request on the invitation. If there is a formal RSVP you should use it; if there is a wedding website or email address, then you should use it instead. Usually there will be a deadline for sending your response, so be sure to respond by that date;

although, the earlier you can let the couple know, the better. Even if you're a participant of the wedding you will still receive an invitation and be expected to answer. It's a traditional formality. If you're invited to bring a 'plus one' then you need to indicate the name of who you will bring, as the couple will need to know this for their seating plans etcetera.

The Wedding Gift

The couple will let you know whether they have a registry somewhere, or if they have a wedding website the information will be there. Although less common, at some traditional weddings the gifts are brought to the wedding and opened after the apéro. If you're unsure what to do, the best thing is to ask someone else. The cost of the wedding gift should relate to the nature of your relationship and cover at least the cost of the meal. It's quite common in Switzerland for colleagues and friends to group together to buy a larger gift.

Dress Code

Your invitation will be a guide as to the correct dress code. It should state the dress code clearly; however, if it doesn't, you can use the venue, time and the formality of the invitation as a guide. When in doubt, ask the bride or groom how they would like their guests to be dressed. Whatever the level of formality, it's important to bear in mind that traditionally black and white should be avoided, along with any colours that may be on the invitation as these could be an indication of the wedding theme colours or bridesmaids' dresses. For an evening wedding reception, a black dress would be acceptable. Generally, guests do get quite dressed up for a wedding, but the wearing of wedding hats is less common in Switzerland than other countries.

Punctuality

In Switzerland, punctuality is extremely important. Arriving late to anything is considered rude. In most situations a slightly early arrival of ten minutes is best; however, for a Swiss wedding, it's better to arrive around thirty minutes before the stated time on the invitation. This allows for everyone to be seated, comfortable and ready for the couple's arrival. If it's a particularly large wedding, then arriving even earlier is recommended.

Social Media

Despite everyone always having a mobile phone attached to our hands, now is not the best time to do so! A bride and groom normally will let guests know how they feel about sharing photos and wedding details on social media as usually it's a real no no! It's considered extremely rude to upload photos of the couple or wedding venue before they have had the chance to do so themselves. Usually, they will have paid a photographer and will prefer to wait and share the professional ones. That doesn't mean they won't allow you take photos; perhaps they just won't appreciate you sharing them. When it comes to using mobile phones, they should never be used during the ceremony and be kept off the dining table!

If you find yourself on the guest list for a traditional Swiss wedding, consider yourself honoured and be sure to save the date! It's not something to be missed!

Turkey
By Özgü Ergün

Chapter 1

Cultural Symbols

The Turkic ethnic group represents one of the oldest cultures in the world. History tells us that the race moved from central Asia and settled in Anatolia in the C.11th. The Ottoman Empire embraced a wide territory in the Balkans (the Caucasus, the Middle East and North Africa), and the Turkish culture became a blend of ethnic groups, races, ideologies and religions across three continents.

With this multicoloured heritage, Turkey restored its final borders a few years after the proclamation of The Turkish Republic; this, on the 29th of October 2023, will be celebrating its 100th year anniversary. Nowadays, the terms 'Turkish' and 'Turk' are used to express being a citizen of Turkey according to the Turkish Constitution and differs from the ethnic 'Turk' definition.

The country is divided into seven geographical regions separated mostly according to topography, the climate and the agricultural diversity. It has eighty-one cities, including Istanbul and the capital city of Ankara, the heart of the country's politics, housing the Turkish Grand National Assembly of Turkey.

THE TURKISH FLAG

The Turkish flag's origin derives from the late Ottoman flag and every single detail of it (the measurements and dimensions, the shade of red, and the rules to use the flag etcetera) was legally standardised by the Turkish Flag Law on the 29th of May 1936. The white crescent hugging a white star on a red background means a lot more than being a national symbol for the Turkish people and the Turkish culture.

It is obligatory that all state institutions, from schools to parliament, from stadiums to office buildings, hospitals to hotels, have to display at least one flag visibly, continuously and definitely at the appropriate place.

According to the law, the Turkish flag cannot be used in any way if it is torn, ripped, patchy, punctured, dirty, pale, wrinkled, or in any way that would damage the spiritual value it deserves. Except for official oath ceremonies, it cannot be laid on tables, podiums or as a cover for any purpose. It cannot be placed on places where you can sit or stand. It cannot be worn as a dress or uniform. Emblems, pennants, symbols etcetera from any political party, organisation, association, foundation and institution other than the public institutions and organisations determined by statute, may not be used on the front or back of the flag for any purpose. The Turkish flag cannot be insulted or disrespected verbally, in writing or in any way. The flag cannot be torn, burned, thrown to the ground, or used without proper care.

The flag appears on all printed and displayed presidential, state and ministerial materials as well as the military uniforms.

During national events, such as republic days, battle victories, commemorations, special celebrations, protestations, and respective occasions such as military, police or state funerals, the Turkish flag stands or is carried and is always used appropriately; it usually also has the portrait of Atatürk, the founder of the Turkish Republic. On these special celebration days, one may see the flag is also shown at the corner of each TV channel during their broadcasting. During mourning or after tragic events, the flag may be presented at half-mast.

The Turkish national anthem also mentions the Turkish flag:

Fear not, the crimson flag, waving in these dawns will never fade. Before the last hearth that is burning in my nation vanishes. That is my nation's star, it will shine; That is mine, it belongs solely to my nation. Oh coy crescent, do not frown, for I am ready to sacrifice myself for you! Please smile upon my heroic nation, why that anger, why that rage? If you frown, our blood shed for you will not be worthy. Freedom is the right of my nation who worships God and seeks what is right.

TURKISH COFFEE AND THE COFFEE CULTURE

"Does this coffee come from Yemen?" This humorous expression can be said whenever the coffee service is later than expected. It points out that originally the first coffee was brought from Yemen to Istanbul. By that time consuming anything roasted was forbidden by the Quran. Özdemir Pasha, Yemen's Governor of the Ottoman Empire, carried the first coffee to Istanbul, in the C.15th, and later the first coffee house was opened in the city by two Syrian merchants. Coffee's success was enormous, and it simultaneously entered the Topkapi Palace's Harem kitchens and was presented to the world-famous Hürrem Sultan (Roxelana), the wife of Suleiman the magnificent and the chief consort. She is also known to be the first person in the palace to try the Turkish coffee with '*lokum*' (the Turkish delight) along with a glass of water; these two additions reduced the coffee's hard roasted taste. Thanks to her coffee addiction, the Quran's prohibition was lifted with an official 'ferman' (imperial order).

The coffee's fame spread very quickly, and local coffee shops popped up all round the country. They became the men's gathering places where they met with friends, instead of staying home with their families. On one side, an evolution of the family traditions was on stage, and on the other side, sociocultural development was occurring. Literate people shared news and read books aloud for others to know what was happening around them, merchants were making deals, soldiers were planning riots; they became a hub for all these different activities. These shops still exist, and they are now called '*Kahvehane*' (meaning coffee house) or '*Kıraathane*' (meaning reading house) in Turkish.

The records tell us that Europe became acquainted with coffee thanks to the forgotten coffee sacks belonging to the Ottoman troops when they left after the second Siege of Vienna, and that the Austrian commander Georg Franz Kolscitzky was the first to produce the Vienna Brown coffee (Kleiner Brauner and Großer Brauner) out of this left-behind coffee.

Across the whole country, the different brands of Turkish coffee are sold in packs in grocery shops and markets. It is also available to buy by the gram and freshly ground at '*Kuruyemişçi* shops' (nut shops). 'Decaf' and other blends such as the 'mastic coffee' are also produced. The Turkish coffee is traditionally prepared 'sur measure': sweet (one teaspoon of coffee: two teaspoons of sugar), with sugar (one teaspoon of coffee: one and a half teaspoons of sugar), medium (one teaspoon of coffee: one teaspoon of sugar), low sugar (one teaspoon of coffee: half a teaspoon of sugar), without sugar, with milk. It is always served in porcelain Turkish coffee cups.

When visiting Turkey, one should know that the Turkish coffee can be consumed in the morning, in the afternoon or in the evening, 'whenever one wishes', as there is no 'the right time' to have a cup of Turkish coffee. You can have one, two, three or four cups per day, or until your doctor tells you to stop. It may be served in a business meeting, after a meal, when visiting a friend, or in a shop where you may have to spend some time deciding what to buy (especially the jewellery and carpet shops in the touristic areas etcetera).

When the groom's family makes the 'asking hand' visit to the bride's family, the Turkish coffee service is a customary ceremony; the bride must serve coffee to all the guests and prepare a salty, hot and spicy one for the groom. It is believed that, once he drinks this coffee and displays no reaction, they will be a 'happily ever after' couple!

'A cup of coffee has a sake of forty years' may be the most popular quote about the Turkish coffee, meaning 'whenever you drink a cup of Turkish coffee with someone, you will remember and be remembered for forty years'.

Turkish Coffee

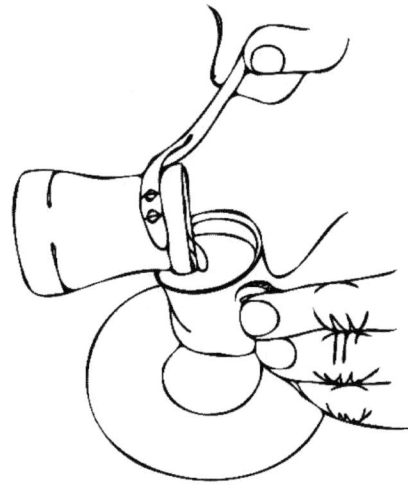

THE BOSPHORUS

The first thing you should know about the Bosphorus is that it is not a river but a strait. Also called the 'Istanbul Strait', Bosphorus is also the only passage between the Mediterranean and the Black Sea.

It is pronounced 'Boga-z', referring to 'Boga' (the bull in Turkish), as its original Greek name Bosporus means the 'strait of cattle'. According to a brief mythological story, the Princess Io was a priestess of the Goddess Hera, Zeus' wife, in Argos. Zeus falls in love with Io, and Hera, out of jealousy, plans to charm away Io. Hearing this, Zeus transforms Io into a cow to protect her from Hera's wrath. Hera captures the cow form of Io and condemns her to wander the earth in this animal body. The only possibility for Io to recover her human body was to cross the strait, which is now called 'the Bosphorus'. She finally managed to do this, as the same mythology tells us that she then gave birth to her daughter 'Kereosa' who then had a child from Poseidon, the God of the Sea, and this child, 'Byzas', would be the founder of the City of Byzantion, where nowadays stands the city of Istanbul. *(Prof Dr Oğuz Tekin-Istanbul of the Old Ages from Byzas to Constantinus Ist)*

The strait has a minimum width of 700 metres (2,300 feet) and a maximum depth of 110 metres (360 feet). There are three bridges connecting the two continents of Europe and Asia, as the city itself has land on both continents. This is what makes Istanbul such a marvellous and unique intercontinental city, as it is embraced on one side by the western world and modernity, and by the magical ancient roots of humanity on the other.

Both sides of the strait are dotted with waterfront houses, 320 today, which are called '*Yalı*' and are specific to the Bosphorus. By taking a local ferry or renting a private boat to cruise along the Bosphorus, beside the *yalıs*, visitors may also have the chance to see the Ottoman palaces and many historical buildings and landmarks such as the Topkapi palace, Beylerbeyi palace, mosques built by the Ottoman sultans, Rumeli and Anatolian castles.

Even the locals are in love with the Bosphorus every time they see it and there are many songs and poems written in the name of it. Perhaps Orhan Veli's poem '*Istanbul's folk song*' is one of the most famous ones. It is reproduced below:

> "In Istanbul, on the Bosphorus, I am a poor Orhan Veli.
> I am Veli's son,
> In an ungrateful sorrow.
> Sat by the Rumeli Fortress,
> Sat here and I am singing this song.
> Istanbul's marble stones,
> and the seagulls are on top of my had."

Chapter 2

Meeting, Greeting, Posture and Body Language

Facial signals and body gestures are commonly used amongst Turkish people, both international types of gestures and some more real 'Turkish style' gestures. These gestures and body language knowledge will help those visiting the country to understand the feelings of the Turkish people.

Anybody visiting Turkey should know that touching (hugging, kissing, holding hands) are the Turkish way of showing care and affection, friendship, respect, love and loyalty; the Turkish people are tactile amongst themselves and also with foreigners.

Kissing on Both Cheeks
Meeting and greeting often happens by kissing on both cheeks and a hug with both arms; it is the same for men to men, men to women, friends, close business colleagues and family members.

Another way for men to greet other men is to toss heads on both sides, a more masculine way with a conservative tendency.

Right Hand on the Chest or Heart
Turkish conservative people and Anatolian locals greet each other by saying 'Selam-ın Alcykum' (peace be with you) and in return 'Aleykum esselam' (also, peace be with you but said in return) and put their right hand on their chest area near to their heart and bow their head a little; this is a widely used greeting in Muslim countries.

Kissing the Hand of Elderly People
The traditional kissing of their right hand and then putting it onto your forehead demonstrates respect, loyalty and love of the elderly by the young. When an old person extends and raises her/his hand towards the other, this is a silent expression of his/her demand of being respected.

Hand Kissing

OFFERING A PAIR OF SLIPPERS
When visiting someone's house, if a pair of slippers is offered to you it means that you should take off your shoes. Although it is still up to you whether you wear the slippers or stay barefoot, you should not enter that house with your shoes on.

POSTURES AND BODY LANGUAGE
Nodding the head up and down is a sign of approval—it can mean 'yes' or 'I understand'. If a mother does this to her child, it means 'I am going to show it to you'. Moving the eyebrows up means 'no'. Another gesture for 'no' is clicking the tongue once. Shaking the head left to right continuously means 'no' also. Clicking the tongue more than once and continuously means 'gosh'. Kissing our fingertips is a common gesture to confirm that something is pleasing and approved.

    Writing in the air is a gesture for asking for the bill when at a restaurant. Whistling can also be used to call someone, more common in the street culture and should never be used in formal situations. To sit with legs crossed or to smoke cigarettes in front of an elderly family member, or to sing whilst having dinner are perceived as 'shameful' traditionally. If a person begins a long journey, a cup of water is poured behind that person or the vehicle carrying the person; this signifies that the journey will flow smoothly, like water, and for that person to get back home sanely and safely.

THE FOLLOWING GESTURES CAN BE COUNTED AS ONES TO BE AVOIDED
- The universal OK sign (making a round shape using the thumb and the forefinger) in Turkey is used to accuse someone of being an LGBTI member; it is slang and may be considered as swearing.
- Pointing the forefinger at someone is rude.

Chapter 3

Conversation Dos and Don'ts

Providing you enact a polite manner towards the Turkish people, you will receive courteous behaviour in return and will be treated with respect, trust, affection, decency, tolerance, serenity, peace, frankness, loyalty, harmony, honesty, helpfulness and thoughtfulness. All these behaviours complete each other; such good manners form the ABC of the Turkish culture.

Turkish people usually show a happy face to their guests. Whatever negative events are happening in life, they do not complain. When two people meet for an occasion, by coincidence or for a business meeting, the first question is always, "how are you?" And 99 % of the time, this will be answered by saying, "I am fine, thank you and you?"

So, whenever you meet someone, this should be your first question too. Most people will express their thankfulness to God by saying either *'Allaha Şükür'* (thank you God) or *'El Hamdullillah'* (praise to God). They believe it is rude to complain about everyday things, as God is always there to help.

Some helpful hints:
- Say, 'thank you' and 'please'—the key to open all doors.
- Learn at least to say 'thank you', 'please', 'yes' and 'no' in Turkish; this will be greatly appreciated.
- Talk about anything but always be honest and decent.
- Say whatever you think but always be respectful.
- Don't talk or laugh in a mosque.
- Do not make comments about the Turkish Flag.
- Do not ever humiliate Mustafa Kemal Atatürk, the father of all Turkish people, the founder of the Turkish Republic.
- Avoid eating in public during the Ramadan period. Please remember that it is not forbidden but it is respectful; additionally, almost all restaurants and cafes are open in this period, so it is advisable to eat there instead.
- Do not haggle unless you are in touristic shops; anywhere else you must pay the stated price.

THE LEGENDARY 'TURKISH HOSPITALITY' AND FAMILY RELATIONS

When you visit Turkey, you are always welcomed and treated as a 'guest sent by the God'; this is called 'the Turkish hospitality'. It never matters who you are, which religion you belong to, which language you speak, or which country you are from.

The Turkish hospitality is no longer a tradition, but a natural way of behaviour. Despite all technological development that keep people apart from each other day by day, this habit still survives in the C.21st. The importance of family ties is passed on from generation to generation. You may notice that most Turkish people have dozens of cousins and a lot of nephews and nieces. Once two families are connected by the marriage of their children, they have the ability to act as if they were the members of the same family since the beginning. Turkish people enjoy large family activities, and they always create a good reason to get together. Female members especially are the ones who build the interactivity between family relations.

The children usually live with their families and are supported financially until they get married. There are very few nursing homes and elderly care homes as the seniors are always respected and taken care by their children, so they are almost never left alone.

DAILY DRESS CODES APPLICABLE IN THE CITIES

- Sports and casual clothes for non-working men and women, the retired, college students.
- All students from primary school until the end of the high school wear uniforms—every school has its own creation.
- Smart casual and casual for freelancers, merchants, service industry workers.
- At hotels uniforms also might be worn by the selected staff.
- Business casual and formal for office workers, those working in banks
- Formal for white and blue-collar workers, senior executives.

There are still people who wear shalwar in the rural areas during the normal day, whereas they prefer to wear more modern but still conservative clothes for special events and celebrations.

Chapter 4

Gift Giving

If you are invited to someone's home, you should never arrive 'empty-handed', to quote a Turkish proverb.

PRIVATE HOME INVITATIONS
Bringing a gift when you are invited shows good manners and respect, you can choose between a bouquet of flowers, a cake, or a pack of pastry desserts are always welcomed. You can also buy a bottle of wine if you are sure your hosts consume alcoholic beverages. You may also try to bring some chocolates or candies/sweets if they have children; the littles ones will appreciate this and they will remember you forever. If you bring glassware or a souvenir, you can present it to your host or simply leave it by the entrance. In the case that there will be other invitees, do not forget to attach a card with your name on it.

PERSONAL CELEBRATIONS (BIRTHDAYS, ANNIVERSARIES, GRADUATIONS, PROMOTIONS)
Be mindful when considering gifts; generally, anything which is not too personal and which would not offend the giftee will be accepted and appreciated. Please keep in mind that both the cheap and the expensive can be rude sometimes. When choosing a gift, always take into consideration the celebrant's life standards and socio-economic level.

SPECIAL DAYS (MOTHER'S DAY, FATHER'S DAY, TEACHER'S DAY)
The second Sunday of May is Mother's Day, and the third Sunday of June is Father's Day. Both Mother's Day and Father's Day are usually celebrated amongst the family members in homes and at restaurants throughout the day. Children buy symbolic but caring gifts for their parents/seniors and a new record is broken every year in that day's flower sales.

Turkey's Teacher's Day has a specific meaning and that is why it is celebrated on November the 24th and not on the universally known October the 5th. In Turkey, this day is more than a commemoration day; it is also to commemorate Mustafa Kemal Atatürk, the founder of The Turkish Republic, who was announced as the 'Head Teacher of the National Schools' on November the 24th 1928. This day is celebrated in schools and even former students buy gifts and flowers for the teachers.

SOUVENIRS

For any family member going abroad for any reason, they are often expected to bring back souvenirs from their destination within their budget: a magnet, a mug, a pencil, a pack of chocolates, any tiny gift is proof that family/friends were remembered. The same is true for close business colleagues.

RELIGIOUS AND NATIONAL HOLIDAYS

There are several important national days which are celebrated in Turkey but there is only one which involves the giving of gifts: the National Sovereignty and Children's Day on the 23rd of April. Many events are held for children and they also receive gifts from their parents on this special day. During religious holidays, the young members of families visit the elder members. Children kiss their grandparents' hands and receive 'pocket money' in return; this tradition makes the young generation a fan of these holidays, as at the end, they get the chance to buy whatever they want. Also, during the Ramadan Feast, as blood sugar levels drop during the fasting period of twenty-nine to thirty days, it is common to bring anything 'sweet' when visiting family members, relatives and friends. It will then be appropriate to buy a box of chocolate and special candies/sweets as well as some Turkish desserts if you are invited to someone's house during this period.

FUNERALS AND COMMEMORATIONS

In Turkey, when someone dies, the house welcomes anybody who wants to express condolences. A short visit to express words of sorrow is more acceptable but you may stay there as long as you wish to give a helping hand. People bring homemade or ready-made easy-to-serve food (Turkish pastries, desserts, boerek, dolma). The visits continue until the end of the first week after the burial. 'Mevlut' is a Quran reading gathering organised in the evening of the burial and every year afterwards on the same day, as a commemoration. During the commemoration event, even though a special Mevlut menu is again prepared by the host, the same tradition of 'never go there empty-handed' stands again.

In fact, Turkish people always take care of their loved ones and never leave each other either in bad days of grief or the happy days of celebrations.

Please note that wedding gift giving is studied in chapter 7 (Wedding Etiquette).

Chapter 5

Dining Etiquette

The ancestors of the Turkish people were the nomads living in the vast steppes of Asia. When it comes to cooking and their culinary habits, it is obvious that things have changed little since then; the men were hunting, and the women were cooking. Every Turkish woman, even if she never cooked when she lived at her parents' home, after getting married becomes a master chef! Men just arrive when it is the barbecue time, with a subconscious 'hunter' instinct. On the other hand, surprisingly enough, 95% of the professional cooks were men until recent years when vocational high schools were opened, and universities included gastronomy in their curriculums. Nowadays, studying gastronomy and culinary arts is very popular and this is a fact which contributes to the further development of the Turkish food culture.

Turkish cuisine has a collection of more than 20,000 dishes which originate from the country's various regions and from the lands which the Ottoman Empire once governed. This rich range of food makes the Turkish cuisine a profound cultural icon. The abundance of fresh vegetables, fruits, spices, different types of herbs, the diversity of cereals and legumes, the fisheries on the four seas (the Black Sea, the Marmara Sea, the Aegean Sea and the Mediterranean Sea), the farming throughout the country, and the importance given to agriculture and livestock make Turkey a paradise of food.

There are two main branches in Turkish cuisine: the Ottoman cuisine and Folkloric cuisine. Whilst the Ottoman Cuisine is a combination of different tastes from the East to the West, the Folkloric cuisine reflects more the local food habits of the territories which stayed within the country's modern-day official border.

Turkish culture is based on 'cooking, eating and sharing'. This is uniquely the Turkish style and is called '*A la Turca*'. Food is a passion, cooking is a daily practice, eating is a ritual and family tables are the naïve and indispensable part of life. Every single detail at a Turkish family table reflects the Turkish etiquette and manners.

Turkish people like to gather for any special occasion, so they are always connected and together. The tables are always prepared with gusto where sharing and unity matter.

Breakfast

Breakfast time is between seven to nine a.m. on weekdays and to after ten a.m. on weekends. Daily regular breakfast menus consist of a selection of cheese, Aegean fresh olives, eggs, butter, homemade fruit jams, cucumber, tomato, parsley and dill leaves and finely sliced fragrant fresh white bread along with a 'tulip shaped glass' of black tea. During weekends, in addition to the regular weekday menu, a special breakfast bun, '*simit* or *açma*', or some '*börek*' (oven-baked or pan-fried patties), fried fermented '*sucuk*' (Turkish pepperoni), '*menemen*' (a delicious and pure Turkish scrambled egg speciality), and some other breakfast specialities are added. Also, don't forget that food is always 'to be shared'.

Lunch

Lunchtime is an hour, between twelve and one p.m. Those who work usually have lunch out at a fast food or an artisan restaurant. The artisan restaurants serve daily vegetable dishes, soups, rice and some chicken or meat dishes, as well as grills, salads and local desserts. Artisan restaurants are usually open only during business hours. The meal finishes with a glass of tea or a cup of Turkish coffee and usually this drink is 'on the house' (not added to the bill).

Children's Menu

In most restaurants, a children's menu is available. It usually consists of some fried potato, grilled meatballs and spaghetti with tomato sauce or mini hamburgers. Children also may prefer doner kebab wraps, which are easier than eating a sandwich, and the '*fındık lahmacun*' (a mini, Turkish flatbread with minced meat—a kind wooden oven-baked soft pizza).

Dinner

Dinner time on weekdays is usually after seven p.m. depending on people's habits, and after eight p.m. on Fridays and Saturdays.

Dinners are times when the family members evaluate their days and exchange ideas, and family relationships are strongly built. In winter, dinner usually starts with soup. Irrespective of the season, the main course is a vegetable dish (with meat or minced meat) or a grill (meat, chicken, meatballs or a steak). A sort of rice or bulgur *'pilav'* or a Turkish pasta is served to complement the main dish. A cold vegetable cooked in olive oil is on the menu especially during the summertime, and this is accompanied by a shepherds' salad, a green leaf salad or a *'cacik'* (diluted mint yoghurt with diced cucumber) which is to be shared in the middle of the table. *'Turşu'* (pickled vegetables which are usually homemade in Anatolia) replaces the salad during the wintertime. Dessert and fruits do not have to be served at the table during a regular evening; instead, they may be served after dinner, whilst watching TV, and perhaps accompanied by some tea or Turkish coffee.

Although homemade food is preferred, dining or lunching out is also very popular, except in more rural areas. The Doner kebab and Lahmacun are the masterpieces of the local fast-food cuisine, as well as the baked potato *'kumpir'*, mussel shells stuffed with rice, and *'kokoreç'* charcoal grilled lamb intestines in a sandwich; please keep in mind that all these go very well with a glass of *Ayran*, the national yoghurt drink. Besides the street food sellers, many small restaurants, patisseries, and cafes exist in every small square. In almost every neighbourhood, takeaway options are available.

In the big cities it is possible to find international cuisine restaurants but when locals dine out, they mainly choose one of these three options: a *Meyhane* (the Turkish tavern), a fish restaurant or a kebab house.

Alcohol is served at all *Meyhanes*, as can be understood by the breakdown of the word, *'mey'* meaning 'wine' and *'hane'* meaning 'house'. Turkey, being a large producer of grapes, has a huge number of wine producers around the country. But still the favourite beverage is *Rakı*, which is also called 'the lion's milk'; this is an alcoholic drink made of twice-distilled grapes and anise. *Rakı* is sold in the markets, in *'Tekel'* shops, and also in grocery shops; it is served at restaurants except those which do not hold an alcohol licence. The seafood restaurants usually offer a variety of fresh seafood meze, served family style, and fish, including the catch of the day.

The kebab restaurants are more frequently used by families dining out and so alcohol may or may not be available. The menu at these restaurants always starts with a special meze and salads, served family style, followed by the main course with a wide selection of charcoal grilled meat and kebabs.

Table Manners

At home, when there is a dish to be served individually, the service starts from the oldest man, followed by the oldest woman. If there is a guest, the guest and the accompanying person are served after the seniors. Usually, the housewife or the oldest daughter serves the meal. Once the elderly person or the host says, "*Afiyet olsun*", meaning "Bon appetit" in Turkish, everybody starts to eat. At a normal daily dinner table, only water is served; however, when there are guests, alcoholic or non-alcoholic beverages may also be available and will be offered before serving the meal.

In restaurants, almost the same sequence is followed but this time the service starts from the oldest woman.

In the small villages and towns, a spoon and a fork are usually enough for a family dinner and the table set up may not contain a knife unless meat is served. In the big cities, restaurants have world-class equipment, and they always perform with the Turkish hospitality manners.

Special Meals and the Service
Ramadan and Ramadan Feast

During the month of Ramadan in the Hijri calendar, the Muslim population (90% of Turkish people are Muslim) fasts for twenty-nine to thirty days, from sunrise until sunset. There are two ritually served meals during these days:

- '*Sahur*' is a meal prepared and eaten before the morning prayer time before the fasting begins. Light breakfast items and some rice pilafs are served. In order to prevent a drop in blood sugar levels, fruit compotes accompany the meal.
- '*Iftar*' is the fast-breaking time. The fast is broken by first drinking water and eating olives. The dinner menu may include some breakfast items and dates followed by a soup, a vegetable and meat dish, rice or bulgur pilaf, a salad, olive oil dishes and any dessert. '*Güllaç*' is Ramadan's special dessert, which is only consumed during the Ramadan period, cooked with thin layers of dough filled with pistachio and topped with a rose water flavoured syrup, usually decorated with pomegranate grains.

• During Ramadan, instead of consuming bread, people prefer eating 'Ramadan Pide'. This wooden oven-baked flatbread is produced only during Ramadan. Not surprisingly, you may notice long queues in front of the bakeries when the *İftar* time approaches.

These thirty days without eating during the daytime finishes by eating sugar and desserts during the Ramadan Feast which endures for three days. 'Baklava' is the queen of this feast. It is made from a minimum of forty very thin layers of pastry, filled with pistachios, walnuts or hazelnuts, oven-baked, with a sugar brown surface topped with a smooth syrup. This sounds really delicious, doesn't it? Because of the high sugar consumption during these days, the Ramadan Feast is also called 'Sugar Feast' in public.

Baklava

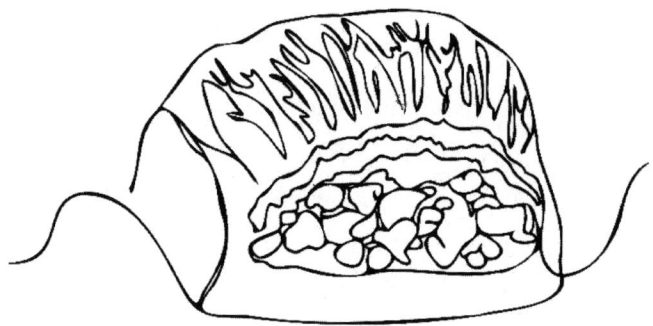

Sacrifice Feast

The Sacrifice Feast is celebrated each year for four days, starting on the 10th day of the month of *Zilhajj* of the Hijri Calendar. This feast's special main dish is '*kavurma*', made by dry-frying the meat of the sacrificed animal (sheep/lamb or calf). The rest of the menu depends on the region but as this is one of the most important family reunions, the table will perhaps be covered by all the family members' favourite dishes and desserts.

New Year's Eve

New Year's Eve is also widely celebrated in Turkey, on December the 31st. The hope of new beginnings brings people together at their homes, at restaurants and at hotels; the main dish is 'oven-baked turkey stuffed with chestnut rice'.

'The Day'
Although there is a huge number of working women in Turkey, a quite big population of 'housewives' still exists. 'Going for the day' is the oldest way of socialising for them and as long as the population of housewives exist, this tradition will always exist too, especially in the rural areas, small towns and villages. 'The Day' refers to a certain day of each week when they all gather at one house (in rotation) to socialise. Usually, homemade patisserie that goes well with the black tea is prepared. It is also a common practice for these women to collectively buy gold and give it to the host of the week for saving. Because of this practice, 'the Day' is something also called 'the Gold Day'. However, in the big cities, this tradition is somehow replaced by luncheons or afternoon coffee breaks at cafes. This way of meeting, at cafes instead of in the home, means every woman pays her share; nobody has to host or prepare for the meeting.

DRESS CODE
The dress code for regular family meals is casual but when it's time for a festive gathering people try to dress 'smart casual' and usually buy new outfits for the children. There is even a generation that spends the Feast Eve with the excitement of their new shoes to wear the next day!

Smart casual or formal is the attire required, depending on the special day's celebrations and feasts. Formal attire is required for business dinners.

SPECIAL NOTES
Formal business dinners are described in the business etiquette chapter.

Wedding and related celebrations are described in the wedding etiquette chapter.

Chapter 6

Business Etiquette

OFFICIAL MEETING AND GREETING

It does not matter whether the person is 'old school' or 'new school', educated or not, from a corporate or a family business, a business owner or a professional, the Turkish businesspeople and the business etiquette will always carry the country's cultural traces and will always be 'one of its kind'.

Check the national and religious holiday periods before arranging a meeting.

For men, a business suit with a tie, and for women, a smart business outfit is acceptable. Guests must not be kept waiting when there is a meeting, although a delay of up to fifteen minutes can be acceptable. In the same way, if they are late themselves, they expect a similar understanding from your side. Business dress is smart casual if the company is neither an international nor local company. Clean socks are a must whenever you are invited to a private house, whether for business meetings or private gatherings, where a pair of home slippers may be offered (please see chapter 2).

Seniors are always very important in Turkish culture. The elderly members should always be greeted first, especially when dealing with a family-owned company. A formal meet and greet always begins with a handshake, unless there is a closer relationship between the parties when it might be appropriate to continue with traditional hugging with both arms and kissing on both cheeks. Between men and women, the handshake should be soft and short, without hugs usually. It is for the woman to offer her hand for a handshake rather than the man to offer his. If a woman does not offer her hand, it means that she is conservative, which is why the man should not be the first one to extend his hand when greeting a woman.

WHEN IN A MEETING

The meeting always starts with small talk; jumping into the business talk before the small talk should be avoided. Modern companies and businesspeople in big cities such as Istanbul, Ankara and Izmir are more used to international business manners, but in smaller cities and rural areas, the Turkish way will always lead the meeting.

There is a common quote which says, 'bargaining is customary' and it is a clear indication of the Turkish business mindset. One should be patient and wait in order to get the desired result. Trust is the driving mechanism for negotiations; as such, before moving forward with meetings and business relationships, first the trust should be built up.

In the Turkish mindset, wealth has a meaning only if it is rightfully 'well earned' and it is going to bring prosperity, blessing and health.

To develop good relations, it is always a good idea to talk about football, Turkish food and culture. Your questions will never be left unanswered if your local counterpart feels your interest in Turkey. The country's political issues are a red line, however, and you should never initiate such a topic unless your counterpart does. Never forget that respect always comes first.

Although most businesspeople have an understanding of foreign languages, you should check beforehand and arrange an interpreter if necessary.

At a business meal, lunch or dinner, the most appropriate method is to leave the topic of the conversation to the host and remember not to talk about business affairs too early. Your host may be conservative, so it would be impolite to ask for alcoholic drink service until it is offered or asked by them. Always remember that the seniors and the ladies are the first to be served, so do not eat or drink before the oldest person at the table or the female guests have been served and have started to eat or drink. If you are the invitee, do not even ask for your share of the bill; just show your appreciation. Remember that you should be the one who pays the total bill if you organised or held the event. It is a tradition to leave an office, a meeting or a shop by saying, "*Hayırlı işler*," meaning, "I wish you an auspicious and blessed business."

Chapter 7

Wedding Etiquette

WEDDING TRADITIONS

'We celebrate weddings for forty days and forty nights' is not only a famous quote but it is also true. The 'big time' story begins with the man proposing. If the answer is 'yes', the first procedure is the 'asking for the lady's hand' visit by the groom's family to the bride's. The groom's side brings the best chocolate basket along with a special bouquet of flowers; the size and the material are chosen in accordance with the man's affection and his family's wealth. Once the Turkish coffee ceremony is completed, the famous phrase is delivered by the oldest family member on the groom's side: 'With the God's commend and the Prophet Mohammed's utterance, we kindly ask your daughter to marry our son'. The woman's father (or the mother, if the father already passed away) gives the official approval, although technically this is granted earlier by the acceptance of the visit.

A few weeks later, a second visit for the 'binding' takes place, again to the parents of the bride-to-be; at this point both families become 'co-in-laws' to-be. These two events are usually held with the core family members and relatives and sometimes with close friends of the young couple.

The next step is the 'engagement', when rings are worn. There will be more people to join this event as this is the official announcement of the soon to-be-married couple. While the number of guests is a joint decision of both parties, the venue selection, the hospitality details and all such related issues regarding this ceremony are organised and financed by the bride-to-be's family. After the engagement event there will be two more visits by the co-in-laws to each other, where the 'engagement packs' containing the special gifts are delivered from one to the other.

The wedding ceremony is usually planned within a year of the engagement, on a date which should never be between the two religious holidays as it is believed that this would bring 'bad luck'. All the wedding expenses are financed by the groom's family. The guest list is generally split fifty-fifty for each side, the venue selection is a joint decision, the wedding dress is chosen by the bride-to-be and paid for by the groom's family. A few days before the wedding, two other events will take place. The 'bachelors party' for the groom and a 'henna night' for the bride. These two events do not have to take place at the same time and it is not a must to use henna but the evening traditionally is still called that name. In the big cities, it is common to have a bachelorette theme event for the bride as well as the henna night, and this is mostly organised by her female friends. There may also be other events such as the '*Hamam* Event' (Turkish Bath ceremony) which was originally organised to ensure the virginity and purity of the bride's body. Things have strongly changed since then, of course, and so this tradition is now replaced by either a full day treatment at a spa or a *Hamam* themed event with special entertainment but still including only the closest female relatives and friends of both parties. The wedding day is a full day celebration at both family houses where the best friends and relatives are gathered. 'Fetching the bride' is such a joyful event; the groom-to-be comes home to pick up the bride, accompanied by a band of drums and clarions playing some folk wedding music. The tears are mixed with laughter; this is where the bride signifies farewell to her childhood home, as a new life for her begins.

Henna Night

Nowadays, the 'asking for her hand' visit and the binding event/engagement ceremony are generally organised as one event, a more efficient way to save time and money. Sometimes the engagement party may be skipped and it is combined with the wedding and the expenses are shared by both families.

In Turkey, only the act of civil marriage is legally binding, not the religious ceremony. The civil marriage is usually organised at one of the wedding halls run by the municipalities. The municipalities are the authority holders in the name of the Republic of Turkey. In accordance with the families' wealth and preference, the wedding may take place at a hotel or an event location other than these civil wedding halls. Then, the appointed wedding officer will be ready at the chosen venue and the marriage contract will be signed in the presence of the guests. A religious wedding is not obligatory as it is not officially recognised but if the couple wishes, this will be organised for after the completion of the civil marriage procedure.

If you are ever invited to an engagement party or to a wedding, please keep in mind that it is uncommon to bring a gift to these events. Gold is the number one gift to offer; you can buy small gold coins or a gram of gold at any jewellery store. The shop will provide a mini velvet pouch and you should place a small name card inside so that the couple knows that this gift is from you. Another option is to contribute to the wedding gift list if it has been previously prepared and announced by the couple.

The neighbours, friends and close relatives may also wish to make a congratulatory visit to the bride's family after the engagement or to both sides of the family after the wedding. There, any household items might be given as a gift such as glassware, silverware, porcelain houseware, furnishings or home textile products, and of course, gold coins are always more than welcome.

'SÜNNET' CIRCUMCISION CELEBRATION

Another ceremony is organised after the circumcision of boys, usually before they are ten or eleven years old. Though nowadays, many parents prefer doing this operation right after the birth or when the boy is still a young child.

Turkish society is patriarchal; the men always are the leaders. The circumcision is the first step for the boy to become a real man, so this has to be announced and celebrated for 'forty days and forty nights'. As for all such events, the most appreciated gifts following the circumcision are gold, cash money, and clothing, but household goods are also common gifts. Recently, it is also very common to buy high-tech materials and toys as a gift.

Event Invitations

The announcement of all types of celebrations and parties is made with an invitation card which includes all necessary details and the itinerary of the event, as well as the venue address. Whether there is an RSVP number or not, you might call to reconfirm your participance.

After the engagement party, the couple will both bring a box of chocolates to their friends and colleagues, to announce this happy new beginning. It is also a tradition to distribute a designed pack of candies/sweets at the end of the wedding, for the sweet memories; this is usually kept as a souvenir.

Nowadays, it is also common to make donation announcements instead of distributing candies, such as planting a tree etcetera.

Dress Code

The dress code for weddings is usually semi-formal or dressy casual if the ceremony is taking place at a municipality wedding hall, as this is always a daytime event. If there is a post-ceremony event, those who wish to may change their outfit to a more formal or cocktail style. Black tie: a formal floor-length gown or a sophisticated cocktail dress for women, and a tuxedo or a business suit for men. If this is a resort wedding or a garden party, women should wear appropriate shoes.

For all other aforementioned events which take place at family houses, a cocktail style or a semi-formal dress code will be chosen by both men and women attending the event.

UAE
By Andreea Stefanescu

Chapter 1

Cultural Symbols

As we travel the world, we end up in places that are so diverse and different to the place we were born and raised in, and from time to time, you end up stumbling upon somewhere that is truly unlike anything we could ever imagine on this planet, which is what most people who visit Dubai feel like. Many people don't even know that Dubai is just a city, not even a capital city, and is not even the largest of the seven emirates that make the country of the United Arab Emirates. That title belongs to Abu Dhabi. The seven emirates that make up the UAE include: Abu Dhabi, Dubai, Sharjah, Ajman, Umm Al Quwain, and Ras Al Khaimah. Dubai, however, has become the main symbol of luxury, famous for the tallest buildings, fancy cars, wealthy people, opulence... and not just compared to this part of the world but for anything that the world has ever seen. What very few people realise is that UAE is the most inspiring real-life result of the power of manifestation that started from the vision of one wise man, also known as 'the father of the nation', Sheikh Zayed bin Sultan Al Nahyan. His vision started less than fifty years ago when the UAE was a deserted area most wouldn't even know existed. Naturally, there is a great sense of honour and gratitude visible from the moment you land in this region, with pictures of Sheikh Zayed displayed everywhere. In general, the UAE holds its rulers in a much greater and genuine level of respect than any other place. Pictures of the rulers are displayed across the country and the members of the ruling family are easily reachable by the residents. Roads are not blocked, nor a long chain of military or police forces surround them. Welcome to a land of tribal democracy, where even the wildest ideas are discussed and supported to become reality.

The region is a unique blend of modern development and traditional values. It is important before you travel to this region to learn a bit about specific values instead of being influenced by the myths spread around in media.

Very Little-Known Facts About This Region That Might Surprise You

Diversity
Over 90% of the population is comprised of expatriates which makes the UAE one of the most cosmopolitan places to be in, with over 200 nationalities living in peace. If you miss a dish from home or have a religious holiday to celebrate, the UAE makes room for diversity in all aspects of life.

Equality
It is one of the leaders in feminism empowerment and equal rights (which I am certain might come as a surprise to most). Women represent 30% of the UAE cabinet and the constitution of the UAE guarantees equal rights for both men and women. Over 70% of HH Sheikh Mohammed bin Rashid Al Maktoum, Vice President and Prime Minister of the UAE and ruler of Dubai's team is made up of women. In addition to that, as an expat woman living in the region, I feel spoiled by the number of special lanes, parking spaces, and benefits which ladies get in this region.

Falcons
Falcons are the only animals in the UAE that are legally allowed to travel inside planes—usually in business, first class or in private jets. There are massive medical facilities and a few hospitals with state-of-the-art technology dedicated strictly to this national bird of the UAE which you will see displayed on everything from currencies to many items originating in this region. Falconry is a traditional national sport practiced for more than 2000 years, and one which clearly holds a lot of interest in this region.

Camels
Camels might be the 'influencers' when it comes to symbols of the region. They've been the main source of income, travel, and nutrition for the Bedouin tribes as well as important players in the camel racing sport. Camels remain a big part of everyday life and economy. These national 'racers' can be more expensive than some of the Formula 1  players nowadays. Prices start from 55k USD and can go higher than ten million USD. In fact, one of the most expensive camels was sold for six million USD (twenty-four million AED, the UAE national currency), and the seller refused any form of bank transfer, so the transaction was in cash.

Pearls
Before tourism and oil (which is wrongfully considered the main and only reason behind the development in the region), fishing and pearl diving were the Emirate's main trades for years. In the early 20th century, there were over 300 pearl diving dhows (traditional sailing boats) with 7000 sailors on board, in Dubai alone. They would free dive ten metres deep fifty times a day, and most members of the local community remain skilled divers.

Wealth
While the world perceives the gold, cars and buildings as symbols of wealth, the UAE perceives green trees and water as symbols of wealth. Companies are required to plant trees equal to the value of their high pollution fines with each sapling worth about $11. In general, across the

region, cutting down trees, shrubs, herbs, or plants will result in severe penalties that in Saudi Arabia can reach an equivalent of seven million USD and/or jail of up to ten years. While the rest of the world is still taking the planet for granted, these countries invest their highest numbers in finding sustainable solutions and protecting their existing flora and fauna. So be mindful of that when bringing up the topic in this region. Do not waste water and drink it with respect when it is offered.

Islam

Islam is a big part of everyday life in this region, and, in fact, the country's laws are governed by what is called 'sharia law'—the Islamic law. Contrary to popular belief though, there is a great sense of inclusion of all religions within the region. There are over forty places of worship across the UAE and, in fact, the land on which most churches were built was donated by the government of the UAE which offers constant support for religious tolerance.

Chapter 2

Meeting, Greeting, Posture and Body Language

If there is one thing to remember when it comes to business or any type of relationships in this region, it is that in the Arab world people do not do business with someone they haven't met in person. Face to face interaction is essential and building a personal relationship with the person before discussing any type of business-related issues is mandatory. That is why gestures and body language can be the element that makes or breaks a success story.

FOLLOW THE LOCAL PERSON'S LEAD WHEN IT COMES TO GREETINGS
If you are offered a handshake, expect a softer one that lingers for a while, sometimes throughout an entire small talk chat. Even if it feels like you are holding hands, avoid withdrawing your hand as that would cause offense. These types of handshakes are much more common than you can imagine and are a sign of the hospitality and warmth of the people.

RIGHT HAND OVER THE HEART GESTURE WITH A SLIGHT BOW
Traditionally, many Muslims only shake hands with someone of the same gender. When greeting someone of the opposite gender, people may keep their hands to the sides politely and just give a verbal greeting. In case you are caught with an extended unreciprocated handshake in the air, do not pretend to brush the awkwardness off by pretend combing your hair, but follow the lead of the local and use this gesture instead. It is a sign of consideration, sincerity, and gratitude which says that even if I can't touch you (which in times of pandemic we all understood better), I am still deeply honoured to know you.

WHEN THE NORMAL VICTORY SIGN WON'T DO: THE THREE-FINGER SALUTE OR DUBAI'S OWN VICTORY SIGN
The gesture was originally introduced during the government summit in Dubai in 2013, when Sheikh Mohammed wanted to create a logo for himself and his country and has taken off since then. Using the thumb,

forefinger and middle finger of the right hand, it consists of three initials that stand for a very important message: W for Win, the V for Victory and the L for Love. This greeting is commonly referred to as Sheikh Mohammed's three-finger salute. You can see this gesture used by various people across the UAE, and there is even a statue depicting it next to Burj Khalifa, the tallest building in the world.

Burj Al Arab & Burj Khalifa

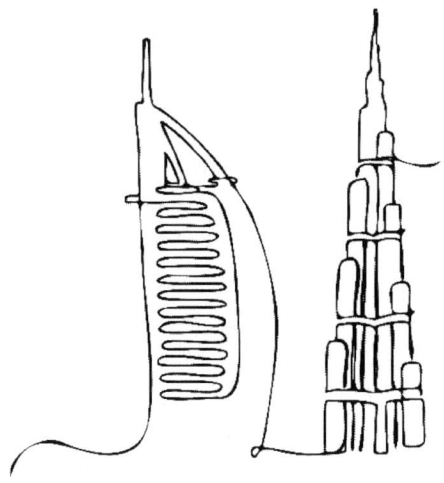

NOSE KISSES

The *Khashm-makh* (nose kiss or nose touch) is a form of greeting among people of the same gender. You will often see UAE male nationals touch noses as they shake hands during their greetings. This is a traditional Bedouin tradition similar to the Maori of New Zealand or Eskimo greetings; it is a sign of friendship, and it is common amongst male friends. The *Khashm-makh* is a tribal custom and way of greeting that represents the values of respect, pride and Bedouin identity upheld by most Arabs in the Gulf region. Women from traditional families also practice this, especially grandmothers, towards their daughters and grandchildren, but it is less common to witness. As a foreigner you are not expected to partake in this local greeting; however, it is good to acknowledge it as you will most likely witness it. Avoid misinterpreting it and remember that the body language and gestures in this region are completely different to the ones you might be used to see in the Western world.

CHEEK KISSES
These come in a pack of three. So, if you or someone else initiated a kissing greeting in this region, do not stop until you count to cheek kiss number three.

SHWAY SHWAY GESTURE
From the moment you land in this region, this might be the most common gesture you'll see, where a person is collecting the fingers of their right hand into a steeple and gently moving the hand up and down. This might look to you exactly like they are asking for food or an Italian asking what you want but actually it is a sign that you need to wait, to calm down, to be patient, to slow down.

BE AWARE OF CROSSED LEGS AND FEET SOLES
Be aware when sitting down of not pointing the sole of the shoe to a local. The sole of the shoe is seen as dirty by many Arabs and therefore efficient for giving offence. That is also a reason for which shoes are removed when entering a house or the mosque. There is another gesture involving crossed legs that is lesser known and most Westerners make unconsciously: bouncing the upper leg on the lower knee with the foot pointed in the general direction of an Arab counterpart. This can cause discomfort as it indicates feeling impatient or being dismissive, both big offenses in the region if we are talking about cross-cultural business etiquette.

ALWAYS AVOID USING THE LEFT HAND
It is perceived as unclean, so avoid passing anything with the left hand, using it to eat with, gifting something or even tip someone with it.

Chapter 3

Conversation Dos and Don'ts

Bedouin Arabs, nomadic by nature, could not and did not collect significant possessions. It was their reputation as hospitable, generous, noble, and brave people that mattered, and it still does. That is why when it comes to topics of conversation, 'showing disrespect' or making someone 'lose face' is one of the gravest offenses.

TOPICS OF CONVERSATION TO STAY CLEAR OF AT ALL COSTS
- *Criticizing the rulers* – Contrary to any other countries around the world, people in this region, as previously mentioned, genuinely love, and respect their rulers. That is not because they are forced to, is not because they do not have a choice, it is because they have a lot they owe and respect when it comes to the people that rule their country. As a rule of thumb, most locals first identify as part of their respective emirate (tribe) and each emirate has their respective ruler, and second with the country as a unit, for which the ruler of Abu Dhabi is considered a president, the ruler of Dubai, prime minister and so on. There is a great level of esteem and pride in tribal democracy. In general, as a rule of thumb, even when it comes to discussing political issues outside of UAE, criticizing your own government should be avoided unless the relationship is very well established.
- *Female members of the family* – This is a sensitive topic. Even among friends, it is best to avoid asking a male Arab about his wife—how she is, if she works, what her job is, etcetera. A male foreigner in the UAE can know someone for years and never meet his wife, daughters, sisters. One can ask about the family, just not go into specific questions of interest about female members of the family. At most you would extend your wishes from a female member from your own family.
- *Avoid criticising local culture, even if locals are expressing negative opinions* – This, in my opinion, should come as a common sense, regardless of which country you find yourself in. Locals can sometimes express or

share challenges. No country is perfect. Acknowledge it but rest assured this is not an invitation to join in. Similarly, to a friend criticizing or complaining about their spouse/children/significant other, the wisest thing to do is to remain neutral—like Switzerland. Follow the manner of the penguins in Madagascar… just smile and wave.

- *Alcohol* – Even if saw your Arab friend drinking, avoid bringing this up in the middle of a meeting or, even worse, with the family. Avoid questioning the person why they do or do not drink. Avoid lingering on the subject unless you know the people around very well. Read the room and be considerate. And before you jump to judgmental mode, remember we are all saints when it comes to someone else's sins. This is a very intimate and personal subject in the region, and it costs nothing to show consideration to people who might feel insulted or uneasy.

- *Israel* – It's complicated and even if a lot has been done in this region to overcome the conflict, the subject remains a very sensitive one. Stay away from bringing this up, respect whatever opinion is shared with you but avoid pursuing the subject. While awareness of the subject and a level of self-education on the topic is highly recommended, debating this in a conversation will bring no value to anyone unless you are a leader of the forces, and the conversation is happening during a summit on the topic.

- *Arranged marriages / multiple wives* – This is foreigners' most delicious topic of conversation when it comes to this region on gossip FM. In general, this is a very intimate subject. It is like someone asking you if you got married because of pregnancy, whether you still love your spouse, who paid for the wedding, or whether you started trying to get pregnant as soon as you got married! Imagine a stranger asking you these questions! Not an enjoyable experience. Just like anything else in this world, when it comes to intimate choices, just because it is different to the way you perceive normality, doesn't make it worthy of an exhibit in *Ripley's Believe it or not!* People never sold you a ticket for your own entertainment, so nothing gives anyone the right to intrude. Be considerate.

- *Labour camps* – Unfortunately, it is a very difficult and sensitive reality. Yes, labour camps do exist. There are many laws in place aiming at improving the situation and protecting the laborers' physical and mental well-being. Sometimes it is a challenging reality to face. Building and maintaining these cities requires a lot of labourers that come from very poor countries. Again, before you judge, no country is perfect… we all have things in our country's past or current situation we are not proud of. Remember that before you comment. There is a lot of good and bad to this story and awareness and education is essential before forming or ever expressing an opinion.

- *Admiring somebody's possessions* – I personally learned this the hard way when I was part of a team where one of my colleagues admired a Sheikha's watch. In most countries this would be nothing but a lovely compliment, a way to bond over small talk. In this region, if you admire something, they traditionally feel obliged to gift it to you. Now before you jump for joy, thinking 'great, I will just come and admire everyone's possessions and get rich', there is an unwritten rule that you should reciprocate with something of equal value. So, in our circumstance, the Sheikha gifted the very expensive watch, but the cabin crew member could not keep such an expensive gift without losing her job; therefore, the watch was handed to the company and the company had to go through an entire protocol process to compensate for the faux pas. So, it is better to stay away from over emphasizing and complimenting someone's possessions.

- *Intimate relationships* – These are intimate for a reason. PDAs like holding hands, hugs, or even a kiss are not going to get you in jail as Gossip FM loves to dramatise. Usually, when it comes to articles where you read that the embassy got involved when a couple on honeymoon hugged and were sent to jail, it is more of a political movement than a reality. Of course, Dubai is a bit more open minded than the other six emirates; however, as a rule of thumb, even in our own countries we would keep certain types of full-blown PDAs outside of the public eyes. This is not a show I paid for regardless of where I am. So, it is nothing out of the ordinary to be considerate. While love is wonderful, keep it PG as much as possible in public spaces where families are around you. Love and consideration do go together.

- *Sarcasm or wit that can make them lose face* – We all love a sense of humour. Keep in mind that humour doesn't always translate well. Therefore, avoid using it as a bonding conversational tool. I especially caution becoming a live comedian sarcastically picking on an Arab in public. That might not be welcomed with your expected response.

- *Gossip / religious debates / money / politics / health (fertility, vaccines, surgeries etcetera) / appearance (weight, looking tired) / intimate relationships* – These are topics that are considered universally bad topics of conversation to be avoided across any nationalities, especially here, since the UAE is home to so many nationalities.

SAFE TOPICS

Since most of us naturally revert to the above list, you might wonder what there is left to talk about! So, here is just the beginning of a very long list of topics that can bring you so much more knowledge, value and improve your relationships:

- Enquiries about mutual friends.
- Their special or favourite blend of perfume—Arabic perfumes.
- Medicine and traditional medicine.
- Horse racing, camel racing.
- Falconry.
- Charisma of the leaders of UAE—books they wrote, history, projects.
- Positive aspects of the economy and development.
- Positive experiences you have made visiting the UAE and recommendations.
- Interesting festivals (Ramadan, Eid).
- Customs you should know.
- Food and restaurants.
- Local handcrafts (pearls, gold, pottery, Arabic calligraphy, rugs, henna).
- Information about Hajj (pilgrimage to Mecca).
- Travel (yours and theirs).

Chapter 4

Gift Giving

When receiving a gift, a Gulf Arab may or may not express thanks to the person that offered the gift. They might receive it, smile, and put it away without a comment. That is not to say that they are ungrateful or rude, just that many traditional Muslims consider that everything received is from the mercy of God. That is where gratitude should go and that is the expression most commonly used in their vocabulary. That is also the source of Arab generosity. This follows the humility of human nature: that no matter how much you have in life, you are just a vessel, that God is the source of everything.

So, you might find some Arabs becoming uncomfortable if excessively thanked for their own gifts, their hospitality and generosity, as they identify these values with their duties. In Bedouin etiquette, if a guest/a stranger passes by, they would cook their best meals and leave their entire home/tents for the comfort of their guests alone. That is how far the hospitality goes and that is something that I hope you will all learn to respect before considering that etiquette is something we've arrogantly assumed to have more of in the West as opposed to Bedouins. On the contrary.

Another reason why, even if thanked for, gifts are not opened immediately but rather in private, is related to losing face. Avoid opening a gift in public so as to avoid that discomfort of having people see what you received and compare it to other potential gifts or items.

Gifts should be offered and received *always* with the right hand or with both hands if needed, but *never with the left* as that hand is considered unclean (it is the hand used to clean yourself).

When it comes to what gifts to give, concentrate on items which can help you bond, something from your own country and culture ideally. It is a really nice gesture if you bring someone a special element of your own culture or childhood, your favourite translated book from European folklore, for example, or traditional clothing from the region where you were raised.

Some other generic gifts would be a nice compass (showing the direction of prayer at all times), a basket of sweets and fruits (usually brought when visiting someone's home—very common in this region), or a personalised luxury pen or agenda. A personalised gift shows that you know the person well and that you care. An important point to remember is that the value of the item is considered to reflect the value of the person you are gifting to; therefore, quality matters.

As a rule of thumb, it is better to stay away from alcoholic liquids, dog representations, non-halal items, gold necklaces or jewellery for men, and things that have 'made in Israel' written on them. Also, if you are a male, avoid gifting items to female members of the family. Instead suggest that the gift is sent by a female member of your family (a spouse, mother, sister). Once again, these are general rules; individuals do not all fit in the same box and for that you need to learn to respect each family's individual values.

If one family is much more open than these guidelines, it does not mean that all families are. So, always be considerate and do your homework when it comes to gifts.

Chapter 5

Dining Etiquette

When it comes to generosity and hospitality, there is nowhere that expresses it better than the opulence of food in the Gulf. A meal without options and abundance can be an offense. This applies also in restaurants, where over-ordering is usual, as is having a lot of food left over—this is a sign of the host's generosity. A host typically makes sure to offer more food several times – not just once – to the guests. The belief is that, if you refuse once, you might have done it out of politeness so the host will rarely take that as a final answer. Equally, if you are the one serving someone from the Gulf, ensure you keep filling their plate until they ask you to stop, otherwise they might feel like you are stingy, or they are not welcomed. The general Arab hospitality guideline suggests that it is a good sign if the person had more than they could finish on their plate as opposed to wiping the plate clean.

When it comes to dining settings, although many families have the option in their daily lives and homes to dine around the table, in the Gulf the preference remains in the traditional *Majlis* type of dining etiquette where everyone sits cross legged on the floor in a circle around the food. The sharing element of Gulf dining is a big part of the etiquette guidelines that define it:

- Always use your right hand to eat, never the left. Cutlery will also be available if requested but it is considerate to at least try to respect the culture if you find yourself in that kind of local setting.
- Use the three fingers of your right hand, ideally. Using all five fingers or your entire hand to grab food might make you come across as greedy, which is one element of difference in etiquette between this region and other parts of the world when it comes to eating with your hands.
- Eat from your side of the shared dish only, collecting the food near you; do not go around the plate or in the centre trying to get the best pieces of food.
- If you add any kind of sauce, ensure you do not add it to the entire dish, just the portion you are about to eat from on your side of the plate.

- Wait for the most elderly to start first as a sign of respect.
- Traditionally, women and children eat separately but it is not the universal rule nowadays. Just follow the lead of the local host before sitting down anywhere.
- Contrary to guidelines of business dining in the West, business is only discussed after Arabic coffee and desserts are served, at the very end of the meal, not from the appetiser! Therefore, if you assume a quick business lunch for business in the Gulf, think again. An entire day might be a better fit to reach that topic. Food is a good opportunity to build the relationship required for a local to trust you enough to want to discuss any business opportunities further.
- During the month of Ramadan, be considerate of people fasting and respect their *Iftar* timings. During these Islamic holy months, fasting, limited working hours in certain departments and several other restrictions are followed during the hours between sunrise and sunset when everyone breaks their fast with an '*iftar*' meal. It is considered rude to eat, drink, smoke in public during this month and in most regions for a long time it was even illegal.
- Pork is a well-known forbidden type of food when it comes to Muslims; however, very few people are aware about the term 'halal' and how in fact any type of meat that comes from an animal that was not slaughtered in the Islamic manner, will be avoided. The Islamic manners (*Dhabihah*) is a method of slaughter for all meat sources, excluding fish and other sea-life (which is a safe option if you are creating a menu and have no certainty of halal meat options). The criteria for non-pork meat options are that the animal was sacrificed in a way that caused no suffering, facing *Qiblah*, 'in the name of Allah' and all blood must be drained. It is important to note these guidelines and importance of halal across many industries outside of food and beverage; for instance, when certain cosmetics are gifted, remember that pharmaceuticals can contain non-halal items and will not be well received.
- Arabic coffee is an essential part of the dining experience and in general of any social interaction. Arabic coffee and dates are offered at the beginning of any visit and end of any meal. The etiquette states that you should at least have one to two offerings of Arabic coffee. The cup is not offered filled and that is not because they do not have enough to go around, but because they try to communicate that they are there to cater to you, they

do not want you to simply drink your coffee and go away. This is a social experience. For that reason, be mindful that if you just hand the cup back empty, it will be refilled with another sip of coffee and given back for you to drink. Many get confused and stuck into a loop of having their cup refilled and returned with no way of escaping. Welcome to the Arabic matrix. The answer is that if you do not want your cup refilled, you should shake the Arabic coffee  cup side to side. Imagine having a ball inside the cup and you want it to make some noise and that is when you found the right wrist motion. Alternatively, you can cover the opening of the cup with two fingers when giving it back. The person collecting the cup should place the cup underneath the rest of the cups or cup in their hand and not on top. That is a clear sign you won't be refilled.

- In general, it is wise to avoid refusing food completely as it is seen as a 'rejection of hospitality'.
- When it comes to ordering or consuming alcohol when you are unsure whether your dining partners drink or not, it is better to abstain.
- When it comes to dining in a restaurant, there is no confusion of the bill. If invited to a restaurant, Gulf Arabs rarely, if ever, understand the concept of going Dutch. A shared meal means that if you are the host, you pay, and if they are the host, they pay.
- Emiratis generally do not introduce the people around the table and are comfortable with silence around the table. It is also common if a Gulf Arab is invited to dinner to show up ten to fifteen minutes late and sometimes accompanied by two to three people. Do not take that as a sign of offence. To them it is the concept of dining being a social event, in which numbers are less important. The more people who join, the better. Similarly, if anyone shows up unannounced at their place, they will always invite them to eat.

When it comes to Arabic meals, the variety is quite vast. Some traditional dishes to expect in this part of the world are:

- *Harira soup:* made out of chickpeas, lentils and Arabic spices, usually served with lemon slices. Don't worry! Soup is not something eaten with the hands also; you do have a spoon!
- *Full Medames:* a breakfast dish cooked with fava beans.
- *Arabic Mezze:* maybe the most internationally popular dish outside the region, they come as a selection of small dishes (samosas, kibbeh, *warak enab*, hummus, *moutabel*, baba ghanouj, *labaneh*, tabbouleh, Fattoush salad) served as appetisers in many parts of the Middle East, Balkans, Greece, and North Africa.
- *Chicken Machboos:* chicken (sometimes meat/lamb) boiled with a distinctive blend of spices served on top of cooked rice with saffron.
- *Camel Meat:* stuffed camel is a delicacy only enjoyed at special occasions by the elite. Also, camel hump is considered a delicacy that only royalties and the elite enjoy during very special ceremonies or weddings.

Chapter 6

Business Etiquette

If there is one thing you need to keep in mind when it comes to business etiquette in the Gulf, it is that *business is very personal.* There is no such thing as doing business over email, video call, phone, or social media unless you previously met and managed to build a relationship with the person. Expect to spend a significant amount of time and effort building personal relationships before getting down to business in this region. Avoid scheduling more than one important client meeting in a day in order to avoid coming across as rushed if you are pursuing a business opportunity in UAE.

In the business world, Gulf Arabs will first and foremost seek out those they trust; that is why 'wasta' can be everything when it comes to success in business. 'Wasta' derives from the Arabic word '*wasat*' meaning 'middle' and that defines exactly what this means: 'the middleman'/ that right person to introduce you (and your project) to the right person. In other terms, who you know that the client trusts is more important than what you know.

Reputation in general is a great asset in the Gulf business world, so ensure you showcase courtesy, respect, and consideration even with people that you might not need anything from at a given time or even people that you found difficult to work with. Because of the emphasis on personal relationships in the UAE, it is highly recommended that you invest time in building good relationships and developing an extensive network in which you build your reputation and credibility. Being connected and having good introductions is essential to doing business in the UAE. Do your homework, learn about the company, the client, respect the culture, the religion, listen more than you talk, show interest and it will pay off in the long run more than any other investment.

One thing to keep in mind, especially when having a rushed, short-tempered mentality is that impatience or a loss of temper is seen as extremely offensive, and it will be the end of your business. So, avoid pointing fingers during or after a meeting, raising your voice, forcing a direct confrontation or showcasing non-verbal signals of impatience like shaking your legs, drumming fingers, avoiding eye contact, or nervous ticks.

Silence in business negotiations is just one of the elements that can be triggering for a businessman from the West. Many Gulf Arabs know and see how stressed and uncomfortable most Westerners get when sitting in silence with others and use it to their advantage when it comes to business negotiations. It is an art of confidence and power to be able to remain calm, discuss non-business-related subjects without becoming agitated and staying silent when needed. It might seem to most like you are not going anywhere but in fact a lot of data is registered about who you are as a professional and how the business will go in the future.

Be mindful that unfortunately the great level of hospitality and can-do attitude in the region comes with a downside in business: saying 'no' or 'I don't know' in this region is considered rude. So, many times, people will choose to leave an open door as they consider you a guest and saying a straight no to a guest, goes against their natural instincts as hosts. Unless you are getting a definitive yes and a signed agreement, avoid celebrating too soon. The best course of action is to follow-up on your meetings, maintain the relationship and ensure there are no misunderstandings.

When it comes to business, presentation matters a lot. So please remember to dress conservatively and appropriately. Hygiene, fitting, pressed and clean clothes, and the quality of your dress showcases not just a level of self-respect and trustworthiness but will make a difference in how you are received and perceived as a professional. A poor presentation can go so far as to be offensive to a business representative from UAE. Keep in mind that their formal business wear is the white Kandura, and they sometimes change it a few times during the day just to ensure it is perfectly crisp, immaculately white and looking professional. And that is for a fully white garment. You can keep up with wearing a tidy suit for the meeting in response.

Punctuality is also very important even though meetings may not start at the appointed time. This means that while time is quite flexible in the UAE, that is not a green light for you to be late, and punctuality will be a noted point of professionalism.

Most business etiquette specialists or books I've come across would recommend having business cards that have a reverse side translated in Arabic. Personally, I do not think this is mandatory nor recommended. While it shows consideration, it might sometimes make your Arab counterparts assume you speak Arabic and create a confusing moment during follow-ups. However, business cards are still customary in certain business settings after every meeting, so have some ready. Using many or all your degrees and honorary titles on your business card is not perceived as bragging and it can be a plus. Do not be surprised if you see it on their business card as well (example: *His Excellency Engineer Shaikh Mohammad bin Salim al-Malaki BSc (Hons)* is the correct form of address in UAE). Titles like Dr/Engineer are important, even if you are merely studying for your PhD.

Avoid leaving business cards on tables and ideally always hand them to the person using your right hand or both hands, never the left. Even more importantly, ensure you receive a business card with the right hand as well and never with the left.

Chapter 7

Wedding Etiquette

It is uncommon for a non-Muslim/person outside the intimate circle to be invited to the actual Islamic wedding ceremony, but you might be invited to all or some of the up to seven days of different stages of an Arabic wedding. Gulf wedding parties are extremely elaborate celebrations with an opulence of food, drinks, decorum, and festivities expanded over the course of a minimum of two days. Hundreds of people not limited to family members and friends, but sometimes even distant acquaintances can partake in the event.

The first stage is the engagement party which is a more intimate event at the bride's home, when the groom's father asks for the hand of the bride from her father and an official contract is signed in front of a court official. This is followed by setting the actual date of the wedding ceremonies and a month of pampering and gifts for the bride. The bridal shower is less about bachelorettes gone wild and more about girls henna night when the bride and her girlfriends and female relatives get henna tattoos, enjoying music, food, and the bride receives gifts and blessings from the attendees. This is the moment when the bride is presented with gifts, as traditionally it is not considered proper etiquette to present gifts at the bride's wedding reception and overwhelm her.

Flower arrangements go above and beyond when it comes to decorating all wedding events from the bridal shower to the wedding reception. Fresh flowers in decorations do hold an utmost level of importance so expect to be amazed.

After the Islamic religious ceremony, which is an intimate event, the receptions start. In traditional Emirati weddings, there are separate receptions for men and women, so that women can celebrate without the restriction of wearing a hijab and cover in front of men. There is a moment in the wedding when the groom comes to the women's reception and this is announced before he enters, so all women that cover, can do so. Also, when it comes to the ladies' party, it is considered a form of respect to avoid dancing until the elder ladies leave, but this guideline differs according to the family. To remain safe, always follow the lead of the local ladies and avoid getting the party started yourself.

Dancing, showcasing expensive dresses and jewellery are important elements, but once again, nothing can compete with the opulence of food. It wouldn't be an Arab festivity if you leave hungry. The feasting never ends. Of course, all these elements will differ depending on the financial status or individual preferences of the family, but in most cases, Emirati weddings are events which are hard to forget once experienced.

When it comes to dress codes and gifts, once again, showing off your wealth is not seen as a negative, on the contrary. So, dress to impress, to say the least. For most Arab women, less is not more when it comes to female-only wedding receptions.

For the male reception, most men will be wearing their traditional white dress called Kandura and while as a foreigner you are not expected to wear the same, that would still be considered a minimum of business formal type of dress code. Pay attention to the way you present yourself as it will communicate the value you put on the event and the host.

If you dislike weddings with children, Wi-Fi, mobile phones taking videos and photos of you, then Emirati weddings are your go to. It is quite common to have these specified on the invitation: no phones, no cameras, no children.

Contrary to popular beliefs, not all Emiratis can afford these lavish events and the rulers of UAE often organise mass wedding events when tens of couples are married in one gathering. The mass weddings also include a large celebratory dinner for all who attend the wedding and if the bride and groom are both locals, the government pays a cash incentive to the newlyweds.

United Kingdom
By Sophia Lingham

Chapter 1

Culture Symbols
Eng;ish Afternoon Tea

AFTERNOON TEA

With roots dating back to the 1840s and the wishes of the Duchess of Bedford, nowadays, one can partake in this delightful British tradition between two p.m. and five- thirty p.m. at selected high-end hotels, restaurants and cafes. There are two main forms of afternoon tea: the cream tea and the traditional afternoon tea.

Cream tea involves a pot of tea of your choice, although it is normally English Breakfast tea, and scones with clotted cream and jam. One breaks a scone in half before adorning condiments. There is an ongoing debate regarding the correct order of condiments. In Devon, cream is put on the scone first followed by jam. In Cornwall, the jam precedes the cream. The choice is yours!

The traditional afternoon tea is served on tiered platters. Generally, there are many teas to choose from and a tea menu is usually supplied. This is a rather special occasion where the chef likes to exhibit his baking skills so expect delectable and original sweet and savoury delicacies!

Traditionally, the lowest tier holds finger-sized sandwiches, then scones with clotted cream and jam are displayed on the tier above, followed by small, sweet delicacies on the highest tier.

For an even more decadent experience, there is also the Royal afternoon tea. This is similar to the traditional afternoon tea but tea is replaced with champagne!

This is a real treat to partake in. Despite common belief, the British do not do this every day or even every month! It is a treat for a special occasion as it is commonly rather expensive, although well worth it! Although, going out for a cup of tea and a slice of cake between either ten to eleven-thirty a.m. or two-thirty p.m. and five p.m. is more commonplace.

THE UNION JACK

The British flag may seem unnecessarily complicated but each part denotes a country of the kingdom.

Flags of UK:
- England (the St George's Cross is red and looks like an addition sign).
- Scotland (the St Andrew's Cross is white, diagonal and on a blue background).
- Northern Ireland (the St Patrick's Cross is red and diagonal).

Although Wales is part of the UK, its flag does not show within the Union Jack. This is because when the flag was designed, Wales was part of England.

The difference between the UK, Great Britain and the British Isles:

In 1707, England and Scotland united to from Great Britain. Thus, Great Britain is Scotland, England and Wales.

Until 1801, Ireland had been an English colony, but then joined Great Britain as an individual political entity. This lasted until 1922 when it became Great Britain and Northern Ireland.

The British Isles include: England, Ireland, Northern Ireland, Scotland and Wales. Along with other islands such as the Hebrides, the Isle of Mann, the Isles of Scilly and the Channel Islands.

The United Kingdom of Great Britain and Northern Ireland is comprised of: England, Wales, Scotland and Northern Ireland.

Then there is the republic of Ireland which is southern Ireland. This, with Northern Ireland, makes Ireland.

THE ROYAL FAMILY

The royal family personify tradition and heritage in the UK. Although generally supported, a few disagree with the idea of the monarchy. However, many believe they create role models for society, shown through their dedication to and sacrifices made for their country. On 8th September 2022, Queen Elizabeth II died at her home in Scotland, Balmoral Castle, after a 70 year reign. She is succeeded by her eldest son, King Charles III. She became the longest reigning monarch in British history on the 9th of September 2015, celebrated her sapphire jubilee in 2017 (sixty-five years on the throne), and her platinum jubilee (70 years on the throne) on 6th February 2022, with celebrations continuing until summer 2022. She was defined by her sense of duty and resilience, providing a constant figurehead and inspiration to her people and others throughout the world during many turbulent times, enhancing peace between nations, imparting wisdom to many, and still managing to retain her wit and dedication to her family. Her presence was felt in many aspects of life, being linked with over six hundred charities, from environmental concerns to sports and health. An image of the queen's head printed on British stamps and coins; she faced to the right and her successor, King Charles III, will face left on currency and stamps, part of a tradition of alternating between monarchs.

The royal family supported the queen, and will continue to support Charles III, in carrying out official duties such as charitable services, supporting the armed forces, international visits strengthening diplomatic relations and occasions and duties strengthening national stability. Their interest and support for environmental causes, sustainability, and tackling climate change are also notable. In all, they carry out over two thousand official engagements a year!

Apart from the UK, there are fifteen other countries who had the queen, and will now have the King, as their monarch, and head of state. These are Australia, New Zealand, Canada, Jamaica, Antigua and Barbuda, Belize, Papua New Guinea, St Christopher and Nevis, St. Vincent and the Grenadines, Tuvalu, Barbados, Grenada, the Solomon Islands, St. Lucia and The Bahamas.

Buckingham Palace has been the London residence of the monarchy since 1837 and is well worth a visit, but you must book! Other notable residences of the royal family include Windsor Castle, Kensington Palace and Clarence House in London, and Holyrood House and Balmoral in Scotland.

British Bulldog

The origins of the British bulldog as a symbol stem from a fictional comical character invented by political Scottish satirist, John Arbuthnot, back in $C17^{th}$-$C18^{th}$. The character, John Bull, was supposed to depict the typical Englishman, demonstrating the qualities of honesty, boldness and being ready to stand up for his beliefs. He is dressed in Regency period clothing with a Union Jack decorated waistcoat. He was plump, wore a topper hat and was usually accompanied by a bulldog.

The phrase alludes to the idea of the 'British Bulldog spirit': the idea of strong courage, fearlessness and determination. It is mainly associated with Winston Churchill's tenacity during World War II and determination never to give in. The UK is very proud of its wartime history throughout the First and Second World Wars and many modern adverts are based on wartime ones, such as 'Your Country Needs You' adverts.

Of course, the English bulldog itself is a short, stocky, muscular dog with a strong jaw set into an oversized head. Historically they were bred for bull baiting, a bloodthirsty sport involving bulldogs and a defenceless bull, abolished in the 1800s.

A Traditional English Pub

According to Samuel Johnson, 'there is nothing which has yet been contrived by man, by which so much happiness is produced as a good tavern or inn'. Most British people, of all ages, would agree with this, many visiting multiple times per week, it being a place to meet friends and bring family.

They appear all over the UK; nearly every village has one or multiple. Traditionally they serve beer, local ales, cider, wine and serve traditional British food, often heavy, stodgy and with a lot of gravy! Examples include sausage and mash, pie and mash, fish and chips, full English breakfast, a ploughman's (a wedge of bread, either cheese or ham and chutney) and a Sunday roast. Many pubs have developed their food to include less traditional and more inventive cuisine; these were first known as gastropubs to differentiate between them and the traditional but nowadays they are simply also called pubs.

Different counties have their own delicacies. For instance, Cornwall has its famous Cornish pasty—a semicircular shaped pastry case filled with steak chunks, potato, swede and onion, although now there are many flavour variations. Cheddar, in Somerset is famous for its cheddar cheese, Wiltshire for its ham, Devon for its Devonshire cream, and Scotland for its whisky and Scottish shortbread.

Ironically, this British culture symbol has the Romans to thank for its roots as they built Roman *tabernae* when they invaded, which were essentially shops which sold wine. They quickly changed to ale and the British pub was born!

Traditional pub games are popular, including the pub quiz, a darts board, pool table or a skittles ally. They can become the hub of the community, especially in villages. For advice and recommendations on where to visit, look for *The Good Pub Guide* and *The Good Food Guide*.

British Humour
Self-depreciation
Much of British humour involves making fun of oneself, and to outsiders it may seem like we are insulting ourselves or each other, whereas in fact, we are joking. For instance, saying 'I could not run a bath, let alone a race' is comical; it self-depreciates by saying how bad they are at running that they could not run a bath. Obviously, running a bath does not involve movement,

so it is also a play on words (a pun) on the word 'run'.

The British like to make fun of everyday life, with notable popular comedies including *Outnumbered, The Vicar of Dibley, Only Fools and Horses, Faulty Towers,* and *Gavin and Stacey*. The class system also has entertainment value, with comedies including *To The Manor Born, Yes, Minister, Dad's Army, Blackadder* and *Jeeves and Wooster*.

Despite how it sounds, the British are generally very supportive of each other and come together in times of need.

Sarcasm

Sarcasm is another form of humour, although according to Oscar Wilde, is the lowest form of wit (humour). It is when a person says one thing but means the opposite and is usually directed at an individual. For example, when you expect something to happen (usually bad) and when it does, you say 'well, what a surprise'. It is sarcastic as clearly you expected it to happen and so it was not a surprise. It is also usually said with a 'straight face' (where there is no expression given), so it can be hard to detect. Internationally, many struggle to understand the humour, or indeed the point of it, especially when it can sometimes be rude. Yet, it is a staple in British humour.

The British find humour in everything, when perhaps in other countries, it might be seen as being in bad taste. For instance, gallows humour, or black humour as it is sometimes called, makes fun of awful situations. For instance, an example from Adam Smith's book *Black Humour*:

Patient: 'Doctor, I am feeling nervous—this is my first operation!'
Doctor: 'Don't worry, mine too.'

UNITY AND DIVERSITY

Our heritage is built from an amalgamation of many countries; even our language is made up of words from many different languages; hundreds of other languages are represented in English including Latin, French, Greek, Italian, Portuguese, German, Scandinavian, Hindi, Hebrew, Arabic, Afrikaans, Norwegian, the list continues. For instance, the word 'anonymous' comes from the Greek word '*Ανώνυμος*' meaning something without a name. The word 'terrain' in English comes from the Latin '*terra*', meaning land.

Then we have 'loan words' which are taken directly from another language without translation, like *'sushi'* from Japanese, *'pizza'* from Italian, *'tai chi'* from Chinese, and *'RSVP'* from French.

The UK has been recipient to nationals from many nations since time immemorial. The Romans, the Vikings, Anglo-Saxons, the Normans, the Dutch, and the French all have their claims to invasion of Britain. Britain itself has invaded all but twenty-two of the world's countries at some point in history and developed the largest empire in history, in 1913 covering over 20% of the world's population. Added to this the following atrocities and more positive relationships developed by history:

- The development of the East India Company.
- The slave trade.
- International Jewish persecution leading many to come to Britain.
- The reliance of Britain on its empire during the wars and the offer of British citizenship after the war to those who fought for Britain.
- The continuing relationships of commonwealth countries since their independence from the empire.
- The British Nationality Act 1948 to encourage commonwealth workers to UK.
- The membership of the European Union since 1973 making cross-border migration easy (until recently).
- International wars creating refugees.

There are many more examples but from these alone, it is easy to see how, through many different drastic historical factors, British culture has developed richly to include such an incredible variety of people, traditions, foods, languages!

QUEUEING

Queueing is possibly the most internationally famous British ritual, one which sparks disbelief and humour globally. Queueing is quite simply a line of individuals, one behind the other, generally when waiting for something. For instance, one can witness queueing occurring outside any ticket booth, outside a kiosk or in shops, with waiting to get on a train/bus etcetera or waiting to walk into a venue. If one happens to need to join the queue, one must join the back of the queue and wait ones turn to be served. Anyone pushing in front of someone in a queue or generally not waiting their turn will receive a hostile reception from queue participants who will probably tell you to move to the back of the queue; you may even be refused service!

LITERARY GIANTS

The UK is lucky enough to boast many highly regarded and internationally renowned authors and poets. A few are listed below:

- Jane Austen (1775–1817)—female writer specialising in romantic novels, such as *Pride and Prejudice* and *Sense and Sensibility*.
- Oscar Wilde (1854–1900) – Playwright and composer of poems. Notable works include *The Picture of Dorian Gray*, *The Importance of Being Earnest* and *An Ideal Husband*. He was imprisoned late in his life for two years for homosexuality.
- William Shakespeare (1564–1616) – Perhaps the most famous of our literary contributors, famous for his tragedies, comedies, histories and sonnets. His most notable works include *Romeo and Juliet*, *Macbeth* and *Hamlet*.
- Charles Dickens (1812–1870) – Novelist whose most famous works include *A Christmas Carol* (a classic read and performed every year since, to this day), *Oliver*, *Great Expectations* and *David Copperfield*.
- William Wordsworth (1770–1850) – Poet who, with Samuel Taylor-Coleridge, wrote lyrical ballads. *Tintern Abbey*, *The Prelude* and *Daffodil* are some of his most famous works.
- Sir Arthur Conan Doyle (1859–1930) – As well as becoming a distinguished author, famous for works such as *Sherlock Holmes*, he was also a medical doctor and was knighted in 1902 for his work in a South African field hospital during the Boer War.
- Other notable authors include Samuel Taylor-Coleridge (famous for *The Rime of the Ancient Mariner*), John Keats, Lord Byron, Percy Shelley (all romantic poets) and Wilfred Owen (WW1 poet).

Some more modern ones include JK Rowling (most famous as being the creator of the *Harry Potter* series), Jeffrey Archer (politician turned author), Anthony Horowitz (novelist and screenwriter), Ian McEwan, Hilary Mantel and John Le Carre.

Chapter 2

Meeting, Greeting, Posture and Body Language

CORRECT POSTURE

If standing, one's shoulders should be back, arms by your side and with no fiddling of hands.

If sitting down, women should sit with their back straight, legs in front and together or to the side with one leg tucked behind the other; hands should lay neatly in the lap. Men should sit with back straight, shoulders back, with legs in front and together, not widely splayed apart. Hands again loose in the lap.

BODY LANGUAGE

Generally, the British are not ones for much physical contact. Shaking hands when greeting is generally sufficient. Hugs and kisses are left only for close friends and family.

It is bad etiquette to display too much affection for a partner in public, kissing and touching each other for example. Simply holding hands is acceptable, as is a kiss on the cheek for friends or a peck on the lips for a partner.

The British like their personal space; some humorously name it their 'personal bubble'. If one approaches too close, it is common for a British person to recoil slightly. This itself does not display good etiquette of the person who steps back but stepping back is generally not meant as an insult to the person who came too close. It is because the British like to have their own space between themselves and others.

The British dislike the act of staring. Sometimes one cannot help but stare if one is in a daze or thinking about something else, but once you realise you are staring at someone, stop it. It is considered rude to stare at someone; even if you are staring because someone is beautiful and it is for good reasons, it is generally still seen as rude. If you found yourself being stared at, politely smile and look away, and the person staring should stop.

Holding eye contact cannot be for too long, although long enough so as not to be a slight.

WHEN MEETING SOMEONE NEW

Shaking hands for greeting and meeting people: shaking hands has five main constituents:

- Shoulders back and stand tall.
- Hold your arm out but not completely straight and maintain a gap between you both.
- A firm handshake has more respect in the UK, rather than a limp one, even for women, but not too strong. This may require practice to get the strength right. Let the woman hold her hand out first, not the man.
- Express pleasure at meeting them by saying 'I'm x, how do you do?'. This is a rhetorical question and does not require an answer, but it is not bad manners to answer if you forget this. If the company are less formal then saying 'I'm x, pleasure to meet you' is sufficient.
- The most important thing is to make eye contact for about three seconds and compliment the other person before finishing the handshake.

Hugging occurs between people who know each other well. Men often handshake and hug at the same time, followed by a pat on the back afterwards—watch out if one of you is left-handed though! Generally, a handshake, even when you know someone well, is sufficient. This was a fashionable gesture before the pandemic, but fashions change and it remains to be seen what the lasting effects of the pandemic will be on this method of greeting. Women more regularly hug in public than men, although this is generally supplemented by a kiss on the cheek.

During the current pandemic, other greeting options are touching elbows or a slight bow. Some turn it into a humorous action when they know the recipient well and try greeting with one's feet, whereby one must balance on one leg whilst you touch the other persons foot with yours a little off the ground. A slight wave may suffice but can sometimes look awkward. However, if you both wish to shake hands then always carry hand sanitiser with you so you can both use it afterwards—it somewhat breaks the ice!

BODY LANGUAGE AND ACTIONS TO AVOID

- If you cannot stifle a yawn in public or when with company, always hold your hand you're your mouth when you yawn, cough, or sneeze.
- In public places, touching accidentally requires an apology, for instance if you bump into someone on a street, or brush past them on a train. Train situations have their own etiquette.
- Swearing with one's hands in the UK constitutes very bad

etiquette. The following hand signals are to be avoided: putting your hand into a fist shape, with your arm raised, palm facing towards yourself, with your middle finger raised; the same as previously, but with both your index finger and your middle finger raised towards someone.
- Chewing gum is generally not a very polite action, especially in public, but if you must do so, then do so with your mouth closed—nobody wishes to see the contents of your mouth!

Body Language and Actions Which Are Acceptable
- Crossing your index and middle finger, however, is acceptable as this is often used as a sign that you wish someone good luck. Both the person wanting the luck and the luck giver may give this gesture. It is a well-meaning gesture.
- If in conversation a British person very obviously taps the side of their nose whilst looking at you, it generally means 'it's a secret', or they are not going to tell you for some reason.

Can You Be Too Polite?
Some may think the British go too far with their manners. For instance, a British person will apologise almost as a default response when something amiss occurs even when it is not their fault. They will apologise for the following amongst many others:
- Bumping into, brushing against or touching someone in any way, however slight, accidently in any situation.
- When in a shop, and walking in between someone and the object of their attention (example: in between a person and the wall of books they are looking at, or array of foods they are choosing from).
- Walking towards someone and not knowing which side to pass them on—there is often an awkward 'sorry' as each person moves the same way, followed often by a slight laugh and sometimes will even apologise for apologising!

Other Useful Guides:
- Stand to the right on escalators etcetera.
- Let people out of lifts etcetera first before entering.
- When driving (we drive on the left-hand side of the road), thank

drivers who let you out/in in a queue, or waited for you in a passing place. A simple wave will suffice, or a quick flash of the lights at night (although not main beams).

- Likewise, if you are a pedestrian walking across the road, thank the drivers for stopping for you.
- When at a pub with friends, each person in the party must buy a round of drinks. If this would constitute too many rounds in one evening, then remember if you have not bought a round then it is your turn next time.
- You can generally never say 'please', 'thank you', or 'sorry' enough times!
- For the gentlemen reading this book, something to bear in mind… some women like men to be gentlemen and some prefer to be treated equally. Therefore, it is best to hold door open for any person you are with, rather than just single out women, for instance. Judge the situation as you see fit; the better acquainted you become, the more you will understand their opinions on the subject. Some women will not take kindly to you carrying something for them, holding an umbrella for them or opening the car door for them, whereas others will appreciate it greatly.

Chapter 3

Conversation Dos and Don'ts

When first meeting someone, one engages in 'small talk' which is useful to make those first crucial connections between you. However, many have difficulty mastering it and find it embarrassing; as such, practice is key. It will soon become second nature.

When introducing yourself, follow the guidelines set out in chapter 2.

If you are being complimented, say thank you sincerely and do not self-depreciate. Use their name in conversation so it implants it into your memory, and it gives the feeling of personal conversation. If they have introduced themselves as an abbreviated name, don't then use the long version, use the name they stated.

The aim of small talk is to find common ground. Topics to talk about:
- How far have they travelled?
- The weather—if it is particularly sunny for the time of year, then this can be a good place to start.
- State of the roads.
- Sport or recent events that are general knowledge.
- Food—but not detrimental comments about food at an event if that is where you meet someone.
- If at a party or event, you can comment on scene or programme for the evening.
- If you have been introduced to someone by another person, then continue that lead as they should have commented on how they know each of you when introducing you both and something you both might have in common.

As in many of the countries represented in this book, avoiding the following topics is wise if you do not know someone well:
- Politics.
- Religion.

- Money—this is in bad taste.
- Relationships.
- Backstabbing other people.
- Also, don't be too direct—'what do you do'? Or 'are you married'? is generally too direct to start with but can be included further into the conversation once rapport has been developed.
- The conversation is not a competition, thus do not try and show off, partake in 'one-upmanship', or name drop. It will not portray you in a good light.
- Try not to be overfamiliar on first meetings as the British take a while to trust, so keep conversation light to start with. Also, if you notice a lack of emotive facial expressions or hand gestures whilst listening or talking, this is normal as the British are not hugely emotive in this sense compared to more Mediterranean cultures!

Don't forget:

- Make eye contact—this is most important as develops trust and rapport. Obviously, not to the extent of staring.
- Don't talk non-stop, give the other person chance to comment and answer. Don't talk too much or too little.
- Listen to what the other person says. If their name is hard to remember, then think of a way to remember it. For instance, my name is pronounced 'So-fire' rather than 'So-fear'. Make sure you remember these details for your next meeting; write them down if you need to. Don't just wait until they have finished, without listening, and then say something you have wanted to butt in and say. Really listen and make your response relevant to their comment.
- Don't let your eyes wander obviously around the room as this shows you are not listening to them and not giving them due respect.
- If in a business context, don't forget to follow up the meeting with an email the next day/within a few days to offer your services. This is all about what you can do for someone else, not what they can do for you.
- If you need to leave the conversation, say 'excuse me' at an appropriate moment.
- Include everyone in the conversation when talking in groups.
- If you offend someone, apologise quickly and sincerely. If you feel insulted, don't hold a grudge and don't take offence too easily.

- If the other person says something rude or inappropriate, don't correct, just move the conversation on.
- When you have got to know someone a little better, especially in a personal situation rather than in business, then you can test the waters with more familiar conversation and gestures. You may kiss on the cheek, as discussed in chapter 2, to greet them, or perhaps hug after a few meetings. Obviously, the more you get to know someone, the less rigid you can be sticking to the above topics. However, talking about money is generally always considered indelicate.

And finally... *It's all about making people feel at ease in your company!*

Chapter 4

Gift Giving

DINNER PARTY ETIQUETTE
When visiting someone's house for dinner, or for an overnight stay or weekend event, presenting the host with a gift is a polite gesture although not essential (however, many consider it fundamental etiquette to arrive with a gift of some kind). The grandeur of the gift depends on the occasion; for a dinner party, a good bottle of wine or chocolates may suffice; such a bottle is a gift however, and not a meal accompaniment so don't expect it to be served with the meal. For a weekend stay, a good bottle of whisky or champagne and a large bouquet of flowers is appropriate—remember to include something for both hosts. If you brought an expensive bottle of champagne and the host decides to open it, do not brag that it was you who brought it or how much it cost. For a weekend or few days' stay, taking your hosts out to lunch or dinner is necessary, other gifts might include a wine hamper, a food hamper etcetera. For more informal dinners between friends, asking what would be useful to bring is acceptable, as well as bringing a contribution to dessert perhaps and an inventive liqueur. Giving a gift does not replace the necessity of writing a thank you note after the event, however.

WEDDING PRESENT ETIQUETTE
All who attend a wedding should give the bride and groom a wedding present; not to do so is bad etiquette. It is reasonable that not all guests will be able to afford an expensive present, but a thoughtful token for the occasion is necessary. Even if you cannot attend a wedding, you have been invited to in person, it is good etiquette to send the couple a present anyway. Although historically, presents were brought to the bride and groom on the wedding day and were placed into an admirable spectacle, nowadays, try and send/give the present before the wedding rather than take it to the event

so a pile of presents does not become an inconvenience at the location on the day. Letting the couple open the presents together at their leisure after the event ensures each gift is appreciated and each guest thanked appropriately in due course.

Traditionally, the wedding gift list corresponded to the necessities and luxuries required when setting up a first home together; cutlery sets, tea sets and china, bathroom towels, etcetera were all commonplace on such a list. However, as many couples already live together or at least have lived away from their parents by the time they marry, they have these items already. As such, the list has expanded. Generally, along with the wedding invite, a gift list or details of where a gift list can be found will also be sent to guests. Nowadays an online list is normal, often from a large department store. Guests can then pick a gift they wish to purchase, and this then removes it from the online list. If not, then asking for the list of the betrothed couple when entering the mentioned store, is required. Having such a list makes it easier for guests and ensures the couple don't receive many of the same present! More recently, many couples often ask for donations to their honeymoon or a charity instead of a gift. If guests are sending money instead of a gift, they generally like to know what it will be spent on—so bear this in mind when writing to thank people who have sent you money!

The bridegroom traditionally should give something to his mother and the bride's mother, the bridesmaids, the best man and the ushers. The gift is a sign of appreciation, so giving each something they will appreciate is important. Jewellery for the women and a decent whisky for the men may be appropriate, but the best man requires something more memorable.

OTHER OCCASIONS

Christmas

Send a small gift to children of your friends until their eighteenth birthday. It is unnecessary to send a gift to all friends each year, although a card is usual (and nowadays 'e-cards' are fashionable too). Each family member should receive a gift other family members, whether individually or collectively.

Births

Before a birth, baby showers are an American rather than British tradition; if invited to one it may be more prudent to give a gift for the mother rather than the baby. Visiting the new mother in hospital is less common if you are not a family member, but if you do visit check beforehand that the hospital allows the gift you wish to give. Flowers would be appropriate, but some wards do not allow them due to pollen issues. Keep in mind that the mother will be shattered so do not stay long. Sending a card to the new parents suffices at this stage. Keep more expensive presents for the baby's first Christmas/birthday/christening. It is easy at this stage to just concentrate on the new baby, however, a thoughtful gift for the new parents will be hugely appreciated, even if just a food hamper—after all, they are the ones who have the hard work!

Christenings/baptisms
If you have been given the honour of being the child's godparent then you must provide a lasting present to the child; gold chains and bracelets, premium bonds, setting up a savings account are all commonplace. As a godparent it is also good etiquette to send a present at Christmas and birthday until the child's eighteenth birthday. Being a guest at a christening generally requires a present for the child; it is traditional to gift something long-lasting although any present will be appreciated.

Coming of age ceremonies
For confirmations, chains and crosses are appropriate, but in order for the child not to receive many of the same gift, it is thoughtful to be more inventive.

For bar and bat mitzvahs, a donation to the child's favourite charity, The Jewish star of David in pendant form or a travel sized Hanukkah *Mennorah* would be appropriate, as would a monetary gift in increments of eighteen.

Both eighteenth and twenty-first birthdays are important birthday milestones in the UK; however, it is unusual to celebrate both with a large celebration. Whichever they choose to celebrate more, requires a more generous present. You should send a present irrespective if you attend the formal celebration. This is generally the last big present you will give regularly, so make it a special one; a good quality watch, jewellery, a monetary donation to any upcoming travels, paying for a course they want to attend etcetera. Equally memorable would be a handmade photo album or scrapbook, personalised for the recipient.

Special birthdays—often friends send presents to celebrate special birthdays: thirtieth, fortieth, fiftieth, sixtieth, seventieth etcetera; for these, a bottle of champagne and a generous food hamper would be appropriate, as would a handmade photo album or personalised symbolic present. Think of the personality and interests of the person to make the gift appropriate and appreciated.

Meeting future in-laws by visiting their house: this is very similar to the gift etiquette for a dinner party. Ask your partner what their parents enjoy and take inspiration from this; this may include a culinary treat or particular liqueur, for example. If in doubt, a nice bouquet of flowers/a potted plant and a bottle of wine is appropriate.

Engagements

As friends of the engaged couple, sending champagne and flowers is acceptable, as is a wedding planner book. As family of an engaged couple, something more substantial; contributing to the cost of the wedding, a family heirloom, silver cutlery sets, candelabras etcetera are all appropriate but take heed of the personality and character of the couple to decide on what would be appropriate. The old wedding saying: 'something old, something new, something borrowed and something blue' can provide inspiration to family.

House-warming

Buying a gift for a house-warming event can be tricky, as buying a long-lasting decoration gift may not be to the receiver's taste or may not go with the colour scheme. Asking them beforehand what they would like saves wasting money on something not entirely appropriate. Normal gifts include picture frames, candles, soaps etcetera, but try and be more inventive. Perhaps buy a book about the local pubs/restaurants in the area or provide a food hamper of essentials. Thinking back to what you would have found useful when you moved house may provide inspiration.

Special anniversaries

In the UK, each anniversary year has a material to represent it; the main ones are listed below. Although it is unnecessary to send a gift corresponding to the material of the year, it is good to acknowledge the year in a card. However, cards with too many words are of bad taste, so keep it personal but classy.

- First anniversary – paper; a scrapbook to fill with photos and memories would be appropriate, or a framed photograph of the couple/scene important to them.
  - Fifth – wood – a nice wooden cheeseboard perhaps.
  - Tenth – tin.
  - Fifteenth – crystal.
  - Twentieth – china.
  - Twenty-fifth – silver.
  - Thirtieth – pearl.
  - Thirty-fifth – coral.
  - Fortieth – ruby.
  - Fiftieth – gold.
  - Sixtieth – diamond.
  - Sixty-fifth – blue sapphire.
  - Seventieth – platinum.
- Mother's Day/Father's Day: here a card from children to their parent is generally a must. Gift-wise, taking the recipient out for a meal, finding a good and appropriate book, making dinner, a framed photograph of you both are all good examples.

THANK YOU ETIQUETTE

After receiving a gift, thank the person who gave the gift by letter, handwritten, within two weeks of receiving the gift. Children should learn to write 'thank you' notes as early as possible. If someone has taken the time to choose and give you/your child a gift, then the least you can do is write to thank them for it.

After attending an event/dinner etcetera, if the invite was formal, printed on engraved card for instance, then your 'thank you' letter must be formal too. If it was an informal dinner invite (such as a text message or phone conversation), then a short informal note suffices or a phone call. Treat like with like; if the invite was by phone, then the thank you can be also.

After a wedding, it is good etiquette to thank the hosts of the wedding for their hospitality, usually the parents of the bride.

Chapter 5

Dining Etiquette

USUAL DINING PLACE SETTING
For normal dining occasions, where very formal place settings are not required, there will usually be only two knives on the right side of the plate, and two forks on the left. The outer knife and fork will be smaller than the inner, as these are starter cutlery. There will usually be a spoon and fork above the plate for dessert. You will have a water glass and a wine glass already set at the table, above the knives. The bread plate will be situated to the left of the forks and will support a bread knife. The positioning of the napkin is generally at the restaurant/pub's discretion.

For formal occasions, the table is set to resemble the picture below:
As you may notice, the fork tines are placed upwards. This was traditionally so the hallmark or family crest were visible. The positioning of knives, with blade facing inwards, was originally to reduce aggression at the table, so blades did not point towards your neighbouring diner.

ATTIRE AND TIMING
For informal occasions, a 'smart casual' dress code is normal: chinos and a shirt for the men, and smart trousers/skirt and a shirt or a dress for women

are possibilities. If you are with people for the weekend, then change out of your day clothes before dinner—always put in effort to your appearance.

If you are attending an informal dinner at a friend's house, then being a few minutes late is advised, to give the hosts time to prepare. More than twenty minutes will be considered 'late' and a little rude.

For formal occasions, the dress code might be 'black tie', so dress accordingly. Be prompt when arriving for a formal occasion.

BEHAVIOUR AT THE TABLE
Wherever you dine, it is as well to maintain formal dining etiquette as best practice, some aspects of which have health benefits. Your posture, for example, aids core strength by requiring you to sit with your back straight throughout the entire meal duration, being mindful not to lean on the table nor lean back in your chair. As such, elbows should not be placed on the table; if you must lean temporarily or to rest your arms, you may place your forearm at the edge of the table.

SOME SIMPLE BEHAVIOURAL RULES TO OBSERVE
Refrain from using cutlery as a conversational prop; do not wave any cutlery about whilst talking. When not preparing your next mouthful of food and when not en route to your mouth, cutlery should remain on the plate, forming a triangle shape, fork resting above the knife, tines down.

Do not start eating until everyone has their meal in front of them.

If you are offered a bread roll before your meal, always break the bread, rather than cut it, above your bread plate. If you have butter with your bread, take some butter from the butter dish with the butter knife and put it on the side of your plate. You may then butter each bit of bread separately from your plate each time you break off a piece of bread.

Never eat/chew with your mouth open and never attempt to talk whilst eating.

Refrain from adding salt or pepper to your food until you have tasted it first as this is considered rude and that you assume the food will be lacking in taste before you start.

Do not prepare your next mouthful of food with your cutlery whilst chewing the last mouthful. Instead, once you are chewing a mouthful of food, place your cutlery on the plate, as stated above, and do not start gathering food onto your cutlery again until you have finished chewing. This slows the process of eating, ensuring better digestion.

Place your napkin in your lap during the meal; if you leave the table at any point, leave it on the table next to your plate or on your chair.

Make polite conversation with everyone at the table; if someone has been left out of a conversation, then ensure you include them.

Do not use your phone at the table or indeed have it visible on the table; keep it in your bag or jacket pocket.

When dining out, always treat staff with respect.

Do not get up from the table when others are still eating, unless absolutely necessary for a bathroom break. If this occurs, excuse yourself quietly from the table.

It is also useful to remember that dogs are allowed in many pubs in the UK (although not in restaurants generally). Therefore, don't be surprised to see them; sometimes the pub has biscuits on the bar counter for dogs and dog water bowls. In some areas they are treated as just as important as the human, although this varies county by county!

USUAL MEALS

Breakfast during the week usually consists of cereal, toast, or porridge, accompanied by a glass of fruit juice and tea or coffee. It is usually eaten between seven and eight a.m. Weekend breakfasts can be more special, often including eggs on toast, a 'fry up' (consisting of a mix of or all of the following: eggs, bacon, sausage, baked beans, grilled tomato, hash browns, fried bread, mushrooms, black pudding), or pancakes, accompanied by fruit juice and tea/coffee. The timing for this is more leisurely and may be eaten at 'brunch', somewhere between breakfast and lunch (eight a.m. to twelve p.m.).

Lunch is a light meal between midday and two p.m. such as a salad, soup, or a sandwich. Sunday is the special day for lunch, where traditionally the family eats a 'Sunday roast' together, one of the few times of the week where there is chance for all to sit down together and chat. A Sunday roast usually consists of roast potatoes, a least two types of vegetables, stuffing, a Yorkshire pudding, with either beef, pork, lamb, or chicken. If lamb is the meat, then mint sauce accompanies the meal; if it is pork, then apple sauce is the accompaniment. Gravy is served with each option.

Dinner is the main meal generally, however, in the north of the country the main meal was traditionally at lunchtime, but generally, now most of the country have their main meal in the evening due to lunchtime time constraints. Imagination, time constraints, cost and the time of year are the limitations for what is eaten at dinner time. Being such a multicultural country, dinner can consist of recipes from all over the world. Timing for dinner is usually from six-thirty p.m. to nine p.m. depending on schedules, children etcetera.

THERE ARE A FEW SPECIAL OCCASION MEALS IN THE UK
Burns Night – This is the celebration of the life and works of the Scottish poet, Robert Burns. It is celebrated in Scotland on the day of his birth, the 25th of January, the first being held in 1801. Whiskey and haggis are the two main culinary constituents of a Burns night, accompanied by a few traditional recitals such as the '*Address to a Haggis*', and '*Immortal Memory*'. Tartan is a must-wear for such parties!

Shrove Tuesday, often referred to as 'pancake day'. Traditionally, this is the last feast day before the start of lent on Ash Wednesday. It starts the forty days leading up to Easter. In the UK, the pancakes are thin and large in diameter, often served rolled up with either lemon juice and sugar, or golden syrup. There are pancake day races across the country, but for the most part it contributes a special treat for dessert.

Easter Sunday – A traditional Sunday lunch, followed by a chocolate inspired dessert. Easter eggs are widely consumed throughout the day after an easter egg hunt for the children.

Christmas – The UK celebrates Christmas on the 25th of December. On Christmas eve (the 24th), children leave a glass of sherry or suchlike beverage and a mince pie on the mantelpiece for Father Christmas, for when he comes down the chimney. Midnight mass is also well patronised, with services starting at around ten-thirty p.m. on Christmas Eve. On Christmas Day, traditional breakfast foods include a cooked ham, smoked salmon, with toast, or a traditional fry up. This may be accompanied by a glass of champagne. Lunch is the main meal, with a light starter of smoked salmon salad or a soup perhaps. The main meal comprises the normal components of a Sunday roast, with the addition of 'pigs in blankets' (cocktail sausages wrapped in bacon), chestnut stuffing, honeyed parsnips, and sprouts. The meat choice varies from the traditional Sunday roast, with turkey and goose being a popular choice. A three-bird roast is also popular, consisting of turkey, pheasant, duck or chicken. The meat is served with cranberry sauce. Dessert is equally decadent, with Christmas pudding being the tradition. This is a rich, dark and alcoholic cake filled with fruit, drizzled with brandy and set alight. It is served when the flames have subsided and with a helping of brandy butter. Traditionally, a sixpence was placed within the mixture, giving good luck to the person lucky enough to have it in their portion! There is also a Christmas cake (which has been three months in the making) and mince pies on hand in the eventuality anyone becomes peckish between meals during the Christmas period!

Boxing Day – This is often revered as even more special than Christmas day, food wise, as lunch constitutes all the leftovers from the previous day. The meat/poultry carcass is also boiled and made into stock or soup, and the leftover meat is made into sandwiches etcetera. There are often also meat pies, smoked salmon, a ham on the bone, Christmas cake, a chocolate yule log (a chocolate cake shaped like a branch of a tree, decorated like bark and with holly leaf garnish). Many families have their own Christmas food traditions which all differ slightly.

Chapter 6

Business Etiquette

DRESS CODES

Whether going for a job interview or dressing for work each day, always put effort into your appearance. You do not know with whom you might meet during the day and so making a good impression is vital. More importantly, taking pride in your appearance and being dressed well gives you confidence in yourself, and confidence and self-respect are noticeable in a person even before conversation begins (this is worth remembering also for non-work-related attire and presentation).

General attire advice for women in business settings:
No skirts or dresses finishing above the knee; knee length is short enough whilst still being classy.

Mind your undergarments—if you are wearing a white shirt, make sure your bra is also white, or even better, wear a white camisole underneath the shirt.

No low-cut tops or revealing styles; keep it professional.

Make sure you can walk in the shoes you wear. If you cannot walk in your work shoes, then there is nothing wrong with wearing different shoes to reach work in and changing them when you arrive. However, wearing trainers with a skirt or dress is not acceptable; a pair of simple comfortable pumps is fine. A smart, classic style jacket finishes the ensemble.

Remember that the impression you give outside work is equally as important to the one you give when at work.

For gentlemen: Check with the type of establishment/business you are working at, as the advice can range widely. These days chinos and a smart shirt are suitable for most work environments; in some businesses even jeans are permitted. In other workplaces, a jacket may be required.

However, when there is an important meeting or if you have a guest visiting the office, then a suit may be more appropriate; although, a tie is usually unnecessary. Although there is a trend to not wear a tie to work, it is a smart addition to a suit and properly finishes the ensemble. A waistcoat can also be a good addition for those wishing to exhibit more unique style.

If working in London or in any more formal job such as lawyers, government workers, headteachers, accountants, etcetera, jeans are inappropriate. For this sort of work environment more formal attire is required in the form of a smart suit with a tie and smart leather shoes, dark brown or black. Oxfords are preferable, with dark coloured socks. Oxford brogues are another option for those looking to impress. If you are particularly eccentric in your attire and like to dress to impress, then the Monk Strap could be an option with a very well-made suit.

It is as well to remember, whatever the dress code of your workplace, always to dress smartly. Dressing slovenly at work, whether you are the CEO or an intern, demonstrates a lack of respect for your work, of yourself, but also of your colleagues. Mentally, also it is as well to differentiate your work clothes from others. Ensure your clothes are ironed, clean, and you have good bodily hygiene.

Advice for Meetings and Interviews

Respect

Time is precious to everyone. Arrive at meetings at least five minutes before the allotted time. If you know you will be a few minutes late, phone ahead to inform them. If you are going to be later than this, they may wish to reschedule.

Unless you know the person well or have been invited to call them by their first name, always address people by their title and surname, example: Mr Piper, Miss Piper or even Dr Piper.

If you are the host, respect that your guest has taken the time to visit you for the meeting; the journey may have been difficult or long. As such, always provide tea, coffee, water and some biscuits for the meeting. Always be attentive and offer refills when necessary.

Conversation and body language

The British are rather reserved in their language and flamboyancy and tend to be less direct in conversation than other nations. Saying this, after initial small talk, they like to get straight to business matters early in the meeting. They are generally quiet speakers and feel awkward when someone talks too loudly or makes great arm displays whilst conversing. This is not to say that you need to hide your personality, but some may need to tone down if they are particularly confident. Remember, the most important rule of etiquette is to make others feel at ease, whoever you are!

Remember the handshake rules! Wait for the person with higher seniority, or women, to offer their hand first.

In meetings, or any social situation where you are meeting someone for the first time or are new acquaintances, always start a conversation with some small talk. There is no such excuse as 'I am not good at small talk'; it takes practice and confidence. It is a polite necessity to ease into further conversation and breaks the ice. The weather, traffic, holidays are all good standbys. Stand a couple of feet away from someone as the British value their personal space; this holds for business or normal social occasions, unless you know someone well.

Be always polite; if someone is rude to you, do not sink to his or her level. Just be kind, polite and move on. They may be having a bad day. Do not interrupt if someone else is talking, wait your turn. Judge the mood of the meeting, but humour may be a good option as it shows you do not take yourself too seriously, providing it is respectful and appropriate.

Try not to rush your words; speak plainly, clearly and concisely. Enunciating words correctly may help your confidence with this.

GENERAL ADVICE

Prepare appropriately ahead of the meeting, whether it be an interview or follow up of an ongoing project. As above, nobody likes to feel their time has been wasted, so do not insult your co-workers/meeting members by not researching sufficiently or not having anything to show them. For instance, if you are going to an interview with a company, research everything the company does, what role the person who is interviewing you has in the company, familiarise yourself with recent projects they have completed. In short, research to form the base of an in-depth conversation about the company and in order to prepare questions you wish to ask. Always have a question or two handy; others may develop during the interview.

- Always thank people for their time, whether you are the MD/CEO or the intern; it demonstrates you respect their time and the effort they have made in attending the meeting.

- People of all nationalities, ethnicities, disabilities, and sexualities in the workplace should be treated equally, and there is a huge drive in the UK to ensure this is the case. Although there are still a few areas where this may not be the case, it is the ideal which the UK is working towards. Therefore, you judge someone purely on their ability to do their job.

Networking

In networking situations especially, after meeting with someone, send them an email to express your pleasure at meeting them, and to offer your services. Remember, your focus should always on what you can do for them, not what they can do for you.

Do not underestimate the importance of business cards. In some sectors in the UK, they have become less commonly used, but having a smart, well thought out business card is always a good aid. It also gives you something to give others to remember you by. If your card is particularly eye-catching (for the right reasons), this will help the other person remember you. Plus, in many countries (as you have read in this book, business cards are a must and are respected as a form of mutual reciprocation; therefore, having a business card handy is useful if you have international counterparts.

The date in the UK is traditionally written in this form: dd/mm/yyyy; although, increasingly one sees the American version of mm/dd/yyyy. As you can imagine, this can be terribly confusing and sometimes it is best to check with your counterpart which date is meant, whether 02/05/2021 means the 2nd of May or the 5th of February, for instance. Traditionally, in the UK, it would mean the former.

When giving a gift in business settings, spend no more than £50, as otherwise it could be construed as bribery. There are HMRC bribery laws in the UK which prohibit the giving of gifts above this amount. The gift cannot include food, alcohol or tobacco.

Chapter 7

Wedding Etiquette

Whilst this chapter concentrates on traditional British wedding etiquette, it is important to appreciate that every wedding is different, and many modern weddings do not adhere to traditional etiquette. It entirely depends on preferences of bride and groom.

Traditionally, the wedding is a one-day celebration.

Whilst there used to be a specific division of costs for the bride's parents and the groom, in more modern times the bride and groom may pay for their own wedding, or the cost may be shared by both sets of parents.

Family members or friends should remember that whilst the bride and groom may ask for advice or help with wedding planning, this is their day, and whilst you might not agree with aspects of it, you must respect their wishes and support as much as possible.

BEFORE THE WEDDING
Once deciding on the guest list, which can be a rather political or challenging debate if one side's family is larger than the other, 'save the date' cards may be sent. These are not invitations and do not require a response, although it is prudent to make the cards memorable, so potential guests do not lose them and book something else for the same day!

Wedding invitations should be sent a few months before the wedding day and should be printed, not written, giving all details relevant. Keep it formal and classy. Include a list of places nearby for guests to stay with contact details. Close friends or relatives may have rooms reserved for them by the bride and groom, especially if the wedding venue has accommodation; such arrangements will be made informally with guests and not appear on the invitation. Invitations can be sent for either the whole day's celebrations or just for the reception or evening entertainment. Be mindful that due to costs and number restrictions at many venues, many friends/associates may not be able to attend the whole day. If inviting people for the evening only event, ensure you state whether there will be food served, so the guests can plan ahead.

The invitation traditionally follows a set sample, sent out by the bride's parents asking guests to join them for the wedding of their daughter to the intended. Nowadays the bride and groom might send the invitations out themselves and an RSVP is usually enclosed with the invitation. Respond as soon as possible, out of respect and organisation.

Details regarding the wedding lists is generally sent out with the invitations. Traditionally, it included presents for the new marital home. Nowadays, the bride and groom more likely to live together already and have what they require, and so it is more common to have an online list for people to choose what to buy or from a specific shop. It is increasingly common for couples to ask for donations towards their honeymoon, although this is still a delicate subject to broach. Using any information provided by the bride and groom or associated families is preferable; it is possible to find an alternative gift, although choose carefully to avoid giving something the couple already have or is not to their taste. The amount you spend on the gift is less important, it is more the gesture which is important. It is useful to note also that even if you cannot attend a wedding you have been invited to, you ought to send a gift. For those attending, organise to have the present sent to the couple's house or the bride's parents' house before the wedding, to save you bringing it on the day.

In such times as we have experienced recently with the Covid-19 pandemic, it may be necessary to postpone the wedding. If the invitations had already been sent out, then cards may be sent out to all guests informing them of the change. A telephone call may be prudent to accompany this.

Whist traditionally, the best man, ushers, the maid of honour and bridesmaids may all have specific roles, nowadays generally the bride's party help more with the organisation of the wedding with the bride, and the groom's party aid more on the day, making sure all runs smoothly, showing guests to their seats for the service, and talking to guests/making everyone feel at ease.

TRADITIONS

The night before the wedding, the bride and groom will traditionally not see one another, and it is bad luck for the groom to see the bride's dress at any point before the ceremony.

There is an old tradition (not etiquette based) in the UK which states that brides should have 'something old, something new, something borrowed and something blue'. Collecting these items before the wedding provides a light-hearted activity for family and friends to become involved with.

The wedding cake was traditionally a tiered fruit cake decorated with white royal icing, the first tier of which was saved for the christening of their first child. However, this tradition is generally unsupported nowadays, with peoples' preference for different cake flavours or changes to family planning desires.

When it comes to dancing, the etiquette can become rather complicated. However, traditionally, the bride and groom dance together, the groom should dance with his and the bride's mother, the bride should dance with both her and the groom's father, the mother of the bride dances with the father of the groom and the father of the bride with the mother of the groom.

DRESS CODE

The bridesmaids traditionally have matching dresses and flowers of the bride's choice, whilst the groom's party and the bride's father generally wear morning dress. Top hats are at the discretion of the bride and groom. More recently, smart suits have been preferred. Buttonholes for either form of suit are required and should reflect the colours of the bridesmaids' flowers.

There are so few occasions on the modern calendar which require one to dress up and really make an effort in one's outfit, but a wedding is certainly one of them. Gentlemen should be smartly and formally dressed in a suit. Morning suit for guests is generally unnecessary but if required you will be informed on the invitation or in person. Military uniform or Highland dress is also permitted. Ladies should dress smartly and may wear a hat, although think carefully about the practicalities of wide-brimmed hats. Avoid white or black dresses however, and style the attire for the weather/season and location. Classy and elegant is the key. And above all, do not try to upstage the bride.

WEDDING CEREMONY

The ceremony can be either religious or civil, with the former being more traditional. However, increasingly couples are adopting for the latter or a venue which can host both the ceremony and reception. A comprehensive overview of each ceremony type is beyond the scope of this chapter and could easily constitute a book in itself! Suffice is to give a few pointers.

An order of service will be prepared and available for each guest in the ceremony. It will include details of the ceremony and the lyrics to the hymns to be sung.

The bride travels with her father or other selected individual to the ceremony, traditionally from her parents' house. The groom travels from the couple's house or family home with the best man.

The ceremony will be the first event guests will attend, although traditionally the families or close friends of the couple will join the bride and groom in a dinner celebration before the wedding, but not the night before.

For either ceremony option, the bride arrives with her father, or another chosen by her to walk her down the aisle, preceded by the bridesmaids. The groom and best man will be standing at the front with the vicar or registrar. Guests should stand whilst the procession is occurring and sit when bride and groom are standing at the front.

After a church ceremony, when the party has relocated outside the church, the guests throw confetti over the newlyweds. Increasingly, this is either biodegradable or in the form of petals.

A special wedding car, often a classic or vintage British car, takes the bride and groom to the reception venue and guests follow in their own cars or in transport provided by the wedding party.

RECEPTION

Receptions are entirely dependent on the couples' wishes. They can vary from a seated lunch or dinner to a buffet or hog roast, or even just drinks and canapes. However, ensuring guests have enough to eat and feel welcome is the main aim.

Organising who sits where is politically tricky and whilst the bride and groom will try and ensure a peaceful table, there is the possibility that you may not see eye to eye with your fellow table diners. Here, etiquette is very important, respecting different views, and not drinking too much. Generally, you will sit next to a person of the opposite gender and most likely know some of the people at your table. Traditionally, the 'top table' will be rectangular and placed where all the guests can see; sat at it will be the bride and groom, both their parents, the maid of honour and the best man. There will usually be a board showing the seating plan at the entrance to the dining area, and place cards on the tables provide a backup should you become lost!

Wedding 'favours' at the table place settings of guests are still a supported tradition. They are a small and ideally inexpensive reminder of the occasion from the bride and groom to the guests. A more recent addition is the provision of ice breakers, for guests at the table to get to know one another better.

After the meal, the speeches occur and in the following order: father of the bride, the groom, and then the best man. Each guest will be given a glass of champagne before these start, ensuring they are ready to toast the bride and groom.

Cake cutting by bride and groom is announced by the toastmaster and usually occurs after the speeches. They cut the first slice together. Often two cakes are made, one to be cut by the couple and another ready and pre-cut by waiting staff to be served as soon as couple cut the cake.

When it comes to the evening reception, the first dance may start things off. This is traditionally between the bride and groom, the music to which is entirely dependent on their wishes. After this dance, the wedding party may join in the dancing.

Traditionally, the bride and groom will leave the reception before their guests so the latter can see them off and wish them good luck. Before departing, the bride will turn away from the guests and throw her bouquet up into the air to be caught by someone in the party. It is meant to be good luck if an unmarried woman in the party catches the bouquet as it means she will be the next to marry—another light-hearted tradition in British wedding etiquette!

GENERAL ETIQUETTE RULES TO REMEMBER
For the bride and groom:
Being invited to a wedding can be a costly affair, with new outfits, accommodation, travel and possibly time off work. Thus, the bride and groom must make all the guests feel very welcome; the ushers and best man can help with this.

Talk with and have photos with *all* guests, with no exceptions, and have separate photos with family. Do not leave people out. If you do not want to talk to a guest, then you should not have invited them; it is the height of bad manners not to make all guests feel welcome.

For guests:
Do not forget good posture, manners, dining, and conversation etiquette.

Make polite conversation even if you do not like the person sitting next to you. It is not about you and is not your day. Make everything as easy for bride and groom as possible as it was very stressful for them to reach that moment with so much to organise!

Although weddings usually operate an open bar, this is no excuse to take advantage of the generosity of who is paying. Plus, judge your intake by the amount of food you eat. Whilst becoming slightly tipsy is acceptable, full intoxication is not. It is both bad manners, bad etiquette and disrespectful to the bride and groom.

Do not post photos on social media without the permission of the bride and groom and especially not before they have had time to post them first.

United States of America
By Nancy Hoogenboom

Chapter 1

Culture Symbols

THE AMERICAN DREAM

Since its beginning, America has been known as the land of opportunity. Regardless of where you were born or what class you were born into, you are able to attain your own version of success in a society where upward mobility is possible for everyone. The American dream is achieved through hard work, sacrifice, and risk-taking, rather than by chance.

The founding fathers of America wrote into law the revolutionary idea that the 'pursuit of happiness' is not just self-indulgence. Rather, it drives ambition and the desire to contribute to the well-being and success of society as a whole. The American dream provides the opportunity to pursue one's own happiness under an equal, fair, and just democracy.

'The American dream is that dream of a land in which life should be better and richer and fuller for everyone, with opportunity for each according to ability or achievement'. This is the first public American dream definition from historian James Truslow Adams' best-selling book *Epic of America*, published in 1931.

With each new generation, the definition of 'the American dream' evolves. As the millennials are thriving in the workplace, they choose to place more emphasis on values, opportunities, experiences, and especially equality. Cassity Brown, MBA, researched millennials and the American dream at Chapman University in Orange, CA, and found that 'the American dream is always relative to the dreamer, but one thing is certain—everyone deserves an equal opportunity to work towards and achieve their dream. In response to the vast inequalities in America today, the millennial American dream is an equally accessible American dream'.

One person who has made a huge and creative impact in America and around the world is Walt Disney, 'The man behind the magic', who was born on the 5th of December 1901 in Chicago, Illinois, and died on the 15th of December 1966. Known as an American film producer, entrepreneur, animator, creator of Mickey Mouse and the Disney theme parks, and much more, the Disney brand has a huge following (fun fact: I grew up going to the original 'Magic Kingdom' of Disneyland in Anaheim, California as a young child). The world has enjoyed the hard work, determination and creative work of Walt Disney, as he followed his American dream.

One of the most inspiring women in America today is founder of SPANX, Sara Blakely. She was getting ready for a party when she realised she did not have the right undergarments to provide a smooth look under white trousers. Armed with scissors and sheer genius, she cut the feet off her control top tights/pantyhose, and the SPANX revolution began. With Sara's sheer determination, she used her $5000 savings and started her business, now worth over one billion dollars.

When answering the question 'In your own words, what is the American dream'? Jamie Hadfield answered, "It is a way of life achieved through hard work, sacrifice, and risk-taking rather than by chance or relying on the government to give you everything for free. In sum, the American dream is not about a land that provides you with stuff, but a land that provides you with opportunity." (Jamie Hadfield, Mrs Utah United States 2020).

Mickey Mouse

AMERICAN FLAG

The national flag of United States represents American freedom. The original flag was created by Betsy Ross in 1776; the current flag, with fifty stars and thirteen stripes, was designed by a high school student in 1958, Robert G Heft. President Dwight D Eisenhower chose his design out of 1,500 entries.

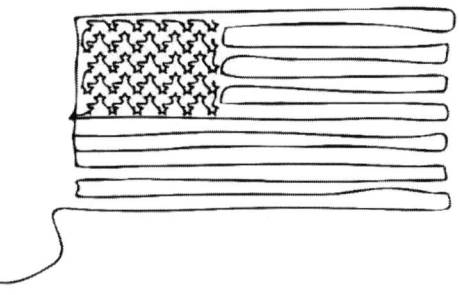

The American flag symbolises freedom, pride, honour, and responsibility.

The stripes on the American Flag represent the original thirteen colonies and the stars represent the fifty states of the union.

The colours on the American Flag are symbolic:
- Red symbolises hardiness and valour.
- White symbolises purity and innocence.
- Blue represents vigilance, perseverance and justice.

The American Flag symbol captures the power and glory of America.

Independence Day, known as the Fourth of July, is a national holiday in the United States. Patriotic displays of fireworks accompanied by patriotic songs such as '*God Bless America*', '*America the Beautiful*', and of course our national anthem, '*The Star Spangled Banner*', are regular parts of the celebrations.

AMERICAN CUISINE

American Cuisine is a mix of all different cultural foods, blending all the various people groups and their culinary contributions together. Many different foods are highlighted in United States. Below are just a few:
- Apple pie is at the top of the list.
- Hamburger, fries and a Coke (or milkshake) would be the all-time favourite meal of Americans. One of the top burgers known is the 'In-N-Out', which started in 1948 by Harry Snyder. Harry introduced California's first drive-through hamburger stand in a space barely ten square feet. Now, with over 300 restaurants, you can enjoy a 'double-double animal style' burger, which is our family's favourite, and do not forget the animal style fries… oh, so tasty!
- New York is known for many foods: hotdogs, bagels and lox, pastrami, pizza, to name a few.
- Clam Chowder in Boston, New England area is tasty.

- Chicago's deep-dish pizza is a must, filled with cheese, tomato sauce and your favourite topping.
- Biscuits and gravy are a highlight in the south.
- Texas barbecue is a way of life in Texas, from brisket, pulled pork, pork links, to beef or pork ribs.
- Chicken and waffles from the south are oh so tasty.
- Tacos are a favourite throughout America. In the Los Angeles area where I live, there are a wide variety of taco stands and Mexican restaurants at which to enjoy tacos.

Bonus: ice cream may have not originated here in America, but we have many incredible and unique ice cream flavours from coast to coast. Make sure you treat yourself along your travels and enjoy some American ice cream.

FASHION

New York is on the east coast of the United States and is one of the top fashion capitals in the world. New York is the world's culture centre in every way, but when it comes to fashion, much of the world is inspired by famous designers who were born in or reside in New York. Ralph Lauren, Donna Karan, Marc Jacobs, Tom Ford, Vera Wang, Betsey Johnson, Carolina Herrera, Jason Wu, Tory Burch, Anna Sui, Bill Blass, Isaac Mizrahi, and Geoffrey Beene are just a few.

New York Fashion is home to a number of the top fifty fashion schools in the world. Parsons School of Design, Fashion Institute of Technology (FIT), and Pratt Institute School of Design are the most sought after in New York.

New York 'Fashion Week' is a highlight in the fashion world. Started in 1943, this was the very first fashion show of its kind. Fashion Week takes place twice a year: February and September.

Los Angeles is on the west coast of the United States and is at the forefront of innovation and design with designers. Los Angeles produces unique, immersive, and state of the art experiences to showcase the newest collections of LA-based and international designers.

Levi Blue Jeans

In 1873, blue jeans were born, with Levi Strauss & Co and Jacob Davis receiving a US patent for an 'Improvement in Fastening Pocket-Openings'. Blue jeans were known as stronger trousers for working men.

In 1934, the first women jeans were designed, called 'Lady Levi's', and in 1935, these jeans were shown in Vogue magazine. In the 1950s, the famous 501 jean was designed and became a glamourous fashion icon.

Fun Fact: in 1964, Levi jeans became part of the permanent collections of the Smithsonian Institution in Washington, DC.

Denim jeans have been a fashion icon for over eighty-five years, highlighting the small but mighty famous red Levi's tag.

Tommy Hilfiger

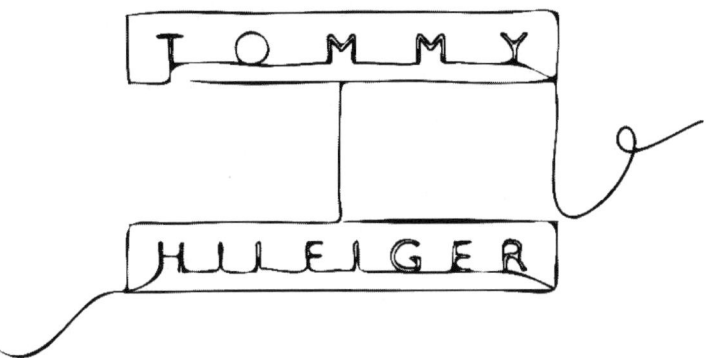

TIPPING

The most unexpected etiquette habit in United States is tipping. When dining in restaurants and in the hospitality industry, tipping is definitely part of the American culture. Tipping has been part of America for many years, though in the 1960s the 'service industry' formalised it, and it became a status quo. The minimum wage in the service industry is very low; for those working in this industry, the tips are part of their pay.

Tipping can be tricky; many other services expect a tip, such as assistance with luggage at the airport and hotels, spa, nail and hair services, and housekeeping, to name a few. Below are suggested tips while travelling to America.

- Dining at a sit-down restaurant: 15%–20% before tax of bill.
- Sommelier comes to your table: 20%–30%.
- Sitting at a bar: $1–2 per drink plus 15%–18% of food bill.
- Coffee and Tea cafe (similar to a Starbucks): not required but much appreciated.

- Meal deliverer to office or home: 10%–20%, not less than $3–$5 for a small order.
- Airport luggage by skycap: $1–$2 per bag.
- Car services (Taxi, Uber): 10%–15%.
- Tour guides: $1/hour per person, or for an all-day tour, 10%–20% of the tour price.
- Hotel housekeeping: $2–$5 room, $5–$10 for a suite.

Tip housekeeping daily as housekeepers are rotated frequently.
Leave a note with the money so they know it is for them.

- Hotel concierge service: $5–$10 for exceptional service.
- Valet parking: $3–$10.

If you receive bad service, people say you do not need to tip. Remember, everyone has a bad day sometimes; my personal feeling is that the tip says more about you than the person who serves you, so tip graciously.

ENTERTAINMENT

The United States of America (USA) is known throughout the world for many forms of entertainment, from coast to coast. Below are a few:

Hollywood, California is the symbol of entertainment, movies, and television. Glamorous, edgy, hip, and eccentric lifestyles make Hollywood a unique place to visit. Whilst in Hollywood, visiting the Walk of Fame (public monuments of famous people in the entertainment industry) is a highlight for guests, and the famous Hollywood sign, and universal studios are also a must.

Sports play a huge part in America's entertainment. American football, baseball (known as the national game of the USA), basketball, soccer, tennis, golf, and ice hockey are a few. The sport of gaming (video games) is one of the biggest in the USA.

New York City's Broadway theatres are known in the USA as simply 'Broadway', with the live theatrical performances located in Midtown Manhattan, New York City. People from in the USA and the world travel to see performances, many being Broadway musicals.

Popular Music in American Culture: many types of music got their start in the United States—from hip hop and rap to country, blues and rock n' roll. Immigrant groups who settled in the United States also influenced many styles of music and made them a part of American music history, like bluegrass, gospel, and Cajun. Many incredible artists are from America; a few examples: Frank Sinatra, Whitney Houston, Michael Jackson and Aretha Franklin.

Chapter 2

Meeting, Greeting, Posture and Body Language

Posture and body language play a large role when meeting people in America. Before we even speak a single word, our posture and body language speak for us.

Americans like their personal space or 'personal bubble'. Personal space represents the distance that Americans feel others need to keep away from them physically. People prefer to keep their distance when talking, walking, and while waiting in line. Typical personal space rules in the United States are:
- One and a half to three feet for good friends and family members.
- Three to five feet for casual acquaintances and co-workers
- More than four feet for strangers.

Albert Mehrabian (pioneer researcher on staff in the psychology department at The University of Los Angeles, California (UCLA) developed a communication model in which he demonstrated that 7% of what we communicate consists of the literal content, 38% is vocal (tone and volume), and 55% of communication consists of body language. Our body language is the first impression people see before we even speak a word.

Good posture is essential to demonstrate positive body language. Below are examples of body language postures and their meanings.
- Leaning or bending forward while sitting down usually means that you are interested by what the other person is saying; this shows engagement.
- Leaning back in your chair while sitting down usually indicates that you are relaxed.
- Crossing your arms, more often than not, denotes anger, frustration, or insecurity. Although, crossed arms may also indicate feeling chilly.
- Slouching indicates laziness and bad posture.

Hand Gestures
- Thumbs up means 'okay' and thumbs down means 'not good'.

- High five means excitement for something well done.
- Waving is a way of greeting someone from afar.

GREETING PEOPLE IN AMERICA

Stand when greeting others as this shows respect to them. Handshakes are the most common way of greeting. Shake with your right hand. Your handshake should be firm, though not extra firm. In business, shake with two pumps, and three pumps for social greetings.

Handshakes are a form of non-verbal communication that says so much about a person.

- An overpowering handshake indicates dominance and control.
- A weak handshake indicates insecurity, disinterest, secretiveness, and shyness.
- An awkward handshake indicates nervousness or a lack of social skills.

A light hug is common in social groups, though this is reserved for close friends and family. The air kiss is also common in social groups, one kiss, right cheek to right cheek. Hugs and kisses are saved for social time and not used in business.

Note: During a pandemic, handshakes, hugs, and air kisses are not common; you may smile with a slight nod or smile while placing your hand over your heart, to keep a non-contact greeting for safety purposes.

PUBLIC INTERACTIONS

Opening Doors

When walking into a building and someone in front of you holds the door for you, the polite response to say is 'thank you'. If you are the first one entering a building, the polite action is to keep the door open for the person coming behind you. In business, opening doors is non-gender, whilst for social settings the man opens the door for a lady.

'Please' and 'Thank you'

Most Americans say 'please' when they want something. For example, if you are ordering food at a restaurant, you may say, "I will have the salad, please." If you ask for something and do not say 'please', Americans will think you are rude.

'Thank you' is commonly used. In the United States, it is common to say 'thank you' or 'thanks' even for small gestures. For example, if you hand someone a book, they might thank you. Remember to say, 'thank you', especially to anyone who is helping or trying to help you.

Saying sorry / apologising:
Americans say 'sorry' more than people in other cultures. For example, if someone accidentally bumps into you on the street, they may apologise with 'excuse me' or 'sorry'.

Using Bus/Taxi/Uber
When using city transportation for travelling, it is good manners to thank the driver. The general etiquette rule is if someone does any favour for you, you thank them; if not, it is considered rude.

Seating
If seating is limited in public transportation or waiting areas, it is proper for people in good health to offer their seats to an elderly person and to those with special needs, such as the disabled, people with infants, and pregnant women.

Covering your mouth
Many Americans consider it impolite to make bodily noises in front of others. They try not to pass gas, burp or make other bodily noises in public or in front of people they do not know well.

Driving
- Drive on the right-hand side of the road (except in the US Virgin Islands).
- Stop at all *stop* signs.
- You must stop for stopped school buses with flashing lights and a stop sign.
- The driver and all passengers must wear seatbelts.

In general, Americans have a 'heart of gold' and welcome travellers to the United States. My mom has said many times, 'people have kind hearts and want to help you', I personally have found this to be an extremely true statement.

Chapter 3

Conversation Dos and Don'ts

THE ART OF CONVERSATION
Small talk is the first step to deeper conversations and new friendships. Here you will find ideas for conversation starters, the etiquette of what to ask and not to ask, and many more of the manners of conversations while enjoying conversations with Americans.

Conversations in the USA are in general the same across the country, although a few minor differences in conversations may be seen in the different areas of the USA. For example, on the east coast people are likely to be more straight forward with conversations. Typically, in the south, proper manners are a way of life so people may speak more correctly. The west coast has beach vibes and so people in general are more casual and easy-going, thus more casual in conversation.

Small Talk
Most Americans enjoy 'small talk', or you may call it 'casual conversations'.

Here are a few things to keep in mind about most Americans. They are friendly and kind. When spoken to, they will respond. Most people will greet others with 'hello' and 'how are you'? The other person almost always says, 'well', 'Good', or 'fine', even if he or she is sad or unwell.

In the USA, people say if someone allows you to go before them in line, holds a door open for you, or another random act of kindness, it is polite to thank them.

When we are in a conversation with other people, we communicate in two important ways: verbally and non-verbally. Non-verbal communication relates to the way we use our body to communicate.

Forms of Non-verbal communication:
- Hand gestures.

- Facial expressions.
- Eye contact.
- Posture (how we stand or sit).
- Tone of voice.

Some people think non-verbal communication is more important than the actual words we say. It helps people decide if they like and trust others. Different cultures use different types of non-verbal communication. Here are some of the ways Americans use non-verbal communication:

Eye contact

Most Americans make eye contact during important conversations. If you do not make eye contact, people may think you are lying, or something is wrong. People who look directly into your eyes are often viewed as more trustworthy, intelligent, and kind. If you come from a culture where people do not look into each other's eyes, this can be difficult to adjust to.

Smiling

Americans smile a lot to be polite and to show that everything is okay. When you meet someone new, they expect you to smile at them.

Posture

If you stand up straight, people tend to give you more respect; it is also better for your health.

Touch

Most Americans shake hands when they meet. Sometimes people will hug each other if they already know each other. During the pandemic, most people feel uncomfortable shaking hands, and even after the pandemic, do not feel you have to shake hands.

Space

In the USA, people have more 'personal space' than most countries. This means when you are talking with someone you should be least a foot away from each other. On a personal note, when my family visited Bilbao, Spain, I found immediately that the personal space was much closer than Americans, so I choose to adapt to the country's personal space version.

VERBAL COMMUNICATIONS
Sensitive subjects:
- Political discussions should be 'politically correct'. Being politically correct means not saying things that will offend a particular group of people. For example, many Americans do not tolerate racist or sexist jokes or comments as this is impolite and disrespectful.
- Most Americans do not like to talk about their weight, their age, or how much money they make, so it is best to keep away from these topics.

Stay away also from topics regarding sex, personal finance, religion, gossip, and health issues.

Safe topics
Now, on the flip side, some topics are easier to talk about. Common areas across cultures are current news, favourite books, hobbies, travel plans, favourite foods or restaurants, and sports. If you are having a hard time talking with someone, talk about these topics.

MISTAKES
Etiquette mistakes during a conversation:
Making your phone more important than the person you are speaking with (constantly checking or using your phone, even text messages).

Interrupting or monopolizing the conversation. Give the other person or people a chance to shine.

Humour in communication can be hard when you are adjusting to a new culture. You may make a joke that people around do not understand, or someone might make a joke that you do not understand. Since humour is cultural, keep this to a minimum until you know someone well.

Remember, no matter where you live in the world, the most important part of a conversation is respect; the key to the art of conversation is not in the *talking*, but in the *listening*.

Chapter 4

Gift Giving

Gift giving is an expression of gratitude. Celebrations and special occasions (weddings, birthdays, birth of a baby) are a time of gift giving to show others how happy you are to be part of their lives and celebrate with them. Holiday gifting is a wonderful time to celebrate a religious or national holiday, such as Christmas, New Year's Eve and Valentine's Day. Americans enjoy celebrating, and below you will find helpful ideas for gifts, sprinkled with a few fun stories from my life. Let us start with the celebration of life…

Baby gifts:
Gifts shared when attending a baby shower, or to celebrate a baby's birth and welcome them into the family: items of their registry, books, soft toys, swaddles, diapers/nappies, musical toys, rattles, clothing, personalised items, and gifts for the new parents.

Baptism/Christening:
Example gift ideas: a personal baby blanket, the Bible, an engraved compass, a personalised book, an engraved baby spoon, a frame, or a keepsake box.

Coming of Age:
Bar Mitzvahs: in Jewish culture, the number eighteen is special, and gifts are often given in multiples of eighteen. This is called giving 'chai', meaning life.
    Religious Confirmations: The Bible, jewellery, money, a watch, or a keepsake box.

Birthday gifts:
Children: books, creative toys for aspiring writers, artists, and scientists, imaginative play games. A great idea is to ask the parents for ideas.
    Adults: Gift something you know your friend would enjoy; for

example, I enjoy wearing accessories, so many times I receive fun, fashionable, and thoughtful accessories. Candles, gift cards, journals, chocolate, travel accessories, games, plants, gourmet foods, wine and experiences (this is one of my favourite items to give my mother, as she loves our fun dining adventures).

ANNIVERSARY GIFTS

With each anniversary that passes, you strengthen your relationship. The gifts start out simple and strengthen as the years pass.

One-Year Anniversary Gifts:
Traditional gift: paper.
Modern gift: clocks.

Five-Year Anniversary Gift:
Traditional gift: wood.
Modern gift: silverware.

Ten-Year Anniversary Gift:
Traditional gift: aluminium or tin.
Modern gift: diamond jewellery.

Twenty-Year Anniversary Gift:
Traditional gift: china.
Modern gift: platinum.

Thirty-Year Anniversary Gift:
Traditional gift: pearl.
Modern gift: diamond.

Forty-Year Anniversary Gift:
Traditional and modern gift: ruby.

Fifty Year Anniversary gift:
Traditional and modern gift: gold.
Sixty Year Anniversary Gift:
Traditional and modern gift: diamond.

Dinner Parties

It is customary to give a gift when attending a dinner party, and it is a good idea not to show up empty-handed. When you RSVP to a dinner party, ask the host/hostess if you may bring something. If nothing is suggested, you arrive with a gift. Ideas for gifts are home-baked goods (a sweet bread for breakfast the next morning to enjoy with their coffee or tea), a candle, chocolates, jam or artisan condiments. At one New Year's Eve party we attended, one guest brought homemade cinnamon rolls for the host and hostess and for each couple who attended to enjoy in the morning with coffee or tea. This was such a delightful and thoughtful hostess gift for all!

House-Warming

Personalised coasters, a monogram mug, a return address stamp, plant, lightly scented candles, personalised dishtowels, personalised home portrait ornaments, specialty foods, home-baked goods.

Add some personality to your gifts with unique or traditional gift wrapping. Be creative with ribbon and wrapping paper, and gift bags always add a special touch to any gift.

Chapter 5

Dining Etiquette

CUISINE

American cuisine reflects the history of the United States, blending the culinary contributions of cultures from around the world. Most American cuisine is developed as home cooking rather than haute cuisine. The millennials are shifting to focus on taste and prioritization of healthy eating. Many of these popular foods are being modified by using healthier ingredients because nutrition is of upmost importance to this generation. Below you will read an overview of the best-known American types of food.

FOODS

All-American cookout: during summer fun and holidays, Memorial Day, July the 4th, or Labour Day, families across the U.S. fire up their grills and invite friends and families for a good old-fashioned cookout or barbecue. American favourites like hamburgers, hot dogs, potato salad, potato chips and coleslaw are the traditional meal.

Southern cooking: traditional fried chicken, biscuits, chicken and dumplings, chicken-fried steak and gravy, and fried green tomatoes are popular dishes from California to Maine.

Meat and potatoes: America is known for its steak houses serving extra-large cuts of meat, served sizzling on a plate with a side of potatoes and vegetables.

Comfort Food: each family has their own favourite comfort food; here are a few: macaroni and cheese, chicken pot pie, chili, meatloaf and pot roasts. Enjoying these comfort foods on a cold day around the dinner table usually takes Americans right back to their mother's kitchen.

Seafood: With the surrounding oceans, Americans have enjoyed New England clam chowder (a creamy way to enjoy the flavours of the sea), Maine lobster, crab boils and many fresh fish dishes.

PB&J: this classic sandwich is a staple amongst Americans. Spread one slice of bread with peanut butter and the other slice with jam; join the two together and enjoy an American go-to. Potato chips are often paired with a PB&J.

Hamburgers: are a staple item in all of the United States, coast to coast.

Each American has their favourite hamburger, from fast food on the west coast (In-N-Out Burger) to fine dining in New York (The Spotted Pig). Hamburgers consist of a round patty of ground beef (fried or grilled), served on a bun and garnished with various condiments.

Fried Chicken: was found in early American cookbooks in the 1860s and 1870s. The Scottish immigrants brought to America the tradition of deep-frying chicken.

Pizza: American pizza today is distinctly different from its original pizza from Italy. 'New York style' is a thin dough made with less oil than the hearty dough of the 'Chicago-style'. The traditional topping is pepperoni, and many unique combinations are well loved in America.

Tacos: are a small hand-sized corn or wheat tortilla topped with a seasoned meat, beans, lettuce and tomatoes with hot sauce. The tortilla is then folded around the filling and eaten by hand. Other popular Mexican foods are the burrito, tostada, beans, and rice.

Buffalo chicken wings: are a favourite of many, and a popular bar food. The wings are deep-fried and covered completely in a tangy and spicy hot sauce.

Hot Dogs: complement a summer cookout or a baseball game better than any other food. Baseball hotdogs are famous in America, served at each baseball park claiming the 'best hot dog'. As I live in Los Angeles, California, I am biased and think the Dodger Dog (as they are referred to) are the best. You will find regional and traditional variations of hot dogs such as a 'Chili Hot Dog', 'Philly Combo', and many more.

Barbecue Ribs: Barbecuing food is one of the country's oldest traditions. You will find many different types of sauces to choose from, to accompany ribs, and chicken.

Biscuits and Gravy: are a Southern favourite; the original biscuit was brought to the country by the British. American biscuits are traditionally made with butter (or lard) and buttermilk and are topped off with the gravy made from meat juices/drippings.

Meatloaf: is comfort food at its best. Most American households will have a family recipe for their version. Typically, it involves ground meat and seasonings, made into a loaf shape, and topped with sauce, ketchup or, my favourite, barbecue sauce. Enjoying meatloaf will usually take Americans right back to their mother's kitchen!

Grits: this Southern American staple is made from coarsely ground corn kernels and is extremely versatile. Typically, this is savoury, although it can also be made sweet.

Chicken and Waffles: this Southern dish is a sweet, savoury, crispy goodness. The fluffy waffles are topped with a piece of crispy fried chicken and topped with maple syrup.

Pot Pies: are a stew mix of chicken or beef, sauce/gravy and vegetables, cooked inside a pastry shell.

Side dishes: some of America's favourites are French fried potatoes, mashed potatoes, egg noodles, rice, baked beans, macaroni salad, coleslaw, potato salad, green salads and vegetables.

Avocado Toast: is a healthy alternative and an American food trend for this decade. Spread mashed avocado over toast with lemon juice, topped with salt and pepper. Many add fun toppings such as fresh herbs, vegetables and eggs. It can be made gluten free and vegan, full of nutrients and yet ever so slightly indulgent. Avocado toast is a staple in our home.

DESSERTS

Apple Pie: (added bonus: topped with vanilla ice cream) is the traditional American dessert along with cherry pie, pecan pie and key lime pie.

Chocolate Chip Cookies: are a close second, and personally my all-time favourite American dessert. The chocolate chip cookie was invented by American chef, Ruth Graves Wakefield in the late 1930s working at the Toll House restaurant in Whitman, Massachusetts.

S'mores: a campfire tradition; roast marshmallows around the campfire and place the marshmallow and chocolate between graham crackers and enjoy this tasty dessert. Sticky fingers are part of the experience.

Root Beer Float: an American diner staple, put a few scoops of vanilla ice cream in a glass and pour a root beer on top. The result is a frothy chilled drink which is sweet and tasty to eat—do not forget the straw and spoon.

DRINKS

Carbonated soft drinks: the largest consumed drink in America, second only to bottled water. Coke is the number one soft drink (also known as 'soda pop' in some areas), with Pepsi close behind. Many new healthy alternative carbonated drinks are becoming more popular to consume.

Wine: America has wineries in every state, though about 90% of wine comes from California. The Napa Valley and Sonoma reign in California have a perfect combination of climate, soil, and terrain ideally equipped for growing wine grapes.

Beer: the fourth most popular beverage in America. Craft breweries are becoming more popular, the number of which operating in the U.S. reaches more than 7,000, according to the Brewers Association.

MEALTIMES FOR AMERICANS
- Breakfast: seven to nine a.m.
- Lunch: noon to one p.m.
- Happy Hour: five to seven p.m.
- Dinner: six to eight p.m.

Breakfast varies from one part of the country to another. An American breakfast menu will include some of the following items: eggs, bacon, pancakes, cold and hot cereal, baked foods (bagels, donuts, and muffins), yogurt, and fruit. Coffee, tea, milk, and juice are the preferred drinks, coffee being number one drink for breakfast.

The typical American *lunch* consists of sandwiches/wraps, soup and salads. Most popular sandwiches are Deli (meats and cheese), tuna salad, peanut butter and jelly, and toasted cheese. American favourite soups are chicken noodle, tomato, and clam chowder. Salads are a favourite especially during the spring and summer months. Many salads are enjoyed by Americans, and Chef Salad is definitely one of the favourites. A Chef Salad consists of chopped greens, tomato, crisp bacon, grilled or roasted chicken breast, hard-boiled eggs, avocado, chives, and cheese, served with a red-wine vinaigrette or ranch dressing. Hamburgers, hot dogs, tacos and burritos are also a common lunch meal.

Dinner (sometimes called supper) is the most substantial meal of the day. An all-American dinner consists of a protein, starch and vegetable (meat, potato, and vegetable) served with a roll and salad. Many other types of dinners are served from cultures around the world; to name a few: Italian, Mexican, Chinese, Korean barbecue. The diversity of food here in America is wonderful and inviting.

Dining Etiquette

American dining etiquette is similar to the rest of the world with a few minor differences.

When using your utensils, pick your fork up using your left hand and the knife with your right hand and assume a cutting position with the fork tines turned down. After cutting your food, place the knife at the top of the plate, blade facing you. Switch the fork from your left hand to your right hand for eating (if you are left-handed simply keeping the fork in your left and turn over so the tines are facing up). If you choose to set your fork down, place it at four o'clock on your plate if you are right-handed, eight o'clock if you are left-handed. The knife should remain at the top of the plate facing towards you. When you are finished with your meal, place the fork and knife at a quarter past three position. Left-handed people may place the knife and fork at the quarter to ten position. Continental dining is also welcomed here in America.

Knowing the correct etiquette and manners shows respect for you and the person(s) you are with.

Below are some important etiquette and manners dining basics:
- Do not talk with your mouth full of food.
- Electronics such as phones are best kept on your lap, pocket, or in your handbag.
- No grooming at the dining table; use the powder room or restroom.
- When not eating, keep your hands on your lap.
- No elbows on the table; you may rest your forearms on the table if no food is present. Mirror yourself with guests when eating, and pace yourself so you finish at similar times. Place your napkin on the seat of the chair if you are returning to your seat after leaving the table. Place your napkin to the left of your plate when you are leaving and have finished eating. Thank the host for the meal and follow up with a 'thank you' note.

Thanksgiving

Thanksgiving Day is an annual national holiday celebrated on the fourth Thursday of November. It celebrates the harvest and blessings from the past year. In 1621,
the Plymouth colonists and Wampanoag Native Americans shared a

harvest celebratory feast. This is known as the first Thanksgiving. The Thanksgiving meal typically consists of turkey, bread stuffing, potatoes, cranberries, and pumpkin pie. For our Thanksgiving dinner, we have all of the above and also cream corn, sweet potato casserole, and barbecue ribs. This is a huge tradition our family looks forward to all year.

Whether you are enjoying a cup of coffee and muffin for breakfast at a local coffee shop or dining at an exclusive restaurant, manners matter. Americans enjoy life; showing kindness, smiles, and respect are what is most important when dining.

Chapter 6

Business Etiquette

Americans in general are friendly and willing to help others. America has fine nuances from different regions across the USA. The east coast is more formal compared to the west coast which is more casual. With this in mind, I will share some differences when considering business etiquette.

The first area in which you will see a difference is *business dress*. The east coast is more formal in their dress code and follows these dress code guidelines:

Business:
Men: suit (jacket and slacks) with a tie.
   Women: suit (trousers or dress/skirt), top (with sleeves) with skirt/trousers, the dress/skirt being mid-length.

Business casual:
Men: collared shirt, tucked in, with slacks or Dockers, or possibly nice jeans with no rips or holes. Sport coat optional.
   Women: day dress, mix and match jacket with skirt/slacks and shirt.

Casual:
Men: slacks, Dockers, jeans, with a button-down shirt or polo shirt.
   Women: day dress, skirt/slacks, with a top or blouse, jeans with no rips or holes.

The west coast takes the dress code more casual; reading the guidelines above you will find the west coast is predominantly business casual and casual, especially within the tech industry. Most of the tech industry does not have a dress code, and is very casual, wearing jeans/shorts and T-shirts.

Working in the fashion industry for years as a buyer for west coast women's clothing stores, the style is more casual, relaxed, with beachy vibe fashions. The warm weather also plays a part in the dress code for the west coast. The east coast tends to be sleeker, polished, and classic. This shows up in the unique fashions sold from coast to coast.

WHETHER CASUAL OR FORMAL, THESE ARE ESSENTIALS FOR PROFESSIONALS:

Hair: keep it clean and well groomed (men, facial hair included).

Clothing: clean and wrinkle free.

Fit: make sure your clothing fits well, a tailor is your best friend.

Nails: clean, filed and neatly cut, without chipped nail polish. In formal business environments, keep your nail polish neutral.

Accessories: simple and classic are the best choice for jewellery, belts, and handbags; shoes should be in pristine condition. Mobile phones and their cases, notebooks, pens, the business card holder, and briefcase should all be business chic and in good condition. All these important accessories are part of your professional look.

Social media plays a big role regarding business etiquette. Most businesses (universities and colleges also) screen candidates' social media before granting an interview. Make sure social media is not negatively influencing your interviewing and career.

The handshake is the proper greeting here in America. Standing when shaking hands shows you are a trusted and confident person. Your eye contact and smile add warmth to the handshake. Shake with two pumps when shaking hands for business, and three pumps for social situations. A firm handshake is the best, not a bone crusher though. An air kiss, hug and cheek kiss are saved for close friends and family, not for business.

Introductions in business are crucial. Say the most important person first, followed with 'May I introduce Suzie', then give a quick comment about Suzie. Example: 'Mr Smith, may I please introduce you to Suzie; she is a new hire here at XYZ business'. The reason for the little bit of information when you give introductions is so they have something to discuss with each other.

Ethics in business are extremely important to protect the company's brand, reputation and you personally. Respect, honesty, integrity, trustworthiness, leadership, law abiding behaviour, and concern for others are some of the top ethics in business. Promise-keeping is most important not only in business, but in personal ethics also.

Modern manners in business have changed through the years, adding a few new manners in 2020 with the world pandemic. Here are a few important manners:

Proofread correspondence for example: emails, written notes, social media, and texting.

Punctuality is critical, arriving on time to work, to in-person meetings, online meetings, and dining meetings.

Inviting a guest to a business meeting is your treat. The rule of thumb is that the person who extends the invitation also covers the bill.

Table manners are of upmost importance. I personally know an owner of a financial business who, after interviewees have passed two interviews, takes the potential new hire to dinner. If they pass the manners test of treating everyone the same with utmost respect, including serving staff, they are hired. If they do not pass the manners test, they are not hired because it is crucial in business to treat everyone with respect, regardless of what job you have within the company.

Following the guidelines of *face masks* within a company is of utmost importance. Check with each company regarding their policies. *Dining manners:* when not wearing your face masks, place them on your lap (using a paper bag or envelope to place them in) with the napkin over the face mask, or place it in your handbag/pocket; never place it on the table.

Mobile devices are kept on silent and not placed on the dining table. If using the phone for meetings, keep it on your lap when not using it.

Mirror your guest's timing whilst eating; slow down or speed up if needed. It is best to finish the meal at similar times.

Thank you notes are always in style; email or handwritten are wonderful.

Enjoy business in America. People are friendly, kind and generally want to help you.

Chapter 7

Wedding Etiquette

Weddings around the world are unique to each culture, religion, and country. Here in the USA, you will find traditional weddings, traditional and modern mixes, and more modern variations to represent the uniqueness of the couple. Thinking back to our wedding thirty-eight years ago, my husband and I had a traditional wedding, mixed with fun touches to represent our personality. I chose white dresses for my bridesmaids which were designed by a dear friend, and my husband and I both love ice cream so we had an ice cream cart for guests to enjoy at our reception.

Below you find etiquette, traditions, and information to help you have a fabulous time at an American wedding. When invited to a wedding here are some helpful tips:

WEDDING INVITATIONS
When receiving an invitation (by mail or electronically) return the RSVP card by mail or electronically in a timely manner to say whether you will or will not be attending. It is best to reply before the RSVP required date. If you are uncertain or need time, communicate this with who sent you the invitation.

PLUS ONES AND CHILDREN
If you receive a 'plus one' on your invitation, include the person's name in your RSVP, to aid the creation of a guest list or placement cards. If the wedding invitation did not specifically name your child/children or your family, then assume they are not invited. Only those whose name (names) is on the invitation are invited.

PHOTOGRAPHY
Look for signs as you enter the wedding regarding photography. Be respectful when taking pictures during the ceremony as you may block the professional photographer the couple hired to document their day.

Wedding Gifts

Most Americans use a gift registry. This is where you will find items the couple have chosen for gift ideas you may purchase. People often ask how much money is appropriate to spend on a wedding gift, so here is a guideline. How close you are to the happy couple is important to consider; if you are social friends: $50, close friend or close relatives: $100–$150+, friend or relative: $75–$125, co-worker, distant family-friend or relative: $50–$100. Important to consider also is what your budget can afford.

It is best not to bring a gift to the wedding location; instead, send physical gifts to the bride in advance of the wedding. Cards can be given at the wedding directly to the couple or placed at the designated spot during the reception.

Mobile Devices

Turn the sound off and all ringer, alarms, vibration, and disruptive alerts.

Arriving at the Appropriate Time

The time stated on wedding invitations is the time when the ceremony begins. Arrive early (no more than thirty minutes, as you may interrupt prewedding activities) as this is a common courtesy to the couple and their family.

Attire

What to wear to the wedding is important; look for dress code information or guidelines on the invitation and if you do not see anything shared, look on the website. If all else fails, communicate with the bride or mother of the bride and ask about the dress attire. Below are helpful descriptions on dress codes:

White-Tie: For the elite formal attire, women wear a formal floor-length evening gown, long gloves are optional. Men wear a tuxedo with tails, a formal white shirt, white vest and bow tie, white or grey gloves, and formal footwear.

Black-Tie: A black-tie event is the epitome of formal. Women wear a formal floor-length gown or may wear a bit less formal, sophisticated cocktail dress. An elegant trouser suit/pantsuit is suitable also. Men wear a tuxedo which may include a black bow tie, black vest or cummerbund, and patent leather shoes. For summer weddings, a white dinner jacket and black tuxedo trousers are also acceptable.

Formal or Black-Tie optional: A black-tie-optional event is still dressy but gives a few more options to wear. Women may wear a floor-length gown, a fancy cocktail dress, dressy separates, or dressy pantsuit. Men may wear a tuxedo, or a formal dark suit, white shirt, and conservative tie.

Cocktail: Women wear a tea-length, midi (mid-calf), knee-length dress, or nice pantsuit/trouser suit. Men wear a suit and tie.

Semi-Formal: Women wear dresses, or pantsuits (more formal fabrics and colours for an evening wedding and light colours and fabrics for a daytime event). Men should wear dress shirt and slacks (dark or light depending on the time of day) with the option to wear a tie and jacket.

Casual: This indicates the wedding will be casual and most likely outside. Women may wear a sundress, top and skirt or trousers (no jeans or tank tops). Men wear dress trousers or khaki trousers with a collared shirt. You may add a sports jacket or sweater if chilly.

Wearing white no matter what dress code is required to a wedding is not recommended unless specifically requested by the couple.

My husband and I were at a formal wedding in Los Angeles years ago; my husband took off his coat to dance and was politely asked by the server to please keep his coat on throughout the evening. Nowadays we have the internet, so you may look online and read about the venue you will be attending and look for dress code specifics of the place the wedding or reception will be held at; this will be helpful to avoid any faux pas.

THE DAY
The exciting day has arrived. Here are some guidelines to make you feel comfortable attending an American wedding:
Wedding Ceremony: most weddings will follow the similar general flow:

Take your seat at least ten minutes (earlier if you would like a specific place to sit) prior to the ceremony. Seating is usually not assigned, though the first few rows are designated for the family.

The Processional
This begins with parents and grandparents are escorted to their seats. Then the bridesmaids and groomsmen walk down the aisle, followed by a flower girl and ring bearer. Traditionally, the father escorts his daughter down the aisle as the groom waits at the altar.

The Ceremony
This may include opening remarks, readings from the officiant who also shares the significance of marriage and vows. The couple exchange their vows (these may be personal vows the couple have written themselves or traditional vows), followed by the couple exchanging rings. Often, there may be a unity candle (or other unique idea), and then officiant will have closing remarks which may include a blessing. The officiant will end the ceremony by introducing the couple to the guests.

After the ceremony has ended, you may be ushered out of the venue, or may exit on your own; watch for clues from the ushers.

Cocktail Hour
Often after the ceremony a cocktail hour will be available to enjoy whilst the couple takes pictures. This is a wonderful time to mix and mingle with other guests.

Meal
The meal most likely will be served or be a buffet style, and you may be assigned a table or seat for dining. Look for place cards or a table plan board, as these will have the table numbers on them. When the food is served or you arrive to the table from the buffet, make sure to wait until the people around you have their meal before beginning to eat. Read about dining etiquette from the dining etiquette chapter.

Dancing
Many weddings have dancing. Wait to dance until you are invited onto the dance floor. The first dance will be for the bride and groom, followed by a father-daughter dance and a mother-son dance. The wedding party will then be welcomed to the dance floor and then the guests are invited also to dance. Speeches and toasts will occur throughout dinner and possibly during the party phase of the evening. A grand exit may be planned as guests line up outside to create a pathway for the couple to walk through as they say their final goodbye.

During or upon leaving the reception, remember to thank the host of the wedding for a special time, and a handwritten note is always a nice gesture.

After writing this chapter, I am ready to attend the next wedding we are invited to and wear my dancing shoes to celebrate! How about you?

Vietnam
By Mai O'Donnell

Chapter 1

Cultural Symbols

Vietnam is a country located in the centre of Southeast Asia, bordered by China, Laos, Cambodia, the East Sea and the Pacific Oceans.

Vietnam is also famously as an S-shaped country, with a long coastline measuring more than 3200 kilometres. Vietnam is located in tropical and subtropical climates, with high humidity and abundant rainfall.

I would like to introduce some interesting things about Vietnam to a large number of readers around the world.

NATIONAL FLAG

The flag of each country is always a sacred symbol and the pride of the people of that country.

Particularly for Vietnam, the flag, with a red background and a yellow star in the middle has a very special meaning. The red colour is a symbol of enthusiasm, patriotism, the colour of the blood of the soldiers who sacrificed their lives to defend the country, gaining independence and freedom.

The yellow star represents the whole nation of Vietnam with five main classes in Vietnamese society: intellectuals, farmers, workers, soldiers, and entrepreneurs who have united to build the country.

AO DAI (TRADITIONAL LONG DRESS)

The *Ao Dai* is a traditional Vietnamese national costume. They can be worn by both women and for men. In modern life, women wear *Ao Dai* on important occasions quite often. Men usually wear suits and rarely wear an *Ao Dai*. The *Ao Dai* is the pride of the Vietnamese people because it honours the beauty that is both shy, discreet, graceful, and elegant.

Vietnam's *Ao Dai* is a set piece consisting of a long dress which flows down to the heel with wide-leg trousers worn underneath. The dress has a waist cut to honour the curves of Vietnamese women. It is suitable for people of all ages. The *Ao Dai* is always worn in Vietnam on the Lunar New Year, to weddings, festivals, graduation ceremonies or simply when friends gather and want to take memorable photos together wearing the *Ao Dai*.

The *Ao Dai* for girls in high schools was formerly white, but now it can be worn in all colours and innovative designs.

Visitors to Vietnam often choose to buy *Ao Dai* as gifts for themselves, their wives, daughters or friends.

CONICAL HAT

The conical hat is a perfect match with the *Ao Dai*, showing the grace and tenderness of Vietnamese women. The hat is made of coconut leaves or palm leaves, combined with bamboo stalks and thread and provides useful protection to the wearer from the sun. It is still used today by many women in rural areas of Vietnam, when doing farm work under the hot summer sun.

This is also an interesting souvenir that tourists visiting Vietnam often buy for themselves or as a gift for family and friends.

CUISINE

I am always so proud of Vietnamese cuisine when I talk about Vietnam to international friends. I can confidently say that Vietnam is one of the countries with the most diverse culinary culture in the world. Vietnamese food is health-oriented because there are a lot of vegetables. All these vegetables have medicinal uses. Vietnamese people also eat little butter, sugar, milk and instead eat rice, noodles, and vegetables. Vietnamese dishes are famous for the combination of many different ingredients and spices that help to enhance the taste and attractiveness of each dish.

When you visit Vietnam, you must try the famous street food. There are many street foods that have been passed down from ancestors to descendants. Interestingly, each shop has only one dish, but believe me, each is very delicious, even more than the food in fancy restaurants.

Let me tell you a secret. In Vietnam, if you want to show off, you must know which street food restaurant is good for each dish.

VIETNAMESE WAR

I studied in Japan in 2002. When I introduced myself as being from Vietnam, everyone asked me about the Vietnam War.

It has been forty-six years since the Vietnamese war was officially ended. Vietnam is now a peaceful, independent and free country, transforming itself from one of the poorest countries in the world into a low middle-income country. Vietnam has seen remarkable economic growth rate in recent years and attracts a lot of foreign investment. Currently in Vietnam there are still many museums dedicated to the Vietnamese war and there are still war remnants in many parts of Vietnam.

LOTUS

The Lotus flower is considered by many Vietnamese as a national symbol.

Vietnam has a famous proverb:

'In a lake, what is more beautiful than the lotus

Green leaves with white flowers and yellow stamens.

Even though the yellow stamens, white flowers and green leaves

grow in mud they still smell sweet'.

The lotus is a symbol of perfection, purity, unaffected by external influences. For Vietnamese people who live far away from their motherland, wherever they go, seeing lotus flowers evokes peace in their hearts and the feeling of seeing their homeland.

BAMBOO

Bamboo is also a plant very close to the Vietnamese peoples' hearts. In ancient times, bamboo was used as a weapon to fight foreign invaders and protect villages. In addition, bamboo is a raw material with which Vietnamese people make many tools.

Bamboo symbolises resilience, determination and an ability to face many difficulties, hardships and adversities. This embodies what the Vietnamese people are.

VIETNAMESE PEOPLE

Vietnam is a country that experienced many years of war. It is because of this, that Vietnamese people are famous for their stamina, toughness, passion, patriotism and solidarity.

Vietnamese people are also famous for being studious, hardworking and skilful. The skilful hands of many Vietnamese people have created many beautiful handicrafts that are sold all over the world.

HA LONG BAY

Ha Long Bay is a famous Vietnamese tourist spot, a place of amazing beauty, recognised by UNESCO as a natural world heritage site. Visitors are never disappointed here. Visitors cannot help but be surprised when they witness the beautiful calm waters, and hundreds of small rocky islands with caves and beaches.

If you come to Vietnam, be sure to visit Ha Long Bay and definitely choose a night tour on a yacht; you can watch the sunrise and the sunset amidst the beautiful calm waters of the bay. It is a once in a lifetime experience.

OTHERS

Some other less prominent symbols of Vietnam are The Bronze drum, the Lac bird, The One-pillar Pagoda, The buffalo, and the rice plant.

There are some world-famous movies about Vietnam you would love to watch such as:

Good Morning, Vietnam
The Scent Of Green Papaya
The Quiet America
Indochine

I hope you visit Vietnam at least once to experience the wonders that I have described. You will certainly have an enjoyable time exploring the beautiful landscapes of Vietnam and experiencing its unique culture.

Chapter 2

Meeting, Greeting, Posture and Body Language

POSTURES AND BODY LANGUAGE

Vietnamese people are shy and rarely touch other people's bodies or have strangers touch theirs, so they do not hug or kiss on the cheeks when socialising.

In Vietnamese culture, Vietnamese people rarely look directly into the eyes of the person they are talking to, but slightly lower their heads and look down to show humility and respect.

Many Vietnamese people don't know how to use body language in communication to express what they want to say, or their feelings.

MEETING AND GREETINGS

Greetings are very important in Vietnamese culture. There are many Vietnamese sayings about greetings, such as 'a polite greeting is better than a good meal', 'learn manners first and then learn to read and write', 'respect the elders, yield to the younger'. From times gone by, for the Vietnamese people, politeness, humility and especially greetings have been considered as an initial measure of whether a person has a good family and education or not.

I would like to give you some tips about meeting and greeting in Vietnam which will be very helpful to you when you travel to Vietnam or do business with Vietnamese people.

o Vietnamese people often address a person by their title, the personal pronoun, accompanied by the first name, not by surname, no matter how old or high in authority the person is. In the Vietnamese language, there is a very clear distinction between personal pronouns such as grandfather, uncle, aunt, brother, sister and so on. Sometimes when greeting, if you do not know how a person relates to you in age, it can create an awkward situation. Because of this, even if it is the first time you meet someone, they may ask your age to make sure they address you with the correct pronoun. This is very common in Vietnamese culture, although can commonly be misunderstood as rudeness by visitors.

    o Vietnamese people have a tradition of respecting the elderly, so when meeting elders, they must greet them out loud, hold their hands or hug them, help them walk, and enthusiastically inquire about their health.

In Vietnamese, when young people talk to the elders, they must also use the word 'ạ' at the end of the sentence as a mark of respect.

Children greet their elders with their arms crossed, bowing and saying: 'I greet you'. Adults respond to children's greetings by smiling affectionately and patting their heads. But with older children, fifteen years old and above, adults will treat them like adults and don't pat their heads any more but nod their heads in return.

- Normally when adults meet, they will greet each other depending on how close they are to each other.

If they are not too close, they will greet each other with eye contact, wave and ask: "Where are you going?" This is not a question but actually a greeting that requires no answer.

If they are closer, the younger person will smile slightly, bow their head, the older person will pat them on the shoulder or on the back, asking them questions such as: "Where are you going?" "How are you?" "Still in the same place?" "Are you doing good at work?" "How is your business these days?" "Come to visit me for a few drinks tomorrow," and so on.

Nowadays, with internationalization, especially when young people meet, they often use the English words such as 'hi', 'hello', 'bye' to greet each other.

- When you meet someone at a business meeting, you can shake hands. But usually, it is only men who shake hands; Women shake hands less often.

When younger people shake hands with older people, they will usually use both hands, grabbing the partner's right hand with their right hand, and placing the left hand lightly on the partner's left hand. Or in some cases, they use the right hand to shake the partner's right hand and put their left hand up to support under their right elbow.

- When meeting Vietnamese people, you should prepare mentally, maybe in the first meeting, for questions such as: "What do you do for living?" "Do you have a family?" "Are you married yet?" "How many children do you have?" "How old are you?" "Do you still have parents?" Even more personal questions, more difficult to answer such as, "How much do you earn?" "Why are you not married?" And, "Why do you have no children?"

In that case, you should just think of it as some Vietnamese, especially the elders, want to get to know about you rather than as rudeness.

- When you meet a baby in the presence of their parents, often when you want to compliment, "You're so cute" "You're chubby." "You're so pretty." "You look so healthy." You should add the words 'touch wood' because the baby's parents are afraid that if saying so then the opposite unlucky things would happen.

Chapter 3

Conversation Dos and Don'ts

Vietnamese people are friendly, affectionate, and care a lot about each other's lives. They especially have great national pride and patriotism. When talking to Vietnamese people, if you understand what you should talk about and what should not, it will make the conversation smoother and more cohesive.

TOPICS THAT YOU SHOULD TALK ABOUT WHEN MEETING VIETNAMESE PEOPLE

Vietnamese cuisine:
Street food is the pride of Vietnam, an attraction for international tourists. When you express your desire to enjoy Vietnamese dishes from various regions, Vietnamese people will be happy to share with you what and where to eat. You can talk about typical Vietnamese dishes that any foreigner wants to try when coming to Vietnam such as bun cha, pho, fried spring rolls, summer rolls, cha ca etcetera. All Vietnamese would be very happy and excited about this topic.

Vietnam travel:
Vietnam is a very beautiful country with a long beach from south to north. Any Vietnamese person would be very proud to hear from you about the places you have visited in Vietnam and your enjoyment and amazement at the beautiful nature of the places you went.

Cultural history of Vietnam:
Vietnam has a long history associated with many wars to protect and build the country. Many generations of Vietnamese people carry with them the desire for freedom, the will to fight, and a high tolerance to overcome all difficulties and challenges. With a passionate patriotism, the Vietnamese are proud to have won every war to protect their motherland.

Che Lan Vien, a famous Vietnamese poet wrote:
We love our country as much as our blood,
as our parents, our wife, our husband
If need be, we would die for our country
For every house, mountain and river.

In Vietnam, you will see the names of national heroes, or places associated with the country's struggle throughout history named on many roads throughout the provinces and cities on this S-shaped country. When you visit Vietnam, you will find history remembered everywhere, from the monuments in the city centres, to the famous war museums. Therefore, it should be nice if you learn more about Vietnam and talk to Vietnamese people with your all heart and show respect for their historical values.

Football:
The most popular sport in Vietnam is football. Football players who put on their international tournament kits are considered to put on the faith and pride of the Vietnamese. After each victory of the national football team, Vietnamese people pour into the streets to celebrate with flags, singing and chanting "Vietnam is the champion." At this time, there is no distinction between rich and poor, there is no daily hustle and bustle, but all ninety million Vietnamese hearts are like one, jumping up and down, hugging each other, laughing in tears. When welcoming the Vietnamese football team back home after important victories, people go to the airport to welcome the players, standing on both sides of the packed road waving flags to greet the players as returning heroes.

Family:
Family is very important to Vietnamese people. Family members in Vietnam are very close to each other. There are many Vietnamese families with three generations living in the same house. Parents give all their love to raise their children and children are responsible for taking care of their parents in their old age. In Vietnam, when a girl gets married, she will move to live in her husband's house, in many cases living with the parents-in-law. She does not change her last name to her husband's last name, but their children are given the father's last name. When a boy gets married, he and his wife live with his parents until he can buy a house, or his parents give him money to buy one. The grandparents normally help to look after the small children when their parents go to work.

When you talk to Vietnamese people, a very good topic for you to start the conversation with is talking about your family and asking about their family. This will create more trust and cohesion with Vietnamese people.

TOPICS THAT YOU SHOULDN'T TALK ABOUT

Loss in war:
Vietnamese people are very proud to have won all wars to protect the country's independence and freedom. However, the Vietnam War ended only forty-six years ago, so a lot of pain is still there; many people have suffered from the war both physically and mentally. So, you can still talk about the Vietnamese war, but don't talk too deeply about war losses and tragedies.

Politics:
According to international etiquette, politics in general is always a topic you should avoid, but especially in Vietnam, it should be completely avoided. Do not comment on the government, policies, or political views with Vietnamese people in Vietnam.

Personal privacy:
Many Vietnamese people, especially the elderly, will ask you somewhat personal questions such as, "How old are you?" "Are you married?" "Do you have any children?" "How much do you earn?" If you don't want to answer, you can just give a friendly smile and then talk about other things. But you should not be the one to ask these questions, because it will make many Vietnamese feel uncomfortable.

NO MATTER WHAT THE TOPIC IS, THE MOST IMPORTANT THINGS ARE:
- Be respectful of the person you talk to.
- Show that you have spent time researching information and you are eager to learn more about the country and people.
- Express admiration for their accomplishments.
- Know how to control your emotions; do not say words that might hurt other people's feelings; do not raise your voice or point your finger at other people's faces.
- Show humility in your words.

Chapter 4

Gift Giving

Not only in Vietnam but also in other countries, giving gifts on a variety of occasions is very important. In particular, Vietnamese people attach great importance to family, social, and neighbouring relationships, so gift giving plays very important part in their life.

The Vietnamese have a saying, 'The gift you give is not as important as the way it is given', which shows that the value of the gift is not as important as the sincere intention of the person giving it. The gift includes the content, and the way it is wrapped expresses the giver's affection and wish to bring luck to the recipient.

Vietnamese people do not open gifts in front of the giver. When you receive a gift just say, 'thank you', and leave it on display. Maybe it is because the Vietnamese culture is reserved; they don't want to show off, and they fear there might be a comparison of gifts between the givers that will make the giver feel uncomfortable.

In Vietnamese culture, black is an unlucky colour, but red and yellow are considered lucky colours, so Vietnamese people often prefer bright colours. Therefore, it is not advisable to give gifts that are black.

You should especially avoid giving chrysanthemums to Vietnamese people because it is a flower only for worship or for the deceased.

There are beliefs that couples should not give handkerchiefs to each other because it is a sign of breaking up.

In terms of numbers, many Vietnamese people do not like the numbers three, four, or thirteen. To contrast, the numbers six and eight bring luck and are loved.

Vietnamese people are very humble, so when giving gifts, even if it is valuable, the giver still says, "I only have a small gift to give you."

When it comes to gift giving in Vietnam, people often talk about the 'envelope' culture. That is, instead of thinking how to find the right gift, they will put an amount of money in the envelope, depending on how close they are to the recipient. It's quite convenient because the recipient can use that money to buy whatever they like. But please note that this is only used in close or family relationships. Finding out the perfect gifts for the recipient has always been a cultural feature of Vietnam, showing concern for others.

OCCASIONS FOR GIVING GIFTS IN VIETNAM:
- Birthdays.
- Congratulating someone on their longevity.
- When visiting someone's house.
- Congratulating someone on their new home.
- Congratulations on a newborn baby.
- Lunar New Year.
- Weddings.
- Meeting business partners.
- Other celebrations: International Women's Day on March the 8th, Vietnamese Women's Day on October the 20th, Vietnamese Teacher's Day on November the 20th, Valentine's Day on February the 14th.
- Christmas.
- Returning from a long holiday.

BIRTHDAY GIFTS
On someone's birthday, it is most common to give flowers and a gift which that person likes. If the relationship is quite close, you can ask what that person likes, or pay attention to his/her preferences to give a gift that they love.

LONGEVITY GIFTS
longevity is also considered a birthday occasion for the elders aged seventy years or above. therefore, the gift will show your sincere heart, wishing the recipient good health and long life. you can give flowers, wall art, wine, flower baskets or even an envelope of money.

GIFTS WHEN VISITING SOMEONE'S HOUSE
When you visit someone's house, if you only come for a quick meet up, and don't eat or drink, you don't really need to give gifts. If you are invited to a meal, you should bring a gift such as fruit, food, wine or decorations to give to the host.

Gifts to Congratulate Someone on Their New Home, or for an Opening Ceremony

Vietnamese people often invite each other to visit a new home, or to an opening ceremony. At this time, guests will bring gifts such as decoration accessories, paintings, vases, and flower baskets with the name of the guest. Gifts are given that express congratulations to the host due to his efforts, and especially that bring luck and good feng shui to the host.

Gift for a Newborn Baby

Vietnamese people often pay a visit when someone has a newborn baby. But you should avoid visiting the baby before it is one month old. Vietnamese people believe that when the baby is less than one month old, it is still weak. If someone outside the family visits and the person is not suitable, the baby may cry all night, or get sick. In that case, family members will have to 'burn the astral' by taking a few sheets of paper to burn and then holding the baby walking back and forth, muttering, "The good ones stay, the bad ones go." Therefore, when you want to visit a new baby, you should be aware about the timing to make it after one month of the baby's birth. The best gifts for a newborn baby are clothes, safe toys, or even some money in an envelope with a card; you can ask family members to use the money to buy suitable gifts for their baby.

Gifts for the Lunar New Year

The Lunar New Year, also called Tet, is the most important occasion of the year for Vietnamese people. Tet for Vietnamese people is like Christmas in European countries. This is an opportunity for those who are far away from home to return home and reunite with their loved ones. This is also an opportunity for Vietnamese people to express their gratitude to their parents, relatives, to their superiors at work and to the people who have helped them.

Therefore, about one or two weeks before Tet, Vietnamese people prepare Tet gifts. Common gifts are baskets of sweets, flowers, fruit, wine, or special foods.

On New Year's Day, Vietnamese people have a custom of giving lucky money to the elderly and children. Everyone prepares red envelopes with new money inside so that when visiting parents, friends and relatives, they give them to the elderly and to the children. This is considered a lucky gift at the beginning of a new year to hope that the elderly will be healthy and live long, and that children will be obedient, study well, and not become ill.

GIFT FOR A BUSINESS PARTNER

In order to create a good relationship with business partners, Vietnamese people choose gifts of traditional Vietnamese culture if their business partners are foreign. If the business partner is Vietnamese, it should be a gift to bring luck and fortune to the recipient.

GIFTS FOR OTHER CELEBRATIONS

There are two occasions for men in Vietnam to express their affection, gratitude, and respect for women in the family and in society. It could be their mother, sister, wife, daughter, female colleagues, or female friends on March the 8th, which is called International Women's Day, or October the 20th which is called Vietnamese Women's Day. On these days, Vietnamese women receive flowers and gifts from men. If at work, male colleagues are willing to do all the work for female colleagues, if at home, the husband and children are willing to do all the housework for their wife or mother.

One more occasion where Vietnamese people give gifts is on November the 20th. It is Teacher's Day. All the teachers receive gifts and flowers from their students or the students' parents as a thank you for their teaching and hard work. In recent years, when Vietnam opened its doors to integrate with the world, Vietnamese people have developed a habit of giving gifts on Valentine's Day on February the 14th between lovers and couples. Christmas is also a celebration imported from abroad into Vietnam, and regardless of religion, many people give gifts on this occasion, such as gift giving between lovers, spouses, adults giving to children, or amongst friends. However, Christmas is not an important holiday for Vietnamese people, so it is not obligatory.

GIFTS WHEN RETURNING FROM A LONG HOLIDAY

When you travel somewhere for a long holiday, it is nice to buy small souvenir gifts for your family, relatives, and close friends. Although a small souvenir does not have much material value, it shows that you remembered and care about the recipient.

Chapter 5

Dining Etiquette

MEALS

Breakfast:
The Vietnamese rarely have breakfast at home. Quickly prepared dishes such as instant noodles and fried rice are some of the dishes that the Vietnamese make when they do have breakfast at home. Usually, Vietnamese people will have breakfast out. Favourite breakfast dishes are pho, sticky rice, vermicelli, *banh mi, banh cuon,* balut and so on. Breakfast is eaten between seven a.m. and eight a.m. because schools and offices usually start at eight a.m.

Lunch:
Lunch usually takes place from twelve p.m. to one p.m. Many people like to use lunch to meet friends, so it can be eaten later, from two p.m. to three p.m. There are many dishes. If you gather with friends, hot pot and grilled dishes are popular.

Dinner:
Dinner is considered as the main daily meal in Vietnamese families. This is the heartiest meal, gathering almost everyone in the family. A typical Vietnamese family dinner consists of soup, boiled or stir-fried vegetables, and one or two main dishes such as meat and fish, especially indispensable rice. Many people have rice in every meal, just as some Westerners cannot live without bread. Then there is fruit or cake for dessert. Dinner is usually at around six p.m. to eight p.m.

Many visitors to Vietnam comment that Vietnamese food is very healthy with lots of fresh vegetables and lots of soup, rarely using fatty foods such as butter, milk, and sugar.

EATING UTENSILS

During meals, Vietnamese people use chopsticks, rather than the knives and forks found in European countries. There is also a non-stick spoon to stir the rice, and a large spoon to scoop the soup into the bowl.

The Vietnamese also use bowls, rather than plates, to eat rice and other foods. Plates are just for sharing food and for discarded food.

TYPICAL VIETNAMESE DISHES

Pho: consisting of broth, rice noodles, traditional herbs, and pork meat or chicken. Broth is well-cooked with cinnamon, anise, bones, and onions.

Banh mi: baguette with butter, sausages, salted shredded pork meat, and herbs.

Bun Cha: rice noodles (round-shaped noodles, not flat like pho), charcoal-grilled pork meatball and pork belly slices, dipping sauce, and served with raw vegetables. In 2015, when former US President Obama visited Vietnam, he went to a bun cha restaurant in Hanoi, the capital of Vietnam, with famous chef, Anthony Bourdan. Since then, bun cha and that bun cha restaurant have become famous throughout Vietnam and the world. People forget the original name of the restaurant and call it 'Obama bun cha'.

Other popular Vietnamese dishes you may know are summer rolls, fried spring rolls, and cha ca.

Pho

Important Holidays

For Vietnamese people, the Lunar New Year (Tet) is the most important occasion of the year. Everyone hopes that in the new year they will have a good business, have delicious food, have beautiful clothes, and good health. There is a saying in Vietnam, "A good beginning makes a good ending." Therefore, at the beginning of the year, every household must prepare a lot of food to make sure there is more than enough. Before Tet, everyone goes to buy a lot of food – enough for a whole month – even though supermarkets only have five to ten days off for Tet, and some shops, even less.

There are many typical dishes for Tet, which differ depending on the region, but there are dishes that are indispensable on every Tet table such as *banh chung*, boiled chicken, fried spring rolls, bamboo shoot soup, sticky rice, fried spring rolls, and pickled onions.

Some Avoided Dishes During Tet or the Beginning of the Month

Dog meat: Vietnamese people eat dog meat. However, everyone avoids eating it at the beginning of the year or the beginning of the month because it is believed to bring bad luck.

Squid: squid is a popular seafood in Vietnam, but there is a saying, 'black as ink', and 'ink' is a homophone for squid in Vietnamese. That is why eating squid at the beginning of the year, or the beginning of the month will bring bad luck in Vietnamese culture.

Shrimp Paste: shrimp paste is made from shrimps and salt, fermented. It has a very specific smell, and no one wants this smell in their house in the New Year.

Vietnamese Dining Etiquette

Of course, Vietnamese dining etiquette has elements similar to international etiquette, but also has some unique ones. I would like to introduce some Vietnamese dining etiquette that will be very useful when you visit a Vietnamese family to dine with them.

- When inviting guests to the house, because of their modesty, Vietnamese people often say, "I would like to invite you to my small home." Or, "I would like to invite you to have a simple meal with us." But in fact, they always prepare a lot of food, even more than enough. They want to see the guests have a nice meal. The

guests must feel very full, with some food left after the meal. When you are invited to eat with the Vietnamese, you should eat all the food in your bowl, but don't empty all the food on the table because the host will think they have not prepared enough food for the guest.
- It is quite an old school tradition, but many Vietnamese families still do it: before you touch the bowl and start dining, you have to say out loud, "I invite you to have a meal." In some families, you can say once to everyone, "I invite everyone to have meal." But in some other families, you have to invite each person in order of age, eldest first. Those who are younger will have to initiate the invitation first.
- When sitting at the table, do not use chopsticks or spoons to knock on the bowl, or make noise.
- If you want to keep food for someone, you must put it on a separate plate at the beginning of the meal; you should not eat the whole meal and leave the leftovers.
- When helping yourself to rice, do not take only one spoon and put it into the bowl; you should take more than one spoon. And you also should not squeeze the rice into the bowl too tightly.
- Vietnamese families often share food from the same dishes. You should not use your chopsticks to stir the soup bowl and poke the food plate many times to choose a delicious piece; only pick it up once.
- When picking up food, don't put it straight from the shared food plate into your mouth; put it into your own bowl and then bring it to your mouth.
- When eating, you must hold the bowl of rice with your left hand and hold the chopsticks in your right hand; do not put the bowl on the table and then bend over the table.
- When sharing food with others from a platter in the centre of the table, and you want to take food from the platter to place in a guest's bowl, always use either the large end of your own chopsticks (i.e., the end you don't put in your mouth) or another set of clean chopsticks Do not connect chopsticks when serving food for other people; pick it up with chopsticks and put it in a bowl.
- A shared spoon to scoop soup from a large bowl can only be used to pour the soup into your bowl; do not scoop the soup from the bowl and then sip from that spoon.

- After scooping the soup, the spoon must be placed upside down in the soup bowl or upside down at the side of the bowl.
- Do not put chopsticks upright in a bowl of rice as this is considered very rude.
- Do not bite your teeth into or lick your chopsticks, spoons, or bowls.
- Vietnamese people often dip the food into sauce, so when dipping, only dip the part you haven't bitten and don't dip your chopsticks into the shared bowl of sauce.
- Vietnamese people are very hospitable. The host is always worried that the guests are too shy to help themselves to food, so they often refill guests' bowls. When receiving food, try to eat all the food in your bowl to respect the host's kindness.
- Vietnamese people have a saying, "When you eat, check the pots, when you sit, check the direction." This means when eating, it is necessary to pay attention to whether the pot has a lot of rice or is about to run out, and whether there is still food left on the plates or not. If there is little food left on the sharing plate, you should not finish the contents but save some for others. When sitting, you need to pay attention to your position—are you obscuring others? And ensure that your elbows are not catching the person next to you.
- Don't talk, drink, or sip soup while you have rice or other food in your mouth.
- Do not rest your chest on the dining table or put your hands and chin on the dining table. There are many Vietnamese families sitting on the ground when dining. In that case, do not sit too close or too far from the tray.
- You should compliment the host's food and also show your enjoyment and that you ate well. After the meal say thank you to the host for the meal.

Chapter 6

Business Etiquette

Vietnam, like some other Asian countries, has a special business etiquette. If you know the secrets about doing business in Vietnam, you will easily succeed when working with Vietnamese people. If, on the other hand, you do not understand the Vietnamese business etiquette, your business may fail due to some small reasons.

TRUST AND RELATIONSHIP BUILDING IN BUSINESS
It is very important to have 'trust' in business in Vietnam. When Vietnamese people trust you, they are willing to do business with you or support you with their best. In some cases, they will even lend large amounts of money without a contract.

DEVELOP PERSONAL RELATIONSHIPS WITH PARTNERS
If you want to do business with someone, you need to develop a personal relationship with them, such as being close to their family, and understanding their hobbies. Therefore, many contracts are signed on the dining table, when drinking, or at the golf club, after considering each other as brothers or family members. Even if you are the boss, building personal relationships with employees such as asking about their family, helping their children, and congratulating them on their special occasions will foster their loyalty.

DRESS CODE
In Vietnam, in doing business, many people often look at the clothes you wear, the accessories you put on, the car you drive, and the house you live in to evaluate your financial ability, as well as how much they can trust you. Therefore, do not forget to wear formal and polite clothes when working with Vietnamese people.

In business meetings, suits and one-coloured shirts are perfect for men. You should avoid wearing too colourful clothing and casual trousers. Suits or formal dresses are perfect for women. The weather in Vietnam is quite hot, so you may not need to wear a suit on hot days, but you need to look sharp in nice clothes. The more luxurious and professional your clothes and accessories are the better impression you will make.

Business Party

When you attend a business party, you need to greet everyone on your arrival, especially those who have a higher position than you.

When the party has started, you should go to each person and toast with them, especially with important partners.

You should say cheers to others every time you want to sip your drink, not only when you start.

Building a Network

When doing business in Vietnam, building your own network is extremely important. That will make it easier for you to book an appointment or build trust with the person you need to reach if you have a third person introducing you. During the meeting, it is also to your benefit if you are able to mention the names of some reputable people.

Save Face

Most Vietnamese people do not want to lose face, so when communicating in business, you should pay attention to the order of age and position. You should not humiliate anyone in front of the crowd, whether it be your partner, boss, or employee. If there is a conflict, resolve it privately. That also leads to the fact that sometimes in a meeting, many people are silent and do not voice their objections for fear of losing face.

Decision Making

In many companies, decision making power is concentrated in one person, so you need to find out who is the decision maker and find ways to approach them. But there are also places, especially state-owned companies, where decisions have to go through many layers of approval. Therefore, don't be surprised if the decision is delayed. You should understand that the process of decision making in Vietnam is long, so you must be patient.

Giving Business Cards

You need to bring your business card when you come to meet your

Vietnamese business partners. It is a criterion for assessing your professionalism in Vietnam.

When giving business cards, documents or anything else, hand them over with two hands to show respect to the other people, especially if they are your important business partner, or older or of a higher rank than you.

GIFT GIVING

When you go to meet your Vietnamese business partner, you should prepare a small gift, which can be a traditional gift of your country, or a special product of your company, with the company's logo. It is even better if the gift is specially designed just for the recipient. Gifts are usually given at the end of the meeting or party with a commemorative photo shoot.

Before the Lunar New Year celebrations, Vietnamese people bring gifts to business partners, including wine, cake, fruit and so on. After the Lunar New Year, they visit to wish each other good luck at the beginning of the new year. In many cases, people exchange lucky money in red envelopes.

Currency

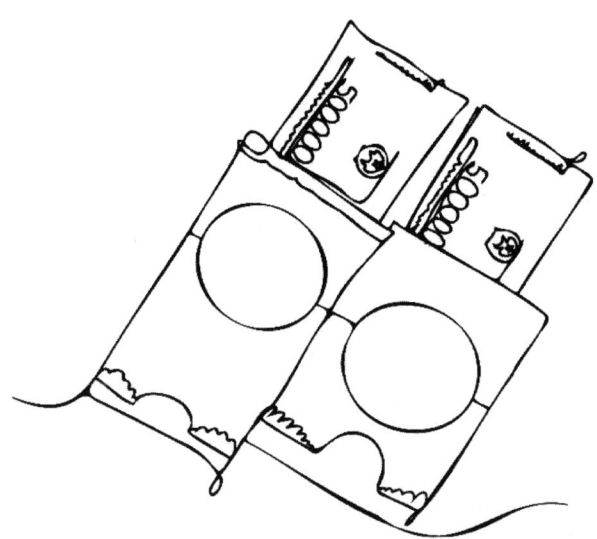

GREETING

In normal social communication, Vietnamese people greet by bowing slightly – but not as low as the Japanese – or shaking hands. In business, they usually shake hands with their business partners. However, if the business partner is a woman, only shake hands when the woman extends her hand first. Otherwise, greeting with a slight bow is appropriate. Shaking hands or bowing occurs both before the start of the meeting and after it ends.

Hierarchy at Work

Hierarchy is very important in business in Vietnam. When entering a room, the younger person or person of lower position must open the door and hold it open for the older person or person of higher position; let them enter the room first and sit in the most central seat.

In formal meetings, you need to address people using Mr/Mrs then first name and title, but normally you can use the personal pronoun plus the first name.

Punctuality

Vietnamese people are sometimes a bit late when meeting friends or family, but at work, especially for important meetings, it is necessary to be on time.

Chapter 7

Wedding Etiquette

In Vietnamese traditional culture, a wedding is a very important occasion in a person's life. That is why there are many customs for the bride, groom, their families, as well as guests, when attending a wedding.

DRESS CODE
The south and the north of Vietnam have many differences in wedding planning. In the south, weddings are often held in the evening, so guests can have gorgeous make-up and wear evening gowns to attend. In the north, many people believe that organising a wedding for the evening or weekends will disturb guests because it is time for families. You will be surprised to learn that many weddings in the north are held on weekdays at noon. Because the wedding is held at noon, the guests attend the wedding in office wear. The guests take advantage of lunchtime to congratulate the bride and groom, so they eat and drink quite quickly, and then they go back to work. Usually, they will ask permission to extend their lunch break by one to two hours to attend the wedding.

Of course, in the north, there are still many evening or weekend wedding parties. In those cases, the guests have more time to dress up. However, they do not have gorgeous make-up and wear evening gowns like they do in the south, often wearing smart casual clothes.

THERE IS A DRESS CODE WHEN ATTENDING A WEDDING IN VIETNAM
Do not wear clothes that have the same design as the bride, groom or involve more prominent colours and designs than the bride and groom's attire. Remember, this is their day.

Do not wear black to the party or if you do, then add other coloured accessories such as scarves, earrings, bracelets and so on.

Bright colours like red, blue, yellow, purple and so on are popular. You can wear white but don't try to stand out or take attention from the bride.

Do not attend the wedding if someone has recently passed away in your family because it is believed that this will bring bad luck to the bride and groom.

At the wedding party in Vietnam, the guests are often invited to drink a lot, but be careful not to get drunk, disturb others and ruin the party.

CONGRATULATIONS GIFTS

Gift: If you are very close to the bride and groom and want to give them a gift, you should contact them in advance, find out or ask for their wish list. The gift should be given before the wedding day.

Cash: Only very close friends or family of the bride and groom give them gifts; most guests give money, which should be put in a beautiful envelope. It is even better if it is a red envelope because red is a lucky colour in Vietnam. You should write your full name on the envelope. You can add more notes to help the bride and groom, or their family know that the envelope is from you because in some cases there are many people with the same name. For example, you can write on the envelope your name plus the name of the person accompanying you, if any, (ABC company) or (friend of XYZ).

The usual amount to give is about 500,000 VND (equivalent to about 25 USD) but the amount can be flexible depending on whether you are accompanied or if the wedding party is held in a more expensive venue, or if your relationship with the bride, the groom, or the family is close.

THE DAY

Reception

When you enter the wedding party, you will see a reception desk. Many families organise one party for guests of the groom's parents, guests of the bride's parents and guests of bride and groom, but some families organise separately, probably two or three parties on different days. When you arrive at the wedding, you should pay attention to see if there are one or two boxes. If there are two boxes, one may have 'The bride's family' and the other box may have 'The groom's family' written on them. You need to be careful to find the right box to put the envelope in.

After that, a representative of the bride and groom will lead you into the room and arrange the table for you. Normally, a group of six to eight people go to the party together and sit at the same table. It would be good for you if you have a partner to go with, so you don't feel lost when sitting at a table full of strangers. If you see someone you know and want to move to the same table with them, you must ask the person who arranges the tables. If that table still has an available seat, you can move, otherwise you must sit at the assigned table.

At the party
Although the food is brought to the table, you are not allowed to touch it until the official wedding ceremony is complete, and that means after the bride and groom have exchanged rings, cut the wedding cake, and made a toast with everyone.

Whilst you are eating, the bride and groom and their family will come to each table to say 'thank you'. At that time, everyone at that table must stand up, toast, and take a photo with the bride, the groom, and the family.

You should only say happy words, bless the bride and groom, and not say anything unlucky, or bad words even if you are joking.

End of the party
After the party is over, everyone starts to leave. Before leaving, don't forget to say goodbye to the groom and bride and have your photo taken with them.

About the Authors

AUSTRALIA:

Victoria Thomas is an image management specialist who is a member of the association of image consultants international. Victoria has gained qualifications through the International Image Institute, The British School of Etiquette in London and International Leadership and Management London (ILM). Prior to establishing her image consultancy, Victoria was a customer service manager and training facilitator for an international airline, in addition to owning and operating a number of successful businesses. This success has allowed her to follow her passion to create positive personal transformations for her valued clients globally.

ARGENTINA:

Mabel Di Michele is an etiquette consultant, founder and CEO of MdM Ceremonial. She developed her experience in etiquette and hospitality by studying International Diplomacy at the University of London, and working in Spain, Wales and England, as a hotel manager. She has over thirty years' experience as a teacher in Argentina. All these experiences with such professionals have led her to impart her acquired knowledge to help everyone be the best they can be in this globalised world.

Social media:
@mabeldimichele
www.mdmceremonial.com.ar

BOTSWANA:

Samantha Matlhagela is a qualified and accredited trainer from The Protocol School of Washington (USA) where she completed her trainer course in intercultural etiquette and protocol, and The Etiquette School of New York where she studied essential manners and social skills. She runs personal refinement classes through Etiquette With Sammy. In October 2020, she released her first duo of books, titled *Behind the Scenes No More, Thanks to Etiquette*. In May 2021 she released journals with the themes of Botho (humility), Lerato (love), and *Tlotlo* (respect), these being the values she lives by and a celebration of her Setswana culture which is built in the value of Botho (humility).

Social media:
@etiquette.with.sammy

BRAZIL:
Expert in social, dining, and organisational etiquette, Mery Siqueira Reis has been a consultant for large social and corporate events for over fifteen years. Celebrity weddings and formal dinners are part of her specialty. She is the owner-partner of the company Santeh Mesa Posta, founded in 2006 and operating in Brazil and abroad. She is a business administrator specialising in strategic marketing, and is a scholar in topics such as dining etiquette, having trained at Étiquette et Savoir Vivre à la Française in Paris, France, and The English Manner Etiquette in New York, USA. She is part of an elite group of international teachers who are experts in etiquette.

Social media:
    @mery.siqueira.santeh
    www.santeh.com.br

CARIBBEAN:
Alice Thomas-Roberts is a protocol and etiquette training consultant and author from Grenada, a tri-island state in the Caribbean. She has served in the Grenada Foreign Service for several years as chief of protocol and senior foreign service officer, as clerk of the houses of parliament, and executive director of the Grenada Hotel and Tourism Association. With her broad experience representing her country in the Caribbean and beyond, Mrs Thomas-Roberts is well placed to write on etiquette in the region.

Social media:
    @alicethomasroberts
    www.protocolcaribbean.com

CHINA:
Ellyna He was born and raised in China. After completing her undergraduate studies, Ellyna pursued a career path overseas holding key positions in several renowned international brands. It is here than Ellyna established her vision to bridge the understanding between eastern and western cultures. With this in mind, Ellyna founded La Fleur Academy, the first etiquette, social skills and image training institute tailored for international new starters. She is a qualified international etiquette consultant and holds double Master's degree from the University of Sydney.

Social media:
    www.lafleur.com.au

FRANCE:
France de Heere is the founder of L'Atelier du Savoir-Vivre. Living in Versailles for more than twenty years, France fell in love with the city and its history: 'Versailles, cradle of the French art of living and etiquette'! As such she decided to create a space in Versailles to learn (or revise) good manners, and to transmit with passion this cultural heritage, inherited from her childhood by education and environment. She finds it a real pleasure to give advice on French savoir-vivre to foreigners and French people alike!

Social media:
@atelierdusavoirvivre
www.ateliersavoirvivre.com

GHANA:
Sasha Seleisha Bayack-Oquaye is the founder and CEO of Poised Etiquette Consultancy, located in Ghana. She provides formal training in business etiquette, social and dining etiquette, customer, and hospitality etiquette. She aims to change the perception of etiquette by continually introducing new perspectives and modern frameworks to the field. She has been a professional in the financial regulatory/compliance industry in the UK for over fifteen years and continues to work within the legal and compliance field. She has degrees from the University of Kent, and Queen Mary University of London. She is originally from Trinidad and Tobago in the Caribbean, and now divides her time between Accra and London. Additionally, she is an experienced compliance and regulatory professional, having worked in the banking and finance industry in London for over fifteen years.

Social media:
@sashabayack
www.poisedetiquette.com

HUNGARY:
Gabriella Kanyok is a diplomatic protocol, etiquette and communication expert with more than ten years' experience in working with EU institutes, NGOs, international organisations, and supporting professionals. She does not only master the subject of diplomatic protocol and etiquette, but she

also leads the communication department of an international organisation. She holds two master's degrees in her fields of expertise, and speaks Hungarian, English and French, and is currently learning Mandarin Chinese.

Social media:
@kgetiquette
www.etiquette.hu

INDIA:

Niraalee Shah is the founder of Image Building and Etiquette Mapping India. After becoming a certified international etiquette trainer from the British School of Excellence (BSE) in England, Niraalee decided to share the training, vision and mission of BSE with India and founded BSE India where she is the CEO. Niraalee aims to share her extensive knowledge to corporates and organisations in India, help entrepreneurs embrace change and add value to the customer experience. As an image consultant and branding strategist, Niraalee Shah is certified by the Indian School of Image Management (Mumbai) and The International Image Counselle (Canada).

Social media:
@niraalee_shah
www.niraaleeshah.com

IRAN:

Farno Rezaei is the director and founder of the Farsse School of Etiquette, the first international school of social etiquette in Iran. She graduated as an etiquette consultant from the IAP College of Canada and the Etiquette Depond School in the UK. Farsse helps women who want to succeed in life and achieve their goals. Farno helps women transform themselves, teaching them about self-esteem as well as luxury, fashion and beauty to help them become the best version of themselves.

Social media:
@farsse.co
www.farsse.com

ITALY AND POLAND:
Dobrochna Aleksandra Giedwidz is the founder of Etiquette Now. Born in Poland, Dobrochna has spent her career in notable cities such as London, Milan and Barcelona. She began her work in public relations and later her ability to truly connect with people and understand their needs led Dobrochna to manage teams and coordinate projects, as well as build and maintain relationships with high-profile clients. As an etiquette trainer and image consultant certified by the British School of Etiquette, she dedicates her time to helping professionals and aspiring individuals improve their image, build confidence and develop soft skills to prepare for success in any field.

Social media:
    @etiquette_now
    etiquette-now.com

LEBANON:
Irma Vartanian Balian is an intercultural consultant, with a background in protocol and soft diplomacy and a focus on diversity, equity and inclusion. Irma is a trusted adviser to global corporate leaders and professionals on developing their cultural intelligence, motivational drive, as well as interpersonal and corporate protocol skills. She has also a particular interest in training women executives in leadership and negotiation skills across cultures. Irma speaks five languages, has lived and worked in North America, Europe and the Middle East, and is a tea champion. Irma serves on several boards, volunteers as a mentor, and is the founder of ProtocolWise.

Social media:
    @protocolwise
    protocolwise.com

MOROCCO:
After twenty-one years in the business world Mariam Filali became an accredited trainer from 'L'école internationale d'Etiquette et de protocole' of Québec and certified by ProtocolToday.

    Mariam also holds a certification from 'la Haute école de Coaching' of

Paris as a counsellor in personalised image. In 2016, she founded a consulting firm specializing in image consulting 'Business Etiquette et Protocol'. She supports professionals and individuals to enhance their image while respecting their personality. Mariam works with passion which pushes her to train at the international level. Her qualifications are multiple and are constantly being updated to share the latest techniques. Her slogan is: "success is in your hands, react!"

Social media:
   @businessetiquetteetprotocole72
   businessetiquetteetprotocole.com

PAKISTAN:

Dr Sadia Javed Rajput holds the position of CEO at the British School of Excellence Pakistan. As a paediatrician, she strongly believes that the best performance of the human body and brain is linked to a person's physical and mental training. Moreover, she believes one can acquire the habit of excellence by cultivating teachability, adaptability, flexibility, creativity, and sensitivity. Dr Sadia graduated from Allama Iqbal Medical College. She has worked in various institutions such as Agha Khan University Hospital Karachi (paediatrics unit), Services Hospital and Children Hospital Lahore, Paediatric Gastroenterology Unit at Southampton General Hospital NHS and Salisbury District Hospital in the UK where she completed her MRCPCH training.

Social media:
   @thebritishschoolofetiquettepak
   thebritishschoolofetiquettepakistan.com

PORTUGAL:

Maria Campos has more than twenty-five years of experience in hospitality. She is a flight attendant with a passion for etiquette. Her professional life demands discipline, pride and professionalism. While this has never been a problem for Maria, etiquette helps her to permanently build the best version of herself. Hence, she has no hesitation in saying that etiquette has always been her greatest ally in her work in commercial aviation. She has always guided her life, both personal and professional, by what she considers to be the basic elements of etiquette, emotional intelligence and good manners, as well as the principle of treating others well. "Etiquette makes you fly!" she says.

Social media:
@myfairmanners

RUSSIA:
Anastasia Martel, the founder of Anastasia Martel Etiquette, is British School of Etiquette and the Sisi Elisabeth Austrian Higher School of Etiquette in Saint Petersburg, Russia qualified etiquette and protocol consultant. She enjoys delving into the rich culture, national customs and traditions of Russian people, covering all the dos and don'ts of this proud nation with her students.

Social media:
@anastasia_martel_etiquette
www.ametiquette.com

SLOVENIA:
Simona Lečnik Očko, Master of Diplomacy and international affairs, born in Bosnia and Herzegovina, escaped as a teenager from war to Slovenia. Since childhood, she was a passionate lover of etiquette. Her father read her an etiquette book before bedtime instead of fairy tales. She proudly founded Lumia-Academy of Values, to bring a fresh and modern perspective to the industry. Highly motivated and qualified, she offers innovative and empowering courses of soft skills and etiquette for everyone and for all ages.

Social media:
@simonalecnikocko

SWITZERLAND:
Julia Esteve Boyd, the etiquette consultant, provides private training in international corporate and social etiquette and VIP protocol. She coaches clients in a variety of lifestyle situations, the ultimate goal being able to present oneself, one's business and one's household in the best possible way.

Social media:
    @the_etiquetteconsultant
    theetiquetteconsultant.com

TURKEY:
Özgü Ergün has certificates for Life coaching, and is an NLP practitioner, an etiquette and manners practitioner, a bioenergy practitioner, and is currently taking a mindfulness practitioner course with Achology Ltd. She is the owner and managing partner at ProLongé Venue Marketing, and since 2020 has also set up Boutiquette Etiquette and Life Coaching. She speaks French, English, Spanish fluently, and is a beginner in Greek and Italian. She is a member of SITE Turkey, I-MICE International, and ODD (School Support Association) which is where she is a volunteer English teacher.

Social media:
    @boutiquette_coaching

UAE:
Andreea Stefanescu is the founder of The School of Manners and has been a resident of UAE for eleven years. She is an internationally certified etiquette trainer under three of the most prestigious institutions in the field: The English Manner in London; The Protocol School of Washington, and Institut Villa Pierrefeu in Switzerland. Andreea has over twelve years of international experience in the field, having personally lived and studied in eight different countries including Ethiopia, France, Switzerland, England, Spain, UAE, USA and Romania and travelled to over ninety-three countries globally, with six years of experience working and flying alongside royal families and VVIPs around the world.

Social media:
    @theschoolofmanners
    www.theschoolofmanners.com

UK:

Sophia Lingham is the founder of The Great British Etiquette Co. Having lived in Asia, the Middle East and Europe, Sophia is no stranger to being catapulted into a totally new country and way of life. Understanding different countries and cultures and being able to adapt successfully into each of them, both professionally and personally, is a skill which she enjoys sharing with her students. An etiquette trainer certified by The British School of Etiquette, she provides 3D, all-encompassing and sustainable etiquette and emotional intelligence training. Sophia is also a PhD researcher specialising in food policy and security at the Royal Agricultural University in England. She holds a first class degree in law and a MSc in sustainable agriculture and food security.

Social media:
@sophialingham
www.thegreatbritishetiquetteco.co.uk

USA:

Nancy Hoogenboom is the founder of Daily Etiquette, Southern California School of Etiquette and Protocol. In addition to being a certified etiquette trainer, she is a speaker, author, consultant, and coach. Nancy makes etiquette relevant for today's society in social media, personal interaction, and social and professional settings. She brings the basics of etiquette into the day-to-day activities of our lives. Nancy enjoys her family, friends, and travelling. Also known as 'Fancy Nancy', her charismatic personality drives her flair for decorating and entertaining.

Social media:
@daily.etiquette
www.dailyetiquette.com

VIETNAM:

Mai Doan O'Donnell is an entrepreneur and manners and etiquette trainer originally from Vietnam, and now based in London, UK. She graduated from one of the most famous Universities in Vietnam, the Hanoi Foreign Trade University, with an excellent result and received a full scholarship from the Japanese Government to study at Osaka University. She has supported many foreign companies to understand Vietnamese culture, find their business partners, train the staff, and build their business successfully in Vietnam for more than fifteen years. With her experience working in manners and etiquette education, hospitality consultancy and business consultancy, Mai is invited to speak as a guest speaker at many events for business clubs and organisations.

Social media:
@maiodonnelluk